A Reader for Developing Writers

THIRD EDITION

$\mathcal{A}$ Reader for Developing Writers

Santi V. Buscemi
Middlesex County College

The **McGraw-Hill** Companies, Inc.

New York   St. Louis   San Francisco   Auckland   Bogotá   Caracas   Lisbon
London   Madrid   Mexico City   Milan   Montreal   New Delhi
San Juan   Singapore   Sydney   Tokyo   Toronto

McGraw-Hill

A Division of The **McGraw·Hill** *Companies*

A Reader for Developing Writers

Acknowledgments appear on pages 568–570, and on this page by reference.

This book is printed on acid-free paper.

1 2 3 4 5 6 7 8 9 0   DOC   DOC   9 0 9 8 7 6 5

ISBN   0-07-009484-5

This book was set in Berkeley by ComCom, Inc. The editors were Tim Julet, Laura Lynch, and John M. Morriss; the text was designed by Paradigm Design; the cover was designed by Joan Greenfield; the production supervisor was Annette Mayeski. Project supervision was done by Tage Publishing Service, Inc. R. R. Donnelley & Sons Company was printer and binder.

Library of Congress Cataloging-in-Publication Data
Buscemi, Santi V.
    A reader for developing writers / Santi V. Buscemi.—3rd ed.
        p.   cm.
    Includes index.
    ISBN 0-07-009484-5
    1. College readers.   2. English language—Rhetoric.   I. Title.
PE1417.B8555   1996
808'.0427—dc20

For   **Joseph** and **Theresa Buscemi**

and for all the other Sicilian heroes
who came to this country to make a better
life for their children

About the Author

Santi V. Buscemi chairs the English Department
and teaches reading and writing at
Middlesex County College in Edison, NJ.

CONTENTS

PREFACE TO THE INSTRUCTOR

When I wrote the proposal for what later became *A Reader for Developing Writers,* I hoped the text would serve as a useful tool for my own students and for those of a few colleagues in my own college and perhaps in a few others. Thus, the enthusiasm, encouragement, and kindness with which it has been received by students and faculty across the United States and elsewhere have been both unexpected and overwhelming. No matter what the future brings, I will always be grateful for your support.

As in its first and second editions, the text's primary purpose is to help students read carefully, to react thoughtfully, and to use these reactions as creative springboards for writing. Research in the theory of reading and writing continues to affirm the close and natural connections between these two skills. Beginning writers need a program of critical and committed reading that increases their appreciation of language, that provides inspiration for their own creative efforts, and that reinforces the teaching of basic rhetorical strategies. In short, no basic-skills program in English makes sense without the integration of reading and writing.

As in the past, the reading selections have been chosen with an eye toward helping students use their own experiences and perceptions as sources of information and insight in writing that explores questions suggested by—if not drawn directly from—the reading. In the second edition, selections by and about Native-Americans, Latino/Caribbean-Americans, Asian-Americans, Arab-Americans and African-Americans widened the text's appeal and enriched its texture, as did pieces depicting cultures and lifestyles that will be unfamiliar to some student readers. Selections for the third edition were chosen with an eye toward maintaining this diversity. As always, introductory materials illustrate important principles and techniques, and reading selections demonstrate variety in length, subject matter, and purpose. Included in most chapters is at least one short, readily accessible piece designed to promote confidence in beginning writers/readers and to prepare them for longer, more challenging selections.

In addition, the third edition continues to emphasize the notion that writing is a process of discovery to be approached with care, commitment, and energy. As in the past, the "Getting Started" section, which opens the text, traces the evolution of an essay from prewriting through the editing of a final draft, with each stage fully explained and illustrated via samples taken from the work of a first-year college student. However, something new has been added to reinforce the idea that students should approach writing as a process. In the third edition, the introduction to each chapter (except the one on the short story) compares excerpts from rough and revised drafts of a student essay that appears a few pages later. Comments in the margins, relevant to techniques and skills covered in the chapter, demonstrate the riches revising can yield.

As in the second edition, the belief that writing is a process is reinforced in the Suggestions for Sustained Writing, which appear at the end of each chapter. Most suggestions refer to journal entries students make after reading the selections, and they encourage the use of this information to begin and develop full-length essays and letters. Each and every Suggestion for Sustained Writing also reminds students that composing is more than simply gathering information and arranging it on a page. Indeed, woven into the fabric of each item is a reminder that successful writing demands careful planning, the creation of multiple drafts, frequent reorganization and revision, and painstaking editing.

Other important features of the third edition include introductions to the reading process and to taking notes. These have been added to the "Getting Started" section, which begins the text. A form of the SQ3R (Survey, Question, Read, Recite, Review) method, taught in many developmental reading classes, is explained clearly and concisely. This new material also offers students suggestions—complete with easy-to-follow illustrations—on how to keep a double-entry notebook and to make notes in the margins. There are even some special tips on how to read this text.

The emphasis on careful reading and thinking is carried through the rest of the text in Thinking Critically, a new pedagogical subsection accompanying each selection. Thinking Critically offers students questions for writing and discussion by which they can practice a variety of important critical skills. For example, some items ask students to practice techniques learned in the reading and note-taking sections of "Getting Started." Others ask them to extend or respond to the discussion of ideas or opinions found in what they have just read. Still others require them to make comparisons between two or more selections in the text.

The table of contents continues to address a variety of academic disciplines and a wide range of social, political, economic, and scientific concerns. As in the first two editions, I have chosen selections appropriate to the reading abilities of developmental students, but I have also included several that promote healthy intellectual stretching. The text continues to offer easy-to-follow aids designed to foster comprehension. While most selections are nonfiction, prose, poetry, and fiction play a prominent role. More important, student writing has an increased presence in the third edition. Indeed, every chapter now boasts at least one student piece. Several are new to the text; others have been revised and expanded. All are the products of careful, sustained effort through which the writers' forceful and distinctive voices address engaging topics through various modes of discourse.

Behind the design of *A Reader for Developing Writers* remains a belief that there should be a natural and clear connection between what students are asked to read and what they are asked to write. This is not to say that reading selections must serve as blueprints for student writing. They should certainly illustrate important principles and techniques clearly, but they should also inspire students to use writing as a way to explore ideas, emotions, and issues they find meaningful. This essential connection is fostered by the text's instructional apparatus. Section and chapter introductions discuss fundamental principles of composition and rhetoric illustrated in the reading selections that follow. In addition, the third edition includes graphic illustrations, whenever possible, to help students see as well as read important principles and techniques they can apply to their own writing.

Of course, each selection is again accompanied by materials that help students learn and practice techniques explained in chapter introductions and illustrated in the selections. Apparatus for each selection includes Looking Ahead (comments to help students preview reading selections); Vocabulary; Questions for Discussion; Thinking Critically; and Suggestions for Journal Entries. As mentioned earlier, Suggestions for Sustained Writing (prompts for full-length essays and letters) appear at the end of each chapter.

Since developmental students often find collecting detail difficult, special attention is paid to the early stages of the writing process. In this regard, perhaps the most useful piece of apparatus is "Getting Started." As in the second edition, this introduction to the text delineates the evolution of a student essay from beginning to end. It also explains prewriting strategies that are recommended in Suggestions for Journal Entries and that help students gather information they can use to launch longer projects described in Suggestions for Sustained Writing. Finally, as indicated above, Getting Started now addresses questions and techniques important to reading and note-taking as well.

Once again, the instructional apparatus is fully integrated. Items under Looking Ahead and Vocabulary help students preview the contents and structure of the paragraph, essay, poem, or short story they are about to read. At the same time, they prepare students for the Questions for Discussion and the Thinking Critically sections, which follow. The clear connection between the Suggestions for Journal Entries and the Suggestions for Sustained Writing has been maintained. The latter make direct reference to details, insights, and ideas students have recorded in their journals, and they encourage the use of such materials as springboards for longer projects.

No textbook is the product of one person alone, even one that carries a single byline. I am indebted to several good friends and fellow teachers whose counsel, direction, and encouragement helped make this book what it is. For their careful reviews and helpful suggestions, I would like to thank several colleagues from across the country: David Davis, Johnson County Community College; Elizabeth Dupe Ojo, Tennessee Technical College; Judith Funston, State University of New York, Potsdam; Maureen Hoag, Witchita State University; and Douglas Johnson, Highline Community College.

Among my friends and colleagues at Middlesex County College, I want to extend my deepest gratitude to Connie Alongi, Betty Altruda, Gert Coleman, Sallie Del Vec-chio, Virve Ettinger, Barry Glazer, Jim Keller, Jane Lasky-MacPherson, Jack Moskowitz, Georgianna Planko, Renee Price, Yvonne Sisko, Sonia Slobodian, Matthew Spano, and Richard Strugala for their support and counsel. Special thanks must go to Emanuel di Pasquale and Albert Nicolai, splendid colleagues and even better friends who brought me advice, comfort, and light. I also want to express my gratitude to members of my McGraw-Hill family, especially Bob Redling, who believed in this book from the very start, and Tim Julet and Laura Lynch, who guided me through the third edition.

Finally, I thank my wife, Elaine, for putting up with my "imperfections" and for granting me her patience and support during the many times she had to vie with this and with other projects for my time and affection.

Santi V. Buscemi

GETTING STARTED

A Reader for Developing Writers is a collection of short reading selections by professional and student authors. Each paragraph, essay, poem, and story is accompanied by discussion questions, suggestions for short and sustained writing, and other instructional aids. The reading selections use techniques you will want to learn as you develop your reading and writing skills. Some will even serve as models for writing you do in other college courses.

Most important, the reading selections will act as springboards to your own writing. Some supply facts and ideas you can include and make reference to in your own work. Others will inspire you to write paragraphs, letters, or essays about similar subjects by drawing details from what you know best—your own experiences, observations, and reading. In short, this book will help you make connections between your reading and your writing, and it will show you ways to improve both.

The rest of this introduction offers advice about getting started. It discusses:

How to Use This Book
Making the Most of Your Reading
Taking Notes
Learning the Writing Process
Gathering Information
The Making of a Student Essay: From Prewriting to Proofreading

HOW TO USE THIS BOOK

The most important parts of this book are the reading selections—paragraphs, essays, poems, and stories—which your instructor will assign. These are accompanied by instructional aids such as discussion questions and Suggestions for Sustained Writing. They will help you make the most of your reading and get started on your own writing projects. Here's one way to use *A Reader for Developing Writers* (your teacher may suggest others):

1. The book is divided into five sections; each contains several chapters. Always begin a section by reading the introduction. Section introductions aren't long, but they provide important information. The introduction to Section I begins on page 17.
2. Next, read the chapter introduction. It explains principles and strategies illustrated by the reading selections that follow. The introduction to Chapter 1 begins on page 19.
3. When you get to the reading selections in a chapter, you will see that each is preceded by an author's biography, a preview section called Looking Ahead, and a

vocabulary section. These are instructional aids. Read them first; then read the selection itself at least twice. The first selection begins on page 28.

4. Read and answer the Questions for Discussion that follow the selection. It's a good idea to put your answers in writing, perhaps in a notebook reserved for this class.

5. Now, respond to the Suggestions for Journal Entries, which follow Questions for Discussion. Write your responses in a notebook (journal) kept for this purpose only. Making regular journal entries is critical to developing your skills. First, like any skill, writing is mastered only through frequent practice, and keeping a journal provides this practice. Second, a journal contains your responses to the readings, so it helps you understand and use what you read. Finally, responding to Suggestions for Journal Entries is an easy way to gather information for longer projects. In fact, almost all of the Suggestions for Sustained Writing (found at the end of each chapter) refer to journal entries. So, keeping a journal means you will have already taken the first step in completing major writing assignments.

6. Next, read and complete the short Thinking Critically exercise following Suggestions for Journal Entries after each selection. In most cases you can write your responses to the exercises in the text itself—on blank pages or in the margins. Completing these exercises will also provide you with ideas for longer writing projects.

7. Finally, respond to one of the Suggestions for Sustained Writing at the chapter's end. Read each suggestion carefully; then, choose one you know a lot about. Almost all Suggestions for Sustained Writing refer to earlier journal suggestions. If you haven't made a journal entry like the one referred to, go back and do so.

8. Important terms are defined in a glossary at the end of the book. Refer to it if you have questions about a term used to define a writing technique, rule, or principle.

MAKING THE MOST OF YOUR READING

READING IN COLLEGE

Reading and writing are closely related. The more you read, the better writer you will become. The more you write, the easier reading will be.

Like writing, reading is an active process. It should be done conscientiously—with a questioning and curious mind. Don't just accept what someone else writes. Don't just ignore what at first you don't understand. Reading is a struggle, but it will make you a better thinker and writer.

Some students get frustrated when they read challenging material. Fortunately, there are many simple methods to make reading more successful and, simultaneously, to use it as a tool for improving writing. **However, all require careful preparation and review.** Here's a five-step process based on one developed by Professor Francis P. Robinson of Ohio State University. Apply it to any text and especially to paragraphs and essays in this book:

Survey: First, pay special attention to the title carefully. Next, scan the entire selection. Look for words or phrases in bold; they reveal important ideas and give clues about organization. Then, read the introduction (first few sentences or paragraphs); try to spot the central or main idea.

Question: Now, ask yourself questions like these:

- What is the author's subject?
- What main point is he or she making about the subject?
- How is the piece organized? What major points will the author make and in what order?
- What do subheadings and words in bold or italics reveal?

You don't have to answer such questions immediately. However, asking intelligent questions (try making up some of your own) is a good way to warm up the mind, just as stretching is a good way to warm up the body before exercising.

Read: Questions like those above will give your reading purpose and focus. Try to answer them as you read through the material.

Reread   You will learn that the key to good writing is rewriting. The same is true
and Take   of reading. Never read an assignment just once. The second time around,
Notes: make sure to take notes. (You will soon learn two good ways to take notes for selections in this book.)

Review: Always read your notes at least once. If possible, write a short response based on them. You can summarize what you have read, question, add to, argue against, or make some other response. The Suggestions for Journal Entries after each selection will help you do this.

SPECIAL TIPS FOR READING SELECTIONS IN THIS BOOK

1. Prepare for a selection by first reading the author's biography, the vocabulary words, and the Looking Ahead section, which come before it.
2. Take notes while you read. You can do this in many ways, such as listing or outlining ideas on a note pad. Two especially good methods are to make notes in the margins of the text and to keep a double-entry notebook. Both are explained below.
3. Answer the Questions for Discussion that appear after each selection in this textbook. Then, complete at least one of the Suggestions for Journal Entries and the Thinking Critically exercise.

TAKING NOTES

Two good ways to take notes are by making them in the margins and by keeping a double-entry notebook. Try these techniques as you read this book:

MAKING NOTES IN THE MARGINS

A simple but effective way to react to what you read is by jotting down short notes anywhere in the text you can find space. Doing so will help you better understand what you read and inspire you to write on similar subjects. The left and right margins are convenient places to put a note, but the bottom of the page or a blank page will also do. Here are tips for making notes in the margins:

- Never read a textbook without a pen or marker in your hand. Your college books are your own; mark them up. Francis Bacon said, "Some books are to be tasted, others to be swallowed, and some few to be chewed and digested." So "chew," "digest," and enjoy them.
- Underline central ideas of essays and paragraphs. (You will learn more about central ideas later.) If the central idea isn't stated, make one up and write it in the margin.
- Circle or highlight words, phrases, or sentences that are moving, convincing, or otherwise effective.
- Ask questions about the writer's ideas or opinions.
- Agree/disagree with the author's facts and opinions.
- Place a question mark (?) next to an unfamiliar word, phrase, name, or fact. You can look it up later.
- Most important, add information of your own. Relate ideas to yourself or people you know. This will inspire you to write on this subject yourself.

Now read the introduction to Gina K. Louis-Ferdinand's *Is Justice Served?* (You can read the complete essay in Chapter 2.) Note the comments a reader has made in the margins.

Americans love a (juicy) story. We want intimate **grabs your attention!**

details, and the media is happy to comply, but what

we forget is that people's lives are at stake. A

crime is not a form of (macabre) entertainment from   **? (look up in dictionary)**

which to derive perverse pleasure. It is the failure

of a person to live up to his or her obligations as a

could be essay's central idea law-abiding citizen, and the media should report it

as such.

And how! Remember the Tanya Harding case.   Recently, several crimes have been   **Yes! Especially TV.**

sensationalized. As far as the media is concerned,

the more gruesome the crime, the better. Take the

Menendez brothers' case or the trial of the

policemen who beat Rodney King. If a famous person

is accused, members of the press appear to smack

their lips and wring their hands in anticipation. *Too strong an accusation ?*

Insert sex or race, as in the O.J. Simpson murder

trial, and the journalist's fondest dreams come *All journalists?*

effective word true. But such (exploitation) is not harmless *I agree 100%*

entertainment; it tears at the core of the American

judicial system: a fair trial by an impartial jury.

This is central idea.

KEEPING A DOUBLE-ENTRY (SUMMARY/RESPONSE) NOTEBOOK

There are several ways to keep a double-entry notebook. Here's one of the easiest:

1. Before you begin a selection, draw a line from top to bottom down the middle of a notebook page.
2. Label the left column *Summary;* the right column, *Response.*
3. As you read the poem, story, or essay, summarize the major ideas in each paragraph or stanza (a paragraph in a poem) under the left column. A summary condenses (puts briefly) what you have read into your own words.
4. After you have finished reading and made summary comments, write brief responses to those summaries in the right column. (You may have to reread sentences or even whole paragraphs to do this.) Your personal responses can take any form you want, but they will probably be similar to notes you might write in the margins. For example:

- Ask a question.
- Agree/disagree with an opinion.
- Identify the central and other important ideas.
- Identify a word or phrase you especially like.
- Add information to show how the reading relates to you or your world. Doing this might inspire you to write on a similar subject.

As an example, here is Alfred Lord Tennyson's poem "The Eagle," followed by a sample notebook entry:

He clasps the crag with crooked hands;
Close to the sun in lonely lands,
Ring'd with the azure world, he stands.

The wrinkled sea beneath him crawls;
He watches from his mountain walls,
And like a thunderbolt he falls.

SUMMARY	RESPONSE
Stanza 1—Grasping a large rock, an eagle stands on a high and lonely cliff.	The eagle is so high he is surrounded by sky. He is given human qualities—"hands."
Stanza 2—The eagle looks down at the sea and drops quickly, furiously.	He is so high the sea seems wrinkled. What is he going after? Food? An enemy? "Thunderbolt" is a great word. This is a wonderful picture of a majestic animal.

LEARNING THE WRITING PROCESS

Like reading, writing is a process. It can be divided into four steps: prewriting, drafting, revising, editing/proofreading. The next five paragraphs outline the process. To understand it fully, read Gathering Information on pages 7–10 and The Making of a Student Essay on pages 10–15.

PREWRITING

Don't skip this most important stage. Also called "invention," prewriting helps you gather information and ideas. It also helps overcome *writer's block*—the problem of staring at a sheet of paper and going blank, as if everything you wanted to say had rushed out of your head. Five prewriting techniques are fully explained in Gathering Information.

WRITING A WORKING DRAFT

Drafting involves using what you have recorded in your journal to begin a simple outline and the first version of your paragraph, essay, or letter. In this stage, you will also decide on your purpose and on a preliminary or working central idea. More about these concepts is presented later in "Getting Started" and in Chapter 1.

REVISING THE WORKING DRAFT

Revising means rewriting, rewriting, and then rewriting some more. With each revision, your writing will improve. Revising helps you clarify your purpose and central idea, reorganize confusing sentences and paragraphs, add details, combine short choppy sentences, and improve word choice.

EDITING AND PROOFREADING

Editing means reading the best of your rough drafts to correct errors in grammar, punctuation, sentence structure, and mechanics. Proofreading involves the final check for spelling, punctuation, and typographical errors.

These steps seem neatly defined, but they are not always distinct from each other. For example, while editing, you might have to make major revisions to correct important language or organizational problems. If this happens, don't worry. It's the way the process is supposed to work.

GATHERING INFORMATION

Earlier you read about prewriting, the process of gathering information. You can use the five prewriting techniques discussed below to gather information for any assignment, especially journal entries. A good way to start a journal entry is to read the notes you made on a reading selection. This should get you mentally set for writing. Then, follow the Suggestions for Journal Entries, which often recommend using the prewriting techniques that follow.

LISTING

You can use your journal to make a list of details by recording what you think is most important, most startling, or most obvious about your topic. Sometimes, in fact, you can compile a useful list of details simply by putting down whatever comes to mind about your topic. Here's a list that student writer Aggie Canino made when she was asked to describe a recent storm and its effects on her community:

```
Cloged rain sewers overflowing
Giant tree limbs across the road
Flooding
Strong winds
Birch trees bent duble in the wind
Cracked utility poles
Downed power lines
Loss of electric
Lasted only one hour
Dog hidding under bed
Flooded basements
Thunder/lightening
Loss of power
Frightning sounds—howling of the wind, crash of
    thunder
Complete darkness in the middle of the day
Old oak on corner struck by lightening—bark ripped
    off
```

This list is repetitious and has spelling errors, but don't worry about such problems at first; you can correct them later. Just concentrate on your topic and record the details as fast as they pop into your head.

Make sure to read your list after—but only *after*—you run out of things to say. Doing so will allow you to eliminate repetition and correct obvious errors. More important, it will help you make various items more specific and even come up with a few new details. For instance, Aggie expanded her mention of "cracked utility poles" by describing the "white sparks that flew from downed power lines" and by detailing the terror she felt as she heard the "splintering of a utility pole struck by lightning."

BRAINSTORMING

This method of gathering details is like making a list. Usually, however, brainstorming results in a collection of words and phrases scribbled across the page just as they come to mind. Another difference is that brainstorming is usually done with friends or classmates. As the saying goes, "two (or more) heads are better than one." Brainstorming will help the group come up with the number and kinds of questions and answers about a topic that would have been impossible had each of you worked alone.

You can begin brainstorming by asking questions to help you understand why your topic is important to you and what you want to say about it. Various kinds of questions can be used to generate details. Among the most common are those journalists use to decide what to put into a news story: "What happened?" "When did it happen?" "Where did it happen?" "How and why did it happen?" "Who was involved?"

Questions like these work best if you want to tell a story or explain how or why something happens or should happen. However, you will probably have to think of different kinds of questions if you have other purposes in mind. Say you want to describe Uncle Charlie. You might ask: "What does he look like?" "How old is he?" "What details best describe his personality?" "What are his friends like?" "What kinds of clothes does he wear?" "What does his car look like?" "What kind of work does he do?" In any case, remember that prewriting is also called "invention," so invent as many kinds of questions as you like.

Not all the questions you ask will yield useful details—the kind that best describe Uncle Charlie, for example. However, the answers to only one or two might suggest other thoughts and opinions among the people in your brainstorming group. In a little while, a kind of mental chain reaction will occur, and you will find yourself discussing facts and ideas that seem to pop up naturally. Working together, then, you can inspire each other to come up with information for a fine journal entry and even for a more formal assignment based on that entry.

FOCUSED FREEWRITING

Freewriting is a very common technique to help overcome *writer's block,* a problem that results in staring at a blank piece of paper while trying unsuccessfully to come up with something to say. Freewriting involves writing nonstop for five or ten minutes, and simply recording ideas that come into your mind at random. Focused freewriting is similar, but it involves concentrating on a predetermined topic.

Let's say that you want to do some focused freewriting on a storm. The results might look like this:

```
    The clogged rain sewers were overflowing, and there
was a lot of flooding with strong winds knocking down
power lines. Thunder crashed, and lightning flashed.
Giant tree limbs fell across the road and a birch was
bent double, and there were lots of flooded basements.
Even though the storm lasted only one hour. Several
downed power lines threw threatening sparks and flashes
across the road. My street was blocked; a large oak had
fallen across it. We lost our electricity. The crash of
thunder shook me to my bones. My dog hid under the bed.
We were terrified.
```

Again, don't worry about grammar and other such errors at this point in the process. Simply try to focus on your topic and record your ideas quickly and completely.

As always, read your journal entry as soon as possible after you've recorded your ideas. Doing so will help you cut out repetition, rework parts that require clarification, and add more details that come to mind in the process.

INTERVIEWING

Asking appropriate questions of people who know about your topic is an excellent way to gather detail. Like brainstorming, interviewing gives you other perspectives from which to view your topic, and it often yields information that otherwise you might never have learned.

The kinds of questions you ask should be determined by your purpose. If you are trying to learn why something happened, what someone did, or how something works, for example, you might begin your interview with a group of questions like those journalists rely on and that you read about under Brainstorming. As you just learned, they have to do with the *who, what, when, where, why,* and *how* of a topic. Again, however, you might have to decide on your own set of questions.

Just make sure that the person you interview is knowledgeable about your subject and willing to spend enough time with you to make your interview worthwhile. People who can give you only a few minutes might not be good sources of information. When you make the appointment to meet with the person you want to interview, tell him or her a little about your topic, your purpose, and the kinds of questions you will ask. This will give your subject a chance to think about the interview in advance and prepare thoughtful responses to your questions.

Finally, come to the interview prepared. Think carefully about the questions you need answered ahead of time. Write them down—at least those you feel are most important—in your journal or on a piece of notebook paper. Bring them to the interview, and use them to get your subject talking. If your questions are clear and interesting, you should gather more information than you bargained for. On the other hand, don't get upset if the interview doesn't go exactly as you planned. Your subject might not answer any of your questions but simply discuss ideas as they come to mind. Such interviews sometimes provide a lot of useful information. Just take good notes!

SUMMARIZING

This prewriting method involves condensing another writer's ideas and putting them into your own words. It is especially effective if you want to combine information found in your reading with details you have gathered from your own experiences or from other sources. Just be sure to use your own language *throughout* the summary. In addition, if you plan to use any of this information in an essay, make certain to tell your readers that it comes from the work of another writer by mentioning the writer's name. For instance, if you decide to summarize the paragraph from Rachel Carson's *The Sea Around Us* (a selection in Chapter 1), you might begin: "As Carson explains in her study of the ocean's origins . . . ."

THE MAKING OF A STUDENT ESSAY: FROM PREWRITING TO PROOFREADING

The rest of Getting Started traces the writing of a full-length essay by Deborah Diglio, who was a first-year nursing student when she wrote it. Diglio's work shows that she sees writing as a process of four important steps:

- Prewriting to Gather Information
- Writing a Working Draft
- Revising the Working Draft
- Editing and Proofreading

PREWRITING TO GATHER INFORMATION

The process began when Diglio was inspired by Carl Sandburg's "Child of the Romans," a poem in Chapter 11 about the difficult life of an immigrant laborer. So, she responded to one of the Suggestions for Journal Entries that recommended using focused freewriting to gather details about a job she once held. Here's what she wrote in her journal about waitressing:

> People ordering food. The night was going by fast.
> Nervous. First nights can be scarry. Keep a pleasant
> attitude. I could do the job easily. Training period
> over, I was on my own. I needed this job. We needed the
> money. I felt confident, too confident. I can now laugh
> at it. Not then. Society may not place waitressing high

on the social ladder, but you have got to be sure-
footed, organized, you have to have a sense of humor,
and a pleasant personality. You have to be able to learn
from your mistakes. Eventually, I did learn but then I
thought I would die. This old woman left her walker in
the corner. How did I know it wasn't a tray stand? Still
I should have! Why didn't I just look more closely. Why
did'nt my brain take over. And the old folks didn't
mind. We should look back at ourselves and laugh sometimes.

As you can see, there is no particular order to Diglio's notes and, like most freewriting, it contains errors in spelling, sentence structure, and the like. Nonetheless, an event
that might make interesting reading is coming through. So is the idea that Diglio learned
something from the experience and can now look back at it with a smile.

WRITING A WORKING DRAFT

After discussing her journal entry with her teacher, Diglio decided to tell her story
in a full-length essay. She reviewed her notes and thought more about her central idea,
the point she wanted her essay to make. After taking more notes, she made a plan, or
outline, to organize and write the working draft of her essay.

As she began writing this first draft, more and more ideas and details came to mind;
she put them into the draft wherever she could. After she stopped writing, she read her
work and began squeezing even more information between paragraphs and sentences
and in the margins of her paper.

The result was messy. So she made a clean copy of her first draft. This is the version
you are about to read. It contains more detail than her journal entry and is better organized. Still, it is only a first, or working, draft.

Waitressing

1
It was a typical Saturday night. I was standing
there, paying no attention to the usual racket of the
dinner crowd. The restaurant was crowded. I was waiting
for my next table. I try to listen to the sounds around
me. I hear the stereo.

2
In come my eight oclock reservation, fifteen minutes
late. There is an elderly woman with them. She reminded
me of something that happened when I started working
there many years before. Recalling that story taught me
to look back and laugh at myself.

3
When my second child was born, it became clear that
I needed to find a part-time job to help make ends meet.
A friend said I should waitress at the restaurant where
she worked. I thought about it for a few days. I decided

to give it a try. I bluffed my way thru the interview. A
new chapter in my life began. Since then, I have learned
from many mistakes like the one I am going to describe.
My friends told me that, someday, I would look back and
laugh at that night. I guess after fifteen years that
day has come!

I followed another waitress for a few days and then   4
I was released on my own. All went well that first week.
When Saturday night came, I had butterflies in my stom-
ache. I was given four tables not far from the kitchen.
It was an easy station. Oh, God, was I happy, however I
still felt awkward carrying those heavy trays. Before I
new it, the restaurant was packed resembling mid-day on
wall street. I moved slowly organising every move. I
remember the tray stand in my station. It looked a little different then the one I was trained on. It had nice
grips for handles of which made it easier to move
around. I was amazed at how well things were going. I
was too confident. I remember thinking that I was a born
natural. Than, this jovial looking old man came over,
and taped me on the shoulder, and said "Excuse me, dear,
my wife and I loved watching you work. It seems your
tray stand has been very handy for you, but we are getting ready to leave now, and my wife needs her walker
back." I wanted to crawl into a hole and hide. What a
fool I made of myself. I was so glad when that night
ended.

Since then, I have learned from many mistakes such   5
as the one I just described.

REVISING THE WORKING DRAFT

The essay above makes for entertaining reading. But Diglio knew it could be
improved, so she revised it *several times* to get to the last draft of her paper, which
appears below. Although this draft is not perfect, it is more complete, effective, and polished than the one you just read.

Lessons Learned

It was a typical Saturday night at Carpaccio's   1
Restaurant. I was standing there, paying no attention to
the usual merrymaking of the dinner crowd. Just two of
the restaurant's twenty-five tables were vacant. As I
waited for my next table, I absorbed a few of the sounds
around me: clanging trays, the ringing of the cash reg-

ister. I could even hear Dean Martin belting out a
familiar Italian song in the background.

Finally, in come my eight o'clock party. As they   2
were seated, my attention was drawn to an elderly woman
with a walker slowly shuffling behind the others. She
brought back a memory I had locked away for fifteen
years.

After the birth of my second child, I needed a part-   3
time job to help make ends meet. A friend suggested I
apply for a waitressing job at a new restaurant where
she worked. After considering it for a few days, I
decided to give it a shot. I bluffed my way through the
interview and was hired. A new chapter in my life began
the next evening.

After trailing an experience waitress for a few   4
days, I was allowed to wait tables on my own. All went
well that first week. When Saturday night came, the butterflies in my stomach were set free. I was given the
apprentice station that night, four tables not far from
the kitchen. Oh, God, was I relieved, however I still
felt awkward carrying the heavy trays.

Before I new it, the restaurant was packed; it   5
resembled mid-day on wall street. I moved slowly, organising every step. I remember how impressed I was with
the tray stand in my station, it looked different than
the one I was trained on. It had nice grip-like handles
on it, of which made it easier to manuver. I was amazed
at how well things were going, I began to believe I was
a natural at this job.

Then, a jovial, old man approached, tapped me on the   6
shoulder, and said, "Excuse me, dear, my wife and I
loved watching you work. It seems your tray stand has
been very handy for you, but we are getting ready to
leave now, and my wife needs her walker back."

At first his message did not register. "What was he   7
talking about!" Then, it sank in. I had set my trays on
his wife's orthopedic walker. I stood there frozen as
ice, but my face was on fire. I wanted to crawl into a
hole; I wanted to hibernate.

Since then, I have learned from many mistakes such   8
as the one I just described. I have learned to be more
observant and more careful. I have learned to guard
against overconfidence, for no matter how well things
are going, something will come along eventually to gum
up the works. Most of all, I have learned that the best

```
way to get over honest embarrassment is to look back and
laugh at yourself.
```

As this last draft shows, Diglio made several important changes to improve her essay:

1. She changed the title to make her purpose clearer; "Waitressing" didn't say much about the point of her story.
2. She moved the central idea—the point she wants it to make—to the end. This allows her to tell her story first and then to explain its importance in a way that is both clear and interesting. It also makes her conclusion more effective and memorable.
3. She added details to make her writing exact and vivid. Just compare the beginnings of each draft. In the later version, Diglio names the restaurant, and she explains that just two of its "twenty-five tables were vacant," not simply that it was "crowded." She even mentions that "Dean Martin [was] belting out a familiar Italian song."
4. She reorganized paragraph 4 into several new paragraphs. Each of these focuses on a different idea, makes a new point, or tells us another part of the story. Thus, the essay becomes easier to read.
5. She removed unnecessary words to eliminate repetition and make her writing more direct.
6. She replaced some words with more exact and interesting substitutes. In paragraph 1, the dinner crowd's "racket" is changed to "merrymaking"; in paragraph 4, "I was happy" becomes "I was relieved."
7. She combined short choppy sentences into longer, smoother ones to add variety and interest.
8. She corrected some—but not all—problems with spelling, verb tenses, punctuation, sentence structure, and mechanics.

EDITING THE FINAL DRAFT

Although Diglio's last version is much better than the draft with which she began, she owed it to her readers to review her paper once more. She wanted to remove annoying errors that could interfere with their appreciation of her work. Using a pencil, a dictionary, and a handbook of college writing skills recommended by her instructor, she corrected problems in grammar, spelling, punctuation, capitalization, and style in her final draft. Here's what just two paragraphs from that draft looked like after she edited them. (If you want to practice your own editing skills, you can go back and correct the rest of Diglio's paper after you review her changes in what follows.)

```
                                    d
    After trailing an experience⌄waitress for a few days.

I was allowed to wait tables on my own. All went well

that first week. When Saturday night came, the butterflies

in my stomach were set free. I was given the apprentice
```

station that night, four tables not far from the kitchen.
Oh, God, was I relieved/ ; however, I still felt awkward
carrying the heavy trays.

    Before I knew it, the restaurant was packed; it resembled
mid-day on Wall Street. I moved slowly, organizing every
steps. I remember how impressed I was with the tray stand in
my station/ ; it looked different ~~than~~ from the one I was trained
on. It had nice grip-like handles on it, ~~of~~ which made it
easier to maneuver. I was amazed at how well things were
going, and I began to believe I was a natural at this job.

Of course, an entire paper full of such corrections is too sloppy to submit in a college composition class. Therefore, after correcting her final draft in pencil, Diglio prepared one last, clean copy of her paper. It was this copy that she gave her instructor.

Each of us is unique in the way he or she writes. The methods you use to put together a paper may be different from those Deborah Diglio used. They also may be different from the ways your friends or classmates choose to write. And no one says any of the steps outlined above has to be done separately from the others. In fact, some folks revise while they edit. Some continue to gather information as they write their second, third, and even fourth drafts. Nevertheless, writing is serious business. Completing just one or two drafts of an essay will never allow you to produce the quality of work you are capable of! You owe it to your readers and to yourself to respect the process of writing and to work hard at every step in that process, regardless of the way or the order in which you choose to do so. (If you want to learn more about the process of writing, read Richard Marius's "Writing and Its Rewards" in Chapter 2.)

ORGANIZATION
AND
DEVELOPMENT

In "Getting Started" you learned several ways to gather facts, ideas, and opinions about the subjects you choose to write about. Collecting sufficient information about your subject—making sure that you know as much about it as you need to—is an important first step in the writing process.

Next, you will need to determine what it is about your subject that you wish to communicate and how to use your information to get your point across clearly and effectively. Learning how to make such decisions is what the four chapters of Section One are all about.

In Chapter 1 you will learn that two of the most crucial steps early in the writing process are *focusing* and *limiting* the information you've collected so that you can begin to decide upon a *central idea*. Sometimes referred to as the "main" or "controlling" idea, the central idea of a paragraph or essay expresses the main point its writer wishes to develop.

The process of deciding on a central idea begins with a review of information you collected in your journal through focused freewriting, brainstorming, and the other prewriting techniques explained in "Getting Started." You can then evaluate these details to determine what they say about your subject and to decide exactly what you want to tell your readers about it. Always keep your journal handy. The more information you collect about a subject, the easier it is to find an interesting central idea. Once you have found it, the central idea will help you choose the kinds and amounts of detail needed to develop your writing effectively.

Chapter 2 introduces you to *unity* and *coherence*, two key principles to observe in organizing information. The section on unity explains how to choose details that best accomplish your purpose and relate most directly to your central idea. The section on coherence shows you how to create connections in and between paragraphs in order to maintain your reader's interest and to make your writing easy to follow.

Chapter 3, "Development," shows you how to determine the amount of detail a paragraph or essay should contain. It also explains ways to arrange these details and develop ideas. Chapter 4, "Introductions and Conclusions," suggests techniques to create effective openings and closings in essays.

The reading selections in Section One contain examples of the important principles of organization and development explained in the chapter introductions. They are also a rich source of interesting topics to develop in your own writing. However, like the other selections in *A Reader for Developing Writers,* each has a value all its own. Whether written by professionals or by college students like you, these paragraphs and essays discuss people, places, or ideas you are sure to find interesting, informative, humorous, and even touching. Here's hoping they will inspire you to continue reading and writing about a variety of subjects, especially those you care about most!

THE CENTRAL IDEA

An important concern for any writer is the ability to organize information in a form that is easy to follow. The best way to do this is to arrange, or focus, the details you've collected around a central idea.

IDENTIFYING THE CENTRAL IDEA

The central idea is often called the "main idea" because it conveys the writer's main point. It is also called the "controlling idea," for it controls (or determines) the kinds and amounts of detail that a paragraph or essay contains.

The central idea is the focal point to which all the other ideas in an essay or paragraph point. Just as you focus a camera by aiming at a fixed point, you focus your writing by making all the details it contains relate directly to the central idea. Everything you include should help prove, illustrate, or support the central idea. You might also think of a central idea as an umbrella. It is the broadest or most general statement in an essay or paragraph; all other information fits under it.

Read these next two paragraphs; their central ideas (in italics) act as focal points to which everything else points. Notice that the central ideas are broader than the details that support them. The diagrams that follow illustrate these two concepts:

> *Talk about bad days: today is a classic.* First, I woke up to hear my parents screaming in my ear about a bill I have to pay. Then I went to school to find out I had failed my art project. After that, I called home to learn that I might have my license revoked, and the accident wasn't even my fault. Finally, while walking out of the cafeteria, I tripped over somebody's book bag and made myself look like an ass. And it's only two in the afternoon! (Donna Amiano, "Bad Days")

> *My life is full of risks.* As a stair builder who works with heavy machinery, I risk cutting off a finger or a limb every day. Each Monday and Thursday, I risk four or five dollars on the state lottery. Every time I take my beat-up, 1981 Chevy Caprice Classic for a drive, I risk breaking down. However, the biggest risk I've ever taken was my decision to attend DeVry Institute this year. (Kenneth Dwyer, "Risks")

In most cases the central idea of a paragraph is expressed in a *topic sentence,* and the central idea of an essay is expressed in a *thesis statement.* In some pieces of writing, how-

Central idea = focal point.

Supporting details
point to central idea

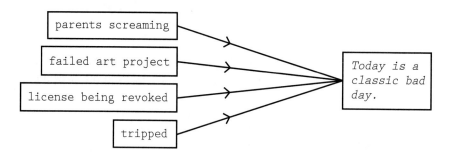

Central idea = umbrella under which supporting details fit.

ever, the central idea is so obvious that the author does not need to state it in a formal topic sentence or thesis statement. In such cases, the central idea is said to be implied. This is often true of narration and description, the kinds of writing you will read in Sections Three and Four. However, it can apply to all types of writing. In this chapter, for example, a paragraph in which the central idea is only implied appears on page 37; it is entitled "Women in Early Islam."

Nonetheless, as a developing writer, you should always state the central idea outright—as a topic sentence when you write a paragraph or as a thesis statement when you tie several paragraphs together in an essay. Doing so will help you focus on specific ideas and organize information.

Often, authors state the central idea early, placing the topic sentence or thesis at the very beginning of a paragraph or essay. However, this is not always the best place for it. For example, you first might have to give readers explanatory details or background materials. In such cases, you can place your topic sentence or thesis somewhere in the middle or even at the end of a paragraph or essay. Delaying the central idea can also create suspense. Finally, it is a good way to avoid offending readers who at first may be opposed to an opinion you are presenting.

WRITING A PRELIMINARY TOPIC SENTENCE OR THESIS STATEMENT

As a developing writer, make sure you have a good grasp of the central ideas that will control the paragraphs and essays you write. You can do this early in the writing process by jotting down a working version of your central idea on a piece of scratch paper or in your journal. This will be your *preliminary* topic sentence or thesis statement. It is called "preliminary" because you can and often should make significant changes in this version of your topic sentence or thesis statement after you've begun to write your paragraph or essay.

Of course, before you draft a preliminary topic sentence or thesis, you must choose a subject to write about. Keep in mind that by its very nature a subject represents a kind of thinking that is abstract, general, and incomplete. A central idea, on the other hand, is a concrete, specific, and complete expression of thought. For example, notice how much more meaningful the subject "waterskiing" becomes when you turn it into a central idea: "Waterskiing can be *dangerous.*"

In order to turn any subject into a central idea, whether it winds up as the topic sentence of a paragraph or the thesis of an essay, you will have to *focus* and *limit* your discussion of a subject by saying something concrete and specific about it. Focusing and limiting are important thinking processes that will help you begin to organize the information you've collected about your subject. Here's how they work.

FOCUS YOUR DISCUSSION

A good time to think about focusing on a central idea and drafting a working thesis or topic sentence is immediately after you have reviewed your journal for facts, ideas, and opinions that you gathered through prewriting as explained in "Getting Started." While these important details are still fresh in your mind, ask yourself three questions:

1. *Purpose:* What do I want this piece of writing to accomplish?
2. *Main Point:* What is the main point I wish to communicate about my subject?
3. *Details:* What details can I use to develop this main point?

PURPOSE   As well as you can at this stage in the writing process, determine your purpose—what you want your essay or paragraph to do. For instance, it may be to entertain the reader with a humorous story, to explain a natural process, to compare two types of music, to warn readers of a health hazard, or to convince them to adopt your position on a social issue.

Once you have determined your purpose, you will be able to decide on your main point more easily, for you will already have begun determining which of the details you have gathered will be useful and which will not.

Let's say your purpose is to describe a forest you hiked through last fall. You review your notes and decide to include details about the colors—brilliant reds, burnt oranges, bright yellows—against which you saw a small herd of white-tailed deer. You also consider describing other things you saw, such as the old truck tire dumped on the side of the trail or the two hunters dressed in green and orange camouflage gear. On the other hand, you decide not to tell readers that you traveled three hours in an old pickup to get there, that you bumped into a high school friend as you were leaving, or that you met a forest ranger who had dated Aunt Bertha. None of these facts describe the forest.

MAIN POINT   The next step is to determine exactly what you want to say about your walk through the woods. Ask yourself what for *you* is the most interesting or important aspect of the subject. This will be your *main point*, the point that will help you tie all the details together logically.

In short, you can turn a subject into a central idea by making a main point about the subject. If you decide that the most interesting or important aspect of your walk in the forest is that it was *inspiring,* your central idea might read: "The forest I hiked through this autumn was inspiring."

As you learned earlier, focusing lets the writer turn an abstract, general, incomplete subject into the central idea for a paragraph or essay. Notice how much clearer, more specific, and more complete the central ideas on the right are than the abstract subjects on the left:

SUBJECT	CENTRAL IDEA
My fall walk in the forest	My fall walk in the forest was inspiring.
Aunt Isabel	Aunt Isabel was a hero.
Rock music	Rock music can damage your hearing.
Electric cars	Electric cars can replace gasoline models.
The Battle of Gettysburg	The Battle of Gettysburg was the turning point of the Civil War.
Homeless children	The government should guarantee homeless children proper nutrition, education, and health care.

As you can see, focusing on a main point helps change an abstract idea into something specific and concrete—into a central idea.

DETAILS   Focusing also provides a starting point for a first draft of an essay because it helps you choose between the details to include and those to discard. If you decide to focus on the inspirational aspects of the forest, for example, you ought to include a description of the changing leaves and of the deer, but should you also mention the old tire and the hunters? They are certainly part of the experience, but do they relate to the notion that your hike was inspirational? Probably not.

LIMIT YOUR DISCUSSION TO A MANAGEABLE LENGTH

Typically, students are asked to write short essays, usually ranging between 250 and 750 words, with paragraphs seldom longer than 75 words. That's why one of the most important things to remember when writing a thesis statement or topic sentence is to limit your central idea as much as you can. Otherwise, you won't be able to develop it in as much detail as will be necessary to make your point clearly, effectively, and completely.

Let's say you are about to buy a car and want to compare two popular makes. In a short essay it would be foolish to compare these automobiles in more than two or three different ways. Therefore, you might limit yourself to cost, appearance, and comfort, rather than discuss their performance, handling, and sound systems as well. You might even limit your central idea to only one of these aspects—cost, for instance. You can then divide cost into more specific subsections, which will be easier to organize when it comes time to write your first draft. The thesis for such an essay might read:

I chose the 1996 Mountain Marauder over the 1996 Cross-Country Schooner because it costs less to buy, to operate, and to repair.

CONTROLLING UNITY AND DEVELOPMENT

At the beginning of this chapter, you read that the central idea can be called the "controlling idea" because it helps the writer determine the kind and amount of information a paragraph or essay contains. This is explained further in Chapters 2 and 3.

For now, remember that the kinds of details a piece of writing contains determine whether it is unified. A paragraph is unified if its sentences relate directly to its central idea, whether or not that idea is expressed formally in a topic sentence. An essay is unified if its paragraphs relate directly to its central idea, whether or not that idea is expressed in a thesis statement.

The amount of detail a piece of writing contains determines whether it is well developed. A paragraph or essay is well developed if it contains all the detail it needs to prove, illustrate, or otherwise support its central idea.

REVISING THE CENTRAL IDEA

One last and very important bit of advice. Always revise the working, or preliminary, versions of your thesis statements and topic sentences during the writing process. Like taking notes or writing a first draft of a paper, writing a preliminary version of a thesis statement or topic sentence is intended only to give you a starting point and a sense of direction. Don't be afraid to reword, edit, or completely rewrite your central idea at any point. Like all processes, writing involves a series of steps or tasks to be completed. However, there is no rule that prevents you from stopping at any point along the way, looking back upon what you've done, and changing it as thoroughly and as often as you like. What's more, the process of writing always includes discovery. The more you discover about your subject, the more likely you are to understand it better and to revise what you *thought* you had wanted to say about it.

As an example, study three drafts of the introductory paragraphs from Maria Cirilli's essay "Echoes." Each time she revised her work, Cirilli came to a clearer understanding of her subject and of what she wanted to say about it. This can be seen best in the last sentence, which is Cirilli's thesis statement. A complete version of "Echoes" appears at the end of this chapter.

Cirilli—Draft #1

I hardly remember my grandmother except for the fact that she used to bounce me on her knees by the old-fashioned brick fireplace and sing old songs. I was only four years old when she died. Her face is a faded image in the back of my mind.

In contrast, I remember my grandfather very well. He was 6'4" tall. He possessed a deep voice, which distinguished him from others whether he was in the streets of our small picture-perfect town in southern Italy or in the graciously sculptured seventeenth century church. He appeared to be strong and powerful. In fact he used to scare all my girlfriends away when they came to play or do homework. Yet, I knew that there was nothing to be afraid of.

Is this thesis clear? Does it tell what the essay will say about Cirilli's grandfather?

Cirilli—Draft #2

I hardly remember my grandmother except for the fact that she used to bounce me on her knees by the old-fashioned brick fireplace and sing old songs. I was only four years old when she died.

The last sentence of Version #1 has been removed.

In contrast, I remember my grandfather very well. He was 6'4" tall, a towering man with broad shoulders and a pair of mustaches that I watched turn from black to grey over the years. He possessed a deep voice, which distinguished him from others whether he was in the streets of our small picture-perfect town in southern Italy or in the graciously sculptured seventeenth century church. He appeared to be strong and powerful. <u>In fact he used to scare all my girlfriends away when they came to play or do homework, yet he was the most gentle man I have ever known</u>.

Detail added to describe him better.

The thesis is clearer. But, will essay also discuss fear?

Cirilli—Draft #3

I hardly remember my grandmother except for the fact that she used to bounce me on her knees by the old-fashioned brick fireplace and sing old songs. I was only four years old when she died. <u>Her face is a faded image in the back of my mind.</u>

Cirilli reuses this sentence from Draft #1.

In contrast, I remember my grandfather very well. He was 6'4" tall, a towering man with broad shoulders and a mustache that I watched turn from black to grey. He voice was deep, distinguishing him from others in the our small picture-perfect town in southern Italy. To some, my grandfather appeared very powerful, and he used to scare my girlfriends away when they came to play or do homework. <u>In fact, he</u>

Detail about church removed; not needed

was strong, but he was the gentlest and most

understanding man I have ever known.

**Thesis is expanded.
Now includes
"most understanding."**

**Thesis stands
alone in its
own sentence.
Much clearer**

PRACTICING WRITING CENTRAL IDEAS

To turn a subject into a central idea, you must express a main point about the subject. In the left column are subjects you might discuss in a paragraph or essay. Turn them into central ideas by writing your main point in the spaces provided. To think of an effective main point, ask yourself what is most interesting or most important about the subject. When you join your subject and main point, be sure to create a complete sentence. A complete sentence has a subject and a verb. The first item is done for you as an example.

┌──────── **CENTRAL IDEA** ────────┐
SUBJECT   **MAIN POINT**

1. A successful diet   _requires much will power._

2. College textbooks   _____

    _____

3. Computers   _____

    _____

4. My family   _____

    _____

5. Noise pollution   _____

    _____

6. Listening to music   _____

    _____

7. Professional athletes   _____

    _____

8. AIDS (or another disease) _____

    _____

9. Learning to drive (swim, play tennis,   _____

    use a computer, cook, fix cars, etc.)   _____

10. Studying mathematics (science,   _____

    accounting, a foreign language, etc.)   _____

                                         _____

The reading selections that follow illustrate the organizational principles just discussed. Read them carefully, take notes, and respond to the Questions for Discussion and the Suggestions for Journal Entries that accompany them. Doing so will give you an even better understanding of the central idea and its importance to organization.

From *The Sea Around Us*

Rachel Carson

Rachel Carson (1907–1964) was one of the founders of the American environmental movement and one of its most eloquent spokespersons. It was she, more than anyone else, who helped convince people of the terrible effects of chemical pollution. In 1951 she won the National Book Award for The Sea Around Us, *from which this paragraph is taken.*

LOOKING AHEAD

1. Carson begins with a statement of her central idea. As you read this paragraph, ask yourself what main point she is making about the sea in her topic sentence.
2. You've learned that before deciding on a central idea you must ask yourself what you want to accomplish. Try to determine Carson's purpose when she wrote this paragraph from *The Sea Around Us.*

VOCABULARY

accounts	Reports, stories.
cosmic	Of the world, of the universe.
testimony	Written or spoken evidence.

*From The Sea
Around Us*   *Rachel Carson*

Beginnings are apt to be shadowy, and so it is with the beginnings of that great mother of life, the sea. Many people have debated how and when the earth got its ocean, and it is not surprising that their explanations do not always agree. For the plain and inescapable truth is that no one was there to see, and in the absence of eyewitness accounts there is bound to be a certain amount of disagreement. So if I tell here the story of how the young planet Earth acquired an ocean, it must be a story pieced together from many sources and containing whole chapters the details of which we can only imagine. The story is founded on the testimony of the earth's most ancient rocks, which were young when the earth was young; on other evidence written on the face of the earth's satellite, the moon; and on hints contained in the history of the sun and the whole universe of star-filled space. For although no man was there to witness this cosmic birth, the stars and the moon and the rocks were there, and, indeed, had much to do with the fact that there is an ocean.

QUESTIONS FOR DISCUSSION

1. What is the paragraph's subject? What is the author's purpose?
2. Reread Carson's topic sentence. What one word in that sentence establishes her focus and reveals her main point about "Beginnings"?
3. What details does she use to develop or explain her main point later in the paragraph?

THINKING CRITICALLY

Carson pieces together the story of how the ocean was formed from many sources. Reread the paragraph and underline as many sources as you can. Then, in your journal, write a complete sentence that mentions each of them. You might start it this way: "Carson says we learned about the origin of the sea from . . . ."

SUGGESTIONS FOR JOURNAL ENTRIES

1. Think about a subject you know well. Then list some points that make the subject interesting or important to you. Here are two examples of what your list might look like:

SUBJECT	IMPORTANT POINTS ABOUT THE SUBJECT
Swimming	good aerobic workout strengthens heart and lungs inexpensive fairly safe helps lose weight
Waiting tables at Benny's Pizza	pays tuition requires talent reason I hate pizza meet interesting folks

2. Review the list you made for Suggestion 1. Then write two topic sentences, each of which combines the subject and one of the points you made about it. Here are some examples:

Swimming strengthens the heart and lungs.
Swimming can help you lose weight.

Waiting tables at Benny's Pizza requires talent.
Waiting tables at Benny's Pizza allows me to meet interesting people.

Remember: A topic sentence is a complete sentence. Make sure it has a subject and a verb and expresses a complete idea.

Four Paragraphs for Analysis

The selection by Rachel Carson you just read shows the importance of focusing on a central idea. The same is true of the four paragraphs that follow. Written by various authors, they discuss four different ideas, but each focuses clearly on a main point developed through detail.

Gilbert Muller and Harvey Wiener are English professors and scholars. "On Writing" first appeared in a textbook they wrote for college students.

Richard Marius, the author of "Writing Things Down," is the director of Harvard University's expository writing program. Another selection by Marius appears in Chapter 2.

Ernest Albrecht is a professor of English, a drama critic, and the author of two books on the circus.

Naila Minai is the author of Women in Early Islam, *a full-length history in which the last of these four paragraphs appears.*

L O O K I N G   A H E A D

As the following paragraphs show, a writer who wants to express a central idea in a topic sentence need not put that sentence first. Depending upon the paragraph's purpose, the author might provide a few sentences of background or explanation first. He or she might even wait until the end of the paragraph to reveal the central idea and, thus, create suspense or emphasis. In fact, as you will see in "Women in Early Islam," the last paragraph, writers sometimes choose not to express central ideas in topic sentences at all. Instead, they allow readers to draw their own conclusions. In such cases, the central idea is implied.

V O C A B U L A R Y

caravan	Line of pack animals used to transport goods across the desert.
conjured	Called up, imagined.
debris	Waste, litter.
discipline	Academic subject, area of study.
hippodrome	Arena for horses.
lathe	Machine for shaping wood.

liberal arts	Branch of academic study including language, literature, philosophy, and history.
Mecca	Place of Mohammed's birth and Islam's holiest city.
random	By chance.
roustabouts	Workers, laborers.
rifle through	Search through vigorously.

On Writing | *Gilbert Muller and Harvey Wiener*

Few writers begin without some warm-up activity. Generally called prewriting, the steps they take before producing a draft almost always start with thinking about their topic. They talk to friends and colleagues; they browse in libraries and rifle through reference books; they read newspaper and magazine articles. Sometimes they jot down notes and lists in order to put on paper some of their thoughts in very rough form. Some writers use free-association: they record as thoroughly as possible their random, unedited ideas about the topic. Using the raw, often disorganized materials produced in this preliminary stage, many writers try to group related thoughts with a scratch outline or some other effort to bring order to their written notes.

Writing Things Down*

Richard Marius

In our zeal to think of writing as communication, we may forget how much writing helps us know things—to arrange facts, to see how they are related to one another, and to decide what they mean. Nothing helps the mind and memory more than writing things down. Everyone who has taught a discipline such as history, literature, economics, or philosophy has had at least one student who protests, "I *know* it; I just can't *write* it." In fact, a person who cannot write about a discipline in the liberal arts rarely knows anything about it except a disconnected jumble of useless facts.

*Editor's title

Sawdust | *Ernest Albrecht*

As a ten year old, I watched as miniature mountains of the magical debris took shape around my father's lathe or his table saw, and with hardly any effort at all I imagined three rings and a hippodrome track sprinkled with the stuff in various colors. Having once conjured that, it didn't take much more effort to envision the ropes and cables that the circus roustabouts spun into a fantastic web transforming the old Madison Square Garden on Eighth Avenue and 49th Street (New York) into an exotic world of wonder and fantasy. That is why, of all the changes that progress has wrought upon the circus, I lament the loss of the sawdust the most. Rubber mats may be practial, but they have no magic.

*Women in Early
Islam* | *Naila Minai*

Khadija, an attractive forty-year-old Arabian widow, ran a flourishing caravan business in Mecca in the seventh century A.D., and was courted by the most eligible men of her society. But she had eyes only for an intelligent and hard-working twenty-five-year-old in her employ named Muhammad. "What does she see in a penniless ex-shepherd?" her scandalized aristocratic family whispered among themselves. Accustomed to having her way, however, Khadija proposed to Muhammad and married him. Until her death some twenty-five years later, her marriage was much more than the conventional Cinderella story in reverse, for Khadija not only bore six children while co-managing her business with her husband, but also advised and financed him in his struggle to found Islam, which grew to be one of the major religions of the world.

QUESTIONS FOR DISCUSSION

1. What are the topic sentences in the first three paragraphs?
2. What, in your own words, is the central idea in the fourth paragraph, "Women in Early Islam"?
3. Would "On Writing" have been as effective and easy to read if the topic sentence appeared in the middle or at the end of the paragraph?
4. What important information does Marius provide before the topic sentence in "Writing Things Down"?
5. What is the main point of "Sawdust"? Why does Albrecht wait until the end of the paragraph to reveal it?

THINKING CRITICALLY

Remember that a central idea acts as an umbrella under which all the details and other, more limited, ideas in a paragraph or essay fit. The central idea for the following paragraph is unstated. Read the paragraph; then, in your journal, write your own central idea for it in a complete topic sentence. Remember, the idea in a topic sentence is broader than any other idea in a paragraph.

> The planet Mars takes its name from the Roman god of war. Mercury is the Roman god of commerce; and Venus, the goddess of love. Pluto is named for the Greek god of the underworld, Neptune rules the sea, and Jupiter reigns as king of the gods. Even the planets Saturn and Uranus borrow their names from ancient deities.

SUGGESTION FOR A JOURNAL ENTRY

This journal entry is in three parts:

First, pick a limited subject you know a lot about. Here are some examples: waiting on tables, last year's Fourth of July picnic, your bedroom at home, feeding a baby, your car, studying math, your Uncle Mort, going to a concert, watching baseball on television.

Second, decide what are the most interesting or important points you can make about that subject. Choose *one* of these as the main point of a central idea. Write that central idea down in the form of a topic sentence for a paragraph you might want to write later.

Third, do the same with three or four other limited subjects you know about. Here's what your journal entry might look like when you're done:

1. Limited Subject: Feeding a baby
   Main Points: Sometimes messy, always fun
   Topic Sentence: Feeding a baby can be messy.
2. Limited Subject: Uncle Mort
   Main Points: Old, handsome, outgoing, considerate
   Topic Sentence: My Uncle Mort was one of the most considerate people in my family.
3. Limited Subject: Last year's Fourth of July picnic
   Main Points: Much food, many people, lots of rain
   Topic Sentence: Last year's Fourth of July picnic was a washout.

Three Passions I Have Lived For

Bertrand Russell

One of the most widely read philosophers and mathematicians of the twentieth century, Bertrand Russell (1872–1970) is even better remembered as a social and political activist. For many years, he was considered an extremely unorthodox thinker because of his liberal opinions on sex, marriage, and homosexuality. Politically, Russell was a socialist and pacifist. In the 1950s and 1960s he became one of the leaders of the ban-the-bomb movement in Europe, and later he helped organize opposition to U.S. involvement in Vietnam.

Among his most famous works are Principles of Mathematics, A History of Western Philosophy, *and a three-volume autobiography in which the selection that follows first appeared. Russell won the Nobel Prize in literature in 1950.*

LOOKING AHEAD

1. The first paragraph contains Russell's thesis. Read it carefully; it will give you clues about the topic sentences on which he develops three of the paragraphs that follow.
2. The word "passions" should be understood as deep, personal concerns that Russell developed over the course of his life and that had a significant influence on the way he lived.

VOCABULARY

abyss	Deep hole.
alleviate	Lessen, soften, make less harsh or painful.
anguish	Grief, sorrow, pain.
consciousness	Mind, intelligence.
mockery	Ridicule, scorn.
prefiguring	Predicting, forecasting.
reverberate	Resound, repeatedly echo.
unfathomable	Unmeasurable.
verge	Edge.

Three Passions I Have Lived For | *Bertrand Russell*

Three passions, simple but overwhelmingly strong, have governed my life: the longing for love, the search for knowledge, and unbearable pity for the suffering of mankind. These passions, like great winds, have blown me hither and thither, in a wayward course over a deep ocean of anguish, reaching to the very verge of despair. 1

I have sought love, first, because it brings ecstasy—ecstasy so great that I would often have sacrificed all the rest of my life for a few hours of this joy. I have sought it, next, because it relieves loneliness—that terrible loneliness in which one shivering consciousness looks over the rim of the world into the cold unfathomable lifeless abyss. I have sought it, finally, because in the union of love I have seen, in a mystic miniature, the prefiguring vision of the heaven that saints and poets have imagined. This is what I sought, and though it might seem too good for human life, this is what—at last—I have found. 2

With equal passion I have sought knowledge. I have wished to understand the hearts of men. I have wished to know why the stars shine. . . . A little of this, but not much, I have achieved. 3

Love and knowledge, so far as they were possible, led upward toward the heavens. But always pity brought me back to earth. Echoes of cries of pain reverberate in my heart. Children in famine, victims tortured by oppressors, helpless old people a hated burden to their sons, and the whole world of loneliness, poverty, and pain make a mockery of what human life should be. I long to alleviate the evil, but I cannot, and I too suffer. 4

This has been my life. I have found it worth living, and would gladly live it again if the chance were offered me. 5

QUESTIONS FOR DISCUSSION

1. The title gives us a clue about why Russell wrote this selection. What was his purpose?
2. Russell expresses the central idea—the thesis—in paragraph 1. What is his thesis?
3. In your own words, explain each of the central ideas—topic sentences—in paragraphs 2, 3, and 4. In other words, what three passions did Russell live for?
4. How do these three passions relate to the thesis?
5. What details does Russell use to develop the topic sentence in paragraph 2? In paragraph 3? In paragraph 4? Explain how these details relate to their topic sentences in each case.
6. You've learned in this chapter how to limit your discussion to a manageable length. In what ways did Russell make sure to limit his essay's length?

THINKING CRITICALLY

Russell lists reasons for seeking love and knowledge. What *other* reasons might someone have for seeking them? In your journal, write a paragraph of between 50 and 100 words explaining why you are seeking love, knowledge, or some other personal "passion." Focus on only one of these. Start your paragraph with a topic sentence modeled after the ones Russell uses.

SUGGESTIONS FOR JOURNAL ENTRIES

1. In your own words, summarize the three reasons Russell has "sought love."
2. In Looking Ahead you read that Russell used the word "passions" to describe the deep, personal concerns that determined the way he lived. Using Russell's essay as a model, write a series of topic sentences for paragraphs that describe the passions—at least three of them—that *you* live for. The kinds of passions you mention should be personal and real. Remember to limit each topic sentence to one and only one passion. If you're embarrassed to write about yourself, write about someone else's passions. Here are some examples:

One of the most important concerns in my life is getting a good education.
My religion is the cornerstone of my existence.
My brother lives to eat.
My grandmother's most important concern was her children.
Mother Teresa's sole purpose in life is to serve the poor.

Echoes

Maria Cirilli

Born in a small town in southern Italy, Maria Cirilli immigrated to the United States in 1971. She earned her associate's degree in nursing from a community college and is now an assistant head nurse at the Robert Wood Johnson University Hospital in New Brunswick, New Jersey. Cirilli has completed her bachelor's in nursing from the University of Medicine and Dentistry of New Jersey. Since writing "Echoes" for a college composition class, she has revised it several times to add detail and make it more powerful.

Looking **A**head

Cirilli chose not to reveal the central idea of this essay—her thesis statement—in paragraph 1. However, the first paragraph is important because it contains information that we can contrast with what we read in paragraph 2.

Vocabulary

distinguished	Made different from.
exuberance	Joy, enthusiasm.
manicured	Neat, well cared for.
mediator	Referee, someone who helps settle disputes.
negotiating	Bargaining, dealing.
placate	Pacify, make calm.
siblings	Sisters and brothers.
solemnly	Seriously.
tribulation	Trouble, distress.
vulnerable	Open, without defenses.
with a vengeance	Skillfully, earnestly.

Echoes | *Maria Cirilli*

I hardly remember my grandmother except for the fact that she used to bounce me   1
on her knees by the old-fashioned brick fireplace and sing old songs. I was only
four when she died. Her face is a faded image in the back of my mind.

In contrast, I remember my grandfather very well. He was 6´4˝ tall, a towering man   2
with broad shoulders and a mustache that I watched turn from black to grey. His voice
was deep, distinguishing him from others in our small picture-perfect town in southern
Italy. To some, my grandfather appeared very powerful, and he used to scare my girlfriends away when they came to play or do homework. In fact, he was strong, but he was
the gentlest and most understanding man I have ever known.

I still see him weeping softly as he read a romantic novel in which his favorite   3
character died after many trials and much tribulation. And I will never forget how carefully he set the tiny leg of our pet bird, Iario, who had become entangled in a fight with
frisky Maurizio, our cat. Once, my brother and I accompanied him to our grandmother's grave at a nearby cemetery that was small but manicured. As we approached
the cemetery, my tall grandfather bent down from time to time to pick wild flowers
along the road. By the end of the journey, he had a dandy little bouquet, which he
placed solemnly at my grandmother's grave while bountiful tears streamed down his
husky, vulnerable face.

My grandfather was always available to people. Mostly, he helped senior citizens   4
apply for disability or pension benefits or file medical-insurance claims. Several times,
however, he was asked to placate siblings who had quarreled over a family inheritance.
Many angry faces stormed into our home dissatisfied with what they had received, but
they usually left smiling, convinced by my grandfather that their parents had, after all,
distributed their possessions fairly.

At times, he could even play Cupid by resolving disputes between couples   5
engaged to be married. Whether the problem concerned which family would pay for
the wedding or who would buy the furniture, he would find a solution. As a result,
our family attended many weddings in which my proud grandfather sat at the table of
honor.

On Sundays, there was always a tray of fresh, homemade cookies and a pot of coffee   6
on our oversized kitchen table for visitors who stopped by after Mass. Seeking advice
about purchasing land or a house, they asked my grandfather if he thought the price
was fair, the property valuable, the land productive. After a time, he took on the role of
mediator, negotiating with a vengeance to obtain the fairest deal for both buyer and
seller.

I remember most vividly the hours we children spent listening to our grandfa-   7
ther's stories. He sat by the fireplace in his wooden rocking chair and told us about the
time he had spent in America. Each one of us kids would aim for the chair closest to
him. We didn't want to miss anything he said. He told us about a huge tunnel, the
Lincoln Tunnel, that was built under water. He also described the legendary Statue
of Liberty. We were fascinated by his stories of that big, industrialized land called
America.

As I grew up and became a teenager, I dreamt of immigrating to America and seeing 8 all the places that my grandfather had talked about. His exuberance about this land had a strong influence on my decision to come here.

A few months before I arrived in America my grandfather died. I still miss him very 9 much, but each time I visit a place that he knew I feel his presence close to me. The sound of his voice echoes in my mind.

QUESTIONS FOR DISCUSSION

1. What important information does Cirilli give us in paragraph 1?
2. What is her thesis? Why does she wait until paragraph 2 to reveal it?
3. Pick out the topic sentences in paragraphs 4 through 7, and explain what each tells us about Cirilli's grandfather.
4. What evidence does the author give to show that her grandfather was "gentle"? How does she prove he was "understanding"?
5. What about Cirilli's grandfather scared her girlfriends? Why does the author give us this information?
6. Why is "Echoes" a good title for this essay?

THINKING CRITICALLY

1. Reread the three versions of Cirilli's introduction, which appear earlier in this chapter (pages 24–26). Then, in your journal, write a paragraph that explains the major differences you see among each version. Use the notes in the margins as guides, but write the paragraph in your own words. If you read carefully, you will find even more differences than those described in the margins.
2. Cirilli tells us that her grandmother's "face is a faded image in the back of [her] mind." Why did she put this line back into the third version after taking it out of the second (page 25)? Explain in two or three sentences why keeping this line is important to Cirilli's essay.

SUGGESTIONS FOR JOURNAL ENTRIES

1. Use focused freewriting to gather information that shows that someone you know practices a particular virtue. Like Cirilli's grandfather, your subject might be gentle or understanding. Then again, he or she might be charitable, hard-working, generous, or considerate of others. Reread paragraph 3 or 4 in "Echoes" to get an idea of the kind of details you might put in your journal.
After completing your entry, read it carefully and add details if you can. Finally, write a sentence that expresses the main point you have made and that might serve as a topic sentence to a paragraph using this information.
2. Think of someone special in your life, and write down a wealth of details about this person. Use brainstorming, interviewing, or any other information-gathering techniques discussed in "Getting Started." Then, discuss this special person in three or four well-written sentences. Like the topic sentences in "Echoes," each of yours should focus on only one main point you want to make about your subject or about your relationship with this person.

SUGGESTIONS FOR SUSTAINED WRITING

1. You may have responded to item 2 of the Suggestions for Journal Entries after the paragraph from Carson's *The Sea Around Us*. If so, you wrote two topic sentences on a particular subject, each of which was to explain a reason you found that subject interesting or important.

   Write one paragraph each for these topic sentences. Make sure that the details you include support or explain the central idea expressed in the paragraph's topic sentence. Here's what a paragraph like the ones you are being asked to write might look like (the topic sentence is in italics):

   > *Preparing a Thanksgiving dinner takes a lot of work.* First you'll have to prepare the stuffing. This means peeling and cutting up the apples, chopping up and soaking the bread, mixing in the raisins and the spices. After you're done, you'll have to stuff the turkey with this gooey mixture. While you're waiting for the bird to roast, you should peel, boil, and mash the potatoes, and cook any other vegetables you will serve. You'll also have to bake the biscuits, set the table, pour the cider, and put the finishing touches on the pumpkin and apple pies you spent three hours preparing the night before.

   As you learned in "Getting Started," don't be satisfied with the first draft of your work; rewrite it several times. Then, correct spelling, grammar, punctuation, and other distracting problems.

2. If you haven't done so already, complete the Suggestion for a Journal Entry after "Four Paragraphs for Analysis." Use *each* of the topic sentences you were asked to write as the beginning of a paragraph in which you explain the main point you are making in that topic sentence. You should wind up with the rough drafts of four or five paragraphs, each of which is several sentences long.

   Rewrite these rough drafts until you are satisfied that your topic sentences are clear and that you have included enough information to help your readers understand the main point in each paragraph easily. Complete the writing process by editing your work just as student writer Deborah Diglio did with her paper in "Getting Started."

3. In "Three Passions I Have Lived For," Bertrand Russell explains three deep, personal concerns that have "governed" his life. If you responded to item 2 in the Suggestions for Journal Entries following this essay, you have probably written a few topic sentences about the passions you or someone you know well lives for.

   Use each of your topic sentences as the basis or beginning of a fully developed paragraph about each of these passions. Next, take the main points expressed in your topic sentences and combine them into a sentence that might serve as the thesis statement to an essay made up of the paragraphs you have just written.

Refer to Russell's essay as a model. Remember that his thesis statement mentions three passions: "the longing for love, the search for knowledge, and unbearable pity for the suffering of mankind." These three passions are used individually as the main points in each of the topic sentences of the paragraphs that follow and develop his thesis.

You should end up with the draft of an essay that contains a thesis statement followed by a few paragraphs, each of which develops one of the points mentioned in that thesis. Don't forget to revise and edit this draft.

4. Write a short essay in which you explain three reasons that you are doing something important in your life. Include these three reasons in a central idea that you will use as your thesis statement. Let's say that you decide to explain three of your reasons for going to college. You might write: "I decided to attend Metropolitan College to prepare for a rewarding career, to meet interesting people, and to learn more about music and literature." Put this thesis somewhere in your introductory paragraph.

Next, use *each* of the reasons in your thesis as the main point in the topic sentences of the three paragraphs that follow. In keeping with the example above, you might use the following as topic sentences for paragraphs 2, 3, and 4. The main point in each topic sentence is in italics:

Paragraph 2: The most important reason I decided to attend Metropolitan College was *to prepare myself for a rewarding career.*
Paragraph 3: *The opportunity to meet interesting people* was another reason I thought that going to college would be a good idea.
Paragraph 4: My decision to continue my schooling also had a lot to do with my desire *to learn more about literature and music.*

Try to develop each of these in a paragraph of three or four sentences that will help you explain the main point of your topic sentence completely and effectively. Finally, as with other assignments in this chapter, revise and edit your work thoroughly.

5. In item 2 of the Suggestions for Journal Entries after Maria Cirilli's "Echoes," you were asked to write three or four sentences, each of which was to focus on a single aspect or characteristic of someone special in your life. Make each of these the topic sentence of a paragraph that describes or explains that aspect or characteristic. If necessary, reread "Echoes." Many of the paragraphs in the body of this essay will serve as models for your writing.

Next, write an appropriate thesis statement for an essay containing the three or four paragraphs you've just written. Make sure that your thesis statement somehow reflects the main points found in the topic sentences of the three or four paragraphs in your essay. Make this thesis part of your essay's first or introductory paragraph.

Again, approach this writing assignment as a process. Complete several drafts of your paper, and don't submit your final product until you are satisfied that you have dealt with problems in grammar, spelling, punctuation, and the like.

UNITY AND COHERENCE

Chapter 1 explained the importance of focusing on a central idea. The central idea is also called the controlling idea. It controls, or determines, the kind of information a writer uses in an essay or paragraph.

Deciding how much information to include in a piece of writing has to do with development, a principle discussed in the next chapter. Deciding what kinds of information to include and making sure such information fits together logically relates to two principles of organization discussed in this chapter: unity and coherence.

CREATING UNITY

A piece of writing is unified if it contains only those details that help develop—explain or support—the central idea. You probably remember from Chapter 1 that a central idea contains both a subject and a main point the writer wishes to make about that subject. In the following paragraph, student Craig Pennypacker uses every detail to explain that "love and infatuation" (his *subject*) are "quite different" (his *main point*):

> *Many people feel that they are in love when they are really only infatuated, but love and infatuation are quite different.* First, infatuation leaps into being, while love takes root and grows one day at a time. Second, infatuation is accompanied by a sense of uncertainty; one is stimulated and thrilled but not really happy. Love, on the other hand, begins with a feeling of security; the lover is warmed by a sense of nearness even when the beloved is away. Third, infatuation tells us to "get married right away." Meanwhile, love advises: "Don't rush into anything; learn to trust each other." These are important differences. Unfortunately, too many people overlook them and wind up getting hurt in the end.

In contrast to what you read in Craig's paragraph, beginning writers sometimes mistakenly include information that is irrelevant—information that does not help explain or support the central idea. Guard against this problem. Including irrelevant material only sidetracks the reader, drawing attention away from your main point and toward details unimportant to your central idea. With such unrelated material, your writing will lack unity, and your reader will have difficulty determining exactly what it is you want to say.

The following paragraph about seventeenth-century Moscow is from Robert K. Massie's biography of Czar Peter the Great. However, it has been rewritten so it now contains many details unrelated to its central idea. This material was added to show that irrelevant details destroy the focus of a piece of writing.

> [1]Not unnaturally in a city built of wood, fire was the scourge [devastation] of Moscow. [2]In winter, when primitive stoves were blazing in every house, and in summer when the heat made wood tinder-dry, a spark could create a holocaust. [3]Some of the homes had beautiful carved porches, windows, and gables, which were unknown in other parts of Europe, where buildings were made of stone. [4]Caught by the wind, flames leaped from one roof to the next, reducing entire streets to ashes. [5]Moscow was also subject to terrible Russian winters, which often caused severe damage to the city's wooden structures. [6]In 1571, 1611, 1626, and 1671, great fires destroyed whole quarters of Moscow, leaving vast empty spaces in the middle of the city. [7]These disasters were exceptional, but to Muscovites the sight of a burning house . . . was a part of daily life. [8]So were the heavy wooden planks that covered the streets, which had become filled with mud after the heavy autumn rains.

Massie establishes his focus—states his central idea—in a topic sentence at the very beginning. His subject is "fire"; his main point about that subject is that it was "the scourge of Moscow." This is what he sets out to develop in the paragraph. Therefore, each detail *should* relate directly to that point. With the added material, however, this is *not* the case.

Let's analyze the paragraph to see which details belong and which do not.

- Sentence 1, the topic sentence, expresses the central idea.
- Sentence 2 details the causes of the fire, so it relates to the central idea in the topic sentence.
- Sentence 3 explains that some homes in Moscow displayed carvings seen nowhere else in Europe. It tells something about the city, but it doesn't explain the topic sentence's main point that "fire was the scourge of Moscow." Sentence 3 must be removed.
- Sentence 4 shows how fire spread, so it relates to the central idea.
- Sentence 5 explains that Russian winters were severe, but it doesn't relate to the point that "fire was the scourge of Moscow." It must be removed.
- Sentences 6 and 7 show how often and to what extent fire endangered the city. They contain relevant information and thus help develop the central idea.
- Sentence 8 discusses another aspect of life in Moscow, but it doesn't mention the threat of fire. It must be removed.

This analysis demonstrates that the details added to Massie's original paragraph are irrelevant. Compare the disunified version above with his original version below:

> Not unnaturally in a city built of wood, fire was the scourge of Moscow. In winter, when primitive stoves were blazing in every house, and in summer

when the heat made wood tinder-dry, a spark could create a holocaust. Caught by the wind, flames leaped from one roof to the next, reducing entire streets to ashes. In 1571, 1611, 1626, and 1671, great fires destroyed whole quarters of Moscow, leaving vast empty spaces in the middle of the city. These disasters were exceptional, but to Muscovites the sight of a burning house . . . was a part of daily life.

MAINTAINING COHERENCE

The second principle important to organization is coherence. A paragraph is coherent if the sentences it contains are connected clearly and logically in a sequence (or order) that is easy to follow. An essay is coherent if the writer has made sure to create logical connections between paragraphs. The thought expressed in one sentence or paragraph should lead directly—without a break—to the thought in the following sentence or paragraph.

Logical connections between sentences and between paragraphs can be created in two ways: (1) by using transitional devices and (2) by making reference to words, ideas, and other details the writer has mentioned earlier.

USE TRANSITIONAL DEVICES

Transitional devices, also called "transitions" or "connectives," are words, phrases, and even whole sentences that establish or show definite relationships in and between sentences and paragraphs. As seen in the following, transitional devices can be used for many different purposes.

TO INDICATE TIME You would be describing the passage of time if you wrote: "Henry left home just before dawn. *After a short while,* sunlight burst over the green hills." Other connectives that relate to time include:

After a few minutes	During
Afterward	Immediately
All the while	In a few minutes (hours, days, etc.)
Already	In a while
As soon as	In the meantime
At that time	Meanwhile
Back then	Now
Before	Prior to
Before long	Right away
Before that time	Soon
Still	Thereafter
Subsequently	Until
Suddenly	When
Then	While

TO INDICATE SIMILARITIES OR DIFFERENCES   You can also use transitions to show that things are similar or different: "Philip seems to be following in his sister's footsteps. *Like* her, he has decided to major in engineering. *Unlike* her, he doesn't do very well in math." Other transitions that indicate similarities and differences include:

SIMILARITIES	**DIFFERENCES**
And	Although
As	But
As if	Even though
As though	However
In addition	In contrast
In the same way	Nevertheless
Like	Nonetheless
Likewise	On the other hand
Similarly	Still
	Though
	Unless
	Yet

TO INTRODUCE EXAMPLES, REPEAT INFORMATION, OR EMPHASIZE A POINT
You would be using a transition to introduce an example if you wrote: "Mozart displayed his genius early. *For example,* he composed his first symphony when he was only a boy."

You would be using a transition to repeat information if you wrote: "At the age of 21, Mozart was appointed court composer for the emperor of Austria. This event was *another* indication of how quickly the young man rose to fame."

You would be using a transition to emphasize a point if you wrote: "The end of Mozart's career was hardly as spectacular as its beginnings. *In fact,* he died in poverty at age 35."

Other transitional devices useful for these purposes include:

INTRODUCING EXAMPLES	**REPEATING INFORMATION**	**EMPHASIZING A POINT**
As an example	Again	As a matter of fact
For instance	Once again	Indeed
Specifically	Once more	More important
Such as		To be sure

TO ADD INFORMATION   If you wanted to add information by using a transition, you might write: "When Ulysses S. Grant and Robert E. Lee met at Appomattox Courthouse in 1865, they brought the Civil War to an end. *What's more,* they opened a whole new chapter in U.S. political history." Here are some other connectives you will find useful when adding information:

Also	Furthermore
And	In addition
As well	Likewise
Besides	Moreover
Further	Too

TO SHOW CAUSE AND EFFECT   If you wanted to explain that an action or idea led to or was the cause of another, you could indicate this relationship by using a transitional device like "consequently," the word that draws a connection between the two thoughts in these sentences: "During the early days of the Revolution, General George Washington was unable to defend New York City. *Consequently,* he was forced to retreat to Pennsylvania." Other transitional devices that show cause-effect relationships are:

As a result	So that
Because	Then
Hence	Therefore
Since	Thus

TO SHOW CONDITION   If you need to explain that one action, idea, or fact depends on another, you might create a relationship based on condition by using words like "if," as in these sentences: "Professor Jones should arrive in a few minutes. *If* she doesn't, we will have to go on without her." Some other transitions that show condition include:

As long as	In order to
As soon as	Provided that
Even if	Unless
In case	When

MAKE REFERENCE TO MATERIAL THAT HAS COME BEFORE

Two other effective ways to connect details and ideas in a sentence or paragraph with what you have discussed in earlier sentences or paragraphs are (1) to use pronouns to link details and ideas and (2) to restate important details and ideas.

USING PRONOUNS TO LINK DETAILS AND IDEAS   A good way to make reference to material that has come before is to use *linking pronouns,* pronouns that point clearly and directly to specific names, ideas, or details you've mentioned earlier. Such pronouns direct the reader's attention to nouns in earlier sentences or paragraphs; these nouns are called "antecedents." Relying on pronouns to maintain coherence also helps you avoid mentioning the same noun over and over, a habit that might make your writing repetitious.

The most important thing to remember about using linking pronouns is to make sure they refer directly and unmistakably to the nouns you want them to. In other words, all pronouns of reference should have antecedents that the reader will be able to identify easily and without question.

Notice how well freshman Helen Giannos uses pronouns (shown in italics) to establish coherence in the opening paragraph of "AIDS: An Epidemic?":

> In the winter of 1981, Dr. Michael Gottlieb, an immunologist at the Harbor-UCLA Medical Center near Los Angeles, was among the first physicians . . . to notice that something strange was going on. In just three months, *he* treated four patients with an unusual lung infection. Each of *these* men was approximately 30 years old, and *they* were avowed [declared] homosexuals. *Their* immune systems were extremely depressed, although *they* had previously enjoyed excellent health. "I knew that I was witnessing medical history, but I had no comprehension of what this illness would become," commented Dr. Gottlieb. *He* was talking about a new virus, *which* was later named AIDS (Acquired Immune Deficiency Syndrome).

Helen's paragraph includes only a few of the pronouns you might want to use to make your writing more coherent. Here are others:

PERSONAL PRONOUNS   These are pronouns that refer to people and things:

I (me, my, mine)	We (us, our, ours)
He, she, it (him, his; her, hers; its)	You (your, yours)
	They (them, their, theirs)

RELATIVE PRONOUNS   These are pronouns that help describe nouns by connecting them with clauses (groups of words that contain nouns and verbs):

Who (whose, whom)	Whatever
That	Which
What	Whichever

DEMONSTRATIVE PRONOUNS   These are pronouns that precede and stand for the nouns they refer to. Sentences like *"Those* are the best seats in the house" or *"That* is my worst subject" make use of demonstrative pronouns. The most common demonstrative pronouns are:

This	These
That	Those

INDEFINITE PRONOUNS   These are pronouns used for general rather than specific reference. You can make good use of these pronouns as long as you are sure the reader can identify their antecedents easily. For instance: "Both Sylvia and Andrew were released from the hospital. *Neither* was seriously injured." In this case, the antecedents of "neither" are Sylvia and Andrew. Here are other indefinite pronouns:

All	Neither
Another	Nobody
Both	No one
Each	None
Either	Several
Everybody	Some
Everyone	Someone

RESTATING IMPORTANT DETAILS AND IDEAS The second way to make reference to material that has come before is to restate important details and ideas by repeating words and phrases or by using easily recognizable *synonyms*, terms that have the same (or nearly the same) meaning as those words or phrases.

In the following paragraph from "How the Superwoman Myth Puts Women Down," Sylvia Rabiner repeats the word "women" three times but for the sake of variety also uses easily recognizable synonyms:

> *Women* are self-critical creatures. We can always find reasons to hate ourselves. Single *women* believe they are failing if they don't have a loving, permanent relationship; *working mothers* are conflicted about leaving their children; divorced *women* experience guilt over the break-up of their marriages; *housewives* feel inadequate because they don't have careers; *career women* are wretched if they aren't advancing; and *everyone* is convinced she is too fat!

VISUALIZING UNITY AND COHERENCE

The following paragraph is from Gerald Parshall's "Freeing the Survivors," which tells what U.S. soldiers saw in 1945 when they liberated inmates of Nazi concentration camps, where millions of people had been murdered.

Notes in the margins explain how the paragraph is unified. Shaded words and phrases show how the writer maintained coherence.

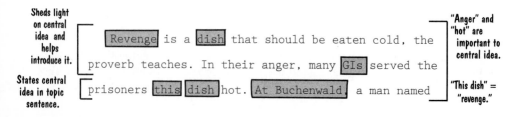

Sheds light on central idea and helps introduce it.

States central idea in topic sentence.

Revenge is a dish that should be eaten cold, the proverb teaches. In their anger, many GIs served the prisoners this dish hot. At Buchenwald, a man named

"Anger" and "hot" are important to central idea.

"This dish" = "revenge."

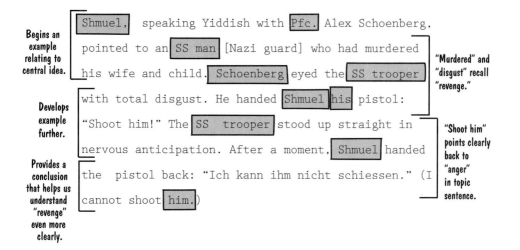

Begins an example relating to central idea.

Shmuel, speaking Yiddish with Pfc. Alex Schoenberg, pointed to an SS man [Nazi guard] who had murdered his wife and child. Schoenberg eyed the SS trooper

"Murdered" and "disgust" recall "revenge."

Develops example further.

with total disgust. He handed Shmuel his pistol: "Shoot him!" The SS trooper stood up straight in nervous anticipation. After a moment, Shmuel handed

"Shoot him" points clearly back to "anger" in topic sentence.

Provides a conclusion that helps us understand "revenge" even more clearly.

the pistol back: "Ich kann ihm nicht schiessen." (I cannot shoot him.)

REVISING TO IMPROVE UNITY AND COHERENCE

Read these two versions of paragraphs from "Is Justice Served?" which appears later in this chapter. Then read notes in the margins of the second version to see how student author Gina K. Louis-Ferdinand revised her essay to improve unity and coherence.

Louis-Ferdinand—Rough Draft

Today, the big story is the OJ Simpson murder trial, which has been splashed across newspapers and televisions all over the world. The media has made it nearly impossible to select an impartial jury because of its lack of

Needs a transition.

responsibility in reporting this case. The press reported that a sock soaked with Nicole Simpson's blood had been found in OJ's bedroom. The judge, defense, and prosecution

Add transitions?

all denied that any such evidence existed. The media stood by the story. They retracted the story without the fanfare that had accompanied the first report. An explosive book was published by Nicole Simpson's self-proclaimed best

New idea. Create new paragraph?

friend. The author discusses her second-hand knowledge of

Add transitions?

Nicole and OJs life. She claims Nicole told her that one day OJ would kill her. The author has become a highly

Add information? ⌐ sought-after commodity on the talk-show circuit. The judge

in the case personally contacted the networks airing shows

that were scheduled to interview her and asked that the

interviews be postponed until after a jury had been

selected and sequestered. All but one refused.

When the media treats crimes in this manner, how can

an impartial jury be found? In a trial, a judge has the   **Is this relevant to central idea?**

power to allow or disallow information based on the

legality of the item. His job is to make sure a trial

is fair for all parties involved and that it is based

on fact and not hearsay or false information. The media

have no such restrictions and can report practically

anything they wish, fact or fiction.

Louis-Ferdinand—Final Draft

Today, the big story is the OJ Simpson murder

trial, which has been splashed across newspapers and

televisions all over the world. The media has made it

nearly impossible to select an impartial jury because of

Adds transitions to introduce example and indicate time. ⌐ its lack of responsibility in reporting the case. For

example, early in the investigation, the press reported

that a sock soaked with Nicole Simpson's blood had been

found in OJ's bedroom. The judge, defense, and

prosecution all denied that any such evidence existed.

Add transitions to indicate time. ⌐ At first, the media stood by the story. Two days later,

they retracted it but without the fanfare that had   **Adds transition to show difference.**

accompanied the first report.

Adds transition to show time and introduce another example. ⌐ More recently, an explosive book was published by

Nicole Simpson's self-proclaimed best friend, who claims   **Creates new paragraph to discuss second example.**

Nicole told her that one day OJ would kill her. As a

Adds transition to show cause/effect.

result, the author has become a highly sought-after

commodity on the talk-show circuit. In fact, upon

Adds transition to emphasize a point.

learning of her intent to be interviewed, the judge in

the case personally contacted the networks airing such

shows and asked that the interviews be postponed until

after a jury had been selected and sequestered. All but

one network refused. When the media treats crimes in

this manner, how can an impartial jury be found?

Unnecessary information about the judge has been removed.

PRACTICING UNITY AND COHERENCE

Read this paragraph—written by Stacy Zolnowski for a first-year writing class—to learn more about paragraph unity. Then, using complete sentences, answer the questions that follow in the spaces provided:

[1] Throughout history, left-handedness has been deemed a nasty habit, a social infraction, a symptom of neurosis, or even a sign of mental retardation. [2] More recently, however, its social, educational, and psychological implications have acquired a more enlightened appreciation. [3] Nonetheless, left-handers continue to be discriminated against in an environment that conforms to the needs and prejudices of a right-handed society. ("The Left-Handed Minority")

1. Assume that the paragraph's topic sentence is the third sentence. What, in your own words, is the paragraph's central idea?

_____

_____

_____

_____

2. How do sentences 1 and 2 relate to the central idea?

_____

_____

_____

3. What transitional devices does the writer use to maintain coherence?

_____

_____

_____

4. In what other ways does the writer maintain coherence?

_____

_____

_____

This chapter has introduced you to two important principles of organization: unity and coherence. A paragraph or essay is _unified_ if all its ideas and details relate to and contribute to the central idea. A paragraph or essay is _coherent_ if the reader can move from sentence to sentence and paragraph to paragraph easily because the writer has connected the ideas logically.

Look for signs of unity and coherence as you read the following selections. More important, apply these principles in your own writing as you respond to the Suggestions for Journal Entries and the Suggestions for Sustained Writing.

From *People of the Deer*

Farley Mowat

Farley Mowat was born in Ontario, Canada, lived two years in the Arctic, and writes about the people and creatures of the northern Canadian wilderness. His most famous work is Never Cry Wolf, *a study of Arctic wolves upon which a popular film was based.* People of the Deer, *from which this paragraph is taken, describes the Ihalmiut people and tells of Mowat's travels.*

LOOKING AHEAD

1. Mowat states his central idea clearly. As you read the paragraph, ask yourself what general impression or main point he communicates about his subject. Then, pick out the sentence that best expresses that main point.
2. The writer maintains coherence in this paragraph well. Look for linking pronouns and connective words and expressions.
3. About the middle of the paragraph, Mowat mentions the "Barrens," a subarctic area of Canada.

VOCABULARY

bleak	Harsh, gloomy, empty.
caribou	Large deer of the North American Arctic.
evading	Escaping, getting away from.
frantic	Desperate.
hordes	Swarms, masses.
malevolent	Evil, harmful.
surcease	End.

From *People of the Deer* | *Farley Mowat*

Equipped with pack dogs, it took us better than a week to cover the same sixty miles that the Ihalmiut cross in two days and a night. I shall not soon forget the tortures of that march. While the sun shone, the heat was as intense as it is in the tropics, for the clarity of the Arctic air does nothing to soften the sun's rays. Yet we were forced to wear sweaters and even caribou skin jackets. The flies did that to us. They rose from the lichens at our feet until they hung like a malevolent mist about us and took on the appearance of a low-lying cloud. *Milugia* (black flies) and *kiktoriak* (mosquitoes) came in such numbers that their presence actually gave me a feeling of physical terror. There was simply no evading them. The bleak Barrens stretched into emptiness on every side, and offered no escape and no surcease. To stop for food was torture and to continue the march in the overwhelming summer heat was worse. At times a kind of insanity would seize us and we would drop everything and run wildly in any direction until we were exhausted. But the pursuing hordes stayed with us and we got nothing from our frantic efforts except a wave of sweat that seemed to attract even more mosquitoes.

QUESTIONS FOR DISCUSSION

1. What is Mowat's topic sentence? What word in that sentence expresses his main point?
2. Where in the paragraph does the author echo his main point by repeating that word or by using other words that relate to it?
3. Why does Mowat say that he and his companions had to wear sweaters and jackets? Does this fact make the paragraph less unified, or does it help explain his main point?
4. What linking pronouns do you find?
5. What connective words and phrases does Mowat use?

THINKING CRITICALLY

1. What question or questions might you ask Mowat about the purpose of his trip into the "Barrens"?
2. Why didn't Mowat and his companions simply turn back to avoid the "tortures of that march"? Can you think of any logical reasons why they didn't?
3. What conclusions can you draw about Mowat's opinion of the wilderness from this paragraph? Is it fair to draw conclusions from such little evidence?

SUGGESTION FOR A JOURNAL ENTRY

Think of a time when you felt physical discomfort or even pain. Using the journalists' questions you learned about in "Getting Started," gather details that describe that experience. For example, you might ask yourself:

1. When did this happen?
2. What or who caused the discomfort or pain?
3. What kind of discomfort or pain did I feel?
4. How did I react?

Say you had a difficult time getting to sleep last night because of all the noise in your house. Here's how you might answer those questions:

1. When did this happen?

Between midnight and 3:00 A.M. last night

2. What or who caused the discomfort or pain?

Sister's stereo blasting

Dad slams front door at midnight
Neighbor's dog attacks my cat—barks/squeals

3. What kind of discomfort or pain did I feel?

Loud pounding rhythm in my ear
Walls throbbing

4. How did I react?

Covered my head with pillows, blankets
Started to doze off; got knocked out of bed when I heard and felt door slam
Wide awake, I heard animals fighting, rushed outside to save cat, got scratched, bitten, fell in the bushes

Your answers will contain words, phrases, and even sentences that might be the makings of a good paragraph because they relate to the same main point. Read the details you have recorded carefully. Then, ask yourself what the main point is. Put that main point into what could be the preliminary topic sentence of a paragraph you might write later. For example, the details above might lead to a topic sentence like one of these (the main point is in italics):

Getting to sleep last night was *impossible.*
Trying to fall sleep in my house last night was *like being tortured.*
Loud music, doors slamming, and animals fighting made trying to get to sleep last night a *nightmare.*

Waste

Wendell Berry

Writer, teacher, and Kentucky farmer, Wendell Berry is concerned about our effect on the natural environment. He is also a champion of simplicity, arguing that relying on "labor-saving" gadgets like personal computers and power tools can make life less fulfilling than using simpler devices. Berry's works include a book of poems, The Wheel; *a book of short stories,* The Wild Birds; *and a collection of essays,* Home Economics. *"Waste" is from another book of essays,* What Are People For?

LOOKING AHEAD

1. The author expresses his feelings about the way we manage our waste in a strong topic sentence. Look for this topic sentence and identify its main point.
2. Berry uses transitional devices and repeats words and ideas to make connections between sentences. Underline or write down words and phrases you think help maintain coherence.

VOCABULARY

abundance	Great amount of.
imperishable	Not able to decay.
Iroquois	North American Indians and their language.
precipitation	Flow, rush, fall.
subside	Ease, dwindle, get weaker.

Waste | Wendell Berry

As a country person, I often feel that I am on the bottom end of the waste problem. I live on the Kentucky River about ten miles from its entrance into the Ohio. The Kentucky, in many ways a lovely river, receives an abundance of pollution from the Eastern Kentucky coal mines and the central Kentucky cities. When the river rises, it carries a continuous raft of cans, bottles, plastic jugs, chunks of styrofoam, and other imperishable trash. After the floods subside, I, like many other farmers, must pick up the trash before I can use my bottomland fields. I have seen the Ohio, whose name (*Oyo* in Iroquois) means "beautiful river," so choked with this manufactured filth that an ant could crawl dry-footed from Kentucky to Indiana. The air of both river valleys is seriously polluted. Our roadsides and roadside fields lie under a constant precipitation of cans, bottles, the plastic-ware of fast food joints, soiled plastic diapers, and sometimes whole bags of garbage. In our county we now have a "sanitary landfill" which daily receives, in addition to our local production, fifty to sixty large truckloads of garbage from Pennsylvania, New Jersey, and New York.

QUESTIONS FOR DISCUSSION

1. What is Berry's topic sentence? What main point does he express in that sentence?
2. How does the sentence beginning "Our roadsides and roadside fields" relate to the topic sentence?
3. Why does telling us that *Oyo* means "beautiful river" help Berry prove his main point?
4. Find examples of words and ideas the author repeats to maintain coherence.
5. What transitional devices does he use to make connections between sentences?
6. Why does Berry put quotation marks around the term *sanitary landfill?*

THINKING CRITICALLY

1. What can one person do to help solve the kinds of pollution problems Berry talks about in this paragraph? What changes can *you* make in *your* lifestyle to do this?
2. Some people believe that the best way to overcome pollution is to limit large-scale manufacturing, do away with nonbiodegradable materials, eat organically grown foods, and, in general, adopt a totally natural lifestyle. Think about the implications of this suggestion. How would it change *your* lifestyle?

SUGGESTIONS FOR JOURNAL ENTRIES

1. Use the focused freewriting or listing techniques explained in "Getting Started" to gather information in your journal about pollution in your town. Is it similar to the kind you read about in Berry's paragraph? Do you see trash littering roadsides and fields? What do you find in streams and lakes? Can you describe the sights and smells of smokestacks, buses, trucks, and cars as they foul the air? How about giving examples of noise pollution? Mention as many types of pollution as you can.
2. In Chapter 1 you learned it is a good idea to review your notes and write a preliminary topic sentence or thesis before drafting a paragraph or essay. Read the journal entry you made for Suggestion 1 above. Then do the following:
   a. Write a preliminary topic sentence that expresses the central idea for the details you have just gathered.
   b. Underline the main point in that topic sentence.
   c. Read the journal entry for Suggestion 1 once more.
   d. Do you find information that doesn't relate to your preliminary topic sentence? If so, cross out that information and keep only what relates directly to the main point in your topic sentence.

Finally, share your two journal entries with other students. Do they think the main point in your topic sentence expresses the general impression they get from reading your journal notes? If not, ask for suggestions about how to revise your topic sentence. Also ask them to provide other examples of pollution. The better your journal entries, the greater your chance of using these details for an assignment described in Suggestions for Sustained Writing at the end of this chapter.

Writing and Its Rewards

Richard Marius

Richard Marius directs the expository writing program at Harvard University. He began his career as a historian and has authored biographies of Thomas More and Martin Luther. He also has written four novels and several books on writing, including The McGraw-Hill College Handbook, *which he co-authored with Harvey Wiener. "Writing and Its Rewards" is from* A Writer's Companion, *Marius's splendid guide for both experienced and developing writers.*

LOOKING AHEAD

1. Writing is a process of drafting and revising, Marius tells us. As you probably learned in "Getting Started," *drafting* means putting down facts and ideas in rough form, no matter how disorganized your paragraph or essay might seem at first. *Revising* involves rewriting, reorganizing, adding to, deleting from, and correcting earlier drafts to make them more effective and easier to read.
2. In paragraph 5, Marius mentions three writers whose work you may want to read: Geoffrey Chaucer, Leo Tolstoy, and W. H. Auden. To learn more about them, look up their names in an encyclopedia or reference book recommended by your college librarian.

VOCABULARY

eighteenth century	The 1700s.
embodied	Contained.
enduring	Lasting.
lexicographer	Writer of a dictionary.
parable	Story with a lesson or moral.
profound	Deep, extreme.
weighing	Carefully considering.

Writing and Its Rewards

Richard Marius

Writing is hard work, and although it may become easier with practice it is sel- 1
dom easy. Most of us have to write and rewrite to write anything well. We try
to write well so people will read our work. Readers nowadays will seldom struggle to
understand difficult writing unless someone—a teacher perhaps—forces them to do so.
Samuel Johnson, the great eighteenth-century English writer, conversationalist, and lex-
icographer, said, "What is written without effort is in general read without pleasure."
Today what is written without effort is seldom read at all.

Writing takes time—lots of time. Good writers do not dash off a piece in an hour 2
and get on to other things. They do not wait until the night before a deadline to begin to
write. Instead they plan. They write a first draft. They revise it. They may then think
through that second draft and write it once again. Even small writing tasks may require
enormous investments of time. If you want to become a writer, you must be serious
about the job, willing to spend hours dedicated to your work.

Most writers require some kind of solitude. That does not mean the extreme of the 3
cork-lined room where the great French writer Marcel Proust composed his huge works
in profound silence. It does mean mental isolation—shutting yourself off from the dis-
tractions around you even if you happen to be pounding a computer keyboard in a noisy
newspaper office. You choose to write rather than do other things, and you must concentrate on what you are doing.

In a busy world like ours, we take a risk when we isolate ourselves and give up 4
other pursuits to write. We don't know how our writing will come out. All writers fail
sometimes. Successful writers pick themselves up after failure and try again. As you
write, you must read your work again and again, thinking of your purpose, weighing
your words, testing your organization, examining your evidence, checking for clarity.
You must pay attention to the thousands and thousands of details embodied in words
and experience. You must trust your intuitions; if something does not sound right, do it
again. And again. And again.

Finally you present your work to readers as the best you can do. After you submit a 5
final draft, it is too late to make excuses, and you should not do so. Not everybody will
like your final version. You may feel insecure about it even when you have done your
best. You may like your work at first and hate it later. Writers wobble back and forth in
their judgments. Chaucer, Tolstoy and Auden are all on record for rejecting some of
their works others have found enduring and grand. Writing is a parable of life itself.

QUESTIONS FOR DISCUSSION

1. Reread Marius's introduction. What is his thesis? What is the main point in this thesis?
2. This essay is unified because each paragraph clearly develops the essay's central idea (thesis). Explain how each topic sentence in paragraphs 2, 3, and 4 relates to Marius's thesis.
3. Reread paragraphs 2 and 3. What techniques does Marius use to maintain coherence?
4. Reread paragraph 4. What words and phrases are used to repeat ideas and, thus, to maintain coherence?
5. What does Marius mean by writing "is a parable of life itself" (paragraph 5)? Why is this conclusion effective?

THINKING CRITICALLY

One assumption Marius makes is that all educated people need to be competent writers. Is that true of you? Will you need strong writing skills for the job you take after college? Contact someone practicing in that field or profession. Ask her or him about the need for good writing skills. Then write a short report of your interview.

SUGGESTIONS FOR JOURNAL ENTRIES

1. Marius says "Most writers require some kind of solitude." Do you? Use your journal to describe the place in which you write or study most often. Is it comfortable? Can you concentrate there? Should you find another place to work?
2. "Writing and Its Rewards" contains advice to make us better writers. Use your journal to list three or more specific pieces of advice to help you or a classmate become better at an important activity you know a lot about. Here are examples of such an activity: studying or doing homework; dressing for school or work; driving in heavy traffic or bad weather; communicating with parents, children, teachers, or classmates; maintaining a car; losing weight; sticking to a nutritious diet; or treating members of a different race, age group, religion, or sex with respect.

   Express each piece of advice in a complete sentence, the kind that can serve as the topic sentence to a paragraph you might write later on to explain that piece of advice more fully.

Is Justice Served?

Gina K. Louis-Ferdinand

Gina K. Louis-Ferdinand grew up in Southfield, Michigan and is planning to pursue a career as a writer. She works full-time and takes college courses in the evening. When the instructor of her first-year composition class invited students to write on a topic about which they had strong feelings, Louis-Ferdinand knew immediately that she would explain her concern over the effects of the media on our justice system.

LOOKING AHEAD

1. Louis-Ferdinand organizes her essay around examples relating to three of the crimes she believes the media has sensationalized. She mentions these three cases early in the essay, then develops each one in detail in the body paragraphs. This pattern makes her essay easy to follow:

   Paragraph 1: Provides introductory information and gets the reader interested.
   Paragraph 2: Expresses the essay's central idea in a thesis statement. It also introduces three examples that support the thesis and that are developed in the essay's body paragraphs, which follow.
   Paragraph 3: Fully discusses the first example mentioned in paragraph 2: the Menendez case.
   Paragraph 4: Fully discusses the second example mentioned in paragraph 2: the Rodney King incident.
   Paragraph 5: Uses an example from the O.J Simpson trial to support the thesis.
   Paragraph 6: Uses a second example from the O.J. Simpson trial to support the thesis.
   Paragraph 7: Concludes the essay by reminding us of the thesis.

2. This essay is fairly easy to read because Louis-Ferdinand has done a masterful job of maintaining coherence by using transitions and other devices discussed in this chapter. Look for them especially in paragraphs 3, 4, 5, and 6.

VOCABULARY

allegations	Charges.
commodity	Object, article of trade.
exploitation	Abuse, unethical or unfair use of.
impartial	Fair, objective.
perverse	Evil, distorted, sinful.
preconceived	Biased, having been made before the evidence was heard.
retracted	Took back, corrected.
sequestered	Isolated, separated.

Is Justice Served? | *Gina K. Louis-Ferdinand*

Americans love a juicy story. We want intimate details, and the media is happy to   1
comply, but we forget that people's lives are at stake. A crime is not a form of
entertainment from which to derive perverse pleasure. It is the failure of a person to
live up to his or her obligations as a law-abiding citizen, and the media should report it
as such.

Recently, several major crimes have been sensationalized. As far as the media is   2
concerned, the more gruesome the crime, the better. Take the Menendez brothers' case
or the trial of the policemen who beat Rodney King. If a famous person is accused, members of the press appear to smack their lips and wring their hands in anticipation. Insert
sex or race, as in the O.J. Simpson murder trial, and the journalist's fondest dreams
come true. But such exploitation is not harmless entertainment; it tears at the core of the
American judicial system: a fair trial by an impartial jury. A juror is supposed to be
objective and have no preconceived opinion about the guilt or innocence of the accused.
However, the media's bombarding the public with information about a crime—true or
otherwise—makes finding twelve people who have no opinion about it nearly impossible.

In the Menendez case, for example, two brothers were accused of murdering their   3
parents. Initially, this case received media attention because the victims' children were
accused of the murders. However, when the brothers claimed they killed their parents
because they had been molested by them, the press really went wild. For months before
the trial, every paper and news program contained something about the crime. Only
then was the jury selected. Thus, even though no proof was ever found to support the
brothers' allegations of molestation, their trials ended in hung juries.

The Rodney King incident gained national attention when a videotape of the racially   4
motivated beating was shown on television. In the beginning, just the facts about the
incident were reported, but as time went on information on Rodney King's personal life
was publicized. Mr. King was portrayed as a sleazy ex-convict from the ghetto who
deserved what happened to him because he had resisted arrest. In reality, Rodney King
was the victim in this crime, and his personal life had nothing to do with his being so
severely beaten. However, the press chose to make his personal life an issue. As a result,
at the end of the first trial, the police officers, who had been caught on videotape kicking and punching Mr. King and against whom a fellow police officer had testified, were
set free.

Today, the big story is the O.J. Simpson murder trial, which has been splashed   5
across newspapers and televisions all over the world. The media has made it nearly
impossible to select an impartial jury because of its lack of responsibility in reporting the
case. For example, early in the investigation, the press reported that a sock soaked with
Nicole Simpson's blood had been found in O.J.'s bedroom. The judge, defense, and prosecution all denied that any such evidence existed. At first, the media stood by the story.
Two days later, they retracted it but without the fanfare that had accompanied the first
report.

More recently, an explosive book was published by Nicole Simpson's self-pro-   6
claimed best friend, who claims Nicole told her that one day O.J. would kill her. As a
result, the author has become a highly sought-after commodity on the talk-show cir-

cuit. In fact, upon learning of her intent to be interviewed, the judge in the case personally contacted the networks airing such shows and asked that the interviews be postponed until after a jury had been selected and sequestered. All but one network refused. When the media treats crimes in this manner, how can an impartial jury be found?

Though our judicial system is far from perfect, it is the best one in the world. Our 7 Constitution seeks fairness for all citizens, victim and accused alike, and what makes this system so effective is the jury. Our legal system cannot work if a jury makes a decision based upon anything other than simple facts, and that is not what happens when the media reports a crime as if it were dramatic entertainment. Did Rodney King or Mr. and Mrs. Menendez receive justice? Can O.J. Simpson get a fair trial? Those are the kinds of questions a journalist should ask before exploiting a story just to "scoop" another network or paper. Those are the kinds of questions we as a society should ask before we get taken in by one of these "juicy" stories. And, if we find ourselves answering such questions with anything other than a resounding "yes," we should not say "shame on the media" for publishing them. Rather, we should say "shame on ourselves" for listening.

QUESTIONS FOR DISCUSSION

1. What sentence in this essay best expresses Louis-Ferdinand's central idea? In other words, what is her thesis?
2. Why does the author introduce the Menendez brothers, Rodney King, and O.J. Simpson early in the essay (paragraph 2)? Why didn't she simply introduce them when discussing their cases later on?
3. The central idea in paragraph 3 is not stated in a topic sentence. It is only implied. How would you express that central idea in your own words?
4. Is this essay unified? If so, explain how paragraph 4 relates to the thesis?
5. What is the topic sentence in paragraph 5?
6. Reread paragraph 4. Circle transitions and other elements the author uses to maintain coherence.
7. Reread paragraph 6. Circle transitions and other elements the author uses to maintain coherence.

THINKING CRITICALLY

1. The policemen accused of beating Rodney King were tried a second time in federal court for violating King's civil rights. Two of them were given long-term jail sentences. Write a paragraph that explains the effect this fact has on Louis-Ferdinand's argument that the media's treatment of Rodney King interfered with justice. Does it strengthen or weaken her argument? Does it have any effect at all? Why or why not?
2. Some say the O.J. Simpson murder trial captured the public's attention like no other trial since the Lindbergh kidnapping case in the 1930s. What are the causes of the public's fascination with the Simpson case? What has the media done to keep our attention? What other factors account for the public's interest in this trial?
3. Different people have different opinions about O.J. Simpson's guilt or innocence. Is it fair to judge Simpson when you are not in the courtroom hearing arguments from both the defense and the prosecution? Why or why not?

SUGGESTIONS FOR JOURNAL ENTRIES

1. Think of a crime, trial, scandal, or other incident that the news media has sensationalized. (Try not to pick one of the examples Louis-Ferdinand used.) Then use listing to gather facts and ideas that might later help you discuss the media's handling of this event. If possible, do some brainstorming with a friend or classmate about the topic before you begin putting down information.

2. Use freewriting or listing to gather information about a sensitive event you believe the media reported accurately, fairly, and professionally. To get started on this assignment, recall what you learned about the event from television or radio; then read three or four accounts of it in different newspapers or magazines.

Gambling

Michael Witt

Michael Witt wrote "Gambling" in an advanced composition class. When the instructor asked students to interview someone with a unique problem and to write a character sketch, Witt knew whom to call. "Richie Martin" (the name is an alias) provided material to draw this touching portrait of a young man in agony. Witt's essay is a record of "Richie's" battle with an evil as strong and destructive as drug addiction or alcoholism.

Looking Ahead

1. Witt's thesis statement, the first sentence in his essay, contains two parts, each of which helps define his idea of gambling. Read it carefully.
2. One of the reasons for Witt's success is that he did a thorough job of gathering important facts in his interview with "Richie Martin." Another is that he organized the material about his subject in unified and coherent paragraphs, each of which is introduced with a clear, distinct, well-written topic sentence. Examine these topic sentences carefully.
3. Still another reason this essay is so successful is that each of the topic sentences in the body (paragraphs 2 through 7) relates directly to the thesis, keeping the essay unified.

Vocabulary

affliction	Disease, illness, misfortune.
attest	Bear witness to.
doldrums	Depression.
exhilarating	Exciting.
profound	Deep, significant.
rehabilitate	Make healthy, make sound.
suppress	Control.
transcend	Go beyond.

Gabling | *Michael Witt*

Though most people don't seem to realize it, it's a disease, akin to alcoholism 1
and drug addiction, and it has ruined more families and more relationships than
statistics can accurately define. It's gambling—and it's one of the most underrated problems in America today.

Richie Martin can attest to this fact. As he speaks, his eyes tell the story as they 2
transcend the excitement of a racetrack photo finish and the disappointment of losing
this month's rent on a solitary basketball game. He's excited, then subtle. His mood
changes reflect a man whose very life goes from ecstatic highs to severe doldrums—
depending on Sunday's games.

Richie bets on anything, from the World Series to the presidential election. Hours 3
before his sister delivered her first child, he attempted to bet his brother-in-law thirty
dollars it would be a boy. But mainly he gambles on sports and, when playoff time
arrives, Richie's money usually departs. "Over the last five years, I've lost at least twenty-
five thousand dollars," he admitted, "and even though it hasn't really broke me, I feel
like I'm always chasing what I've lost."

His obsession with gambling has also had a profound effect on several relationships. 4
"I used to bring my ex-girlfriend to the racetrack and Atlantic City all the time," he
remembered, "but when I'd lose I'd snap at her all the way home. She couldn't take it
any more." His gambling habits started early when, as a young boy, he'd bet nickels
with his father on TV bowling tournaments. "We'd bet on every ball that went down
the alley," he recalled. "It was just for fun." Though it seemed harmless at the time, it led
to a more serious and distressing involvement in gambling. And this, he feels, has thrust
upon his father strong feelings of guilt. "I've never blamed him for my problem and he
knows it, but I don't think he'll ever be satisfied until I quit."

He freely admits his affliction, which he feels is an important step towards recovery, 5
but the exhilarating world of taking chances is not an easy place to leave. "When I win,
it's like everything I touch turns to gold, but when I lose, I wanna dig a hole and crawl
right in it," he said. It's these sensations, these extremes of emotion, that give his life a
sense of meaning and keep him in constant touch with his bookie.

At times, the stench of losing becomes so unbearable he vows to rehabilitate him- 6
self. Every Monday morning, after a weekend of gambling away half of Friday's pay-
check, he takes an oath to change his destructive ways—so far without success. "Every
time I'm ready to quit, I win a good buck. Then I'm right back where I started."

Lately, however, he has taken some drastic steps towards rehabilitation. He has quit 7
his day job and taken a night one in the hope of isolating himself from the world of
racetracks and ballparks, which operate primarily at night. "What I don't know won't
hurt me," he says with a sad smile. He also hopes the change in "work friends" will
influence his habits.

"It's a no-win situation, just like alcohol and drugs," he concludes. "And I'm tired of 8
it." The world of sports will never go away, nor will the excitement of winning and losing, but with a little luck and a lot of self-control he may suppress his disease—but don't
bet on it.

QUESTIONS FOR DISCUSSION

1. In his thesis, Witt says that gambling is "a disease" and that it has "ruined more families and more relationships than statistics can accurately define." In which paragraphs does he describe gambling as a disease? In which does he talk about the relationships it has destroyed?
2. Explain how each topic sentence in paragraphs 2 through 7 relates to Witt's thesis or helps the reader understand his central idea better.
3. Make a list of transitions, linking pronouns, and repeated words and ideas in paragraphs 2 through 7.
4. What transitions and linking pronouns does the author use to create coherence between paragraphs? Does he ever repeat words or ideas to do this?

THINKING CRITICALLY

1. What advice would you give to someone like "Richie Martin"?
2. What advice would you give to a person dating or married to someone addicted to drugs, alcohol, gambling, or any other substance or activity?

SUGGESTIONS FOR JOURNAL ENTRIES

1. If you know someone who is suffering from an addiction, write a paragraph that discusses the addiction and its effect on this individual. Start with a topic sentence that names the addiction (such as alcoholism, drug abuse, gambling, or even an addiction to money), and make sure that the topic sentence also explains how the addiction has affected this person's life.

    Both the topic sentence and the paragraph's development must be specific. Limit your discussion to one aspect or part of your subject's life; for instance, you might say that "Martha's drinking problem is affecting her performance on the job." Then provide details that support or prove your topic sentence: explain that Martha has been late three mornings this week because of severe hangovers, that she didn't make it to work the day after a holiday party, and that she never returns to the office if she has a drink with lunch.

    In addition, be sure that your paragraph is unified. Check to see that each detail helps explain how the addiction has affected your subject's life. Finally, maintain coherence throughout the paragraph. Include transitional expressions, repeat words and ideas, and use synonyms and linking pronouns whenever you can to connect one sentence with the next.

2. If you know a person who is suffering from a serious illness, write a paragraph in which you identify the illness and describe *one* and *only* one of the effects it is having on this individual. For instance, your topic sentence might read: "Aunt

Clara's diabetes has caused her to make radical changes in her diet." Develop and organize your paragraph by following the advice in Suggestion 1.

SUGGESTIONS FOR SUSTAINED WRITING

1. Review the journal entries you made after reading the selections by Farley Mowat or Wendell Berry in this chapter. If you responded to the suggestion after the paragraph from Mowat's *People of the Deer,* you wrote a preliminary topic sentence and gathered details about a painful or uncomfortable experience. If you responded to the suggestions after Berry's "Waste," you wrote a preliminary topic sentence and collected details about pollution in your town. Now, write a paragraph beginning with *one* of these preliminary topic sentences. Develop that paragraph using details from your journal. Keep the paragraph unified; focus your information on the main point of your topic sentence. If you want to refresh your memory about unity, read pages 50–52.

    After completing your first draft, reread the paragraph. Is it coherent? Do you use linking pronouns and repetition to draw logical connections between sentences? Should you add transitional words and expressions? If you are writing about a painful or uncomfortable experience, you can use transitional devices that indicate time, like those you read about on pages 52–53. If you are describing pollution in your town, you can use transitions that introduce examples, that emphasize a point, or that add information, like those you read about on pages 53–54.

    In any event, make several more drafts of your paragraph. Stop revising only when you are satisfied that it is easy to follow and that the information it contains relates to and explains your topic sentence clearly. Then, review your work once more to correct problems with grammar, sentence structure, punctuation, capitalization, and spelling.

2. If you responded to item 2 in the Suggestions for Journal Entries after Marius's "Writing and Its Rewards," you have probably listed three or four sentences that give advice on a particular activity you know a lot about. Use *each* of these sentences as the topic sentence of a paragraph that explains the advice you are giving in detail. For example, if you are trying to help a friend lose weight, one thing you might suggest is that he or she "get a lot of exercise." That would make a good topic sentence of a paragraph that goes like this:

    Get a lot of exercise. Wake up early and jog two or three miles. Use the weight room in the college gymnasium several times a week or ride one of the stationary bicycles you will find there. If all else fails, walk the three miles to school every day, do sit-ups in your room, or jump rope in your backyard.

    After you have written three or four such paragraphs, decide on a thesis statement that might express the central idea of the essay in which these paragraphs will appear. Make your thesis broad enough to include the main points you made in all three or four of your topic sentences. Use the thesis statement as the basis of a paragraph that comes before and introduces the three or four body paragraphs you have just completed.

Now, rewrite your paper several times. Make sure it is clear and well organized. Check to see that you have included enough transitional devices to maintain coherence as explained in this chapter.

3. Read the journal entry you made after completing Louis-Ferdinand's "Is Justice Served?" (If you haven't responded to this essay in your journal, do so now.)

What does your journal tell you about your opinion of how the news media handles sensitive events? Make your answer to this question the thesis statement of a short essay discussing at least three events, like those used by Louis-Ferdinand, to support that thesis.

If you followed the suggestions for journal entries after "Is Justice Served?" carefully, you already have one of the three examples you will use in your essay. Now, do some prewriting to gather information about two other events the media has handled badly or well.

As you draft your essay, make sure that all three events relate to and help prove your thesis. Place your thesis in your introductory paragraph. Then, following Louis-Ferdinand's model, explain each example in a body paragraph. End your essay with a short paragraph that reminds your readers of your thesis.

Here's an outline you might follow:

Paragraph 1: Contains thesis; captures readers' interest.
Paragraph 2: Discusses first example, which you wrote about in your journal.
Paragraph 3: Discusses second example.
Paragraph 4: Discusses third example.
Paragraph 5: Reminds readers of your thesis.

As you revise your first draft, make sure to check coherence. Repeat ideas and insert transitions and linking pronouns as needed. Finally, edit and proofread your work.

4. The Suggestions for Journal Entries following Michael Witt's "Gambling" involve writing about a person who is suffering from an addiction or serious illness. If you responded to either suggestion, you have probably written a unified and coherent paragraph that discusses one of the ways the addiction or illness has affected his or her life.

Review this paragraph carefully. Then, write several more well-organized paragraphs, each of which explains another way in which the person's life has been changed by this addiction or illness. Next, turn these separate paragraphs into a unified essay by providing an appropriate thesis statement that will appear at the beginning of your essay and serve as its introduction. Then, check to see that you have maintained coherence in and between paragraphs by using techniques explained in the introduction to this chapter. As with other writing assignments, remember that the best papers are those that are revised thoroughly and edited carefully.

DEVELOPMENT

By now you know from practice that you use the central idea to focus your writing on a main point and to keep it unified. You do so by making sure that all the information in your paragraphs and essays relates clearly to the central idea. This chapter explains how the central idea also controls *development*—how much information a piece of writing contains and how this information is organized.

A paragraph or essay is well developed if it contains all the details it needs to prove, support, or illustrate its central idea. You should provide enough details to make your point clearly and convincingly. You should also arrange these details in a way that fits your purpose and that allows readers to follow your train of thought easily.

DETERMINING HOW MUCH A PARAGRAPH OR ESSAY SHOULD CONTAIN

It is not always easy to determine how much detail is enough to develop a particular point, and there is no simple rule to tell how long a piece of writing should be. Depending upon your thesis, you might be able to develop an essay in only a few paragraphs. But in some cases, your central idea will require that you write several paragraphs of explanation and support.

Something similar is true for paragraphs. In some, you will have to supply many concrete details, illustrations, and other information important to your topic sentence. In other paragraphs, you will be able to make your point clearly with only one or two supportive details. In a *few,* you might find that one sentence is all you need to achieve your purpose. (Keep in mind, however, that using too many one-sentence paragraphs can make your writing seem choppy and incomplete.)

In any event, it is a good idea to rely on your central idea as a guide for development. After all, the central idea contains the main point you want to make. Therefore, it can give you a good clue about the kinds and amount of detail you should use to develop that point effectively.

Let's say you want to explain that there are *several* career opportunities for people majoring in biology. To develop your paragraph adequately, you might start by discussing teaching and medicine. But you will also have to include other fields (such as laboratory research, environmental management, and forestry) if you want your reader to understand all of what you meant when, in your topic sentence or thesis, you wrote, "Majoring in biology can provide a good foundation for *several* careers."

You already know that in order to come up with a good central idea, you need to focus on the main point you want to make about your subject. The subject in the sentence above is "Majoring in biology." The main point you want to make about this subject is that it can lead to "*several* careers." In order to write a paragraph or essay that develops this point fully, therefore, you will have to discuss *several*—at least three—careers.

In short, you can think of the central idea as a promise you make to your readers at the beginning of a paragraph or essay—a promise to discuss your main point in as much detail as is appropriate. If you start off by writing that "Three types of birds visit your backyard regularly during the winter," make sure to discuss all *three* birds. If you set out to explain that "There are many ways to decrease cholesterol in the bloodstream," discuss *many* ways, not just one or two. If you want to prove that your brother is not neat, don't be content to describe his closet and leave it at that. Talk about the mess of papers and books he often leaves scattered across the floor, and mention the jumble of sporting equipment and dirty clothes on the back seat of his car.

As you have learned, deciding how many details are enough to develop a paragraph or essay fully is not always easy. However, the more experienced you become, the easier it will be to determine how much to include. For now, remember that providing too much detail is better than not providing enough. Too much information might bore your readers, but too little might leave them unconvinced or even confused. The first of these sins is forgivable; the second is not.

Just how much detail to include is what physician Lewis Thomas had to decide when he wrote a paragraph illustrating (giving examples of) the idea that computer errors have become commonplace:

> Everyone must have had at least one personal experience with a computer error by this time. Bank balances are suddenly reported to have jumped from $379 into the millions, appeals for charitable contributions are mailed over and over to people with crazy-sounding names at your address, department stores send the wrong bills, utility companies write that they're turning everything off, that sort of thing. If you manage to get in touch with someone and complain, you then get instantaneously typed, guilty letters from the same computer, saying, "Our computer was in error, and an adjustment is being made in your account." ("To Err Is Human")

Obviously, Thomas could not include an example of every computer error he had ever heard of. So, he limited himself to those that he thought would make his point most effectively and that his readers would recognize. His decision to include a specific number of examples—four in this case—is not important. We know without counting that Thomas has provided enough information to get his point across. We also know that he might not have made his point so clearly and convincingly had he used fewer examples.

CHOOSING THE BEST METHOD OF DEVELOPMENT

You can develop an idea in many ways. The method you choose depends on your purpose—the point you wish to make and the effect you want your writing to have on your readers. Your purpose can be descriptive, narrative, explanatory, persuasive, or any combination of these.

DESCRIPTION

If your purpose is to introduce your reader to a person, place, or thing, you might *describe* your subject in concrete detail. The easiest way to gather detail for this kind of paragraph or essay is to use your five physical senses. Sight, smell, hearing, taste, and touch provide details that make writing vivid and effective. Description is also discussed in Chapters 8 and 9.

NARRATION

If you want to tell a story—to explain what happened—you will likely *narrate* a series of events as they occurred in time, explaining each event or part of an event in the order it took place. Narration is also discussed in Chapters 10, 11, and 12.

EXPLANATION AND PERSUASION

If your purpose is to *explain* an idea (expository writing) or to *persuade* your reader that an opinion or belief is correct (persuasive writing), you can choose from several methods to develop your ideas. Among these, of course, are narration and description, as well as the simple method called "conclusion and support," which allows you to defend an opinion or explain an idea by using concrete and specific details that relate to it directly. However, you may want *to explain* or *to persuade* by choosing from seven other methods:

• Illustration: develop an idea with examples
• Definition: explain a term or concept
• Classification: distinguish between types or classes
• Comparison and contrast: point out similarities and differences
• Analogy: compare an abstract or difficult idea to something that is concrete and that the reader knows; usually, the subjects being compared seem unrelated at first
• Cause and effect: explain why something happens
• Process analysis: explain how something happens or how to do something

Deciding which method of development is best for your purpose depends on the idea you are explaining or the point you are making. Let's say you want to persuade your readers that the best way to clean up the rivers in your town is to fine polluters. The cause-and-effect method might work well. If you decide to explain that the daily routine you followed in high school is quite different from the one you follow in college, you might choose contrast. If want to prove how serious a student you are, you can support your opinion with specific details that show how often you visit the library, how infrequently you miss class, or how seldom you go to parties on nights before important tests.

Various methods of development appear in the sample paragraphs and essays that follow in this chapter. You will learn even more about exposition and persuasion in Section Five of this book. There you will find separate chapters on three very common and useful methods of development: illustration, comparison and contrast, and process analysis. Section Five also contains a chapter on techniques useful in persuasive writing. For now, just remember that any method of development can be used by itself or in combination with others to develop paragraphs and essays that explain, that persuade, or that do both.

DECIDING HOW TO ARRANGE THE IDEAS AND DETAILS IN A PARAGRAPH

FOR NARRATIVE AND DESCRIPTIVE WRITING

Often, the best way to organize narration or description is simply to recall details naturally—just as you saw or experienced them. When *narrating,* you can arrange events in the order they happened, from beginning to end; this is called "chronological order," or order of time. In the following narrative paragraph, John Steinbeck tells of a young man who is being chased by the police in the wilderness. Words that relate to time or that show action are in italics:

> Pepé *stumbled* down the hill. His throat was almost closed with thirst. *At first* he *tried to run,* but immediately he *fell* and *rolled. After that* he *went* more carefully. The moon *was just disappearing* behind the mountains *when* he *came* to the bottom. He *crawled* into the heavy brush *feeling* with his fingers for water. There was no water in the bed of the stream, only damp earth. Pepé *laid* his gun down and *scooped* up a handful of mud and put it in his mouth, and *then* he *spluttered* and *scraped* the earth from his tongue with his finger, for the mud *drew* at his mouth like a poultice [plaster dressing]. He *dug* a hole in the stream bed with his fingers, *dug* a little basin to catch water; but *before* it was very deep his head *fell* forward on the damp ground and he *slept.* ("Flight")

When *describing,* you can put concrete details into a *spatial* pattern, according to any arrangement you think best. For example, you might describe a place from east to west or from left to right; an object from top to bottom or from inside to outside; and a person from head to toe. In the following paragraph, John Steinbeck introduces a character from his short story "The Chrysanthemums" by telling us about both her facial and physical characteristics and then by describing what she wore:

> Elisa watched [the men] for a moment and then went back to her work. She was thirty-five. Her face was lean and strong and her eyes were as clear as water. Her figure looked blocked and heavy in her gardening costume, a man's black hat pulled low down over her eyes, clodhopper shoes, a figured print dress almost completely covered by a big corduroy apron with four big pockets to hold the snips, the trowel and scratcher, the seeds and the knife she worked with. She wore heavy leather gloves to protect her hands while she worked.

FOR EXPOSITORY AND PERSUASIVE WRITING

Again, several choices are available when trying your hand at exposition—writing that explains—and at persuasion—writing that proves a point or defends an opinion. Here are a few patterns of arrangement you can use.

FROM GENERAL TO SPECIFIC   Starting with a general statement and supporting it with specific details or ideas is a common way to organize a paragraph. Each of the following paragraphs has a different purpose and uses a different method of development. However, all begin with a general statement (the topic sentence) that is followed and developed by specific information.

ILLUSTRATION: DEVELOP AN IDEA WITH EXAMPLES

Bizarre [strange], sometimes tragic events checker [mark] the history of aviation in New Jersey. Charles and Anne Lindbergh built their estate at Somerville to be near a test facility; their son's kidnapping and murder exiled [drove] them from America for years. The *Hindenburg,* largest rigid airship ever built, crashed and burned at Lakehurst; that ended the use of dirigibles for passenger service. In his radio version of *War of the Worlds,* Orson Wells landed "Martians" at Grover's Mill—a hamlet just south of Princeton—and panicked thousands of listeners into fleeing the imaginary spacecraft. (William Howarth, *The John McPhee Reader*)

COMPARISON AND CONTRAST: POINT OUT SIMILARITIES AND DIFFERENCES

Grant and Lee were in complete contrast, representing two diametrically opposed elements in American life. Grant was the modern man emerging: behind him, ready to come on the stage, was the great age of steel and machinery, of crowded cities and a restless, burgeoning [blossoming] vitality. Lee might have ridden down from the old age of chivalry, lance in hand, silken banner fluttering over his head. Each man was the perfect champion of his cause, drawing both his strengths and his weaknesses from the people he led. (Bruce Catton, "Grant and Lee: A Study in Contrasts")

CLASSIFICATION: DISTINGUISH BETWEEN TYPES OR CLASSES

In general, there are seven basic signals that get communicated from the [baseball] manager . . . to the players. The batter may be ordered to take a pitch on a three-and-zero count, or to hit away. He may be asked to protect a base runner on a hit-and-run by trying to slug the ball on the ground. On a run-and-hit, the batter is ordered to swing at a pitch only if it is in the strike zone; however, on the bunt-and-run, the batter must try to bunt to protect the breaking runner. . . . The batter can be told to sacrifice bunt, which means he should try for the ball only if it is in the strike zone. There are signs for squeeze bunts, and finally, there is the sign to steal a base. (Rockwell Stensrud, "Who's on Third?")

DEFINITION: EXPLAIN A TERM OR CONCEPT

It's hard to imagine what under-development means until you have experienced it. Last year we had to queue [line up] on the road from Medellin to Barranquilla because a landslide had swept part of it away. The road, the only link between Colombia's main industrial city and its principal port, had been closed all weekend. Now it was open again, but only just. We sat in the Jeep, dwarfed by the huge *tractomulas* [tractor trailers] that haul Colombia's freight. . . . Three hours it took, inching forward through the rain, before we came to what they had managed to rebuild of the road; a single lorry's [truck's] width of gravel and mud, shelving precariously [dangerously] on a steep hillside. (Roger Garfitt, "Bogotá, Colombia")

ANALOGY: COMPARE AN ABSTRACT OR DIFFICULT IDEA TO SOMETHING THAT IS CONCRETE AND THAT THE READER KNOWS

Time is like a river made up of the events which happen, and a violent stream: for as soon as a thing has been seen, it is carried away, and another comes in its place, and this will be carried away too. (Marcus Aurelius, "Meditations")

FROM SPECIFIC TO GENERAL   Beginning with specific details and moving toward a general conclusion (the topic sentence) that relates to these details is another way to arrange information. Although the following paragraphs use different methods of development, all move from specific to general.

CONCLUSION AND SUPPORT: USE DETAILS THAT EXPLAIN OR PROVE

A New York taxi driver . . . is licensed to operate, and thereby earn his living, by the city. One of the rules in the taxi code stipulates that the cabdriver must take his customer to any point within the city limits that the rider requests. Never mind that the driver makes more money operating in Manhattan; is lost when he enters the precincts of Brooklyn; is frightened by the prospect of a trip to Harlem at night. The rules are clear. He must go where the customer asks. (Willard Gaylin, *The Rage Within*)

COMPARISON AND CONTRAST: POINT OUT SIMILARITIES AND DIFFERENCES

Just today I talked to a big blond bruiser of a football player who wants to learn the basics of grammar. I didn't tell him it was too late. You see, he was a very, very good football player, so good that he never failed a course in high school. He had written on a weekly theme [essay], "I wants to go to the prose and come fames." He may become a pro, may even become famous, but he will probably never read a good book, write a coherent letter or read a story to his children. I will, however, flunk him if he does not learn the material in the course. My job means too much to me to sacrifice my standards and turn soft. Suppose that every time my student played football badly, the coach said it was "just a game." Suppose the coach allowed him to drink booze, stay up all night, eat poorly and play sloppily. My student would be summarily [quickly] dismissed from the team or the team would lose the game. So it goes with academic courses. (Suzanne Britt, "I Wants to Go to the Prose")

(You learned earlier that various methods of development can be used together. The paragraph you just read uses both comparison and narration. Britt begins with an anecdote, a very brief story that makes a point. She then compares the standards she demands of a student with those a coach expects of football players.)

I had always thought of stingrays, with their broad wings and graceful movements, as almost mythological [legendary] beasts: part bird, part fish. These creatures have long been feared for their whiplike tails bearing a spine that can deliver an excruciatingly painful wound. Now, as a crystalline [clear] wave washes over my camera—half in, half out of the water—I watch in fascination as two stingrays cruise the shallows of North Sound off Grand Cayman [Island]. I have come to join divers who, amazingly, have been feeding large groups of southern stingrays . . . in waters protected by a barrier reef. As they gather around me, the rays lose their fearsome [frightening] reputation. I find them to be gentle, wondrous birds of the sea. (David Doubilet, "Ballet with Stingrays")

(The paragraph above uses both contrast and description.)

ANALOGY: COMPARE AN ABSTRACT OR DIFFICULT IDEA TO SOMETHING THAT IS CONCRETE AND THAT THE READER KNOWS

. . . imagine a loaf of raisin bread baking in the oven. Each raisin is a galaxy [group of millions of stars]. As the dough rises in the oven, the interior of the loaf expands, and all the raisins move apart from one another. The loaf of bread is like our expanding Universe. Every raisin sees its neighbors receding [moving away] from it; every raisin seems to be at the center of the expansion; but there is no center [to the Universe]. (Robert Jastrow, *Journey to the Stars*)

FROM QUESTION TO ANSWER   A good way to begin a paragraph is with an interesting question. You can then devote the rest of your paragraph to details that develop an effective answer to that question.

DEFINITION: EXPLAIN A TEAM OR CONCEPT

A weasel is wild. Who knows what he thinks? He sleeps in his underground den, his tail draped over his nose. Sometimes he lives in his den for two days without leaving. Outside, he stalks rabbits, mice, muskrats, and birds, killing more bodies than he can eat warm, and often dragging the carcasses home. Obedient to instinct, he bites his prey at the neck, either splitting the jugular vein at the throat or crunching the brain at the base of the skull, and he does not let go. One naturalist refused to kill a weasel who was socketed into his hand deeply as a rattlesnake. The man could in no way pry the tiny weasel off, and he had to walk half a mile to water, the weasel dangling from his palm, and soak him off like a stubborn label. (Annie Dillard, "Living Like Weasels")

ANALOGY: COMPARE AN ABSTRACT OR DIFFICULT IDEA TO SOMETHING THAT IS CONCRETE AND THAT THE READER KNOWS

How can a telescope provide information about the beginning of the Universe? The answer is that when we look out into space, we look into the past. If a galaxy is five billion light-years away, it takes five billion years for the light from this galaxy to reach the earth. Consequently, our telescopes show the galaxy not as it is today, but as it was five billion years ago, when the light we are receiving now had just left that galaxy on its way to the earth. A telescope is a time machine; it carries us back to the past. (Robert Jastrow, *Journey to the Stars*)

(The paragraph above is another that uses more than one method of development. Here, analogy combines with process analysis.)

FROM PROBLEM TO SOLUTION   Organizing a paragraph by stating a problem and explaining how to solve it in the sentences that follow is much like asking a question and answering it. It is especially effective when you are explaining a process or analyzing causes and effects. But it can be used with other methods of development as well.

PROCESS ANALYSIS: EXPLAIN HOW TO DO SOMETHING

For most people, being overweight is not simply a matter of vanity. Excess weight is a threat to health and longevity. You should start losing weight by getting a thorough physical examination, then begin following a regular exercise program prescribed by your doctor. Next, start counting calories; read labels or look up the caloric content of your favorite foods in diet guides available at most supermarkets and drugstores. Finally, stay away from high-fat animal products and rich desserts. Fill up on fruits, vegetables, natural grains and other high-fiber foods. (Diana Dempsey, "Tightening Our Belts")

BY ORDER OF IMPORTANCE Writers of fiction often place the most important bit of information last. This makes their work suspenseful and creates a more effective climax. If arranged in this pattern, an expository or persuasive paragraph can help you create emphasis by guiding your readers to the details and ideas you believe are most important. For example, Anthony Lewis waits until the end of the following paragraph to mention the right to vote—the most important of all rights—which had been denied black people in the South before 1954.

ILLUSTRATION: DEVELOP AN IDEA WITH EXAMPLES

It is hard to remember, now, what this country was like before May 17, 1954 [the day the U.S. Supreme Court outlawed racial segregation in public schools]. More than a third of America's public schools were segregated by law. And not just schools: In the Southern and Border states, black men and women and children were kept out of "white" hospitals, and parks, and beaches, and restaurants. Interracial marriage was forbidden. In the deep South, law and brutal force kept blacks from voting. (Anthony Lewis, "The System Worked")

AROUND A PIVOT The pivoting pattern begins with one idea, then changes direction—pivots—by presenting a different or contrasting idea. The topic sentence normally appears in the middle of the paragraph and announces the shift. Often, but not always, the topic sentence is introduced by a transition such as *but, however,* and *nonetheless.*

CAUSE AND EFFECT: EXPLAIN WHY SOMETHING HAPPENS

In the early 1980s, a young doctor named Barry Marshall was a medical laughingstock: He argued that ulcers were caused by a bacterium, not by stress. He even drank a vial of bacteria to prove his point. No one is laughing now. Today, experts agree that most stomach ulcers are caused by a tiny organism called *Helicobacter pylori*. As a result, many doctors no longer prescribe drugs that reduce stomach acid. They advise ulcer sufferers to take antibiotics. (Traci Watson, "Germs and Chronic Illness")

ILLUSTRATION: DEVELOP AN IDEA WITH EXAMPLES

I sometimes hear people who should know better saying that we would be healthier if we depended solely on herbal remedies and refused to take the synthetic drugs purveyed by modern scientific medicine. Nonsense! A large part of modern medicine *is* herbal medicine. Browse through a pharmacopoeia and see how many of the medicines prescribed by doctors and sold by druggists are prepared from plants. Quinine for malaria, ephedrine for asthma, cascara for constipation, digitalis for heart conditions, atropine for eye examinations and a great host of other valuable medicines in constant use came directly from folk herbal medicines, and are still prepared from wild plants or those recently brought under cultivation. (Euell Gibbons, *Stalking the Wild Asparagus*)

VISUALIZING PARAGRAPH DEVELOPMENT

The following paragraphs are from "Which Side of the Fence?" freshman Dan Roland's essay that recalls a honeymoon trip to Jamaica. The first uses the conclusion-and-support method of development and a general-to-specific pattern of organization. The second, which is arranged in the specific-to-general pattern, illustrates three methods of development: description, cause/effect, and contrast.

Topic sentence expresses a conclusion.

Paragraph moves from general to specific.

¶ Arriving at the resort is like stepping into another world. This ultra-modern hotel is surrounded by a golf course; tennis courts; a huge swimming pool; outdoor lounges complete with palm trees, calypso bands, and elegant bamboo cages that hold parrots and other exotic birds; and a beach that features water skiers, wind surfers, yachts, and hundreds of tourists wearing the latest summer fashions and sipping numerous fruit and rum drinks with little umbrellas in them.

Specific details support conclusion.

Paragraph moves from specific to general.

All of the luxury in this hotel is surrounded by a barbed-wire fence, with only one entrance on each side patrolled by armed security guards. This protects the tourist from a constant bombardment of sales pitches from native Jamaicans, who can feed their families for weeks by selling just a few of their homemade souvenirs. Hotel guests are allowed to go out through the gate, but natives may not come in. Many of them live in small shacks right next to the fence, so as never to miss a

Description

Cause/effect

Contrast

selling opportunity. The symbolism is staggering; on one

side are wealth and luxury, on the other poverty and

hunger. The fence is a barrier to the good life.   **Topic sentence**

REVISING TO IMPROVE DEVELOPMENT

Read these two versions of paragraphs from "Exile and Return," an essay appearing later in this chapter, which discusses the author's return to his high school after many years. Compare the second version with the first to learn how James Keller added to, corrected, and clarified his rough draft to improve the effectiveness of his essay.

Keller—Rough Draft

¶Eventually my eyes come to rest on the chalkboards. I

remember staring at them bored at what I was listening   **Why was he "bored"?**

Whose faces?   to. Faces turn and face me from seats in front and to my

side. They are only shadows from the past, only

memories. They're looking for me. And through me.   **Choppy, vague and weak. Needs detail.**

They've left. Some gone to school, some gone to the

Check meaning?   world. Others gone quite literally to hell, not soon to

return.

Out of the building I walk on grassy playing fields

Vague. What "places" are these?   that were greener whend.l.l| Places where many of us found   **Explain this term?**

brief, insignificant glory. I no longer remember who won

and who lost. Only that somehow we all walked away

winners and losers to the same heart. It is more than I

can bear.

I leave now, maybe forever, if I ever 𝒳 existed at

all.

Keller—Final Draft

¶Eventually my eyes come to rest on the chalkboards. Old
habits die hard. I remember staring at them through
teachers whose words "had forked no lightning." My
teachers and classmates are gone, but many faces remain.

Identifies "faces".

Adds quotation to explain why he was "bored."

Adds narrative and descriptive details.

From seats in front and to my side, they turn and stare.
They are shadows of the past, bloodless visions,
returned from long exile to mock my exile and return.

They're looking for me and through me. But they're only
memories. They've left, you know—some gone to school,
some gone to the world, others gone to their own
private hells. Faces that laughed, young and innocent,
now cry, worn and haggard. Their expressions hide lives
that were true and alive but now are neither.

Has removed "literally."

Smoother and developed more fully. Adds information about classmates.

Out of the building, I walk on grassy playing fields
where so many of us found brief insignificant glory.
They were greener in another spring. The empty stands
play sentinel to the lonely track and football field,
and a thousand ghosts applaud a hundred athletes only I
can see. I no longer remember who won and lost, only
that somehow we all walked away winners and losers to
the same heart, veterans of so much happiness and so
much pain. It is more than I can bear.

Identifies "places" with specific information.

Adds information to explain "insignificant glory."

A stronger conclusion: adds detail to convey his emotional reaction.

I leave now, maybe forever. I wonder if I ever
existed and was ever here at all. To say good-bye is to
die a little. And so I do.

PRACTICING METHODS OF DEVELOPMENT

Complete the paragraphs begun below. Include information based on your own observations and experiences. Use whatever method of development you think the topic sentence, which begins each paragraph, calls for.

1. My family provides me with a great deal of emotional support. For example, _____

_____

_____

_____

_____

_____

_____

2. There are three types of students at my college. The first _____

_____

_____

_____

_____

_____

3. If you want to flunk a test, do the following:

_____

_____

_____

_____

_____

4. Most people gain weight because _____

_____

_____

_____

_____

_____

5. My sister (brother, best friend) is a _____ type of person. I, on the other hand, am

_____

_____

_____

_____

_____

As you read the following selections, remember what you've just learned about (1) the methods that writers use to develop their ideas and (2) the patterns they use to organize their paragraphs. Approach each selection carefully, and devote as much effort to determining *how* the author has organized and developed the material as you do to understanding what the essay means. Doing so will help you develop your own writing more effectively.

The Last Safe Haven

Joannie M. Schrof

"The Last Safe Haven" appeared in the December 26, 1994 issue of U.S. News and World Report, *a weekly news magazine. It analyzes the spread of violence to the small town, once considered a refuge from the kinds of crime found in the city.*

Looking Ahead

1. This essay was printed in an end-of-year column called "Farewells: "Faces We Knew, Ways We Were: Now They Are Gone." This information is important in understanding the author's purpose.
2. Schrof makes good use of transitions and other devices to maintain coherence. Read her essay twice. The second time, circle words and phrases that make it coherent.

Vocabulary

hamlet	Small town, village.
maelstrom	Storm.
mayhem	Violence.
palpable	Obvious, plain, evident.
seared	Burned.
recital	Speech, reading, presentation.
refuge	Safe place, shelter.
relentless	Without end, unceasing.
sanctuary	Holy place, haven, refuge.

The Last Safe Haven

Joannie M. Schrof

Nineteen ninety-four seared a series of disturbing images into the American 1 memory: a mother drowning her sons, children shooting each other, a 5-year-old boy thrown from a high-rise window. The relentless recital of mayhem added to the fear, to the feeling—however illusory—that there was once true refuge, and that it has disappeared.

Nowhere is this sense more palpable than in the nation's small towns. While cities 2 have always battled crime, the small town has been celebrated as a sanctuary, where doors are left unlocked and children roam freely. But even the smallest towns are growing more dangerous, often at the hands of the very children they are famous for protecting.

Geneseo, Ill. (population 5,990), is one such place. A decade ago its quiet streets 3 won the state's "Hometown Award." This year, after a series of violent incidents, the police department created a gang investigation unit. Every other week now, it seems, a teenager is badly beaten in gang-related violence: Recently, a local boy was clubbed to death in a nearby town. Stolen cars, burglarized homes and vandalism are on the rise. And nightfall brings the sound of doors locking all around town.

City dwellers have long imagined that if things got too bad, they could pack up and 4 move to a place like Geneseo, a cozy, self-enclosed hamlet far from the maelstrom. It was probably always a fantasy. Now that we know it, the only alternative left is to stand and fight back.

Questions for Discussion

1. Identify the essay's thesis.
2. In Looking Ahead, you read that the subtitle of the column in which this essay appeared, "Faces We Knew, Ways We Were: Now They Are Gone," tells us something about the author's purpose. Explain.
3. What is the chief method of development used in paragraphs 1 and 4?
4. What is the chief method of development used in paragraphs 2 and 3?
5. What pattern of organization does Schrof use in paragraphs 2 and 4? In paragraph 3?
6. Explain the function of paragraph 2's first sentence in terms of maintaining coherence.
7. Find places in which Schrof uses transitions to maintain coherence.

Thinking Critically

1. In paragraph 2, Schrof writes: "even the smallest towns are growing more dangerous, often at the hands of the very children they are famous for protecting." Are children getting more and more violent? If so, what do you think is causing this?
2. Schrof concludes by saying that "the only alternative left is to stand and fight back." What are some ways we can combat the growing trend toward violence?

Suggestions for Journal Entries

1. Whether you come from a city or small town, do you think your community is a safe haven? Ask yourself whether or not you feel safe walking the streets at night, leaving the front door unlocked, carrying around a lot of cash, parking your car on the street, and so on. Try asking and answering a variety of questions that will help you determine how safe your community is.
2. Many of us have "safe havens," places where we can feel safe and at ease. There we seek advice, safety, sympathy, or encouragement, or just a peaceful atmosphere where we can relax and rejuvenate ourselves ("recharge our batteries"). Where is your "safe haven"? Freewrite for about ten minutes to describe this place.

Exile and Return

James Keller

As managing editor for his college newspaper, James Keller wrote many news and feature stories that attracted the attention of professors and fellow students. Today he is the head tutor in a college computer writing lab, and is pursuing graduate work in English. He plans a career as a teacher and writer. "Exile and Return" recalls his visit to his suburban high school several years after graduation. This before-and-after portrait reveals as much about the author as it does about his school.

Looking Ahead

1. Keller's thesis statement appears at the end of his first paragraph. Identify the main point he makes in this essay as you read this sentence.
2. "Had forked no lightning" (paragraph 5) is from "Do Not Go Gentle into That Good Night," a poem by Dylan Thomas.

Vocabulary

arcane	Secret, known only by a few.
asbestos	Insulating material now considered a health hazard.
banality	Boring quality.
predicting	Giving signs of, foretelling.
stifling	Suffocating.

Exile and Return | *James Keller*

It's all different, quiet and grey now, like the sun reflecting on the previous night's 1 darkness or predicting the afternoon's storm. On this stifling summer morning, I scarcely recognize the school I had attended for four years. The life and laughter have died. It is another world.

I walk down the vacant halls, and what light there is shines a path on the mirrored 2 beige floors, leading me past imposing grey lockers that stand erect in columns. At one time, they woke the dead in closing but now remain closed in silence. I remember the faces of people who stood and sometimes slumped before them at day's end. They were friendly faces that looked up and nodded or said "Hello" as I galloped past. Now there are other faces, faces of people I never got to know.

The lockers soon give way to the classrooms, cement cells we once lived in, learned 3 in, and often slept in. Steel I-beams I had once hardly noticed now hang like doom over cracked and peeling walls. The architect left them exposed, for want of talent, I assume. From the color scheme of putrid green to the neutral asbestos ceiling and steel rafters, the banality of the classrooms overwhelms me.

The rooms are empty now save the ancient desks. They are yellow clay and steel 4 and much smaller than I remember. I can still read arcane graffiti, its meaning forgotten, on their dull surfaces. The handwriting is my own. I recognize the doodles drawn as every minute ran past like a turtle climbing up a glass wall. Back then, they killed the time. They didn't do much for the furniture either.

Eventually my eyes come to rest on the chalkboards. Old habits die hard. I remem- 5 ber staring at them through teachers whose words "had forked no lightning." My teachers and classmates are gone, but many faces remain. From seats in front and to my side, they turn and stare. They are shadows of the past, bloodless visions, returned from long exile to mock my exile and return. They're looking for me and through me. But they're only memories. They've left, you know—some gone to school, some gone to the world, others gone to their own private hells. Faces that laughed, young and innocent, now cry, worn and haggard. Their expressions hide lives that were true and alive but now are neither.

Out of the building, I walk on grassy playing fields where so many of us found brief 6 insignificant glory. They were greener in another spring. The empty stands play sentinel to the lonely track and football field, and a thousand ghosts applaud a hundred athletes only I can see. I no longer remember who won and lost, only that somehow we all walked away winners and losers to the same heart, veterans of so much happiness and so much pain. It is more than I can bear.

I leave now, maybe forever. I wonder if I ever existed and was ever here at all. To 7 say good-bye is to die a little. And so I do.

QUESTIONS FOR DISCUSSION

1. What is Keller's thesis statement? What words in that thesis express his main point? In short, what is he telling us about his high school?
2. In which paragraphs does the topic sentence not appear at the very beginning? Can you find a paragraph in which the central idea is only implied?
3. The author's purpose is to contrast his memories of a place with its present reality. However, he uses other methods of development as well. In which paragraph or paragraphs does he use cause and effect?
4. Where in this essay can you find examples of narration and description?
5. Find an instance in which Keller has used analogy.
6. Which pattern of organization discussed earlier in this chapter does Keller use in paragraph 2?
7. Which pattern of organization does he use in paragraphs 6 and 7?

THINKING CRITICALLY

The biographical note on Keller, which appears before the essay, claims that this selection reveals as much about the author as about the place he is discussing. What have you learned about Keller's personality from this essay?

SUGGESTIONS FOR JOURNAL ENTRIES

1. Take a mental stroll through the hallways, classrooms, or athletic fields of your high school. What do you remember most about it and about your classmates, your teachers, and yourself? Use focused freewriting or listing to record these memories in your journal.

   Next, read your journal entry. What main impression about your high school experience can you draw from these details? Did you enjoy it? Were you happy and secure around the teachers and students you met each day? Is the opposite true? Or do you have mixed feelings? Put your main impression into a preliminary thesis statement that might get you started on a longer assignment described in the Suggestions for Sustained Writing at the end of this chapter.
2. "To say good-bye is to die a little," Keller writes. Recall an incident in which you had to say good-bye to someone, something, or some place. Use focused freewriting to write a brief story about the event. Try to reveal why saying good-bye was so hard.

Condolences, It's a Girl

Sandra Burton

Written while Burton was in Beijing, capital of the People's Republic of China, this article appeared in a special edition of Time *magazine devoted to issues facing women in the 1990s. Because of its large population, China has a "one-child-per-couple" policy, which, as Burton explains, "has inflamed age-old prejudices against females."*

LOOKING AHEAD

1. Burton's title is a twist on what we expect to hear at the birth of a child: "Congratulations, it's a . . ."
2. The paragraphs in this selection use some methods of development you just read about. Look for contrast, cause and effect, and illustration.
3. In paragraph 3, we learn that the "Communists sought to change" the status of women in China in 1949. That was the year the Communist revolution led by Mao Tse-tung took control of the country.
4. Burton uses "feudal" to explain traditional Chinese thinking about having children. Feudalism was a male-dominated political and economic system in medieval Europe.

VOCABULARY

amniocentesis	Medical procedure to determine the health of a fetus.
bastion	Stronghold.
cadre	Group, association.
condolences	Expressions of sympathy.
draconian	Tyrannical, rigid, strict.
enlightened	Well-educated, forward-thinking, progressive.
infanticide	Murder of a baby.
inflamed	Aroused, made stronger.
scion	Offspring, child.
wistful	Sad, melancholic.

Condolences, It's a Girl

Sandra Burton

The letter from a Chinese woman to her American friend reflected her torment 1 and tears. "I told you I wish a baby girl, because nothing can compare with one's love of a baby, especially mother and daughter," she wrote in broken English. Instead of bringing joy, however, the birth of a daughter was destroying her family. "My husband wants to divorce me," she continued. "When he knew the baby was a girl, he left quickly." Reluctant to blame only her husband, she pointed to her in-laws. "He is the only boy, so his having a son is more important for his parents," she explained. "Although he had been hoping for a boy, I never thought he would act like this."

Old attitudes die hard in a society that has been a bastion of male chauvinism for 22 2 centuries. Until a few decades ago, the drowning of infant girls was tolerated in poor rural areas as an economic necessity. A girl was just another mouth to feed, another dowry to pay, a temporary family member who would eventually leave to serve her husband's kin. A boy, on the other hand, meant more muscle for the farm work, someone to care for aged parents and burn offerings to ancestors.

The Communists sought to change all that in 1949 by freeing women from the 3 household, putting them to work in fields and factories and giving them the right to inherit property. Suddenly a girl could have positive economic value. Still, feudal tradition has resisted change in many regions, and the government's draconian one-child-per-couple population policy, begun in 1979, has inflamed age-old prejudices against females. Rural and minority families routinely lie, cheat or pay fines in order to try a second pregnancy in the hope of having a son. And female infanticide—plus its modern variation, the misuse of amniocentesis to identify female fetuses in order to abort them—continues. The problem is so extensive that government campaigns urge parents to "Love your daughter" and allow girl babies to live.

Even in enlightened circles, condolences are in order for a couple whose new-born 4 is a girl. Over dinner in the Beijing apartment of a liberal-party cadre, a young guest proudly passes around color photos of her infant son, lying spread-eagled on a blanket, his genitals prominently displayed. Seated beside her, the new mother of a baby girl looks on in wistful silence. She carries no pictures. Jiang Junsheng, a senior engineer in a Beijing auto-parts factory, says he wasn't upset when his only child, a daughter, was born, but "my mother did not like it." That's an understatement, says his wife Chen Yiyun, 50, a well-known sociologist. "His mother would not take care of our daughter," she says. "Yet when my husband's brother had a boy, she showered him with attention."

Social observers believe a daughter's lot will improve as women become more valu- 5 able to China's growing economy and as the one-child policy eventually makes every scion—male and female—precious to parents. Chen's own daughter Jiang Xu, 19, reflects changing attitudes when she expresses her preference for a daughter: "To have a boy means happiness for a moment. To have a girl means a lifetime of good fortune."

QUESTIONS FOR DISCUSSION

1. What is Burton's thesis statement?
2. Contrasting a mother's and father's reactions to the birth of their daughter (paragraph 1) is a good way to arouse the reader's interest. Where else does Burton use contrast to develop her ideas?
3. In what paragraph is the cause-and-effect method used?
4. What is the central idea in the last paragraph? What method that you learned about earlier does Burton use to develop this idea?
5. Which paragraphs are arranged according to the general-to-specific pattern? Does Burton ever use the specific-to-general pattern? Where?

THINKING CRITICALLY

"Old attitudes die hard," says Burton at the beginning of paragraph 2. Make a list of old attitudes you wish would "die." Focus on attitudes about men, women, families, religion, education, government, or any other topic or topics important to you.

SUGGESTIONS FOR JOURNAL ENTRIES

1. Use the focused freewriting method you learned about in "Getting Started" to describe your reaction to the birth of a sister, brother, niece, nephew, cousin, or child of your own. Did the sex of the child matter to you or to anyone else?
2. Does your family treat boys and girls differently? If you are female, think of ways in which your parents, grandparents, aunts, uncles, and other family members have treated your brother(s) or male cousins. If you are male, think of ways they have treated your sister(s) or female cousins. Were they different from the ways they treated you? If so, list as many of these differences as you can.

A Brother's Dreams

Paul Aronowitz

Paul Aronowitz was a medical student at Case Western Reserve University when he wrote this very sensitive essay comparing his dreams, hopes, and ambitions with those of his schizophrenic brother. Schizophrenia is a mental illness characterized by withdrawal from reality.

Aronowitz's love, compassion, and understanding come across clearly as he unfolds the story of how he learned to deal with the fact that his brother's strange, sometimes violent behavior was the symptom of an illness and not a defect in character. This essay is also Aronowitz's admission and unselfish affirmation that, however "elusive" and "trivial," his brother's dreams might be even more meaningful than his own.

"A Brother's Dreams" first appeared in "About Men," a weekly column in The New York Times Magazine.

LOOKING AHEAD

1. Aronowitz's central idea concerns how he came to understand his brother's illness and to accept the fact that his brother's dreams were meaningful and important. However, the author does not begin to reveal this central idea until near the end of this essay, and he never puts the idea into a formal thesis statement.
2. Many of the paragraphs in this selection are developed through narration and description, but Aronowitz also makes good use of cause and effect, comparison and contrast, illustration, and conclusion and support.
3. Josef Mengele, whom Aronowitz mentions in paragraph 5, was a Nazi medical researcher who conducted unspeakable experiments in which he tortured and maimed or killed thousands of human beings.

VOCABULARY

acrid	Bitter, harsh, sharp.
aimlessly	Without purpose.
alienate	Make enemies of, isolate oneself from.
delusions	Misconceptions, fantasies.
depravity	Immorality, corruption.
elusive	Hard to grasp, intangible.
paranoid	Showing unreasonable or unwarranted suspicion.
prognosis	Prediction about the course or outcome of an illness.
resilient	Able to bounce back.
siblings	Sisters and brothers.

A Brother's Dreams | *Paul Aronowitz*

Each time I go home to see my parents at their house near Poughkeepsie, N.Y., 1
my brother, a schizophrenic for almost nine years now, comes to visit from the
halfway house where he lives nearby. He owns a car that my parents help him to maintain, and his food and washing are taken care of by the halfway house. Somewhere,
somehow along the way, with the support of a good physician, a social worker and my
ever-resilient parents, he has managed to carve a niche for himself, to bite off some inde-
pendence and, with it, elusive dreams that, to any healthy person, might seem trivial.

My brother sits in a chair across from me, chain-smoking cigarettes, trying to take 2
the edge off the medications he'll be on for the rest of his life. Sometimes his tongue
hangs loosely from his mouth when he's listening or pops out of his mouth as he
speaks—a sign of tardive dyskinesia, an often-irreversible side effect of his medication. 3

He draws deeply on his cigarette and tells me he can feel his mind healing—cells
being replaced, tissue being restored, thought processes returning. He knows this is happening because he dreams of snakes, and hot, acrid places in which he suffocates if he
moves too fast. When he wakes, the birds are singing in the trees outside his bedroom
window. They imitate people in his halfway house, mocking them and calling their
names. The birds are so smart, he tells me, so much smarter than we are.

His face, still handsome despite its puffiness (another side effect of the medications 4
that allow him to function outside the hospital), and warm brown eyes are serious.
When I look into his eyes I imagine I can see some of the suffering he has been through.
I think of crossed wires, of receptors and neurotransmitters, deficits and surpluses,
progress and relapse, and I wonder, once again, what has happened to my brother.

My compassion for him is recent. For many years, holidays, once happy occasions 5
for our family of seven to gather together, were emotional torture sessions. My brother
would pace back and forth in the dining room, lecturing us, his voice loud, dominating,
crushing all sound but his own, about the end of the world, the depravity of our exis-
tences. His speeches were salted with paranoid delusions: our house was bugged by the
F.B.I.; my father was Josef Mengele; my mother was selling government secrets to the
Russians.

His life was decaying before my eyes, and I couldn't stand to listen to him. My 6
resentment of him grew as his behavior became more disruptive and aggressive. I saw
him as being ultimately responsible for his behavior. As my anger increased, I withdrew
from him, avoiding him when I came home to visit from college, refusing to discuss the
bizarre ideas he brought up over the dinner table. When I talked with my sister or other
two brothers about him, our voices always shadowed in whispers, I talked of him as of
a young man who had chosen to spend six months of every year in a pleasant, private
hospital on the banks of the Hudson River, chosen to alienate his family with threats,
chosen to withdraw from the stresses of the world. I hated what he had become. In all
those years, I never asked what his diagnosis was.

Around the fifth year of his illness, things finally changed. One hot summer night, 7
he attacked my father. When I came to my father's aid, my brother broke three of my
ribs and nearly strangled me. The State Police came and took him away. My father's
insurance coverage had run out on my brother, so this time he was taken to a locked

ward at the state hospital where heavily sedated patients wandered aimlessly in stockinged feet up and down long hallways. Like awakening from a bad dream, we gradually began talking about his illness. Slowly and painfully, I realized that he wasn't responsible for his disease any more than a cancer patient is for his pain.

As much as I've learned to confront my brother's illness, it frightens me to think 8 that one day, my parents gone from the scene, my siblings and I will be responsible for portions of my brother's emotional and financial support. This element of the future is one we still avoid discussing, much the way we avoided thinking about the nature of his disease and his prognosis. I'm still not capable of thinking about it.

Now I come home and listen to him, trying not to react, trying not to show disap- 9 proval. His delusions are harmless and he is, at the very least, communicating. When he asks me about medical school, I answer with a sentence or two—no elaboration, no revelations about the dreams I cradle in my heart.

He talks of his own dreams. He hopes to finish his associate's degree—the same one 10 he has been working on between hospitalizations for almost eight years now—at the local community college. Next spring, with luck, he'll get a job. His boss will be understanding, he tells me, cutting him a little slack when he has his "bad days," letting him have a day off here or there when things aren't going well. He puts out his cigarette and lights another one.

Time stands still. This could be last year, or the year before, or the year before that. 11 I'm within range of becoming a physician, of realizing something I've been working toward for almost five years, while my brother still dreams of having a small job, living in his own apartment and of being well. As the smoke flows from his nose and mouth, I recall an evening some time ago when I drove upstate from Manhattan to tell my parents and my brother that I was getting married (an engagement later severed). My brother's eyes lit up at the news, and then a darkness fell over them.

"What's wrong?" I asked him. 12

"It's funny," he answered matter-of-factly. "You're getting married, and I've never 13 even had a girlfriend." My mother's eyes filled with tears, and she turned away. She was trying her best to be happy for me, for the dreams I had—for the dreams so many of us take for granted.

"You still have us," I stammered, reaching toward him and touching his arm. All of 14 a sudden my dreams meant nothing; I didn't deserve them and they weren't worth talking about. My brother shrugged his shoulders, smiled and shook my hand, his large, tobacco-stained fingers wrapping around my hand, dwarfing my hand.

QUESTIONS FOR DISCUSSION

1. If you wanted to write a formal thesis statement for this essay, what would it be?
2. "A Brother's Dreams" contains at least two paragraphs that are developed through description. Identify one of them. What important idea does this paragraph communicate?
3. The purpose of paragraph 6 is to explain a cause and an effect. What is the paragraph's topic sentence (cause)? What details (effect) does Aronowitz provide to develop the paragraph fully?
4. Which paragraphs use narration?
5. Aronowitz gets specific about his brother's dreams in paragraph 10, which he develops by stating a conclusion and then supporting this conclusion with details. Identify these details.
6. Paragraph 11 contrasts some of Aronowitz's dreams to some of his brother's. In what other paragraph do we see their dreams contrasted?
7. Most paragraphs in this essay are organized in the general-to-specific pattern. However, paragraphs 11 and 13 are organized according to order of importance. What is the most important idea in each of these paragraphs?
8. This is a powerful essay. Which paragraph affects you most strongly? What do the details in this paragraph tell you about the author or his brother or both?

THINKING CRITICALLY

1. Explaining how he came to terms with his brother's illness, Aronowitz says his compassion for his brother is only "recent." Pretend you are interviewing Aronowitz. What would he say is the reason for not feeling compassion earlier? What caused his change in attitude?
2. Reread Michael Witt's "Gambling" in Chapter 2. In what way are these two essays similar?

SUGGESTIONS FOR JOURNAL ENTRIES

1. Aronowitz writes about a person whose lifestyle and dreams are very different from those of most other people. Do you know someone like this? If so, write a paragraph showing how this person's lifestyle or dreams differ from those of most others. Use one major method of development; for instance, you might *describe* what this individual looks like (much in the way Aronowitz describes his brother in paragraphs 2 and 4), or you might use *narration* to tell a story about the kind of behavior you have come to expect from the person (as Aronowitz does in paragraphs 3, 5, and 7). You might even want to try your

hand at the cause-and-effect method by telling your reader how you normally react to or deal with this person and then explaining what causes you to react in this way.

2. Aronowitz's essay contrasts his brother's dreams to his own. Write a paragraph in which you show how different you are from your brother, sister, or other close relative by contrasting a major goal in your life to one of his or hers.

   Clearly identify the two different goals in your topic sentence, and fill the rest of your paragraph with details showing how different they are; that is, develop the paragraph by contrast. Your topic sentence might go something like this: "My sister Janet intends to move to the city and find a high-paying job, even if she hates every minute of it; I'll be happy earning the modest income that comes with managing our family farm."

SUGGESTIONS FOR SUSTAINED WRITING

1. Write a paragraph that uses the cause-and-effect method to explain why you do something habitually. For instance, explain why you are late for work every day, why you take the same road home, why you frequent a particular restaurant or bar, or why you study in the same place every night.

   Arrange the paragraph in a general-to-specific or specific-to-general pattern, provide enough details to develop your central idea clearly and convincingly, and check for unity and coherence. You will find examples of effective cause-and-effect paragraphs in "Exile and Return" and "A Brother's Dreams."

   As with other assignments, revise your work as necessary; never be satisfied with an early draft! Add or remove detail as appropriate, and insert transitions that will make your ideas easy to follow. Then edit carefully for mechanical errors that might reduce your writing's effectiveness.

2. If you responded to the first of the Suggestions for Journal Entries after "The Last Safe Haven," you have begun to gather information on whether or not you believe your community is safe. If you think it isn't, use what you have written thus far as the basis of a longer essay that supports your opinion. Here's a *sample* outline for the first draft of such an essay:

   Paragraph 1: Thesis: *An increase in serious crime is making my hometown unsafe.* (You might include general information about kinds of crime you have seen, read about, or heard about.)
   Paragraph 2: Discusses specific examples of criminal acts you know about. A good way to organize this paragraph is the general-to-specific pattern.
   Paragraph 3: Uses cause and effect to explain the increase in crime. A good way to organize this paragraph is the question-to-answer pattern.
   Paragraph 4: Uses process analysis to explain what your community should do to combat crime. A good way to organize this paragraph is the order-of-importance pattern.
   Paragraph 5: Concludes the essay by referring to the thesis and expressing hope that things will get better.

   Make sure to revise your rough draft several times. As you do, practice the techniques for maintaining coherence and unity discussed in Chapter 2. Whenever possible, add detail to make your ideas more convincing. Finally, edit and proofread the final version carefully.

3. After you read Keller's "Exile and Return," you might have used your journal to take a "mental stroll" through your high school and to write a preliminary thesis statement for an essay explaining your main impression or opinion of the time you spent there. If so, you might also have begun collecting memories that explain that impression.

   Read your journal notes carefully. Add information if you can. Then, use your preliminary thesis as the beginning of an essay on your high school experience. Express your main impression or opinion of the experience through the thesis statement's main point.

Next, write three or four paragraphs that explain or support your thesis. Give each paragraph a topic sentence about one aspect of your experience. Make sure the topic sentence expresses a main point, and focus the information in your paragraph on that point.

Here's what an outline for such an essay *might* look like:

Paragraph 1
Thesis: *The thing I appreciate most about Valley High is that it helped me gain confidence as a student.* (This paragraph might also include information about the kind of high school you attended, your overall impression of the place, and things you most remember about it.)

Paragraph 2
Topic Sentence: *My classmates were supportive*
Method of Development: Illustration
Pattern: General to Specific

Paragraph 3
Topic Sentence: *My teachers taught me to study for tests.*
Method of Development: Process Analysis or Contrast
Pattern: Order of Importance

Paragraph 4
Topic Sentence: *With the help of math tutors, I finally overcame my fear of algebra.*
Method of Development: Cause and Effect or Contrast
Pattern: Pivot

Paragraph 5:
Conclusion: This paragraph makes reference to the thesis. It also explains that the confidence you developed in high school will help you in college.

Read your rough draft carefully. Add details as needed to make your essay complete and convincing. After completing several drafts, edit and proofread the best of them.

4. Review your journal notes after Burton's "Condolences, It's a Girl." You may have described important differences in the ways your family treated boys and girls. Focus on one such difference based upon personal experience, and express it in a topic sentence. Here are two examples of what that sentence might say:

In my house, I spent Saturdays doing housework while my brother played baseball or went fishing.
When I was a boy, Saturdays meant getting up early to wash the car, mow the lawn, or clean up the basement while my sisters slept until noon!

Now provide specific examples of what your family expected of you. Talk about having to scrub the bathroom sink or vacuum the rug as you saw your brother stroll out of the house with a baseball bat over his shoulder. Or explain how hard it was to lug garbage up the cellar steps while your sister was still in dreamland. Then talk about the other things you had to do while your brother(s) or sister(s) relaxed! You should wind up with a paragraph developed through both comparison and contrast and illustration. As always, revise and edit your work carefully as you learned in "Getting Started." In the process, check for unity and coherence.

5. After completing Paul Aronowitz's "A Brother's Dreams," you might have written a paragraph in your journal explaining how different your goal in life is from that of your brother, sister, or other close relative. If so, the method by which you developed this paragraph was contrast.

Reread this paragraph. What does it tell you about your subject's character? What kind of person is he or she? Turn your answer into the central idea (thesis statement) of an essay in which you continue to discuss this relative. In fact, make the paragraph you've already written the introduction to your essay.

As you plan this essay, consider writing a paragraph or two in which you describe this individual—the way he walks, the way she dresses, and so on. You might also want to include a narrative paragraph, one in which you tell a story that helps support what you say about him or her in your thesis. Finally, think about using additional methods of development—illustration, and conclusion and support, for example—in other paragraphs to develop your thesis further.

Once again, remember that writing is a process. You owe it to yourself and your readers to produce the most effective paper you can through painstaking rewriting and editing.

Chapter 4

INTRODUCTIONS AND CONCLUSIONS

In the previous chapters you learned a number of important principles to help you focus on the central idea of a paragraph or essay and to express this central idea in a topic sentence or thesis statement. You also learned how to develop paragraphs adequately and to make sure that each paragraph in an essay clearly develops the essay's thesis.

Most effective essays begin with an interesting and informative introduction—a paragraph or a series of paragraphs that reveals the essay's thesis and captures the reader's attention. Similarly, most successful essays end with a paragraph or a series of paragraphs that brings the writer's discussion of the subject to a timely and logical conclusion. Effective conclusions always leave the reader satisfied that everything the writer set out to discuss from the very beginning has been discussed.

Clearly, then, introductions and conclusions have special uses and are important to the success of an essay. That's why this entire chapter is devoted to explaining how to write them.

WRITING INTRODUCTIONS

Before deciding exactly what to include in an introduction, how to organize it, or even how to begin it, ask yourself whether the essay you're writing actually calls for a formal introduction. If you're writing a narrative, for instance, you might simply want to start with the very first event in your story. Of course, you can always begin with colorful details, exciting vocabulary, or intriguing ideas that will spark your reader's interest. But you need not provide a thesis statement, background information, explanatory details, or other introductory material before getting into the story proper. If you feel the need to express your central idea in a formal thesis statement, you can do so later, at a convenient point in the body of your essay or even in its conclusion.

On the other hand, you might decide that your essay needs a formal introduction. If so, remember that the *most important* function of an introduction is to capture the attention of the readers and make them read on. However, you can also use an introduction to:

- Reveal the essay's central idea as expressed in the thesis.
- Guide readers to important ideas in the body of the essay.
- Provide background or explanatory information to help readers understand the essay's purpose and thesis.

Consider these four objectives when you plan your introduction. But if you are unable to decide how to begin, simply write out a preliminary thesis statement and go directly to the body of your essay. You can always get back to your introduction later in the writing process. It certainly does not have to be the very first part of the essay you write!

However you choose to get started, remember that an exciting part of writing is deciding *exactly* what you want to say about your subject. You usually won't make this discovery until after you have completed at least one draft—and often more than one draft—of the middle or body paragraphs of your essay. Once you have done that, your chances of going back and drafting a clearer, more substantial thesis will have improved. So will your chances of writing an interesting and effective introduction.

The simplest and sometimes best way to write an introductory paragraph or series of introductory paragraphs is to place your thesis at the very beginning and to follow it with explanatory details that prepare readers for what they will find in the body of the essay. However, depending on your purpose, your thesis, and your audience, this may not always be the best way to begin. In Chapter 3 you learned several methods to develop and organize the middle paragraphs in a piece of writing. Similarly, there are many methods for developing and organizing an introduction. Here are eight:

1. Use a startling remark or statistic.
2. Ask a question or present a problem.
3. Challenge a widely held assumption or opinion.
4. Use a comparison, a contrast, or an analogy.
5. Tell an anecdote or describe a scene.
6. Use a quotation.
7. Define an important term or concept.
8. Address your readers.

Often, beginning writers limit their introductions to one paragraph. Doing so will help you get to the point quickly. On the other hand, you can—and sometimes must— spread your opening remarks over two or three short paragraphs. This may help you increase your readers' interest because it allows you to use a variety of methods to write your introduction. Each method is described below and illustrated by one or more sample paragraphs. In some samples, the central idea is expressed in a formal thesis statement (shown in italics); in others, the central idea is only implied, and no formal thesis statement can be identified.

USE A STARTLING REMARK OR STATISTIC

Some pieces of writing begin with statements or statistics (numbers) that, while true to the author's intent, have an effective shock value—one sure to make readers want to continue. Take this example of a lead paragraph from an essay on the state of the American family:

Divorce and out-of-wedlock childbirth are transforming the lives of American children. In the postwar generation more than 80 percent of children grew up in a family with two biological parents who were married to each other. By 1980 only 50 percent could expect to spend their entire childhood in an intact family. If current trends continue, less than half of all children born today will live continuously with their own mother and father throughout childhood. *Most American children will spend several years in a single-mother family.* (Barbara Dafoe Whitehead, "Dan Quayle Was Right")

You might find this technique particularly effective if you have to take an unpopular stand on a well-known subject, as did former Philadelphia Phillies pitcher Robin Roberts in the opening of "Strike Out Little League":

In 1939, Little League baseball was organized by Bert and George Bebble and Carl Stotz of Williamsport, Pa. What they had in mind in organizing this kids' baseball program, I'll never know. But *I'm sure they never visualized the monster it would grow into.*

A startling statement is often followed by details—some of them statistics—that explain the writer's point. Such is the case with the introduction to "The Nuclear Winter," in which Carl Sagan warns of nuclear destruction:

Except for fools and madmen, everyone knows that nuclear war would be an unprecedented [never having happened before] human catastrophe. A more or less typical strategic warhead has a yield of 2 megatons, the explosive equivalent of 2 million tons of TNT. But 2 million tons of TNT is about the same as all the bombs exploded in World War II—a single bomb with the explosive power of the entire Second World War but compressed into a few seconds of time and an area 30 to 40 miles across.

In *Victims of Vanity,* a book criticizing laboratory tests on animals, Lynda Dickinson decided that spreading startling remarks and statistics over three short paragraphs would be a better way to capture the readers' attention and prepare them for her thesis than using one long unit:

Lipstick, face cream, anti-perspirant, laundry detergent . . . these products and hundreds of other personal care and household items have one common ingredient: the suffering and death of millions of animals.

An average of 25 million animals die every year in North America for the testing of everything from new cosmetics to new methods of warfare. Five hundred thousand to one million of these animals are sacrificed each year to test new cosmetics alone.

Of all the pain and suffering caused by animal research, cosmetic and household product testing is among the least justifiable, as it cannot even be argued that [these] tests are done to improve the quality of human life.

ASK A QUESTION OR PRESENT A PROBLEM

If you begin by asking a question or presenting a problem, you can devote the rest of your essay to discussing that question or problem and, perhaps, to providing answers or solutions. For example, this introduction to a chapter in a book by Euell Gibbons begins with a question the rest of the chapter answers:

> Why bother with wild food plants in a country which produces a surplus of many domestic food products? With as much reason, one might ask, why go fishing for mountain trout when codfish fillets are for sale in any supermarket? Or why bother with hunting and game cookery when unlimited quantities of fine meat can be purchased at every butcher counter? (Euell Gibbons, *Stalking the Wild Asparagus*)

The same technique can be seen in this two-paragraph introduction to a *USA Today* editorial:

> After 30 years of acceptance, the wisdom of affirmative action is up for recall. From California to Congress, the clamor is growing to revamp or to eliminate activist policies designed to deter gender and race discrimination.
> Why now? Has the ultimate goal—a society where color or sex shouldn't matter when it comes to opportunity—radically changed? Has it been realized? ("Affirmative Action: Not an All-or-Nothing Issue")

In the first paragraph of "The Ambivalence of Abortion," Linda Bird Francke introduces the problem she and her husband faced over an unplanned pregnancy, thus preparing us for her discussion of abortion later in the essay:

> We were sitting in a bar on Lexington Avenue when I told my husband I was pregnant. It is not a memory I like to dwell on. Instead of the champagne and hope which had heralded [announced] the impending [coming] births of the first, second and third child, the news of this one was greeted with shocked silence and Scotch. "Jesus," my husband kept saying to himself, stirring the ice cubes around and around, "Oh Jesus."

CHALLENGE A WIDELY HELD ASSUMPTION OR OPINION

This can be a quick, direct way to state your thesis and stir the reader's interest. In most cases it will take only a few sentences for you to deny the assumption or opinion and to state your own views. Notice how smoothly Roger D. McGrath does this in the introduction to "The Myth of Frontier Violence":

It is commonly assumed that violence is part of our frontier heritage. But *the historical record shows that frontier violence was very different from violence today.* Robbery and burglary, two of our most common crimes, were of no great significance in the frontier towns of the Old West, and rape was seemingly nonexistent.

Use a Comparison, a Contrast, or an Analogy

Comparison points out similarities; contrast points out differences. Both methods can help you provide important information about your subject, clarify or emphasize a point, and catch the readers' attention.

Donald M. Murray offers students good advice by contrasting the way they sometimes complete writing assignments with the more thorough and careful process used by professionals:

> When students complete a first draft, they consider the job of writing done—and their teachers too often agree. *When professional writers complete a first draft, they usually feel that they are at the start of the writing process.* When a draft is completed, the job of writing can begin. ("The Maker's Eye")

In the following paragraph, student Dan Roland uses both comparison and contrast. He begins by likening Kingston, Jamaica, to any city the reader might recognize, only to follow with a stark contrast between the extremes of wealth and poverty found there. The effect is startling and convincing. Roland has prepared his readers well for the thesis at the end of the paragraph.

> From my seat on an American Airlines 727, Kingston, Jamaica, looks like any other large urban center to me: tall buildings dominate the skyline, traffic weaves its way through roadways laid out like long arteries from the heart of the city. But Kingston is not like other cities, for it is here that some of the most extreme poverty in the world exists. The island of Jamaica was founded as a slave colony to help satisfy Europe's great demand for sugar cane, and its inhabitants are the descendants of slaves. Despair and poverty are part of everyday life and have been for centuries. The leading industry is tourism; every year thousands of well-to-do vacationers, mostly Americans and Canadians, come to stay in the multitudes of luxurious hotels and resorts. *Jamaica is one of the most beautiful places on Earth; it is also one of the most destitute [poorest].* ("Which Side of the Fence?")

Analogy serves the same purposes as comparison or contrast; the most important of these is, once again, to keep the readers' attention. But analogy also helps explain ideas that are hard to grasp by allowing you to compare them with things the reader can understand more easily. Analogy points out similarities between subjects that are unrelated. This is what happens in "The Tapestry" when student Steven Grundy compares his family to a fine wall hanging:

> *My family is an ancient tapestry,* worn in places, faded by the passage of time, its colors softened by accumulated dust. It has hung there for so long that we rarely stop to appreciate its value. Yet beneath the dusty coating lies a precious masterpiece, a subtle composition of woven thread.

TELL AN ANECDOTE OR DESCRIBE A SCENE

Anecdotes are brief, interesting stories that illustrate or support a point. An anecdote can help you prepare readers for the issues or problems you will be discussing without having to state the thesis directly. For example, this anecdote, which begins a *Wall Street Journal* editorial, makes the essay's central idea clear even though it does not express it in a thesis statement:

> We don't know if Janice Camarena had ever heard of *Brown v. Board of Education* when she enrolled in San Bernadino Valley College in California, but she knows all about it now. Mrs. Camarena was thrown out of a class at her public community college because of the color of her skin. When she sat down at her desk on the first day of the semester in January 1994, the instructor asked her to leave. That section of English 101 was reserved for black students only, she was told; Mrs. Camarena is white. ("Affirmative Reaction")

Another way to prepare readers for what follows is to describe a scene in a way that lets them know your feelings about a subject. Take the introduction to "A Hanging," an essay in which George Orwell reveals his view of capital punishment. Orwell does not express his opinions in a thesis statement; the essay's gloomy setting—its time and place—does that for him:

> It was Burma, a sodden [soggy] morning of the rains. A sickly light, like yellow tinfoil, was slanting over the high walls into the jail yard. We were waiting outside the condemned cells, a row of sheds fronted with double bars, like small animal cages. Each cell measured about ten feet by ten and was quite bare within except for a plank bed and a pot for drinking water. In some of them brown silent men were squatting at the inner bars, with their blankets draped around them. These were the condemned men, due to be hanged within the next week or two.

USE A QUOTATION

Quoting an expert or simply using an interesting, informative statement from another writer, from someone you've interviewed formally, or even from someone with whom you've only been chatting can lend interest and authority to your introduction. If you use this method, however, remember to quote your source accurately. Also be sure that the quotation relates to the other ideas in your paragraph clearly and logically.

Philip Shabecoff uses a quotation from world-famous scientist and writer Rachel Carson to lead us to his thesis in the introduction to his essay on pesticides:

> "The most alarming of all man's assaults upon the environment is the contamination of air, earth, rivers, and sea with dangerous and even lethal materials," Rachel Carson wrote a quarter of a century ago in her celebrated book *Silent Spring.* Today there is little disagreement with her warnings in regard to such broad-spectrum pesticides as DDT, then widely used, now banned. *But there is still hot debate over how to apply modern pesticides—which are designed to kill specific types of weeds or insects—in ways that do not harm people and their environment.* ("Congress Again Confronts Hazards of Killer Chemicals")

DEFINE AN IMPORTANT TERM OR CONCEPT

Defining a term can explain aspects of your subject that will make it easier for readers to understand and agree with your central idea. But try not to use dictionary definitions. Because they are often limited and rigid, they can make the beginning of an essay flat and uninteresting. Instead, rely on your own knowledge and ingenuity to create definitions that are interesting and appropriate to your purpose. This is what student Elena Santayana has done in the introduction to a paper about alcohol addiction:

> Alcoholism is a disease whose horrible consequences go beyond the patient. Families of alcoholics often become dysfunctional; spouses and children are abandoned or endure physical and emotional abuse. Co-workers suffer too. Alcoholics have high rates of absenteeism, and their work is often unreliable, thereby decreasing office or factory productivity. Indeed, alcoholics endanger the whole community. One in every two automobile fatalities is alcohol-related, and alcoholism is a major cause of violent crime. ("Everybody's Problem")

ADDRESS YOUR READERS

Speaking to your readers directly is an excellent way to get their attention. Notice how effective Claudia Wallis does this at the very beginning of an article from *U.S. News and World Report:*

> To grasp what it means to be 120 years old, consider this: a woman in the U.S. now has a life expectancy of 79 years. Jeanne Calment of Arles, France, reached that advanced age back in 1954, when Eisenhower was in the White

House and Stalin had just passed from the scene. Twenty-two years later, at age 100, Calment was still riding her bicycle around town, having outlived both her only child and grandchild. And 20 years after that, she was charming the photographers and reporters who arrived in droves last week, . . . to mark her 120 birthday. ("How to Live to Be 120")

In "What Is Poverty?" Jo Goodwin Parker has also chosen to address her readers directly, but she begins with a question. Her introduction is both urgent and emphatic:

You ask me what is poverty? Listen to me. Here I am, dirty, smelly, and with no "proper" underwear on and with the stench of my rotting teeth near you. I will tell you. Listen to me. Listen without pity. I cannot use your pity. Listen with understanding. Put yourself in my dirty, worn out, ill-fitting shoes, and hear me.

WRITING CONCLUSIONS

Make sure your essay has an effective conclusion. Sometimes, it is on the basis of your conclusion alone that your readers respond to your essay and remember the point it tries to make.

The conclusion's length depends on the essay's length and purpose. For a very short essay, you can simply end the last paragraph with a concluding sentence, which might itself contain details important to developing your thesis. Such is the case in Kenneth Jon Rose's "2001 Space Shuttle." Rose's last paragraph, a description of the shuttle's landing on its return to Earth, also contains his conclusion (shown in italics):

. . . the sky turns lighter and layers of clouds pass you like cars on a high-way. Minutes later, still sitting upright, you will see the gray runway in the distance. Then the shuttle slows to 300 mph and drops its landing gear. Finally, with its nose slightly up like the Concorde SST and at a speed of about 225 mph, the shuttle will land on the asphalt runway and slowly come to a halt. *The trip into space will be over.*

While one-sentence conclusions are fine for short essays, you will often need to close with at least one full paragraph. Either way, a conclusion should bring your discussion of the thesis to a timely and logical end. Try not to conclude abruptly; always give a signal that you are about to wrap things up. And never use your conclusion to introduce new ideas—ideas for which you did not prepare your readers earlier in the essay.

There are many ways to write conclusions. Here are just eight:

1. Rephrase or make reference to your thesis.
2. Summarize or rephrase your main points.
3. Offer advice; make a call to action.
4. Look to the future.

5. Explain how a problem was resolved.
6. Ask a rhetorical question.
7. Close with a statement or quotation readers will remember.
8. Respond to a question in your introduction.

REPHRASE OR MAKE REFERENCE TO YOUR THESIS

In Chapter 1 you learned that it can be appropriate to place the thesis statement not in the introduction, but in a later paragraph or even in the conclusion. As a beginning writer, however, you might want to use the more traditional pattern of organization, which is to place your thesis at the beginning of the essay. Of course, this doesn't mean that you shouldn't rephrase or refer to the thesis in your conclusion. Doing so can be an excellent way to emphasize your central idea.

Notice how well the conclusion to Donald M. Murray's "The Maker's Eye" recalls the central idea in this essay's introduction (see page 117).

> A piece of writing is never finished. It is delivered to a deadline, torn out of a typewriter on demand, sent off with a sense of accomplishment and shame and pride and frustration. If only there were a couple of more days, time for just another run at it, perhaps then. . . .

SUMMARIZE OR REPHRASE YOUR MAIN POINTS

For long essays, restating your thesis can be combined with summarizing or rephrasing each of the main points you have made in the body paragraphs. Doing so will help you write an effective summary of the entire essay and emphasize important ideas. This is exactly what Robin Roberts has done in his two concluding paragraphs of "Strike Out Little League" (see his introduction on page 115):

> I still don't know what those three gentlemen in Williamsport had in mind when they organized Little League baseball. I'm sure they didn't want parents arguing with their children about kids' games. I'm sure they didn't want young athletes hurting their arms pitching under pressure. . . . I'm sure they didn't want young boys . . . made to feel that something is wrong with them because they can't play baseball. I'm sure they didn't want a group of coaches drafting the players each year for different teams. I'm sure they didn't want unqualified men working with the young players. I'm sure they didn't realize how normal it is for an 8-year-old boy to be scared of a thrown or batted baseball.
>
> For the life of me, I can't figure out what they had in mind.

OFFER ADVICE; MAKE A CALL TO ACTION

An example of a conclusion that offers advice appears in Elena Santayana's "Everybody's Problem," the introduction to which appears on page 119.

> If you have alcoholic friends, relatives, or co-workers, the worst thing you can do is to look the other way. This disease and its effects are simply not theirs to deal with alone. Try persuading them to seek counseling. Describe the extent to which their illness is hurting their families, co-workers, and neighbors. Explain that their alcoholism endangers the entire community. Above all, don't pretend not to notice! Alcoholism is everybody's problem.

Along the same lines, a good way to end an essay that discusses a problem or controversial issue is to make a call to action, as in a *USA Today* editorial on affirmative action. As you read its two-paragraph conclusion, keep in mind the editorial's introduction, which appears on page 116.

> . . . a majority of blacks and whites believe in the continued need for job training, special education and recruiting for minorities and women.
>
> This country and its ideals will not be served by an all-or-nothing shouting match on affirmative action. Let's debate its method, update its mechanics. Let's not lose sight of its ultimate goal—a colorblind land of opportunity. ("Affirmative Action: Not an All-or-Nothing Issue")

LOOK TO THE FUTURE

If you believe the future can bring significant changes or new developments in regard to a topic you have discussed in your essay, you might end by discussing those changes. This is what Barbara Dafoe Whitehead does in "Dan Quayle Was Right." (You will find her introduction on pages 114–115.)

> People learn; societies can change; particularly when it becomes apparent that certain behaviors damage the social ecology, threaten the public order, and impose new burdens on core institutions. Whether Americans will act to overcome the legacy of family disruption is a crucial but as yet unanswered question.

EXPLAIN HOW A PROBLEM WAS RESOLVED

In "The Ambivalence of Abortion" (see page 116 for the introduction to this essay), Linda Bird Francke writes about the difficulty she and her husband had in deciding whether to have or abort their fourth child. Francke's conclusion tells us how they resolved the question and, like many effective endings, reveals the author's feelings:

My husband and I are back to planning our summer vacation and his career switch. And it certainly does make sense not to be having a baby right now—we say to each other all the time. But I have this ghost now. A very little ghost that only appears when I'm seeing something beautiful, like the full moon on the ocean last weekend. And the baby waves to me. And I wave at the baby. "Of course, we have room," I cry to the ghost. "Of course, we do."

ASK A RHETORICAL QUESTION

A rhetorical question (a question whose answer is obvious) asks your readers to participate in your essay's conclusion by answering the question. If you believe the essay has made the answer so obvious that all readers will indeed respond to the question as you want them to, ending with a rhetorical question can be a fine way to make your essay memorable. As a reader, it's hard to forget an essay when you've answered its question in your own words.

Jo Goodwin Parker uses this device to emphasize the seriousness of the problem she describes in "What Is Poverty?" (See her introduction on page 120.):

I have come out of my despair to tell you this. Remember I did not come from another place to another time. Others like me are all around you. Look at us with an angry heart, anger that will help you help me. Anger that will let you tell of me. The poor are always silent. Can you be silent too?

CLOSE WITH A STATEMENT OR QUOTATION READERS WILL REMEMBER

Deciding whether a statement or quotation will stick in readers' memories isn't easy. Just trust your instincts. If a particular remark has made a strong impression on you, it may work for others. As always, however, make your conclusion relate directly to your essay's content. In "How to Live to Be 120," Claudia Wallis closes her discussion with a direct quotation from her fascinating subject, which you read about in the introduction to her essay on pages 119–120.

As for Jeanne Calment, she seems to embody the calm resilience associated with long life. "I took pleasure when I could," she said. . . . "I acted clearly and morally and without regret. I'm very lucky."

RESPOND TO A QUESTION IN YOUR INTRODUCTION

After asking a question in your introduction, you can fill your essay with information that explains your question and/or prepares the reader for an answer in your conclusion. In his first paragraph of a chapter in *Stalking the Wild Asparagus,* which appears on page 116, Euell Gibbons asks "Why bother with wild food plants in a country which produces a surplus of many domestic food products?" Here's how he answers that question in the chapter's conclusion:

> I know of no other outdoor sport which can furnish me with as much pleasure as foraging wild food, which can be made into exquisite dishes to share with family and friends. If your interest has been aroused, then let me welcome you into the growing array of neoprimitive food gatherers who are finding new fascination and meaning in America's great outdoors.

VISUALIZING WAYS TO WRITE INTRODUCTIONS AND CONCLUSIONS

Read the introduction and conclusion to Michael Ryan's "They Track the Deadliest Viruses," which appear below. Comments in the margins identify effective techniques you might use in your own introductions and conclusions.

Ryan—Introduction

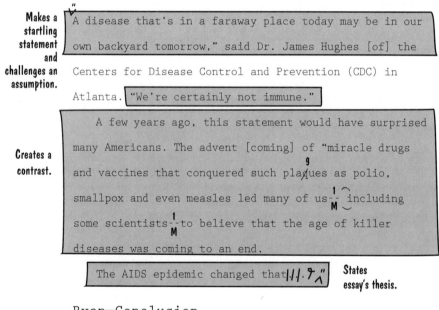

Makes a startling statement and challenges an assumption.

"A disease that's in a faraway place today may be in our own backyard tomorrow," said Dr. James Hughes [of] the Centers for Disease Control and Prevention (CDC) in Atlanta. "We're certainly not immune."

Creates a contrast.

A few years ago, this statement would have surprised many Americans. The advent [coming] of "miracle drugs and vaccines that conquered such plagues as polio, smallpox and even measles led many of us—including some scientists—to believe that the age of killer diseases was coming to an end.

The AIDS epidemic changed that.

States essay's thesis.

Ryan—Conclusion

On my visit to Atlanta I met with the associate director of the CDC, Dr. James Curran. He has been involved in the fight against AIDS since 1981.

"The first five years, through 1985, was the age

of discovery ͼ.ᴵ.ᴵ.ᴵ We discovered the global extent

of the epidemic, the virus, antibody tests, AZT.

Refers to thesis.

It was an exciting time, but when it ended, half a million people in the U.S. already were infected."

Today, Dr. Curran said, the Centers for Disease

Control and Prevention's response to the AIDS

epidemic has changed. "We're trying to help the

country evaluate the blood supply, develop test

Looks to the future.

kits and work on prevention and counseling

strategies ͼ.ᴵ.ᴵ.ᴵ Information alone isn't sufficient.

We have to find ways to change behavior --
¹∕M

Makes a call to action.

Uses a quotation readers will remember.

especially in young people, who sometimes think

they're invulnerable."

REVISING INTRODUCTIONS AND CONCLUSIONS

Later in this chapter, you will read Anita DiPasquale's "The Transformation of Maria Fernandez." DiPasquale knew that the first version of her essay was not the best she could do, so she rewrote her paper several times. Compare the rough and final drafts of the paragraphs she used in her essay's introduction and conclusion.

DiPasquale's Introduction—Rough Draft

Maria's story is a very shocking testimony to a brutal

A good first try; add stronger details?

war. Her country is Nicaragua. This impoverished yet

beautiful land is the site in which the Reagan Adminis-

tration became involved in a series of actions known as

the Iran-Contra fiasco. The only good that has come from

Is this essay's thesis?

our country's involvement in this dreadful war is that

the apathetic American, hopefully, has finally realized

that Kansas does not mean Central America, *Contra* does

not mean freedom fighter, and *Sandinista* does not mean repressive regime.

We met Maria on a trip through hell. The month was June; the year was 1988. Maria is seventeen, no longer a child, no longer a woman. She is a soldier in the FSLN.

Is author with someone, or does "we" include her readers?

Maria is a thin girl with shoulder-length raven hair, which she keeps in a braid and tucks away under her camouflage hat. Her nose is long, her chin is proud.

Will this move the reader?

She is olive in color, and her cheekbones are high like those of a *Vogue* model.

DiPasquale's Introduction—Final Draft

Final draft combines sentences for smoothness.

Maria's story is testimony to the horror of war. Her country is Nicaragua, one of America's greatest embarrassments and yet another battle ground in what the superpowers called the "cold" war. In this

Adds detail; improves word choice.

impoverished, merciless, yet beautiful land, the Reagan Administration became mired in series of covert operations known as the Iran-Contra fiasco. Ironically, our shame over this dreadful incident may be the only good thing to come from our presence in Nicaragua. Perhaps Americans who were once parochial and apathetic will realize that Kansas is not Central America, that *Sandinista* and "repressive" are not synonymous, that

Focuses her essay on a revised, more specific thesis.

Contra may not mean "freedom fighter," and that all wars, no matter who the adversaries, are barbarous!

My friend Michael and I meet Maria on a trip through

Adds information to clarify a point.

hell in Nicaragua's capital, Managua. The month is June,

the year 1988. Maria is seventeen, no longer a child,

Explains important historical information and abbreviation. no longer a woman. She is a soldier in the FSLN (*Frente Sandinista de Liberacion Nacional*), the national liberation front named for Augusto Sandino, a guerilla fighter martyred in an earlier war of liberation.

Maria is thin, with shoulder-length raven hair, which she braids and tucks away under her camouflage hat. Her nose is long and straight, her chin prominent and proud. A silky olive complexion and cheekbones straight out of *Vogue* magazine reveal a face that is

Adds a question that startles reader and sets essay's tone. truly delicate. How, then, has it come to harbor the deadest eyes I have ever seen?

DiPasquale's Conclusion—Rough Draft

My stomach grew heavy and sank to a depth I did know was possible. A truck pulled into the street. It was filled with dead Contra bodies on the way to burial. Another truck pulled up behind, and this one was filled with Sandinista soldiers. My heart sank in desperation. These soldiers were children: eight, ten, fifteen. All toting — **Sentences are choppy.** rifles, passing cigarettes among the crowd. When I

Needs to describe in more detail. looked in the other truck, I grew ill with fear. This truck was also filled with children, men, and women, but all were dead.

Needs expansion, stronger detail. It is practically impossible to tell the Contras and Sandinistas apart. Their youth, their camaraderie, and dead have a lot in common.

DiPasquale's Conclusion—Final Draft

Uses present tense to create excitement.

As Maria finishes her story, my stomach grows heavy and sinks to a depth I did not think was possible. Suddenly, a truck pulls onto the street. It is filled with dead Contras on the way to burial. Another truck pulls up behind; this one is filled with Sandinista soldiers, none of whom look over twenty. Most are between ten and fifteen. Some might be eight. They are all toting rifles, passing cigarettes out among the crowd.

Combines sentences to correct and smooth out sentence structure.

Uses stronger vocabulary and adds stark details.

When I look into the first truck, I become desperate with fear. Piled one on top of another are men, women, and children. They are all dead.

Adds a new paragraph that refers to someone mentioned earlier in the essay.

Back at the ledge, I slump against Michael. Maria emerges from the daze of her horrid memory and kisses Michael on the cheek. She points to the trucks. "If he [Maria's younger brother] were here, his world would be all too real."

Sometimes it is nearly impossible to tell Contra soldiers and Sandinistas apart. They have a lot in common: their youth, their camaraderie, their mortality. When Salvadoran Archbishop Rivera y Damas spoke of the role of the superpowers in his country's civil war, he could have been describing the tragedy of Nicaragua:

Expands this paragraph with stronger smoother wording.

Adds quotation readers will remember.

"They supply the weapons, and we supply the dead."

PRACTICING WRITING INTRODUCTIONS

Write a one-paragraph introduction for an essay you might compose on one of the following topics. Try using one of the methods for writing introductions suggested with each topic.

1. TOPIC: A terrifying, tragic, or emotionally charged experience.
   METHOD: Use a startling remark or statistic.

   _____

   _____

   _____

   _____

   _____

2. TOPIC: Dealing with an allergy or other common health problem.
   METHOD: Ask a question or present a problem.

   _____

   _____

   _____

   _____

   _____

3. TOPIC: The benefits (or dangers) of physical exercise.
   METHOD: Tell an anecdote or use contrast.

   _____

   _____

   _____

   _____

   _____

4. TOPIC: Ways to overcome pain other than using drugs.
   METHOD: Challenge a widely held opinion, use contrast, or present a problem.

   _____

   _____

   _____

   _____

5. TOPIC: What your clothes (car, home, or room) say about you.
   METHOD: Describe a scene, use a quotation, or address your readers.

   _____

   _____

   _____

   _____

6. TOPIC: The role of a father or mother in a young family.
   METHOD: Ask a question or challenge a widely held opinion.

   _____

   _____

   _____

7. TOPIC: Overcoming a fear of math (heights, closed-in places, water, etc.).
   METHOD: Address your readers, ask a question, or define a term.

   _____

   _____

   _____

8. TOPIC: Practicing safe sex.
   METHOD: Present a problem, define a term, or address your readers.

   _____

   _____

   _____

   _____

Read the introductions and conclusions to the following four essays carefully, and take some time to respond to the Questions for Discussion and the Suggestions for Journal Entries that follow each selection. As always, you will also want to try your hand at the Suggestions for Sustained Writing at the end of the chapter. Doing so will help you develop the skills needed to write good introductions and conclusions of your own—the kind that will capture your readers' attention and make them look forward to more and more of your writing.

How to Keep Air Clean

Sydney Harris

Sydney Harris was born in London in 1917 and began writing as a regular columnist for the Chicago Daily News *in 1941. Models of interesting and effective prose, Harris's newspaper columns, such as "How to Keep Air Clean," have proved him to be an important American essayist and earned him thousands of devoted readers over the years. Many of these columns have been used in college textbooks and gathered in book-length collections of his work.*

Looking Ahead

1. The essay's introduction consists of the first three paragraphs. Read these paragraphs carefully, and try to determine what technique Harris relies on most to open this essay.
2. Harris uses two terms from meteorology, the study of the earth's atmosphere. The *troposphere* (paragraph 4) is the bottom layer of the atmosphere, where clouds, rain, snow, and other weather phenomena occur. Directly above the troposphere is the *stratosphere* (paragraph 2), which extends to about 30 miles up.
3. In his conclusion (paragraph 9), Harris calls our attention to the Industrial Revolution, which occurred in the eighteenth and nineteenth centuries in Europe and North America. Not an armed conflict, the Industrial Revolution was a series of technological developments that led to the modern factory system, mass production, and automation.

Vocabulary

infinitely	Without end.
irreversible	Not reversible or repairable.
noxious	Toxic, dangerous, harmful.
particulates	Small particles.

How to Keep Air Clean
Sydney Harris

Some months ago, while doing research on the general subject of pollution, I 1 learned how dumb I had been all my life about something as common and familiar—and essential—as air.

In my ignorance, I had always thought that "fresh air" was infinitely available to 2 us. I had imagined that the dirty air around us somehow escaped into the stratosphere, and that new air kept coming in—much as it does when we open a window after a party.

This, of course, is not true, and you would imagine that a grown man with a decent 3 education would know this as a matter of course. What is true is that we live in a kind of spaceship called the earth, and only a limited amount of air is *forever* available to us.

The "walls" of our spaceship enclose what is called the "troposphere," which 4 extends about seven miles up. This is all the air that is available to us. We must use it over and over again for infinity, just as if we were in a sealed room for the lifetime of the earth.

No fresh air comes in, and no polluted air escapes. Moreover, no dirt or poisons 5 are ever "destroyed"—they remain in the air, in different forms, or settle on the earth as "particulates." And the more we burn, the more we replace good air with bad.

Once contaminated, this thin layer of air surrounding the earth cannot be cleansed 6 again. We can clean materials, we can even clean water, but we cannot clean the air. There is nowhere else for the dirt and poisons to go—we cannot open a window in the troposphere and clear out the stale and noxious atmosphere we are creating.

Perhaps every child in sixth grade and above knows this, but I doubt that one adult 7 in a hundred is aware of this basic physical fact. Most of us imagine, as I did, that winds sweep away the gases and debris in the air, taking them far out into the solar system and replacing them with new air.

The United States alone is discharging *130 million tons of pollutants a year* into the 8 atmosphere, from factories, heating systems, incinerators, automobiles and airplanes, power plants and public buildings. What is frightening is not so much the death and illness, corrosion and decay they are responsible for—as the fact that this is an *irreversible process*. The air will never be cleaner than it is now.

And this is why *prevention*—immediate, drastic and far-reaching—is our only hope 9 for the future. We cannot undo what we have done. We cannot restore the atmosphere to the purity it had before the Industrial Revolution. But we can, and must, halt the contamination before our spaceship suffocates from its own foul discharges.

QUESTIONS FOR DISCUSSION

1. What technique discussed earlier in this chapter does Harris rely upon most to open his essay?
2. In paragraph 3, Harris also makes use of an analogy, another of the techniques for beginning an essay discussed earlier. What is this interesting analogy? In what other paragraph does Harris make reference to it?
3. Reread paragraph 3 of "How to Keep Air Clean." What is Harris's thesis?
4. What techniques does he use to conclude this essay?
5. The title suggests that Harris has used process analysis to develop his ideas. Identify one paragraph in which he uses this method of development. (Process analysis was discussed in Chapter 3.)
6. The essay is very well developed and organized. What techniques does the author use to maintain coherence in and between paragraphs? (For ways to maintain coherence, see Chapter 2.)

THINKING CRITICALLY

1. As you have learned, Harris uses an analogy when he compares earth to a spaceship. Write a short paragraph in which you develop three or four specific comparisons between earth and a spaceship.
2. List some ways in which you might help in the fight to prevent further pollution of the atmosphere.
3. Read Berry's "Waste," a short paragraph in Chapter 2. On what points might Berry and Harris agree?

SUGGESTIONS FOR JOURNAL ENTRIES

1. Summarize in a paragraph of your own the three paragraphs Harris uses to introduce his essay. Make sure to use your own words throughout.
2. To introduce his essay, Harris challenges a widely held opinion or assumption. Think of a widely held opinion or assumption that you believe is incorrect. In a sentence or two, write this idea in your journal. Then, using one of the prewriting techniques described in "Getting Started," write down your major reasons for disagreeing. Here are a few examples of the kinds of opinions or assumptions you might want to correct:

Someone who has had only one or two drinks shouldn't be prevented from driving a car.
Breaking an alcohol or drug addiction is relatively easy.
Women have no aptitude for math.
Reading poetry, listening to opera, and going to the ballet aren't things that "real" men do.

I Was Just Wondering

Robert Fulghum

Robert Fulghum wrote All I Really Need to Know I Learned in Kindergarten, *the best-selling collection of essays from which this one is taken. The contents of this funny book are summed up by its subtitle:* Uncommon Thoughts on Common Things. *Fulghum has worked as a cowboy, IBM sales representative, bartender, teacher, artist, and minister. Judging from this selection, he has a curiosity and love for life that make it easy to understand why his writing is so popular.*

LOOKING AHEAD

1. As you read this essay, ask yourself why Fulghum's introduction and conclusion are effective. Identify methods for writing beginnings and endings you learned earlier in this chapter.
2. In paragraphs 1, 5, and 8, Fulghum intentionally uses incomplete sentences, known as fragments, to create emphasis and establish a conversational tone. They are part of a carefully considered style that this experienced writer chose for his essay. As a rule, however, developing writers should avoid fragments.

VOCABULARY

curry	Groom.
epidemic	Widespread occurrence.
meditate	Think, ponder, contemplate.
oracle	Advisor, prophet. (Here, "oracle" is used figuratively; Fulghum describes the habit some folks have of questioning themselves as they look in the mirror.)
Ph.D.	Advanced academic degree, also known as a doctorate.
potions	Liquid medicines, remedies.
preen	Make ready, prepare.
unguents	Salves, ointments.
spelunking	Cave exploring.

*I Was Just
Wondering* | *Robert Fulghum*

I was just wondering. Did you ever go to somebody's house for dinner or a party or 1
something and then use the bathroom? And while you were in there, did you ever
take a look around in the medicine cabinet? Just to kind of compare notes, you know?
Didn't you ever—just look around a little?

I have a friend who does it all the time. He's doing research for a Ph.D. in sociology. 2
He says lots of other people do it, too. And they aren't working on a Ph.D. in sociology,
either. It's not something people talk about much—because you think you might be the
only one who is doing it, and you don't want people to think you're strange, right?

My friend says if you want to know the truth about people, it's the place to go. All 3
you have to do is look in the drawers and shelves and cabinets in the bathroom. And
take a look at the robes and pajamas and nightgowns hanging on the hook behind the
door. You'll get the picture. He says all their habits and hopes and dreams and sorrows,
illnesses and hangups, and even their sex life—all stand revealed in that one small room.

He says most people are secret slobs. He says the deepest mysteries of the race are 4
tucked into the nooks and crannies of the bathroom, where we go to be alone, to confront ourselves in the mirror, to comb and curry and scrape and preen our hides, to
coax our aging and ailing bodies into one more day, to clean ourselves and relieve ourselves, to paint and deodorize our surfaces, to meditate and consult our oracle and
attempt to improve our lot.

He says it's all there. In cans and bottles and tubes and boxes and vials. Potions and 5
oils and unguents and sprays and tools and lotions and perfumes and appliances and
soaps and pastes and pills and creams and pads and powders and medicines and devices
beyond description—some electric and some not. The wonders of the ages.

He says he finds most bathrooms are about the same, and it gives him a sense of 6
the wondrous unity of the human race.

I don't intend to start an epidemic of spelunking in people's bathrooms. But I did 7
just go in and take a look in my own. I get the picture. I don't know whether to laugh or
cry.

Take a look. In your own. And from now on, please go to the bathroom before you 8
visit me. Mine is closed to the public.

QUESTIONS FOR DISCUSSION

1. What two ways of writing introductions discussed in this chapter did you find in paragraph 1?
2. Which of the methods for concluding discussed earlier best describes Fulghum's approach in paragraph 8?
3. What method of development that you learned about in the previous chapter does Fulghum use in paragraph 3?
4. What techniques does Fulghum use to maintain coherence in and between paragraphs?

THINKING CRITICALLY

1. Pretend you caught someone snooping around in your bathroom, bedroom, closet, or other private part of your home. Write this person a letter explaining your reaction.
2. What does Fulghum mean when he says that bathrooms are places where we go "to meditate and consult our oracle and attempt to improve our lot"?

SUGGESTIONS FOR JOURNAL ENTRIES

1. Are most people "secret slobs"? What about you? Think of a particular place you call your own. Does the way you keep it show how neat or sloppy you are? If so, use focused freewriting to describe what it looks like. A place to write about might be your bedroom, bathroom, car, closet, area in which you study, or location where you spend most of your time at work.
2. Like Fulghum, do some wondering. Focus on someone you know very well. Can you describe or at least imagine what the inside of his or her room, closet, apartment, house, refrigerator, garage, basement, or bathroom looks like? What might you see in such places that would describe this individual's personality?

Pain Is Not the Ultimate Enemy

Norman Cousins

This selection is an excerpt from Anatomy of an Illness: As Perceived by the Patient, *the story of how the author helped direct his recovery from a disease some doctors said would cripple him for life. The theme of this book, Cousins tells us, is that within each of us lies an enormous self-curing power, which doctors are only now beginning to tap. The book began as an article in the* New England Journal of Medicine; *it is one of the few articles written by a layperson that that professional journal has ever published.*

LOOKING AHEAD

1. Cousins' introduction runs for three paragraphs. As you read it, look for techniques such as making a startling remark, creating a contrast, and challenging a widely held opinion.
2. The essay's conclusion comes in the last two paragraphs. Look for at least two of the methods for concluding essays that you read about earlier.
3. Paragraphs 7 and 8 are important to Cousins' message. Read them twice.

VOCABULARY

alleviating	Relieving.
analgesics	Sedatives, tranquilizers.
antagonistic	Against, harmful to.
boomeranged	Backfired, had an effect opposite of the one intended.
boon	Advantage, important tool.
clamorous	Noisy, confusing.
correlation	Parallel, match, connection.
hypochondria	Irrational worry about one's health.
indignant	Angry, insulted.
lethal	Deadly.
malaise	Illness.
morbidly	Deathly.
promiscuous	Careless, indiscriminate.
psychogenic	Produced by the mind.
self-limiting	Not going beyond itself.
ultimate	Extreme, worst.
unremitting	Unending.

Pain Is Not the Ultimate Enemy | *Norman Cousins*

Americans are probably the most pain-conscious people on the face of the earth. 1
For years we have had it drummed into us—in print, on radio, over television, in everyday conversation—that any hint of pain is to be banished as though it were the ultimate evil. As a result, we are becoming a nation of pill-grabbers and hypochondriacs, escalating the slightest ache into a searing ordeal.

We know very little about pain and what we don't know makes it hurt all the more. 2
Indeed, no form of illiteracy in the United States is so widespread or costly as ignorance about pain—what it is, what causes it, how to deal with it without panic. Almost everyone can rattle off the names of at least a dozen drugs that can deaden pain from every conceivable cause—all the way from headaches to hemorrhoids. There is far less knowledge about the fact that about 90 percent of pain is self-limiting, that it is not always an indication of poor health, and that, most frequently, it is the result of tension, stress, worry, idleness, boredom, frustration, suppressed rage, insufficient sleep, overeating, poorly balanced diet, smoking, excessive drinking, inadequate exercise, stale air, or any of the other abuses encountered by the human body in modern society.

The most ignored fact of all about pain is that the best way to eliminate it is to elim- 3
inate the abuse. Instead, many people reach almost instinctively for the painkillers—aspirins, barbiturates, codeines, tranquilizers, sleeping pills, and dozens of other analgesics or desensitizing drugs.

Most doctors are profoundly troubled over the extent to which the medical profes- 4
sion today is taking on the trappings of a pain-killing industry. Their offices are overloaded with people who are morbidly but mistakenly convinced that something dreadful is about to happen to them. It is all too evident that the campaign to get people to run to a doctor at the first sign of pain has boomeranged. Physicians find it difficult to give adequate attention to patients genuinely in need of expert diagnosis and treatment because their time is soaked up by people who have nothing wrong with them except a temporary indisposition or a psychogenic ache.

Patients tend to feel indignant and insulted if the physician tells them he can find 5
no organic cause for the pain. They tend to interpret the term "psychogenic" to mean that they are complaining of nonexistent symptoms. They need to be educated about the fact that many forms of pain have no underlying physical cause but are the result, as mentioned earlier, of tension, stress, or hostile factors in the general environment. Sometimes a pain may be a manifestation of "conversion hysteria" . . ., the name given by Jean Charcot to physical symptoms that have their origins in emotional disturbances.

Obviously, it is folly for an individual to ignore symptoms that could be a warning 6
of a potentially serious illness. Some people are so terrified of getting bad news from a doctor that they allow their malaise to worsen, sometimes past the point of no return. Total neglect is not the answer to hypochondria. The only answer has to be increased education about the way the human body works, so that more people will be able to steer an intelligent course between promiscuous pill-popping and irresponsible disregard of genuine symptoms.

Of all forms of pain, none is more important for the individual to understand than 7 the "threshold" variety. Almost everyone has a telltale ache that is triggered whenever tension or fatigue reaches a certain point. It can take the form of a migraine-type headache or a squeezing pain deep in the abdomen or cramps or a pain in the lower back or even pain in the joints. The individual who has learned how to make the correlation between such threshold pains and their cause doesn't panic when they occur; he or she does something about relieving the stress and tension. Then, if the pain persists despite the absence of apparent cause, the individual will telephone the doctor.

If ignorance about the nature of pain is widespread, ignorance about the way pain- 8 killing drugs work is even more so. What is not generally understood is that many of the vaunted pain-killing drugs conceal the pain without correcting the underlying condition. They deaden the mechanism in the body that alerts the brain to the fact that something may be wrong. The body can pay a high price for suppression of pain without regard to its basic cause.

Professional athletes are sometimes severely disadvantaged by trainers whose job it 9 is to keep them in action. The more famous the athlete, the greater the risk that he or she may be subjected to extreme medical measures when injury strikes. The star baseball pitcher whose arm is sore because of a torn muscle or tissue damage may need sustained rest more than anything else. But his team is battling for a place in the World Series; so the trainer or team doctor, called upon to work his magic, reaches for a strong dose of butazolidine or other powerful pain suppressants. Presto, the pain disappears! The pitcher takes his place on the mound and does superbly. That could be the last game, however, in which he is able to throw a ball with full strength. The drugs didn't repair the torn muscle or cause the damaged tissue to heal. What they did was to mask the pain, enabling the pitcher to throw hard, further damaging the torn muscle. Little wonder that so many star athletes are cut down in their prime, more the victims of overzealous treatment of their injuries than of the injuries themselves.

The king of all painkillers, of course, is aspirin. The U.S. Food and Drug Adminis- 10 tration permits aspirin to be sold without prescription, but the drug, contrary to popular belief, can be dangerous and, in sustained doses, potentially lethal. Aspirin is self-administered by more people than any other drug in the world. Some people are aspirin-poppers, taking ten or more a day. What they don't know is that the smallest dose can cause internal bleeding. Even more serious perhaps is the fact that aspirin is antagonistic to collagen, which has a key role in the formation of connective tissue. Since many forms of arthritis involve disintegration of the connective tissue, the steady use of aspirin can actually intensify the underlying arthritic condition.

· · ·

Pain-killing drugs are among the greatest advances in the history of medicine. Prop- 11 erly used, they can be a boon in alleviating suffering and in treating disease. But their indiscriminate and promiscuous use is making psychological cripples and chronic ailers out of millions of people. The unremitting barrage of advertising for pain-killing drugs, especially over television, has set the stage for a mass anxiety neurosis. Almost from the moment children are old enough to sit upright in front of a television screen, they are being indoctrinated into the hypochondriac's clamorous and morbid world. Little wonder so many people fear pain more than death itself.

It might be a good idea if concerned physicians and educators could get together to 12
make knowledge about pain an important part of the regular school curriculum. As for
the populace at large, perhaps some of the same techniques used by public-service agencies to make people cancer-conscious can be used to counteract the growing terror of
pain and illness in general. People ought to know that nothing is more remarkable about
the human body than its recuperative drive, given a modicum of respect. If our broad-
casting stations cannot provide equal time for responses to the pain-killing advertisements, they might at least set aside a few minutes each day for common-sense remarks
on the subject of pain. As for the Food and Drug Administration, it might be interesting
to know why an agency that has so energetically warned the American people against
taking vitamins without prescriptions is doing so little to control over-the-counter sales
each year of billions of pain-killing pills, some of which can do more harm than the
pain they are supposed to suppress.

QUESTIONS FOR DISCUSSION

1. What method for writing introductions did you find in paragraph 1?
2. Where in Cousins's introduction does he contradict a widely held opinion?
3. Where does he use contrast?
4. What sentence in the first three paragraphs best expresses the central idea of this essay?
5. What methods of concluding an essay, which you learned about earlier, did you find in the last two paragraphs?
6. What are the central ideas in paragraphs 7 and 8? Would the essay have been as effective had these paragraphs been left out?

THINKING CRITICALLY

1. Reread paragraph 9. Do you know of anyone from sports or another field whose experiences would help prove Cousins's point in this paragraph? Explain in writing how drugs—prescribed by a doctor or bought over the counter—actually caused this person harm.
2. In recent years, we have heard much from the media and our schools about the dangers of illegal drugs. If you were head of your state's department of health, what would you do to educate people about the dangers of legal drugs?

SUGGESTIONS FOR JOURNAL ENTRIES

1. Have you ever had a serious illness or knew someone suffering from one? Spend five or ten minutes freewriting about the symptoms of this illness. Then, spend another five or ten minutes describing the treatment.
2. Do you know anyone who was or is addicted to a legal drug? Use listing or freewriting to describe the results of the addiction.
3. Have you ever treated a wound or an illness yourself, or have you known anyone who did? Use any method of prewriting to gather information about this treatment.

The Transformation of Maria Fernandez

Anita DiPasquale

Anita DiPasquale had the rare opportunity to visit Nicaragua near the end of the civil war that devastated that Central American country in the 1980s. She went there with a friend to bring news to relatives of a Nicaraguan child who had been adopted by a family in California. When a college writing instructor asked DiPasquale to narrate an unforgettable experience, she had no trouble deciding what to write about.

L O O K I N G   A H E A D

1. The Iran-Contra affair (paragraph 1) involved the sale of arms to Iran as part of an illegal plan to provide American military aid to the Nicaraguan *Contras,* the group trying to overthrow that country's *Sandinista* government. The "super-powers," mentioned twice in this essay, are the United States and the former Soviet Union.
2. Like the introduction by Sydney Harris, DiPasquale's is longer than one paragraph, and it uses several methods for beginning essays discussed in this chapter.
3. Although her story takes place in the past, DiPasquale writes in the present tense. In paragraph 2, for example, she tells us that Michael and she "meet," not "met" Maria. Using the present tense often adds excitement to a narrative essay and makes it more convincing.
4. The author kept an informal journal of her conversations with Maria by recording what she remembered of their talks from time to time. What we read may not be exactly what she and Maria said, word for word, but it is a fair re-creation of their conversations.

V O C A B U L A R Y

adversaries	Opponents, enemies.
apathetic	Unconcerned, uninterested.
communal	Having to do with a community.
covert	Secret, hidden.
defiled	Dirtied, violated.
diverse	Various, assorted.
eking out	Struggling to make or get.

eradicate	Destroy, annihilate.
ironically	Contrary to what is expected.
meager	Poor, little.
mired	Stuck.
parochial	Isolated, provincial.
raven	Black.
repressive	Tyrannical, dictatorial.
synonymous	Similar in meaning.

*The Transformation
of Maria Fernandez* | *Anita DiPasquale*

Maria's story is testimony to the horror of war. Her country is Nicaragua, one of   1
America's greatest embarrassments and yet another battleground in what the
superpowers called the "cold" war. In this impoverished, merciless, yet beautiful land,
the Reagan Administration became mired in a series of covert operations known as the
Iran-Contra fiasco. Ironically, our shame over this dreadful incident may be the only
good thing to come from our presence in Nicaragua. Perhaps Americans who were once
parochial and apathetic will realize that Kansas is not Central America, that *Sandinista*
and "repressive" are not synonymous, that *Contra* may not mean "freedom fighter," and
that all wars, no matter who the adversaries, are barbarous!

My friend Michael and I meet Maria on a trip through hell in Nicaragua's capital,   2
Managua. The month is June, the year 1988. Maria is seventeen, no longer a child, no
longer a woman. She is a soldier in the FSLN *(Frente Sandinista de Liberacion Nacional),*
the national liberation front named for Augusto Sandino, a guerrilla fighter martyred in
an earlier war of liberation.

Maria is thin, with shoulder-length raven hair, which she braids and tucks away   3
under her camouflage hat. Her nose is long and straight, her chin prominent and proud.
A silky olive complexion and cheekbones straight out of *Vogue* magazine reveal a face
that is truly delicate. How, then, has it come to harbor the deadest eyes I have ever seen?

Maria, Michael and I make our way along the gray and blue cobblestone street and   4
sit on a curb so large it would be considered a ledge in the United States. The masonry
buildings around us are old, bruised, and defiled. Bullet holes and political graffiti have
stained the faces of these tired shelters. Some still lie battered and tormented by the
earthquake that devastated Nicaragua on December 23, 1972.

A young woman bathes in rain water that has collected in an old metal drum across   5
the street. No one notices; people walk by as if she were invisible. Maria catches me
staring: "It's a way of life here; so many people are without water, without homes."

She is safer here on the street than at the river, I am told. "Listen, haven't you heard   6
the gunfire or seen the blood?" asks Maria.

"Have my eyes and ears deceived me?" I wonder. I have seen no blood and heard no   7
shooting. I know there is a war, but not until many days later will I fully realize what she
means.

Michael pulls a photograph from his shirt pocket and hands it to Maria. It is a pic-   8
ture of her brother Alberto; he is seated on a bright red Big Wheel. Alberto is seven and
lives in Log Angeles with Michael's uncle. The child is smiling; he knows his world is
make-believe, like that of most children in countries free of war.

"I remember," she proclaims, as she stares at the photo. "I remember when I was a   9
child; we lived in the north, in Matagalpa." Matagalpa is known for its mountains and its
hard living. Aside from the small towns every five miles or so, nothing but small shacks
dot the landscape. The people of Matagalpa work alone on small plots of land, eking
out a meager existence. There are no real communities here as there are in the Pacific
culture, which is known for its communal involvement with the land.

Maria lights a cigarette and sighs. "We were very poor and lived close to the earth.   10

I can still smell Mama's tortillas cooking in the oven. Our house had two rooms, and the roof was made of corrugated tin. The floor was dirt except for a small area which Papa dug out and covered with wood in order to hide us when the soldiers came through."

Her face grows solemn for a moment. But she lifts her strong chin and continues 11 proudly. "As a small girl, I would wear pretty dresses that Mama made from spare pieces of cloth. They always had flowers on them, pink and yellow. I never had a pair of shoes; there was no need for them. My job on the land was to spread the fertilizer." Maria's nose crinkles as if she can still smell the manure.

"Once we went on a trip to Puerto Cabezas; Alberto was so small he had just 12 learned to walk. There the Miskito Indians were catching giant sea tortoises on the shore. The tortoises were larger than Alberto," she chuckles. "A Miskito woman gave us a ride on her boat. It was made from a hollowed out tree. That was the last family outing I remember."

"How did Alberto come to live in America?" I ask. Michael has never told me, and 13 I know by the look on his face that I should not have asked the question. The story Maria tells is more horrifying than any horror film. It makes the ravages of war real to me. I no longer look on them as someone else's problems. It also explains how a happy little girl in flowered dresses could have become a soldier, a killer, how her eyes can be so dead.

"I must go back a few years to help you understand what led to Alberto's depar- 14 ture," began Maria. "In August of 1978, when I was a very small child, before Alberto was born, our world changed forever. The FSLN had seized the National Palace, taking 1,500 hostages. When the attackers and 59 newly freed prisoners drove to the airport to get a flight to Panama, thousands of people lined the streets and cheered their victory. After the Palace assault, there were many attacks on the National Guard throughout Nicaragua—in Matagalpa, Leon, Masaya, Esteli, and Chinandega. The people lifted up arms against President Anastasio Somoza Debayle. So, to stop the rebels, the Guard destroyed our cities from the air. It took about two weeks and left over 4,000 dead. As the Sandinistas withdrew, they took thousands of newly recruited soldiers. My father was one.

"Later, in 1979, Somoza was driven into exile, to America's Miami. We thought 15 there was hope for our country. Your President Carter worked with us, but then Reagan came. He reorganized Somoza's National Guard, which became the Contras. They were given haven in Honduras. The 75,000 Sandinistas had few weapons and little money, so they could not eradicate the 10,000 Contras, who were well equipped with U.S. weapons and money.

"Back to Alberto. The last day I saw my brother started like any other. I was four- 16 teen or so, Alberto about four. We were home alone with my mother. Papa was off fight-ing in the jungle. It was September, and a wonderful rain had fallen the night before, leaving the air fragrant with a lush tropical scent. However, smoke hovered over the vil-lage, casting shadows on houses and streets and plunging the land into a deep, damp calm.

"Suddenly, I heard our neighbor Guillermo run into our house. He was covered 17 with blood. 'Contras,' he screamed before darting into the mist. Mama moved the heavy trunk that covered the hiding place my father had made. She was eight months pregnant, so I helped. First we placed Alberto into the hole, and I climbed on top of him. Mama placed the wood back on top and threw a rug over the floor.

"Just then the soldiers must have arrived. They were yelling and laughing. I covered Alberto's ears and tried to muffle his crying. I heard my mother's screams; I still hear her screams. They were finally silenced by gunfire. 18

"The soldiers must have stayed about an hour; it felt like an eternity. The house grew quiet. 'I dare not move,' I thought, so we lay there for several hours. Before I climbed out of the hole, I tied a piece of my dress around Alberto's eyes and around his hands so he wouldn't remove the blindfold. When I entered the daylight I was instantly sick. Mama was dead; they had cut my baby sister from her stomach; they lay there in a pool of blood. Both bodies were riddled with bullets. 19

"The soldiers had stayed there with their dead bodies long enough to eat our breakfast. There was blood everywhere. I don't know how long I stood motionless when a shadow crossed the doorway. It was Chris, a U.S. reporter who often came by to feed his stories and his belly. He buried Mama and the baby, Isabel. That would have been her name. 20

"Chris told me my father had died the week earlier in a battle in Jinotega. He said he could get Alberto out of Nicaragua, away from the Contras. He knew someone who was smuggling small, light-skinned children into California. He promised he would personally get him a good home as repayment for the help my family had given him. He was crying when he said I was too big to go. I had forgotten how to cry. Right then, at that moment, I was reborn into this world all alone. You do what you have to do in order to survive. I now know the meaning in the smoke. You do what you have to do to survive." 21

As Maria finishes her story, my stomach grows heavy and sinks to a depth I did not think was possible. Suddenly, a truck pulls onto the street. It is filled with dead Contras on the way to burial. Another truck pulls up behind; this one is filled with Sandinista soldiers, none of whom look over twenty. Most are between ten and fifteen. Some might be eight. They are all toting rifles, passing cigarettes out among the crowd. When I look into the first truck, I become desperate with fear. Piled one on top of another are men, women, and children. They are all dead. 22

Back at the ledge, I slump against Michael. Maria emerges from the daze of her horrid memory and kisses Michael on the cheek. She points to the trucks. "If he were here, his world would be all too real." 23

Sometimes it is nearly impossible to tell Contra soldiers and Sandinistas apart. They have a lot in common: their youth, their camaraderie, their mortality. When Salvadoran Archbishop Rivera y Damas spoke of the role of the superpowers in his country's civil war, he could have been describing the tragedy of Nicaragua: "They supply the weapons, and we supply the dead." 24

QUESTIONS FOR DISCUSSION

1. A transformation is a very significant change. What significant change has Maria experienced? Has the author experienced a change as a result of meeting Maria?
2. What is DiPasquale's thesis? What events in the story support or develop that thesis best?
3. The introduction to the essay includes several startling remarks. Identify two or three.
4. Where in the introduction does DiPasquale challenge widely held assumptions or opinions?
5. How does the question at the end of paragraph 3 help us understand her thesis?
6. This essay closes with quotations and statements that might stick in your mind long after you have read them. Which of these do you think is most memorable?
7. In what way does the scene described in paragraph 22 support the essay's thesis?
8. In paragraph 24, DiPasquale mentions the "superpowers," which we recall from paragraph 1. What is she trying to accomplish by repeating this word at the end of the essay?

THINKING CRITICALLY

1. Do a little reading on Nicaragua in a recently published encyclopedia or other reference work. Your college librarian can help you find such resources. Then, write a short explanation of DiPasquale's first paragraph. Make sure to identify the *Sandinistas* and the *Contras* and to explain the significance of her hope that Americans will no longer confuse Central America with Kansas.
2. Read "Growing Up in Rumania," another student essay, which appears in Chapter 13. What does it have in common with DiPasquale's work?

SUGGESTIONS FOR JOURNAL ENTRIES

1. Recall a horrifying or dangerous event that showed you the sad or dark side of life. Ask the journalists' questions (you can find these in "Getting Started," under Brainstorming) to collect as many details about it as you can. Examples of such an incident include military combat; a bad automobile or industrial accident; a building fire; a tornado; a bout with a serious illness; a violent crime; a fall from a ledge or down a stairs; a mishap at sea, in a lake, river, or other body of water; or a fight in which someone was seriously hurt. Whatever event you write about, make sure to show why it was horrifying or dangerous.
2. Do you know someone who experienced a tragic or horrifying event like those mentioned above? If so, interview him or her using the techniques described in

"Getting Started." Gather as much information as you can about the incident, and determine how it affected the person you interview.

3. Do you have a friend or relative who went through a drastic and sudden personality change as a result of an important event or development in his or her life? Write about this person by making three lists: one that contains details describing your subject before the change; one that describes him or her after the change; and one that explains what caused the change.

SUGGESTIONS FOR SUSTAINED WRITING

1. Reread any one of the college papers you've written this semester. Try to pick the one you or your instructor liked best, but don't limit your choice to papers you've completed for English class. Then, rewrite the beginning and ending to that essay by using any of the techniques for writing effective introductions and conclusions discussed in this chapter.

2. In one of the Suggestions for Journal Entries after Sydney Harris's "How to Keep Air Clean," you were asked to write a number of reasons that have led you to disagree with a widely held assumption or opinion. If you responded to this item, read over what you recorded in your journal. Then, do the following:

   a. Turn your notes into an introductory paragraph—complete with a formal thesis statement—that challenges this assumption and briefly explains your reasons for disagreeing.

   b. Make each of your reasons for disagreeing the topic of a well-developed paragraph. Use these paragraphs to develop the body of your essay.

   c. Write a concluding paragraph that:

   • Rephrases your thesis and summarizes your major points;
   • Uses an anecdote to illustrate those ideas;
   • Makes a call to action, as Harris does at the end of his essay; **or**
   • Uses one of the other methods for writing effective conclusions discussed in this chapter.

   Incidentally, although you follow the steps above, you need not complete them in the same order that they are listed. For example, writing the body paragraphs and the conclusion before you write the introduction might be an easier and more effective way for you to proceed.

   In any case, remember that writing is a process of discovery. Often you might have to revise one part of the essay in light of what you said in another. Therefore, if you begin the assignment by drafting your introduction, don't be afraid to rewrite it later if what you put into the body of the paper demands a change—major or minor—in your thesis or in other parts of the introduction. Finally, no matter how many times you revise a paper, make sure to edit the final draft carefully.

3. Do you agree with Robert Fulghum that people's bathrooms tell a lot about them? How about their cars, bedrooms, closets, or refrigerators? Write an essay in which you introduce your readers to a close friend or relative by describing his or her room, home, apartment, car, work area, or the like. Include details that focus on one and only one aspect of your subject's personality. For example, to show that this person has expensive tastes, mention the brand names and estimate the costs of clothes you saw in his or her closet. Then talk about the luxurious furniture and expensive stereo equipment in his or her living

room, and so on. If you responded to the second suggestion for journal writing after "I Was Just Wondering," you have already gathered useful details for this assignment.

When you write your introduction, you might use a startling statement or, like Fulghum, ask a question that helps reveal your thesis. Here's an example of such a question: "How do I know Andy has expensive tastes?"

You can conclude by summarizing your main points, offering advice, or looking to the future. For example:

Andy spends money faster than he can make it. Unless he gets a better-paying job, cuts back on expensive purchases, or inherits money from a rich relative, the finance company will repossess his furniture.

As with any assignment, begin with a rough draft, and revise your work several times. Make sure your essay is well developed, unified, and coherent. Then edit for grammar, spelling, punctuation, and so on.

4. Perhaps you responded to one of the items under Suggestions for Journal Entries after Cousins' "Pain Is Not the Ultimate Enemy." If so, you might have gathered information to use in an essay on **one** of the following:
   a. The symptoms and treatment of a serious illness you or someone you know has suffered from.
   b. The effects of an addiction to a legal drug on you or someone you know.
   c. What you or someone you know did to treat a wound or an illness.
      (You might have also gathered information for this assignment if you completed Practicing Writing Introductions on page 128.)
      Before you begin, read these tips on organizing and writing your essay:

   • Open your essay by using one of the techniques for writing introductions explained earlier.
   • Make sure your introduction includes a thesis statement.
   • As you learned in Chapter 2, make sure your essay is unified and coherent.
   • Close by using one of the methods of concluding essays that you just learned.
   • Make several drafts of your paper. Edit your best version to make sure that spelling, sentence structure, grammar, and punctuation are correct.

5. "The Transformation of Maria Fernandez" tells of tragic events that Anita DiPasquale witnessed or that she learned about from someone else. If you responded to either of the first two suggestions for journal writing after this essay, you have collected information about a terrifying incident you experienced directly, witnessed, or heard about from another person. Turn these notes into a full-length essay that tells your story in detail. Like the author of "The Transformation of Maria Fernandez," you might quote yourself or others in your story.

DiPasquale opens by making startling statements, challenging popular assumptions, and asking a rhetorical question. Any of these methods is a good way to introduce your essay, but you can also describe a scene, use a quotation, or explain a problem. When concluding, try a memorable quotation from someone in the story, make a call to action, or look to the future.

You can tell from the final product that DiPasquale wrote several drafts of her essay and edited it quite well. Do the same with yours.

6. Have you ever known anyone who, because of a single experience, went through a drastic and sudden change in personality, lifestyle, or attitude like the one you read about in "The Transformation of Maria Fernandez"? Write the story of this transformation by telling your readers about the experience and by explaining how it changed the person you are writing about. First, however, review the notes you made after reading DiPasquale's essay. If you responded to the third journal suggestion, you may have gathered details you can use in this assignment.

A startling statement, an interesting question or analogy, or the vivid description of a place might make an interesting introduction to your story. Quoting your subject, looking to the future, or asking a rhetorical question might make an effective conclusion.

Once again, remember that writing is a process, so draft, revise, and edit!

WORD CHOICE
AND SENTENCE PATTERNS

In Section One you learned how to approach a subject, to focus on a purpose and central idea, and to organize and develop the information you collected. The three chapters in Section Two explain how to use language and sentence structure to make your writing clearer, more interesting, and more emphatic.

What you will learn in Section Two is just as important as what you learned earlier. In most cases, however, the techniques discussed in this section—refining word choice, creating figures of speech, and reworking sentence structure for emphasis and variety— are things you will turn your attention to after having written at least one version of a paper, not while you are focusing on a central idea, organizing details, or writing your very first rough draft.

Keep this in mind as you read the next three chapters. Chapter 5 explains how to choose vocabulary that is concrete, specific, and vivid. You will learn even more about using words effectively in Chapter 6, which explains three types of figurative language: metaphor, simile, and personification. Finally, Chapter 7 will increase your ability to create variety and emphasis through sentence structure.

Enjoy the selections that follow. Reading them carefully and completing the Questions for Discussion, the Suggestions for Journal Entries, and the Suggestions for Sustained Writing will not only help you learn more about the writing process but should also inspire you to continue developing as a writer.

WORD CHOICE: USING CONCRETE, SPECIFIC, AND VIVID LANGUAGE

A writer has three ways to communicate a message: by (1) implying it, (2) telling it, or (3) showing it. Of course, all three types of writing serve specific and important purposes. Usually, however, writing that is the clearest and has the greatest impact uses language that shows what you wish to communicate. Words that show are more concrete, specific, and usually more interesting than those that simply tell the reader what you want to say, and they are always more direct than language that only implies or suggests what you mean.

Although the following two paragraphs discuss the same subject, they contain very different kinds of language. Which of the two will have the greater impact on the reader?

WRITING THAT TELLS

Smith's old car is the joke of the neighborhood. He should have gotten rid of it years ago, but he insists on keeping this "antique" despite protests from his family and friends. The car is noisy and unsafe. What's more, it pollutes the environment, causes a real disturbance whenever he drives by, and is a real eyesore.

WRITING THAT SHOWS

Whenever Smith drives his 1957 Dodge down our street, dogs howl, children scream, and old people head inside and shut their windows. Originally, the car was painted emerald green, but the exterior is so covered with scrapes, dents, and patches of rust that it is hard to tell what it looked like when new. His wife, children, and close friends have begged him to junk this corroded patchwork of steel, rubber, and chicken wire, but Smith insists that he can restore his "antique" to its former glory. It does no good to point out that its cracked windshield and bald tires qualify it as a road hazard. Nor does it help to complain about the roar and rattle of its cracked muffler, the screech of its well-worn brakes, and the stench of the thick, black smoke that billows from its rusty tail pipe.

As you will learn in the chapters on narration and description, language that shows makes for effective and interesting writing, especially when your purpose is to describe

155

a person or place or to tell a story. But such language is important to many kinds of writing, and learning how to use it is essential to your development as a writer.

There are three important things to remember about language that shows: It is concrete, it is specific, and it is vivid.

MAKING YOUR WRITING CONCRETE

Concrete language points to or identifies something that the reader can experience or has experienced in some way. Things that are concrete are usually material; they can be seen, heard, smelled, felt, or tasted. The opposite of *concrete* is *abstract*, a term that refers to ideas, emotions, or other intangibles that, while very real, exist in our minds and hearts. That's why readers find it harder to grasp the abstract than the concrete.

Compare the nouns in the following list. The ones on the left represent abstract ideas. The ones on the right stand for concrete embodiments of those ideas; that is, they are physical representations, showing us what such ideas as "affection" and "hatred" really are.

ABSTRACT	CONCRETE
Affection	Kiss, embrace
Hatred	Sneer, curse
Violence	Punch, shove
Anger	Shout
Fear	Scream, gasp
Joy	Laugh, smile

Here are three ways to make your writing concrete.

USE YOUR FIVE SENSES TO RECALL AN EXPERIENCE

Giving your readers a straightforward, realistic account of how things look, smell, sound, taste, or feel is one of the most effective ways to make your writing concrete. There are several examples in this book of how authors appeal to the five senses, especially in the chapters on description. For now, read the following passage from "Once More to the Lake," in which E. B. White recalls concrete, sensory details about arriving at the camp in Maine where he spent his summer vacations as a boy. The only sense that White does not refer to is taste; see if you can identify details in this paragraph that appeal to the other four:

> The arriving . . . had been so big a business in itself, at the railway station the farm wagon drawn up, the first smell of the pine-laden air, the first glimpse of the smiling farmer . . . and the feel of the wagon under you for the long ten-mile haul, and at the top of the last long hill catching the first view of the lake after eleven months of not seeing this cherished body of water. The shouts and

cries of the other campers when they saw you, and the trunks to be unpacked, to give up their rich burden.

USE YOUR FIVE SENSES TO CREATE A CONCRETE IMAGE

An *image* is a mental picture that expresses an abstraction in concrete terms and, therefore, helps readers understand that idea more easily. You can create images by packing your writing with details, usually in the form of nouns and adjectives, that show your readers what things look, sound, smell, taste, or feel like.

The word "image" is related to the word "imagine"; a good time to create an image is when you write about something that your readers have never experienced or that they can only imagine from the information you provide. This is what happens in *A Portrait of the Artist as a Young Man,* when novelist James Joyce puts a startling image into the mouth of a priest who wants to describe his personal vision of hell to a group of schoolboys. Like White, Joyce relies on the senses. Notice the many nouns and adjectives used to create an image of what the speaker thinks eternal damnation is like, an idea that would otherwise have remained very abstract:

> Hell is a strait [narrow] and dark and foulsmelling prison, an abode [home] of demons and lost souls, filled with fire and smoke. The straitness of this prisonhouse is expressly designed by God to punish those who refused to be bound by His laws. In earthly prisons the poor captive [prisoner] has at least some liberty of movement, [if] only within the four walls of his cell or in the gloomy yard of his prison. Not so in hell. There, by reason of the great number of the damned, the prisoners are heaped together in their awful prison, the walls of which are said to be four thousand miles thick: and the damned are so utterly bound and helpless that . . . they are not even able to remove from the eye a worm that gnaws it.

The paragraphs by White and Joyce communicate abstract ideas so concretely that we can understand what the writer is explaining even though we haven't actually experienced it. White's recollection of his arrival makes us feel his personal excitement and anticipation, emotions we could not have appreciated fully had he not used details that appeal to our senses. But such information is even more important in Joyce's paragraph. Unlike that earthly camp in Maine, hell is not part of the world we know. To show us what hell looks like, Joyce must rely on concrete details we recognize from other experiences, details that will help us imagine the scene because they appeal to our senses.

USE EXAMPLES

Using easily recognizable examples is a very effective way to help your readers grasp abstract ideas, which might otherwise seem vague or unclear. For instance, if you want to explain that your Uncle Wendell is eccentric, you can write that "he has several quirks," that "he is odd," or that "he is strange." But such synonyms are as abstract and as hard to grasp as "eccentric." Instead, why not provide examples that your readers are sure to understand? In other words, *show* them what "eccentric" means by explaining that Uncle Wendell never wears the same color socks, that he often cuts his own hair, that he refuses to speak for days at a time, and that he sometimes eats chocolate-covered seaweed for dessert.

In "Less Work for Mother?" Ruth Schwartz Cowan uses a number of examples we are certain to recognize as she explains the idea that technology has transformed the American household:

> During the first half of the twentieth century, the average American house-hold was transformed by the introduction of a group of machines that pro-foundly altered the daily lives of housewives. . . . Where once there had been a wood- or coal-burning stove there now was a gas or electric range. Clothes that had once been scrubbed on a metal washboard were now tossed into a tub and cleansed by an electrically driven agitator. The dryer replaced the clothesline; the vacuum cleaner replaced the broom; the refrigerator replaced the ice box and the root cellar. . . . No one had to chop or haul wood anymore. No one had to shovel out ashes or beat rugs or carry water; no one even had to toss egg whites with a fork for an hour to make an angel food cake.

MAKING YOUR WRITING SPECIFIC

As you've learned, writing that shows uses details that are both specific and con-crete. Writing that lacks specificity often contains language that is general, which makes it difficult for the writer to communicate clearly and completely. One of the best ways to make your language more specific is to use carefully chosen nouns and adjectives. As you probably know, nouns represent persons, places, and things; adjectives modify (or help describe) nouns, thereby making them more exact and distinct. In the following list, compare the words and phrases in each column; notice how much more meaning-ful the items become as you move from left to right:

GENERAL	MORE SPECIFIC	MOST SPECIFIC
Automobile	Sports car	Corvette
Residence	House	Three-bedroom ranch
Fruit	Melon	Juicy cantaloupe
School	College	University of Kentucky
Tree	Evergreen	Young pine
Baked goods	Pastries	Chocolate-filled cream puffs
Airplane	Jetliner	Brand-new Boeing 777
Beverage	Soft drink	Caffeine-free diet cola
Television show	Situation comedy	*Seinfeld*
Public transportation	Train	*Orient Express*

You probably noticed that several of the "Most Specific" items contain capitalized words. These are proper nouns, which name specific persons, places, and things. Use proper nouns that your readers will recognize whenever you can. Doing so will show how much you know about your subject and will increase the readers' confidence in you. More important, it will help make your ideas more familiar and easier to grasp.

At first, you might have to train yourself to use specifics. After a while, though, you will become skilled at eliminating flat, empty generalizations from your writing and at filling it with details that clarify and focus your ideas.

Notice the differences between the following two paragraphs. The first uses vague, general language; the second uses specific details—nouns and adjectives—that make its meaning sharper and clearer and that hold the readers' interest better.

GENERAL

The island prison is covered with flowers now. A large sign that is visible from a long way off warns visitors away. But since the early 1960s, when they took the last prisoners to other institutions, the sign has really served no purpose, for the prison has been abandoned. The place is not unpleasant; in fact, one might enjoy the romance and solitude out there.

SPECIFIC

Alcatraz Island is covered with flowers now: orange and yellow nasturtiums, geraniums, sweet grass, blue iris, black-eyed Susans. Candytuft springs up through the cracked concrete in the exercise yard. Ice plant carpets the rusting catwalks. "WARNING! KEEP OFF! U.S. PROPERTY," the sign still reads, big and yellow and visible for perhaps a quarter of a mile, but since March 21, 1963, the day they took the last thirty or so men off the island . . . the warning has been only *pro forma* [serving no real purpose]. It is not an unpleasant place to be, out there on Alcatraz with only the flowers and the wind and the bell buoy moaning and the tide surging through the Golden Gate. (Joan Didion, "Rock of Ages")

The differences between these two paragraphs can be summed up as follows:

- The first calls the place an "island prison." The second gives it a name, "Alcatraz."
- The first claims that the prison is covered with flowers. The second shows us that this is true by naming them: "nasturtiums, geraniums," and so on. It also explains exactly where they grow: "through the cracked concrete" and on "rusting catwalks."
- The first tells us about a sign that can be seen "from a long way off." The second explains that the sign is "visible for perhaps a quarter of a mile" and shows us exactly what it says.
- The first mentions that the last prisoners were removed from Alcatraz in the 1960s. The second explains that they numbered "thirty or so" and that the exact date of their departure was March 21, 1963.

• The first tells us that we might find "romance and solitude" on Alcatraz Island. The second describes the romance and solitude by calling our attention to "the flowers and the wind and the bell buoy moaning and the tide surging through the Golden Gate."

MAKING YOUR WRITING VIVID

Besides using figurative language (the subject of the next chapter), you can make your writing vivid by choosing verbs, adjectives, and adverbs carefully.

1. Verbs express action, condition, or state of being. If you wrote that "Jan *leaped* over the hurdles," you would be using an action verb. If you explained that "Roberta *did not feel* well" or that "Mario *was* delirious," you would be describing a condition or a state of being.

2. Adjectives describe nouns. You would be using adjectives if you wrote that "the *large, two-story white* house that the *young Canadian* couple bought was *old* and *weather-beaten.*"

3. Adverbs modify (tell the reader something about) verbs, adjectives, or other adverbs. You would be using adverbs if you wrote: "The *easily* frightened child sobbed *softly* and hugged his mother *very tightly* as she *gently* wiped away his tears and *tenderly* explained that the knee he had *just* scraped would stop hurting *soon.*"

Choosing effective verbs, adjectives, and adverbs can turn dull writing into writing that keeps the readers' interest and communicates ideas with greater emphasis and clarity. Notice how much more effective the rewritten version of each of the following sentences becomes when the right verbs, adjectives, and adverbs are used:

1. The old church needed repair.

   The pre-Civil War Baptist church cried out for repairs to its tottering steeple, its crumbling stone foundation, and its cracked stained-glass windows.

2. The kitchen table was a mess. It was covered with the remains of peanut butter and jelly sandwiches.

   The kitchen table was littered with the half-eaten remains of very stale peanut-butter sandwiches and thickly smeared with the crusty residue of strawberry jelly.

3. A pathetic old homeless person was in an alley among some garbage.

   The body of a homeless man, his face wrinkled and blistered, lay in a pile of oil-covered rags and filthy cardboard boxes piled in the corner of a long alley devoid of life and light.

VISUALIZING CONCRETE, SPECIFIC, AND VIVID DETAILS

In the following paragraphs from "Where the World Began," Margaret Laurence describes her small hometown on the Canadian prairie. Comments in the margins of the first paragraph point to examples of the kinds of language you just learned about. After studying the first paragraph, find and circle similar examples of effective language in the second.

Adjectives appeal to senses.

Summers were scorching, and when no rain came and the wheat became bleached and dried before it headed, the faces of farmers and townsfolk would not smile much, and you took for granted, because it never seemed to have been any different, the frequent knocking at the

Startling image.

back door and the young men standing there, mumbling or **Vivid verbs.**

thrusting defiantly their requests for a drink of water **Vivid adverb.**

and a sandwich if you could spare it. They were riding

Specific type of train.

the freights, and you never knew were they had come from, or where they might end up, if anywhere. The Drought and Depression were like evil deities which had **Proper nouns.**

been there always. You understood and did not understand.

Yet the outside world had its continuing marvels. The poplar bluffs and the small river were filled and surrounded with a zillion different grasses, stones, and weed flowers. The meadowlarks sang undaunted [courageously] from the twanging telephone wires along the gravel highway. Once we found an old flat-bottomed scow [small boat], and launched her, poling along the shallow brown waters, mending her with wodges [chunks] of hastily chewed Spearmint, grounding her among the tangles of yellow marsh marigolds that grew succulently along the banks of the shrunken river, while the sun

made our skins smell dusty-warm.

REVISING TO INCLUDE CONCRETE, SPECIFIC, AND VIVID LANGUAGE

Read these two versions of a paragraph from Nancy J. Mundie's ironic (tongue-in-cheek) essay that proposes to use the mentally ill in scientific experimentation. It is clear that, by revising her work, Mundie was able to make her language more concrete, specific, and vivid. You will find a complete version of Mundie's essay—"The Mentally Ill and Human Experimentation: Perfect Together"—later in this chapter.

Mundie—Rough Draft, Paragraph 2

This proposal would have an immediate impact on the condition of our cities. For the homeless a dirty, litter-strewn corner would be replaced by a clean living environment. Tourism would become more attractive to out-of-towners, for the mentally ill would be off the streets. Public transportation would flourish as bus, train, and subway stations would be devoid of ranting vagabonds. Houses of worship would see an increase in membership, for the "street-corner preacher" would be unavailable. Crime would decrease, for police could concentrate on serious offenders as opposed to acting as street sweepers of the homeless.

Mundie—Final Draft, Paragraphs 2 and 3

Added detail causes author to create two paragraphs from one.

This proposal would have an immediate impact on the homeless, many of whom are afflicted with mental disorders. For them, a filthy, litter-strewn street

Adds concrete details, vivid language. corner would be replaced by a sterile environment in a research hospital, sheltered from rains, sleet and snow, from the heat of summer and the biting winds of winter.

Of course, their absence would improve our cities' landscapes as well. Tourism would increase

Adds detail that appeals to senses; creates an image. dramatically, for the mentally ill, many of whom walk around encrusted with filth and reeking of their own excrement, would be off the streets. Public transportation would flourish as bus, train, and subway stations would be devoid of ranting vagabonds.

Houses of worship would see an increase in membership, for "street-corner preachers" would be hauled off to hospitals where, while undergoing

Adds specifics and a quotation. extensive neurological observation, they could shout that the "world is coming to an end" to their heart's content. Crime would decrease, for police would concentrate on serious offenders as opposed to acting as

Expands original to create a startling image. street sweepers of the homeless, of beggars, and of vagrants shouting obscenities to passersby or mumbling incoherently to themselves as they lay in dark and dirty doorways.

PRACTICING USING CONCRETE, SPECIFIC, AND VIVID LANGUAGE

In the spaces provided rewrite the following sentences to improve word choice. Use techniques you have just read about to turn language that *tells* into language that *shows*. The first item has been completed for you as an example.

1. When the proud, old woman graduated, her classmates showed their approval.

When the eighty-year-old chemistry major strutted across the stage to get her diploma, her classmates stood up and cheered.

2. A construction worker hung from a beam above the street.

_____

_____

_____

3. The woman was overjoyed to be reunited with her lost son.

_____

_____

_____

4. The exterior of the house needed painting.

_____

_____

_____

5. His desk was cluttered.

_____

_____

_____

6. The garden contained a variety of beautiful flowers and trees.

_____

_____

_____

7. The children became frightened when the dog came into the room.

_____

_____

_____

8. The bus was crowded.

_____

_____

_____

0 9. The supermarket was doing a brisk business.

_____

_____

_____

10. The Greasy Spoon Restaurant was a breeding ground for bacteria.

_____

_____

_____

Word choice is extremely important to anyone who wants to become an effective writer. Using the right kind of language marks the difference between writing that is flat, vague, and uninteresting and writing that makes a real impact on its readers. The following selections present the work of poets and essayists who have written clear and effective explanations of very abstract ideas, ideas they would have been unable to explain without language that is concrete, specific, and vivid.

Those Winter Sundays

Robert Hayden

Robert Hayden (1913–1980) taught English at Fisk University and at the University of Michigan. For years, the work of this talented black writer received far less recognition than it deserved. Recently, however, his reputation has grown, especially since the publication of his complete poems in 1985.

"Those Winter Sundays" uses the author's vivid memories of his father to show us the depth and quality of love that the man had for his family. Unlike much of Hayden's other work, this poem does not deal with the black experience as such, but it demonstrates the same care and skill in choosing effective language that Hayden used in all his poetry.

If you want to read more by Hayden, look for these poetry collections in your college library: A Ballad of Remembrance, Words in Mourning Time, Angle of Ascent, *and* American Journal.

L OOKING A HEAD

1. Hayden's primary purpose is to explain his father's love for his family. Look for details that are physical signs of that love.
2. The author says his father "made/banked fires blaze." Wood and coal fires were "banked" by covering them with ashes to make them burn slowly through the night and continue giving off heat.
3. The word "offices" isn't used in its usual sense in this poem. Here, it means important services or ceremonies.

V OCABULARY

austere	Severe, harsh, difficult, without comfort.
chronic	Persistent, unending, constant.
indifferently	Insensitively, without care or concern.

*Those Winter
Sundays* | *Robert Hayden*

Sundays too my father got up early
and put his clothes on in the blueblack cold,
then with cracked hands that ached
from labor in the weekday weather made
banked fires blaze. No one ever thanked him.   5

I'd wake and hear the cold splintering, breaking.
When the rooms were warm, he'd call,
and slowly I would rise and dress,
fearing the chronic angers of that house,

Speaking indifferently to him,   10
who had driven out the cold
and polished my good shoes as well.
What did I know, what did I know
of love's austere and lonely offices?

QUESTIONS FOR DISCUSSION

1. What details in this poem appeal to our senses?
2. In line 2, Hayden uses "blueblack" to describe the cold in his house on Sunday mornings. What other effective adjectives do you find in this poem?
3. Hayden shows us his father in action. What were some of the things this good man did to show his love for his family?
4. What was Hayden's reaction to his father's "austere and lonely offices" when he was a boy? How did he feel about his father when he wrote this poem?

THINKING CRITICALLY

Hayden mentions that he feared "the chronic angers of that house." What might he mean by that? Do you associate any "chronic angers" with your home?

SUGGESTIONS FOR JOURNAL ENTRIES

1. In Looking Ahead, you read that Hayden describes his father's love by using language that is concrete, specific, and vivid. In your own words, discuss the kind of love that Hayden's father showed his family.
2. Do you know someone who demonstrates love for other people day in and day out, as Hayden's father did? In your journal, list the offices (services, tasks, or activities) that he or she performs to show this love. Include as many concrete and specific terms as you can. Then expand each item in your list to a few short sentences, showing that these activities are clearly signs of love.

Going Home

Maurice Kenny

Maurice Kenny is a Native American poet who lives and teaches in rural New York State. Among his most important publications are The Mama Poems *and* Between Two Rivers. *"Going Home" expresses the writer's sense of loss and isolation when he comes home after a long absence.*

LOOKING AHEAD

Kenny uses nouns, both common and proper, to create a picture of the land to which he returns. As you know, nouns name persons, places, and things. Proper nouns, like "Greyhound" and "Syracuse," name specific persons, places, and things.

VOCABULARY

privies   Toilets.

Going Home | *Maurice Kenny*

The book lay unread in my lap
snow gathered at the window
from Brooklyn it was a long ride
the Greyhound followed the plow
from Syracuse to Watertown   5
to country cheese and maples
tired rivers and closed paper mills
home to gossipy aunts . . .
their dandelions and pregnant cats . . .
home to cedars and fields of boulders   10
cold graves under willow and pine
home from Brooklyn to the reservation
that was not home
to songs I could not sing
to dances I could not dance   15
from Brooklyn bars and ghetto rats
to steaming horses stomping frozen earth
barns and privies lost in blizzards
home to a Nation, Mohawk
to faces, I did not know   20
and hands which did not recognize me
to names and doors
my father shut

QUESTIONS FOR DISCUSSION

1. "The book lay unread in my lap," the poet says in line 1. What does this tell us about his state of mind?
2. How would you describe the image that closes this poem? What emotion does it show?
3. What do the adjectives "tired" and "closed" in line 7 tell us about Kenny's home? Find other adjectives that make his writing vivid.
4. What details does the writer use to contrast the two places he has called home?
5. What nouns, common and proper, do we find in "Going Home"? What effect do they have on you?

THINKING CRITICALLY

What is Kenny referring to when he tells us about doors his "father shut"? There is no correct answer to this question, but thinking and writing about it will help you to appreciate the poem more and to exercise your mental muscles.

SUGGESTIONS FOR JOURNAL ENTRIES

1. Kenny does not say exactly how long he has been away or what has happened during that time. What do you imagine happened to him or to the place and people he left since he was home last? Use brainstorming or focused freewriting to make up details that could explain why he feels so separated from the people and land he is returning to.
2. Think of a town, community, or neighborhood in which you once lived and have been away from for a long time. Would you like to live there again? Why or why not? Answer this question by listing concrete details about the place. Rely on your senses; explain what it looked like, smelled like, and so on. Like Kenny, include nouns, both common and proper, to create images that will reveal your feelings about your subject.

From "No Name Woman"

Maxine Hong Kingston

Born in 1940 to newly arrived immigrants, Maxine Hong Kingston has become one of our most celebrated Chinese-American writers. "No Name Woman" is the first chapter of The Woman Warrior: Memoirs of a Girlhood Among Ghosts *(1978), a collection of autobiographical essays about the female members of her family.*

LOOKING AHEAD

1. The story in these four paragraphs is being told to the author by her mother; thus, they appear in quotation marks.
2. The setting is China, 1924. Neighbors, who have learned that Hong Kingston's aunt has conceived a child not her husband's, condemn her and express their outrage by attacking her home.
3. It may seem strange that an illegitimate pregnancy would draw violence from neighbors. But the story is from a time and place different from our own. In this poor village, Hong Kingston later says, "adultery is extravagance." The villagers use the aunt as an example to discourage such behavior in others, for having children out of wedlock brings economic hardship to all.

VOCABULARY

acrid	Pungent, having a harsh smell.
flared	Rose up.
torrents	Floods.

*From "No Name
Woman"* | **Maxine Hong Kingston**

"At first they threw mud and rocks at the house. Then they threw eggs and began slaughtering our stock. We could hear the animals scream their deaths—the roosters, the pigs, a last great roar from the ox. Familiar wild heads flared in our night windows: the villagers encircled us. Some of the faces stopped to peer at us, their eyes rushing like searchlights. The hands flattened against the panes, framed heads, and left red prints.

"The villagers broke in the front and the back doors at the same time, even though we had not locked the doors against them. Their knives dripped with the blood of our animals. They smeared blood on the doors and walls. One woman swung a chicken, whose throat she had slit, splattering blood in red arcs about her. We stood together in the middle of our house, in the family hall with the pictures and tables of the ancestors around us, and looked straight ahead.

". . . The villagers pushed through both wings [of the house] . . . to find your aunt's [room]. . . . They ripped up her clothes and shoes and broke her combs, grinding them underfoot. They tore her work from the loom. They scattered the cooking fire and rolled the new weaving in it. We could hear them in the kitchen breaking our bowls and banging the pots. They overturned the great waist-high earthenware jugs; duck eggs, pickled fruits, vegetables burst out and mixed in acrid torrents. The old woman from the next field swept a broom through the air and loosed the spirits-of-the-broom over our heads. 'Pig.' 'Ghost.' 'Pig,' they sobbed and scolded while they ruined our house.

"When they left, they took sugar and oranges to bless themselves. They cut out pieces from the dead animals. Some of them took bowls that were not broken and clothes that were not torn. Afterward we swept up the rice and sewed it back up into sacks. But the smells from the spilled preserves lasted. Your aunt gave birth in the pigsty that night. The next morning when I went for the water, I found her and the baby plugging up the family well."

QUESTIONS FOR DISCUSSION

1. Where in this piece does Hong Kingston appeal to our senses?
2. You learned earlier that using verbs, adjectives, and adverbs carefully can make writing vivid. Find a paragraph in which the author uses verbs well. Underline these verbs.
3. Find a paragraph in which the author uses adjectives well. Underline these adjectives.
4. This selection ends with a startling image. Find other effective images in this piece.
5. In paragraph 1, Hong Kingston does not *tell* us that the villagers' hands are bloodied; she *shows* us that. Explain.

THINKING CRITICALLY

1. In paragraph 2, we learn that the villagers broke in the doors even though they were unlocked. In paragraph 4, we learn that some "took bowls that were not broken and clothes that were not torn." What does this information tell us about them?
2. What do you make of the villagers' condemning the woman and not the man who made her pregnant? What does this reveal about the society in which the story occurs? Can you find any parallels in the way contemporary society treats this issue?

SUGGESTIONS FOR JOURNAL ENTRIES

1. Use freewriting to express your reaction to the villagers' behavior.
2. What would you say to the man who impregnated Hong Kingston's aunt? Use freewriting or listing to gather information you might later use in a letter to this man.
3. Have you ever witnessed or seen television coverage of mob or gang violence comparable to what you read about in "No Name Woman"? If so, record concrete, specific, vivid details about this incident in your journal. Use any prewriting method you want, but be as complete as you can. You might want to use this information in a formal essay later on.

The San Francisco Earthquake

Jack London

One of the world's best-known adventure writers, London (1876–1916) held a number of colorful jobs that took him around the world and supplied material for his stories. When only a boy, he left his native San Francisco on a commercial steamer to Japan. Several adventures later, he traveled to the Klondike to prospect for gold. In 1904, he returned to the Orient as a journalist to report on the Russo-Japanese War, and in 1914, he found himself in Mexico to cover that country's revolution. Among his best-known novels are The Call of the Wild, White Fang, *and* The Sea Wolf.

LOOKING AHEAD

1. London makes his writing concrete and specific by choosing nouns carefully. In paragraph 1, he calls the blaze that followed the earthquake a "conflagration," not simply a fire. In paragraph 2, he tells us about the "hotels and palaces of the nabobs" when he could simply have mentioned their "houses."
2. In paragraph 3, London uses the adjective "lurid" to describe the tower of smoke from the burning city. In paragraph 6, he makes use of an interesting adverb when he explains that dynamite was used "lavishly." Pick out other effective adjectives and adverbs as you read this selection.
3. London was a master at creating concrete visual imagery. One of his best can be found in paragraph 3, but there are others in this essay. Find them.

VOCABULARY

colossal	Gigantic.
conflagration	Large and very destructive fire.
contrivances	Inventions.
cunning	Skillful.
debris	Fragments, remains.
enumeration	Listing.
lavishly	Generously, in great amounts.
lurid	Glaring, shocking.
nabobs	People of wealth and power.
vestiges	Traces.
wrought	Caused.

The San Francisco Earthquake

Jack London

The earthquake shook down in San Francisco hundreds of thousands of dollars 1
worth of walls and chimneys. But the conflagration that followed burned up
hundreds of millions of dollars worth of property. There is no estimating within hundreds of millions the actual damage wrought.

Not in history has a modern imperial city been so completely destroyed. San Fran- 2
cisco is gone. Nothing remains of it but memories and a fringe of dwelling houses on its
outskirts. Its industrial section is wiped out. Its social and residential section is wiped
out. The factories and warehouses, the great stores and newspaper buildings, the hotels
and palaces of the nabobs, all are gone. Remains only the fringe of dwelling houses on
the outskirts of what was once San Francisco.

Within an hour after the earthquake shock, the smoke of San Francisco's burning was 3
a lurid tower visible a hundred miles away. And for three days and nights this lurid tower
swayed in the sky, reddening the sun, darkening the day, and filling the land with smoke.

On Wednesday morning at quarter past five came the earthquake. A minute later the 4
flames were leaping upward. In a dozen different quarters south of Market Street, in the
working class ghetto and in the factories, fires started. There was no opposing the flames.
There was no organization, no communication. All the cunning adjustments of a twentieth century city had been smashed by the earthquake. The streets were humped into ridges
and depressions, and piled with the debris of fallen walls. The steel rails were twisted into
perpendicular and horizontal angles. The telephone and telegraph systems were disrupted.
And the great water mains had burst. All the shrewd contrivances and safeguards of man
had been thrown out of gear by thirty seconds' twitching of the earth-crust.

By Wednesday afternoon, inside of twelve hours, half the heart of the city was gone. 5
At that time I watched the vast conflagration from out on the bay. It was dead calm.
Not a flicker of wind stirred. Yet from every side wind was pouring in upon the city.
East, west, north, and south, strong winds were blowing upon the doomed city. The
heated air rising made an enormous suck. Thus did the fire of itself build its own colossal chimney through the atmosphere. Day and night this dead calm continued, and yet,
near to the flames, the wind was often half a gale, so mighty was the suck.

Wednesday night saw the destruction of the very heart of the city. Dynamite was lav- 6
ishly used, and many of San Francisco's proudest structures were crumbled by man himself into ruins, but there was no withstanding the onrush of the flames. Time and again
successful stands were made by the firefighters, and every time the flames flanked around
on either side, or came up from the rear, and turned to defeat the hard won victory.

An enumeration of the buildings destroyed would be a directory of San Francisco. 7
An enumeration of the buildings undestroyed would be a line and several addresses. An
enumeration of the deeds of heroism would stock a library and bankrupt the Carnegie
medal fund. An enumeration of the dead—will never be made. All vestiges of them were
destroyed by the flames. The number of the victims of the earthquake will never be
known.

QUESTIONS FOR DISCUSSION

1. Pick out a few examples of the effective nouns that make the writing in this essay concrete.
2. One reason London's works are still popular is that they are filled with interesting adjectives. Identify those you find especially vivid.
3. London is famous for creating brilliant visual images like the one in paragraph 3. What other effective images do you find in this selection?
4. In paragraph 4, we read "All the cunning adjustments of a twentieth century city had been smashed by the earthquake." What were these "cunning adjustments"? What examples does London use to explain this idea?
5. What caused the strong wind described in paragraph 5?
6. This essay is well organized. Discuss a few techniques London uses to maintain coherence in and between paragraphs. (Such techniques are explained in Chapter 2.)
7. Did you ever read about, view on television, or experience firsthand the results of an earthquake? What "cunning adjustments" of a modern city did that earthquake destroy? In what ways were its effects different from what London describes?

THINKING CRITICALLY

1. Explain what causes the phenomenon that London describes in paragraph 5. (You may have to rely on principles you learned in a high school science class.)
2. Consider what might happen if a huge earthquake struck your hometown or your college campus. Make a list of the specific changes you would be forced to experience. For example, the earthquake would probably knock out all electrical power and telephone service. How would this affect your food supply, your drinking water, your ability to communicate? What would you do without television?

SUGGESTIONS FOR JOURNAL ENTRIES

1. Have you ever seen the results of a great natural disaster (a flood, an earthquake, a forest fire, a tornado, or a hurricane)? If so, write down as many concrete, specific, and vivid details about the scene as you remember. Use the focused-freewriting method discussed in "Getting Started."
2. Take your journal with you as you walk along one of the main streets of a town or city near your college or your home. Spend a half hour or so gathering details

about what you see, hear, feel, smell, and even taste. Don't bother listing these sensory details in any specific order; just jot them down as you walk along, journal in hand. When you complete your short outing, find a quiet place to read your notes. Then write a paragraph or two explaining your impression of and reaction to what you just experienced.

The Mentally Ill and Human Experimentation: Perfect Together

Nancy J. Mundie

Mundie wrote this essay in a composition class after reading Jonathan Swift's "A Modest Proposal," an eighteenth-century essay that uses irony to expose the abuse of the Irish poor by the rich. Irony is a technique writers use to state the opposite of what they really mean. Often, it adds sting to social criticism. For example, Swift suggested ironically that poor children be bred like cattle and sold for food to the rich. His point was that the poor were being "eaten alive" by the economic practices of the powerful and wealthy.

Mundie uses irony to condemn society's treatment of the mentally ill. Thus, although she seems to suggest we use the mentally ill for experimentation, she is arguing just the opposite. As she makes clear at the essay's end, she is a strong advocate for the mentally ill. In fact, Mundie is majoring in psychological/social rehabilitation.

LOOKING AHEAD

Mundie refers to Willowbrook and Salem in paragraph 1. Willowbrook is a psychiatric hospital on Staten Island, New York, which was criticized for its treatment of patients in an investigation by Geraldo Rivera in the 1970s. Salem, Massachusetts, is often remembered for its seventeenth-century trials, as a result of which several people accused of being witches were burned at the stake.

VOCABULARY

advocates	Supporters.
afflicted	Adversely affected by, hurt by.
consistent	Compatible with, conforming to.
diverse	Varied.
incompetent	Unfit, incapable.
paramount	Most important.
pesky	Annoying, troublesome.
psychotropic	Affecting one's behavior, changing one's psychological state or mood.
squalor	Misery, poverty, filth.
suffice	Be enough.

*The Mentally Ill and
Human
Experimentation:
Perfect Together* | *Nancy J. Mundie*

The human race has always failed at attempting to solve the problem of the men- 1
tally ill. In previous generations, this segment of society had been handled in
ways consistent with the thinking of the times. However, whether burned at the stake in
Salem, Massachusetts, or condemned to live in squalor at Willowbrook, the mentally ill
have never fulfilled a constructive purpose. Therefore, I propose that we begin using
the mentally incompetent as test subjects for scientific and social research.

This proposal would have an immediate impact on the homeless, many of whom are 2
afflicted with mental disorders. For them, a filthy, litter-strewn street corner would be
replaced by a sterile environment in a research hospital, sheltered from rains, sleet and
snow, from the heat of summer and the biting winds of winter. Of course, their absence
would improve our cities' landscapes as well. Tourism would increase dramatically, for
the mentally ill, many of whom walk around encrusted with filth and reeking of their
own excrement, would be off the streets. Public transportation would flourish as bus,
train, and subway stations would be devoid of ranting vagabonds.

Houses of worship would see an increase in membership, for "street-corner preach- 3
ers" would be hauled off to hospitals where, while undergoing extensive neurological
observation, they could shout that the "world is coming to an end" to their heart's content. Crime would decrease, for police would concentrate on serious offenders as
opposed to acting as street sweepers of the homeless, of beggars, and vagrants shouting
obscenities to passersby or mumbling incoherently to themselves as they lie in dark and
dirty doorways.

Those classified as mentally ill (except women with children, for their behavior 4
mimics that of the unstable) would be housed in a common area close to the hospital or
research center. Public homeless shelters—notorious for filth, crime, and vermin—
would suffice, for the patients' stay would not be long. This would keep housing costs
down.

Moreover, only short-term, unskilled care would be required, for research on 5
patients would be unmonitored and as such would probably result in high fatality rates.
Since the patients' stay would be brief, the use of psychotropic drugs would be unnecessary; hence, another cost savings. At the same time, the housing industry would be
stimulated by the need to build more low-quality public shelters, the medical professions given yet another opportunity to grow and profit as a result of the need for more
research.

The advantages of this proposal to the scientific community are numerous. Human 6
experimentation is usually preferred over experimenting with animals to determine a
procedure's or product's effectiveness. However, in much research as we know it, animal
experimentation must precede work on human beings. Using the mentally ill as guinea
pigs, so to speak, would eliminate this requirement, thereby saving much time, effort,
and money. In addition, a diverse test pool is paramount to reliable and accurate scien-

tific research. Using the mentally ill will enable us to create a large and varied pool, for mental illness knows no social, economic, ethnic, or gender boundaries. Finally, researchers will not be forced to contend with pesky animal-rights activists such as members of the ASPCA. Moreover, there is no need to worry about civil-rights advocates, for American Civil Liberties Union's attorneys and the like will make up a large portion of the "research pool."

This proposal is of course preposterous and inhumane at best. The mentally ill 7 have a right to decent living conditions and proper care. Because their illness is largely "unseen" in the physical realm and misunderstood in the intellectual sense, they are often undiagnosed, misclassified, or ignored. But the mentally ill are our beloved family members and friends: the aging grandfather with Alzheimer's disease, the teenager battling depression, the daughter suffering from bulemia, the uncle addicted to alcohol, the neighbor victimized by schizophrenia. Mental illness is so widespread, so close to us, that we would do well always to remember the saying "there but for the grace of God go I."

QUESTIONS FOR DISCUSSION

1. Mundie begins by saying that we have "failed at attempting to solve the problem of the mentally ill." Why didn't she write "failed at attempting to solve the problem of mental illness"? Would this have meant the same thing?
2. What is Mundie's thesis (or supposed thesis)?
3. Where in this essay do you find proper nouns?
4. Find and explain at least one image Mundie creates.
5. Discuss the language in paragraph 4. Which words contribute most to the effect of this paragraph?
6. What is Mundie proposing at the end of paragraph 6?
7. What type of conclusion does Mundie use? (Recall various types of conclusions you read about in Chapter 4.)

THINKING CRITICALLY

1. This proposal is "preposterous," Mundie admits. However, many of the social problems she describes are all too real. Focus on one such problem—say the one mentioned at the end of paragraph 3—and offer a solution you think is both practical and humane. Put your "proposal" in a paragraph of between 75–100 words.
2. Reread Paul Aronowitz's *A Brother's Dreams* in Chapter 3. Explain how that selection helps us understand Mundie's essay, especially her conclusion.

SUGGESTIONS FOR JOURNAL ENTRIES

1. Are you concerned about the way victims of poverty, disease, or a social problem are treated by others? If so, use your journal to list your complaints about the way society treats members of any *one* of these groups.
2. Reread Mundie's last paragraph. Do any of the people she mentions remind you of people you know? If so, use freewriting to describe the effects of their illnesses on themselves or on their families.

Suggestions for Sustained Writing

1. Hayden's "Those Winter Sundays" praises a man who demonstrates his love for others. If you responded to the second journal suggestion after this poem, you have probably made a list of the offices (activities, tasks, or services) that someone you know performs to show his or her love.

   Focus on at least three offices that mean the most to you, and expand your discussion into an essay in which you show how much this individual does for others. Begin with a preliminary thesis that expresses your feelings about your subject, but remember once again that you will probably want to revise this statement after you write your first draft.

   Limit each of the body paragraphs to only one of the offices in your list. Try developing these paragraphs by using methods described in Chapter 3; narration, description, conclusion and support, illustration, and process analysis might work well in such an assignment. Whatever you decide, follow Hayden's lead and use language that is concrete and specific.

   Express your revised thesis in an effective introduction that uses one or more of the techniques for effective openings explained in Chapter 4. Close with a conclusion like one you read about in that chapter. As usual, write several drafts of your paper and edit it carefully.

2. After reading Kenny's "Going Home," you might have made a journal entry about a town, neighborhood, or community that you once lived in and that you may or may not wish to return to. Use your notes and any other important information you can remember about the place to write an essay that describes it in language that is concrete, specific, and vivid.

   Begin with a preliminary thesis statement that clearly expresses your fondness or distaste for the place, your intention to return or to stay away. Use the rest of the essay to explain what about the place makes you feel this way.

   If you have trouble deciding how to introduce or conclude your essay, try one or more of the methods for beginning and ending explained in Chapter 3. As with all assignments, remember that you might have to rewrite your thesis after you draft and revise your paper. As a last step in the process, edit your work for mechanical errors that might reduce your essay's effectiveness.

3. If you read Hong Kingston's "No Name Woman" and responded to the second of the Suggestions for Journal Entries that followed it, you may have already begun to express your opinions of the man who fathered a child with the author's aunt. Write this man a letter in which you explain what you think of his actions. Ask him why he was not present to protect the mother of his child when she was attacked? Ask him why he did not take on the responsibility that was his as a father?

   This is an emotional subject, but try to make your letter as logical and common-sensical as you can. At the same time, include language that is concrete, vivid, and specific to convey your reaction to his behavior. Reread Hong Kingston's essay to gather startling details your reader will need to hear. If necessary, retell parts of the story in your own, carefully chosen words in order to show him how much pain he has caused.

As you have learned, make sure to revise your letter a number of times. If the language seems abstract, flat and unexciting, change it. Then edit and proofread the letter carefully.

4. If you have written about the third of the journal suggestions after "No Name Woman," you might have gathered information about mob or gang violence you witnessed in person or on television. Tell the story of this incident in an essay of about 500 words.

In your first draft, simply put down the facts. Then, as you rewrite your paper, revise it to include language that appeals to the senses. Try to create images. Identify places and people by using proper nouns. Insert verbs and adjectives that will make your writing vivid. As always, add relevant detail as you go along.

Edit the final draft carefully for spelling, punctuation, grammar, and other important matters. Finally, check your introduction and conclusion. Are they effective? If not, try rewriting them using methods you learned about in Chapter 4.

5. In the second suggestion for journal entries after Nancy Mundie's "The Mentally Ill and Human Experimentation: Perfect Together," you were asked to describe the effects of an illness on someone you know or on his or her family. Turn this journal entry into a full-length essay by explaining the causes and/or symptoms of the illness. Then, in language that is concrete, specific, and vivid, show to what degree it has changed the lives of the people it touches. If appropriate, conclude your essay by looking to the future. Try to predict what will become of the people you are writing about.

As you revise the first drafts of your paper, include language that will show your reader what you mean by using the techniques discussed in this chapter. In other words, try to create forceful images, to use concrete and specific nouns, and to fill your writing with lively verbs, adjectives, and adverbs.

After you are satisfied with the result, edit and proofread your work. A great paper deserves a final polishing!

6. If you responded to the first of the Suggestions for Journal Entries after Jack London's "The San Francisco Earthquake," you have already begun gathering details to describe the results of a natural disaster you witnessed recently. Use your notes as the starting point of an essay about the effects of this fire, tornado, earthquake, flood, or the like. Like London, rely on your senses to create effective images, and use verbs and adjectives to make the experience come alive for your readers.

You can add excitement to your essay by beginning with specific details about the disaster itself. In any case, be sure your introduction explains where and when it occurred. Also, try fitting your thesis into your first or second paragraph as London does.

Most important, take your time as you go through the process of describing the effects of this terrible event. Revise the early drafts of your paper by adding important details and improving word choice. Check to see that you have included appropriate transitions to maintain coherence and that you have organized your information well. Finally, edit your paper to remove errors that might detract from the fine work you have produced!

WORD CHOICE: USING FIGURATIVE LANGUAGE

In Chapter 5 you learned that you can clarify abstract ideas by using concrete language. One way to do this is to fill your writing with specific details or to create verbal images (pictures in words) that appeal to the readers' senses. You also learned that using effective verbs, adjectives, and adverbs can help make your writing vivid. All of these techniques will help you *show*—and not simply tell—your reader what you mean.

Another way to make your writing clearer and more vivid is to use figurative language. Such language is called "figurative" because it does not explain or represent a subject directly. A figure of speech works by creating a comparison or other relationship between the abstract idea you want to explain and something concrete that readers will recognize easily. In that way, it can help you explain an idea more clearly and emphatically than if you used literal language alone.

In fact, figures of speech provide a way to create images, mental pictures that allow readers to *see* what you mean. Notice how effective your description of a "clumsy" friend becomes when you compare him to a "bull in a china shop." The concrete image of a "bull in a china shop"—complete with shattered teacups, bowls, and plates—is sharper and more dramatic than an abstraction like "clumsy" can ever be.

The most common figures of speech take the form of comparisons. The three discussed in this chapter are simile, metaphor, and personification.

SIMILE

A simile creates a comparison between two things by using the word "like" or "as." For example, say that you're writing your sweetheart a letter in which you want to explain how much you need him or her. You can express your feelings literally and directly by writing "I need you very much." Then again, you can *show* how strongly you feel by writing that you need him or her "as a great oak needs sunlight," "as an eagle needs the open sky," or "as the dry earth needs spring rain."

Read the following list carefully. Notice how much more concrete, exciting, and rich the ideas on the left become when they are expressed in similes:

LITERAL EXPRESSION	SIMILE
She arrived on time.	She arrived as promptly as the sunrise.
Snerdly's face was sunburned.	Snerdly's face was as red as the inside of a watermelon.
Eugene is a fancy dresser.	Eugene dresses like a peacock.

The tires made a loud noise.	The tires screeched like a wounded animal.
The dog moved slowly.	The dog moved like corn syrup on a cold day.

Finally, look at a passage from "Java Jive," an essay in which Al Young recalls a hot Mississippi afternoon from his childhood. Pick out the two effective similes Young uses in this passage:

The sun—like a hot, luminous magnet—happened to be shining powerfully that antique afternoon. My father was busy being his auto mechanic self, and I could see him through the dusty window screen out there in the grass and dirt and clay of the sideyard driveway, fixing on our dark blue Chevy coupe, grease all over his face and forearms; black on black. Pious as a minister or metaphysician [philosopher], he was bent on fixing that car.

Metaphor

A metaphor also uses comparison to show the relationship between things in order to make the explanation of one of these things clearer and livelier. In fact, a metaphor works just like a simile except that it does not make use of "like" or "as." For instance, you can turn the simile "Eugene dresses like a peacock" into a metaphor by writing "Eugene is a peacock." In neither case, of course, do you actually mean that Eugene is a bird; you're simply pointing out similarities between the way he dresses and the showiness we associate with a peacock.

Remember that, like all figures of speech, similes and metaphors turn abstract ideas (such as "Eugene is a fancy dresser") into vivid, concrete images. In other words, they communicate more emphatically and clearly than if the writer had used literal language alone. Study the following list of similes and metaphors. What effect do they have on you, especially when compared with the literal expressions on the left?

LITERAL EXPRESSION	SIMILE	METAPHOR
My old car is hard to drive.	My old car drives like a tank.	My old car is a tank!
She works too hard for her family.	She works like a slave for her family.	She is a slave to her family.
During holidays, shopping malls are crowded and noisy.	During holidays, shopping malls are so crowded and noisy that they seem like madhouses.	During holidays, shopping malls are so crowded and noisy that they become madhouses.
The hayloft was hot.	The hayloft was as hot as a blast furnace.	The hayloft was a blast furnace.

Finally, read the following excerpt from Martin Luther King's "I Have a Dream," a speech he delivered at the Lincoln Memorial during the 1963 march on Washington. Identify the metaphors and similes that Dr. King used to captivate the thousands in his audience and to make his message more concrete, vivid, and effective:

> Five score years ago, a great American, in whose symbolic shadow we stand today, signed the Emancipation Proclamation. This momentous decree came as a great beacon light of hope to millions of Negro slaves who had been seared in the flames of withering injustice. It came as a joyous daybreak to end the long night of their captivity.
>
> But one hundred years later, the Negro still is not free. One hundred years later, the life of the Negro is still sadly crippled by the manacles of segregation and the chains of discrimination.

PERSONIFICATION

Personification is the description of animals, plants, or inanimate objects by using terms ordinarily associated with human beings. Like metaphor and simile, personification is an effective way to turn abstract ideas into vivid and concrete realities that readers will grasp easily and quickly.

One common example of personification is Father Time, the figure of an old man trailing a white beard and carrying a scythe and hourglass. Another is the Grim Reaper, the representation of death pictured as a skeleton holding a scythe. Shakespeare often used personification to enrich the language of his poems and plays. In "Sonnet 18," for example, he described the sun as "the eye of heaven." William Least Heat Moon does something similar when, in *Blue Highways,* he describes the saguaro cactus of the southwestern U.S.:

> Standing on the friable slopes . . . saguaros mimic men as they salute, bow, dance, raise arms to wave, and grin with faces carved in by woodpeckers. Older plants, having survived odds against their reaching maturity of sixty million to one, have every right to smile.

VISUALIZING FIGURATIVE LANGUAGE

You may recall reading two paragraphs from Margaret Laurence's "Where the World Began" in Chapter 5. Here are two more paragraphs from that essay. Read the first paragraph, which is accompanied by notes that identify figures of speech. Then, read the second paragraph and circle or box examples of figurative language you find.

In winter we used to hitch rides on the back of the milk sleigh, our moccasins squeaking and slithering on the hard rutted snow, our hands in ice-bubbled mitts **metaphor** hanging onto the box edge of the sleigh for dear life. Those mornings, rising, there would be the perpetual fascination of the frost feathers on windows, the ferns **metaphor** **metaphor** and flowers and eerie faces traced there during the night by unseen artists of the wind. Evenings, coming **personification** back from skating, the sky would be black but not dark for you could see a cold glitter of stars from one side of the earth's rim to the other. And the sometime astonishment when you saw the Northern Lights flaring across the sky, like the scrawled signature of God. **simile**

My best friend lived in an apartment above some stores on Main Street (its real name was Mountain Avenue, goodness knows why), an elegant apartment with royal-blue velvet curtains. The back roof, scarcely sloping at all, was corrugated tin, of a furnace-like warmth on a July afternoon, and we would sit there drinking lemonade and looking across the back lane at the Fire Hall. Sometimes our vigil would be rewarded. Oh joy! Somebody's house was burning down. Then the wooden tower's bronze bell would clonk and toll like a thousand speeded funerals in a time of plague, and in a few minutes the team of giant black horses would cannon forth, pulling the fire wagon like some scarlet chariot of the Goths, while the firemen clung with one hand, adjusting their helmets as they went.

REVISING TO INCLUDE FIGURATIVE LANGUAGE

Read these two versions of a paragraph from Louis Gonzalez's "Music," a student essay that appears at the end of this chapter. As you will see, the revision process has enabled Gonzalez to make his writing stronger, livelier, and more interesting.

Gonzalez—Rough Draft

As I became a little older and entered high school, my interests shifted toward learning to play a musical instrument. After a little experimentation, the bass guitar became my love. It produced warm, confident tones. They danced around my head. The guitar became the implement of my creativity. It soon became the center of my existence. I felt naked and insecure without it. Its weight was a lover's hand upon my shoulder.

Gonzalez—Final Draft

When I entered high school, my interests shifted towards learning to play a musical instrument. After a

Adds personification by comparing guitar to lover. Creates an image; personifies "tones."

little experimentation, I fell in love with the bass guitar. It covered me with warm, confident tones-- blankets of pure ecstasy. They were poised ballroom dancers waltzing elegantly around my head. The guitar

Adds a metaphor; compares guitar to a painter's brush.

became the implement of my creativity, the brush with which I painted portraits of candid love and dark emotion. I was naked and insecure without it. Its weight

Adds detail to continue personifying guitar as lover.

was a lover's hand upon my shoulder and its smooth hourglass body was a pleasure to hold. It whispered sweet kisses in my ear.

PRACTICING CREATING SIMILE, METAPHOR, AND PERSONIFICATION

In the spaces provided, put the idea you find in the literal expressions into a simile, metaphor, or personification as indicated. The first item is done for you as an example.

1. **Literal Expression:** The two men fought hard through the night.

   Simile: <u>The two men fought like gladiators through the night.</u>

2. **Literal Expression:** Cheryl treats her mother well.

   Simile: _____

   _____

   _____

3. **Literal Expression:** He ran to the end of the street and jumped over the barricade.

   Simile: _____

   _____

   _____

4. **Literal Expression:** Modern appliances have made our homes more comfortable and convenient than ever before.

   Simile: _____

   _____

   _____

5. **Literal Expression:** I enjoy the sounds of robins in the morning.

   Metaphor:

   _____

   _____

6. **Literal Expression:** The small boat was overloaded.

   Metaphor: _____

   _____

   _____

7. **Literal Expression:** In the last twenty years, medical researchers have produced wondrous cures.

   Metaphor: _____

_____

_____

8. Literal Expression: The wind was strong.

   Personification: _____

   _____

   _____

9. Literal Expression: We did not feel welcome as we entered the dark house.

   Personification: _____

   _____

   _____

10. Literal Expression: The front-page photograph contained a warning about driving drunk.

    Personification: _____

    _____

    _____

The following selections demonstrate very careful uses of language, both literal and figurative. As you read them, identify their similes, metaphors, and personifications and ask yourself if these figures of speech have made the selections clearer, more vivid, and more effective than if their authors had relied on literal language alone.

From "A Visit to Belfast"

Mary Manning

This selection is the introduction to an article Manning published in The Atlantic *magazine of May 1972. Belfast is the capital of Northern Ireland, the site of civil strife between Protestants and Catholics that lasted for many years.*

L O O K I N G
A H E A D

Manning uses both figures of speech and the kinds of nouns and adjectives you learned about in Chapter 5 to make her writing concrete and vivid.

V O C A B U L A R Y

discothèques   Nightclubs where people dance to recorded music.

From "A Visit to Belfast"

Mary Manning

It is a dying city, a broken city, a city almost without hope, for where do we go from here? The heart still beats faintly in the University, in beautiful outlying suburbs, in the brave little Lyric Theater, in the few discothèques where the students, girls and boys, line up for hours in the wintry nights just to get in—to have a drink, to listen to the music of the outside world. The few visitors must stay in guesthouses. Hotels, because of the bombings, are increasingly dangerous. But the heart is still beating faintly. Like a patient in intensive care, Belfast, having survived several heart attacks, may survive, for Belfast has a tough Northern heart; it may just make it.

QUESTIONS FOR DISCUSSION

1. Where in this paragraph does Manning use personification? What about simile?
2. Explain one of the images that the author creates in this selection. What details make that image effective?
3. What does Manning see in Belfast to make her believe this city "may just make it"?

THINKING CRITICALLY

Read a little about the violence in Northern Ireland in your college library. Your librarian can help you find sources. Then, compare the strife between Protestants and Catholics in that country with conflicts between members of opposing ethnic, religious, political, or cultural groups in the United States or any other country. Write a paragraph or two showing the similarities between these conflicts.

SUGGESTIONS FOR JOURNAL ENTRIES

1. A writer personifies an inanimate object by giving it human qualities. Manning has done this with an entire city. Think about a town or city you have lived in or visited recently. Use focused freewriting to collect details that make the place seem human in one way or another. For example, describe the activity at the center of town as the beating of a heart, the flow of traffic as the flow of blood through veins (streets) or arteries (highways); compare the community to a healthy young child or to a sick old person; or give the place a distinct personality based on your opinion of the kind of people who live there.
2. Cities can be wonderful places to live in, filled with opportunities to work, play, and grow. But they can also be nightmarish and bleak. What image comes to mind when you think about the city you know best? Use listing or answer the journalists' questions to gather concrete details about this place. As you learned in Chapter 5, rely on your five senses. At the same time, try your hand at creating figures of speech—metaphor, simile, and personification—that will show why you would or would not choose to live there permanently.

January Wind

Hal Borland

Journalist, nature writer, playwright, novelist, and poet, Hal Borland (1900–1978) was trained as an engineer, an experience which may account for the precision and concreteness of his writing. "January Wind" is one of hundreds of articles on the outdoors he wrote for The New York Times.

LOOKING AHEAD

Borland uses personification to describe the wind. To do this, he makes good use of vivid adjectives and verbs like those you learned about in Chapter 5. He also includes nouns that are concrete and specific.

VOCABULARY

hieroglyphics	Ancient Egyptian writing that used figures or pictures.
lichen	Fungus found on rocks and tree trunks.

January Wind | *Hal Borland*

The January wind has a hundred voices. It can scream, it can bellow, it can whisper, and it can sing a lullaby. It can roar through the leafless oaks and shout down the hillside, and it can murmur in the white pines rooted among the granite ledges where lichen makes strange hieroglyphics. It can whistle down a chimney and set the hearth-flames to dancing. On a sunny day it can pause in a sheltered spot and breathe a promise of spring and violets. In the cold of a lonely night it can rattle the sash and stay there muttering of ice and snowbanks and deep-frozen ponds. 1

Sometimes the January wind seems to come from the farthest star in the outer darkness, so remote and so impersonal is its voice. That is the wind of a January dawn, in the half-light that trembles between day and night. It is a wind that merely quivers the trees, its force sensed but not seen, a force that might almost hold back the day if it were so directed. Then the east brightens, and the wind relaxes—the stars, its source, grown dim. 2

And sometimes the January wind is so intimate that you know it came only from the next hill, a little wind that plays with leaves and puffs at chimney smoke and whistles like a little boy with puckered lips. It makes the little cedar trees quiver, as with delight. It shadow-boxes with the weather-vane. It tweaks an ear, and whispers laughing words about crocuses and daffodils, and nips the nose and dances off. 3

But you never know, until you hear its voice, which wind is here today. Or, more important, which will be here tomorrow. 4

QUESTIONS FOR DISCUSSION

1. Where in the essay does the author appeal to the senses?
2. Pick out two or three sentences in which verbs picture the wind as a person.
3. Find several examples of nouns and adjectives that make Borland's writing concrete and specific.
4. What does "lichen makes strange hieroglyphics" mean? What other images do you find in this essay?
5. What is the essay's thesis?

THINKING CRITICALLY

Write a paragraph that uses personification to describe the March wind, the July wind, the October wind, or the December wind.

SUGGESTIONS FOR JOURNAL ENTRIES

1. Use listing, brainstorming, or focused freewriting to capture the sounds, sights, feel, smell, and/or taste of wind, rain, snow, hail, thunder, lightning, fire, or another natural phenomenon. Try to remember a particularly vivid experience involving this phenomenon, and compare what you saw, heard, smelled, felt, and/or tasted to sights, sounds, smells, and so on that a reader would recognize easily. In other words, explain the experience by relying on metaphor, simile, and personification.
2. "The January wind has a hundred voices," claims Borland. Explain the different ways in which a natural object, place, or phenomenon can be experienced. For example, write about two or three kinds of wind, rain, and snow you've seen, heard, and felt; describe different types of cacti, evergreen trees, mountains, deserts, or seashores; or discuss the kinds of water you swim in—river, lake, ocean, pool. Like Borland, use figures of speech, especially personification, whenever you can to create distinct and effective images of your subject.

"Joy of an Immigrant, a Thanksgiving" and "Old Man Timochenko"

Emanuel di Pasquale

Emanuel di Pasquale immigrated to the United States from Ragusa, Sicily, when he was fourteen. An accomplished poet and a teacher of composition, creative writing, and children's literature, di Pasquale has published in several important periodicals, including The Nation *and* The Sawanee Review. *His work has been anthologized in college textbooks and in several collections of children's poems.* Genesis, *a full-length collection of his poetry, was published in 1989.*

"Joy of an Immigrant, a Thanksgiving" and "Old Man Timochenko" reveal di Pasquale's intense love of nature and his talent for creating powerful figures of speech that make his writing clear and captivating.

LOOKING AHEAD

1. "Joy of an Immigrant, a Thanksgiving" contains an extended metaphor in which di Pasquale compares himself to a wandering bird. It is an "extended" metaphor because the writer develops the comparison *throughout* the poem.
2. "Old Man Timochenko" is a brilliant portrait of an old man the poet spotted regularly during drives along a country road in eastern Pennsylvania. Identify the many similes and metaphors that di Pasquale uses to reveal important things about Timochenko's character.

VOCABULARY

lineaments   Lines.

"Joy of an Immigrant, a Thanksgiving" and "Old Man Timochenko" | *Emanuel di Pasquale*

JOY OF AN IMMIGRANT, A THANKSGIVING

Like a bird grown weak in a land
where it always rains
and where all the trees have died,
I have flown long and long
to find sunlight pouring over branches   5
and leaves. I have journeyed, oh God,
to find a land where I can build a dry nest,
a land where my song can echo.

OLD MAN TIMOCHENKO

Winds scratch his hands
and his sharp bones
deeply assert
their lineaments.
He stands like a   5
trembling leaf
on the branch
of an evergreen,
and will not fall.

Careful,   10
by the road's edge,
silent as a sunray,
he waves
as I drive by.
Like birds' wings,   15
loose as they coast
in the high air,
his eyes
soften and expand.

He moves in slow waves,   20
like an ancient snake,
knowing the end can wait.

QUESTIONS FOR DISCUSSION

1. In "Joy of an Immigrant, a Thanksgiving," di Pasquale compares himself to a bird through an extended metaphor. What details does he use to develop this comparison?
2. Why does di Pasquale subtitle the first of these poems "a Thanksgiving"?
3. What do the metaphors "where I can build a dry nest" and "where my song can echo" show us about the poet's feelings for his new "land"?
4. What is your emotional reaction to the words in the first three lines of "Joy of an Immigrant, a Thanksgiving"? What do they tell you about the place the poet has left?
5. What do the metaphors and similes in "Old Man Timochenko" show us about the old man?
6. In Looking Ahead you learned that di Pasquale uses figures of speech to create vivid and effective images. Describe the verbal pictures you see in his poems.
7. Recall what you learned about concrete details in Chapter 5. What concrete details, other than those which appear in the similes and metaphors you have identified, does di Pasquale include in "Old Man Timochenko"?

THINKING CRITICALLY

From what you have read, explain di Pasquale's attitude toward either of his subjects: his new homeland or Mr. Timochenko. Put your ideas into a paragraph or two.

SUGGESTIONS FOR JOURNAL ENTRIES

1. Have you ever experienced a change—any change—in your life that was as dramatic or as important as the one di Pasquale describes in "Joy of an Immigrant, a Thanksgiving"? It need not involve moving from one country or even from one town to another, but it should be something that has had an effect on the person you have become. Describe how this change affected you by listing as many concrete details about it as you can. Try to create similes and/or metaphors that will help you describe its effects more vividly.
2. Is there some interesting person in your life who, like Timochenko, would make a good subject for a short descriptive paragraph or poem? Begin gathering details that will help show your readers how you feel about this individual.

The Death of Benny Paret

Norman Mailer

Norman Mailer established his reputation in 1948, when he published The Naked and the Dead, *a popular and influential novel about World War II. Since then, he has produced a number of important works, both fiction and nonfiction, many of which have been critical of modern American society. Mailer has won Pulitzer prizes for* Armies of the Night, *his account of the 1967 peace march on Washington, D.C., and for* The Executioner's Song, *the story of convicted murderer Gary Gilmore.*

LOOKING AHEAD

1. Mailer was at ringside on the night of March 25, 1962, when Emile Griffith knocked out Benny Paret in the twelfth round of a welterweight championship bout in New York City's Madison Square Garden. The beating that Paret took that night led to his death. He was twenty-four.

2. "The Death of Benny Paret" contains good examples of all three of the figures of speech discussed earlier in this chapter. Look for places in which Mailer uses simile, metaphor, and personification in this frank and vivid account of one of the most brutal episodes in sports history.

VOCABULARY

irrevocably	Irreversibly.
maulings	Beatings.
orgy	Spree, wild party.
psychic	Mental, spiritual.

The Death of Benny Paret
Norman Mailer

On the afternoon of the night Emile Griffith and Benny Paret were to fight a third time for the welterweight championship, there was murder in both camps. "I hate that kind of guy," Paret had said earlier to Pete Hamill about Griffith. "A fighter's got to look and talk and act like a man." One of the Broadway gossip columnists had run an item about Griffith a few days before. His girl friend saw it and said to Griffith, "Emile, I didn't know about you being that way." So Griffith hit her. So he said. Now at the weigh-in that morning, Paret had insulted Griffith irrevocably, touching him on the buttocks, while making a few more remarks about his manhood. They almost had their fight on the scales.

The rage in Emile Griffith was extreme. I was at the fight that night, I had never seen a fight like it. It was scheduled for fifteen rounds, but they fought without stopping from the bell which began the round to the bell which ended it, and then they fought after the bell, sometimes for as much as fifteen seconds before the referee could force them apart.

Paret was a Cuban, a proud club fighter who had become welterweight champion because of his unusual ability to take a punch. His style of fighting was to take three punches to the head in order to give back two. At the end of ten rounds, he would still be bouncing, his opponent would have a headache. But in the last two years, over the fifteen-round fights, he had started to take some bad maulings.

This fight had its turns. Griffith won most of the early rounds, but Paret knocked Griffith down in the sixth. Griffith had trouble getting up, but made it, came alive and was dominating Paret again before the round was over. Then Paret began to wilt. In the middle of the eighth round, after a clubbing punch had turned his back to Griffith, Paret walked three disgusted steps away, showing his hindquarters. For a champion, he took much too long to turn back around. It was the first hint of weakness Paret had ever shown, and it must have inspired a particular shame, because he fought the rest of the fight as if he were seeking to demonstrate that he could take more punishment than any man alive. In the twelfth, Griffith caught him. Paret got trapped in a corner. Trying to duck away, his left arm and his head became tangled on the wrong side of the top rope. Griffith was in like a cat ready to rip the life out of a huge boxed rat. He hit him eighteen right hands in a row, an act which took perhaps three or four seconds, Griffith making a pent-up whimpering sound all the while he attacked, the right hand whipping like a piston rod which has broken through the crankcase, or like a baseball bat demolishing a pumpkin. I was sitting in the second row of that corner—they were not ten feet away from me, and like everybody else, I was hypnotized. I had never seen one man hit another so hard and so many times. Over the referee's face came a look of woe as if some spasm had passed its way through him, and then he leaped on Griffith to pull him away. It was the act of a brave man. Griffith was uncontrollable. His trainer leaped into the ring, his manager, his cut man, there were four people holding Griffith, but he was off on an orgy, he had left the Garden, he was back on a hoodlum's street. If he had been able to break loose from his handlers and the referee, he would have jumped Paret to the floor and whaled on him there.

And Paret? Paret died on his feet. As he took those eighteen punches something 5 happened to everyone who was in psychic range of the event. Some part of his death reached out to us. One felt it hover in the air. He was still standing in the ropes, trapped as he had been before, he gave some little half-smile of regret, as if he were saying, "I didn't know I was going to die just yet," and then, his head leaning back but still erect, his death came to breathe about him. He began to pass away. As he passed, so his limbs descended beneath him, and he sank slowly to the floor. He went down more slowly than any fighter had ever gone down, he went down like a large ship which turns on end and slides second by second into its grave. As he went down, the sound of Griffith's punches echoed in the mind like a heavy ax in the distance chopping into a wet log.

QUESTIONS FOR DISCUSSION

1. Powerful similes appear in paragraph 4. Find one or two and explain why they work so well.
2. What metaphors does Mailer use in paragraph 4?
3. What examples of personification can be found in paragraph 5?
4. In paragraph 3, Mailer writes that Paret had "started to take some bad maulings." Is "maulings" a more effective noun than "beatings"? In paragraph 4, he tells us that Paret began "to wilt." Is this verb better than "to weaken"? What other effective nouns and verbs does Mailer use?
5. This selection begins with an anecdote (brief story) about what passed between Griffith and Paret before the fight. Does this anecdote make for a good introduction? How does it help prepare us for what is to follow?

THINKING CRITICALLY

Mailer tells us that Paret's death "reached out to us" (paragraph 5). Write about a recent event covered by the media that had an emotional or psychological impact on the community, state, or country. Begin by explaining what happened. Then, explain its effect. For example, write about the 1995 bombing of the federal building in Oklahoma City, which killed nearly 170 people. On the other hand, you might choose something positive such as your city's being selected as the site of the Olympics or World's Fair.

SUGGESTIONS FOR JOURNAL ENTRIES

1. Think about a serious or significant event you recently witnessed: a car accident, a natural disaster, or perhaps an important ceremony. Use one of the strategies for prewriting discussed in "Getting Started" to gather details that will help you describe this incident and discuss its impact on you or on anyone else who may have seen it. Include figures of speech in your list of details.
2. Whether physical or verbal, violence always leaves us shaken and disturbed. Think about a fight you saw or were involved in recently. Do some focused freewriting for about five or ten minutes in which you explain how you felt during or after the incident. Include figures of speech that *show* what you were feeling at the time.

The Gift

Li-Young Lee

Li-Young Lee is a Chinese-American poet born in Indonesia, where his father had been imprisoned by the government of Sukarno, that country's dictator. After his father's escape, the family left Indonesia and eventually made their home in Pennsylvania. Lee's reputation has grown rapidly over the last several years. He is the author of Rose, *a book of poems published in 1986.*

L O O K I N G
A H E A D

1. Lee's title is especially significant. Keep it in mind as you read this tender poem.
2. Look for examples of both metaphor and personification in "The Gift."

V O C A B U L A R Y

christen	Give a name to.
shard	Fragment of metal or glass.

The Gift | *Li-Young Lee*

To pull the metal splinter from my palm
my father recited a story in a low voice.
I watched his lovely face and not the blade.
Before the story ended he'd removed
the iron sliver I thought I'd die from.   5

I can't remember the tale
but hear his voice still, a well
of dark water, a prayer.
And I recall his hands,
two measures of tenderness   10
he laid against my face,
the flames of discipline
he raised above my head.

Had you entered that afternoon
you would have thought you saw a man   15
planting something in a boy's palm,
a silver tear, a tiny flame.
Had you followed that boy
you would have arrived here,
where I bend over my wife's right hand.   20

Look how I shave her thumbnail down
so carefully she feels no pain.
Watch as I lift the splinter out.
I was seven when my father
took my hand like this,   25
and I did not hold that shard
between my fingers and think,
Metal that will bury me,
christen it Little Assassin,
Ore Going Deep for My Heart.   30
And I did not lift up my wound and cry,
Death visited here!
I did what a child does
when he's given something to keep.
I kissed my father.   35

QUESTIONS FOR' DISCUSSION

1. What "gift" has Lee received? Is it simply the skill to remove a splinter? Or is there more to it than that?
2. Why does he tell us about removing the shard from his wife's hand? What point does this image help him make about his father? About himself?
3. What other image do you see in this poem?
4. To which of the five senses does Lee appeal?
5. What examples of metaphor do you find in this poem? Of personification?
6. Why does Lee tell us that he didn't "christen" the splinter "Little Assassin" (line 29)? What does *"Death visited here!"* mean (line 32)?

THINKING CRITICALLY

Reread Hayden's "Those Winter Sundays" (page 167), which is also about a father's love. In what ways is it similar to Lee's poem? In what ways is it different? Explain these similarities and differences in two or three paragraphs. Before you begin, consider the titles of the poems and the stories they tell. What do they reveal about the authors and their purposes?

SUGGESTIONS FOR JOURNAL ENTRIES

1. Think back to a time when your father, mother, or family member comforted you or made you feel good about yourself. Use freewriting to explain what happened and to discuss your reaction.
2. What Lee is "given . . . to keep" is not material; it is an attitude, an emotional treasure, made plain in his father's voice and gentle touch. Think about similar gifts that your mother, father, or other relative has given you by example and that you will pass on to others. Your father may have shown you a love for gardening, your great-aunt may have taught you to love animals, and through her actions your mother may have taught you that all people, regardless of race or sex, deserve respect. Use focused freewriting to describe one or more of these gifts. Include figures of speech to make your ideas concrete and vivid.

Music

Louis Gonzalez

When asked by his professor to define a concept, idea, or activity that was important to him, Louis Gonzalez knew immediately what he would write about. The challenging part came in making this abstraction real to his readers. He did this by choosing concrete, specific, and vivid vocabulary and by filling his writing with powerful figures of speech. In other words, he showed the reader what he meant.

Gonzalez writes musical reviews for a local magazine and is considering a career as a writer. He was a first-year liberal-arts student when he wrote this essay.

L O O K I N G   A H E A D

1. Pay special attention to paragraph 4. You will recall that the rough draft of this paragraph appears earlier in the chapter with the author's revisions, which show how much care he puts into the process of writing.
2. Gonzalez uses all three figures of speech discussed in this chapter. He also uses hyperbole, or exaggeration. Look for an example of this technique at the end of paragraph 7.

V O C A B U L A R Y

cathartic	Cleansing, purifying.
chaotic	Confusing, disorderly.
licks	A musical phrase created when improvising.
mesmerizing	Absorbing, hypnotizing.
obsession	Passion, fixation.
orgasms	Sexual climaxes.
oscillating	Moving from side to side.
poised	Balanced.
preoccupied	Absorbed in, wrapped up in.
reverberates	Echoes.
tangible	Able to be touched, felt.
tenacity	Determination, persistence.
venues	Places where events take place.
yoke	Shackle, chain.

Music | *Louis Gonzalez*

Music is my obsession. It reverberates across every fiber of my being. I have 1
spent endless hours of my life creating music, performing it, or even just
dreaming about it. My thoughts are filled with the angelic sigh of a bow kissing the
string of a violin, or the hellish crash of batons torturing the skin of a kettle drum. But
my favorite instrument is the vociferous world around us. The scuff of a penny loafer
against a wood floor, the clinking of Crayolas across a child's desk, or the mesmerizing
hum of an oscillating fan are all part of this chaotic symphony. It is within this sonic
spectrum that I exist.

I have long been preoccupied with the audible world. When I was younger, any- 2
thing and everything that made a sound became a musical instrument. My mother's
pots, empty soda bottles, even the railing on my front porch became part of my private
symphony orchestra. Then, for my ninth birthday, I received a Fisher-Price record
player. A single tin speaker was built into the base, and the needle was attached to a
wooden lid, which I had to shut in order to make the thing work. More often than not,
the lid would fall accidentally and cut deep scratches into the record. But to my young
ears, it made the sounds of heaven.

Armed with my record player and some old jazz 45's I liberated from my dad's col- 3
lection, I locked myself in the garage and entered another world. Instead of remaining
surrounded by tools and half-empty paint cans, I lowered the lid of that cheap Fisher-
Price and transported myself to a smokey club somewhere in the city. As the music
played, wrenches became saxophones, boxes became a set of drums, and the workbench
became a sleek black piano. I played 'em all, man! I wore those old 45's down until there
was nothing left but pops, cracks, and the occasional high note. I spent most of my
childhood in that smelly garage listening to Miles Davis and my other patron saints,
while other kids played football and video games. Even though my parents said I wasted
my time there, the experience instilled in me a burning desire to become a musician.

When I entered high school, my interests shifted towards learning to play a musical 4
instrument. After a little experimentation, I fell in love with the bass guitar. It covered
me with warm, confident tones—blankets of pure ecstasy. They were poised ballroom
dancers waltzing elegantly around my head. The guitar became the implement of my
creativity, the brush with which I painted portraits of candid love and dark emotion. I
was naked and insecure without it. Its weight was a lover's hand upon my shoulder,
and its smooth hourglass body was a pleasure to hold. It whispered sweet kisses in my
ear.

As my skills increased, so did my yearning to play those old jazz songs of my youth. 5
But the harder I tried, the less I succeeded. It seemed as though I was simply incapable
of playing those songs. All those wild bass licks that poured out of that Fisher-Price
record player were ripped from my dreams.

My lust for jazz was then replaced by the desire to perform in a live rock band. So, 6
I joined a local college group and began to play small venues. The shows were like
cathartic orgasms of sweaty bodies undulating as the sensation of music overwhelmed
them. While I was on stage, the power of the music pierced through the air like a volley
of arrows falling upon the flannel-clad flesh whirling below me. But I felt as though the

music was in control and I was just letting it happen. That feeling began to consume my spirit and destroy my sense of oneness with the music.

There was definitely something missing. Even though what I played was structurally powerful, it lacked a soul. I also realized that my style of playing lacked a human quality. So when I came upon my old jazz records, I listened to them with new ears. I dropped all of my preconceived notions of song structure. As the records popped and scratched their way around the turntable, the secrets of the universe were finally revealed to me.

I realized that my approach had been all wrong. All my songs were suffocated under the weight of formality. Harnessed to the yoke of "proper" song structure and arrangement, they were never allowed to grow fully. So, I picked up my bass with a fresh tenacity and dropped all my inhibitions. Not, surprisingly, those old jazz songs started to pour out. I played them as if I had known them all of my life.

I look back on that day and realize that I did know how to play those songs all along. It wasn't a tangible lack of something—like talent or effort—that held me back. I just needed to *feel* the music—to feel the sweet life a musician blows into, to feel it the way that innocent child felt in the garage all those years ago.

QUESTIONS FOR DISCUSSION

1. What is Gonzalez's thesis? Has he proved it?
2. How would you describe the introduction of this essay? Is it like one or more of the types you learned about in Chapter 4? Which one or ones?
3. Find examples of metaphor in paragraphs 3 and 4.
4. Where in this essay does Gonzalez use simile?
5. Find two paragraphs in which the author makes good use of personification. Explain these figures of speech.
6. Paragraphs 1, 2, and 3 show that Gonzalez has a talent for using concrete and specific nouns, like those you read about in Chapter 5. Find examples of such nouns in these paragraphs.
7. Vivid verbs make paragraph 7 especially interesting. Identify a few of them.

THINKING CRITICALLY

1. In Looking Ahead, you learned that Gonzalez uses a hyperbole, another figure of speech, at the end of paragraph 7. Write a paragraph that explains what he means. Is his use of exaggeration effective?
2. If you could speak to Gonzalez face to face, what would you ask him about aspects of his experience with music that you would like to know more about? Write these questions in the margins of the essay.
3. In what way is Gonzalez's obsession with music different from "Richie Martin's" obsession with gambling in "Gambling," an essay that appears in Chapter 2?

SUGGESTIONS FOR JOURNAL ENTRIES

1. "Music is my obsession" begins this brilliant essay. What is your obsession? Use freewriting or brainstorming to record some facts about your love for a particular activity or idea that will show how much you are committed to it.
2. Create a list of metaphors, similes, or personifications that might describe how you feel when you are doing a particular activity you really enjoy. For inspiration reread paragraphs 1, 3, 4, and 6 of "Music."

SUGGESTIONS FOR SUSTAINED WRITING

1. After reading the paragraph from "A Visit to Belfast," you may have used your journal to gather concrete details and figures of speech expressing an opinion about the city you know best. Use this information to draft two or three paragraphs, each of which explains *one* reason you would or would not choose to live there permanently. Then, set this work aside.

   On another piece of paper, explain the reasons that some people hold an opposing opinion about this city. (Come on; you can do it!) Turn these notes into a unified and coherent paragraph. Then, at the end of the paragraph, add a sentence that denies what these other folks think and that states *your* opinion clearly. For example, if you hate the city, the last sentence might read: "However, despite the wonderful things my friends say about Dismalville, I wouldn't live there for the world." On the other hand, if you like the city, you might write: "However, the nasty things my friends say about Dismalville don't impress me, and I am looking forward to living there for many years." Either way, use this paragraph as the introduction to your essay. Make its last sentence your preliminary thesis statement.

   Now turn to the paragraphs you set aside. Each should focus on and fully develop one reason you hate or like "Dismalville." If not, rewrite them by adding, removing, or rearranging detail. Place these paragraphs after your introduction. Next, write a conclusion that explains what "Dismalville's" citizens should do to improve their city or that sums up what you think is good about the place.

   Now, revise the entire essay—introduction, body, and conclusion. Ask yourself whether your writing can be improved by adding concrete details and figures of speech like those discussed in this chapter. Finally, make sure to edit your last draft.

2. After reading di Pasquale's "Joy of an Immigrant, a Thanksgiving," you might have made journal notes to begin explaining how a dramatic change in your life affected you. Tell the story of what caused this change. Using "Joy of an Immigrant, a Thanksgiving" as an example, include effective metaphors and similes to help your readers understand the full effect of the change. This is also a good time to continue using concrete nouns—both common and proper—and vivid adjectives like those you read about in Chapter 5. They will help you create powerful images to communicate your feelings.

   When you finish your story, write an introductory paragraph, complete with a formal thesis statement that states the importance of this change in your life. Describe a scene, use a startling remark, create a contrast or analogy, or try any other method explained in Chapter 4 to write an introduction that captures the readers' attention. Conclude your paper by making reference to your thesis, looking to the future, or using a memorable statement or quotation.

   Now review the completed draft of your essay. Is it the best you can do, or can you add detail, strengthen your focus, and improve your word choice? Write at least one more draft. Then revise and edit this version thoroughly before submitting your work to your instructor.

3. In "Joy of an Immigrant, a Thanksgiving," the poet expresses human feelings by comparing himself to a bird. In "Old Man Timochenko," he uses "a leaf," "a sunray" "birds' wings," and "an ancient snake" to help describe his subject. Write an essay in which you create an extended metaphor comparing a person you know to a flower, tree, animal, or other natural object. That object should somehow reflect your subject's personality.

   For example, compare your worst enemy to a snake or worm by describing that creature's most obvious characteristics and by showing that your subject has similar qualities. Use concrete details, figures of speech, and examples to explain his habit of sneaking behind people's backs or to describe the way she squirms out of taking responsibility. Of course, you might want to take a more positive approach and, like di Pasquale, make comparisons that will flatter your subject.

   Whatever you decide, have fun with this project. It's a good chance to create entertaining images of a person about whom you have strong feelings. As usual, check your journal notes for information that will help you get started. Revise your essay several times, and edit it closely.

   A word of caution: If your essay criticizes a person, keep his or her real identity secret.

4. If you have ever seen a fight close up, you know how frightening physical or verbal violence can be. Recall a heated argument or fight you witnessed or were involved in. What important point did this incident reveal about other people, about yourself, or about life in general? Put the answer to this question into a preliminary thesis statement. Then, narrate the events that led up to and that occurred during this incident. Explain what caused the problem, and describe the people who took part.

   Before you begin your essay, review the notes you made after reading "The Death of Benny Paret," especially those in response to item 2 of the Suggestions for Journal Entries. When you draft your paper, use the concrete details and figures of speech you have already collected. Try adding more of them as you tell your story.

   After you complete this rough draft, turn back to your preliminary thesis. Is it right for the essay you have just written? If not, revise the thesis or make changes in your essay so that your thesis will clearly state your main point and prepare readers for what follows. Put your thesis into an introductory paragraph that captures the readers' attention. Next, write a logical and natural conclusion by using methods explained in Chapter 4.

   Once you are satisfied that you have produced a well-organized and well-developed final draft, edit that draft carefully for grammar, punctuation, spelling, and other important considerations.

5. "The Gift" by Li-Young Lee explains how the poet received an emotional treasure that enriched his life and that he can pass on to others. If you read this poem, you may have made journal notes about similar gifts your parents or others have passed along to you through example. For instance, seeing your sister work hard at her studies may have motivated you to do the same; watching your aunt tend her roses may have made you love flowers; or noticing how cheerful your father remains on bad days may have inspired you to keep smiling through sorrow or adversity.

   Use your journal notes as the basis of an essay that discusses one emotional treasure or gift someone in your family (or your family as a whole) has given you. A good way to begin is to explain what that gift is. You might even compare it to the gift Lee discusses in his poem. Then, in the body of your paper, you can provide three or four examples of how your father, mother, or other relative revealed the gift to you. In any case, be specific. Show what difficulties your father has had to face, or describe the long hours and hard work your sister devotes to studying for an exam or completing a paper. A good way to conclude is to explain how you intend to share your gift with someone else.

   Use figures of speech to create images that, like those in Lee's poem, will help readers see what you are trying to explain. As always, write several versions of your paper and edit it carefully. Make sure it is fully developed, easy to follow, and free of distracting errors.

6. Read the journal notes you made after completing Louis Gonzalez's "Music." If you responded to either or both of the Suggestions for Journal Entries, you have a good start on an essay that will discuss an "obsession" of your own.

   Begin with an introduction that, like Gonzalez's, explains the extent to which you are committed to a particular pursuit, idea, study, activity, hobby, art form, or sport. Then go on to explain how this "obsession" developed in you. End your essay by looking to the future or by using any of the other types of conclusions discussed in Chapter 4.

   As always, remember that one draft is never enough. When you write your second draft, include concrete and specific nouns and adjectives. Add vivid verbs, adjectives, and adverbs as well. When you revise this draft, try to add figures of speech like those discussed in this chapter. Then, revise your third draft to improve organization, sentence structure, and grammar. The final step is, of course, to edit and proofread your work carefully.

CHAPTER 7

SENTENCE STRUCTURE: CREATING EMPHASIS AND VARIETY

In Chapters 5 and 6 you learned to express your ideas more effectively by using language that is concrete, specific, and vivid. In this chapter you will learn how to use sentence structure to give your writing emphasis and variety, making it even more interesting and effective.

EMPHASIS

Communicating ideas clearly often depends on the ability to emphasize, or stress, one idea over another. By arranging the words in a sentence carefully, you can emphasize certain ideas and direct your readers' attention to the heart of your message.

A good way to emphasize an idea is to express it in a short, simple sentence of its own. But you will never develop your writing skills if you stick to a steady diet of such sentences. Even the shortest writing projects require sentences containing two or more ideas. In some cases, these ideas will be equally important; in others, one idea will need to be emphasized over the other or others.

CREATE EMPHASIS THROUGH COORDINATION

Ideas that are equal in importance can be expressed in the same sentence by using coordination. The sentence below coordinates (makes equal) three words in a series: "found," "pitched," and "started."

We *found* a clearing, *pitched* the tent, and *started* a small fire.

You can also use coordination to join two or more *main clauses*. A main clause contains a subject and verb and, even when standing by itself, expresses a complete idea. You can join main clauses with a comma and a coordinating conjunction, such as "and," "but," "or," "nor," "for," or "so." Here are some examples; the main clauses are shown in italics:

Wild ponies gallop through the surf, and *eagles soar quietly overhead.*
Robert Frost is famous for poetry set in rural New England, but *he was born in San Francisco.*

The raccoons have not been near our house in days, nor *have they been missed.*
Marlin will take the final exam, or *he will fail the course.*
The area was contaminated with a strange virus, so *the medical team wore protective gear.*
I floss my teeth daily, for *I want to avoid gum disease.*

Another way to coordinate main clauses within a sentence is to join them with a semicolon:

Alice's car is an antique; it was built in 1927.

You can use both a semicolon and a conjunction when you want to make sure your readers see the relationship between the ideas you are emphasizing. This is especially important in long sentences:

Hoping to reach Lake Soggy Bottom by noon, we left our house by 6:00 A.M. and took Interstate 90; but traffic was so heavy that we soon realized we would be lucky to reach the lake before dark.

CREATE EMPHASIS THROUGH SUBORDINATION

The sentences above contain complete ideas—main clauses—that are equal in importance. But what if you decide that one of your ideas is more important than the other? Sometimes, putting the less important idea into a *phrase* or *subordinate clause* helps emphasize the other. A phrase is a group of words without a subject or predicate; a subordinate clause contains a subject and predicate, but, unlike a main clause, it does not express a complete idea. Say you wrote these sentences:

Ethel turned the corner, and she noticed a large truck in her lane.
She was frightened, but she avoided the truck.

When revising, you decide that in each sentence the second idea is more important than the first. Therefore, you *subordinate* the first idea to the second:

Turning the corner, Ethel noticed a large truck in her lane.
(The first idea has been put into a phrase.)

Although she was frightened, she avoided the truck.
(The first idea has been put into a subordinate clause.)

Here are three of many ways to subordinate ideas.

USE PARTICIPLES   *Participles* are adjectives formed from verbs. They describe nouns and pronouns. Each sentence below has been revised by turning one of its main clauses into a phrase that begins with a participle. Doing so helps put emphasis on the main clause that remains.

> **Original**   Charlotte was visiting her Uncle in Knoxville, and she decided to drive through the Great Smoky Mountains.
> *(The sentence contains two main clauses of the same importance.)*
>
> **Revised**   Visiting her uncle in Knoxville, Charlotte decided to drive through the Great Smoky Mountains.
> *(The first idea is expressed in a phrase that begins with the participle "Visiting." It is less important than the second idea, which remains in a main clause, "Charlotte decided" . . .)*

> **Original**   Angel planned to visit Moscow, so he began to study Russian.
> *(The ideas are equally important.)*
>
> **Revised**   Planning to visit Moscow, Angel began to study Russian.
> *(The first idea is now less important than the second because it is expressed in a phrase, which begins with the participle "Planning.")*

USE SUBORDINATE CONJUNCTIONS   You can turn a main clause into a subordinate clause with words like "although," "after," "as," "because," "even though," "if," "since," "unless," "until," and "while."

> **Original**   The French military leader Joan of Arc was condemned as a witch, so she was burned at the stake.
> *(The ideas are equally important.)*
>
> **Revised**   Because she had been condemned as a witch, the French military leader Joan of Arc was burned at the stake.
> *(The second idea, expressed in a main clause, is emphasized. The first idea is now in a subordinate clause, which begins with "Because.")*

USE RELATIVE PRONOUNS   Using pronouns like "who," "whom," "whose," "that," and "which" is another way to subordinate one idea to another. Subordinate clauses beginning with relative pronouns describe nouns in the sentence's main clause.

> **Original**   My friend's parents once lived in Corsica; Corsica is the birthplace of Napoleon.
> *(The ideas are equally important.)*
>
> **Revised**   My friend's parents once lived in Corsica, which is the birthplace of Napoleon.
> *(The first idea, expressed in a main clause, is more important than the second idea, which is now in a subordinate clause introduced by "which.")*

Original   Audrey Davis has spent two years in the Marine Corps; she was
sent to Saudi Arabia.

Revised   Audrey Davis, who has spent two years in the Marine Corps, was
sent to Saudi Arabia.
*(The subordinate clause, introduced by "who," comes in the mid-
dle of the main clause.)*

CREATE EMPHASIS BY USING PERIODIC SENTENCES

You can create emphasis by putting the strongest or most important word or idea at the end of the sentence. Such sentences are called "periodic" because the emphasis comes just before the period. Here are three examples:

Mario forgot the tomato sauce's most important ingredient, garlic!
India, where over half a billion people have the right to vote, is the world's largest democracy.
Zora Neale Hurston is remembered not for her work in anthropology, the field in which she was trained, but for her novels.

CREATE EMPHASIS BY USING A COLON

A colon can be used in place of a semicolon in a compound sentence when the second main clause explains the first. The effect is similar to the one created by a periodic sentence.

Toni Morrison has been busy: she has written seven novels and several books of criticism over the last twenty years.

The second main clause, which follows the colon, explains what the writer means by "busy." Notice that, as with a periodic sentence, emphasis is placed on information at the end of the sentence.

CREATE EMPHASIS BY USING THE ACTIVE OR PASSIVE VOICE

Sentences that use the *active voice* contain subjects—persons, places, or things—that perform an action. Sentences that use the *passive voice* contain subjects that are acted upon. Notice how the structure of a sentence changes when it is put into the passive voice.

Active
The enthusiastic listeners applauded the young guitarist.
Passive
The young guitarist was applauded by the enthusiastic listeners.

Generally, using the active voice rather than the passive voice makes it easier to stress the subject of a sentence. For instance, if you wanted to report that the president of your college announced her decision to resign, it wouldn't make much sense to write, "Her decision to resign was announced by President Greenspan." A clearer and more emphatic version would be "President Greenspan announced her decision to resign."

However, there are times when using the passive voice can create emphasis. In some cases, you might decide that the receiver of an action is more important than the person, place, or thing who completes that action. For example,

> Ann was elected to the Monroe City Council.

is more emphatic than

> The residents of Monroe elected Ann to the City Council.

Sometimes, in fact, you might not know who or what is responsible for an action, and you will have to use the passive voice:

> Doors and windows were left open; books, furniture, and clothing were scattered across the room; and curtains, sheets, and blankets were torn to shreds.

CREATE EMPHASIS BY REPEATING KEY WORDS AND PHRASES

Repeating important words and phrases, carefully and sparingly, can help you stress important ideas over those that deserve less emphasis. This technique is used in the speeches of President John F. Kennedy and of Reverend Martin Luther King, Jr.

In his inaugural address, Kennedy gave a special meaning to his plans for the nation when he said:

> All this will not be finished in the first one hundred days. Nor will it be finished in the first one thousand days, nor in the life of this administration, nor even perhaps in our lifetime on this planet. But let us begin.

Dr. King used repetition to communicate a sense of urgency about civil rights to a massive audience at the Lincoln Memorial when he delivered the speech now known as "I Have a Dream":

> Now is the time to make real the promises of democracy. Now is the time to rise from the dark and desolate valley of segregation to the sunlit path of racial justice. Now is the time to lift our nation from the quicksands of racial injustice to the solid rock of brotherhood. Now is the time to make justice a reality for all of God's children.

CREATE EMPHASIS THROUGH PARALLELISM

Parallelism is a way to connect facts and ideas of equal importance in the same sentence and thereby give them added emphasis. Sentences that are parallel list items by expressing each of them in the same grammatical form. For instance, Adlai Stevenson's eulogy of Winston Churchill, the great British prime minister, contains several examples of parallelism:

> The voice that led nations, raised armies, inspired victories and blew fresh courage into the hearts of men is silenced. We shall hear no longer the remembered eloquence and wit, the old courage and defiance, the robust serenity of indomitable faith. Our world is thus poorer, our political dialogue is diminished, and the sources of public inspiration run more thinly in all of us. There is a lonesome place against the sky.

In the first sentence, Stevenson placed equal emphasis on Churchill's accomplishments by expressing each through a verb followed by a direct object: "led nations," "raised armies," "inspired victories," and "blew fresh courage into the hearts of men." He created parallelism in the second sentence in a series of adjectives and nouns that describe Churchill's best qualities: "the remembered eloquence and wit," "the old courage and defiance," "the robust serenity of indomitable faith." In the third sentence, he explained the effects of Churchill's death in a series of main clauses: "Our world is thus poorer," "our political dialogue is diminished," and "the sources of public inspiration run more thinly in all of us."

Here are three other examples of how parallelism creates emphasis:

> The President enjoys *reading* mystery novels, *fishing* in Maine, and *speaking* with young people.
> *(The sentence contains gerunds, nouns formed from verbs by adding "ing"; gerunds show activity.)*

> To master the piano, to compose beautiful music, and to lead a symphony orchestra seemed to be her destiny.
> *(The sentence contains infinitives, which are formed by placing "to" before the present tense of the verb. Infinitives act as nouns, adjectives, or adverbs.)*

> They vowed to battle the invaders on the land, on the sea, and in the air.
> *(The sentence contains prepositional phrases; a preposition is a short word—such as "at," "in," or "on"—that shows the relationship of a noun or pronoun to the rest of the sentence.)*

Consistency is the key to making sentences parallel. Express every idea in a list in the same grammatical form. Without a doubt, the eulogy you just read would have sounded awkward and been less emphatic had Stevenson written that Churchill's voice "led nations, raised armies, inspired victories, and it blew fresh courage into the hearts of men." The first three items are verbs followed by objects; the fourth is a main clause.

VARIETY

One sure way to make your readers lose interest in what you have to say—no matter how important—is to ignore the need for variety. Good writers try not to repeat vocabulary monotonously, and they vary the length and structure of their sentences whenever possible.

CREATE VARIETY BY CHANGING SENTENCE LENGTH

A steady diet of long, complicated sentences is sure to put your readers to sleep. On the other hand, relying solely on short, choppy sentences can make your writing seem disconnected and even childish. Therefore, one of the most important things to remember about the sentences you write is to vary their length. You can do this by combining some of them into longer, more complex units and by leaving others short and to the point.

Reread the passage from President Kennedy's Inaugural Address on page 220. One reason it holds our interest is that it contains sentences of different lengths. The last of these leaves a lasting impression, not simply because it comes at the end but because it is so much shorter than the others and carries a special punch.

You can combine two or three short sentences into a longer unit in three ways: coordination, subordination, or compounding.

COORDINATION   This method is useful if you want to write a longer sentence in which all the main ideas receive equal emphasis. The easiest way to do this is to combine sentences with a comma and the appropriate coordinating conjunction or to use a semicolon, as explained on pages 216–217.

SUBORDINATION   As you know, subordination lets you combine two or more sentences in order to emphasize one idea over another. It also helps you vary sentence length and make your writing more interesting. Say you've just written:

> I had been waiting at the bus stop for twenty minutes. The afternoon air was hot, thick, and humid. I became uncomfortable and soon began to perspire. I wished I were home. I thought about getting under the shower, cooling off, and relaxing. My day at work had been long and hard. I looked up from the newspaper I was reading. I saw a huge truck. It sped by, and it covered me with filthy exhaust. I prayed the bus would come soon.

As you read this paragraph, you realize that you haven't emphasized your most important ideas and that your style is choppy and monotonous. Therefore, you decide to rewrite by combining sentences through subordination (you can review ways to do this by rereading pages 217–219):

I had been waiting at the bus stop for twenty minutes. Because the afternoon air was hot, thick, and humid, I became uncomfortable and soon began to perspire. Wishing I were home, I thought about getting under the shower, cooling off, and relaxing. My day at work had been long and hard. As I looked up from the newspaper I was reading, I saw a huge truck, which sped by and covered me with exhaust. I prayed the bus would come soon.

In combining some sentences, you've made your writing smoother and more interesting because you've created sentences of different lengths. What's more, some ideas have gained emphasis.

COMPOUNDING   This method involves putting subjects, verbs, adjectives, and adverbs together in the same sentence as long as they relate to one another logically.

Sometimes, ideas that are very similar seem awkward and boring if expressed in separate sentences. For example: "Egbert has been transferred to Minneapolis. Rowena has also been transferred to that city." Notice how much more interesting these short sentences become when you combine their subjects to make a compound sentence: "Egbert and Rowena have been transferred to Minneapolis." Here are a few more examples:

Original	The doctor rushed into the emergency room. She went immediately to a patient who had been bitten by wasps.
Compound verb	The doctor rushed into the emergency room and went immediately to a patient who had been bitten by wasps.
Original	The weather around here is sometimes unpredictable. Sometimes it becomes treacherous.
Compound adjective	The weather around here is sometimes unpredictable and treacherous.
Original	Grieving over the loss of her child, the woman wept openly. She wept uncontrollably.
Compound adverb	Grieving over the loss of her child, the woman wept openly and uncontrollably.

CREATE VARIETY BY CHANGING SENTENCE PATTERNS

As you know, all complete sentences contain a subject, a verb, and a complete idea; many also contain modifiers (adjectives, adverbs, prepositional phrases, and the like) and other elements. However, there is no rule that all sentences must begin with a subject, that a verb must follow the subject immediately, or that everything else must be placed at the end of a sentence. Depending on their purpose, good writers create as many patterns as they need to make their writing interesting and effective. Here are a few ways you can vary the basic patterns of your sentences.

BEGIN WITH AN ADVERB   *Adverbs* modify verbs, adjectives, or other adverbs. They help explain *how, when, where,* or *why.* The following examples begin with adverbs or with groups of words that contain and serve as adverbs (shown in italics):

> *Soon* the rain stopped and the sun reappeared.
> *High above the spectators,* the hot air balloon drifted peacefully.
> *Slowly* and *confidently,* Maria rose to the speaker's platform.
> *Near the ancient Egyptian city of Thebes,* pharaohs built monuments to their wealth and power.

BEGIN WITH AN INFINITIVE   As you learned earlier, an *infinitive* is the present tense of a verb with the word "to" in front of it. Infinitives acting as nouns often make good beginnings for sentences:

> *To study* archaeology was her childhood dream.
> *To defend* unpopular ideas takes courage.
> *To call* him a coward is unfair and inaccurate.

BEGIN WITH A PREPOSITION OR PREPOSITIONAL PHRASE   *Prepositions* connect or show relationships between nouns or pronouns and the rest of a sentence. *Prepositional phrases* contain prepositions, a noun or pronoun, and any words that modify that noun or pronoun.

> *Without love,* life is empty.
> *Between the mountains* ran a bright, clear stream.
> *Before the spectators* stood a Mayan priest ready to perform the harvest ritual.
> *To a large temple,* the worshippers carried flowers, candles, and statues.
> *Inside the barn,* Freda found tools that dated from the Revolution.

BEGIN OR END WITH A PARTICIPLE OR PARTICIPIAL PHRASE   A *participle* is a verb turned into an adjective. Many participles end in "ed" or "ing." But words like "caught," "lost," "found," "brought," and "drawn," which are formed from irregular verbs, can also be participles. A *participial phrase* is a group of words containing a participle.

> *Screeching,* the infant birds told their mother they were hungry.
> *Exhausted,* I fell asleep as soon as my head touched the pillow.
> *Caught in the act,* the thief gave up easily.
> I stayed home that night, *having nowhere else to go.*
> Suddenly, the old bicycle broke apart, *scattering spokes and bits of chain everywhere.*
> Jamie wept openly, *his dream destroyed.*

ASK A RHETORICAL QUESTION   You learned in Chapters 3 and 4 that asking a question is a good way to begin a paragraph or an essay. Rhetorical questions—those to which the writer knows the answer or to which no answer is expected—can also empha-size important points and create variety. Take this example from a speech condemning television by Federal Communications Commission head Newton Minnow at a meeting of television executives in 1961:

> You will see a procession of game shows, violence, audience participa-tion shows, formula comedies about totally unbelievable families, blood and thunder mayhem, violence, sadism, murder, Western badmen, Western good men, private eyes, gangsters, more violence and cartoons. And endlessly, commercials—many screaming, cajoling, and offending. And, most of all boredom. . . .
>
> Is there one person in this room who claims that broadcasting can't do better?

REVERSE THE POSITION OF THE SUBJECT AND THE VERB Say that you write, "Two small pines grew at the crest of the hill." When you read your rough draft, you realize that this is the kind of pattern you've used in many other sentences. To vary the pattern, simply reverse the position of your subject and verb: "At the crest of the hill grew two small pines."

USE A COLON AFTER AN INDEPENDENT CLAUSE TO INTRODUCE INFORMATION THAT NAMES OR EXPLAINS SOMETHING IN THAT CLAUSE

Such information can be expressed in a word or phrase, a list of words, or even a sentence.

> **Word:** He was motivated by one thing and one thing only: greed.
> *("Greed" names "thing.")*
> **List:** He has three loves: his dog, his car, and his stomach.
> *("His dog, his car, and his stomach" name his "loves.")*
> **Sentence:** Please follow these instructions: Find the nearest exit, walk to it quickly, and help other passengers who need assistance.
> *(The sentence after the colon explains "instructions.")*

USE A COLON TO INTRODUCE A QUOTATION

Using a colon is a good way to introduce someone else's words and at the same time use a different sentence pattern. Let's say you wanted to quote from President Kennedy's Inaugural Address. You might write:

Today we would do well to remember JFK's exhortations to his fellow Americans: "Ask not what your country can do for you—ask what you can do for your country."

VISUALIZING SENTENCE STRUCTURE

To see how some of the principles you have just learned work in professional writing, read these paragraphs from Pete Hamill's autobiography, *A Drinking Life*. Comments in the left margin explain how Hamill created emphasis. Those on the right discuss variety. Hamill is writing about World War II.

EMPHASIS

Colon introduces list explaining "special way."

Repeats "our" for emphasis, parallelism.

We lived in the rhythms of the war. Years later, we even marked time in a special way: Before the War, During the War, After the War. The war was in our comics, our movies, our dreams. The radio was filled with it. Every evening, my mother listened to Edward R. Murrow and Gabriel Heatter, and in school we followed the war on

Divides sentence into segments to increase emphasis.

maps. There was North Africa. And Tobruk. And somewhere in all that yellow emptiness El Alamein.

At Holy Name, I heard about the war from new teachers every year, each of them rolling down the maps and showing us the places that were in the newspapers

Subordinates one idea to another.

and on the radio. There was so much excitement when the Allies landed in Sicily because the parents of most of the Italian kids were from that island. They wanted the

Coordinates two equally important ideas.

Americans to win. They had brothers in our army, and some of the brothers died in those first battles. All of them said their parents were worried. I got an aunt

Creates emphasis through repetition.

there, said Vito Pinto. My grandmother is there, said Michael Tempesta. I got an uncle over there, said George Poli. The war went on and on.

VARIETY

Varies sentence length.

Follows a simple sentence with a compound sentence.

Ends sentence with participial phrases.

Follows long sentence with short one.

Follows simple sentence with compound sentence.

REVISING TO CREATE VARIETY AND EMPHASIS

Read these two versions of paragraphs from Alice Wnorowski's "A Longing," which appears in this chapter. Although the rough draft is correct, Wnorowski knew that revising it would allow her to give important ideas the appropriate emphasis and to bring variety to her writing style.

Wnorowski—Rough Draft, Paragraphs 3 and 4

Vary length?

Vary structure?

The morning dew chilled my naked feet. I stopped on the sandy lane. From out of the corner of my eye, I suddenly caught a movement. Something was moving in the wide, open hay field that lay before me. Five deer, three does and two fawns, were grazing in the mist-filled dips of the roller-coaster landscape. I sat down in the damp earth to watch them. I got my white nightdress all brown and wet.

What is being emphasized in this one-sentence paragraph?

The deer casually strolled through the thigh-high grass, stopping every other step to dip their heads into the growth and pop them back up again with long, tender timothy stems dangling from the sides of their mouths.

Too long?

Wnorowski—Final Draft, Paragraphs 3 and 4

Combines sentences through coordination, subordination, and compounding.

The morning dew chilled my naked feet, and I stopped on the sandy lane. From out of the corner of my eye, I suddenly caught a movement in the wide, open hay field that lay before me. In the mist-filled dips of the roller-coaster landscape grazed five deer: three does and two fawns. I sat down in the damp earth to watch them and got my white nightdress all brown and wet.

Creates variety by reversing subject and verb. Uses a colon to introduce a list.

Divides paragraph into two sentences; emphasizes both ideas.

The deer casually strolled through the thigh-high grass, stopping every other step to dip their heads into the growth and pop them back up again. Long, tender timothy stems dangled from the sides of their mouths.

PRACTICING COMBINING SENTENCES

The two paragraphs below lack emphasis and variety because the sentences they contain are similar in length and structure. Use techniques explained in this chapter to rewrite the paragraphs in the spaces that follow them. Combine sentences, remove words, add details, choose new vocabulary, or make any other changes you wish in order to make the paragraphs more interesting and effective.

```
Ramses II

    Ramses II was a pharaoh [ruler] of Egypt. He lived
approximately 3300 years ago. He took the throne when he
was only 24. He ruled for 66 years. He died at about age
90. He had a huge family. He had more than 100 children.
He is thought to be the pharaoh when Moses led the
Hebrews from bondage in Egypt. He is also remembered for
his many important building projects. He was an indus-
trious and resourceful king. He left his mark on the
Egyptian landscape. He built temples and other magnifi-
cent monuments in every major city of his kingdom. His
projects included expanding the famous temples at Karnak
and at Luxor. He is buried in the Valley of the Kings.
This place is near Luxor. Luxor used to be called
Thebes.
```

_____

_____

_____

_____

_____

_____

_____

_____

_____

_____

_____

_____

_____

_____

_____

Trinity

The prefix "tri" means three. Traditional Christianity teaches that God exists in a trinity, three persons. These are the Father, the Son, and the Holy Spirit. Christianity is not the only religion that has a trinity. Hinduism also has a trinity. It is called the Trimurti. "Murti" means shape in Sanskrit. Sanskrit is the ancient language of India. Many classical religious and literary works are written in this language. The Hindu trinity has three members. They are Brahma, Vishnu, and Shiva. Brahma is the creator. Vishnu is the preserver. Shiva is the destroyer.

_____

_____

_____

_____

_____

_____

_____

_____

_____

_____

The following selections will help you develop the ability to create sentences that are both varied and emphatic. As you read on, try to apply the techniques you're learning in this chapter to your own writing. Don't hesitate to reread important sections in the introduction to this chapter when you need to.

From *America and Americans*

John Steinbeck

Nobel Prize–winning novelist, short story writer, and essayist, John Steinbeck (1902–1968) wrote The Grapes of Wrath, *an American classic that describes the suffering of an Oklahoma family forced from their land by severe drought during the great depression of the 1930s. All of Steinbeck's work shows a deep respect for nature. However, his concern for the environment and his love for the land are expressed no more eloquently than in these two paragraphs from* America and Americans, *a book he published in 1966.*

Looking Ahead

Although some sentences in this selection are relatively short, the author seems to prefer long sentences. Nevertheless, he holds the readers' interest. Look for ways like those you have just learned by which Steinbeck creates variety and emphasis.

Vocabulary

belching	Erupting, gushing forth.
debris	Litter, junk, rubbish.
exhausted	Used up, consumed.
pillaged	Looted, plundered, robbed.
scythe	Tool with a large blade used for mowing or reaping.
uninhibited	Uncontrolled, indiscriminate.

From *America and*
Americans | John Steinbeck

I have often wondered at the savagery and thoughtlessness with which our early 1
settlers approached this rich continent. They came at it as though it were an
enemy, which of course it was. They burned the forests and changed the rainfall; they
swept the buffalo from the plains, blasted the streams, set fire to the grass, and ran a
reckless scythe through the virgin and noble timber. Perhaps they felt that it was limit-
less and could never be exhausted and that a man could move on to new wonders end-
lessly. Certainly there are many examples to the contrary, but to a large extent the early
people pillage the country as though they hated it, as though they held it temporarily
and might be driven off at any time.

This tendency toward irresponsibility persists in very many of us today; our rivers 2
are poisoned by reckless dumping of sewage and toxic industrial wastes, the air of our
cities is filthy and dangerous to breathe from the belching of uncontrolled products
from combustion of coal, coke, oil, and gasoline. Our towns are girdled with wreckage
and the debris of our toys—our automobiles and our packaged pleasures. Through uninhibited spraying against one enemy we have destroyed the natural balances our survival
requires. All these evils can and must be overcome if America and Americans are to survive; but many of us still conduct ourselves as our ancestors did, stealing from the future
for our clear and present profit.

QUESTIONS FOR DISCUSSION

1. Which sentences place equal emphasis on ideas through coordination? What methods discussed in this chapter does Steinbeck use to coordinate these ideas?
2. Does Steinbeck use subordination? Where?
3. What examples of parallelism do you see? In which sentences does Steinbeck use repetition to create emphasis?
4. What figures of speech has he included?
5. Explain what he means by calling America an "enemy" to early settlers.
6. Why will the "uninhibited spraying" mentioned in paragraph 2 destroy "the natural balances our survival requires"?

THINKING CRITICALLY

1. Read (or reread) "Waste" by Wendell Berry in Chapter 2. What similarities do you see in this piece and the selection by Steinbeck?
2. What is the most important environmental problem of our day? Is it air pollution? The dumping of toxic waste? The destruction of the ozone layer? The mounting garbage problem? Draw ideas and examples from your experiences, observations, or reading that will explain your answer in two or three paragraphs.

SUGGESTION FOR A JOURNAL ENTRY

The two paragraphs you have just read were written in the late 1960s. Have we made progress in protecting our environment since then? List two or three things you do or could do to safeguard the air, water, or land that you will pass on to future generations. Then make two other lists: In the first, explain what your community does or could do; in the second, explain what the nation as a whole is or should be doing to save the environment.

The Vices of Age*

Malcolm Cowley

Poet, critic, historian, and literary editor of The New Republic *magazine, Malcolm Cowley (1898–1989) remained energetic and productive well into old age. He is the author of* Exile's Return, *an important book about the "lost generation" of American writers, such as Hemingway and Fitzgerald, who lived in Paris during the 1920s. The paragraphs that follow are taken from "The View from 80," an article that Cowley wrote for* Life *magazine in 1978 and that he later used in a book of the same title.*

Looking Ahead

One of the people discussed in this selection was an "admiralty lawyer." He practiced law governing naval, shipping, and other maritime matters.

Vocabulary

avarice	Greed.
dismantled	Took apart.
dismaying	Disappointing.
immoderate	Extreme, unreasonable.
intruders	Trespassers.
lethargy	Sluggishness, lack of energy.

*Editor's title

The Vices of Age | Malcolm Cowley

Among the vices of age are avarice, untidyness, and vanity. . . .   1

Untidiness we call the Langley Collyer syndrome. To explain, Langley Collyer was 2 a former concert pianist who lived alone with his 70-year-old brother in a brownstone house on upper Fifth Avenue. The once fashionable neighborhood had become part of Harlem. Homer, the brother, had been an admiralty lawyer, but was now blind and partly paralyzed; Langley played for him and fed him on buns and oranges, which he thought would restore Homer's sight. He never threw away a daily paper because Homer, he said, might want to read them all. He saved other things as well and the house became filled with rubbish from roof to basement. The halls were lined on both sides with bundled newspapers, leaving narrow passageways in which Langley had devised booby traps to catch intruders.

On March 21, 1947, some unnamed person telephoned the police to report that 3 there was a dead body in the Collyer house. The police broke down the front door and found the hall impassable; then they hoisted a ladder to a second-story window. Behind it Homer was lying on the floor in a bathrobe; he had starved to death. Langley had disappeared. After some delay, the police broke into the basement, chopped a hole in the roof, and began throwing junk out of the house, top and bottom. It was 18 days before they found Langley's body, gnawed by rats. Caught in one of his own booby traps, he had died in a hallway just outside Homer's door. By that time the police had collected, and the Department of Sanitation had hauled away, 120 tons of rubbish, including, besides the newspapers, 14 grand pianos and the parts of a dismantled Model T Ford.

QUESTIONS FOR DISCUSSION

1. What sentences in this selection are periodic? Explain the ideas they emphasize.
2. What other methods discussed in this chapter does Cowley use to create emphasis? For instance, find an example of parallelism.
3. These paragraphs illustrate ways to create variety. Where does Cowley use participial phrases? In what other way(s) does he create variety?
4. Identify one or two of the vivid images the author uses to show us the kind of life Langley and Homer Collyer led. What words make these images effective?
5. Is Cowley's attitude toward the aged negative? Explain by making reference to specific words and sentences.

THINKING CRITICALLY

1. In the first sentence, Cowley mentions three vices of age. Name three vices of youth. Then explain one of these by using examples of people you know or have read about. Put your ideas in writing.
2. What kind of old age will you have? Before you answer, consider your personality—your habits, your virtues, your faults, your temperament, the people and things with which you surround yourself, the kinds of things you save, and so on. Then, use this information to predict the kind of person you will be at age 80 or 90. Take notes as you go through this process. Then, put the results into a paragraph or two.

SUGGESTIONS FOR JOURNAL ENTRIES

1. People of all ages have vices. Do you know someone who is particularly greedy, sloppy, vain, lazy, or jealous, or who suffers from another bad quality or habit? What does this person say or do to illustrate this vice? Use brainstorming or focused freewriting to record these details. If possible, recall incidents from your subject's life to show how seriously he or she has been affected by this vice. Incidentally, a good subject for this assignment might be a relative, a close friend, or even yourself.
2. Are all elderly people like those Cowley describes? Think about someone about age 80 whom you admire. List details to show that, far from being eccentric or strange, he or she keeps up with the times, is active and alert, or contributes much to the lives of others. Once again, recall an incident or two that explain why you think highly of this person.

Gettysburg Address

Abraham Lincoln

Abraham Lincoln is one of the best-loved U.S. Presidents. His Second Inaugural Address and the Gettysburg Address are landmarks in American public speaking.

In November 1863, Lincoln came to Gettysburg, Pennsylvania, to dedicate a cemetery at the site of the Civil War's bloodiest contest. The Battle of Gettysburg, which proved to be the turning point of the war, had raged for four days and killed 50,000 Americans before Confederate forces under General Robert E. Lee withdrew.

Lincoln's Gettysburg Address is an eloquent and powerful statement of his grief over the death of his countrymen on both sides and of his belief "that government of the people, by the people, for the people, shall not perish from the earth."

LOOKING AHEAD

1. In his concluding sentence, Lincoln describes a "great task remaining before us." Read this important section of the speech a few times to make sure you understand it fully.
2. "Four score and seven years" equals eighty-seven years. A "score" is twenty.
3. Throughout this speech, and especially in paragraph 3, Lincoln uses parallelism, a technique that makes his sentences more forceful, emphatic, and memorable.

VOCABULARY

conceived	Created.
consecrate	Bless, sanctify.
detract	Take away from, lessen.
hallow	Make holy or sacred.
in vain	For no reason or purpose.
measure	Amount.
proposition	Idea, principle.
resolve	Decide, determine.

Gettysburg Address | Abraham Lincoln

Four score and seven years ago our fathers brought forth on this continent a new 1 nation, conceived in Liberty, and dedicated to the proposition that all men are created equal.

Now we are engaged in a great civil war, testing whether that nation, or any nation 2 so conceived and so dedicated, can long endure. We are met on a great battlefield of that war. We have come to dedicate a portion of that field, as a final resting place for those who here gave their lives that that nation might live. It is altogether fitting and proper that we should do this.

But, in a larger sense, we can not dedicate—we can not consecrate—we can not 3 hallow—this ground. The brave men, living and dead, who struggled here, have consecrated it, far above our poor power to add or detract. The world will little note, nor long remember what we say here, but it can never forget what they did here. It is for us the living, rather, to be dedicated here to the unfinished work which they who fought here have thus far so nobly advanced. It is rather for us to be here dedicated to the great task remaining before us—that from these honored dead we take increased devotion to that cause for which they gave the last full measure of devotion—that we here highly resolve that these dead shall not have died in vain—that this nation, under God, shall have a new birth of freedom—and that government of the people, by the people, for the people, shall not perish from the earth.

QUESTIONS FOR DISCUSSION

1. What words and ideas are repeated in paragraph 3? What ideas does this repetition emphasize?
2. What examples of parallelism do you find in the Gettysburg Address?
3. Most sentences in this speech are long, but Lincoln does vary sentence length. Where does he do this?
4. What two participial phrases does Lincoln use at the end of his first sentence? Do they help make this sentence more interesting than if he had put the information they convey into another sentence?
5. Does Lincoln include a participial phrase in paragraph 2? Where?
6. What is Lincoln's central idea? What devices or techniques does he use to maintain coherence?

THINKING CRITICALLY

1. Lincoln used the words "of the people, by the people, and for the people" to describe the American government. What do each of these three phrases mean to you? In other words, what kind of government do you think they describe?
2. In what ways do you think our government should be "for the people"? What services and guarantees should it provide us?

SUGGESTIONS FOR JOURNAL ENTRIES

1. Many speeches in American history have served as sources of inspiration from decade to decade, from generation to generation. With the help of your instructor or your college librarian, locate a speech that you'd like to read or reread. Then analyze this speech. Pick out examples of parallelism, repetition, and other techniques the writer has used to create emphasis. Here are a few speeches you might choose from:
   Abraham Lincoln, Second Inaugural Address
   Franklin Delano Roosevelt, First Inaugural Address
   Adlai Stevenson, Eulogy for Eleanor Roosevelt
   Dwight D. Eisenhower, Farewell Address
   John F. Kennedy, Speech at the Berlin Wall
   Martin Luther King, Jr., Speech at the Lincoln Memorial ("I Have a Dream")
   Ronald Reagan, Speech at Moscow State University
2. Using as many paragraphs as you like, rewrite Lincoln's speech in your own words. Make sure that you express his central idea clearly and that you emphasize his other important ideas through parallelism, repetition, or any of the other techniques you've learned for creating emphasis.

A Longing

Alice Wnorowski

"A Longing" is a tender, almost dreamlike recollection of a beautiful childhood experience that continues to haunt the author. Wnorowski wrote this short essay in response to a freshman English assignment designed to help students learn to use concrete detail. However, it also illustrates several important principles about sentence structure discussed earlier in this chapter. Wnorowski began her studies at a community college. She has since earned a B.S. with honors in engineering.

L O O K I N G   A H E A D

1. You've learned that coordination can be used to create sentences in which two or more ideas receive equal emphasis and that subordination can be used to create sentences in which one idea is stressed over others. Look for examples of coordination and subordination in this essay.
2. The author puts variety into her writing by using techniques discussed earlier in this chapter. They include beginning sentences with an adverb and a prepositional phrase and using participles to vary sentence structure and length.
3. Remember what you learned about using details in Chapter 5, especially those that appeal to the five senses. Identify such details in "A Longing."

V O C A B U L A R Y

acknowledge	Recognize.
conceived	Understood.
yearn	Desire, long for.

A Longing | *Alice Wnorowski*

An easy breeze pushed through the screen door, blowing into my open face and 1
filling my nostrils with the first breath of morning. The sun beamed warm rays
of white light onto my lids, demanding they lift and acknowledge the day's arrival.

Perched in the nearby woods, a bobwhite proudly shrieked to the world that he
knew who he was. His song stirred deep feelings within me, and I was overcome by an
urge to run barefoot through his woods. I jumped up so abruptly I startled the dog lying
peacefully beside me. His sleepy eyes looked into mine questioningly, but I could give
him no answer. I only left him bewildered, pushing through the front door and trotting
down the grassy decline of the front lawn.

The morning dew chilled my naked feet, and I stopped on the sandy lane. From 2
out of the corner of my eye, I suddenly caught a movement in the wide, open hay field
that lay before me. In the mist-filled dips of the roller-coaster landscape grazed five deer:
three does and two fawns. I sat down in the damp earth to watch them and got my white
nightdress all brown and wet.

The deer casually strolled along through the thigh-high grass, stopping every other 3
step to dip their heads into the growth and pop them back up again. Long, tender timothy stems dangled from the sides of their mouths.

The fawns were never more than two or three yards behind their mothers, and I 4
knew a buck must not be far off in the woods, keeping lookout for enemies. Suddenly,
a car sped along the adjacent road, disrupting the peace of the moment. The deer
jumped up in terror and darted towards the trees. They took leaps, clearing eight to ten
feet in a single bound. I watched their erect, white puffs of tails bounce up and down,
until the darkness of the woods swallowed them up and I could see them no more.

I don't think that at the simple age of eleven I quite conceived what a rare and beau- 5
tiful sight I had witnessed. Now, eight years later, I yearn to awaken to the call of a bobwhite and to run barefoot through wet grass in search of him.

QUESTIONS FOR DISCUSSION

1. Find a few examples of both coordination and subordination in this essay.
2. Identify some adverbs, prepositional phrases, and participles Wnorowski uses to create variety.
3. In which sentence are the normal positions of the subject and verb reversed?
4. In paragraph 5, the author varies the length and structure of her sentences to make her writing more interesting. What methods discussed in this chapter does she use?
5. To which of our five senses do the details in this essay appeal?
6. What is the meaning of Wnorowski's title? Why is it appropriate?
7. What techniques does the writer use to maintain coherence in and between paragraphs?

THINKING CRITICALLY

1. This selection reveals as much about the writer as about the experience she recalls. From what you have just read, what can you say about Wnorowski's personality?
2. For anyone living in or near a rural area, seeing a family of wild animals is not an unusual event. Why, then, is this event so special to the writer?

SUGGESTIONS FOR JOURNAL ENTRIES

1. Think back to an experience you would like to relive. Make a list of the things that made this experience memorable and that will explain why you have such "a longing" to relive it.
2. Use the brainstorming technique discussed in "Getting Started" to list details about a natural setting (for example, a meadow, mountain, seashore) that you experienced recently or remember vividly.

The Buried Sounds of Children Crying

Harrison Rainie

On a quiet April morning in 1995, terrorists set off a 5,000-pound bomb at a federal office building in Oklahoma City. Among the 170 people killed were many infants and small children. It is a tragedy that has been burned into the American consciousness and that will cause us pain for generations to come. Harrison Rainie writes for US News & World Report, *where this essay was published shortly after the bombing.*

LOOKING AHEAD

1. In paragraph 3, Rainie quotes lines from William Shakespeare's *King John*. In this play, Arthur, the king's nephew, is captured in battle and is killed while attempting to escape. Constance, Arthur's mother, goes mad with grief and kills herself.
2. This essay contains examples of language that "shows," which you learned about in Chapters 5 and 6. Look for concrete and specific nouns, vivid verbs, adjectives, and adverbs. Make a special effort to find figures of speech.

VOCABULARY

distraught	Troubled, upset, worried.
embodiment	Realization, manifestation.
gracious	Gentle, tender, lovely.
implication	Indication, suggestion.
incessant	Without end.
ineffable	Indefinable, indescribable.
instinctive	Inbred, natural.
molecular level	The most basic level, the smallest part of our being.
nourish	Feed.
nurturing	Caring for, feeding, supporting.
pluck	Boldness, nerve, courage.
prevails	Exists, is the rule.
qualifiers	Describers.
riveting	Captivating, engaging.
roguishness	Friskiness.
vacant	Empty.

The Buried Sounds
of Children Crying | *Harrison Rainie*

Almost to a person, the searchers who combed the ruins at the Alfred P. Murrah 1
Federal Building said they had one thought after finishing their work: They
wanted to go home and hug their kids. The most chilling fact about the Oklahoma City
bombing was that it struck at children eating breakfast and playing in a day-care center
one floor above the street. And the only way to respond to the ache the incident created is to clasp all surviving children tightly—even those thousands of miles from harm's
way—and pour out a fearful love.

While there was much talk about the meaning of this attack on "America's heart- 2
land," its biggest impact was on the soul's heartland. We are fixed at the molecular level
to respond to children. Some famous experiments have shown that their faces have been
designed to draw instinctive nurturing from us; their noises are especially riveting to
adult ears. Give a mother a pile of dozens of identical T-shirts, as one researcher did, and
she can pick out the one her child wore by its scent.

The death of such precious beings violates the order and meaning of life. The only 3
way to understand it is to describe the incessant pain of the loss, as the distraught Constance does in Shakespeare's *King John:* "Grief fills the room up of my absent child, / Lies
in his bed, walks up and down with me; / Puts on his pretty looks, repeats his
words, / Remembers me of all his gracious parts, / Stuffs out his vacant garments with
his form." Adults nourish this grief the way they would the child himself, psychologist
Louise Kaplan says.

The tragedy of the children's deaths in Oklahoma City is compounded by the loss of 4
many adult lives and the implications of the bombing's occurrence in a heartland city.
Oklahoma holds a spot in the American imagination as the embodiment of normality, a
gritty wholesomeness, an appealing streak of roguishness and pluck, as a place where a
pretty happy coexistence prevails among American Indians, Northern Methodists whose
ancestors entered through Kansas, Southern Baptists whose kin came from Texas and
many newcomers in the past generation.

Its capital city is a festival of Americana, home of the National Cowboy Hall of Fame 5
and Western Heritage Center, the National Softball Hall of Fame and a nice firefighters'
museum. That, though, did not prevent it from being devastated by an evil force—and
an alien one, no matter what its origin is. "You don't have terrorism in Middle America,"
insisted firefighter Bill Finn. Now we do. And the city will be long haunted by the
sounds described by Red Cross worker Jennifer Harrison: "As we helped people on the
street, we could hear children crying, like blowing in the wind. You couldn't see them.
You just heard their voices."

In our language, we use parental terms in inventive ways as qualifiers: We can live 6
in fatherlands, speak in mother tongues, measure things by Father Time and exist in
Mother Nature. But our attachment to children is so ineffable, we don't use it to describe
other ideas. Child love is the essence of life, and we have all been orphaned by the
slaughter of children in Oklahoma City.

QUESTIONS FOR DISCUSSION

1. What function does the colon serve in the first sentence of paragraph 1?
2. Where else in this essay does the author use a colon? What function does it serve in those places?
3. Find examples of parallelism in this essay.
4. Explain how Rainie maintains variety in paragraph 2.
5. Paragraph 5 contains a three-word sentence. Should this sentence have been combined with another sentence? Why or why not?
6. Find a periodic sentence in paragraph 5.
7. Where does Rainie use images to communicate his feelings? Discuss two examples.
8. Where does Rainie use personification?

THINKING CRITICALLY

1. In your own words write a summary of the quotation from *King John* in paragraph 3.
2. Read (or reread) "The Last Safe Haven," an essay in Chapter 3, which also discusses violence in America. In what way is its message similar to that in "The Buried Sounds of Children Crying"?
3. In paragraph 3, we read: "The death of such precious beings violates the order and meaning of life." Explain this statement.

SUGGESTIONS FOR JOURNAL ENTRIES

1. "We are fixed at the molecular level to respond to children," Rainie says in paragraph 2. He then provides a few brief examples to explain what he means. Reread this paragraph. Then, use freewriting to recall at least one example from your own experience or observation that would support or explain this idea.
2. Use any prewriting method explained in "Getting Started" to discuss your reaction to the Oklahoma City bombing or to any other event that shocked the nation or your community, campus, or family. Don't be content to list a few words such as "Stunned," or "Angry," which will describe your immediate reaction only. Instead, explore the thoughts and feelings you have had about this event since learning about it.

Inaugural Address

John Fitzgerald Kennedy

One of the most popular leaders in American history, JFK took the oath of office as our thirty-fifth President on January 20, 1961. Through more than a quarter of a century, his speeches have served to inspire and to instruct new generations of Americans.

The best-remembered and most frequently quoted of Kennedy's speeches, his Inaugural Address, seems fresh and new even after nearly four decades. Perhaps this has to do with his ability to speak to what is deepest and most universal in the human spirit—the real hopes and problems that all generations and all peoples share.

Looking Ahead

1. Like most Presidents, Kennedy relied on a professional speech writer. Ted Sorenson composed his Inaugural Address.
2. Kennedy begins by recognizing several dignitaries on the platform. Among them are Dwight D. Eisenhower, the thirty-fourth President; Richard Nixon, the outgoing Vice President and later the thirty-seventh President; and the new Vice President, Lyndon B. Johnson, who became President upon Kennedy's death in 1963.
3. Paragraphs 19 and 23 make reference to the Old Testament and especially to the prophet Isaiah, who wrote that someday the armies of the world would "beat their swords into plowshares and their spears into pruning hooks."
4. This selection makes especially good use of parallel structure and repetition.
5. One reason this speech is so spellbinding is that its language and sentence structure are both powerful and varied. The writer was especially successful at changing the length of its sentences at just the right times. As you read JFK's Inaugural Address, identify some of the other methods you've learned for maintaining variety.

Vocabulary

abolish	Eliminate, do away with.
asunder	Apart.
belaboring	Talking about for an unreasonable length of time.
formulate	Create, make.
invective	Verbal abuse, insult.

invoke	Call upon, use.
prescribed	Recommended, directed, dictated.
symbolizing	Representing.
tribulation	Suffering, trouble.
writ	Authority.

Inaugural Address | *J o h n   F i t z g e r a l d   K e n n e d y*

Vice President Johnson, Mr. Speaker, Mr. Chief Justice, President Eisenhower, Vice   1
President Nixon, President Truman, Reverend Clergy, Fellow Citizens: We observe
today not a victory of party but a celebration of freedom—symbolizing an end as well as
a beginning—signifying renewal as well as change. For I have sworn before you and
Almighty God the same solemn oath our forebears prescribed nearly a century and three
quarters ago.

The world is very different now. For man holds in his mortal hands the power to   2
abolish all forms of human poverty and all forms of human life. And yet the same revolutionary beliefs for which our forebears fought are still at issue around the globe—the
belief that the rights of man come not from the generosity of the state but from the hand
of God.

We dare not forget today that we are the heirs of that first revolution. Let the word   3
go forth from this time and place, to friend and foe alike, that the torch has been passed
to a new generation of Americans—born in this century, tempered by war, disciplined
by a hard and bitter peace, proud of our ancient heritage—and unwilling to witness or
permit the slow undoing of those human rights to which this nation has always been
committed, and to which we are committed today, at home and around the world.

Let every nation know, whether it wishes us well or ill, that we shall pay any price,   4
bear any burden, meet any hardship, support any friend or oppose any foe to assure the
survival and the success of liberty.

This much we pledge—and more.   5

To those old allies whose cultural and spiritual origins we share, we pledge the loy-   6
alty of faithful friends. United, there is little we cannot do in a host of cooperative ven-
tures. Divided, there is little we can do—for we dare not meet a powerful challenge at
odds and split asunder.

To those new states whom we welcome to the ranks of the free, we pledge our word   7
that one form of colonial control shall not have passed away merely to be replaced by a
far more iron tyranny. We shall not always expect to find them supporting our view.

But we shall always hope to find them strongly supporting their own freedom—   8
and to remember that, in the past, those who foolishly sought power by riding the back
of the tiger ended up inside.

To those people in the huts and villages of half the globe struggling to break the   9
bonds of mass misery, we pledge our best efforts to help them help themselves, for whatever period is required—not because the Communists may be doing it, not because we
seek their votes, but because it is right. If a free society cannot help the many who are
poor, it cannot save the few who are rich.

To our sister republics south of our border, we offer a special pledge—to convert   10
our good words into good deeds—in a new alliance for progress—to assist free men and
free governments in casting off the chains of poverty. But this peaceful revolution of
hope cannot become the prey of hostile powers. Let all our neighbors know that we
shall join with them to oppose aggression or subversion anywhere in the Americas. And
let every other power know that this hemisphere intends to remain the master of its
own house.

To that world assembly of sovereign states, the United Nations, our last best hope in 11 an age where the instruments of war have far outpaced the instruments of peace, we renew our pledge of support—to prevent it from becoming merely a forum for invective—to strengthen its shield of the new and the weak—and to enlarge the area in which its writ may run.

Finally, to those nations who would make themselves our adversary, we offer not a 12 pledge but a request: That both sides begin anew the quest for peace, before the dark powers of destruction unleashed by science engulf all humanity in planned or accidental self-destruction.

We dare not tempt them with weakness. For only when our arms are sufficient 13 beyond doubt can we be certain beyond doubt that they will never be employed.

But neither can two great and powerful groups of nations take comfort from our 14 present course—both sides overburdened by the cost of modern weapons, both rightly alarmed by the steady spread of the deadly atom, yet both racing to alter that uncertain balance of terror that stays the hand of mankind's final war.

So let us begin anew—remembering on both sides that civility is not a sign of weak- 15 ness, and sincerity is always subject to proof. Let us never negotiate out of fear. But let us never fear to negotiate.

Let both sides explore what problems unite us instead of belaboring those prob- 16 lems which divide us.

Let both sides, for the first time, formulate serious and precise proposals for the 17 inspection and control of arms—and bring the absolute power to destroy other nations under the absolute control of all nations.

Let both sides seek to invoke the wonders of science instead of its terrors. Together 18 let us explore the stars, conquer the deserts, eradicate disease, tap the ocean depths and encourage the arts and commerce.

Let both sides unite to heed in all corners of the earth the command of Isaiah—to 19 "undo the heavy burdens . . . [and] let the oppressed go free."

And if a beachhead of cooperation may push back the jungle of suspicion, let both 20 sides join in creating a new endeavor: not a new balance of power, but a new world of law, where the strong are just and the weak secure and the peace preserved.

All this will not be finished in the first one hundred days. Nor will it be finished in 21 the first one thousand days, nor in the life of this administration, nor even perhaps in our lifetime on this planet. But let us begin.

In your hands, my fellow citizens, more than mine, will rest the final success or 22 failure of our course. Since this country was founded, each generation of Americans has been summoned to give testimony to its national loyalty. The graves of young Americans who answered the call to service surround the globe.

Now the trumpet summons us again—not as a call to bear arms, though arms we 23 need—not as a call to battle, though embattled we are—but a call to bear the burden of a long twilight struggle, year in and year out, "rejoicing in hope, patient in tribulation"— a struggle against the common enemies of man: Tyranny, poverty, disease and war itself.

Can we forge against these enemies a grand and global alliance, North and South, 24 East and West, that can assure a more fruitful life for all mankind? Will you join in that historic effort?

In the long history of the world, only a few generations have been granted the role 25 of defending freedom in its hour of maximum danger.

I do not shrink from this responsibility—I welcome it. I do not believe that any of 26 us would exchange places with any other people or any other generation. The energy, the faith, the devotion which we bring to this endeavor will light our country and all who serve it—and the glow from that fire can truly light the world.

And so, my fellow Americans: Ask not what your country can do for you—ask what 27 you can do for your country.

My fellow citizens of the world: Ask not what America will do for you, but what 28 together we can do for the freedom of man.

Finally, whether you are citizens of America or citizens of the world, ask of us here 29 the same high standards of strength and sacrifice which we ask of you. With a good conscience our only sure reward, with history the final judge of our deeds, let us go forth to lead the land we love, asking His blessing and His help, but knowing that here on earth God's work must truly be our own.

QUESTIONS FOR DISCUSSION

1. Reread any three or four paragraphs in this selection, and identify examples of parallel structure that are used to create emphasis.
2. Reread paragraph 21, which illustrates repetition. Then find other passages in which key words and phrases are repeated to create emphasis.
3. Paragraphs 6, 7, 9, 10, and 11 are introduced by phrases that begin with the preposition "to." This repetition helps the speaker draw connections between and emphasize important ideas in each of these paragraphs. In what other section of this speech does he use repetition to begin a series of paragraphs?
4. The speech writer's ability to vary sentence length is evident throughout this selection. In what paragraphs is this skill most apparent?
5. Near the conclusion, JFK asks two rhetorical questions that add variety and interest to his presentation. What are they?
6. The speech writer often creates coherence between sentences and paragraphs by beginning with a coordinating conjunction: "And," "But," and "For." Find places in which he does so.

THINKING CRITICALLY

1. The most frequently quoted part of this speech is paragraph 27. Is there any connection between the idea in this paragraph and the last line of Lincoln's Gettysburg Address, which appears earlier in this chapter?
2. Throughout our history, young Americans have answered "the call to service" (paragraph 22) by going to war. If you were in government, in what ways—other than through military service—would you suggest that young people serve their country?
3. "If a free society cannot help the many who are poor," says Kennedy in paragraph 9, "it cannot save the few who are rich." What do you think he meant? Does the statement still hold true?

SUGGESTIONS FOR JOURNAL ENTRIES

1. Kennedy's speech seems fresh and current because it touches something universal in the human spirit, the hopes and the problems of all generations and all peoples. In your journal, list the issues (or problems) mentioned in Kennedy's Inaugural Address that you believe are still important today. Begin discussing details that, in a later assignment, might help show your readers how current these problems still are. Draw these details from your own experiences and/or from what you know about current events.

2. Understanding paragraph 2 is important to understanding Kennedy's ideas about government. What is he saying here? Begin analyzing this paragraph by making notes in the margins. Then write out a complete answer in a short paragraph. Vary the structure and length of your sentences by using techniques you learned in this chapter.

SUGGESTIONS FOR SUSTAINED WRITING

1. John Steinbeck may have inspired you to think about what we are doing or should be doing to preserve the natural environment. Read the journal notes you made after reading the selection by Steinbeck. Then, write an essay explaining how well or how poorly we are doing at keeping the environment healthy.

   Focus on a problem you know well: air, land, or water pollution; global warming; and so on. Discuss the causes of the problem first. Then describe its effects. Finally, explain what you and your community are doing or should be doing to solve it.

   Write multiple drafts of your paper and edit it carefully. In the process, use techniques for creating variety and emphasis explained in this chapter.

2. Malcolm Cowley describes the horrible deaths of two old gentlemen as a way to explain one of the "vices" of old age. But we all have vices, whatever our age. Consider someone you care about who suffers from a particular vice, such as laziness, greed, vanity, sloppiness, or even a more serious problem like sexual promiscuity or drug or alcohol abuse. Write this person a letter that recalls two or three startling incidents from his or her life. In other words, show your reader how seriously this vice is affecting him or her.

   You might begin the letter by explaining how much better life could be if your reader overcame the problem. You might conclude by offering your help, advice, and friendship.

   Before you start writing, look at the journal notes you made after reading the Cowley selection; you may have already gathered important information for this assignment. Then, draft the first version of your letter. When you revise this draft, make sure to emphasize important ideas. Like Cowley, for example, use parallelism and include a few periodic sentences. At the same time, try asking your reader a few rhetorical questions.

3. The second item under Suggestions for Journal Entries after "The Vices of Age" asks you to gather information about an elderly person you admire. If you responded to this suggestion, read it now and add any new detail that comes to mind.

   Next, organize what you've written into the paragraphs of an essay. Place your thesis in an introductory paragraph that compares or contrasts your subject with others, that begins with a startling remark, or that uses another technique for writing introductions discussed in Chapter 4. Make sure your thesis states why you admire your subject. Explain that you respect this individual because of his or her accomplishments, or simply name particular character traits you find admirable. Then, in *each* of the paragraphs that follow, discuss one accomplishment or character trait in detail.

   Like Cowley, vary the length and structure of your sentences, use rhetorical questions, and practice parallel structure. Don't forget to revise your paper and to edit it carefully.

4. One of the Suggestions for Journal Entries after Alice Wnorowski's "A Longing" asks you to think about an experience you would like to relive. If you responded to this suggestion, you've made a list of effective details that will help explain why you have such a longing to repeat this experience.

    Add to your notes, and expand them into a short essay that shows your readers what made the experience so memorable. Develop your thesis in concrete detail, and don't forget to make your writing unified and coherent by using techniques discussed in Chapter 2.

    After you've written your first draft, read your essay carefully. Should you do more to emphasize important ideas or to maintain your readers' interest? If so, revise your paper by using some of the techniques for creating emphasis and variety explained in the introduction to this chapter. As usual, edit the final draft of your paper carefully.

5. The second item in Suggestions for Journal Entries after "A Longing" invites you to begin listing details about a natural setting—a forest, meadow, seashore, mountain, river—that you visited recently or remember vividly.

    Follow the advice in item 4 of Suggestions for Sustained Writing, and turn these notes into a short essay.

6. In the first suggestion for journal entries after Rainie's "The Buried Sounds of Children Crying," you were asked to provide an example to support the idea that "We are fixed at the molecular level to respond to children," which appears in paragraph 2. Reread that paragraph. Then, read your journal notes. Next, add at least two other examples that will help prove this point. You should be able to discuss each of these examples in a separate paragraph of an essay that uses the quotation above as its thesis.

    Make sure the quotation and your explanation of it appears in your essay's introduction. You might also use a contrast, a definition, or an anecdote in the beginning of your paper. A good way to conclude is to refer to your thesis or to make a call to action. In any case, review the methods of writing introductions and conclusions in Chapter 4 before you begin to draft your essay. And speaking of drafting, make sure to revise your first draft several times and to edit your final draft carefully.

7. President Kennedy's Inaugural Address mentions serious social and political problems that are still with us. The most obvious of these are poverty and hunger, but there are many others. In fact, you may have already begun writing about such problems in your journal. Focus on the one problem you know most about, either through personal experience or through what you have learned about it from newspapers, television, or other sources. Continue adding details about this problem to your journal.

Then, turn your journal notes into an essay that states the problem in your thesis and explains its effects in the essay's body paragraphs. Your thesis might go something like this: "More than three decades after President Kennedy took office, extreme poverty still plagues even our richest cities."

Take time to revise your rough drafts and to give your sentences both variety and emphasis. Techniques for creating emphasis that might work well in this assignment are parallelism and the repetition of key words and phrases. This is also a good time to use startling images and figures of speech like those discussed in Chapters 5 and 6. Finally, check your writing to make certain it is organized, developed, and edited well.

$\mathscr{S}$ECTION T H R E E

DESCRIPTION

This section's two chapters show how to develop verbal portraits—pictures in words—of people, places, and things you know well. The more specific you make any piece of writing, the more interesting, exciting, and effective it will be. And this is especially true of descriptive writing. Successful descriptions require a lot of specific details.

KNOWING YOUR SUBJECT

Gathering descriptive details becomes easier when you know the person, place, or thing you're describing. If you need to learn more about your subject, spend some time observing it. Use your five senses—sight, hearing, touch, taste, and smell—to gather important information. And don't be afraid to take notes. Write your observations, reactions, and impressions in your journal, on note cards, or at least on scratch paper. They will come in handy as you sit down to put together your verbal portrait.

USING LANGUAGE THAT SHOWS

As you learned in Chapter 5, using language that shows makes any writing you do far more *concrete, specific,* and *vivid* than simply telling your readers what you mean. Such language is vital to description.

For instance, it's one thing to say that your mother "came home from work looking very tired." It's quite another to describe "the dark shadows under her eyes and the slowness of her walk as she entered the house."

In the first version, the writer uses a weak abstraction to get the point across. But "looking very tired" can mean different things to different people. It doesn't show the reader exactly what the writer sees. It doesn't point to things about the subject—the dark shadows under her eyes, the slowness of her walk—that *show* she is tired.

USE CONCRETE NOUNS AND ADJECTIVES

The next thing to remember is to make your details as concrete as possible. For example, if you're describing a friend, don't just say that "He's not a neat dresser" or that his "wardrobe could be improved." Include concrete nouns and adjectives that will enable your readers to come to the same conclusion. Talk about "the red dirt along the sides of his scuffed, torn shoes; the large rips in the knees of his faded blue jeans; and the many jelly spots on his shirt."

The same is true when describing objects and places. It's not enough to claim that your 1979 convertible is "a real eyesore." You've got to *show* it! Describe the scrapes, scratches, dents, and rust spots; mention the cracked headlights, the corroded bumpers, and the bald tires; talk about the fact that the top is faded.

INCLUDE SPECIFIC DETAILS

After you've chosen a number of important details that are concrete—details that show rather than tell something about your subject—make your description more specific. For instance, revise the description of your friend's attire to "Red clay was caked along the sides of his scuffed, torn loafers; his knees bulged from the large rips in his faded Levi's; and strawberry jelly was smeared on the collar of his white Oxford shirt."

When describing that 1979 convertible, don't be content simply to mention "the scratches and scrapes on the paint job." Go on to specify that "some of them are more than an inch wide and a half inch deep." Make sure your readers know that those "corroded bumpers" are made of "chrome" and "are scarred with thousands of tiny pockmarks and rusty blemishes." Finally, don't say that the top is "faded"; explain that "the canvas top, which was once sparkling white, has turned dirty gray with age."

CREATE FIGURES OF SPEECH

In Chapter 6 you learned that one of the best ways to make your writing clear and vivid is to use figures of speech, expressions that convey a meaning beyond their literal sense. Writers rely heavily on figures of speech when they need to explain or clarify abstract, complex, or unfamiliar ideas. Metaphors and similes are the most useful figures of speech for description because they can be used to compare an aspect of the person, place, or thing being described to something else with which the reader may already be familiar. Gilbert Highet makes excellent use of a simile when, in "Subway Station" (Chapter 8), he tells us that the paint is peeling off the station walls "like scabs from an old wound."

In addition, figures of speech make it possible for writers to dramatize or make vivid feelings, concepts, or ideas that would otherwise have remained abstract and difficult to understand. If you read Emanuel di Pasquale's "Joy of an Immigrant, a Thanksgiving" (Chapter 6), you might remember that the poet compares his journey to America with the flight of a bird to a land where he "can build a dry nest" and where his "song can echo."

RELY ON YOUR FIVE SENSES

Earlier you read that a good way to gather information about any subject is through observation. Observation is often thought of as seeing, and the most common details found in description are visual. However, observing can also include information from the other four senses. Of course, explaining what something sounds, feels, smells, or tastes like can be harder than showing what it looks like. But the extra effort is worthwhile. In fact, whether you describe people, places, or things, the greater the variety of details you include, the more realistic and convincing your description will be.

Next to sight, hearing is perhaps the sense writers rely on most. There are many ways to describe sound. In Chapter 9, for example, Carl Sandburg claims that Lincoln's voice had "a log-cabin smack" and that he pronounced "the word 'really' more like a drawled Kentucky 'ra-a-ly'." In Chapter 8, Annie Dillard relies on her readers' knowing "Old MacDonald Had a Farm," a tune with which she serenades a group of children in Ecuador. "I thought they might recognize the animal sounds," she tells us.

When writers describe rain-covered sidewalks as "slick," scraped elbows as "raw" or "tender," or the surfaces of bricks as "coarse" or "abrasive," they appeal to the sense of touch. Another example appears in Mary Ann Gwinn's "A Deathly Call of the Wild," in Chapter 8, when she writes that some of the oil spilled onto the shores of Alaska had the "consistency of chocolate syrup."

Tastes and smells are perhaps the most difficult things to describe. Nonetheless, you should include them in your writing when appropriate. Notice how well Mary Taylor Simeti does this when describing the Easter picnic she and her family make of take-out food from a hillside restaurant in Sicily:

> . . . [our] obliging host produces [brings out] three foil-covered plates, a bottle of mineral water, and a round kilo loaf of fragrant, crusty bread. We drive back along the road a little way to a curve that offers space to park and some rocks to sit on. Our plates turn out to hold spicy olives, some slices of *prosciutto crudo* [cold ham] and of a peppery local salami, and two kinds of pecorino [sheep's milk] cheese, one fresh and mild, the other aged and sharper. With a bag of oranges from the car, the sun warm on our backs, the mountains rolling down at our feet to the southern coast and the sea beyond, where the heat haze clouds the horizon and hides Africa from view, we have as fine an Easter dinner as I have ever eaten. (*On Persephone's Island*)

BEING OBJECTIVE OR SUBJECTIVE

Describing something objectively requires the writer to report what he or she sees, hears, and so on as accurately and as thoroughly as possible. Subjective description allows the writer to communicate his or her personal feelings or reactions to the subject as well. Both types of description serve important purposes.

Most journalists and historians try to remain objective by communicating facts, not opinions about those facts. In other words, they try to give us the kind of information we'll need to make up our own minds about the subject.

This is what student Meg Potter does when she describes one of the thousands of homeless living on the streets of our cities:

> This particular [woman] had no shoes on, but her feet were bound in plastic bags that were tied with filthy rags. It was hard to tell exactly what she was wearing. She had on . . . a conglomeration of tattered material that I can only say . . . were rags. I couldn't say how old she was, but I'd guess in her late fifties. The woman's hair was grey and silver, and she was beginning to go bald.
>
> As I watched for a while, I realized she was sorting out her bags. She had six of them, each stuffed and overflowing. . . . I caught a glimpse of ancient magazines, empty bottles, filthy pieces of clothing, an inside-out umbrella, and several mismatched shoes. The lady seemed to be taking the things out of one bag and putting them into another. All the time she was muttering to herself. ("The Shopping Bag Ladies")

Potter never reveals her feelings about her subject. She simply explains what the shopping bag lady looks like and what she does. Even words like "conglomeration" and "filthy," while vivid, tell us more about what the writer sees than how she feels about her subject. As a result, we are left to make up our own minds about what we read.

In some cases, however, writers find it useful to reveal their feelings about the person, place, or thing they are describing, so they take a subjective approach. Doing so often adds depth and interest to their work. In "The Temptress," for example, student Dan Roland includes details from his senses and creates figures of speech to communicate various feelings about a golf course he visits:

> A friendly sun peeks out from behind the green hills, revealing a giant coat of glistening frost on a silent land. At this hour, even the birds still sleep. The howling wind's savage teeth bite deeply, and the cold air grips me by the throat. The steaming coffee goes down easily, warming my insides and making the frigid environment almost bearable. I peer over an elegant landscape. As far as I can see, all is calm. Manicured fairways reach out across the land, and ponds of glass reflect the sun's red glow. There are trees everywhere, from delicate symmetrical pines that line the fairways to majestic, spiteful oaks that eat my golf balls for breakfast, lunch, and dinner.

Watch for examples of objective and subjective description as you read the poems and essays in Chapters 8 and 9. At the same time, identify concrete and specific details and figures of speech, which will help you better appreciate and understand what goes into the writing of a vivid, interesting, and well-written piece of description.

C HAPTER
8

DESCRIBING PLACES AND THINGS

The introduction to Section Three explained several ways to increase your powers of description regardless of the subject. This chapter presents several selections that describe places and things. It also explains two techniques, introduced earlier, that will help you make your subjects as interesting and as vivid to your readers as they are to you: using proper nouns and effective verbs.

U SING P ROPER N OUNS

In addition to filling your writing with concrete details and figures of speech, you might also want to include a number of *proper nouns,* which, as you know, are the names of particular persons, places, and things. Here are some examples: Arizona, University of Tennessee, Lake Michigan, Farmers and Merchants' Savings and Loan, First Baptist Church, Spanish, Chinese, Belmont Avenue, Singer Sewing Machine Company, Harold Smith, San Francisco Opera House, *Business Week* magazine, and Minnesota Vikings.

Including proper nouns that readers recognize easily can make what you are describing more familiar to them. At the very least, it makes your writing more believable. Notice how Alfred Kazin's recollection of his childhood home is enriched by the names of places and things (shown in italics) he uses in this passage from "My Mother in Her Kitchen":

> In the corner next to the toilet was the sink at which we washed, and the square tub in which my mother did our clothes. Above it, tacked to the shelf on which were pleasantly arranged square, blue-bordered white sugar and spice jars, hung calendars from the *Public National Bank* on *Pitkin Avenue* and the *Minsker Progressive Branch* of the *Workman's Circle;* receipts for the payment of insurance premiums and household bills on a spindle; two little boxes engraved with *Hebrew* letters. One of these was for the poor, the other to buy back the *Land of Israel.*

U SING E FFECTIVE V ERBS

We know how important verbs are to narration, but effective verbs can also add much to a piece of description. Writers use verbs to make descriptions more specific, accurate, and interesting. For instance, "the wind had chiseled deep grooves into the sides of the cliffs" is more specific than "the wind had made deep grooves." The verb "chiseled" also gives the reader a more accurate picture of the wind's action than "made" does.

In the introduction to Section Three, you learned how to enrich the description of a friend's clothing by adding specific details. Notice that lively verbs (in italics) make as much of a difference in that sentence as do concrete nouns and adjectives:

> Red clay *was caked* along the sides of his scuffed, torn loafers; his knees *bulged* from the large rips in his faded Levi's; and strawberry jelly *was smeared* on the collar of his white Oxford shirt.

Something similar can be said about the verbs Robert K. Massey uses in a portrait of the Russian countryside that opens his biography of Peter the Great:

> Around Moscow, the country *rolls* gently up from the rivers *winding* in silvery loops across the pleasant landscape. Small lakes and patches of woods *are sprinkled* among the meadowlands. Here and there, a village *appears, topped* by the onion dome of its church. People *are walking* through the fields on dirt paths *lined* with weeds. Along the riverbanks they *are fishing, swimming* and *lying* in the sun. It is a familiar Russian scene, *rooted* in centuries. (*Peter the Great*)

INCLUDING ACTION AND PEOPLE IN THE DESCRIPTION OF A PLACE

Narration and description are closely related, and they often appear together. Storytellers describe places where their narratives take place. Writers of description often reveal the character or atmosphere of a place by narrating events that occur in it or by describing people who appear in it.

Take the following paragraph from Annie Dillard's "In the Jungle," which appears in this chapter. Effective verbs, like those we associate with narrative writing—and like the ones discussed earlier—reveal something about the jungle's character by telling us about natural processes and events that occur there.

> Green fireflies *spattered* lights across the air and *illumined* for seconds, now here, now there, the pale trunks of enormous, solitary trees. Beneath us the brown Napo River *was rising,* in all silence; it *coiled* up the sandy bank and *tangled* its foam in vines that *trailed* from the forest and roots that *looped* the shore.

Clearly, the jungle is a place of energy, activity, and excitement. Knowing that is as important as learning about the sizes of its trees or the sounds of birds flying overhead.

A selection in this chapter that shows how actions and the people who perform them can help reveal the character of a place is Le Guin's "The Ones Who Walk Away from Omelas." Here are a few sentences from that piece:

Children dodged in and out, their high calls rising like the swallows' crossing flights over the music and the singing. All the processions wound toward the north side of the city, where on the great water-meadow called the Green Fields boys and girls, naked in the bright air, with mud-stained feet and ankles and long, lithe arms, exercised their restive horses before the race.

VISUALIZING DETAILS THAT DESCRIBE PLACES AND THINGS

The following paragraphs are from John Ciardi's essay "Dawn Watch," in which he describes the sights, sounds, and smells of sunrise in his backyard.

The traffic has just started, not yet a roar and stink. *(Appeals to senses)*

One car at a time goes by, the tires humming almost like

(Uses simile) the sound of a brook a half mile down in the crease of a

mountain I know—a sound that carries not because it is

loud but because everything else is still.

The lawns shine with a dew not exactly dew. There is

(Includes action) a rabbit bobbing about on the lawn and then freezing. If

it were truly a dew, his tracks would shine black on the

grass, and he leaves no visible track. Yet, there is

something on the grass that makes it glow a depth of

green it will not show again all day. Or is it something

in the dawn air?

(Relies on concrete, specific nouns) Our cardinals know what time it is. They drop pure

tones from the hemlock tops. The black gang of grackles

(Uses metaphor) that makes a slum of the pin oak also knows the time but

can only grate at it. They sound like a convention of

(Uses simile) broken universal joints grating up hill. The grackles

(Appeals to senses) creak and squeak, and the cardinals form tones that only

occasionally sound through the noise. I scatter

sunflower seeds by the birdbath and hope the grackles

won't find them.

(Reveals subjective reaction to cardinals and grackles.)

REVISING DESCRIPTIVE ESSAYS

Read these two versions of three paragraphs from Jessie Sullivan's "If at First You Do Not See . . . ," a student essay that appears later in this chapter in its entirety. Though the rough draft is powerful, Sullivan's revision smooths out rough spots, improves wording, and provides additional detail that makes her writing even more vivid and effective.

Sullivan—Rough Draft

I live in an apartment on the outskirts of New Brunswick, New Jersey. To the right of my building is Robeson Village, a large low-income housing project with about two-hundred apartments facing each other on opposite sides of a wide, asphalt driveway that runs the length of the complex. In this driveway, drug dealers and buyers ⟧ **Wordy?** congregate daily, doing business in front of anyone who cares to watch. Sometimes, children who have witnessed these transactions look over paraphernalia the dealers ⟧ **What kind of paraphernalia?** and their customers have left in their wake.

   To the left of my building is Henry Street, a street that has grown to be synonymous with illegal drugs over the years. It is truly a pathetic sight. The block consists of a half dozen vacant and condemned buildings, ⟧ **If "vacant," how can** all of which are still inhabited by addicts and dealers ⟧ **they be "inhabited"?** who have have set up store there in much the same way a **Wordy?** ⟦ legitimate business owner decides on a particular location where business will be most profitable.

                              . . .

Whose eye? ⟦ To the eye, the community appears to be in a state of depression. Even trees, which traditionally symbolize ⟧ **Make this more vivid?** **What kinds of** ⟦ life and vitality reflect this. Pungent odors are made ⟧ **Make this image** **"pungent odors"?** worse by the stench of rotting food, spilled from **more active,**

overturned garbage cans onto the sidewalk and cooking in | lively?

the heat of the sun.

Sullivan—Final Draft

I live in an apartment on the outskirts of New

Brunswick, New Jersey. To the right of my building is

Robeson Village, a large low-income housing project with

about two-hundred apartments facing each other on

opposite sides of a wide, asphalt driveway that runs the

length of the complex. Here, drug dealers and buyers | Substitutes one word for three

congregate daily, doing business in front of anyone who

cares to watch. Sometimes, children who have witnessed

these transactions look over the crack vials, hypodermic | Adds specific detail to define "paraphernalia"

needles, syringes, and other paraphernalia the dealers

and their customers have left in their wake.

Uses fewer words than original | To the left of my building is Henry Street, which has become synonymous with illegal drugs. It is a pathetic place. The block consists of a half dozen condemned buildings, all of which are lived in or frequented by addicts and dealers. The latter have set | Changes wording to be more accurate

up stores there in much the same way legitimate

Uses fewer words than original | merchants choose locations where they think business will be profitable.

. . .

Adds effective adjective | To the eye of the visitor, the community appears to be in a chronic state of depression. Even trees, symbols of life and vitality, seem to bow their heads in sorrow. Rather than reaching up in praise, their | Uses personification to create a vivid image.

branches are twisted and ill-formed, as if poisoned by ⌋

the very soil in which they are rooted. The pungent

Uses odors of <u>urine</u>, <u>feces</u> and <u>dead</u>, <u>wet</u> leaves are made

specifics

to explain worse by the stench of rotting food, which <u>spills</u> from ⎤ **Uses verbs**

what kinds   **to make**

of odors. overturned garbage cans onto the sidewalk and <u>cooks</u> in ⎥ **image**

active, lively

the heat of the sun.

PRACTICING TECHNIQUES THAT DESCRIBE PLACES AND THINGS

Write a three- or four-sentence paragraph on each of the topics below. You may want to write the rough draft of each paragraph on a piece of scrap paper first, then write the final draft in the spaces provided.

Ways to make your writing rich and vivid are suggested, but use whatever techniques you think will work best.

1. Topic: An eating area in your student center or a reading area in the library.
   Suggestions: Appeal to the senses; include information about people and their behavior.

_____

_____

_____

_____

_____

_____

_____

_____

_____

2. Topic: A wedding or other type of ceremony.
   Suggestions: Describe the people in attendance; use simile or metaphor.

_____

_____

_____

_____

_____

_____

_____

_____

3. Topic: An animal (or type of animal) you like or dislike.
   Suggestions: Use simile, metaphor, or personification; appeal to the senses.

_____

_____

_____

_____

_____

_____

_____

4. Topic: The inside of a coffee shop, bar, restaurant or other small public place.
   Suggestions: Appeal to the senses; include information about people and their
   behavior.

_____

_____

_____

_____

_____

_____

_____

5. Topic: The inside of your car, your bedroom, your family's kitchen, or any other
   room in which you spend a great deal of time.
   Suggestions: Appeal to the senses; use simile.

_____

_____

_____

_____

_____

_____

_____

Enjoy the six selections in this chapter. Each describes its subject in a unique way, but all will show you how to make your writing more vivid, interesting, and moving.

Filling Station

Elizabeth Bishop

Winner of the Pulitzer Prize and the National Book Award, Elizabeth Bishop (1911–1979) grew up in Nova Scotia, Canada, and in Massachusetts. After graduating from Vassar College and traveling in Mexico and Europe, she settled in Florida and later Brazil. Then, she returned to Massachusetts to teach at Harvard University. Her poetry and fiction are filled with brilliant descriptive detail. Bishop was a master painter who described the world with passion and precision.

LOOKING AHEAD

1. The Exxon Corporation was called *Esso* before it changed its name in the 1970s. This poem was published in 1955. The *Esso* trademark is still used in some countries.
2. Mark concrete nouns and vivid adjectives as you read this poem.

VOCABULARY

doily	Decorative woven covering placed on furniture.
extraneous	Unnecessary, inappropriate.
hirsute	Hairy, shaggy.
impregnated	Drenched, soaked, filled with.
marguerites	Daisy-like flowers.
permeated	Saturated, penetrated.
taboret	Stool.
translucency	Quality of being semitransparent, allowing partial light through.

Filling Station | *Elizabeth Bishop*

Oh, but it is dirty!
—this little filling station,
oil-soaked, oil-permeated
to a disturbing, over-all
5   black translucency.
Be careful with that match!

Father wears a dirty,
oil-soaked monkey suit
that cuts him under the arms,
10   and several quick and saucy
and greasy sons assist him
(it's a family filling station),
all quite thoroughly dirty.

Do they live in the station?
15   It has a cement porch
behind the pumps, and on it
a set of crushed and grease-
impregnated wickerwork;
on the wicker sofa
20   a dirty dog, quite comfy.

Some comic books provide
the only note of color—
of certain color. They lie
upon a big dim doily
25   draping a taboret
(part of the set), beside
a big hirsute begonia.

Why the extraneous plant?
Why the taboret?
30   Why, oh why, the doily?
(Embroidered in daisy stitch
with marguerites, I think,
and heavy with gray crochet.)

Somebody embroidered the doily.
35   Somebody waters the plant,
or oils it, maybe. Somebody
arranges the rows of cans
so that they softly say:

ESSO—so—so—so
40   to high-strung automobiles.
Somebody loves us all.

QUESTIONS FOR DISCUSSION

1. Reread the third and fourth stanzas (paragraphs). What concrete nouns do you find in them? What vivid adjectives do you find in these stanzas?
2. Pick out examples of specific detail in stanza 5.
3. Earlier you learned that writers sometimes describe a place by discussing the people in it. What do the people who run the filling station tell us about it?
4. Does Bishop appeal to our sense of hearing? Where?
5. Where in the second stanza does the author use metaphor?

THINKING CRITICALLY

1. Answer the questions that Bishop asks in stanza 5. Start by making notes in the margins.
2. Why doesn't Bishop tell us the color of the begonia in line 27?
3. How would you classify this description: subjective or objective? Explain your answer by making reference to specific words and lines in the poem. Again, begin by making notes in the margins.

SUGGESTIONS FOR JOURNAL ENTRIES

1. Picture in your mind a public place you know well. Pick one that is fairly small, such as a neighborhood grocery, a corner candy store, a filling station, or a classroom. Then, focus on specific sounds, sights, and smells. List as many of these concrete details as you can in your journal. Be objective; do not include details that reveal your feelings about the place.
2. Use freewriting to gather details that would reveal your feelings about a public place such as the one mentioned in Suggestion 1. In fact, if you responded to Suggestion 1, use this opportunity to express your subjective reactions about the place you focused on in that assignment.

From "The Ones Who Walk Away from Omelas"

Ursula Le Guin

Born in Berkeley, California, Le Guin writes short stories, novels, poems, essays, and children's books. She is best known for her works of science fiction and fantasy, types of writing she uses to discuss important human concerns. Her best-known works include The Dispossessed *and* The Lathe of Heaven *as well as* The Farthest Shore, *for which she won a National Book Award in 1973. The selection you will read is the introductory paragraph to a short story.*

LOOKING AHEAD

You know that explaining what happens in a place can reveal a lot about its character or atmosphere. Look for vivid verbs that tell us as much about what Le Guin is describing as do nouns and adjectives.

VOCABULARY

decorous	Dignified, mannerly, refined.
grave	Serious, staid.
lithe	Flexible, limber.
mauve	Shade of deep violet or purple.
restive	Restless, impatient.

*From "The Ones
Who Walk Away
from Omelas"* | Ursula Le Guin

With a clamor of bells that set the swallows soaring, the Festival of Summer came to the city Omelas, bright-towered by the sea. The rigging of the boats in harbor sparkled with flags. In the streets between houses with red roofs and painted walls, between old moss-grown gardens and under avenues of trees, past great parks and public buildings, processions moved. Some were decorous: old people in long stiff robes of mauve and gray, grave master workmen, quiet, merry women carrying their babies and chatting as they walked. In other streets the music beat faster, a shimmering of gong and tambourine, and the people went dancing, the procession was a dance. Children dodged in and out, their high calls rising like the swallows' crossing flights over the music and the singing. All the processions wound towards the north side of the city, where on the great water-meadow called the Green Fields boys and girls, naked in the bright air, with mud-stained feet and ankles and long, lithe arms, exercised their restive horses before the race. The horses wore no gear at all but a halter without bit. Their manes were braided with streamers of silver, gold, and green. They flared their nostrils and pranced and boasted to one another; they were vastly excited, the horse being the only animal who has adopted our ceremonies as his own. Far off to the north and west the mountains stood up half circling Omelas on her bay. The air of morning was so clear that the snow still crowning the Eighteen Peaks burned with white-gold fire across the miles of sunlit air, under the dark blue of the sky. There was just enough wind to make the banners that marked the racecourse snap and flutter now and then. In the silence of the broad green meadows one could hear the music winding through the city streets, farther and nearer and ever approaching, a cheerful faint sweetness of the air that from time to time trembled and gathered together and broke out into the great joyous clanging of the bells.

QUESTIONS FOR DISCUSSION

1. This passage contains many visual details, but Le Guin describes sounds as well. What words does she use to convey sound?
2. Pick out examples of concrete and specific language (nouns and adjectives) that make her writing crisp and clear.
3. This is as much the description of the "Festival of Summer," an event, as it is of "Omelas," a city. What verbs in this passage help Le Guin capture the atmosphere of the festival?
4. Does the author use figurative language? Where? What types?

THINKING CRITICALLY

1. Where in this paragraph does Le Guin create a contrast? In what way does this contrast make her description richer?
2. Le Guin claims that the horse is "the only animal that has adopted our ceremonies as his own." Do you agree? Are there other animals about whom this can be said? Think of examples of human ceremonies that horses or other animals have adopted as their own.

SUGGESTIONS FOR JOURNAL ENTRIES

1. Focus on a festival, fair, parade, or other large gathering you have been to recently where people came to celebrate an occasion or just to have a good time. List details from your senses that would describe both the event and the place in which it was held. Then, make a second list about the variety of people and activities you observed there.
2. Le Guin's paragraph describes sounds and colors well. Think of a place in which you spend a lot of time: for example, the store, office, or factory in which you work; the student center or union; a classroom building; a shopping mall; a park. Use listing or focused freewriting to gather information about what you might see *and* hear on a typical visit to this place.

Subway Station

Gilbert Highet

Gilbert Highet (1906–1978) came to the United States from Scotland in 1937 to teach Greek and Latin at Columbia University in New York City. A witty and urbane writer and speaker, he served as editor of the Book-of-the-Month Club and was chief book reviewer for Harper's Magazine. *He also hosted* People, Places and Books, *a weekly radio talk show, and published hundreds of essays on life in New York City. What Highet describes in "Subway Station" is typical of the thousands of stations in New York's vast underground rail system.*

LOOKING AHEAD

1. The most important thing "Subway Station" shows us is Highet's ability to create a photograph in words by piling detail upon detail. For instance, he makes it a point to tell us that the "electric bulbs" were "meager"; then he adds that they were "unscreened, yellow, and coated with filth." Look for other examples of his ability to do this.

2. Highet is also famous for using figurative language, especially metaphors and similes. As you learned in the introduction to Section Three, one of the most startling of these comes about midway in this selection, when he describes the "gloomy vaulting from which dingy paint was peeling off like scabs from an old wound." Look for and mark other examples of figurative language as you read this piece.

3. "Subway Station" mixes objective with subjective description. When Highet recalls various "advertisement posters on the walls," he remains objective. He does not explain whether he approves or disapproves of them, whether he finds them attractive or distasteful. When he tells us that "the floor was a nauseating dark brown," on the other hand, he is being subjective. Look for other places in which Highet is particularly subjective or objective.

VOCABULARY

abominable	Disgusting, abhorrent.
congealed	Clotted.
defilement	Filth, dirt, object of disgust.
dubious	Unknown.
encrusted	Covered over, encased with a crusty layer.
laden	Covered with.

leprous	Relating to leprosy, a disease in which parts of the body begin to decay and the skin exhibits sores and severe scaling.
meager	Sparse, skimpy.
nauseating	Sickening.
obscenities	Indecent or offensive language.
perfunctory	Apathetic, without care.
relish	Enjoy.
vaulting	Arched or rounded ceiling.

Subway Station | *Gilbert Highet*

Standing in a subway station, I began to appreciate the place—almost to enjoy it. First of all, I looked at the lighting: a row of meager electric bulbs, unscreened, yellow, and coated with filth, stretched toward the black mouth of the tunnel, as though it were a bolt hole in an abandoned coal mine. Then I lingered, with zest, on the walls and ceiling: lavatory tiles which had been white about fifty years ago, and were now encrusted with soot, coated with the remains of a dirty liquid which might be either atmospheric humidity mingled with smog or the result of a perfunctory attempt to clean them with cold water; and, above them, gloomy vaulting from which dingy paint was peeling off like scabs from an old wound, sick black paint leaving a leprous white under-surface. Beneath my feet, the floor was a nauseating dark brown with black stains upon it which might be stale oil or dry chewing gum or some worse defilement; it looked like the hallway of a condemned slum building. Then my eye traveled to the tracks, where two lines of glittering steel—the only positively clean object in the whole place—ran out of darkness into darkness about an unspeakable mass of congealed oil, puddles of dubious liquid, and a mishmash of old cigarette packets, mutilated and filthy newspapers, and the debris that filtered down from the street above through a barred grating in the roof. As I looked up toward the sunlight, I could see more debris sifting slowly downward, and making an abominable pattern in the slanting beam of dirt-laden sunlight. I was going on to relish more features of this unique scene: such as the advertisement posters on the walls—here a text from the Bible, there a half-naked girl, here a woman wearing a hat consisting of a hen sitting on a nest full of eggs, and there a pair of girl's legs walking up the keys of a cash register—all scribbled over with unknown names and well-known obscenities in black crayon and red lipstick; but then my train came in at last, I boarded it, and began to read. The experience was over for the time.

QUESTIONS FOR DISCUSSION

1. In Looking Ahead you were asked to find examples of Highet's ability to pile detail upon detail to create a verbal picture—a photograph in words—of the scene. What examples did you find?
2. What examples of figurative language, other than those mentioned in Looking Ahead, did you find?
3. Do you believe Highet succeeds in conveying an accurate picture? What overall feeling or impression of the station does he communicate?
4. Which of his concrete details contribute to this impression the most? Which nouns and adjectives have the strongest effect on you?
5. As you know, "Subway Station" contains both subjective and objective description. Where does Highet use subjective description (showing his personal feelings or emotional reactions)?

THINKING CRITICALLY

1. Use the left and right margins of the textbook to write questions you might ask Highet about this experience. For example, ask him why he observed the station's walls and ceiling with "zest."
2. Discuss similarities and differences between Highet's "Subway Station" and Bishop's "Filling Station," which also appears in this chapter. As you consider this question, ask yourself what the authors found so fascinating about these less-than-pretty places.

SUGGESTIONS FOR JOURNAL ENTRIES

1. Review your responses to item 1 of the Questions for Discussion. Then write a one-sentence description of a familiar object or place by gathering details (adjectives and nouns) that give the reader a verbal portrait of your subject. For instance, start with an ordinary piece of furniture—perhaps the desk or table you're working on right now—and then begin adding details until you have a list that looks something like this:

The desk
The wooden desk
The large wooden desk
The large brown wooden desk
The large brown wooden desk covered with junk
The large brown wooden desk covered with junk, which squats in the corner of my room

The large brown wooden desk covered with junk, books, and papers, which squats in the corner of my room.

Repeat this process, adding as many items as you can, until you've exhausted your mind's supply of nouns and adjectives. Then review your list. Can you make your description even more specific and concrete? For instance, the above example might be revised to read:

The four-foot-long dark brown oak desk was covered with my math book, an old dictionary with the cover ripped off, two chemistry test papers, today's French notes, a half-eaten bologna sandwich, and a can of diet cola.

2. Choose an object or place you know quite well and can describe easily. Start with a totally objective description; then write down your subjective reactions to it in a sentence or two. Repeat the process with three or four other places or things.

Whenever possible, use a simile, metaphor, or other figure of speech to get your feelings across. For instance, describe the bedroom your brother has failed to clean out in two years as "his private garbage scow," or compare your home computer to an "electronic maze."

If at First You Do Not See . . .

Jessie Sullivan

When Jessie Sullivan began this essay for a college composition class, she wanted simply to tell her readers what her neighborhood looked like. As she revised and developed her work, however, she discovered that the place in which she lived had a vibrant character beyond what the eye can see. Slowly, she expanded and refined her purpose until description became a tool for exploring the sorrow and the promise of her world. Sullivan majors in liberal arts and business. She plans to study business administration in graduate school.

LOOKING AHEAD

1. As you learned in Chapter 3, narration and description can sometimes be used to explain ideas. Sullivan uses description to explain what is wrong with her neighborhood but also to reveal her hope for the people and place she loves.
2. In creating the contrast explained above, Sullivan reveals much about herself: her courage, her vision, and her desire to make a difference.
3. You know that this essay uses both description and contrast. Look for examples as well.

VOCABULARY

bewilderment	Astonishment, confusion.
condone	Make excuses for.
defaced	Made ugly, disfigured.
diversified	Varied, different.
illicit	Illegal, prohibited.
infamous	Dishonorable, known for evil or wrongdoing.
obscenities	Words or drawings that are indecent and offensive.
oppressive	Harsh, severe, hard to bear.
paraphernalia	Gear, equipment used in a particular activity.
pathetic	Pitiful, wretched, miserable.
preconceived notions	Prejudices, opinions formed before having accurate information about something.
sober	Reliable, serious, steady.
superficial	Quick and careless, shallow, on the surface.

If at First You Do
Not See . . .   *Jessie Sullivan*

Alook of genuine surprise comes over some of my classmates when I mention 1
where I live. My neighborhood has a reputation that goes before it. People who
have never been there tend to hold preconceived notions about the place, most of which
are negative and many of which are true. Those who actually visit my neighborhood
usually notice only the filth, the deterioration of buildings and grounds, and the crime.
What they fail to see isn't as apparent, but it is there also. It is hope for the future.

I live in an apartment on the outskirts of New Brunswick, New Jersey. To the right 2
of my building is Robeson Village, a large low-income housing project with about two-
hundred apartments facing each other on opposite sides of a wide, asphalt driveway that
runs the length of the complex. Here, drug dealers and buyers congregate daily, doing
business in front of anyone who cares to watch. Sometimes, children who have witnessed these transactions look over the crack vials, hypodermic needles, syringes, and
other paraphernalia the dealers and their customers have left in their wake.

To the left of my building is Henry Street, which has become synonymous with ille- 3
gal drugs. It is a pathetic place. The block consists of a half dozen condemned buildings,
all of which are lived in or frequented by addicts and dealers. The latter have set up
stores there in much the same way legitimate merchants choose particular locations
where they think business will be profitable.

It is this area, three blocks in radius, that is infamous for illicit drugs, prostitution, 4
and violence of every sort. Known as the "Vil," it is regarded as the city's hub of criminal activity and immorality.

With the growing popularity of crack, the appearance of the community has gotten 5
worse and worse, as if it were on a collision course with destruction. Fences that once
separated one property from another lie in tangled rusted masses on sidewalks, serving
now only as eyesores. Almost all of the buildings are defaced with spray-painted obscenities and other foul messages. Every street is littered with candy wrappers, cardboard
boxes, balled-up newspapers, and broken beer and soda bottles.

But Henry Street is undeniably the worst. The road is so covered with broken glass 6
that the asphalt is barely visible. The way the glass catches the sunlight at every angle
makes the street look almost magical, but there is nothing magical about it. Henry Street is
a dead-end in more than the literal sense. In front of apartment buildings, the overgrown
lawns, which more closely resemble hay than grass, are filled with old tires, cracked televisions, refrigerators and ovens with missing doors, rusted bikes, broken toys, and worn
chairs and tables without legs. Dozens of abandoned cars, their windows shattered and
their bodies stripped of anything of value, line the curbs. The entire block is so cluttered
with refuse that strangers often mistake it for the junk yard, which is five blocks up.

To the eye of the visitor, the community appears to be in a chronic state of depres- 7
sion. Even trees, symbols of life and vitality, seem to bow their heads in sorrow. Rather
than reaching up in praise, their branches are twisted and ill-formed, as if poisoned by
the very soil in which they are rooted. The pungent odors of urine, feces, and dead, wet
leaves are made worse by the stench of rotting food, which spills from overturned
garbage cans onto the sidewalk and cooks in the heat of the sun.

Most people familiar with the neighborhood are aware that the majority of us residents are virtual prisoners in our homes because of the alarming crime rate. Muggings, rapes, and gang-related shootings, many of which do not get reported in newspapers, are commonplace. Many residents live in such fear that they hide in their apartments behind deadbolt locks and chains, daring to peer out of their peepholes only when a frequent gunshot rings out. 8

Many of my neighbors have adopted an I-mind-my-own-business attitude, preferring to remain silent and blind to the goings-on around them. This is the case for so many of them that many nonresidents believe everyone feels this way. Unfortunately, most outsiders learn about our community from people who have been here only once or twice and who leave with unfair and dangerous misconceptions about us. They see the filth and immorality, and that is all they see. They take one quick look and assume none of us cares about the neighborhood or about the way we live. 9

I see my neighborhood from the inside, and I face all of the terrible things I have mentioned on a day-to-day basis. I also see aspects of my community that cannot be appreciated with a superficial first glance. If you look at the place closely, you will find small strong family units, like my own, scattered amid the degeneration and chaos. Working together, struggling to free themselves from oppressive conditions, these families are worth noticing! We are sober, moral people who continue to live our lives according to the laws of society and, more important, according to the laws of God Himself. 10

Look closely and you will find those of us who pick up the trash when we see it scattered on our small lawns, sidewalks, and doorsteps. We discourage our children from disrespecting the area in which they live, and we see to it that they don't litter or deface public property. We emphasize the importance of schooling, and we teach them about the evils of drugs and crime, making certain that they are educated at home as well. 11

Most important, we practice what we preach. We show the children with our actions that we do not condone the immoral and illegal acts around us, and we refuse to take part in any of them. We call the police whenever we hear gunshots, see drug transactions, or learn of any other unlawful activity. The children know that we care and that we are trying to create a brighter future for them. 12

However, the most visible sign of hope is that young people from my neighborhood—and from many neighborhoods like mine, for that matter—are determined to put an end to the destruction of our communities. It angers us that a minute yet very visible group of negative individuals has come to represent the whole. It saddens us that skills, talents, and aspirations, which are so abundant in our communities, should go untapped. Therefore, we have decided to take matters into our own hands; we will get the education we need and solve the problems of our neighborhoods ourselves. 13

Many of us attend the local county college, where we come together often to share ideas for a better future for our community. We also give each other the moral support we need to achieve our educational goals. Our hope binds us together closely and is itself a sign that things will get better. 14

This May, I was proud to see a number of friends receive associate's degrees and get admitted to four-year colleges and universities for advanced degrees. I hope to do the 15 same soon. We are studying for different professions, but no matter how diversified our goals, we will use our knowledge for the benefit of all. This means returning to the community as doctors, lawyers, teachers, entrepreneurs. We will build programs to assist the people of our community directly: day care centers for children with working mothers; family mental and physical health clinics; job-training and placement facilities; legal service centers; youth centers; and drug/alcohol rehabilitation programs. Given the leadership of educated people like those we will become, such facilities can eventually be operated by community residents themselves. Most important, we intend to serve as visible and vocal role models for our children—for the leaders who will follow us and keep our hope alive. Eventually, we will bring about permanent change and make it impossible for a misguided few to represent a proud and productive community.

When friends visit me in my apartment for the first time, they frequently ask in awe 16 and bewilderment, "How can you live in such a bad place?" I always give the same reply: "It isn't where you live, but how you live and what you live for."

QUESTIONS FOR DISCUSSION

1. What does Sullivan mean in paragraph 1 when she says that her "neighborhood has a reputation that goes before it"? Does this statement help introduce what follows in the rest of the essay?
2. Where in this essay does Sullivan include proper nouns? How do they help her achieve her purpose?
3. One reason this essay is so powerful is that it uses specific details. Find examples of these in paragraphs 5 and 6. Then find more examples in any other paragraph of your choice.
4. What image does Sullivan create in paragraph 7? What figure of speech does she use to develop this image?
5. Does action play a role in this essay? What is it?
6. Sullivan mentions her neighbors. How do they help define the neighborhood?
7. What sense other than sight does Sullivan appeal to?
8. When does she make use of illustration (examples)?

THINKING CRITICALLY

1. Why do you think Sullivan bothers to tell us that many shootings never get reported in the newspapers?
2. Summarize Sullivan's central idea in your own words.
3. This is a thought-provoking essay. What questions might you ask Sullivan about herself or her neighborhood if you were able to interview her? (For example, who or what has been her greatest inspiration?) Write your questions in the right- and left-hand margins.

SUGGESTIONS FOR JOURNAL ENTRIES

1. Make a list of the qualities you admire most about the neighborhood in which you live or grew up. Then make another list of ways it might be improved.
2. Use any of the techniques discussed in "Getting Started" to gather information about what your home, neighborhood, or town might look like to someone seeing it for the first time. Then, go beyond appearances and discuss the real character of the place as you know it. In other words, like Sullivan, describe what's on the "inside."
3. Think of a community, a family, or any group of people struggling to grow, improve, or even survive. What makes their life a struggle? What hope do you see for this place or these people?

A Deathly Call of the Wild

Mary Ann Gwinn

Mary Ann Gwinn was among several reporters at the Seattle Times *who wrote about the effects of the Exxon Valdez oil spill on Prince William Sound in 1989. Their stories were so penetrating that they won a Pulitzer Prize in journalism.*

Gwinn's article shows that, in the right hands, description has uses beyond pure observation. In some ways, "A Deathly Call of the Wild" is the kind of writing scientists do: it explains a serious problem by carefully recording the effects of that problem. At the same time, Gwinn uses what she saw to persuade us that we have a lot to learn from nature. However we look at it, she proves that description is a powerful tool for many purposes.

LOOKING AHEAD

1. "A Deathly Call of the Wild" is an example of narration and description working together. Gwinn tells us what she observed on a trip to Prince William Sound. An expert reporter, she also includes a great many direct quotes from people she spoke with. You will learn more about using quoted material and other narrative techniques in Section Four.

2. Although writing straight news stories demands objectivity, journalists are permitted a more subjective approach in columns, human-interest stories, or feature articles like this one.

VOCABULARY

cause célèbre	Important cause or issue.
compelling	Urgent, demanding.
compulsively	Involuntarily, as if being forced or compelled.
havoc	Ruin, destruction.
intermittently	Now and again.
lacerated	Cut, torn, scraped.
mournful	Sad, heartbreaking.
plumage	Feathers.
provoke	Cause, bring about, induce.
pruned	Trimmed, clipped.
rationality	Reason, intelligence.
sinuous	Curved.
vain	Useless, futile.
vengeance	Revenge.
wreaked	Caused.

A Deathly Call of the Wild

| Mary Ann Gwinn

VALDEZ, Alaska—I had tried to prepare myself for Green Island, but nothing can 1
prepare you for the havoc wreaked on the creatures of Prince William Sound.

From the helicopter that took me there, the 987-foot tanker Exxon Valdez, stuck 2
like a toy boat on Bligh Reef, was dwarfed by the immensity of the sound. It was hard to
believe that we could fly 60 miles, land and walk right into the ruination of a landscape,
so far from that broken boat.

The helicopter landed on the beach of Green Island. Its beaches are broad and slope 3
gently, in contrast to the rocky, vertical shores of many of the other islands in the sound.
For that reason, Green Island is favored by wildlife. Now the oil has turned the gentle
beach into a death trap.

No sooner had the Alaska National Guard helicopter roared away than a black lump 4
detached itself from three or four others bobbing in the oil-streaked water. It was an
old squaw, a sea bird normally recognizable by its stark black-and-white plumage. The
tuxedo plumage had turned a muddy brown and orange.

It staggered up the beach, its head compulsively jerking back and forth, as if trying 5
to escape the thing that was strangling it. Tony Dawson, a photographer for Audubon
magazine, and I watched it climb a snowbank and flap into the still center of the woods.
"They move up into the grass, along the creek beds and into the woods, where they
die," Dawson said. "It's like they're fleeing an invisible enemy."

Dawson used to be a veterinarian. He said documenting the oil spill makes him feel 6
like a photographer in Vietnam: "Every day, a new body count." As in that war, heli-
copters drone across the sky, boats beach on shore, men land, size up the situation and
depart.

Eleven days into the spill, scientists are trying to decide which beaches to clean and 7
which to leave alone, reasoning that disruption would hurt some more than it would
help. Very little actual beach cleanup is taking place. Most of the animals are going to
die, a few dozen or hundred every day, by degrees.

I walked along the beach, which in some places was glutted with oil like brown 8
pudding; in others, streaked and puddled with oil the consistency of chocolate syrup.
The only sounds came from a few gulls and the old squaw's mate, which drifted down
the polluted channel toward its fate. Far away, a cormorant spread its wings and
stretched in a vain attempt to fluff its oil-soaked feathers. A bald eagle passed overhead.

It was then that I heard a sound so strange, for a brief moment all my 20th century 9
rationality dropped away.

Something was crying in the vicinity of the woods, a sound not quite human. I 10
looked into the trees.

Whooooooh. Whooooh. Whoooh. Up and down a mournful scale. Something is 11
coming out of those woods, I thought, and is going to take vengeance for this horror on
the first human being it sees.

Then I saw a movement in the grass at the end of the beach. It was a loon. 12

Loons have become something of a cause célèbre to bird lovers. They are beautiful 13
birds, almost as large as geese, with long, sharp beaks, striking black-and-white striped

wings and a graceful, streamlined head. They are a threatened species in the United States because they need large bodies of water to fish in and undeveloped, marshy shorelines to nest on, and most shoreline in this country has been landscaped and pruned.

The most compelling thing about the loon is its call—something between a cry, a 14 whistle and a sob, a sound so mournful and chilling it provoked the word "loony," a term for someone wild with sorrow, out of their head.

This was an artic loon in its winter plumage, brown instead of the striking black 15 and white of summer. It had ruby-red eyes, which blinked in terror because it could barely move. It was lightly oiled all over—breast, feet, wings, head—destroying its power of flight. Its sinuous head darted here and there as we approached. It flapped and stumbled trying to avoid us, and then it came to rest between two large rocks.

As Dawson photographed it, it intermittently called its mournful call. Its mate swam 16 back and forth, calling back, a few yards offshore.

I could see it tremble, a sign that the bird was freezing. Most oiled birds die because 17 the oil destroys their insulation.

"It's like someone with a down coat falling into a lake," Dawson explained. The 18 breeze ruffled its stiffening feathers. As Dawson moved closer with the camera, it uttered a low quivering cry.

After 10 minutes or so, I just couldn't watch anymore. It was so beautiful, and so 19 helpless and so doomed. We had nothing like a bag, sack or cloth to hold it in. I walked around the point.

Then I heard Dawson calling. He walked into view holding the furious, flapping 20 loon by its upper wings, set it down on the grass and said, "Come here and help me. He won't hurt you."

I was stunned by the rough handling of such a wild thing, but it developed that 21 Dawson, the former veterinarian, knew his birds. He had grasped the loon exactly in the place where his wings would not break. He would tell me later that most bird rescuers are too tender-hearted or frightened of birds to contain them, and let a lot of salvageable birds get away.

We had to wait for the helicopter, and Dawson had to take more pictures, so I 22 grasped the loon behind the upper wings, pinning them together, and took up the loon watch. The bird rose, struggled and fell back to earth, then was still.

I was as afraid of the loon as it was of me in a way that touching a totally wild thing 23 can provoke. But I began to feel its strength. It was warm, it had energy, and it could still struggle. I could hear it breathing, and could feel its pulse. It turned its red eye steadily on me. We breathed, and waited, together.

Dawson returned, took a black cord from a lens case and neatly looped it around 24 the bird's wings. The helicopter dropped out of the sky and settled on the beach. I held the string as the loon, unblinking, faced the terrific wind kicked up by the machine. Then Dawson neatly scooped up the bird and settled into the helicopter. The loon lashed out with its needle beak until David Grimes, a fisherman working with the state on the spill, enveloped it in a wool knit bag he carried with him. The bird stilled.

Dawson and I were both streaked with oil and blood from the loon's feet, lacerated 25 by barnacles on the beach. He gave me a small black and white feather that had fallen from the bird's wing.

We took the loon to the bird-rescue center in Valdez. I don't know if it will live. 26
Dawson thought it had a good chance. I thought of the mate we had left behind in the
water.

Afterward, we talked about whom bird rescues help more, the rescued or the res- 27
cuer. Most rescued birds don't make it. And tens of thousands more from the Valdez
spill will die before they even get a chance.

I know only that the loon told me something that no one other thing about this 28
tragedy could. If only we could learn to value such stubborn, determined life. If only
we could hold safe in our hands the heart of the loon.

QUESTIONS FOR DISCUSSION

1. What makes Gwinn's description of the loon's call disturbing? Why does she say it is "not quite human" (paragraph 10)? Why does she bother to define the word "loony" (paragraph 14)?
2. What is it about the loon's appearance that makes its cry even more "mournful"?
3. To which sense besides sight and hearing does Gwinn appeal?
4. Identify effective verbs she uses to reveal the tragedy in Prince William Sound. Why does she explain how she and her companion reacted; why doesn't she simply focus on the birds?
5. What examples of analogy did you find? How about comparison or contrast?
6. If the article is about the loon, why does Gwinn talk about the "old squaw," the cormorant, and other birds?
7. Does the image in paragraph 23 prepare us for the conclusion of this essay? In what way?

THINKING CRITICALLY

1. Explain what the author is suggesting when she wonders "whom bird rescues help more, the rescued or the rescuer" (paragraph 27).
2. Reread paragraph 28. What has the author learned from the loon?
3. What is the purpose of this essay? Does it go beyond criticizing civilization's assault on the natural environment?

SUGGESTIONS FOR JOURNAL ENTRIES

1. We don't need to fly to Prince William Sound to see pollution, nor can we say that protecting nature is the responsibility of big oil companies alone. Focus on a natural scene near your home or campus—a hillside, forest, lake, park, seashore—whose beauty is diminished because of what careless individuals have done. Are there beer bottles, paper bags, and cigarette wrappers around? Have people carved their initials in trees or spray-painted large rocks? Does the water contain old tires or other junk instead of fish, birds, and other wildlife? Can you hear car horns and loud radios? Brainstorm about this place, if possible with someone else who has been there. Gather details that show the effects of human irresponsibility on the environment you are describing.
2. Have you ever had to help an animal in trouble? Think about a lost dog or cat, an injured bird, or even a larger animal like a cow, sheep, or horse that needed assistance. Use listing or focused freewriting to gather details that (1) describe the animal; (2) explain where, when, and how you tried to help it; and (3) reveal

how both you and it reacted to the problem. For inspiration, reread some of the more moving paragraphs in Gwinn's article, especially paragraph 23.

3. The essay's title is particularly effective. Think back to a time when you found yourself in a wilderness: a forest, mountain range, desert, large state or national park. How did you react to what you saw, heard, felt, and so on? What word best describes your reaction to being there: "excitement," "uneasiness," "fear," "terror," "contentment," "peacefulness," "happiness," "boredom," "discomfort"? Use any method for gathering information discussed in "Getting Started" to begin describing this "wild" place and to explain how you felt about being there.

In the Jungle

Annie Dillard

Born in Pittsburgh in 1945, Annie Dillard worked at Harper's Magazine *from 1973 to 1981 as a contributing editor. Before she was thirty, she had won a Pulitzer Prize for* Pilgrim at Tinker Creek, *a narrative about the Roanoke Valley of Virginia, where she once lived. She has also written a book of poetry entitled* Tickets for a Prayer Wheel.

In 1982 she published Teaching a Stone to Talk, *an anthology of essays, which includes "In the Jungle." In this essay, Dillard describes a jungle village she visited while traveling in Ecuador, South America.*

LOOKING AHEAD

1. Paragraph 3, some of which is quoted in the introduction to this chapter, shows that Dillard enriches her description of the jungle by using verbs that show action. Look for such verbs in other parts of the essay as well.
2. Ecuador is located on the western coast of South America between Colombia and Peru. The Andes Mountains dominate the landscape of Ecuador, but in the eastern portion are jungles through which flow tributaries of the Amazon, the world's second longest river. The Napo is one of these tributaries, or "headwaters."
3. The official language of Ecuador is Spanish, but the Indians speak Quechua or Jarva. The predominant religion is Roman Catholicism.
4. In paragraph 3, Dillard writes: "It was February, the middle of summer." That's not a misprint. When North America is experiencing winter, it's summer in South America.

VOCABULARY

canopies	Coverings or kinds of roofs.
goiters	Swellings of the thyroid, a gland found in the neck.
illumined	Lit up.
impaled	Stuck upon.
Jesuit	Order of Roman Catholic priests.
muted	Quieted, muffled.
nightjar	Jungle bird that is active at night.
opaque	Not reflecting light, dull.
Orion	Constellation.
recorder	Musical instrument resembling a flute.
roil	Stir and become muddy.

swath	Patch.
thatch	Leaves, grasses, reeds, or other natural building materials used as roofing and sometimes as siding.
uncanny	Strange, unexplainable.
wistful	Sweetly sad, melancholic.

In the Jungle | *Annie Dillard*

L ike any out-of-the-way place, the Napo River in the Ecuadorian jungle seems   1
real enough when you are there, even central. Out of the way of *what?* I was
sitting on a stump at the edge of a bankside palm-thatch village, in the middle of the
night, on the headwaters of the Amazon. Out of the way of human life, tenderness, or
the glance of heaven?

A nightjar in deep-leaved shadow called three long notes, and hushed. The men   2
with me talked softly in clumps: three North Americans, four Ecuadorians who were
showing us the jungle. We were holding cool drinks and idly watching a hand-sized
tarantula seize moths that came to the lone bulb on the generator shed beside us.

It was February, the middle of summer. Green fireflies spattered lights across the air   3
and illumined for seconds, now here, now there, the pale trunks of enormous, solitary
trees. Beneath us the brown Napo River was rising, in all silence; it coiled up the sandy
bank and tangled its foam in vines that trailed from the forest and roots that looped the
shore.

Each breath of night smelled sweet, more moistened and sweet than any kitchen, or   4
garden, or cradle. Each star in Orion seemed to tremble and stir with my breath. All at
once, in the thatch house across the clearing behind us, one of the village's Jesuit priests
began playing an alto recorder, playing a wordless song, lyric, in a minor key, that
twined over the village clearing, that caught in the big trees' canopies, muted our talk on
the bankside, and wandered over the river, dissolving downstream.

This will do, I thought. This will do, for a weekend, or a season, or a home.   5

Later that night I loosed my hair from its braids and combed it smooth—not for   6
myself, but so the village girls could play with it in the morning.

We had disembarked at the village that afternoon, and I had slumped on some   7
shaded steps, wishing I knew some Spanish or some Quechua so I could speak with the
ring of little girls who were alternately staring at me and smiling at their toes. I spoke
anyway, and fooled with my hair, which they were obviously dying to get their hands
on, and laughed, and soon they were all braiding my hair, all five of them, all fifty fingers, all my hair, even my bangs. And then they took it apart and did it again, laughing,
and teaching me Spanish nouns, and meeting my eyes and each other's with open
delight, while their small brothers in blue jeans climbed down from the trees and began
kicking a volleyball around with one of the North American men.

Now, as I combed my hair in the little tent, another of the men, a freelance writer   8
from Manhattan, was talking quietly. He was telling us the tale of his life, describing
his work in Hollywood, his apartment in Manhattan, his house in Paris. . . . "It makes
me wonder," he said, "what I'm doing in a tent under a tree in the village of Pompeya,
on the Napo River, in the jungle of Ecuador." After a pause he added, "It makes me
wonder why I'm going *back*."

The point of going somewhere like the Napo River in Ecuador is not to see the most   9
spectacular anything. It is simply to see what is there.

What is there is interesting. The Napo River itself is wide (I mean wider than the   10
Mississippi at Davenport) and brown, opaque and smeared with floating foam and logs
and branches from the jungle. White egrets hunch on shoreline deadfalls and parrots in

flocks dart in and out of the light. Under the water in the river, unseen, are anacondas—which are reputed to take a few village toddlers every year—and water boas, stingrays, crocodiles, manatees, and sweet-meated fish.

Low water bares gray strips of sandbar on which the natives build tiny palm-thatch 11 shelters, arched, the size of pup tents, for overnight fishing trips. You see these extraordinarily clean people (who bathe twice a day in the river, and whose straight black hair is always freshly washed) paddling down the river in dugout canoes, hugging the banks.

Some of the Indians of this region, earlier in the century, used to sleep naked in 12 hammocks. The nights are cold. Gordon MacCreach, an American explorer in these Amazon tributaries, reported that he was startled to hear the Indians get up at three in the morning. He was even more startled, night after night, to hear them walk down to the river slowly, half asleep, and bathe in the water. Only later did he learn what they were doing: they were getting warm. The cold woke them; they warmed their skins in the river, which was always ninety degrees; then they returned to their hammocks and slept through the rest of the night.

The riverbanks are low, and from the river you see an unbroken wall of dark forest 13 in every direction, from the Andes to the Atlantic. You get a taste for looking at trees: trees hung with the swinging nests of yellow troupials, trees from which ant nests the size of grain sacks hang like black goiters, trees from which seven-colored tanagers flutter, coral trees, teak, balsa and breadfruit, enormous emergent silk-cotton trees, and the pale-barked *samona* palms.

When you are inside the jungle, away from the river, the trees vault out of sight. It 14 is hard to remember to look up the long trunks and see the fans, strips, fronds, and sprays of glossy leaves. . . . Butterflies, iridescent blue, striped, or clear-winged, thread the jungle paths at eye level. And at your feet is a swath of ants bearing triangular bits of green leaf. The ants with their leaves look like a wide fleet of sailing dinghies—but they don't quit. In either direction they wobble over the jungle floor as far as the eye can see.

Long lakes shine in the jungle. We traveled one of these in dugout canoes, canoes 15 with two inches of freeboard, canoes paddled with machete-hewn oars chopped from buttresses of silk-cotton trees, or poled in the shallows with peeled cane or bamboo. Our part-Indian guide had cleared the path to the lake the day before; when we walked the path we saw where he had impaled the lopped head of a boa, open-mouthed, on a pointed stick by the canoes, for decoration.

The lake and river waters are as opaque as rain-forest leaves; they are veils, blinds, 16 painted screens. You see things only by their effects. I saw the shoreline water roil and the sawgrass heave above a thrashing *paichi,* an enormous black fish of these waters; one had been caught the previous week weighing 430 pounds. Piranha fish live in the lakes, and electric eels. I dangled my fingers in the water, figuring it would be worth it.

We would eat chicken that night in the village, and rice, yucca, onions, beets and 17 heaps of fruit. The sun would ring down, pulling darkness after it like a curtain. Twilight is short, and the unseen birds of twilight wistful, uncanny, catching the heart. The two nuns in their dazzling white habits—the beautiful-boned young nun and the warm-faced old—would glide to the open cane-and-thatch schoolroom in darkness, and start the children singing. The children would sing in piping Spanish, high-pitched and pure; they would sing "Nearer My God to Thee" in Quechua, very fast. (To reciprocate, we sang for them "Old MacDonald Had a Farm"; I thought they might recognize the animal sounds. Of course they thought we were out of our minds.) As the children became excited by their own singing, they left their log benches and swarmed around the nuns, hopping, smiling at us, everyone smiling, the nuns' faces bursting in their cowls, and the clear-voiced children still singing, and the palm-leafed roofing stirred.

The Napo River: it is not out of the way. It is in the way, catching sunlight the way 18 a cup catches poured water; it is a bowl of sweet air, a basin of greenness, and of grace, and, it would seem, of peace.

QUESTIONS FOR DISCUSSION

1. Dillard mentions some terms that may be unfamiliar to you. From the way she uses them, take a guess at the meaning of "egrets," "anacondas," "manatees," "troupials," "tanagers," and "machete."
2. The author says little about how the Indians looked, but she does explain what they did. In what paragraphs does she tell us about the natives of Pompeya, and what do these anecdotes reveal about them?
3. Why does Dillard bother to mention in paragraph 12 that "the Indians get up at three in the morning" to bathe in the river? Does this help her describe the jungle?
4. Besides the Indians, what inhabitants of the village does Dillard mention? What is her opinion of these other people?
5. Which paragraph in this selection do you find most descriptive? Identify nouns, adjectives, and figures of speech that make it work so well.
6. Where in the essay does Dillard use proper nouns? Pick out a few examples of such words and explain why their inclusion makes "In the Jungle" more effective.
7. As noted earlier, Dillard makes excellent use of descriptive verbs in paragraph 3. Where else did you find such verbs?

THINKING CRITICALLY

1. Overall, the author sees the jungle as lovely and pleasant. Yet, she also includes details that show us a different side of this place. Find and mark such information in the text. In the margins, write notes that explain what these details reveal about the jungle.
2. How does the last paragraph of this essay relate to the first? Has Dillard used any of the methods for introducing and concluding essays discussed in Chapter 3? Which ones?

SUGGESTIONS FOR JOURNAL ENTRIES

1. Think of a natural setting (for example, a park, forest, garden, seashore) that you visited recently, and list its most pleasant (or unpleasant) aspects. Then, in one or two sentences, sum up your overall reaction to (or impression of) the place.
2. Dillard isn't very specific about what the Indians of Pompeya look like, but she gives us enough details to infer certain things about them. Given the climate, for instance, they probably wear little clothing. Try to describe what these people look like from what the author tells us about them. If you run into trouble, use your imagination and make up details that you think might apply.

SUGGESTIONS FOR SUSTAINED WRITING

1. After reading Bishop's "Filling Station" you might have written in your journal about a public place you know well. The suggestions after this poem asked you to collect specifics about a fairly small place such as a neighborhood grocery, a corner candy store, or a filling station.

   Expand your journal notes into the rough draft of an essay that describes your subject objectively. When you rewrite this draft, add details and ideas that reveal your subjective reactions (feelings) about the place as well. Write three or four drafts, each time adding information to make the essay vivid, clear, and convincing. For example, include details that appeal to the senses. If possible, describe the people who frequent this place, and explain what goes on there.

   When you revise your introduction, make sure it contains a thesis statement that clearly indicates how you feel about your subject. Here's an example: *Consuelo's Coffee Corner is my safe haven.* Then, make sure your essay contains details about *Consuelo's Coffee Corner* that will show why you consider it a *safe haven.* Write a conclusion that looks to the future or contains a memorable quotation—perhaps from someone you met at this place.

   At the end of the process, read your best draft. Correct distracting errors in grammar and mechanics, and make certain it is easy to read.

2. Le Guin describes Omelas by telling us what happens in that city during the Festival of Summer. Write a letter inviting out-of-town friends to a fair, festival, parade, carnival, picnic, or other celebration in your town or school. Persuade them to visit by mentioning the exciting sights, sounds, smells, and tastes of the affair. But don't forget to enrich your description with action; describe events they might want to watch or take part in. If you are writing about a Fourth of July celebration, for example, recall the fun of a softball game at last year's picnic or describe the fireworks that ended the day.

   Begin this assignment by looking over the journal notes you made after reading Le Guin's paragraph. You might be able to use this information in your first draft. To make your writing vivid and convincing, add details and figures of speech as you develop ideas from one draft to the next. When deciding how to open or close your letter, consider methods for writing introductions or conclusions discussed in Chapter 4.

   In any case, edit your letter well. If you respect your friends, you will send them something that is clear, correct, and easy to read.

3. Highet describes a subway station both objectively and subjectively. Think of a public place you visit often, such as a bus or train station, the post office, your church or temple, a ball park, a movie theater, a gymnasium, or a shopping mall. Perhaps you have collected information about this place in your journal. Now, write an essay that describes it fully and explains how you feel about it.

   In your first draft, use details that will give readers an objective picture of your subject: talk about its size and shape, the colors of the walls, the furniture it contains, the people who frequent it. In your next draft(s), add other information about what it looks, sounds, smells, and, if possible, feels like. As you do this, begin revealing your subjective reactions. Like Highet, use concrete details, vivid verbs, adjectives and adverbs, and figures of speech to let readers know whether you enjoy the place, find it attractive, and like the people you meet there—or whether the opposite is true.

After completing your second or third draft, write a thesis statement expressing your overall opinion. Put that thesis into an introductory paragraph that captures the readers' attention. Close your essay with a memorable statement or with a summary of the reasons you are or are not looking forward to visiting this place again. Finally, edit your work by checking grammar, spelling, word choice, and other important considerations.

4. If you read "If at First You Do Not See . . . ," follow Sullivan's lead: describe a place you know well by presenting two views of it. For example, one view might be negative, the other positive. Another way to proceed is to describe what newcomers see when they visit this place as opposed to what you see in it. A good place to describe might be your neighborhood or other part of your hometown, your high school or college campus, a run-down but beautiful old building, or the home of an interesting relative or friend.

While your paper need not be as long as Sullivan's, it should use techniques like those found in hers. For example, appeal to the senses, include action, use figures of speech to create images, or describe the people who live in or frequent the place.

Check the journal entries you made after reading Sullivan's essay. They might help you get started. Once you have finished several drafts, write an introduction that captures the readers' attention and expresses your central idea in a formal thesis statement. Put the finishing touches on your writing by correcting errors that will reduce its effectiveness or distract your readers.

5. The three journal suggestions following Gwinn's "A Deathly Call of the Wild" provide good starts for longer assignments.

If you responded to item 1, turn your notes into an essay about the effects of pollution on a natural setting you know well. Explain how civilization has marred or destroyed its beauty, and don't be afraid to give your subjective reaction to what you see, hear, and so on. A good way to begin is to use a startling remark or to contrast what *is* with what *should be*. A good way to conclude is to make a call to action.

If you responded to item 2 in the Suggestions for Journal Entries after Gwinn's essay, use this information to write about an incident in which you had to help an animal in trouble. Explain what happened, describing the animal and the scene vividly and concretely. Like Gwinn, however, focus on one thing: what you learned about the animal, about yourself, *or* about your relationship with nature. In fact, summarize what the experience taught you in your thesis statement.

If you responded to suggestion 3, continue the description of a "wild" place by explaining how you reacted to being there. Again, express the central idea that all of your essay's details will support in a thesis statement. In other words, use your thesis to tell readers how you felt about the experience. Then, in the rest of the essay, include information about the place that will show why you felt that way.

Good luck. Any of these suggestions can lead to an exciting essay. Whichever one you choose, follow a careful process of revising and editing to produce a paper that is well developed, vivid, and free of errors.

6. Annie Dillard and Mary Ann Gwinn draw inspiration from nature. Review the journal notes you made after reading their essays. You have probably put down details and ideas that you can use in a paper describing an outdoor setting like a beach, park, garden or backyard, wood, desert, mountainside, or jungle. Add to these notes by doing more prewriting in your journal. Then turn them into an essay that explains your subjective reaction to the place.

Begin by writing a preliminary thesis statement that sums up that reaction clearly. Here are two examples:

> I never felt more frightened than when I camped overnight at Willow Creek.
> What we saw and heard while hiking in the Cascade Mountains showed us how exciting nature can be.

In the body of your essay, use techniques you learned in this chapter to describe the place and to reveal your reaction to it. But remember to focus on the main point in your thesis. If you want to show how *frightened* you were, describe sights, sounds, and the like; tell of events; and create figures of speech that express your fear. Don't include details about how expensive your trip was or how much fun you had swimming in a cold stream on a hot afternoon.

After completing your first draft, revise the thesis if necessary. Next, write an introduction—if you haven't done so already—in which to place the thesis. Then, decide on a conclusion.

Again, remember that writing is a process. Don't hand in a final version until you have completed several drafts, each one building on, adding to, and refining the one that came before.

DESCRIBING PEOPLE

In Chapter 8, you learned that writers often go beyond physical appearance when describing a place or thing; they reveal its character as well. This is even more true when people are the subjects of description. Writers describe gardens at dawn, summer festivals, or dirty subway stations because they are impressed by what that they see, hear, and so on. More often than not, they describe human beings because they are fascinated by their personalities, values, and motivations as well as by their looks and the sounds of their voices. Of course, many writers start by describing physical appearance—what's on the outside. But they often end up talking about their subjects' characters—what's on the inside.

All the authors represented in this chapter use concrete and specific details (nouns and adjectives) to describe the physical characteristics of their subjects. This is always a good way to begin. You can start off by explaining something about your subjects' physical appearance, the clothes they wear, the sound of their voices, the language they use, or simply the way they walk. Such description might also help you introduce your subjects' personalities to your readers, for someone's physical appearance can reveal a great deal about what he or she is like inside.

You can also communicate a great deal about the people you're describing by telling your reader what you've heard about them from others and even what you've heard them say about themselves; such information is usually conveyed through dialogue (quoted material). Recalling anecdotes about your subjects is still another good way to convey important information about them. Finally, some authors comment directly on their subjects' personalities or use figurative language to make their descriptions more lively and appealing. Remember such techniques when you gather and communicate important information about your subjects.

DESCRIBING YOUR SUBJECT'S APPEARANCE AND SPEECH

Physical appearance can show a great deal about a person's character, and writers don't hesitate to use outward details as signs or symbols of what's inside. For instance, how often have you heard people mention deep-set, shifty eyes or a sinister smile when describing a villain? Aren't heavy people often described as jolly? And often, aren't the clothes people wear or the way they comb their hair seen (fairly or unfairly) as a sign of their character?

Carl Sandburg uses physical appearance to reveal the complexity and depth of Abraham Lincoln's character. Here's just one example you will find when you read Sandburg's portrait of the sixteenth President later in this chapter:

In his eyes as nowhere else was registered the shifting light of his moods; their language ran from rapid twinkles of darting hazel that won the hearts of children on to a fixed baffling gray that the shrewdest lawyers and politicians could not read, to find there an intention he wanted to hide.

As you will see later, Sandburg does a good job of describing Lincoln's face and body, and he even talks about the kind of clothes he wore and the way he combed his hair. But he doesn't limit himself to the President's looks. He also recreates the sound of his voice. To show that Lincoln was a man of the frontier, for example, Sandburg tells us that he pronounced the word "idea" more like "idee."

Another good way to provide insight into someone's personality is to recall what he or she says. In "Mothers and Fathers," for example, Phyllis Rose quotes her mother directly to show that, despite losing her husband and nearly all her eyesight, this woman retains her spunk and sense of humor. When the author praises her mother on being able to apply lipstick perfectly despite her poor vision, the seventy-five-year-old "beauty" replies: "By now I should know where my mouth is."

REVEALING WHAT YOU KNOW ABOUT YOUR SUBJECT

You have learned that narrating events helps capture the character or atmosphere of a place you are describing. Similarly, you can reveal a lot about someone by discussing his or her actions or behavior. One of the best ways to do this is by telling anecdotes, brief stories that highlight or illustrate an important aspect of your subject's personality. For example, Sandburg demonstrates Lincoln's sensitivity and "natural grace" through a story about his open expression of grief at a friend's funeral. Anecdotes like this help us understand how someone reacts to various people, problems, and situations. They say a lot about a person's attitude toward life.

Another good way to reveal character is to tell readers important facts about your subject's life, home, or family. In "Two Gentlemen of the Pines," for example, we learn that Bill's parents abandoned him as a child and that, except for some help from neighbors, he survived alone. This information goes a long way toward accounting for his shyness. In the same selection, we are treated to a good look at the house and yard of Fred Brown, a picture that gives us a more complete understanding of the old man's character than simply learning what he looks or talks like.

REVEALING WHAT OTHERS SAY ABOUT YOUR SUBJECT

One of the quickest ways to learn about someone is to ask people who know this individual to tell you about his or her personality, lifestyle, morals, disposition, and so on. Often, authors use dialogue or quotations from other people to reveal something important about their subject's character. In "Crazy Mary," student Sharon Robertson combines physical description (concrete details) with information she learned from other people (dialogue) to create a memorable and disturbing portrait of an unfortunate woman she once knew:

> She was a middle-aged woman, short and slightly heavy, with jet-black hair and solemn blue eyes that were bloodshot and glassy. She always looked distant, as if her mind were in another place and time, and her face lonely and sad. We called her "Crazy Mary."
>
> Mary came to the diner that I worked in twice a week. She would sit at the counter with a scowl on her face and drink her coffee and smoke cigarettes. The only time she looked happy was when an old song would come on the radio. Then Mary would close her eyes, shine a big tobacco-stained smile, and sway back and forth to the music.
>
> One day an elderly couple came in for dinner. They were watching Mary over their menus and whispering. I went over to their table and asked if they knew who she was. The old man replied, "Aw, dat's just old Mary. She's loonier than a June bug, but she ain't nutten to be afraid of. A few years back, her house caught fire and her old man and her kids got kilt. She ain't been right since."
>
> After hearing this, it was easy to understand her odd behavior.

Other people can make good sources of information. We know from experience, however, that what others say about a person is often inaccurate. Sometimes, in fact, different people express very different—even contradictory—opinions about the same person. In "Abraham Lincoln," Carl Sandburg tells us that some folks saw Lincoln as a cold and crafty politician, others as a "sad, odd, awkward man," and still others as a "superb human struggler."

VISUALIZING DETAILS THAT DESCRIBE PEOPLE

The two short selections that follow use techniques important to describing people. The first, by Dr. Richard Selzer, describes the physical appearance of an AIDS patient in Haiti. The second, by Jade Snow Wong, describes the personality of a man who works in a factory that is run by the author's family and that doubles as their home.

MIRACLE BY RICHARD SELZER

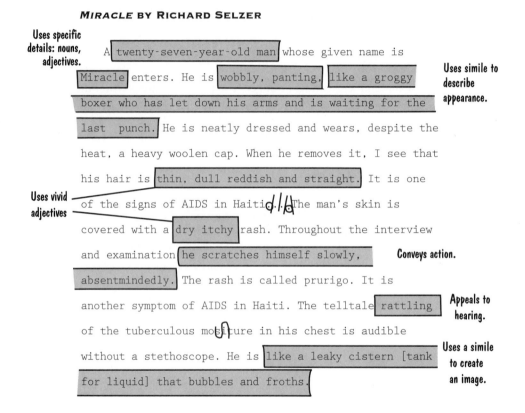

Uses specific details: nouns, adjectives.

A twenty-seven-year-old man whose given name is Miracle enters. He is wobbly, panting, like a groggy boxer who has let down his arms and is waiting for the last punch. He is neatly dressed and wears, despite the heat, a heavy woolen cap. When he removes it, I see that his hair is thin, dull reddish and straight. It is one of the signs of AIDS in Haiti. The man's skin is covered with a dry itchy rash. Throughout the interview and examination he scratches himself slowly, absentmindedly. The rash is called prurigo. It is another symptom of AIDS in Haiti. The telltale rattling of the tuberculous moisture in his chest is audible without a stethoscope. He is like a leaky cistern [tank for liquid] that bubbles and froths.

Uses simile to describe appearance.

Uses vivid adjectives

Conveys action.

Appeals to hearing.

Uses a simile to create an image.

UNCLE KWOK BY JADE SNOW WONG

Recalls a recurring action that tells us about Kwok's personality.

After Uncle Kwok was settled in his chair, he took off his black, slipperlike shoes. Then taking a piece of stout cardboard from a miscellaneous pile which he kept in a box near his sewing machine, he traced the outline of his shoes on the cardboard. Having closely examined the blades of his scissors and tested their sharpness, he would cut out a pair of cardboard soles, squinting critically

Uses vivid adjectives to create an image.

through his inaccurate glasses. Next he removed from both

shoes the cardboard soles he had made the day before and

inserted the new pair. Satisfied with his inspection, he

got up, disposed of the old soles, and returned to his

machine. He had not yet said a word to anyone.

Reveals an important aspect of his personality.

Daily this process was repeated.

Describes his clothing as a clue to his personality.

The next thing Uncle Kwok always did was to put on

his own special apron, homemade from double thicknesses

of heavy burlap and fastened at the waist by strong

denim ties. This long apron covered his thin, patched

trousers and protected him from dirt and draft. After a

half hour had been consumed by these chores, Uncle Kwok

was ready to wash his hands. He sauntered into the Wong

Uses a vivid verb.

kitchen, stationed himself at the one sink which served

both family and factory, and with characteristic

meticulousness [care], now proceeded to clean his hands

and fingernails.

It was Mama's custom to begin cooking the evening

meal at this hour, but every day she had to delay her

preparations at the sink until slow-moving Uncle Kwok's

Recalls an action to describe Kwok.

last clean fingernail passed his fastidious [close]

inspection. One day, however, the inconvenience tried

her patience to its final limit.

Trying to sound pleasantly persuasive, she said,

Explains what someone else thinks of Kwok.

"Uncle Kwok, please don't be so slow and awkward. Why

don't you wash your hands at a different time, or else

wash them faster?"

Uncle Kwok loudly protested $\not{d}./.|.||$ "Mama, I am not

awkward. The only awkward thing about my life is that it

has not yet prospered!" And he strode off, too hurt even

to dry his hands, finger by finger, as was his custom.

> **Allows Kwok to reveal himself in his own words.**

REVISING DESCRIPTIVE ESSAYS

Below are the rough and final drafts of paragraphs from Maria Scamacca's "Oma: Portrait of a Heroine" an essay that describes her husband's grandmother. The complete essay can be found in this chapter. Scamacca knew she was on to something when she wrote a rough draft, but she felt she owed her subject her best effort. Therefore, she revised her essay several times, making excellent use of the descriptive techniques discussed in this and in the previous chapter. If you still have doubts about the importance of revising, compare these two drafts.

Scamacca—Rough Draft

How old? How much over-weight?

When I first met Oma, she looked very old and a bit over-weight. She wore a house dress, an apron, and

Add details?

loafers. She was deaf in one ear, and there was something wrong with the muscles in her face. Oma

What was wrong?

Good, but make more vivid?

shuffled when she walked and had to hold on to the furniture. Despite her disability, and the fact that she lived alone, Oma's house looked neat, but there were signs that her eyes had become weak.

Clarify? What signs?

. . .

Oma was born in Hungary. She was an only child— $\overset{1}{\underset{M}{\frown}}$

What days?

rare in those days. Her mother died when she was in her teens, and she was left alone. At eighteen, she married a widower with a young daughter; the couple eventually had three other children. They lived on a farm near the Rumanian border. Farm life was hard, but Oma took to it well. In addition to cooking and housekeeping, she did

Does this information reveal her personality?

other chores. She often told me how she force-fed geese
by stuffing balls of bread down their long necks.

Scamacca—Final Draft

Provides specifics; makes description more accurate, vivid.

When I first met Oma six years ago, she looked about
eighty years old, was a few pounds over-weight for her
medium frame, and was slightly hunched over. She wore a
flowered house dress, a starched white apron, and old,
scuffed leather loafers. Oma was deaf in one ear from a

Adds specific details.

"Shows" what was wrong.

neglected childhood ear infection, and half of her face
drooped from Bell's palsy. She shuffled her feet and

Explains kind of childhood she had.

held on to the furniture with swollen, scarred hands as
she walked. Despite Oma's disability and the fact that

Adds vivid details.

she lived alone, her house looked neat, but there were
small crumbs and stains on the tables, and particles of
food were stuck to some of the dishes, unnoticed by eyes
weakened with age.

Adds details to clarify what was meant by "signs" that her eyes had become weak.

. . . .

Oma was born in Hungary. She was an only child—
rare in the early days of this century—the only
surviving baby of four pregnancies. Her mother died when

Explains "those days."

Author has added so much information about Oma's personality that she must create 2 paragraphs.

Oma was in her teens, and she was left alone to keep
house for her father. At eighteen, she married a widower
with a young daughter; the couple eventually had three
other children. They lived on a farm near the Rumanian
border on which they grew and raised all their food,
even the grapes from which they made their own wine.

Shows that she has been a hard worker from childhood.

Adds detail to show she is self-sufficient.

Farm life was hard, but Oma took to it well. In

addition to cooking and housekeeping, she had to tend to
the horses and other farm animals, bake bread, make
sausage, and salt the meats the family would eat year

Adds concrete details that make ideas more convincing.

round. Oma was fond of telling me how she force-fed
geese by stuffing balls of bread down their long necks
with her fingers. Her geese got so fat they couldn't
fly, but they brought the best prices at the market, she
often reminds me.

Allows Oma to speak for herself, to reveal her pride.

PRACTICING TECHNIQUES THAT DESCRIBE PEOPLE

1. Write a paragraph that describes your physical appearance. Include details that appeal to the senses and try to use figures of speech. Be specific about your height, weight, hair color, eye color, and so on. Write the rough draft on scratch paper. Put your final draft on the lines below.

_____

_____

_____

_____

_____

_____

_____

_____

_____

2. Write a paragraph that describes your best or worst quality. For example, discuss your patience or impatience, your tolerance or lack of tolerance for differences in people, your ambition or laziness, or your knack for making or losing friends. Show readers what you mean by using examples and by recalling what others have said about you. Write the rough draft on scratch paper. Put your final draft on the lines below.

_____

_____

_____

_____

_____

_____

_____

_____

3. How do others see you? Write a paragraph that explains how someone you know well would describe your best or worst quality. Focus on only one aspect of your personality. Use any of the techniques for describing you have learned so far. Write the rough draft on scratch paper. Put your final draft on the lines below.

_____

_____

_____

_____

_____

_____

_____

_____

_____

Enjoy the selections that follow. Each contains examples of the practices discussed above, and each provides additional hints to help you make your writing stronger and more interesting.

Photograph of My Father in His Twenty-second Year

Raymond Carver

Born in Clatskanie, Oregon, Raymond Carver (1938–1988) was a writer of fiction and poetry and winner of several major literary prizes including a National Book Award. He taught English and creative writing at UCLA, the University of Iowa's Writer's Workshop, the University of Texas at El Paso, Syracuse University, and Goddard College in Vermont. He is best remembered for Cathedral, *a collection of short stories that was nominated for a Pulitzer Prize. His last work was* A New Path to the Waterfall, *a book of poetry completed just before he died.*

Looking Ahead

1. This is both a physical and psychological portrait. Try to figure out what the physical details that Carver includes tell us about his father's personality.
2. At the end of the poem, Carver reveals things about himself. Ask yourself why he does this.

Vocabulary

bluff	Confident, arrogant.
cocked	Tilted or turned up.
dank	Damp, humid.
hearty	Robust, cheerful.
perch	Freshwater fish.
posterity	Descendants, future generations.

Photograph of My Father in His Twenty-second Year | Raymond Carver

October. Here in this dank, unfamiliar kitchen
I study my father's embarrassed young man's face.
Sheepish grin, he holds in one hand a string
of spiny yellow perch, in the other
a bottle of Carlsbad beer.   5

In jeans and denim shirt, he leans
against the front fender of a 1934 Ford.
He would like to pose bluff and hearty for his posterity,
wear his old hat cocked over his ear.
All his life my father wanted to be bold.   10

But the eyes give him away, and the hands
that limply offer the string of dead perch
and the bottle of beer. Father, I love you,
yet how can I say thank you, I who can't hold my liquor either,
and don't even know the places to fish?   15

QUESTIONS FOR DISCUSSION

1. What details does Carver reveal about his father's appearance?
2. Which of these details tell us about his personality?
3. In certain places, Carver interprets the picture from his own point of view. In line 2, for example, he describes his father's face as "embarrassed." Find other places where he does this.
4. Why is it important for us to know what Carver's father is holding?
5. What do we learn about Carver's father in line 14?
6. What has the information in line 15 to do with Carver's father?

THINKING CRITICALLY

1. Why can't Carver tell his father "I love you"? What else can we conclude from this short poem about the relationship between the poet and his father?
2. Why does Carver bother to tell us that the kitchen was "dank" and "unfamiliar"?

SUGGESTIONS FOR JOURNAL ENTRIES

1. Study a photograph of yourself that is at least three years old. Use listing to gather information that will help describe the kind of person you were when the photograph was taken.
2. Study a photograph of a member of your family or a close friend. Use listing or answer the journalists' questions to record information about this person's appearance and character.

From "Mothers and Fathers"

Phyllis Rose

A biographer, literary critic, and essayist, Phyllis Rose is the author of a life of British novelist Virginia Woolf. She has also published in Vogue, The Atlantic, *and* The Washington Post. *The two paragraphs that make up this selection are taken from an essay Rose wrote for "Hers," a regular column of* The New York Times Magazine.

LOOKING AHEAD

1. Like Carver's "Photograph of My Father . . . ," this selection includes some physical description, but its primary purpose is to describe the subject's personality. Identify techniques explained earlier in this chapter as you read Rose's description of her mother.
2. In paragraph 1, the author tells us her mother used the Latin saying "De gustibus non disputandum est." Translated literally, this means that taste is not something to be disputed.

VOCABULARY

enhancer	Something that increases, improves, or intensifies something else.
glaucoma	Eye disease that can result in blindness.

From "Mothers and |
Fathers" | **Phyllis Rose**

M y mother has always said: "The daughters come back to you eventually. When 1
the sons go they're gone." She has other favorite sayings—"A father's not a
mother," "The beginning is the half of all things," and "De gustibus non disputandum
est," which she translated as "That's what makes horse races"—all of which have
become increasingly meaningful to me with time. Recently I told her that she was right
in a fight we had twenty-seven years ago about which language I should study in high
school. This came up because I had just had the same discussion with my son and took
the side my mother took then (French). She laughed when I told her that she was right
twenty-seven years ago. There have been more and more nice moments like that with
my mother as we both grow older.

She is seventy-five, ash blond, blue-eyed, a beauty. When my father died three years 2
ago she suddenly developed glaucoma and lost a lot of her vision. She says she literally
"cried her eyes out." She can read only very slowly, with the help of a video enhancer
supplied by the Lighthouse for the Blind. Nevertheless, her lipstick is always perfect.
She doesn't use a mirror. She raises her hand to her lips and applies it. When I praise her
for this, she says, "By now I should know where my mouth is."

QUESTIONS FOR DISCUSSION

1. Other than quoting the subject directly, what technique for revealing character do you see here?
2. Why is quoting what Rose's mother says about daughters a good way to begin?
3. The author explains that her mother's sayings "have become increasingly meaningful to [her] with time." What does this tell us about their relationship?

THINKING CRITICALLY

1. This is a relatively short passage, yet Rose packs a lot of information into it. Write a paragraph or two in which you describe the kind of person you would discover had you the pleasure of meeting Rose's mother.
2. Compare this piece with Carver's "Photograph of My Father . . . ." In what ways are these selections similar? Then compare Rose's portrait of her mother with Hayden's "Those Winter Sundays," which appears in Chapter 4. In what ways are these two pieces different?

SUGGESTIONS FOR JOURNAL ENTRIES

1. Rose obviously loves and honors her mother for a variety of reasons. Use focused freewriting to write a paragraph or two about a parent, a grandparent, or other older relative whom you love and honor. For now, describe this person by focusing on the one personality trait in him or her that you admire most.
2. Think of a favorite saying your mother, your father, or another relative uses. Explain what it means and what it tells you about the person who uses it.

Two Gentlemen of the Pines*

John McPhee

A productive writer with a wide range of interests, John McPhee has been a long-time essayist for The New Yorker *magazine. Among his latest books are* Rising from the Plains *(1986) and* The Control of Nature *(1989). One of the things McPhee does best is to describe the human character. His portraits of people he meets on his travels are among the most memorable in contemporary American literature. McPhee ran into two of his most interesting subjects on a trip through New Jersey's Pine Barrens, a wilderness whose name he used as the title of a book from which this selection is taken.*

LOOKING AHEAD

1. You know that we can learn a lot about people from what they say. This is very true of Fred, the first of McPhee's subjects, but less true of Bill. Nonetheless, the little that Bill lets slip out provides good clues to his personality.
2. McPhee describes the setting in which he meets his subjects; doing so helps enrich their portraits.

VOCABULARY

cathode ray tubes	Television picture tubes.
dismantled	Taken apart.
eyelets	Holes through which laces can pass.
gaunt	Lean, thin, angular.
mallet	Heavy hammer with a short handle.
poacher	Someone who uses another's land to hunt or fish there illegally.
thong	Strip of leather used as a lace.
"turfing it out"	Digging out the top layer of soil and grass.
understory	Underbrush.
undulating	Changing, varying, fluctuating.
vestibule	Small room at the entrance to a building.
visored	Having a long brim that shades the sun.

*Editor's title

Two Gentlemen of the Pines*

John McPhee

Fred Brown's house is on an unpaved road that curves along the edge of a wide cranberry bog. What attracted me to it was the pump that stands in his yard. It was something of a wonder that I noticed the pump, because there were, among other things, eight automobiles in the yard, two of them on their sides and one of them upside down, all ten years old or older. Around the cars were old refrigerators, vacuum cleaners, partly dismantled radios, cathode-ray tubes, a short wooden ski, a large wooden mallet, dozens of cranberry picker's boxes, many tires, an orange crate dated 1946, a cord or so of firewood, mandolins, engine heads, and maybe a thousand other things. The house itself, two stories high, was covered with tarpaper that was peeling away in some places, revealing its original shingles, made of Atlantic white cedar from the stream courses of the surrounding forest. I called out to ask if anyone was home, and a voice inside called back, "Come in. Come in. Come on the hell in."

I walked through a vestibule that had a dirt floor, stepped up into a kitchen, and went on into another room that had several overstuffed chairs in it and a porcelain-topped table, where Fred Brown was seated, eating a pork chop. He was dressed in a white sleeveless shirt, ankle-top shoes, and undershorts. He gave me a cheerful greeting and, without asking why I had come or what I wanted, picked up a pair of khaki trousers that had been tossed onto one of the overstuffed chairs and asked me to sit down. He set the trousers on another chair, and he apologized for being in the middle of his breakfast, explaining that he seldom drank much but the night before he had had a few drinks and this had caused his day to start slowly. "I don't know what's the matter with me, but there's got to be something the matter with me, because drink don't agree with me anymore," he said. He had a raw onion in one hand, and while he talked he shaved slices from the onion and ate them between bites of the chop. He was a muscular and well-built man, with short, bristly white hair, and he had bright, fast-moving eyes in a wide-open face. His legs were trim and strong, with large muscles in the calves. I guessed that he was about sixty, and for a man of sixty he seemed to be in remarkably good shape. He was actually seventy-nine. "My rule is: Never eat except when you're hungry," he said, and he ate another slice of the onion.

In a straight-backed chair near the doorway to the kitchen sat a young man with long black hair, who wore a visored red leather cap that had darkened with age. His shirt was coarse-woven and had eyelets down a V neck that was laced with a thong. His trousers were made of canvas, and he was wearing gum boots. His arms were folded, his legs were stretched out, he had one ankle over the other, and as he sat there he appeared to be sighting carefully past his feet, as if his toes were the outer frame of a gunsight and he could see some sort of target in the floor. When I had entered, I had said hello to him, and he had nodded without looking up. He had a long, straight nose and high cheekbones, in a deeply tanned face that was, somehow, gaunt. I had no idea whether he was shy or hostile. Eventually, when I came to know him, I found him to be as shy a person as I have ever had a chance to know. His name is Bill Wasovwich, and he lives alone in a cabin about half a mile from Fred. First his father, then his mother left him when he was a young boy, and he grew up depending on the help of various people in the pines. One of them, a cranberry grower, employs him and has given him some acreage, in which Bill is building a small cranberry bog of his own, "turfing it out" by hand. When he is not working in the bogs, he goes roaming, as he puts it, setting out cross-country on long, looping journeys, hiking about thirty miles in a typical day, in search of what he calls "events"—surprising a buck, or a gray fox, or perhaps a poacher or a man with a still. Almost no one who is not native to the pines could do this, for the woods have an undulating sameness, and the understory—huckleberries, sheep laurel, sweet fern, high-bush blueberry—is often so dense that a wanderer can walk in a fairly tight circle and think that he is moving in a straight line. State forest rangers spend a good part of their time finding hikers and hunters, some of whom have vanished for days. In his long, pathless journeys, Bill always emerges from the woods near his cabin—and about when he plans to. In the fall, when thousands of hunters come into the pines, he sometimes works as a guide. In the evenings, or in the daytime when he is not working or roaming, he goes to Fred Brown's house and sits there for hours. The old man is a widower whose seven children are long since gone from Hog Wallow, and he is as expansively talkative and worldly as the young one is withdrawn and wild. Although there are fifty-three years between their ages, it is obviously fortunate for each of them to be the other's neighbor.

QUESTIONS FOR DISCUSSION

1. What do details about Fred's and Bill's physical appearances say about them?
2. Think about the way the older man welcomes his visitor. How do such actions reveal his character?
3. The original shingles on Fred's house are made of cedar "from the stream courses of the surrounding forest" (paragraph 1). In what way is this and other information about the house helpful to understanding Fred?
4. Does Fred's claiming there is "something the matter" with him explain the way he views himself?
5. Bill says he goes into the woods in search of "events." What are these events? Should the author have used a synonym for this word instead of quoting Bill directly? Why or why not?

THINKING CRITICALLY

1. Why is it important for us to learn about Bill's childhood? In a short paragraph that uses information from "Two Gentlemen of the Pines," explain how learning about Bill the child helps us to understand Bill the man.
2. Pretend that you accompanied McPhee into the Pines. What would have been your reaction to Fred and Bill? Reread this selection and make notes in the margins to explain what you might have said or done in response to various events you read about. For example, how would you have reacted to meeting Fred in his undershorts?

SUGGESTIONS FOR JOURNAL ENTRIES

1. As this selection shows, we can learn a lot about people from the places they call home. Use listing to begin describing a place you consider your own: your room, your kitchen, your garage, the inside of your car, for example. You might even describe a place—public or private, indoors or out of doors—that you enjoy visiting. Gather details that show how this place reflects your personality or that explain what draws you to it time and again.
2. Have you ever taken a trip and come upon strangers you found interesting because they were different from most people you know? Use focused freewriting to explain why they captured your attention.
3. McPhee accounts for Bill's shyness by explaining that his parents abandoned him. Do you know someone who experienced an event or set of circumstances that marked his or her personality? Interview this person; learn what in his or

her past contributed to a particular characteristic or personality trait. Say your great uncle is thrifty. When you interview him, you find that he was orphaned at age eight, that he lived many years in poverty, and that he is afraid of being poor again. Good subjects for this assignment include anyone with a distinctive personality trait and a willingness to talk about his or her past.

Oma: Portrait of a Heroine

Maria Scamacca

Maria Scamacca graduated from college with a degree in nursing and is now a critical-care registered nurse at a large hospital. "Oma: Portrait of a Heroine" was written in a freshman composition class in response to an assignment that asked students to describe people they found inspiring. After reading Scamacca's essay, it is easy to understand why she chose to write about Oma.

LOOKING AHEAD

1. *Oma* means grandmother in Hungarian; *Opa* means grandfather.
2. You have learned that description and narration often appear together. Here, stories from Oma's life help shed light on her character.
3. Scammaca mentions events from 20th-century history. During World War II (1939–1945), the Germans conquered much of eastern Europe but were pushed back by the Soviets. At the war's end, Hungary, Rumania, East Germany and other eastern nations became Soviet satellites. In the Korean War (1950–1953), American troops formed the bulk of a United Nations force that defended South Korea from communist North Korea and China.

VOCABULARY

black market	Underground commercial system in which banned or stolen goods are sold or traded.
compensation	Payment.
displaced	Forced to move.
equivalent	The equal of.
humane	Kind, charitable, benevolent.
implores	Begs.
palsy	Paralysis.
provisions	Necessities, supplies.

Oma: Portrait of a Heroine

Maria Scamacca

When I first met Oma six years ago, she looked about eighty years old, was a few 1
pounds over-weight for her medium frame, and was slightly hunched over.
She wore a flowered house dress, a starched white apron, and old, scuffed leather loafers.
Oma was deaf in one ear from a neglected childhood ear infection, and half of her face
drooped from Bell's palsy. She shuffled her feet and held on to the furniture with swollen,
scarred hands as she walked. Despite Oma's disability and the fact that she lived alone,
her house looked neat, but there were small crumbs and stains on the tables, and particles
of food were stuck to some of the dishes, unnoticed by eyes weakened with age.

That's why I was shocked when she led me through the back door to a garden that 2
she boasted of planting and maintaining alone. It was like no garden I had ever seen, an
acre of food and beauty. Ready to be picked and eaten were neat and orderly rows of
potatoes, carrots, asparagus, onions, peppers, lettuce, lima beans, and string beans. Her
garden also boasted strawberries, blueberries, gooseberries, currant, peach trees, water-
melons, and many other fruits. And there were flowers everywhere: zinnias, day lilies,
marigolds, irises, and petunias. I sensed immediately that this paradise was the creation
of a unique energy, courage, and beauty I came to see in Oma.

Each year the impossible garden yields bushels of fruits and berries for the jams and 3
jellies that Oma cooks and jars herself. She also cans fruit and vegetables, and she uses the
fruit in the fillings of luscious pastries that, as I was to learn, have made her famous
among friends, family, and neighbors. She still does all of her own cooking and had been
known, until only recently, to throw holiday dinners for more than twenty people.

From the day I met Oma, I grew to admire her and have looked forward to visiting. 4
Almost every Sunday after church, my husband's family and I gather around her dining
room table for fresh coffee, homemade Prinz Regent Torte (a seven-layer cake),
Schwarzwälder Kirschtorte (Black Forest cherry cake), warm cookies, and good talk.

Oma dominates the conversation, filling us with stories of her childhood and of 5
World War II; she hardly stops to take a breath unless one of us asks a question or
implores her to translate the frequent German or Hungarian phrases that pop out of her
mouth. At such times, we play guessing games as Oma tries to explain in broken English
a word or expression for which she knows no English equivalent.

Oma was born in Hungary. She was an only child—rare in the early days of this 6
century—the only surviving baby of four pregnancies. Her mother died when Oma was
in her teens, and she was left alone to keep house for her father. At eighteen, she married
a widower with a young daughter; the couple eventually had three other children. They
lived on a farm near the Rumanian border on which they grew and raised all their food,
even the grapes from which they made their own wine.

Farm life was hard, but Oma took to it well. In addition to cooking and house- 7
keeping, she had to tend to the horses and other farm animals, bake bread, make
sausage, and salt the meats the family would eat year round. Oma is fond of telling me
how she force-fed geese by stuffing balls of bread down their long necks with her fingers. Her geese got so fat they couldn't fly, but they brought the best prices at the market, she often reminds me.

Her family also raised their own pigs. But when it came time to slaughter the ani-   8
mals, her husband, Opa, asked his neighbor to do it. In return, Opa slaughtered the
neighbor's pigs. "He felt bad, you know, killing his own pig," Oma said. At times, Oma
and Opa hired outside help, whom they paid with bread and salted meat, but they did
most of the work themselves, and they prospered.

Then the war came. First her horses were stolen by Russian soldiers. Then the fam-   9
ily was removed from their farm, and Oma found herself in a Russian concentration
camp. The stories from this period of her life are confusing. I have heard bits and pieces
of them repeatedly over the past six years, and I have had to reconstruct them myself.
Once in a while I ask Oma to clarify the order of events, but she doesn't get very far
until she starts an entirely new story.

After the war, the borders of countries were redrawn, and Oma's family was dis-   10
placed with only a few hours' notice. Allowed to take only the clothes on their backs
and whatever they could carry, they were put into a cattle car on a long freight train. The
new government provided no compensation for their land and told them to leave all of
their possessions behind. The only explanation was that their family had originally come
from Germany and that they were required to leave Hungary and return to the land of
their ancestors. This was not punishment, the authorities explained; it was "humane
displacement."

Before they boarded the train, the family had to collect enough grain and other pro-   11
visions to feed themselves during the long trip. But they saw little of their food; Oma
thinks it was stolen and sold on the black market. "There were no bathrooms on the
train," Oma explained. "If someone had to defecate or urinate, they were held by others
out of the open doors over the side of the moving train. And they call that humane!"

When they arrived in Germany, Oma and her family were placed in a room in a   12
run-down building that had holes in the walls and was full of rats. Her husband developed pneumonia. Sick for months, he almost lost the will to live and just lay in bed.
When he finally recovered, they moved to America, but they had to leave their daughter
behind because she had tuberculosis. Oma still weeps openly whenever she recalls being
forced to abandon her child. Luckily, however, things turned out well for "Tante Vicki,"
who still lives in Germany and now has a family of her own.

In time, the family settled in Millstone, New Jersey, and began to build a new life in   13
what was then a small rural community. In the early 1950s, however, Oma and Opa
lost their oldest son in the Korean War, so when the other two boys married and moved
out of the house, the two old people were on their own.

Several years ago, Opa died of lung cancer contracted from many years of working   14
in an asbestos factory. Oma continues to receive a good pension and health benefits
from his employer. They come in handy, for over the past few years she has been hos-
pitalized several times. Last summer she got so sick she couldn't even plant her garden,
so all of her grandchildren got together to plant it for her. That is the only request she
has ever made of us.

It is hard to see a woman who was once so strong grow old and weak. At times,   15
Oma feels quite useless, but she can still tell wonderful stories, and we listen avidly. I
wonder if there will be a garden this year.

QUESTIONS FOR DISCUSSION

1. What is Scamacca's thesis?
2. Where does the author use details that describe Oma's physical appearance? Do any of these details provide hints about her character?
3. Explain what two or three incidents from Oma's life tell us about her personality.
4. What does Oma reveal about herself?
5. Why does Scamacca tell us about Opa in paragraphs 8 and 12? How does this information help describe Oma?
6. This essay makes fine use of concrete and specific details. Pick out such details in at least two paragraphs.
7. What techniques for writing introductions does Scammaca use? (Review Chapter 4 if you need to.)
8. What technique for writing conclusions does she use? (Review Chapter 4 if you need to.)
9. In Oma, the author sees "energy, courage, and beauty." In what ways is Oma beautiful?

THINKING CRITICALLY

1. If you were able to meet Oma, what would you ask her about her life? As you reread this essay, write questions to her in the margins of the text when they occur to you. Then do some creative guessing. Based upon what you know about Oma, answer your questions in a paragraph or two.
2. Pretend that the government has decided to take almost everything you own and to send you to another country. Would you resist? If so, how? If not, how would you prepare for this drastic change?
3. Reread Maria Cirilli's "Echoes" in Chapter 1. In what ways is this essay similar to Scamacca's? In what ways are these essays different?

SUGGESTIONS FOR JOURNAL ENTRIES

1. Do you have an older relative, friend, or neighbor whose attitude toward life you consider heroic? Choose your own definition of the word *heroic*. Freewrite for about five minutes about an event from this person's life that might show his or her heroism.
2. Interview the person mentioned above. Try to find out more about his or her attitude toward life. A good way to do this is to ask your subject to tell you about a difficult or depressing time and to explain how he or she dealt with it. Record your subject's comments as accurately as you can; use direct quotations when appropriate.
3. Brainstorm with one or two others who know the person mentioned above. Try to gather facts, direct quotations, and opinions that you could use in a paper that describes your subject as heroic.

Abraham Lincoln

Carl Sandburg

One of America's best-loved poets and biographers, Carl Sandburg (1878–1967) had a deep respect for common folk, and he filled his work with images from their simple and sometimes tragic lives. He is remembered chiefly for Corn Huskers *and for* The People, Yes, *a collection of poems published during the Great Depression. He is also known for his six-volume biography of Abraham Lincoln, for which he won one of his three Pulitzer Prizes.*

The following excerpt, from Abraham Lincoln: The Prairie Years, *describes Lincoln at age thirty-seven, about the time he left New Salem, Illinois, and his job as postmaster, lawyer, and storekeeper to enter the U.S. Congress (1847–1849). For a time, Lincoln had served in the Illinois legislature in Springfield, where he certainly would not have won the "best-dressed" award. For Sandburg, however, there's more to a person than his clothing; therefore, he goes well beyond appearances to reveal the inner strength and nobility of our sixteenth President.*

Another selection by Sandburg appears in Chapter 11.

L OOKING A HEAD

1. Sandburg uses a number of interesting anecdotes [brief, sometimes humorous stories] from Lincoln's life to illustrate something about his personality. Look for such anecdotes as you read through this piece.
2. The author also uses specific and concrete details in this early portrait of Lincoln. Many have to do with his physical appearance—his height, the way his eyes looked, the shape of his nose and cheeks, for example. Ask yourself what Lincoln's physical appearance tells you about his character.
3. Sandburg explains in paragraph 1 that by the time Lincoln was thirty-seven, he "had changed with a changing western world." In the 1840s Illinois and Kentucky were still considered the "west." But this concept was changing fast as the United States pushed its borders toward the Pacific. Nonetheless, as the author tells us, there was still a great deal of the simple frontiersman in Lincoln, the *central* idea that ties this essay together and gives it focus.

V OCABULARY

angular	Thin and bony.
broadcloth	Plain, tightly woven wool cloth.
buckskin breeches	Pants made of deer hide.
cravat	Necktie.
dejection	Emotional depression.

falsetto	Tone much higher than the normal range of men's voices.
granitic	Hard as granite.
gravity	Seriousness.
melancholy	Sadness.
modulations	Variations.
niche	Nook, place.
pretenses	False shows.
resolve	Steadfastness, determination.
shambled	Shuffled, walked lazily.

Abraham Lincoln | Carl Sandburg

The thirty-seven-year-old son of Thomas Lincoln and Nancy Hanks Lincoln had changed with a changing western world. His feet had worn deer-skin moccasins as a boy; they were put into rawhide boots when he was full-grown; now he had them in dressed calf leather. His head-cover was a coonskin cap when he was a boy, and all men and boys wore the raccoon tail as a high headpiece; floating down the Mississippi to New Orleans he wore a black felt hat from an eastern factory and it held the post-office mail of New Salem; now he was a prominent politician and lawyer wearing a tall, stiff, silk hat known as a "stovepipe," also called a "plug hat."

In this "stovepipe" hat he carried letters, newspaper clippings, deeds, mortgages, checks, receipts. Once he apologized to a client for not replying to a letter; he had bought a new hat and in cleaning out the old hat he missed this particular letter. The silk stovepipe hat was nearly a foot high, with a brim only an inch or so in width; it was a high, lean, longish hat and it made Lincoln look higher, leaner, more longish.

And though Lincoln had begun wearing broadcloth and white shirts with a white collar and black silk cravat, and a suggestion of sideburns coming down three-fourths the length of his ears, he was still known as one of the carelessly dressed men of Springfield. . . .

The loose bones of Lincoln were hard to fit with neat clothes; and, once on, they were hard to keep neat; trousers go baggy at the knees of a story-teller who has the habit, at the end of a story, where the main laugh comes in, of putting his arms around his knees, raising his knees to his chin, and rocking to and fro. Those who spoke of his looks often mentioned his trousers creeping to the ankles and higher; his rumpled hair, his wrinkled vest. When he wasn't away making speeches, electioneering or practicing law on the circuit, he cut kindling wood, tended to the cordwood for the stoves in the house, milked the cow, gave her a few forks of hay, and changed her straw bedding every day.

He looked like a farmer, it was often said; he seemed to have come from prairies and barns rather than city streets and barber shops; and in his own way he admitted and acknowledged it; he told voters from the stump that it was only a few years since he had worn buckskin breeches and they shrank in the rain and crept to his knees leaving the skin blue and bare. The very words that came off his lips in tangled important discussions among lawyers had a wilderness air and a log-cabin smack. The way he pronounced the word "idea" was more like "idee," the word "really" more like a drawled Kentucky "ra-a-ly."

As he strode or shambled into a gathering of men, he stood out as a special figure for men to look at; it was a little as though he had come farther on harder roads and therefore had longer legs for the traveling; and a little as though he had been where life is stripped to its naked facts and it would be useless for him to try to put on certain pretenses of civilization.

The manners of a gentleman and a scholar dropped off him sometimes like a cloak, and his speech was that of a farmer who works his own farm, or a lawyer who pails a cow morning and evening and might refer to it incidentally in polite company or in a public address. He was not embarrassed, and nobody else was embarrassed, when at the Bowling Green funeral he had stood up and, instead of delivering a formal funeral address on the character of the deceased, had shaken with grief and put a handkerchief to his face and wept tears, and motioned to the body-bearers to take his dead friend away. There was a natural grace to it; funerals should be so conducted; a man who loves a dead man should stand up and try to speak and find himself overwhelmed with grief so that instead of speaking he smothers his face in a handkerchief and weeps. This was the eloquence of naked fact beyond which there is no eloquence.

Standing, Lincoln loomed tall with his six feet, four inches of height; sitting in a 8 chair he looked no taller than other men, except that his knees rose higher than the level of the seat of the chair. Seated on a low chair or bench he seemed to be crouching. The shoulders were stooped and rounded, the head bent forward and turned downward; shirt-collars were a loose fit; an Adam's apple stood out on a scrawny neck; his voice was a tenor that carried song-tunes poorly but had clear and appealing modulations in his speeches; in rare moments of excitement it rose to a startling and unforgettable falsetto tone that carried every syllable with unmistakable meaning. In the stoop of his shoulders and the forward bend of his head there was a grace and familiarity so that it was easy for shorter people to look up into his face and talk with him.

The mouth and eyes, and the facial muscles running back from the mouth and eyes, 9 masked a thousand shades of meaning. In hours of melancholy, when poisons of dejection dragged him, the underlip and its muscles drooped. . . . [However,] across the mask of his dark gravity could come a light-ray of the quizzical, the puzzled. This could spread into the beginning of a smile and then spread farther into wrinkles and wreaths of laughter that lit the whole face into a glow; and it was of the quality of his highest laughter that it traveled through his whole frame, currents of it vitalizing his toes.

A fine chiseling of lines on the upper lip seemed to be some continuation of the 10 bridge of the nose, forming a feature that ended in a dimple at the point of the chin. The nose was large; if it had been a trifle larger he would have been called big-nosed; it was a nose for breathing deep sustained breaths of air, a strong shapely nose, granitic with resolve and patience. Two deepening wrinkles started from the sides of the right and left nostrils and ran down the outer rims of the upper lip; farther out on the two cheeks were deepening wrinkles that had been long crude dimples when he was a boy; hours of toil, pain, and laughter were deepening these wrinkles. From the sides of the nose, angular cheek-bones branched right and left toward the large ears, forming a base for magnificently constructed eye-sockets. Bushy black eyebrows shaded the sockets where the eyeballs rested. . . . In his eyes as nowhere else was registered the shifting light of his moods; their language ran from rapid twinkles of darting hazel that won the hearts of children on to a fixed baffling gray that the shrewdest lawyers and politicians could not read, to find there an intention he wanted to hide.

The thatch of coarse hair on the head was black when seen from a distance, but 11 close up it had a brownish, rough, sandy tint. He had been known to comb it, parting it far on the right side, and slicking it down so that it looked groomed by a somewhat particular man; but most of the time it was loose and rumpled. The comb might have parted it either on the far right or on the far left side; he wasn't particular.

It was natural that Abraham Lincoln was many things to many people; some 12 believed him a cunning, designing lawyer and politician who coldly figured all his moves in advance; some believed him a sad, odd, awkward man trying to find a niche in life where his hacked-out frame could have peace and comfort; some believed him a superb human struggler with solemn and comic echoes and values far off and beyond the leashes and bones that held him to earth and law and politics.

QUESTIONS FOR DISCUSSION

1. As noted in Looking Ahead, Sandburg's central idea is that Lincoln had a great deal of the simple frontiersman in him. Which details develop this central idea best?
2. In paragraph 1, Sandburg gives a brief history of Lincoln's footwear. What do his shoes reveal about him?
3. From the physical details Sandburg provides, what do you think Lincoln looked like?
4. Lincoln's trousers were "baggy at the knees." Look back to paragraph 4. What does this physical description reveal about his character?
5. What other details about Lincoln's appearance help us understand his personality?
6. A number of anecdotes in this selection show us things about Lincoln's personality. What does his sobbing at a friend's funeral reveal about him? Pick out two or three other anecdotes that you find especially revealing.
7. In paragraphs 9 and 10, Sandburg indicates that Lincoln could experience a variety of moods. Describe these moods.

THINKING CRITICALLY

1. Sandburg tells us that the public held differing views of President Lincoln: some people respected him; others thought he was a schemer; still others saw him as sad and lost. In fact, after reading this essay, you probably realized that Lincoln's personality was complex, that there were "several Lincolns." Reread Sandburg's essay and make notes in the margins that might identify at least two different aspects of Lincoln's personality. Then, write a paragraph or two that summarize your notes.
2. Appearances can be deceiving. Did Lincoln look like the kind of person we might elect as President today? How would the media have treated this man? Think of a person you know well whose looks might mislead people about them. For example, have you ever met someone who looked dangerous, frightening, or strange but turned out to be one of the kindest, most supportive of your friends? Write a paragraph or two that make this contrast clear.

SUGGESTIONS FOR JOURNAL ENTRIES

1. Use your journal to list details you found in this selection that build a full portrait of Lincoln's physical appearance.
2. Lincoln's inner nobility, simplicity, and lack of pretense were reflected in the way he dressed. Do you know people whose outward appearance provides clues to what they are inside? Write a short description of one such person, concentrating on only one or two outward features that reveal what he or she is like inside.

SUGGESTIONS FOR SUSTAINED WRITING

1. Describe someone you know by focusing on the strongest or most important feature of his or her personality. Here's an example of a preliminary thesis statement for such an essay: "When I think of Millie, what comes to mind first is her faith in people."

   As you draft the body of your essay, tell of something in your subject's past that accounts for this characteristic. For example, explain that Millie has had an unshakable faith in the goodness of people ever since, as a child, she lost her parents and was raised by neighbors. Then, give examples of that faith. Use what you have learned about Millie from personal experience, from people who know her, or from Millie herself. Tell one or two anecdotes [brief, illustrative stories] to convince readers that what you say is true.

   A good way to learn more about the person you are describing is to interview him or her. Take accurate notes. When it comes time to write your essay, try quoting your subject directly; use his or her own words to explain how he or she feels. Examples of how to put direct quotations into your work appear in Rose's "Mothers and Fathers" and McPhee's "Two Gentlemen of the Pines." In fact, if you responded to the journal suggestions after these selections, you may already have gotten a fine start on the assignment.

   Revise your paper as often as necessary. Make sure it includes enough information and is well organized. As part of the editing process, check that you have used quoted material correctly. If you have doubts, speak with your instructor.

2. The journal suggestions after Carver's "Photograph of My Father in His Twenty-second Year" asked you to make notes about a photograph of a close friend or family member or of yourself. If you responded to either suggestion, turn your notes into an essay.

   Before you begin, review your journal notes, then add details that come to mind as you are reading them. If possible, interview another person who knows your subject well and ask him or her to provide information and quotations that might help describe your subject's character. This is essential if the picture is of you.

   Begin drafting by describing the physical appearance of your subject. Like Carver, you might also describe the setting. Then, use this information as a springboard to discussing your subject's personality. For example, Carver says his father wore "his old hat cocked over his ear" as a sign of his desire to be "bold."

   Read your rough draft carefully. As you revise, try to narrate events that might reveal your subject's character. Include quotations and figures of speech when possible. Double-check word choice when you edit your paper for grammar, spelling, and other matters. A good way to introduce this essay is with a startling remark or a question. A good way to conclude it is by using an anecdote or quotation that will stick in the readers' minds.

3. Both Phyllis Rose and Maria Scamacca write about brave women: one battles eye disease; the other has suffered from war, illness, and the loss of children. Do you know people who have faced hardship and disappointment? What do their reactions tell you about their characters?

Describe one such person by explaining how he or she reacts to difficulty and disappointment. Tell interesting facts from his or her personal history to help readers understand the strength (or weakness) of your subject's character. In addition, explain what other people think of this individual, quote him or her directly, or use anecdotes to tell readers about the way he or she faces misfortune.

Summarize the information you have gathered in a thesis statement that expresses your feelings about this person. Of course, you don't need to place the thesis at the very beginning of your essay. Put it anywhere it fits, even at the end. In fact, you can open your first draft simply by describing physical appearance. If you do this, however, try to follow Scamacca's example: choose details that show what your subject looks like and that provide clues to his or her character.

In any case, before you get started, look over the journal entries you made after reading "From 'Mothers and Fathers' " and "Oma: Portrait of a Heroine." Then, go through the process of writing systematically. Never remain satisfied with an early draft; for best results, always rewrite and edit!

4. If you haven't done so yet, respond to all three of the Suggestions for Journal Entries after Scamacca's "Oma: Portrait of a Heroine." Now, write an essay that explains to readers why you think the subject you are writing about is heroic.

Narrate events from your subject's life that will show his or her heroism, but also try to include comments—perhaps direct quotations—from your subject and from people who know him or her well. Like Scamacca, you might want to start by describing your subject's physical appearance or by taking readers on a tour of his or her home. Just make sure this information contains clues to your subject's character.

As you go through the revision process, improve word choice by substituting vivid verbs and adjectives as well as concrete, specific nouns for less effective language. Try creating figures of speech when appropriate. As always, edit and proofread your work.

5. If you responded to item 2 of the Suggestions for Journal Entries after Sandburg's "Abraham Lincoln," you have begun writing about a person whose appearance is a clue to his or her character. Turn this short sketch into an essay. Focus on the one aspect (part) of your subject's personality that is most obvious or important. Start off with a preliminary thesis that tells how his or her outward appearance reflects what is on the inside. Here's an example: "The bags under Nelson's eyes, the tightness in his face, and the droop of his shoulders tell us he is not happy."

In the first draft, describe what your subject looks and even sounds like. Then, go back and include details about his or her behavior to make the main point in your thesis even clearer. Don't be afraid to describe strange mannerisms you've noticed—perhaps the odd gestures she uses while speaking or the curious way he shuffles down the street.

Once satisfied that you have included enough information, revise your thesis if necessary and make sure your introduction works well. If you haven't written an introduction yet, try a startling remark or an interesting anecdote like the one in paragraph 2 of Sandburg's description of Abraham Lincoln. To conclude, express your personal reaction to the person you have just described or make some predictions about his or her future.

Revise the completed draft once more; check that the details in your paper relate directly to one aspect of your subject's personality—the one mentioned in your thesis. Then, correct punctuation, grammar, spelling, and other types of errors that will reduce the quality of your work.

6. Most people send friends and relatives store-bought greeting cards on their birthdays. Try something different. Write a birthday letter to a friend or relative whom you love and admire! Begin with a standard birthday greeting if you like. But follow this with four or five well-developed paragraphs that explain the reasons for your love and admiration. Use your knowledge of your reader's past— what you have learned firsthand or heard from others—to recall anecdotes that support your opinion. In other words, show what in his or her character deserves love and admiration.

Not everything you say in this letter has to be flattering. In fact, this is a good chance to do some mild kidding. So, don't hesitate to poke good-natured fun at your reader—and at yourself—as a way of bringing warmth and sincerity to your writing. Just remember that your overall purpose is positive.

This assignment is different from most others. Nonetheless, it demands the same effort and care. In fact, the more you love or admire your reader, the harder you should work at revising and editing this tribute.

SECTION FOUR

NARRATION

The selections in the three chapters of this section have a great deal in common. Their most basic and most obvious similarity is that they tell stories. They do this through *narration,* a process by which events or incidents are presented to the reader in a particular order. Usually, this is done in chronological order, or order of time.

The logical arrangement of events in a story is called its "plot." Often, writers begin by telling us about the first event in this series, the event that sets the whole plot in motion. And they usually end their stories with the last bit of action that takes place.

But this is not always the case. Where a writer begins or ends depends on the kind of story he or she is telling and the reason or purpose for telling it. Some stories begin in the middle or even at the end and then recall what happened earlier. A good example is Wagner's "Death of an Officer" in Chapter 10. Other stories are preceded or followed by information the author thinks is important. For instance, in "38 Who Saw Murder Didn't Call the Police" (Chapter 11), Martin Gansberg tells us about the police investigation of a crime before narrating the crime itself.

More than 2300 years ago, the Greek philosopher Aristotle taught that a narrative must have a beginning, a middle, and an end. In other words, a successful story must be complete. It must contain all the information a reader will need to learn what has happened and to follow along easily. That's the single most important idea to remember about writing effective narratives, but there are several others you should keep in mind.

DISTINGUISHING FICTION FROM NONFICTION

Narration can be divided into two types: fiction and nonfiction. Works of nonfiction recount events that actually occurred. Works of fiction, though sometimes based on real-life experiences, are born of the author's imagination and do not recreate events exactly as they happened. The short stories that appear in Chapter 12 are examples of fiction.

DETERMINING PURPOSE AND THEME

Many nonfiction stories are written to inform people about events or developments that affect or interest them. Newspaper articles, like Martin Gansberg's "38 Who Saw Murder Didn't Call the Police" (Chapter 11), are perfect examples. This type of writing is also used by scientists to explain natural processes as they occur step by step over

333

time. In fact, narration can explain complex ideas or make important points about very real situations. Adrienne Schwartz's "The Colossus in the Kitchen" (Chapter 11), for instance, tells a true story that illustrates the evil and stupidity of apartheid, the political system whose effects Schwartz witnessed in South Africa.

On the other hand, fiction is written to entertain people. As the short stories in Chapter 12 prove, good fiction enriches the emotional, spiritual, and intellectual lives of its readers as well.

Whether fiction or nonfiction, therefore, many narratives are written to dramatize or present an important (central) idea, often called a "theme." They portray life in such a way as to reveal something important about people, human nature, society, or life itself. At times, this theme is stated in a "moral," as in Aesop's fables, the ancient Greek stories that teach lessons about living. More often than not, however, the theme or idea behind a story is unstated or implied. It is revealed only as the plot unfolds. In other words, most stories speak for themselves.

As a developing writer, one of the most important things to remember as you sit down to write a narrative is to ask yourself whether the story you're about to tell is important to you in some way. That *doesn't mean* you should limit yourself to narrating events from personal experience only, though personal experience can often provide just the kind of information you'll need to spin a good yarn. It *does mean* the more you know about the people, places, and events you're writing about and the more those people, places, and events mean to you, the better able you'll be to make your writing interesting and meaningful to your readers.

FINDING THE MEANING IN YOUR STORY

As explained above, you won't always have to reveal why you've written your story or what theme it is supposed to present. You can allow the events you're narrating to speak for themselves. Often, in fact, you won't know what the theme of your story is or why you thought it important until you're well into the writing process. Sometimes, you won't know that until after you've finished.

But that's just fine, for writing is a voyage of discovery! It helps you learn things about your subject (and yourself) that you would not have known had you not started the process in the first place. *Just write about something you find interesting and believe is important.* This is the first step in telling a successful story. You can always figure out why your story is important or what theme you want it to demonstrate later in the process, when you write your second or third draft.

DECIDING WHAT TO INCLUDE

In most cases, you won't have much trouble deciding what details to include. You'll be able to put down events as they happened or at least as you remember them. However, in some cases—especially when you are trying to present a particular theme or idea—you'll have to decide which events, people, and so on should be emphasized or talked about in great detail, which should be mentioned only briefly, and which should be excluded from the story altogether.

In "Incident" (Chapter 10), for example, Countee Cullen's purpose is to explain the racism he experienced one day during a long stay in Baltimore. He could have included events from his visit that had nothing to do with racism. But he chose to exclude them and focus on the one event that illustrates his theme.

MAKING YOUR STORIES LIVELY, INTERESTING, AND BELIEVABLE

Once again, good stories dramatize ideas or themes. They do this through actions and characters that seem vivid and interesting, as if they were alive or real.

One of the best ways to keep your readers' interest and to make your writing vivid is to use verbs effectively. More than any other part of speech, verbs convey action! They tell *what happened.* It's important to be accurate when reporting an incident you've experienced or witnessed. You ought to recapture it exactly as you remember and without exaggeration. However, good writing can be both accurate and interesting, both truthful and colorful. You can achieve this balance by choosing verbs carefully.

In "Wanderlust" (Chapter 10), Charles Kuralt chooses to write that his father and he "rolled" along country roads. Of course, words like "traveled" and "drove" would have communicated the same general idea, but "rolled" captures the sensation Kuralt experienced more accurately and it is a far more interesting word.

Similarly, notice how Edgar Lee Masters' verbs and participles—adjectives made from verbs—in "Lucinda Matlock" (Chapter 10) reveal his subject as an energetic, vivacious, and agreeable person. We learn that she *"Rambled* over the fields" and that she could be heard *"Shouting* to the wooded hills, *singing* to the green valleys." How less interesting she would have seemed had we seen her "walking" through the fields and heard her "talking" to the hills.

Using adverbs—words that tell something about verbs, adjectives, and other adverbs—can also add life to your writing and often make it more specific. Consider these two lines from Pickering's "Faith of the Father" (Chapter 11): ". . . Miss Ida was shy. She read poetry and raised guinea fowl and at parties sat *silently* in a corner. Only on Easter was she outgoing; then like a day lily she bloomed *triumphantly."*

A good way to make your writing both more interesting and more believable is to include proper nouns—names of specific persons, places, and things—which will help your readers feel they are experiencing the story as they read it. In "Wanderlust," for example, Charles Kuralt writes that he traveled with his father to towns like *New Bern* and *Swanquarter,* his dad smoking *Tampa Nuggets* and reading *Burma-Shave* signs as they drove along. He also recalls a song from a *Judy Garland* movie (*The Wizard of Oz*), and later he mentions the colorful names of people he met on a baseball road trip.

SHOWING THE PASSAGE OF TIME

Of course, the most important thing in a story is the plot, a series of events occurring in time. Writers must make sure that their plots make sense, that they are easy to follow, and that each event or incident flows into the next logically.

One of the best ways to show time order is to indicate the actual time that an event took place. In "38 Who Saw Murder Didn't Call the Police," for instance, Martin Gansberg introduces the story of Kitty Genovese's murder with "This is what the police say happened beginning at 3:20 A.M." Later on, he tells us that a bus passed the scene at "3:35 A.M." and that an ambulance finally took the body away at "4:25 A.M."

Another way of indicating the passage of time is by using transitions or connectives, the kinds of words and expressions used to create coherence within and between paragraphs. In his popular essay about future trips to outer space, Kenneth Jon Rose uses a number of such transitional devices (in italics) as he explains what it might be like to leave the earth on a tourist shuttle to the stars. Notice how they keep the story moving and make it easy to follow:

> [While] looking out your window, you'll see the earth rapidly falling away, and the light blue sky progressively turning blue-black. You'll now be about 30 miles up, traveling at about 3000 mph. Within minutes, the sky will appear jet black, and only the fuzzy curve of the earth will be visible. Then, at perhaps 130 miles above the surface of the earth and traveling at 17,000 mph, engines will shut down and . . . you'll become weightless. ("2001: Space Shuttle")

If you want to refresh your memory about other effective transitional devices to use in your writing, turn back to Chapter 2.

Describing Setting and Developing Characters

Establishing the setting of your story involves describing the time and place in which it occurs. You've probably done some of that in response to the assignments in Chapter 8, "Describing Places and Things." Developing characters involves many of the skills you practiced in Chapter 9, "Describing People."

In general, the more you say about the people in your narrative and about the time and place in which it is set, the more realistic and convincing it will seem to your readers. And the more they will appreciate what it has to say! Remember that your purpose in writing a narrative is to tell a story. But the kind of characters who inhabit that story and the kind of world in which it takes place can be as interesting and as important to your readers as the events themselves.

As you probably know, an important narrative element is dialogue, the words a writer allows people in the story to speak. You can use dialogue to help reveal important aspects of someone's personality, to describe setting, and even to relate events that move the plot along. In fact, several authors whose selections follow allow their characters to explain what happened or to comment on the story's action in their own words. Usually, such comments are quoted exactly—complete with grammatical errors and slang expressions. So, whether you are writing fiction or nonfiction, try letting your characters speak for themselves. They may be able to tell your readers a lot about themselves, about other characters, and about the stories in which they appear.

CHAPTER 10

PERSONAL REFLECTION AND AUTOBIOGRAPHY

Though different in style and content, the selections in this chapter are similar because they are written in the first person. This is the point of view from which the authors have chosen to tell their stories. In first-person narration, the storyteller, also known as the narrator, participates in the action and recalls the events from his or her personal perspective.

When writers reveal things about other people's lives or talk about events in which they were not involved, they often rely on third-person narration and use the pronouns "he," "she," "it," and "they" to explain who did what in the story. Examples of this kind of writing can be found in Chapter 11, "Reporting Events." However, all the selections in Chapter 10 are intended to reveal something important about the lives or personalities of their storytellers. That's why they can be classified as "personal reflection" or "autobiography" and are written from the first-person point of view, using the pronouns "I" or "we."

This is even true of the two poems from *Spoon River Anthology*. To make his poems more believable, Edgar Lee Masters lets his title characters speak for themselves and tell us about their lives in their own words. As such, Lucinda Matlock and Margaret Fuller Slack become the narrators of the poems that bear their names.

VISUALIZING DETAILS AND TECHNIQUES IMPORTANT TO PERSONAL REFLECTION AND AUTOBIOGRAPHY

This paragraph from Ralph Ellison's "Battle Royal" recalls a strange event in which Ellison and nine other young black men were made to fight one another blindfolded. The scene is a fight ring in the middle of a hotel ballroom filled with spectators—including "some of the most important men of the town"—anxious to see faces bruised and bloodied. The young fighters are just entering the ring. [Other parts of this story appear later in this chapter.]

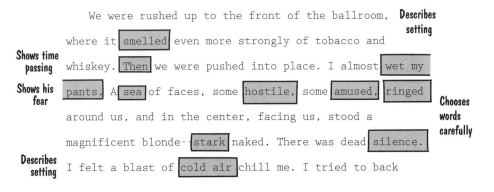

We were rushed up to the front of the ballroom, | *Describes setting*

where it | smelled | even more strongly of tobacco and

Shows time passing | whiskey. | Then | we were pushed into place. I almost| wet my

Shows his fear | pants. | A | sea | of faces, some | hostile, | some | amused, | ringed |

around us, and in the center, facing us, stood a | *Chooses words carefully*

magnificent blonde--| stark | naked. There was dead | silence. |

Describes setting | I felt a blast of | cold air | chill me. I tried to back

away, but they were behind me and around me. Some of the
boys stood with lowered heads, trembling. I felt a wave
of irrational guilt and fear. My teeth chattered, my
skin turned to goose flesh, my knees knocked. Yet I was
strongly attracted and looked in spite of myself. Had
the price of looking been blindness, I would have
looked. The hair was yellow like that of a circus kewpie
doll, the face heavily powdered and rouged, as though to
form an abstract mask, the eyes hollow and smeared a
cool blue, the color of a baboon's butt. I felt a desire
to spit on her. I wanted at one and the same time to run
from the room, to sink through the floor, or go to her
and cover her from my eyes and the eyes of the
others. ¶ / /

Uses action to convey his feelings.

Describes others in the story

Emphasizes his curiosity

Shows his subjective reaction.

Shows his conflicting emotions.

REVISING AUTOBIOGRAPHICAL ESSAYS

Later in this chapter you will read Lois Diaz-Talty's "The Day I Was Fat," which explains how this nursing student turned a painful insult into an occasion for self-reflection. It is no accident that the story is so vivid, convincing, and meaningful. Diaz-Talty revised and edited her work carefully and repeatedly. Compare a few paragraphs from one of her early drafts with those from her final draft.

Diaz-Talty—Rough Draft

I was headed to the pool with Mary Gene and the
children, and I got into an argument with a teenager
driving behind our car. He nearly ran us off the road. I
showed my disapproval, and we began yelling at each
other. He was about 18, with rotten teeth. He pulled into
the pool's parking lot behind us; our argument became
heated. Turning to his friend, he said, "She's fat!"

Once inside the gates to the pool, my friend advised

Who is Mary Gene?

More detail about how he did this?

How did you show it?

When did this occur?

Is that all? Did more take place?

me to forget the whole incident. "He was gross," she said.

Will this convince the readers?
But I couldn't get his words out of my mind. Nobody had ever called me fat before, and it hurt terribly. But it was true.

On that very day, as I sat at the pool praying that nobody would see me in my bathing suit, I promised myself that no one would ever call me fat again.

Diaz-Talty—Final Draft

Makes time reference.
One summer afternoon in 1988, as I was headed to the pool with my sister-in-law Mary Gene and our children, I got into an argument with a teenager who was driving fast and tail-gaiting our car. When he nearly ran us off the road, I turned around and glared at him to show my disapproval and my concern for our safety. Suddenly, we began yelling at each other. He was about 18, with an ugly, red, swollen face. The few teeth he had were yellow and rotten. He followed us to the pool and, as he pulled into the parking lot behind us, our argument became heated.

Adds details to explain how he "nearly ran us off the road."

Identifies Mary Gene.

Explains how she showed disapproval. Provides more information.

Explains when this happened.

"What's your problem, bitch?" he screamed.

"You drive like an idiot! That's my problem, okay?"

When I got out of the car and walked around to get the baby, he laughed to his friend, "Ah, look at 'er. She's fat! Go to hell, fat bitch." And then they drove away.

Adds an effective verb.

Adds details and direct quotations to recreate the argument.

Expands Mary Gene's response.
Once inside the gates to the pool, my sister-in-law advised me to forget the whole incident.

"Come on," she said. "Don't worry about that jerk! Did you see his teeth? He was gross."

Captures author's thoughts through direct quotation.

But I couldn't get his words out of my mind. They stung like a whip. "I'm fat," I thought to myself. "I haven't just put on a few pounds. I'm not bloated. I don't have baby weight to lose. I'm just plain fat."

Paragraph is now more convincing

Nobody had ever called me fat before, and it hurt terribly. But it was true.

Adds sentences to explain the importance of what just happened.

On that very day, as I sat at the pool praying that nobody would see me in my bathing suit, I promised myself that no one would ever call me fat again. That hideous, 18-year-old idiot had spoken the words that none of my loved ones had had the heart to say even though they were true. Yes, I was fat.

PRACTICING SKILLS OF PERSONAL REFLECTION AND AUTOBIOGRAPHY

Here are two more paragraphs from Ralph Ellison's "Battle Royal" (another appears on pages 337-338). Practice your skills by following the instructions for each paragraph below.

a. In this first paragraph, underline effective words or phrases, especially vivid verbs, adjectives, and adverbs.

A glove smacked against my head. I pivoted, striking out stiffly as someone went past. . . . Then it seemed as though all nine of the boys had turned upon me at once. Blows pounded me from all sides while I struck out as best I could. So many blows landed upon me that I wondered if I were not the only blindfolded fighter in the ring. . . .

b. Important words have been removed from this second paragraph. Replace them with words of your own. Use only the kinds of words indicated. Avoid *is, are, was, were, have been, had been,* and other forms of the verb *to be.*

I could no longer control my emotions. I had no dignity. I

_____ about like a baby or a drunken man. The smoke had
VERB

become _____ and with each new blow it seemed to

ADJECTIVE

_____ and _____ my lungs. My saliva

VERB   VERB

_____ like hot bitter glue. A glove _____ my

VERB   VERB

head, filling my mouth with _____ blood. A blow landed

ADJECTIVE

_____ against the nape of my neck. I felt myself going over, my

ADVERB

head hitting the floor. Streaks of _____ light filled the

ADJECTIVE

_____ world behind the blindfold. I lay _____

ADJECTIVE   ADVERB

pretending I was knocked out, but felt myself seized by hands and

_____ to my feet. "Get going, black boy!" My arms were like

ADJECTIVE

_____ , my head _____ from blows. I managed

NOUN   VERB

to feel my way to the ropes and held on. A glove landed in my mid-section, and I

went over _____ , feeling as though the smoke had become a

ADVERB

knife _____ into my guts. Pushed this way and that by the legs

ADJECTIVE

milling around me, I _____ pulled erect and discovered that I

TRANSITION

could see the black, sweat-washed forms weaving in the blue-smokey atmosphere

like _____ dancers weaving to the _____ drum-

ADJECTIVE   ADJECTIVE

like thuds of the blows.

The reading selections that follow are powerful personal statements about the people who speak through them and the worlds they inhabit. Read them carefully. They may inspire you to create articulate and convincing statements about yourself and your world.

Incident

Countee Cullen

Countee Cullen (1903–1946) played a significant role in the Harlem Renaissance, one of the most influential artistic movements in modern America. As a member of this important group of African-American poets, novelists, and playwrights in New York's Harlem during the 1920s, he helped create an authentic voice for black Americans and contributed to a tradition that is among the finest in American literature.

During his brief lifetime he authored several volumes of poetry, was the editor of two important black journals, and at age thirty published Caroling Dusk, *a collection of poetry by important African-American writers.*

LOOKING AHEAD

Although brief, "Incident" contains all the basic narrative elements: plot, setting, character, and dialogue.

VOCABULARY

whit   Bit, small amount.

Incident | *Countee Cullen*

Once riding in old Baltimore,
Heart-filled, head-filled with glee,
I saw a Baltimorean
Keep looking straight at me.

Now I was eight and very small,   5
And he was no whit bigger,
And so I smiled, but he poked out
His tongue, and called me, "Nigger."

I saw the whole of Baltimore
From May until December,   10
Of all the things that happened there
That's all that I remember.

QUESTIONS FOR DISCUSSION

1. What three events make up the plot of "Incident"?
2. What example of dialogue do we find in this selection? How is it important to the poem?
3. Why does the speaker tell us that the "Baltimorean" he met was about his age and size?
4. Cullen does not provide many details about the setting, but he does give us a clue. Where does the poem take place?

THINKING CRITICALLY

In a well-written paragraph, explain what change you see in the speaker's attitude from the beginning to the end of this poem. Be sure to explain what, at the end of the poem, tells us the speaker's attitude has changed.

SUGGESTIONS FOR JOURNAL ENTRIES

1. Think of an incident from your childhood in which someone insulted you, called you names, or tried to degrade you in some way. Briefly recall what happened and explain your reaction to this incident.
2. In your journal, explain your emotional reaction to "he poked out/His tongue, and called me, 'Nigger.' "

Namas-te*

Peter Matthiessen

Peter Matthiessen has explored and written about remote parts of the world like the Amazon River, the Sudan, and New Guinea. Among his best-known works are Far Tortuga, Killing Mister Watson, At Play in the Fields of the Lord, Blue Meridian, *and* In the Spirit of Crazy Horse.*"Namas-te" is taken from* The Snow Leopard, *for which Matthiessen won the National Book Award. It recalls his travels through Nepal, a small country between India and Tibet, where he went to study the blue sheep of the Himalaya Mountains and to find the legendary snow leopard.*

LOOKING AHEAD

1. This piece begins with a sentence fragment. Professional writers create dramatic effects with fragments, but developing writers should avoid them.
2. In paragraph 3, Matthiessen mentions places that he visited and events that happened much earlier in his journey. He even recalls the death of his wife, which took place before he left home. Gorkha and Pokhara are cities in central Nepal, near the site of this story.
3. GS is George Schaller, a zoologist and friend of the author.

VOCABULARY

Annapurna	Mountain of the Himalayas.
luminous	Bright, radiant.
mortality	Certainty of death.
pitiable	Sad, deserving pity.
ravines	Gaps, crevasses.
Sanskrit	Ancient language of India.
subdued	Overcome.
tamper with	Interfere with, disturb.

*Editor's title

Namas-te* | *Peter Matthiessen*

A luminous mountain morning. Mist and fire smoke, sun shafts and dark ravines: 1
a peak of Annapurna poises on soft clouds. In fresh light, to the peeping of
baby chickens, we take breakfast in the village tea house, and are under way well before
seven.

A child dragging bent useless legs is crawling up the hill outside the village. Nose to   2
the stones, goat dung, and muddy trickles, she pulls herself along like a broken cricket.
We falter, ashamed of our strong step, and noticing this, she gazes up, clear-eyed, without resentment—it seems much worse that she is pretty. In [parts of the world], GS
says stiffly, beggars will break their children's knees to achieve this pitiable effect for
business purposes: this is his way of expressing his distress. But the child that lies here
at our boots is not a beggar; she is merely a child, staring in curiosity at tall, white
strangers. I long to give her something—a new life?—yet am afraid to tamper with such
dignity. And so I smile as best I can, and say *"Namas-te!"* "Good morning!" How absurd!
And her voice follows as we go away, a small clear smiling voice—*"Namas-te!"*—a Sanskrit word for greeting and parting that means, "I salute you."

We are subdued by this reminder of mortality. I think of the corpse in Gorkha   3
Country, borne on thin shoulders in the mountain rain, the black cloths blowing; I see
the ancient dying man outside Pokhara; I hear again my own wife's final breath.

QUESTIONS FOR DISCUSSION

1. What is the story's setting, the time and place in which it occurs?
2. How does Matthiessen describe the child's voice? What does this information tell us about her?
3. What else do we learn about the girl?
4. Matthiessen says GS and he are "subdued" by this experience. What does he mean? What else do we learn about these men as a result of their meeting the child?
5. Why does the author include GS's statement about beggars in paragraph 2?

THINKING CRITICALLY

1. In reference to the child, Matthiessen says he is "afraid to tamper with such dignity" (paragraph 2). How would you interpret this statement?
2. Reread paragraph 3. Then, in a well-constructed paragraph or two, answer these questions:
   a. Why does the author believe his meeting with the child is a "reminder of mortality"?
   b. Whose mortality is he talking about?
   c. Why does he mention the "corpse in Gorkha Country" and the "dying man outside Pokhara"?
   d. Why does he bring up the memory of his wife?

SUGGESTIONS FOR JOURNAL ENTRIES

1. Recall the last time you witnessed a pitiable sight. Use listing to record details about what you saw, heard, smelled, and so forth. Describe the setting of the story by recalling when and where it took place. Like Matthiessen, include names of specific people, places, or things. Most of all, recall as much as you can about the events and people you observed. Finally, sum up your reaction to the experience in a sentence or two.
2. Despite her terrible situation, the young child in Matthiessen's story manages to greet the travelers with joy in her voice. Do you know someone who suffers from a severe handicap? Use focused freewriting to explain this person's attitude toward him- or herself, toward the handicap, toward other people, or toward life in general. Briefly recall incidents from his or her life that will help you explain what you mean.

From *Spoon River Anthology*

Edgar Lee Masters

Spoon River Anthology *is a collection of poems spoken by people buried in the cemetery of a fictional nineteenth-century village that Masters based upon recollections of his hometown. One by one, Spoon River's citizens are made to address us from the grave and to reveal important secrets about their relatives and friends, and, most of all, about themselves.*

Born in Kansas in 1869, Masters eventually settled in Chicago, where he practiced law for several years before taking up writing as a career. When Spoon River Anthology *was published, it became a literary sensation. The idea of unraveling the story of a town through the recollections of people lying in its cemetery was unique, and it attracted the attention of thousands of readers and many imitators. "Lucinda Matlock" and "Margaret Fuller Slack," the two poems in this selection, are taken from* Spoon River Anthology.

LOOKING AHEAD

1. Lucinda's and Margaret's very different outlooks on life reveal a great deal about their personalities. Ask yourself what their attitudes tell you about them.
2. Chandlerville and Winchester, which Lucinda mentions, are towns near Spoon River. By including these place names, Masters makes the poem and Lucinda seem more realistic and believable.
3. Margaret claims that she could have been as good a writer as George Eliot. "George Eliot" was the pen name of the nineteenth-century English novelist Mary Ann Evans, who wrote *The Mill on the Floss, Silas Marner,* and *Middlemarch.*

VOCABULARY

celibacy	Life without sex.
degenerate	Not strong in spirit.
ere	Before.
holiday	Vacation.
ironical	Ironic, exactly the opposite of what is expected. Margaret's death as a result of tetanus was "ironical" because one of the disease's first symptoms is lockjaw.
luring	Attracting.
repose	Rest.
unchastity	Sex outside of marriage.
untoward	Unhappy, unlucky.

From *Spoon River Anthology* | *Edgar Lee Masters*

LUCINDA MATLOCK

I went to the dances at Chandlerville,
And played snap-out at Winchester.
One time we changed partners,
Driving home in the moonlight of middle June,
And then I found Davis.   5
We were married and lived together for seventy years,
Enjoying, working, raising the twelve children,
Eight of whom we lost
Ere I had reached the age of sixty.
I spun, I wove, I kept the house, I nursed the sick,   10
I made the garden, and for holiday
Rambled over the fields where sang the larks,
And by Spoon River gathering many a shell,
And many a flower and medicinal weed—
Shouting to the wooded hills, singing to the green valleys.   15
At ninety-six I had lived enough, that is all,
And passed to a sweet repose.
What is this I hear of sorrow and weariness,
Anger, discontent and drooping hopes?
Degenerate sons and daughters,   20
Life is too strong for you—
It takes life to love Life.

MARGARET FULLER SLACK

I would have been as great as George Eliot
But for an untoward fate.
For look at the photograph of me made by Penniwit,
Chin resting on hand, and deep-set eyes—
Gray, too, and far-searching.   5
But there was the old, old problem:
Should it be celibacy, matrimony or unchastity?
Then John Slack, the rich druggist, wooed me,
Luring me with the promise of leisure for my novel,
And I married him, giving birth to eight children,   10
And had no time to write.
It was all over with me, anyway,
When I ran the needle in my hand
While washing the baby's things,
And died from lock-jaw, an ironical death.   15
Hear me, ambitious souls,
Sex is the curse of life!

QUESTIONS FOR DISCUSSION

1. Lucinda seems to have had a very active and productive life. What events in her poem make this clear?
2. Masters uses a number of interesting verbs to describe Lucinda's life. Identify these verbs in the poem. What do they reveal about her?
3. Lucinda's life hasn't been all joy. Which events in the poem reveal that she has experienced great sorrow too?
4. Why does Lucinda call her sons and daughters "degenerate"?
5. What does Lucinda mean when she says that "It takes life to love Life"? What does this tell us about her personality?
6. Margaret Fuller Slack says that she was lured into her marriage "with the promise of leisure for [her] novel." What does this reveal about her attitude toward marriage?
7. What verbs does Masters use in "Margaret Fuller Slack" to keep the story moving and to maintain the reader's interest?

THINKING CRITICALLY

1. Discuss Lucinda's attitude toward life. How does it differ from Margaret's? What does this difference tell us about their characters?
2. How would Margaret and Lucinda react to the same event such as the loss of a child, the death of a husband, the destruction of their home, or some other serious occurrence? If you don't want to dwell on the tragic, pick a more common event like a child's stepping into a mud puddle or spilling a dinner plate on the kitchen floor.
3. How would Lucinda respond to Margaret's claim that "sex is the curse of life!"? How would you respond to it?

SUGGESTIONS FOR JOURNAL ENTRIES

1. Do you know someone like Lucinda Matlock, who has kept smiling and maintained a courageous attitude even though he or she has had a difficult life? Make a list of the difficulties this person has experienced, and explain how he or she manages to remain hopeful and happy.
2. Do you know someone like Margaret, who is resentful about the way his or her life has unfolded? What events in this person's life have caused him or her to adopt this attitude?

The Day I Was Fat

Lois Diaz-Talty

When she isn't waitressing part-time or taking care of her family of four, Lois Diaz-Talty studies nursing and writes interesting essays like the one below. She credits her husband and children for encouraging her academic efforts. Nonetheless, as the essay shows, she is an energetic, determined, and intelligent woman, who is sure to succeed. When asked to write about a pivotal event or turning point in her life, Diaz-Talty recalled an incident that is burned into her memory and that has helped shaped her life.

Looking Ahead

1. The significance of the event narrated in this essay is explained in its thesis, which appears near the end.
2. Diaz-Talty's style is conversational, familiar, and often humorous, but her essay is always clear, correct, and focused. Pay particular attention to her use of dialogue, which helps capture the flavor of the moment.

Vocabulary

condiments	Seasonings, flavorings.
committed	Determined.
ironically	Having an effect opposite the one expected.
limber	Able to bend easily, flexible.
notorious	Shameful, bad.

The Day I Was Fat | *Lois Diaz-Talty*

I was never in great shape. As a child, I was always called "plump," and my friend   1
"Skinny Sherri" was always, well, skinny. I could never sit Indian-style the way
other kids did, and when I made the cheerleading squad in eighth grade it was because
I had a big mouth and a great smile, not because I could execute limber splits or elegant
cartwheels. Although I maintained a respectable weight throughout high school (after
all, my "entire life" depended upon my looks and popularity), there was always a fat
person inside of me just waiting to burst onto the scene.

Adulthood, marriage, and settling down had notorious effects on my weight: I blew   2
up! The fat lady had finally arrived, saw the welcome mat, and moved right in. No one
in my family could tell me I was fat. They knew that I had gained weight, I knew that I
had gained weight, and I knew that they knew that I had gained weight. But to discuss
the topic was out of the question. Once, my mother said, "You're too pretty to be so
heavy"; that was the closest anyone had ever come to calling me fat. Later, my husband
teased me because we couldn't lie on the couch together anymore, and I just cried and
cried. He never dared to mention it again, but I didn't stop eating.

I had just given birth to my first child and was at least fifty pounds overweight.   3
Nonetheless, I remember feeling that that was the greatest time in my life. I had a beautiful new baby, new furniture, a great husband, a lovely house. What more could anyone want? Well, I knew what else I wanted: I wanted to be thin and healthy. I just
didn't care enough about myself to stop my frequent binging. I tried to lose weight
every day, but I couldn't get started. Diets didn't last through lunch, and I got bigger by
the day.

One summer afternoon in 1988, as I was headed to the pool with my sister-in-law   4
Mary Gene and our children, I got into an argument with a teenager who was driving
fast and tail-gaiting our car. When he nearly ran us off the road, I turned around and
glared at him to show my disapproval and my concern for our safety. Suddenly, we
began yelling at each other. He was about 18, with an ugly, red, swollen face. The few
teeth he had were yellow and rotten. He followed us to the pool and, as he pulled into
the parking lot behind us, our argument became heated.

"What's your problem, bitch?" he screamed.   5

"You drive like an idiot! That's my problem, okay?"   6

When I got out of the car and walked around to get the baby, he laughed to his   7
friend, "Ah, look at 'er. She's fat! Go to hell, fat bitch." And then they drove away.

Once inside the gates to the pool, my sister-in-law advised me to forget the whole   8
incident.

"Come on," she said. "Don't worry about that jerk! Did you see his teeth? He was   9
gross."

But I couldn't get his words out of my mind. They stung like a whip. "I'm fat," I   10
thought to myself. "I haven't just put on a few pounds. I'm not bloated. I don't have
baby weight to lose. I'm just plain fat." Nobody had ever called me fat before, and it
hurt terribly. But it was true.

On that very day, as I sat at the pool praying that nobody would see me in my   11
bathing suit, I promised myself that no one would ever call me fat again. That hideous,

18-year-old idiot had spoken the words that none of my loved ones had had the heart to say even though they were true. Yes, I was fat.

From then on, I was committed to shedding the weight and getting into shape. I 12 started a rigorous program of running and dieting the very next day. Within months, I joined a gym and managed to make some friends who are still my workout buddies. However, in the past seven years, I've done more than lose weight: I've reshaped my attitude, my lifestyle, and my self-image. Now, I read everything I can about nutrition and health. I'm even considering becoming an aerobics instructor. I cook low-fat foods—chicken, fish, lean meats, vegetables—and I serve my family healthy, protein-rich meals prepared with dietetic ingredients. The children and I often walk to school, ride bikes, rollerblade, and run. Health and fitness have become essential to our household and our lives. But what's really wonderful is that, some time between that pivotal day in 1988 and today, my self-image stopped being about how I look and began being about how I feel. I feel energetic, healthy, confident, strong, and pretty. Ironically, the abuse I endured in the parking lot has helped me re-gain my self-esteem, not just my figure. My body looks good, but my mind feels great!

I hope that the kid from the pool has had his teeth fixed because I'm sure they were 13 one source of his misery. If I ever see him again, I won't tell him that he changed my life in such a special way. I won't let him know that he gave me the greatest gift he could ever give me just by being honest. I won't give him the satisfaction of knowing that the day he called me fat was one of the best days of my life.

QUESTIONS FOR DISCUSSION

1. Where does Diaz-Talty express the essay's central idea? In other words, which sentence is her thesis?
2. What purpose does the author's quoting herself serve in this essay? Why does she quote her mother?
3. Why did the author quote the exact words of the 18-year-old who harassed her? Would simply telling us what happened have been enough?
4. Why does Diaz-Talty bother to describe this person? Why does she make sure to reveal her attitude toward him?
5. Reread three or four paragraphs, and circle the transitions used to show the passage of time and to create coherence.
6. Find places in which the author uses particularly good verbs, adjectives, and adverbs.

THINKING CRITICALLY

1. Make notes in the margins next to details that reveal important aspects of the author's personality.
2. Were you in the author's place, how would you have reacted to the insult? Now think about an aspect of your personality or lifestyle that needs improvement. Write a paragraph that explains how you might improve it.
3. What similarities do you see between this essay and Cullen's "Incident"?

SUGGESTIONS FOR JOURNAL ENTRIES

1. Recall a painful experience that changed your life for the better. Answer the journalists' questions to collect details about this event and to explain how it helped you. For example, here is the journal entry Lois Diaz-Talty made in preparation for "The Day I Was Fat":

   When? In 1988, shortly after I gave birth to Tommy.
   What? An argument with a teenager who had been driving behind us. He called me fat.
   Who? I and a rude, 18-year-old stranger, who looked "gross."
   Where? On the way to the pool.
   Why Important? Because I *was* fat.
   How? His insult shamed me. Made me work harder to lose weight and helped restore self-esteem.

2. Use focused freewriting to gather details about how you reacted to an incident in which someone hurt, insulted, or cheated you, or did something else unpleasant to you. In the process, analyze your reaction to this event. What did it reveal about your character?

Death of an Officer

Gaye Wagner

The author is an officer with the San Diego Police Department. Before joining the force she had worked for seven years in children and youth services in New Hampshire. Wagner holds both bachelor's and master's degrees. "Death of an Officer" appeared in The American Enterprise *magazine in 1995. Accompanying the article was a list of 161 police officers killed in the line of duty in the United States during 1994.*

LOOKING AHEAD

1. In addition to practicing narrative techniques, the author uses description and verbal images to enrich her story. Look for places where she does so.
2. Included here are letters from children expressing their reactions to the officer's death. Read them carefully.

VOCABULARY

apathy	Indifference, lack of concern.
bizarre	Strange.
counteract	Remedy, work against.
detachment	Separation.
dimension	Aspect.
enamoured	Pleased, enchanted, in love with.
immerse	Plunge into.
invincible	Unbeatable.
mired	Stuck in.
mortality	Certainty of death.
nunchakus	A hand weapon used in martial arts and police work.
ponder	Think about, consider.
preoccupied	Absorbed by, totally concerned about.
prophecy	Prediction.
resuscitating	Reviving, restoring.
shrouded	Covered, concealed.

Death of an Officer | *Gaye Wagner*

When Officer Ron Davis was shot in the dark, foggy pre-dawn of September 1 17, 1991, I momentarily lost my perspective on why I've chosen to do what I'm doing. For a time, I focused on just one dimension of my job as a police officer: the possibility of a violent death, for me or people I care about.

Despite the graphic slides and blow-by-blow descriptions of on-duty deaths that we 2 sat through in the Academy, I still must have believed deep down that I, and those alongside me, were invincible. Then the faceless gloom of mortality took the place of a fallen comrade. The streets became an evil, threatening place.

Before I felt the blow of a co-worker's death, I looked on each shooting, stabbing, 3 and act of violence as any rubbernecker would—with a certain detachment. I was living the ultimate student experience: Social Wildlife 101. What better way to understand problems of crime and justice than to immerse yourself in the 'hood. I was there, but I was still an onlooker peering inside some kind of fence. I watched, probed each tragic or bizarre incident with curiosity, and pondered the problems I faced.

With the death of a comrade, I understood that I was inside the fence. I'm no longer 4 an outsider looking in. The shadow of death stalks all of us who walk in the valley of drugs, guns, alcohol, hopelessness, and hate. Police, addicts, hustlers, parents trying to build futures for their children, good people struggling—we all risk falling into the firing line of desperation, apathy, or corruption.

For a while, my response to the new threats I saw around me was to treat all people 5 like they were the enemy. Since an "us" and "them" mentality can be a self-fulfilling prophecy, some of my contacts with people were a little bumpy. Normally my approach is courteous, in one of several variations: either as sympathizer, "just the facts, Bud" chronicler, or all-ears naïve airhead who can hardly believe that you, yes you, could do a dastardly deed . . . ("how did this all happen my friend?").

But suddenly I just wasn't as enamored with this job as I had been. Let's face it, a 6 sense of contributing to society, the excitement of racing cars with lights and sirens, helping folks, and the drama of never knowing what's next place a poor second to living long enough to count grey hairs and collect Social Security.

I had trouble getting an impersonal all-units bulletin about someone I knew out of 7 my head. I read these bulletins every day, but the words now stung: "187 Suspect . . . Arrest in Public for 187 P.C.—Homicide of a Police Officer . . . Suspect Description: Castillo, Arnaldo . . . On September 17, 1991, at 05:15 hours, Castillo was contacted by two officers in regard to a domestic violence call. As the officers approached, Castillo opened fire with a .45 cal. automatic weapon, fatally wounding one officer."

It was a routine incident that any one of us could have gone to, in an apartment 8 complex that we've all been to. A victim mired in her own problems—a broken collar bone and a life crushing down around her—forgot to tell officers that her crazed, abusive boyfriend had fled with a gun. What followed happened fast. Thick fog and darkness shrouded the complex parking lot where Davis and his partner stopped to contact a driver backing out of the lot.

Ron took a bullet in the neck as he stepped out of his passenger side door. The bul- 9 let bled him faster than any resuscitating efforts could counteract. He died while his partner hopelessly tried to breathe life back into his bloody, weakening body. Medics said that even if they'd been there when it happened, there would have been nothing they could do to save his life.

The next week brought a crush of support for our division. The chief, the field oper- 10 ations commander, psychological services counselors, and peer support counselors all came to our lineups to say we're here man, and we know it doesn't feel good. The lineup room looked like a wake with its display of food, flowers, and cards that showered in from other divisions, other departments, and the citizens of our division.

Ron's squad was placed on leave, so officers came from other divisions to help us 11 cover manpower shortages. And on the day of the funeral, officers volunteered from all over the city to cover our beats so that everyone in our division could go to the service.

The funeral procession filled the three miles from Jack Murphy Stadium to the 12 church with bumper-to-bumper police units flashing red and blue overhead lights. Police cars came from San Diego, the Border Patrol, the U.S. Marshals, El Cajon, La Mesa, Chula Vista, National City, Riverside, Los Angeles, seemingly everywhere. The sight we made sent chills up my spine.

For the breadth of that three-mile procession, for a few minutes at least, drivers 13 couldn't keep racing in their usual preoccupied frenzy. Traffic had to stop. In those frozen freeway moments, a tiny corner of the world had to take time out to notice our mourning at the passing of Ronald W. Davis, age 24, husband, father of two, San Diego police officer. The citizens held captive by the procession responded with heart. There was no angry beeping, there were no cars nosing down breakdown lanes. Drivers turned off ignitions in anticipation of a long wait and watched patiently. Many got out of their cars and waved or yelled words of sympathy.

The pastor's words at the funeral have stayed with me, because he began stretching 14 my perspective back to a more fruitful, hopeful size. "Life is not defined by the quantity of years that we are on this earth, but by the quality of the time that we spend here."

I never cried at the funeral. I cried three weeks later in front of a second grade class. 15

Staring at the bulletin board one day drinking my coffee, I noticed a sheaf of papers 16 with big, just-learned-to-write letters on them. The papers were letters to the Officers of Southeastern from Ms. Matthews's second grade class at Boone Elementary:

Dear Friends of Officer Davis,   17

We hope this letter will make you feel better. We feel sad about what happened to Offi-cer Davis. We know he was a nice man and a good cop. We thank you for protecting our neighborhood. We know you try to protect every one of us. We know Officer Davis was a good father. We're sorry.

Your friend, 18
Jeffrey

Dear Friends of Officer Davis,   19

We feel sorry about Officer Davis. I know you feel sorry for what happened when the 20 bad guy killed your friend, Officer Davis. Thank you for protecting us. I know that he's dead and I know you feel sorry about it. I'm glad you got the bad guy. Do you think this would happen again? I'm sure not. Please protect yourself.

Your friend, 21
Henry
P.S. I live in Meadowbrook apartments. Thank you. 22

Dear Friends of Officer Davis, 23

We feel sad about Officer Davis being killed. The man that killed Officer Davis got killed 24 right behind our house. We live in front of Meadowbrook apartments. It is really sad that Officer Davis got killed. Last year when my brother was in sixth grade and he was playing basketball with his friends, two kids came and took the ball away. They broke his basketball hoop. Officers helped find the two kids. We are thankful you are trying to protect us.

Your friend, 25
Travis

Dear Friends, 26

I hope you will feel better. I know how you feel, sad. Was Officer Davis your friend? 27 Well, he was my friend, too. When I saw the news I felt very sad for him. When I grow up, I might be a police officer. I'll never forget Officer Davis. I know how losing a friend is. When you lose a friend you feel very sad. I know how losing a friend is cause my best friend moved away to Virginia. They wrote to me once and I still miss her and I miss Officer Davis, too.

Your Friend, 28
Jennifer L.

Dear Officers, 29

I hope you feel a little better with my letter. We feel sorry that Officer Davis was killed. 30 I heard that he got shot on his neck when he was just getting out of his car. I also heard that Officer Davis was an officer for two years and that he has two children. That one is one years old and the other five years old. I want to say thank you for protecting us and for helping us. We all wish that Officer Davis was still alive.

Your friend always, 31
Arlene

Dear Officers, 32

We were so sad that your friend Officer Davis died. Last night on 9-17-91 I couldn't 33 sleep because I was thinking all about your friend Officer Davis. When I heard about Officer Davis getting shot I was so sad. I know how it feels when a friend is gone. I wish that Officer Davis could hear this but he can't right now. Officer Davis and the rest of the force do a great job.

Sincerely, 34
Jasper

Those letters brought feelings up from my gut. The next day I visited Room B-17 to 35
deliver thank you notes to the authors. Ms. Matthews was so excited with my visit that
she asked me to speak to the class. She explained that the letters were a class exercise to
help the students deal with fears they had expressed to her after the shooting. Because
many of her students lived in the apartments where Ron was shot, the shooting was
very personal to them. Some couldn't sleep, others were afraid to walk to school, and
some were shocked at the realization that the "good guys" get killed too.

I hadn't expected to give a speech, and wasn't really ready to give one on this par- 36
ticular topic. When I faced the class, I saw 32 sets of Filipino, Latino, white, and African-
American eyes fixed on me. Their hands all sat respectfully in their laps. In those young
faces, I saw an innocence and trust that I didn't want to shake.

I thought of the sympathy in their letters; I pictured them passing by the large, dark 37
stain of Officer Davis's blood that still scarred the parking lot pavement; and I wondered
what young minds must think when a force of blacked-out SWAT officers sweeps
through nearby homes in search of the "bad guy" who shot the "good guy."

I wondered how many of the children had been home looking out their windows 38
when the suspect, Arnaldo Castillo, was shot by a volley of officers' gunfire as he sprung
out of his hiding place in the late afternoon of September 17. I couldn't imagine what
these children must be thinking, because a second grader growing up in rural New
Hampshire in 1962 didn't witness such events. I could only think that second graders of
any generation in any place in the world shouldn't have to witness or ponder the sense-
lessness of human violence.

When I finally opened my mouth to speak, my eyes watered and no words would 39
come out. I could say nothing. Each time I tried to push my voice, my eyes watered
more. I looked helplessly at Ms. Matthews and the vice principal, who had come to listen to me. Ms. Matthews came to my rescue by starting to talk to the class about strong
feelings and the importance of letting feelings out so we don't trap sadness inside ourselves. "Even police officers know that crying can be a strong thing to do." Her reassur-
ances to them reassured me and made me smile at the image of myself, "the big, brave
cop" choked up by a second grade class.

We talked for a time about the shooting, about having someone to talk to about 40
scary things, and about how important their thoughtful letters had been in a time of
sadness. By the time I left, they were more enchanted with my handcuffs and nunchakus
than they were concerned by death. Ahhh, the lure for us kids of all ages conjured up by
cops and robbers, catching bad guys, rescuing good guys, and having a belt full of cop
toys.

Through Ron's death, I grew to have a more mature, realistic view of my job. 41
Through the eyes of the pastor at the funeral and Ms. Matthews's second grade class, I
recovered perspective and belief in the value of what I do. It's important for me to live
my life doing something I believe is important for this thing we call humanity. And I
believe that what I do is important because of people like Henry, Jasper, Jennifer L., Jeffrey, Travis, Arlene, Ms. Matthews, and all of the kids in Room B-17.

QUESTIONS FOR DISCUSSION

1. How does Wagner show the passage of time? Reread paragraphs 5–10 to find good examples.
2. Find verbs, adjectives, and adverbs that keep the essay interesting and believable. Reread paragraphs 6–13 for good examples.
3. What use does Wagner make of proper nouns? What effect do they have on her story?
4. What use does the essay make of description?
5. Before this incident, Wagner had looked on violence as "any rubbernecker would—with a certain detachment" (paragraph 3). What does this image tell us? Where else in this paragraph and the next does she use verbal images?
6. All writers must decide to include some things and to exclude others. Why are the children's letters included?
7. Why does Wagner mention "the citizens held captive" by the funeral procession (paragraph 13)? Why does she use the word "citizens"?
8. How did the officer's death change Wagner's view of herself and of her job?

THINKING CRITICALLY

1. Why were the students asked to write letters? Is the purpose of their assignment similar to the purpose behind Wagner's writing this essay? Point out similarities by writing notes in the margins of the essay.
2. Is it strange that second graders are writing about violence in their community? What does this tell us about our society? Does "Death of an Officer" echo ideas in "The Last Safe Haven," in Chapter 3? If you haven't read that short essay, do so now. Write your response in a paragraph or two that make reference to both selections.

SUGGESTIONS FOR JOURNAL ENTRIES

1. The pastor says that "Life is not defined by the quantity of years that we are on this earth but by the quality of the time that we spend here." Use this idea as the focus of a freewriting exercise. Use examples from your own life and observations to support this idea.
2. Writing is a good tool for dealing with the fear, anger, or sadness that comes from losing someone you care for or respect. Use focused freewriting or listing to explain your immediate and long-term reactions to such a loss. Then explain what the reaction you have just described says about you. Does it reveal something about your personality? Did the experience change you in any way?

3. Because of the death of a fellow officer, Wagner sees herself and her job differently. Recall an event that changed your attitude about your role at school, at work, in your family, in your community, or in any other group or place. Use listing to gather information about the most important aspects of this event.

Wanderlust

Charles Kuralt

A native of North Carolina, Charles Kuralt has long been one of America's most respected journalists and has won almost every major award for television journalism. He was the host of CBS's Sunday Morning, *a television magazine that has earned national acclaim. "Wanderlust" is the first chapter of* A Life on the Road, *the story of Kuralt's travels as a reporter.*

L OOKING
A HEAD

1. The Depression was a severe economic downturn in the 1930s; it caused widespread unemployment and poverty. One way President Roosevelt's administration fought these problems was through public-works and social-services programs that created jobs for people. Often referred to by their initials, the offices that ran these programs were known as the "alphabet agencies."
2. The Washington Senators were a major league baseball team. Farm teams are organizations that train young players for the major leagues.

V OCABULARY

banter	Playful conversation, teasing.
cadre	Small group of people who lead a larger organization.
chaperoneship	Guidance, direction.
contrived	Thought up, imagined.
curfew	Time by which one has to be indoors.
detachment	Group sent to do a job.
enlistees	Ordinary soldiers, nonofficers.
forerunner	Predecessor, something that comes before.
indiscriminately	Without plan or preference.
pith helmet	Light hat that shades the sun.
plug	Fishing lure.
rapture	Joy, ecstasy.
three-stripers	Sergeants.

Wanderlust | *C h a r l e s   K u r a l t*

Before I was born, I went on the road. The road was U.S. 17, south from Jack- 1
sonville, North Carolina, through the Holly Shelter Swamp to Wilmington,
where the hospital was. My father backed the Chevrolet out of its place in the hay barn
next to the farm cart and helped my mother into the front seat on the afternoon of September 9, 1934. He made the trip in little more than an hour, barely slowing down for
the stop signs in Dixon, Folkstone and Holly Ridge. I was born the next morning with
rambling in my blood and fifty miles already under my belt.

We lived on my grandparents' farm off and on for a while there during the Depres- 2
sion. A sandy road passed in front of the house and a logging path through the pine
woods behind it. I always wondered where the roads went, and after I learned that the
one in front went to another farm a mile away, I wondered where it went from there.
Once, playing in the woods, I surprised a flock of wild turkeys, which went flying down
the logging road and out of sight. I remember wanting to go with them. Whenever I
hear the Judy Garland lyric "Birds fly over the rainbow—Why then, oh why can't I?" it's
those turkeys I see flying.

My mother was a schoolteacher and my father was getting started in what seemed to 3
him the right job for the times, helping out poor people. There was no shortage of poor
people to help out in the thirties, of course. My father, who had earned a Phi Beta Kappa
key at the University of North Carolina and had planned to become a big businessman,
became a social worker instead. He found employment in several of President Roosevelt's alphabet agencies, the CCC, the ERA, the WPA, then went back to the university
at Chapel Hill, took some graduate courses in social work, and accepted a job with the
state Department of Public Welfare. We moved from one town to another in eastern
North Carolina, and I loved every move. I began to find out where the roads went.

My father's job as field supervisor for the state required him to travel to the small- 4
town county seats to visit the local welfare offices. Since my mother was busy teaching
school, somebody had to take care of me. The solution—a little troublesome for my
father, I imagine, but perfect for me—was for him to take me with him on his trips.

We rolled along the country roads to the old tidewater towns, Edenton and Ply- 5
mouth and New Bern and Swanquarter, my father smoking Tampa Nuggets and spinning yarns for my amusement. He tried a little history on me, thinking to improve my
mind: "The people here didn't like the British governor, and had a fight with the British
at this bridge." He filled me with local lore: "At Harkers Island over there, they make
wonderful strong boats and go to sea in them." He taught me to read the Burma-Shave
signs: " 'Twould Be More Fun . . . to Go by Air . . . but We Couldn't Put . . . These Signs
Up There. Burma-Shave." We stopped in the afternoons to fish for a few minutes in
roadside creeks turned black by the tannin of cypress trees, my father casting a red-and-
white plug expertly with the old bait-casting rod he carried in the trunk, and patiently
picking out the backlashes that snarled the reel when I tried it. We stopped for suppers
of pork chops, sweet potatoes and collard greens at roadside cafes, and rolled on into the
night, bound for some tourist home down the road, my father telling tales and I listening in rapture, just the two of us, rolling on, wrapped in a cloud of companionship and
smoke from his five-cent cigar.

I wanted never to go home from these trips, and when we did go home, I contrived   6
longer trips to farther-away places, trips of the mind. In a field within walking distance
of our farm, a small detachment of U.S. Marines was setting up a tent camp, forerunner
of what was to become Camp LeJeune, the sprawling Marine base that eventually
changed Jacksonville forever. On hot summer mornings, I used to walk barefoot down
the sandy road to the tent camp towing a red wagon filled with quart jars of milk from
our cows and sugar cookies my grandmother had baked and wrapped in wax paper. It
never took more than a few minutes to sell out my stock of milk and cookies to the
Marines. If they didn't have money, I accepted souvenirs. Somewhere in my folks' attic,
there must still be a cigar box containing sharpshooter medals, uniform buttons and
globe-and-anchor emblems from the pith helmets of those Marines. Most of them were
young enlistees, I suppose, who had never traveled farther than a few miles from home,
but the cadre was composed of old sergeants who told me casual tales of service in
places I had trouble imagining, places where the people spoke other languages entirely,
they told me, places with names like the Philippines and Nicaragua and the Canal Zone.
I learned to seek out the three-stripers when I wanted to hear good traveling stories. I
learned the words of their song, "From the halls of Montezuma to the shores of Tripoli
. . ." More than anything else, I wanted to wear a Marine pith helmet and go to the halls
of Montezuma. I asked a jolly fat sergeant named Carpenter if he had ever been there.
He always called me "Charlie, my boy." "Charlie, my boy," he said, "I'll tell you the
truth. I've never even figured out where Montezuma might be. But if the United States
Marines decide to send me there, I'll send you a penny postcard." I asked Sergeant Carpenter how old he was when he joined the Marines. "Charlie, my boy," he said, "I was a
grand old man of sixteen." You had to be sixteen, he said. I was only six.

In school, I proved to be a below-average student in all forms of mathematics, and   7
later in such subjects as chemistry and biology, but I was good at reading—I had started
early on the Burma-Shave signs—and I was fascinated by history and geography, subjects that were still taught in public school in those days. Indiscriminately, I read the
works of writers who had traveled, including everything I could find of Richard Hal-
liburton's. I knew the capitals of all the states. The ones I most wanted to go to were
Montpelier, Vermont, and Olympia, Washington, for they were the ones that sounded
most distant and wondrous.

I entered contests that promised travel as a prize. In 1947, when I was twelve, to my   8
surprise, I won one of these competitions—or rather, finished second for the second
straight year, which proved to be just as good as winning. We lived in Charlotte, North
Carolina, then, where my father had become the county welfare superintendent. *The
Charlotte News* sponsored an annual baseball writing contest for students on the subject
"My Favorite Hornet." The prize was a road trip with the Charlotte Hornets, our Washington Senators' farm team. Baseball was my passion and regularly I spent my Saturdays
in the old green grandstand watching the Hornets play, but it was the trip I was after. My
essay on "bouncing" Bobby Beal, the third baseman, was judged good enough that I was
invited to accompany the winner, an older boy named Buddy Carrier. We were to ride in
the bus with the team and take turns covering six games in Asheville, North Carolina,
and Knoxville, Tennessee. I loved it. I loved the easy chaperoneship of manager Cal
Ermer, who assigned Buddy and me the same curfew that applied to the team—one

A.M.! I loved listening to the banter of the players on the bus, sitting in the dugout during the games and hanging around the hotel lobbies with my heroes. I loved being away from home, in places I had only heard about. Asheville! Knoxville! A good-natured country pitcher named Sonny Dixon played catch with me on the field before each game began and took to introducing me to players on the other teams as "Flash Kuralt, our traveling big-time sports writer." I loved that, too. But best of all was climbing up to the press box as the game was about to end and pecking out my story on the battered portable typewriter I had borrowed for the trip from a caseworker in my father's office, then, downtown after the game, swaggering into the Western Union office, tossing the copy across the counter and saying to the clerk the words I had been instructed to say by Ray Howe, the *Charlotte News* sports editor. They are words that still give me a little thrill of importance all these years later. I did my twelve-year-old best to growl them like a veteran.

The words were: 9

"*The Charlotte News*. Press rate collect."   10

QUESTIONS FOR DISCUSSION

1. Which type(s) of introduction discussed in Chapter 4 does this essay use?
2. Where in this selection do we learn about the setting, the story's time and place?
3. What techniques does Kuralt use to describe the people in his story? How does telling us about them help him move the plot along?
4. Why does he bother to include so many proper names?
5. Selling milk and cookies to the Marines didn't take young Charles far from home. Should the author have spent as much time as he did recalling this experience?
6. In the introduction to Section Four you read examples of language that makes Kuralt's writing lively and believable. Find other examples of effective verbs, adjectives, and nouns.

THINKING CRITICALLY

1. This is a story about visiting new places, meeting new people, and discovering new realities. What does all this exploration tell us about the boy who did the exploring? Write one or two paragraphs describing this boy's character.
2. Briefly discuss what this story tells us about the character of Kuralt the adult.
3. Briefly discuss what this story tells us about the 1930s in the southeastern United States.

SUGGESTIONS FOR JOURNAL ENTRIES

1. To illustrate his passion for traveling, the author tells us about rambling over country roads, selling milk and cookies to Marines, and going on a trip with the Hornets. Think about a passion you had as a child: raising tropical fish, collecting stamps, dancing, playing video games, playing and/or watching a sport, for example. Use focused freewriting to recall an incident like one of those in Kuralt's essay. Make sure the incident you narrate shows how "passionately" you felt about this activity.
2. Is there someone in your life who inspired a special interest or talent in you much like Kuralt's father encouraged his interest in travel? Use any method for collecting information discussed in "Getting Started" to recall what this person did to inspire or encourage you.

Suggestions for Sustained Writing

1. Use narration to explain what someone did to influence you either positively or negatively. Show how this person encouraged or discouraged you to develop a particular interest or talent; explain what he or she taught you about yourself; or discuss ways he or she strengthened or weakened your self-esteem.

   You need not express yourself in an essay. Consider writing a letter instead. Address it to the person who influenced you, and explain your appreciation or resentment of that influence. Either way, put your thesis—a statement of just how positively or negatively he or she affected you—in the introduction to your essay or letter.

   Before you begin, check the journal entries you made after reading Cullen, Diaz-Talty, or Kuralt. Then, write one or two stories from personal experience that show how the person in question affected you. After completing your first draft, try adding dialogue to your stories. Reveal your subject's attitude toward you by recalling words he or she used when answering your questions, giving you advice or instructions, or commenting on your efforts.

   As you revise your work further, make sure you have explained the results of this person's influence on you thoroughly. Add details as you move from draft to draft. Then, edit for grammar, punctuation, spelling, and other problems that can make your writing less effective.

2. In "Namas-te," Peter Matthiessen explains that the sight of a crippled child dragging herself through the mud was a "reminder of mortality." If you have seen human suffering up close, you know that it can affect people in different ways. Write an essay or a letter to a friend in which you recall a "pitiable" sight or event you recently witnessed.

   Narrate what happened from beginning to end. Include vivid descriptions of the setting and of the people involved. Tell what you and they did and said during this experience; use dialogue when appropriate. Most important, as you conclude, explain how this experience affected you personally. For example, express anger, sadness, or disappointment that human beings are allowed to suffer, or give thanks that life has not been as cruel to you as it has been to the person(s) you are describing. Like Matthiessen, you might even explain why this incident was a "reminder of mortality."

   As you revise and edit, make sure the information you include and the vocabulary you choose clearly reflect your reaction to the incident. A good place to find such details might be the journal entries you made after reading "Namas-te."

3. How we face life's hardships, losses, fears, and emergencies says a lot about the people we are. We can see this clearly in Masters' "Lucinda Matlock" and "Margaret Fuller Slack" and in Wagner's "Death of an Officer." Tell the story of how you, a close friend, neighbor, or relative dealt with a serious personal problem or

concern. As you draft your essay, make sure the events of your narrative reveal the strength or lack of strength in your subject's character.

Begin by reviewing the journal notes you made after reading Masters' poems or Wagner's essay. Your reactions to the Matthiessen's "Namas-te" might also come in handy.

A general overview of your subject's character can make a good introduction to this essay. If you are writing about someone other than yourself, explain how well you know each other or how close you are. Make sure the introduction also includes a statement that clearly expresses the way your subject handles hardship, stress, or adversity. This will be your thesis, the idea that the rest of your essay will illustrate or prove through narration.

After you have completed the second or third draft, read your story carefully and decide whether you have included enough detail to make it convincing. Add information if necessary. At the same time, check that transitions between sentences and paragraphs are clear and logical. As always, polish the final version to catch errors in grammar, spelling, and so on.

4. Cullen and Kuralt tell stories about childhood experiences that had a significant effect on their visions of the world and even on the persons they were to become. What one event in your childhood do you remember most clearly?

Recall this experience in an essay that also explains why it is important to you even today. First, however, review what you wrote in your journal after reading the selections by the authors mentioned above. Your notes might provide both inspiration and information for this assignment. Whether the experience you write about is positive or negative, tell your story vividly by using verbs, adjectives, and adverbs like those in this chapter's poems and essays. Also, include the exact names of places, people, and things to help make your story believable.

After you have written two or three drafts and are convinced your essay is well developed, write a concluding paragraph that explains how the event you have just narrated continues to touch your life today. In other words, explain how it has helped make you the person you are, how it affects the way you view yourself or others, or how it influences the way you now live.

Finally, review the paper as a whole. Have you included enough information, maintained coherence in and between paragraphs, and eliminated distracting errors in spelling, grammar, and the like?

5. The first of the Suggestions for Journal Entries after Diaz-Talty's "The Day I Was Fat" asks you to gather information about a painful experience that changed your life for the better. Use this information to begin drafting a full-length essay that explains what happened.

You might begin the first draft by stating in one sentence how this event changed you; this will be your working thesis. You can then tell your story, including only those materials that help explain or prove the thesis. For example, Diaz-Talty's says that being called "fat" helped her regain her self-esteem and her figure; every detail in her story helps prove this statement.

As you write later drafts, add dialogue and descriptive detail about people in your story, just as Diaz-Talty did. If you are unhappy with your introductory and concluding paragraphs, rewrite them by using techniques explained in Chapter 4.

Before you get to your final draft, make certain your paper contains vivid verbs, adjectives, and adverbs, which will keep readers interested. If it doesn't, add them. Then, edit and proofread your work carefully.

6. Like Gaye Wagner ("Death of an Officer"), write the story of an event that significantly changed your attitude about your role at school, at work, in your family, in your community, or in any other group or place. If you responded to the third of the Suggestions for Journal Entries after Wagner's essay, read your notes before you start writing.

   Begin your rough draft by explaining how the event you are narrating changed your attitude. Next, summarize that explanation in one sentence, which will act as your working thesis statement. Then tell your story as completely as you can, but include only those details that support or explain your thesis.

   Don't hesitate to use dialogue or to describe other people who had important roles in your story. Make sure that your introduction captures your readers' attention and that your conclusion is logical and memorable. If not, rewrite these parts of your essay.

   If you have done a good job of introducing, developing, and concluding your paper, you will want to edit and proofread it with care. Working hard to mine diamonds makes no sense if you are not going to polish them.

7. "Wanderlust" traces Charles Kuralt's passion for travel by recalling incidents in his youth, all the way back to the afternoon *before* he was born! Think back to a time in your childhood or teen years when you seemed to focus your attention on one activity: flying kites, playing basketball, making model airplanes, playing with dolls, collecting baseball cards, teasing a brother or sister, playing video or board games, for example.

   If you responded to the journal entries after Kuralt's essay, you might have done some freewriting about an incident that shows how "passionate" you were about this activity. Turn your journal entry into a full-length essay by narrating two or three more incidents to develop this idea. Try following Kuralt's example by opening your paper with a startling remark, and include a thesis statement that clearly explains how strong your interest was.

   As you revise early drafts, make sure your essay contains enough details to support your thesis, to show how passionate you were about the activity you are discussing. Then, before you begin editing your final version for grammar, spelling, and punctuation, review the language you have used. Is your writing concrete, vivid, and convincing? Will your paper hold the readers' interest as firmly as the passion you are describing held yours?

REPORTING EVENTS

The poems and essays in the preceding chapter are autobiographical; they look inward and explain something important about the narrator, the person telling the story. As you recall, each of them is told from the first-person point of view, using the pronoun "I" or "we."

The poems and essays you will read in this chapter, on the other hand, look outward. Some may reveal important facts and insights about their storytellers. Nevertheless, they tell us more about the worlds their narrators live in than about the narrators themselves.

Several of these selections recreate incidents from personal experience and show their writers involved in the action in some way. As a result, they, too, are written in first person. An example is Adrienne Schwartz's "The Colossus in the Kitchen," a story about racism in South Africa, told from the perspective of its young narrator.

In Gansberg's "38 Who Saw Murder Didn't Call the Police," on the other hand, the storyteller is not part of the action. He learns of the murder only secondhand, after talking with eyewitnesses and police. As such, he tells the story from a third-person point of view, using "he," "she," and "they" to explain who did what. As you can see, then, a story's point of view depends upon whether the narrator is a participant or is an outsider—someone who is actually involved in the action or someone who observes it from a distance or learns about it secondhand.

Whichever point of view the selections in this chapter use, they provide a sometimes touching, sometimes terrifying, and always interesting account of their authors' reactions to the world around them. In the introduction to Section Four, you read that narration can be used for a variety of purposes. The poems and essays that follow prove that reporting events is one way to make a point about the nature of human beings and the worlds in which they live. Indeed, if you have ever taken a course in psychology or sociology, you know how important narration can be to explaining human and social behavior.

Though not always expressed in a formal thesis statement, the main point in each of these selections comes across clearly and forcefully because of the writer's powerful command of language and of other techniques important to telling a story. Use these poems and essays as sources of inspiration for your own work. Reporting events you have heard about, witnessed, or even taken part in is an excellent way to continue growing as a writer. It can also help you discover a clearer and more perceptive vision of the world, at least the world you are writing about.

VISUALIZING NARRATIVE ELEMENTS

The paragraphs that follow are from "Padre Blaisdell and the Refugee Children," René Cutforth's true story of a Catholic priest's efforts to save abandoned children during the Korean War. The place is Seoul; the time, December 1950.

At dawn Padre Blaisdell dressed himself in the little icy room at the top of the orphanage at Seoul. He put on his parka and an extra sweater, for the Siberian wind was fluting in the corners of the big grey barrack of the school. The water in his basin was solid ice.

Describes setting and introduces the main character.

His boots clicked along the stone flags in the freezing passages which led to the main door. The truck was waiting on the snow-covered gravel in the yellow-grey light of sunrise; the two Korean nurses stood as usual, ready for duty—pig-tailed adolescents, their moon faces as passive and kindly as cows'.

Describes other characters.

By the time he reached Riverside Road the padre had passed through the normal first stage of reaction to the wind: he was content now in his open vehicle to lie back and admire the effortless skill of the wind's razor as it slashed him to the bone.

Uses a transition to show passage of time.

Uses metaphor, action verb.

There's a dingy alley off Riverside Street, narrow, and strewn with trodden straw and refuse which would stink if the cold allowed it life enough. This alley leads to the arches of the railway bridge across the Han River. The truck's wheels crackled over the frozen... alley, passed from it down a sandy track and halted at the second arch of the bridge [in front of which] lay a pile of filthy rice sacks, clotted with dirt and stiff as boards. It was a child, practically naked and covered with filth. It lay in a pile of its own excrement in a sort of nest it had scratched out among the rice sacks. Hardly able to raise itself on an elbow, it still had

Uses vivid adjectives and proper nouns to describe setting.

Uses vivid verbs and adjectives.

enough energy to draw back cracked lips from bleeding

gums and snarl and spit at the padre like an angry   **Uses a simile.**

kitten. Its neck was not much thicker than a broom

handle and it had the enormous pot-belly of starvation.

Uses a transition to show passage of time.

At eleven o'clock in the morning, when the padre

returned to the orphanage, his truck was full. "They are

the real victims of the war," the padre said in his

careful/./. colourless voice., "Nine-tenths of them were

Uses dialogue to provide information and explain story's purpose.

lost or abandoned ¶/./. No one will take them in unless

they are relations, and we have 800 of these children at

the orphanage. Usually they recover in quite a short

time, but the bad cases tend to become very silent¶/./. I

have a little boy who has said nothing for three months

now but *Yes* and *No*."

TRACKING THE PASSAGE OF TIME IN "PADRE BLAISDALE AND THE REFUGEE CHILDREN"

We can divide the story roughly into three major sections, each of which is introduced by transitions that relate to time.

At dawn . . .

Padre Blaisdale and the nurses leave the
orphanage in search of orphans.

↓

By the time he reached Riverside Road . . .

They find the child in the alley.

↓

At eleven o'clock in the morning . . .

They return with a truckload of children.

REVISING NARRATIVE ESSAYS

The third selection in this chapter, "The Colossus in the Kitchen," was written by Adrienne Schwartz, a student who recalls the racial prejudice aimed at Tandi, a black woman who worked for her family in her native South Africa. Realizing narrative essays require as much care as any others, Schwartz made important changes to her rough draft and turned an already fine essay into a moving and memorable experience for her readers. Compare these excerpts from her drafts.

Schwartz—Rough Draft

Our neighbors, in conformity with established

thinking, had long called my mother, and therefore all

of us, deviants, agitators, and no less than second

cousins to Satan himself. The cause of this dishonorable

Use a quotation to show this? labeling was the fact that we had been taught to believe

in the equality and dignity of humankind.

That was why I could not understand the apoplectic

reaction of the neighbors to my excited news that Tandi

was going to have a baby. After all, this was not

politics; this was new life. Tandi's common-law husband

lived illegally with her in the quarters assigned to

Connect these ideas better? them; complying with the law on this and many other

petty issues was not considered appropriate in our

household. It was the Group Areas Act that had been

responsible for the breakup of Tandi's marriage. Her

lawful husband, who was not born in the same area as she,

had been refused a permit to work in the Transvaal, a

province in northeastern South Africa, where we lived. **Needed?**

Make smoother? More vivid? In the way of many others, he had been placed in such a

burdensome situation and found the degradation of being

taken from his wife's bed in the middle of the night and

joblessness more often than he could tolerate. He simply

went away, never to be seen or heard from again.

Find a better place for this idea?

> The paradox of South Africa is complex in the extreme. It is like a rare and precious stone set amid barren wastes, and yet it feeds off its own flesh.

Slow down? Show passage of time?

> The days passed, and Tandi's waist got bigger and pride could be seen in her eyes.
>
> The child died after only one day.

Schwartz—Final Draft

Our neighbors, in conformity with established thinking, had long called my mother, and therefore all of us, deviants, agitators, and no less than second cousins to Satan himself. The cause of this dishonorable

Uses a direct quotation to prove an idea.

> labeling was the fact that we had been taught to believe in the equality and dignity of humankind.
>
> "Never take a person's dignity away from him," my mother had said, "no matter how angry or hurt you might be because in the end you only diminish your own worth."

That was why I could not understand the apoplectic reaction of the neighbors to my excited news that Tandi was going to have a baby. After all, this was not

Moves this information to a more logical place.

Adds vivid details in a metaphor.

> politics; this was new life. But the paradox of South Africa is complex in the extreme. The country is like a rare and precious stone set amid barren wastes, and yet close up it is a gangrenous growth that feeds off its own flesh.

Tandi's common-law husband lived illegally with her in the quarters assigned to them; complying with the law on

Adds transition to conect ideas.

> this and many other petty issues was not considered appropriate in our household. It was the Group Areas Act that had been responsible for the breakup of Tandi's

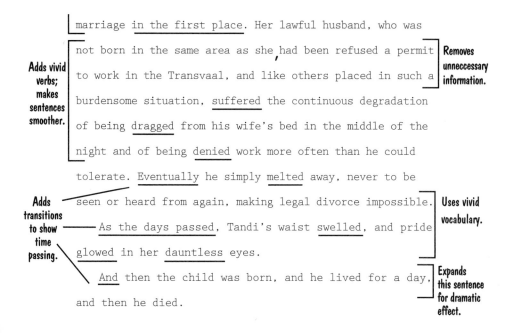

marriage in the first place. Her lawful husband, who was

Adds vivid verbs; makes sentences smoother.

not born in the same area as she had been refused a permit
to work in the Transvaal, and like others placed in such a
burdensome situation, suffered the continuous degradation
of being dragged from his wife's bed in the middle of the
night and of being denied work more often than he could

Removes unneccessary information.

tolerate. Eventually he simply melted away, never to be

Adds transitions to show time passing.

seen or heard from again, making legal divorce impossible.
As the days passed, Tandi's waist swelled, and pride
glowed in her dauntless eyes.

Uses vivid vocabulary.

And then the child was born, and he lived for a day,
and then he died.

Expands this sentence for dramatic effect.

PRACTICING NARRATIVE SKILLS

What follows is an eyewitness account of the last moments of the Titanic, which sank in 1912 after striking an iceberg. The writer views the scene from a lifeboat about two hours after having abandoned ship. Practice your skills by following the instructions for each section of this exercise.

a. Underline words and phrases that make this an effective narrative. Look especially for vivid verbs, adjectives, and adverbs. Also underline transitions.

In a couple of hours . . . [the ship] began to go down . . . rapidly. Then the fearful sight began. The people in the ship were just beginning to realize how great their danger was. When the forward part of the ship dropped suddenly at a faster rate . . . there was a sudden rush of passengers on all the decks towards the stern. It was like a wave. We could see the great black mass of people in the steerage sweeping to the rear part of the boat and breaking through to the upper decks. At a distance of about a mile we could distinguish everything through the night, which was perfectly clear. We could make out the increasing excitement on board the boat as the people, rushing to and fro, caused the deck lights to disappear and reappear as they passed in front of them. [Mrs. D.H. Bishop]

b. Important words have been removed from the following paragraphs. Replace them with words of your own. Use only the kinds of words indicated. Avoid *is, are, was, were, have been, had been,* and other forms of the verb *to be*.

This panic went on, it seemed, for an hour. _____the

underline: TRANSITION

ship seemed to _____ out of the water and stand

underline: VERB

there perpendicularly. It seemed to us that it stood _____ in

underline: ADVERB

the water for four full minutes.

_____it began to_____gently

underline: TRANSITION   underline: VERB

downwards. Its speed increased as it went down head first, so that the stern

_____down with a rush.

underline: VERB

The lights continued to burn till it sank. We could see the people

_____ _____in the stern till it

underline: VERB   underline: ADVERB

was gone. . . .

_____ the ship sank we_____

underline: ADVERB OF TIME   underline: VERB

the screaming a mile away. Gradually it became fainter and fainter and died away.

Some of the lifeboats that had room for more might have_____

underline: VERB

to their rescue, but it would have meant that those who were in the water would

have _____ aboard and sunk them.

underline: VERB

The five selections that appear in this chapter are very different in style, content, and purpose. But they all make their points in interesting and meaningful ways. More important, they illustrate effective techniques important to narrative and other types of writing that you will use in both your college and your professional lives.

Child of the Romans

Carl Sandburg

In the introduction to "Abraham Lincoln" (Chapter 9), you learned that Sandburg is one of America's best-loved poets and biographers. His respect for the common people and his support for labor are evident in "Child of the Romans," a sketch of an Italian immigrant railroad worker. For Sandburg, this "dago shovelman" was typical of the immigrant laborers who built America's factories and railroads.

LOOKING AHEAD

1. "Dago" is an insulting term for an Italian. The poem's title refers to the fact that 2000 years ago Italy was the center of the powerful Roman Empire.
2. Sandburg contrasts the life of the shovelman with those of the people on the train. It is this comparison that serves as the theme of the poem.
3. Verbs and adjectives create a sense of reality in this poem and keep it interesting. Look for them as you read "Child of the Romans."

VOCABULARY

eclairs	Rich, custard-filled pastries topped with chocolate.
jonquils	Garden plants of the narcissus family with lovely yellow or white flowers.

Child of the Romans | *Carl Sandburg*

The dago shovelman sits by the railroad track
Eating a noon meal of bread and bologna.
A train whirls by, and men and women at tables
Alive with red roses and yellow jonquils,
Eat steaks running with brown gravy, 5
Strawberries and cream, eclairs and coffee.
The dago shovelman finishes the dry bread and bologna,
Washes it down with a dipper from the water-boy,
And goes back to the second half of a ten-hour day's work
Keeping the road-bed so the roses and jonquils 10
Shake hardly at all in the cut glass vases
Standing slender on the tables in the dining cars.

QUESTIONS FOR DISCUSSION

1. The poem's plot is very simple. What events take place during the shovelman's lunch?
2. Sandburg gets very detailed in listing the various items that the railroad passengers are dining on. How do these contrast with what the shovelman is eating?
3. Why does Sandburg make sure to tell us that the train "whirls" by as the man eats his lunch? How does his description of the movement of the train contrast with what you read in the last three lines of this poem?
4. How long is the shovelman's day? In what way does his work, "keeping the road-bed," affect the passengers?
5. The poem has two very different settings. What are they, and how does the contrast between the two help Sandburg get his point across?

THINKING CRITICALLY

1. Earlier you read that Sandburg was a friend to labor and the common people. Underline words or phrases in his poem that support this idea. Does the poem tell us anything about Sandburg's attitude toward the wealthy? If so, what is it?
2. "Child of the Romans" was written in 1916. Would the setting be different if Sandburg were writing this poem today? What else might change?
3. Read a little about the Romans in an encyclopedia. Besides being Italian, in what way is the shovelman a "child of the Romans"?

SUGGESTIONS FOR JOURNAL ENTRIES

1. If you know a hardworking immigrant who has come here in search of a better life, write a story about this person's typical workday.
2. If you have ever had a job in which you provided a service for other people (perhaps as a housepainter, waitress, or salesclerk), narrate one or two events from a typical workday.
3. After reading Sandburg's story of the shovelman's difficult life, many readers are inclined to count their blessings. List some things in your life that make it easier and more hopeful than that of the shovelman.

What the Gossips Saw

Leo Romero

A native of New Mexico, Leo Romero is among a growing number of contemporary southwestern writers whose poetry and fiction are becoming popular across the country. Romero studied at the University of New Mexico, where he took a degree in English. His poems have appeared in several recent collections of poetry and prose. "What the Gossips Saw" was first published in 1981 in a collection of his poetry called Agua Negra.

LOOKING AHEAD

1. This is the story of a community's response to a woman who had her leg amputated. What it says about the way society sometimes reacts to those who are "different" can be compared with what we learn from another piece in this chapter: Schwartz's "The Colossus in the Kitchen."
2. Romero chooses to leave out periods and other end marks. Doing so sometimes helps poets create dramatic effects. Nevertheless, developing writers should always include appropriate punctuation.

VOCABULARY

alluring	Appealing, tempting.
conjecture	Guessing, speculation.
hobble	Limp.
in cohorts	In league with, cooperating with.
murmur	Mumble discontentedly.

What the Gossips Saw

Leo Romero

Everyone pitied Escolastica, her leg
had swollen like a watermelon in the summer
It had practically happened over night
She was seventeen, beautiful and soon
to be married to Guillermo who was working   5
in the mines at Terreros, eighty miles away
far up in the mountains, in the wilderness
Poor Escolastica, the old women would say
on seeing her hobble to the well with a bucket
carrying her leg as if it were the weight   10
of the devil, surely it was a curse from heaven
for some misdeed, the young women who were
jealous would murmur, yet they were grieved too
having heard that the doctor might cut
her leg, one of a pair of the most perfect legs   15
in the valley, and it was a topic of great
interest and conjecture among the villagers
whether Guillermo would still marry her
if she were crippled, a one-legged woman—
as if life weren't hard enough for a woman   20
with two legs—how could she manage
Guillermo returned and married Escolastica
even though she had but one leg, the sound
of her wooden leg pounding down the wooden aisle
stayed in everyone's memory for as long   25
as they lived, women cried at the sight
of her beauty, black hair so dark
that the night could get lost in it, a face
more alluring than a full moon

Escolastica went to the dances with her husband   30
and watched and laughed but never danced
though once she had been the best dancer
and could wear holes in a pair of shoes
in a matter of a night, and her waist had been
as light to the touch as a hummingbird's flight   35
And Escolastica bore five children, only half
what most women bore, yet they were healthy
In Escolastica's presence, no one would mention
the absence of her leg, though she walked heavily
And it was not long before the gossips   40
spread their poison, that she must be in cohorts

with the devil, had given him her leg
for the power to bewitch Guillermo's heart
and cloud his eyes so that he could not see
what was so clear to them all   45

QUESTIONS FOR DISCUSSION

1. What words and phrases in this poem show time passing?
2. What figures of speech does Romero include?
3. Pick out a few vivid verbs and adjectives used in "What the Gossips Saw."
4. The story takes place in a village where life is hard. Why is it important for us to know that?
5. The gossips believe Guillermo "could not see/what was so clear to them all." What does Guillermo see that they don't?
6. How do the gossips explain Guillermo's marrying Escolastica even after she loses her leg? What does this say about them?
7. What can we conclude about the gossips' opinion of men in general?

THINKING CRITICALLY

1. Many of us know people like the gossips. Do such people deserve blame or pity? Are they malicious or just ignorant?
2. Schwartz's "The Colossus in the Kitchen," which comes next in this chapter, shows that bad luck can be mistaken by small-minded people as a sign of sinfulness and of God's punishment. Where does this theme appear in Romero's poem? Make notes in the margins to prove your point.

SUGGESTIONS FOR JOURNAL ENTRIES

1. Think of a person or an event that was the subject of gossip in your school or community. Use listing or another method for gathering details discussed in "Getting Started" to explain how much the gossips exaggerated, twisted, or lied about the facts. Try to show how they changed the truth in order to make it seem more sensational, startling, racy, or horrible than it was.
2. Not all communities react badly to people who are different. Do you agree? If so, provide evidence from personal experience, from newspapers, or from other sources to support this idea. For example, talk about how quickly people in your city responded when they heard a neighbor needed expensive medical care, or explain how well students at your school accept newcomers from other cultures.

The Colossus in the Kitchen

Adrienne Schwartz

Adrienne Schwartz was born in Johannesburg in the Republic of South Africa, where she now lives. "The Colossus in the Kitchen" is about the tragedy of apartheid, a political system that kept power and wealth in the hands of whites by denying civil and economic rights to non-whites and by enforcing a policy of racial segregation. Tandi, the woman who is at the center of this story, was Schwartz's nursemaid for several years.

Schwartz wrote this essay in 1988. Since that time, South Africa has abolished apartheid and extended civil rights to all citizens. Today, Nelson Mandela, a black political leader who had been imprisoned by the white minority government during the apartheid era, is South Africa's freely elected president.

LOOKING **A**HEAD

1. The "Group Areas Act," which Schwartz refers to in paragraph 7, required blacks to seek work *only* in those areas of the country for which the government had granted them a permit. Unfortunately, Tandi's legal husband was not allowed to work in the same region as she.
2. The "Colossus" was the giant bronze statue of a male figure straddling the inlet to the ancient Greek city of Rhodes. It was known as one of the seven wonders of the ancient world. More generally, this term refers to anything that is very large, impressive, and very powerful. As you read this essay, ask yourself what made Tandi a colossus in the eyes of young Schwartz.

VOCABULARY

apoplectic	Characterized by a sudden loss of muscle control or ability to move.
ashen	Gray.
bestriding	Straddling, standing with legs spread widely.
cavernous	Like a cave or cavern.
confections	Sweets.
cowered	Lowered in defeat.
dauntless	Fearless.
deviants	Moral degenerates.
disenfranchised	Without rights or power.
entailed	Involved.
flaying	Whipping.

gangrenous	Characterized by decay of the flesh.
nebulous	Without a definite shape or form.
prerogative	Privilege.
sage	Wise.

The Colossus in the Kitchen

Adrienne Schwartz

I remember when I first discovered the extraordinary harshness of daily life for   1
black South Africans. It was in the carefree, tumbling days of childhood that I
first sensed apartheid was not merely the impoverishing of the landless and all that that
entailed, but a flaying of the innermost spirit.

The house seemed so huge in those days, and the adults were giants bestriding the   2
world with surety and purpose. Tandi, the cook, reigned with the authoritarian discipline of a Caesar. She held audience in the kitchen, an enormous room filled with half-
lights and well-scrubbed tiles, cool stone floors and a cavernous black stove. Its ceilings
were high, and during the heat of midday I would often drowse in the corner, listening
to Tandi sing, in a lilting voice, of the hardships of black women as aliens in their own
country. From half-closed eyes I would watch her broad hands coax, from a nebulous
lump of dough, a bounty of confections, filled with yellow cream and new-picked apri-
cots.

She was a peasant woman and almost illiterate, yet she spoke five languages quite   3
competently; moreover, she was always there, sturdy, domineering and quick to laugh.

Our neighbors, in conformity with established thinking, had long called my mother,   4
and therefore all of us, deviants, agitators, and no less than second cousins to Satan himself. The cause of this dishonorable labeling was the fact that we had been taught to
believe in the equality and dignity of humankind.

"Never take a person's dignity away from him," my mother had said, "no matter   5
how angry or hurt you might be because in the end you only diminish your own worth."

That was why I could not understand the apoplectic reaction of the neighbors to   6
my excited news that Tandi was going to have a baby. After all, this was not politics; this
was new life. But the paradox of South Africa is complex in the extreme. The country is
like a rare and precious stone set amid barren wastes, and yet close up it is a gangrenous
growth that feeds off its own flesh.

Tandi's common-law husband lived illegally with her in the quarters assigned to   7
them; complying with the law on this and many other petty issues was not considered
appropriate in our household. It was the Group Areas Act that had been responsible for
the breakup of Tandi's marriage in the first place. Her lawful husband, who was not
born in the same area as she, had been refused a permit to work in the Transvaal, and
like others placed in such a burdensome situation, suffered the continuous degradation
of being dragged from his wife's bed in the middle of the night and of being denied work
more often than he could tolerate. Eventually he simply melted away, never to be seen
or heard from again, making legal divorce impossible.

As the days passed, Tandi's waist swelled, and pride glowed in her dauntless eyes.   8

And then the child was born, and he lived for a day, and then he died.   9

I could not look at Tandi. I did not know that the young could die. I thought death   10
was the prerogative of the elderly. I could not bear to see her cowered shoulders or
ashen face.

I fled to the farthest corner of the yard. One of the neighbors was out picking off   11
dead buds from the rose bushes. She looked over the hedge in concern.

"Why! You look terrible . . . are you ill, dear?" she said.   12

"It's Tandi, Mrs. Green. She lost her baby last night," I replied.   13

Mrs. Green sighed thoughtfully and pulled off her gardening gloves. "It's really not   14
surprising," she said, not unkindly, but as if she were imparting as sage a piece of advice
as she could. "These people (a term reserved for the disenfranchised) have to learn that
the punishment always fits the crime."

QUESTIONS FOR DISCUSSION

1. Why does Schwartz spend so much time describing the kitchen in paragraph 2? Does this help us understand Tandi?
2. What details do we learn about Tandi, and what do they tell us about her character? Why does the author call her a "colossus"?
3. Besides Tandi, who are the characters in this narrative and what do we know about them?
4. Why does Schwartz recall events from Tandi's past (paragraph 7)?
5. The author makes especially good use of verbs in the last half of this essay. Find some examples.
6. Schwartz's use of dialogue allows her to explain important ideas. Where in this essay does she use dialogue, and what does it reveal?

THINKING CRITICALLY

1. Apartheid was not "merely the impoverishing of the landless" but also "a flaying of the innermost spirit," says Schwartz. What does she mean by this? If necessary, use the encyclopedia to do a little research on apartheid.
2. Is Schwartz's message or central idea similar to Romero's in "What the Gossips Saw?" Write a paragraph in which you compare (point out similarities between) the central ideas of these selections.

SUGGESTIONS FOR JOURNAL ENTRIES

1. Have you or anyone you know well ever witnessed or been involved in a case of intolerance based on race, color, creed, or sex? List the important events that made up this incident and, if appropriate, use focused-freewriting to write short descriptions of the characters involved.
2. Schwartz's essay is a startling account of her learning some new and very painful things about life. Using any of the prewriting methods discussed in "Getting Started," make notes about an incident from your childhood that opened your eyes to some new and perhaps unpleasant reality.
3. Were you ever as close to an older person as Schwartz was to Tandi? Examine your relationship with the individual by briefly narrating one or two experiences you shared with him or her.

Faith of the Father

Sam Pickering

Sam Pickering teaches nature writing and children's literature at the University of Connecticut. He has written many scholarly books and articles and has published in the National Review, The Kenyon Review, *and* Sewanee Review, *as well as in other prestigious journals. His essay collections include* The Right Distance, A Continuing Education, *and* May Days.

"Faith of the Father's" humorous tone makes it different from other selections in this chapter. However, its message is just as serious as theirs. Indeed, Pickering is a master at making important ideas come alive through interesting, sometimes hilarious, characters and events. "Faith of the Father" first appeared in The Southwest Review.

L**OOKING AHEAD**

Pickering makes references to the Bible and to the Christian faith throughout this essay. Lazarus (paragraph 2) is a figure from the New Testament, whom Christ brought back from the dead. Solomon (paragraph 6) is a king of Israel; in describing the lillies of the field, St. Matthew says that "Solomon in all his glory was not arrayed [dressed] like one of these." The Resurrection (paragraph 11) is the rising of Christ from the dead.

V**OCABULARY**

analysis	Study of, investigation of.
articled	Formal, made up of regulations and procedures.
ascension	Rise.
chalice	Cup for sacred wine.
deity	A god, divinity.
dispassionate	Unemotional, without feeling.
emblem	Sign.
endured	Lasted through.
erratically	Unevenly, not in any pattern.
irascible	Ill tempered, cranky.
mourning cloak	Butterfly with purplish-brown wings.
pretension	Arrogance, excessive pride.
speculated	Guessed, wondered.
sustenance	Support, nourishment.

Faith of the Father | *Sam Pickering*

On weekdays Campbell's store was the center of life in the little Virginia town in   1
which I spent summers and Christmas vacations. The post office was in a corner of the store, and the train station was across the road. In the morning men gathered
on Campbell's porch and drank coffee while they waited for the train to Richmond. Late
in the afternoon, families appeared. While waiting for their husbands, women bought
groceries, mailed letters, and visited with one another. Children ate cups of ice cream
and played in the woods behind the store. Sometimes a work train was on the siding,
and the engineer filled his cab with children and took them for short trips down the
track. On weekends life shifted from the store to St. Paul's Church. Built in a grove of
pine trees in the nineteenth century, St. Paul's was a small, white clapboard building. A
Sunday School wing added to the church in the 1920s jutted out into the graveyard.
Beyond the graveyard was a field in which picnics were held and on the Fourth of July,
the yearly Donkey Softball Game was played.

St. Paul's was familial and comfortable. Only a hundred people attended regularly,   2
and everyone knew everyone else and his business. What was private became public
after the service as people gathered outside and talked for half an hour before going
home to lunch. Behind the altar inside the church was a stained glass window showing
Christ's ascension to heaven. A red carpet ran down the middle aisle, and worn, gold
cushions covered the pews. On the walls were plaques in memory of parishioners killed
in foreign wars or who had made large donations to the building fund. In summer the
minister put fans out on the pews. Donated by a local undertaker, the fans were shaped
like spades. On them, besides the undertaker's name and telephone number, were pictures of Christ performing miracles: walking on water, healing the lame, and raising
Lazarus from the dead.

Holidays and funerals were special at St. Paul's. Funerals were occasions for remi-   3
niscing and telling stories. When an irascible old lady died and her daughter had "Gone to
Jesus" inscribed on her tombstone, her son-in-law was heard to say "poor Jesus"—or so
the tale went at the funeral. Christmas Eve was always cold and snow usually fell. Inside
the church at midnight, though, all was cheery and warm as the congregation sang the
great Christmas hymns: "O Come, All Ye Faithful," "The First Noel," "O Little Town of
Bethlehem," and "Hark! The Herald Angels Sing." The last hymn was "Silent Night." The
service did not follow the prayer book; inspired by Christmas and eggnog, the congregation came to sing, not to pray. Bourbon was in the air, and when the altar boy lit the candles, it seemed a miracle that the first spark didn't send us all to heaven in a blue flame.

Easter was almost more joyous than Christmas. Men stuck greenery into their lapels   4
and women blossomed in bright bonnets, some ordering hats not simply from Richmond but from Baltimore and Philadelphia. On a farm outside town lived Miss Emma
and Miss Ida Catlin. Miss Emma was the practical sister, running the farm and bringing
order wherever she went. Unlike Miss Emma, Miss Ida was shy. She read poetry and
raised guinea fowl and at parties sat silently in a corner. Only on Easter was she outgoing; then like a day lily she bloomed triumphantly. No one else's Easter bonnet ever
matched hers, and the congregation eagerly awaited her entrance which she always
made just before the first hymn.

One year Miss Ida found a catalogue from a New York store which advertised hats ₅
and their accessories. For ten to twenty-five cents ladies could buy artificial flowers to
stick into their bonnets. Miss Ida bought a counter full, and that Easter her head resembled a summer garden in bloom. Daffodils, zinnias, and black-eyed Susans hung yellow
and red around the brim of her hat while in the middle stood a magnificent pink peony.

In all his glory Solomon could not have matched Miss Ida's bonnet. The congregation ₆
could not take its eyes off it; even the minister had trouble concentrating on his sermon.
After the last hymn, everyone hurried out of the church, eager to get a better look at Miss
Ida's hat. As she came out, the altar boy began ringing the bell. Alas, the noise frightened
pigeons who had recently begun to nest and they shot out of the steeple. The congregation scattered, but the flowers on Miss Ida's hat hung over her eyes, and she did not see
the pigeons until it was too late and the peony had been ruined.

Miss Ida acted like nothing had happened. She greeted everyone and asked their ₇
healths and the healths of absent members of families. People tried not to look at her hat
but were not very successful. For two Sundays Miss Ida's "accident" was the main subject of after-church conversation; then it was forgotten for almost a year. But, as Easter
approached again, people remembered the hat. They wondered what Miss Ida would
wear to church. Some people speculated that since she was a shy, poetic person, she
wouldn't come. Even the minister had doubts. To reassure Miss Ida, he and his sons
borrowed ladders two weeks before Easter, and climbing to the top of the steeple, chased
the pigeons away and sealed off their nesting place with chicken wire.

Easter Sunday seemed to confirm the fears of those who doubted Miss Ida would ₈
appear. The choir assembled in the rear of the church without her. Half-heartedly the
congregation sang the processional hymn, "Hail Thee, Festival Day." Miss Ida's absence
had taken something bright from our lives, and as we sat down after singing, Easter
seemed sadly ordinary.

We were people of little faith. Just as the minister reached the altar and turned to ₉
face us, there was a stir at the back of the church. Silently the minister raised his right
hand and pointed toward the door. Miss Ida had arrived. She was wearing the same hat
she wore the year before; only the peony was missing. In its place was a wonderful sunflower; from one side hung a black and yellow garden spider building a web while fluttering above was a mourning cloak, black wings, dotted with blue and a yellow border
running around the edges. Our hearts leaped up, and at the end of the service people in
Richmond must have heard us singing "Christ the Lord Is Risen Today."

St. Paul's was the church of my childhood, that storied time when I thought little ₁₀
about religion but knew that Jesus loved me, yes, because the Bible told me so. In the
Morning Prayer of life I mixed faith and fairy tale, thinking God a kindly giant, holding
in his hands, as the song put it, the corners of the earth and the strength of the hills.
Thirty years have passed since I last saw St. Paul's, and I have come down from the cool
upland pastures and the safe fold of childhood to the hot lowlands. Instead of being
neatly tucked away in a huge hand, the world now seems to bound erratically, smooth
and slippery, forever beyond the grasp of even the most magical deity. Would that it
were not so, and my imagination could find a way through his gates, as the prayer says,
with thanksgiving. Often I wonder what happened to the "faith of our fathers." Why if it
endured dungeon, fire, and sword in others, did it weaken so within me?

For me religion is a matter of story and community, a congregation rising together   11
to look at an Easter Bonnet, unconsciously seeing it an emblem of hope and vitality,
indeed of the Resurrection itself. For me religion ought to be more concerned with people than ideas, creating soft feeling rather than sharp thought. Often I associate religion
with small, backwater towns in which tale binds folk one to another. Here in a university in which people are separated by idea rather than linked by story, religion doesn't
have a natural place. In the absence of community ceremony becomes important.
Changeable and always controversial, subject to dispassionate analysis, ceremony does-
n't tie people together like accounts of pigeons and peonies and thus doesn't promote
good feeling and finally love for this world and hope for the next. Often when I am discouraged, I turn for sustenance, not to formal faith with articled ceremony but to memory, a chalice winey with story.

QUESTIONS FOR DISCUSSION

1. Where in this essay does Pickering describe setting?
2. What do we learn about Miss Ida's character? Is it important for us to know about her?
3. Why does Pickering mention the names of the hymns the congregation sang at Christmas and Easter?
4. How does he indicate the passage of time in paragraphs 6–9?
5. Does the author include dialogue in this story? Where and for what purpose?
6. What is his purpose in mentioning that, on Christmas Eve at St. Paul's, "Bourbon was in the air" (paragraph 3)?

THINKING CRITICALLY

1. Pickering believes religion has more to do with people than with doctrine. What does he mean?
2. Why is the congregation happy about Miss Ida's return (paragraph 9)? How is her story related to the Easter theme?
3. The author doesn't think religion has a "natural place" in colleges and universities. Do you agree?

SUGGESTIONS FOR JOURNAL ENTRIES

1. Answer the journalists' questions to recall information about a humorous event that happened during a celebration—religious or not—that you attended.
2. In paragraph 10, Pickering tells us that his childhood vision of religion was a mixture of "faith and fairy tale." What was your childhood faith like? Recall an incident from those years that might help answer this question. Use listing or answer the journalists' questions to explain what happened.

38 Who Saw Murder Didn't Call the Police

Martin Gansberg

Martin Gansberg was a reporter and editor at The New York Times *when he wrote "38 Who Saw Murder Didn't Call the Police" for that newspaper in 1964. This story about the murder of a young woman is doubly terrifying, for the thirty-eight witnesses to the crime might very well have saved her life if only they had had the courage to become involved.*

Looking Ahead

1. The setting is Kew Gardens, a well-to-do neighborhood in Queens, New York. One reason Gansberg describes it in great detail is to make his story realistic. Another is to show his readers that the neighbors had a clear view of the crime from their windows. But there are other reasons as well. Pay close attention to the details used to describe the setting.
2. Gansberg begins the story by using dialogue to report an interview he had with the police. He ends it similarly, including dialogue from interviews with several witnesses. Read these two parts of the narrative as carefully as the story of the murder itself. They contain important information about Gansberg's reaction to the incident and his purpose in writing this piece.
3. The story of Kitty Genovese is a comment about the fact that people sometimes ignore their responsibilities to neighbors and lose that important sense of community that binds us together. Identify this central idea, or theme, as you read "38 Who Saw Murder Didn't Call the Police."

Vocabulary

deliberation	Thinking.
distraught	Very upset, nervous.
punctuated	Were clearly heard (literally "made a mark in").
recitation	Speech, lecture.
Tudor	Type of architecture in which the beams are exposed.

38 Who Saw Murder Didn't Call the Police

| Martin Gansberg

For more than half an hour 38 respectable, law-abiding citizens in Queens 1 watched a killer stalk and stab a woman in three separate attacks in Kew Gardens.

Twice their chatter and the sudden glow of their bedroom lights interrupted him 2 and frightened him off. Each time he returned, sought her out, and stabbed her again. Not one person telephoned the police during the assault; one witness called after the woman was dead.

That was two weeks ago today. 3

Still shocked is Assistant Chief Inspector Frederick M. Lussen, in charge of the bor- 4 ough's detectives and a veteran of 25 years of homicide investigations. He can give a matter-of-fact recitation on many murders. But the Kew Gardens slaying baffles him— not because it is a murder, but because the "good people" failed to call the police.

"As we have reconstructed the crime," he said, "the assailant had three chances to 5 kill this woman during a 35-minute period. He returned twice to complete the job. If we had been called when he first attacked, the woman might not be dead now."

This is what the police say happened beginning at 3:20 A.M. in the staid, middle- 6 class, tree-lined Austin Street area:

Twenty-eight-year-old Catherine Genovese, who was called Kitty by almost every- 7 one in the neighborhood, was returning home from her job as manager of a bar in Hollis. She parked her red Fiat in a lot adjacent to the Kew Gardens Long Island Railroad Station, facing Mowbray Place. Like many residents of the neighborhood, she had parked there day after day since her arrival from Connecticut a year ago, although the railroad frowns on the practice.

She turned off the lights of her car, locked the door, and started to walk the 100 8 feet to the entrance of her apartment at 82-70 Austin Street, which is in a Tudor building, with stores in the first floor and apartments on the second.

The entrance to the apartment is in the rear of the building because the front is 9 rented to retail stores. At night the quiet neighborhood is shrouded in the slumbering darkness that marks most residential areas.

Miss Genovese noticed a man at the far end of the lot, near a seven-story apartment 10 house at 82-40 Austin Street. She halted. Then, nervously, she headed up Austin Street toward Lefferts Boulevard, where there is a call box to the 102nd Police Precinct in nearby Richmond Hill.

She got as far as a street light in front of a bookstore before the man grabbed her. 11 She screamed. Lights went on in the 10-story apartment house at 82-67 Austin Street, which faces the bookstore. Windows slid open and voices punctuated the early-morning stillness.

Miss Genovese screamed: "Oh, my God, he stabbed me! Please help me! Please help 12 me!"

From one of the upper windows in the apartment house, a man called down: "Let 13 that girl alone!"

The assailant looked up at him, shrugged and walked down Austin Street toward a 14 white sedan parked a short distance away. Miss Genovese struggled to her feet.

Lights went out. The killer returned to Miss Genovese, now trying to make her way 15 around the side of the building by the parking lot to get to her apartment. The assailant stabbed her again.

"I'm dying!" She shrieked. "I'm dying!" 16

Windows were opened again, and lights went on in many apartments. The assailant 17 got into his car and drove away. Miss Genovese staggered to her feet. A city bus, Q-10, the Lefferts Boulevard line to Kennedy International Airport, passed. It was 3:35 A.M.

The assailant returned. By then, Miss Genovese had crawled to the back of the 18 building, where the freshly painted brown doors to the apartment house held out hope for safety. The killer tried the first door; she wasn't there. At the second door, 82-62 Austin Street, he saw her slumped on the floor at the foot of the stairs. He stabbed her a third time—fatally.

It was 3:50 by the time the police received their first call, from a man who was a 19 neighbor of Miss Genovese. In two minutes they were at the scene. The neighbor, a 70-year-old woman, and another woman were the only persons on the street. Nobody else came forward.

The man explained that he had called the police after much deliberation. He had 20 phoned a friend in Nassau County for advice and then he had crossed the roof of the building to the apartment of the elderly woman to get her to make the call.

"I didn't want to get involved," he sheepishly told the police. 21

Six days later, the police arrested Winston Moseley, a 29-year-old business-machine 22 operator, and charged him with homicide. Moseley had no previous record. He is married, has two children and owns a home at 133-19 Sutter Avenue, South Ozone Park, Queens. On Wednesday, a court committed him to Kings County Hospital for psychiatric observation.

When questioned by the police, Moseley also said that he had slain Mrs. Annie May 23 Johnson, 24, of 146-12 133rd Avenue, Jamaica, on Feb. 29 and Barbara Kralik, 15, of 174-17 140th Avenue, Springfield Gardens, last July. In the Kralik case, the police are holding Alvin L. Mitchell, who is said to have confessed to that slaying.

The police stressed how simple it would have been to have gotten in touch with 24 them. "A phone call," said one of the detectives, "would have done it." The police may be reached by dialing "O" for operator or SPring 7-3100.

Today witnesses from the neighborhood, which is made up of one-family homes in 25 the $35,000 to $60,000 range with the exception of the two apartment houses near the railroad station, find it difficult to explain why they didn't call the police.

A housewife, knowingly if quite casually, said, "We thought it was a lover's quar- 26 rel." A husband and wife both said, "Frankly, we were afraid." They seemed aware of the fact that events might have been different. A distraught woman, wiping her hands on her apron, said, "I didn't want my husband to get involved."

One couple, now willing to talk about that night, said they heard the first screams. 27 The husband looked thoughtfully at the bookstore where the killer first grabbed Miss Genovese.

"We went to the window to see what was happening," he said, "but the light from 28 our bedroom made it difficult to see the street." The wife, still apprehensive, added: "I put out the light and we were able to see better."

Asked why they hadn't called the police, she shrugged and replied: "I don't know." 29

A man peeked out from the slight opening in the doorway to his apartment and rat- 30 tled off an account of the killer's second attack. Why hadn't he called the police at the time? "I was tired," he said without emotion. "I went back to bed."

It was 4:25 A.M. when the ambulance arrived to take the body of Miss Genovese. It 31 drove off. "Then," a solemn police detective said, "the people came out."

QUESTIONS FOR DISCUSSION

1. Catherine Genovese "was called Kitty by almost everyone in the neighborhood" (paragraph 7). What does this fact reveal about her relationship with her neighbors?
2. In Looking Ahead, you learned that there are several reasons for Gansberg's including details to describe the setting of this story. In what kind of neighborhood does the murder take place? What kind of people live in it?
3. In reporting several interviews he had with the police and with witnesses, Gansberg frames the story with dialogue at the beginning and end. What do we learn from this dialogue?
4. The author keeps the story moving by mentioning the times at which various episodes in the attack took place. Where does he mention these times?
5. In addition, what transitional words or expressions does Gansberg use to show the passage of time?
6. The story's verbs demonstrate how brutal and terrifying the murder of Kitty Genovese actually was. Identify a few of these verbs.

THINKING CRITICALLY

1. Make a list of things you might have done to help Kitty Genovese had you witnessed the attack.
2. Ganzburg quotes several witnesses. If you had had the opportunity to interview these people, what would you have asked or told them? Write your questions and comments in the margins alongside their remarks.

SUGGESTIONS FOR JOURNAL ENTRIES

1. This story illustrates what can happen when people lose their sense of community and refuse to "get involved." Use focused freewriting to make notes about one or two incidents from your own experiences that illustrate this idea too.
2. Recall a time when you thought you were in some danger. Briefly describe what it was like. What did you do to try to avoid or escape physical harm?

SUGGESTIONS FOR SUSTAINED WRITING

1. Sandburg's "Child of the Romans" contrasts the shovelman's life with those of the railroad passengers. Show how difficult or easy your life seems when contrasted with the life of someone you know. If you made a journal entry after Sandburg's poem, you might have already gathered details for this paper.

   Focus your essay on the other person; recall events that show the kind of life he or she has led. At the same time, remember that setting is important, so include details that reveal where or when these events took place.

   A good way to introduce the essay is to explain how difficult or easy life seems to you. Then, write a thesis statement that contrasts your life with the life of the other person. Put the thesis at the end of your introduction. For example, say you start by complaining about the difficult courses you are taking, the many hours you work as a cashier, or the fact that you drive an old car. The thesis at the end of this introduction might be: "My life may be hard, but I count my blessings when I think about the sacrifices my cousin made to get through college."

   However you begin, make the events you narrate in the body of your essay illustrate or prove your thesis. If they don't, revise the thesis or rewrite the body of the paper to include details that relate to the thesis more directly. Conclude your essay by explaining what this assignment has taught you about yourself or your society.

   Finally, rewrite and edit the finished product. Make sure your information is well organized, your language is vivid and clear, and your grammar, sentence structure, punctuation, and spelling are correct.

2. Several selections in this chapter are about life's painful realities. "The Colossus in the Kitchen" tells of an encounter with racism; "38 Who Saw Murder Didn't Call the Police" explains how apathy and fear can paralyze a neighborhood; "What the Gossips Saw" and "The Colossus in the Kitchen" show that people can become mean-spirited toward those who appear different from them.

   Use these selections as inspiration, and write the story of an event that taught you something distressing about human behavior or society. Try to include the journal notes you made after reading the works mentioned above.

   There are several ways to organize this narrative. Perhaps the easiest is to tell the story from beginning to end, just as you remember it. You need not write a formal introduction unless, like Gansberg, you want to share important insights or background information with readers before beginning the story itself. In fact, your central idea can wait until you write a concluding paragraph that summarizes what the events you just narrated taught you.

   As always, write several drafts and provide enough details to make your story believable. This is a good time to include proper nouns and write dialogue that will give readers the feeling they are on the scene. As you edit, make sure the story moves smoothly and remains interesting. If not, include words and expressions that show the passage of time, and add vivid verbs and adjectives.

3. In "What the Gossips Saw," Romero shows that people who gossip can exaggerate or twist a story so badly that, in their mouths, the truth becomes unrecognizable. Look back to the journal notes you made after reading this poem. Then, begin drafting an essay that tells what happened when gossips spread rumors about a person or event in your school or community.

    As with other assignments, there are several ways to organize your thoughts. For example, start by revealing the truth of a story and then explain step-by-step how gossips distorted that truth. On the other hand, you might recall how false rumors began, how they spread, and how they affected people. A good way to end this kind of paper is to tell the truth as you know it.

    Whether you use either of these methods or follow one of your own, make the story persuasive. Write several drafts, each of which develops the plot in greater and more vivid detail. In addition, explain what this experience taught you about gossip and about the people who spread it. The best place to do this is in the paper's introduction or conclusion.

    This assignment is a good chance to use dialogue and to practice other techniques discussed in Chapter 9 for describing people and their personalities. As you revise your work, rely on such techniques to make the characters in your story interesting and believable. When the time comes to edit, double-check any dialogue you have included for correct punctuation.

4. The selections by Schwartz and Romero speak of the unfair treatment people sometimes receive. Have you ever been treated unfairly because of your race, religion, nationality, a physical handicap, a personal belief, or any other reason? Tell your story vividly and completely, and reveal your feelings about what occurred. More important, explain what the experience taught you about other people or about society in general. You can express this idea in a thesis statement somewhere in your essay.

    A good example of an essay that uses narration to develop a strong thesis statement is Schwartz's "The Colossus in the Kitchen." In the first paragraph, the author defines apartheid as "a flaying of the innermost spirit." The story she tells in the rest of the essay shows exactly what she means.

    Like Schwartz, you may want to focus on one event. On the other hand, like Romero, you can narrate two or three events to support your thesis. Either way, remember to include details about the people in your story as you write and revise. Describing their personalities by recalling what they said or did is one way to convey your opinion of the world you live in. Then, as you edit for grammar, punctuation, and the like, pay special attention to the vocabulary you have chosen. Include proper nouns as appropriate, and make sure your language is both specific and vivid.

5. Did you respond to the first of the Suggestions for Journal Entries after "Faith of the Father"? If so, use the details you collected to get started on an essay that

tells a humorous event you witnessed or took part in during a religious, political, academic, or other kind of ritual, ceremony, or formal event.

Like Pickering, describe both the setting and the people of your story. Use dialogue whenever you can, and identify specific places and things—like the hymns in "Faith of the Father"—that will make your writing realistic and convincing.

A good way to introduce this essay is to describe a scene or to make a startling remark. You might conclude by using a quotation readers will remember, looking to the future, or offering advice.

When it comes time to rewrite your first draft, replace flat, uninteresting vocabulary with forceful verbs and vivid adjectives. Add transitions to make your story easy to follow. Use as much detail as needed to help your readers see the event as you did. If you write a truly entertaining paper, share it with your friends and family. First, however, remove any mechanical or stylistic errors that would reduce your essay's effect on them.

6. If you responded to the second journal suggestion after Pickering's essay, expand your entry into a full-length essay. Tell a story that will allow your readers to understand what religion meant for you when you were a child. Like Pickering, you need not have had an active role in the event or events you are narrating. Just make sure that what you write will be vivid and clear enough to explain the part religion played (and perhaps still plays) in your life.

If you run short on details, try interviewing others who witnessed or took part in what occurred. Otherwise, follow the advice offered in Suggestion #5.

7. Have you ever witnessed or experienced an automobile accident, a robbery, a mugging, a house fire, serious injury, sudden illness, or other violence or misfortune? Tell what happened during this terrible experience and describe the people involved. However, spend most of your time discussing the reactions of people who looked on as the event took place. Were you one of them? What did they do or say? What didn't they do that they should have done?

You might find inspiration and information for this project in the journal entries you made after reading Romero, Schwartz, and Gansberg. Before you write your first draft, however, think about what the event itself and the onlookers' reactions taught you about human nature. Were you encouraged or disappointed by what you learned? Express your answer in a preliminary thesis statement. Write at least two drafts of your story, and make sure to include details that will support this thesis.

Then revise at least one more time by turning what you have just written into a letter to the editor of your college or community newspaper. Use your letter to explain your approval or disappointment about the way the onlookers reacted, but don't mention their names. If appropriate, offer suggestions about the way your readers might respond if faced with an experience like the one you have narrated. Whether or not you send your letter to a newspaper, edit it carefully, just as if it were going to be published!

CHAPTER 12

THE SHORT STORY

In the introduction to Section Four, you learned the major difference between nonfiction and fiction. The former is based upon fact. The latter is, for the most part, a product of the author's imagination and, as such, does not recreate events as they actually happened.

Whether fiction or nonfiction, the selections in Section Four use important narrative tools like character, setting, dialogue, point of view, and, of course, plot to develop a central idea or theme. In some cases, especially in works of nonfiction, this idea or theme is stated plainly, in a thesis. In fact, writers of nonfiction often use their stories as concrete illustrations or examples of an important principle or idea about themselves, other people, or life in general.

However, in works of fiction, such as the selections you will read in this chapter, the theme is rarely stated openly. What the writer wishes to tell his or her readers about life is revealed through plot, character development, and other narrative elements. In most cases, in fact, it is up to the reader to identify the theme for him- or herself after having read and analyzed the story carefully. This process, known as interpretation, can make reading fiction both challenging and exciting for you, and it is sure to make it more enjoyable.

Before you read the selections in this chapter, study excerpts from two other stories, by William Carlos Williams and James Baldwin. The first illustrates techniques writers of fiction use to convey action and develop plots—their story lines. The second gives you a picture of the way they portray characters—the people in their stories.

VISUALIZING NARRATIVE ELEMENTS IN FICTION

DEVELOPING PLOT—"THE USE OF FORCE"

The narrator of William Carlos Williams's story "The Use of Force" is a doctor who is having a hard time getting a young patient to cooperate as he tries to examine her throat for signs of diphtheria.

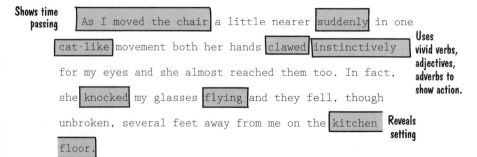

Shows time passing

As I moved the chair a little nearer suddenly in one cat-like movement both her hands clawed instinctively for my eyes and she almost reached them too. In fact, she knocked my glasses flying and they fell, though unbroken, several feet away from me on the kitchen floor.

Uses vivid verbs, adjectives, adverbs to show action.

Reveals setting

Both the mother and the father almost turned themselves inside out in embarrassment and apology. You bad girl, said the mother, taking her and shaking her by one arm. Look what you've done. The nice man...

For heaven's sake, I broke in. Don't call me a nice man to her. I'm here to look at her throat on the chance that she might have diphtheria and possibly die of it. But that's nothing to her.

Uses dialogue to move the story forward. Look here I said to the child, we're going to look at your throat. You're old enough to understand what I'm saying. Will you open it now by yourself or shall we have to open it for you?

Not a move. Even her expression hadn't changed. Her

Builds suspense. breaths however were coming faster and faster. Then the battle began. I had to do it. I had to have a throat culture for her own protection.

. . .

Uses transititons to show time passing. Then I grasped the child's head with my left hand and tried to get the wooden tongue depressor between her teeth. She fought with clenched teeth, desperately! **Uses vivid verbs, adjectives, adverbs to show action.** But now I had grown furious--at a child. I tried to hold myself down but I couldn't. I know how to expose a throat for inspection and I did my best. When finally I got the wooden spatula behind the last teeth and just the point of it into the mouth cavity, she opened up for an instant, but before I could see anything she came down again and gripping the wooden blade between her molars she reduced it to splinters before I could get it out again.

Uses transititons to show time passing.

DEVELOPING CHARACTER—"SONNY'S BLUES"

In this excerpt from James Baldwin's "Sonny's Blues," the narrator, a teacher, has read in the newspapers that his brother has been arrested for heroine abuse. At this point in the story, he is just leaving his school.

The courtyard was almost deserted by the time I got downstairs. I saw this boy standing in the shadow of a

Makes a comparison that reveals character

doorway, looking just like Sonny. I almost called his name. Then I saw that it wasn't Sonny, but somebody we used to know, a boy from around our block. He'd been Sonny's friend. He'd never been mine, having been too

Reveals his opinion of this character

young for me, and anyway, I never liked him. And now even though he was a grown-up man, he still hung around

Reveals negative aspects of his lifestyle

that block, still spent hours on the street corner, was always high and raggy. I used to run into him from time to time and he'd often work around to asking me for a quarter or fifty cents. He always had some real good excuse, too, and I always gave it to him, I don't know why.

Comments on his facial expressions, physical appearance

But now, abruptly, I hated him. I couldn't stand the way he looked at me, partly like a dog, partly like a cunning child. I wanted to ask him what the hell he was doing in the school courtyard.

Uses a vivid verb to reveal character's attitude

He sort of shuffled over to me, and he said, "I see you got the papers. So you already know about it."

"You mean about Sonny? Yes, I already know about it. How come they didn't get you?"

Includes grammatical error to capture his speech patterns

He grinned. It made him repulsive and it also brought to mind what he'd looked like as a kid. "I wasn't there. I stay away from them people."

"Good for you." I offered him a cigarette and I watched him through the smoke. "You come all the way down here just to tell me about Sonny?"

"That's right." He was sort of shaking his head and his eyes looked strange, as though they were about to cross. The bright sun deadened his damp dark brown skin and it made his eyes look yellow and showed up the dirt in his conked hair. He smelled funky. I moved a little away from him and I said. "Well thanks. But I already know about it and I got to get home."

Includes more physical description to develop this negative picture.

"I'll walk you a little ways," he said. We started walking. There were a couple of kids still loitering in the courtyard and one of them said good night to me and looked strangely at the boy beside me.

Explains how others view this character

"What're you going to do?" he asked me. "I mean about Sonny?"

"Look. I haven"t seen Sonny for over a year, I'm not sure I'm going to do anything. Anyway, what the hell can I do?"

"That's right," he said quickly, "ain't nothing you can do. Can't much help old Sonny no more, I guess."

Exposes his negative attitude by letting him speak for himself

Charles

Shirley Jackson

Shirley Jackson (1919–1965) launched her career in the 1940s, when she began to publish short stories in periodicals such as The New Republic *and* The New Yorker. *Her most important short story is "The Lottery." Like most of her other work, it uses ordinary people and places—in this case a typical American farm community—to reveal something strange or terrifying about the human character. The people we meet in "Charles" are also quite recognizable. But in this story Jackson explains human nature by poking us with gentle humor, not by scaring the wits out of us.*

LOOKING AHEAD

1. There seem to be two main characters in this selection, Laurie and Charles. Look for similarities in their personalities by comparing what one says and does with what you learn about the other.
2. To make the plot realistic, Jackson gives the job of telling the story to Laurie's mother, another important character. She is the narrator.

VOCABULARY

cynically	Distrustfully, skeptically.
incredulously	Doubtfully, without believing.
insolently	Disrespectfully.
renounced	Rejected.
unsettling	Disturbing.

Charles   *Shirley Jackson*

The day my son Laurie started kindergarten he renounced corduroy overalls with   1
bibs and began wearing blue jeans with a belt; I watched him go off the first
morning with the older girl next door, seeing clearly that an era of my life was ended,
my sweet-voiced nursery-school tot replaced by a long-trousered, swaggering character
who forgot to stop at the corner and wave good-bye to me.

He came home the same way, the front door slamming open, his cap on the floor,   2
and the voice suddenly become raucous shouting, "Isn't anybody *here?*"

At lunch he spoke insolently to his father, spilled his baby sister's milk, and   3
remarked that his teacher said we were not to take the name of the Lord in vain.

"How *was* school today?" I asked, elaborately casual.   4

"All right," he said.   5

"Did you learn anything?" his father asked.   6

Laurie regarded his father coldly. "I didn't learn nothing," he said.   7

"Anything," I said. "Didn't learn anything."   8

"The teacher spanked a boy, though," Laurie said, addressing his bread and butter.   9
"For being fresh," he added, with his mouth full.

"What did he do?" I asked. "Who was it?"   10

Laurie thought. "It was Charles," he said. "He was fresh. The teacher spanked him   11
and made him stand in a corner. He was awfully fresh."

"What did he do?" I asked again, but Laurie slid off his chair, took a cookie, and   12
left, while his father was still saying, "See here, young man."

The next day Laurie remarked at lunch, as soon as he sat down, "Well, Charles was   13
bad again today." He grinned enormously and said, "Today Charles hit the teacher."

"Good heavens," I said, mindful of the Lord's name, "I suppose he got spanked   14
again?"

"He sure did," Laurie said. "Look up," he said to his father.   15

"What?" his father said, looking up.   16

"Look down," Laurie said. "Look at my thumb. Gee, you're dumb." He began to   17
laugh insanely.

"Why did Charles hit the teacher?" I asked quickly.   18

"Because she tried to make him color with red crayons," Laurie said. "Charles   19
wanted to color with green crayons so he hit the teacher and she spanked him and said
nobody play with Charles but everybody did."

The third day—it was Wednesday of the first week—Charles bounced a see-saw   20
onto the head of a little girl and made her bleed, and the teacher made him stay inside all
during recess. Thursday Charles had to stand in a corner during story-time because he
kept pounding his feet on the floor. Friday Charles was deprived of blackboard privi-
leges because he threw chalk.

On Saturday I remarked to my husband, "Do you think kindergarten is too unset-   21
tling for Laurie? All this toughness, and bad grammar, and this Charles boy sounds like
such a bad influence."

"It'll be all right," my husband said reassuringly. "Bound to be people like Charles   22
in the world. Might as well meet them now as later."

On Monday Laurie came home late, full of news. "Charles," he shouted as he came 23 up the hill; I was waiting anxiously on the front steps. "Charles," Laurie yelled all the way up the hill, "Charles was bad again."

"Come right in," I said, as soon as he came close enough. "Lunch is waiting." 24

"You know what Charles did?" he demanded, following me through the door. 25 "Charles yelled so in school they sent a boy in from first grade to tell the teacher she had to make Charles keep quiet, and so Charles had to stay after school. And so all the children stayed to watch him."

"What did he do?" I asked. 26

"He just sat there," Laurie said, climbing into his chair at the table. "Hi, Pop, y'old 27 dust mop."

"Charles had to stay after school today," I told my husband. "Everyone stayed with 28 him."

"What does this Charles look like?" my husband asked Laurie. "What's his other 29 name?"

"He's bigger than me," Laurie said. "And he doesn't have any rubbers and he doesn't 30 ever wear a jacket."

Monday night was the first Parent-Teachers meeting, and only the fact that the baby 31 had a cold kept me from going; I wanted passionately to meet Charles's mother. On Tuesday Laurie remarked suddenly, "Our teacher had a friend come to see her in school today."

"Charles's mother?" my husband and I asked simultaneously. 32

"Naaah," Laurie said scornfully. "It was a man who came and made us do exercises, 33 we had to touch our toes. Look." He climbed down from his chair and squatted down and touched his toes. "Like this," he said. He got solemnly back into his chair and said, picking up his fork, "Charles didn't even *do* exercises."

"That's fine," I said heartily. "Didn't Charles want to do exercises?" 34

"Naaah," Laurie said. "Charles was so fresh to the teacher's friend he wasn't *let* do 35 exercises."

"Fresh again?" I said. 36

"He kicked the teacher's friend," Laurie said. "The teacher's friend told Charles to 37 touch his toes like I just did and Charles kicked him."

"What are they going to do about Charles, do you suppose?" Laurie's father asked 38 him.

Laurie shrugged elaborately. "Throw him out of school, I guess," he said. 39

Wednesday and Thursday were routine; Charles yelled during story hour and hit a 40 boy in the stomach and made him cry. On Friday Charles stayed after school again and so did all the other children.

With the third week of kindergarten Charles was an institution in our family; the 41 baby was being a Charles when she cried all afternoon; Laurie did a Charles when he filled his wagon full of mud and pulled it through the kitchen; even my husband, when he caught his elbow in the telephone cord and pulled telephone, ashtray, and a bowl of flowers off the table, said, after the first minute, "Looks like Charles."

During the third and fourth weeks it looked like a reformation in Charles; Laurie 42 reported grimly at lunch on Thursday of the third week, "Charles was so good today the teacher gave him an apple."

"What?" I said, and my husband added warily, "You mean Charles?"   43

"Charles," Laurie said. "He gave the crayons around and he picked up the books   44
afterward and the teacher said he was her helper."

"What happened?" I asked incredulously.   45

"He was her helper, that's all," Laurie said, and shrugged.   46

"Can this be true, about Charles?" I asked my husband that night. "Can something   47
like this happen?"

"Wait and see," my husband said cynically. "When you've got a Charles to deal   48
with, this may mean he's only plotting."

He seemed to be wrong. For over a week Charles was the teacher's helper; each day   49
he handed things out and he picked things up; no one had to stay after school.

"The P.T.A. meeting's next week again," I told my husband one evening. "I'm going   50
to find Charles's mother there."

"Ask her what happened to Charles," my husband said. "I'd like to know."   51

"I'd like to know myself," I said.   52

On Friday of that week things were back to normal. "You know what Charles did   53
today?" Laurie demanded at the lunch table, in a voice slightly awed. "He told a little girl
to say a word and she said it and the teacher washed her mouth out with soap and
Charles laughed."

"What word?" his father asked unwisely, and Laurie said, "I'll have to whisper it to   54
you, it's so bad." He got down off his chair and went around to his father. His father
bent his head down and Laurie whispered joyfully. His father's eyes widened.

"Did Charles tell the little girl to say *that?*" he asked respectfully.   55

"She said it *twice,*" Laurie said. "Charles told her to say it *twice.*"   56

"What happened to Charles?" my husband asked.   57

"Nothing," Laurie said. "He was passing out the crayons."   58

Monday morning Charles abandoned the little girl and said the evil word himself   59
three or four times, getting his mouth washed out with soap each time. He also threw
chalk.

My husband came to the door with me that evening as I set out for the P.T.A. meet-   60
ing. "Invite her over for a cup of tea after the meeting," he said. "I want to get a look at
her."

"If only she's there," I said prayerfully.   61

"She'll be there," my husband said. "I don't see how they could hold a P.T.A. meet-   62
ing without Charles's mother."

At the meeting I sat restlessly, scanning each comfortable matronly face, trying to   63
determine which one hid the secret of Charles. None of them looked to me haggard
enough. No one stood up in the meeting and apologized for the way her son had been
acting. No one mentioned Charles.

After the meeting I identified and sought out Laurie's kindergarten teacher. She had   64
a plate with a cup of tea and a piece of chocolate cake; I had a plate with a cup of tea and
a piece of marshmallow cake. We maneuvered up to one another cautiously, and smiled.

"I've been so anxious to meet you," I said. "I'm Laurie's mother."   65

"We're all so interested in Laurie," she said.   66

"Well, he certainly likes kindergarten," I said. "He talks about it all the time."   67

"We had a little trouble adjusting, the first week or so," she said primly, "but now 68 he's a fine little helper. With occasional lapses, of course."

"Laurie usually adjusts very quickly," I said. "I suppose this time it's Charles's influ- 69 ence."

"Charles?" 70

"Yes," I said, laughing, "you must have your hands full in that kindergarten, with 71 Charles."

"Charles?" she said. "We don't have any Charles in the kindergarten." 72

QUESTIONS FOR DISCUSSION

1. How would you describe Laurie's personality? Is the fact that he has created an imaginary friend unusual?
2. What changes do we see in Laurie's personality as the story progresses?
3. There are many things about Laurie's family life that seem quite ordinary. Are there others that strike you as strange?
4. What kind of parents are Laurie's mother and father? Does the fact that they can't see through Laurie's lies seem believable to you? Would you have been able to see through Laurie's lies if you were his parents?
5. Think about your answer to question 4. What is the theme of this story? What does it tell us about human nature?

THINKING CRITICALLY

Though the truth comes as a shock, there are signs throughout the story that Charles is none other than Laurie. Reread "Charles" and mark places in the text where you find evidence of this. Write short notes in the margins to explain what such evidence reveals. For example, compare something Laurie does at home with something Charles does at school.

SUGGESTIONS FOR JOURNAL ENTRIES

1. Write a short character sketch of Laurie. Compare him to children you've known who like to pretend a lot.
2. Sometimes we have difficulty recognizing the truth even when it is right under our noses. Recall an incident from your own experience or from something you've read recently that illustrates this theme. In a brief journal entry, explain in what ways the incident is similar to Shirley Jackson's "Charles."
3. Did you ever have an imaginary friend or classmate as a child? Use the focused-freewriting method explained in "Getting Started" to recall one or two experiences you had with this companion. If you can, explain why you created this person in the first place.

The Hammon and the Beans

Américo Parédes

Born in Brownsville, Texas, in 1915, Américo Parédes began his career as a journalist, then taught English and anthropology at the University of Texas at Austin, where he also directed the Mexican-American studies program. He has published fiction and poetry as well as scholarly works on folklore. This brilliant and prolific writer has also served as editor of the Journal of American Folklore *and has collected several anthologies of Mexican folklore and of literature by Mexican-Americans. His most recent book is* Uncle Remus Con Chile *(1993). "The Hammon and the Beans" was published in* The Texas Observer *(1963).*

LOOKING AHEAD

1. Emiliano Zapata (1879–1919) and Pancho Villa (1877–1923), revolutionary leaders mentioned in the story, are still revered in Mexico. After the revolution, Zapata retired to his home state of Morelos. In 1916, Villa made raids into Texas and New Mexico. Because of these "border troubles" (paragraph 4), the U.S. sent troops to places like "Fort Jones." "The Hammon and the Beans" is set in this fictitious Texas border town in the 1920s, when memories of these men and events were fresh.
2. Colonel Francis Marion, known as the "Swamp Fox," was an American revolutionary who operated near the Santee River in South Carolina.
3. In paragraph 32, the doctor mentions Troy, an ancient city destroyed by the Greeks. The story is told in Homer's *Iliad*.

VOCABULARY

conservative	Someone who wants little change in a country's social, political, or economic systems. Conservative comes from the verb "to conserve."
deprecatory	Offensive, insulting.
hammon	In Spanish, the word for ham is "jamon," pronounced "hammon."
hoary	Old, ancient.
radical	Someone who wants to overhaul a country's social, political, or economic systems. "Radical" comes from the Latin word for "root." Therefore, a radical wants root or fundamental changes.

The Hammon and the Beans

A m é r i c o   P a r é d e s

Once we lived in one of my grandfather's houses near Fort Jones. It was just a 1
block from the parade grounds, a big frame house painted a dirty yellow. My
mother hated it, especially because of the pigeons that cooed all day about the eaves.
They had fleas, she said. But it was a quiet neighborhood at least, too far from the center of town for automobiles and too near for musical, night-roaming drunks.

At this time Jonesville-on-the-Grande was not the thriving little city that it is today. 2
We told off our days by the routine on the post. At six sharp the flag was raised on the
parade grounds to the cackling of the bugles, and a field piece thundered out a salute.
The sound of the shot bounced away through the morning mist until its echoes worked
their way into every corner of town. Jonesville-on-the-Grande woke to the cannon's
roar, as if to battle, and the day began.

At eight the whistle from the post laundry sent us children off to school. The whole 3
town stopped for lunch with the noon whistle, and after lunch everybody went back to
work when the post laundry said that it was one o'clock, except for those who could
afford to be old-fashioned and took the siesta. The post was the town's clock, you might
have said, or like some insistent elder person who was always there to tell you it was
time.

At six the flag came down, and we went to watch through the high wire fence that 4
divided the post from the town. Sometimes we joined in the ceremony, standing at
salute until the sound of the cannon made us jump. That must have been when we had
just studied about George Washington in school, or recited "The Song of Marion's Men"
about Marion the Fox and the British cavalry that chased him up and down the broad
Santee. But at other times we stuck out our tongues and jeered at the soldiers. Perhaps
the night before we had hung at the edges of a group of old men and listened to tales
about Aniceto Pizaña and the "border troubles," as the local paper still called them when
it referred to them gingerly in passing.

It was because of the border troubles, ten years or so before, that the soldiers had 5
come back to old Fort Jones. But we did not hate them for that; we admired them even,
at least sometimes. But when we were thinking about the border troubles instead of
Marion the Fox we hooted them and the flag they were lowering, which for the moment
was theirs alone, just as we would have jeered an opposing ball team, in a friendly sort
of way. On these occasions even Chonita would join in the mockery, though she usually
ran home at the stroke of six. But whether we taunted or saluted, the distant men in
khaki uniforms went about their motions without noticing us at all.

The last word from the post came in the night when a distant bugle blew. At nine it 6
was all right because all the lights were on. But sometimes I heard it at eleven when
everything was dark and still, and it made me feel that I was all alone in the world. I
would even doubt that I was me, and that put me in such a fright that I felt like yelling
out just to make sure I was really there. But next morning the sun shone and life began
all over again. With its whistles and cannon shots and bugles blowing. And so we lived,
we and the post, side by side with the wire fence in between.

The wandering soldiers whom the bugle called home at night did not wander in 7 our neighborhood, and none of us ever went into Fort Jones. None except Chonita. Every evening when the flag came down she would leave off playing and go down towards what was known as the "lower" gate of the post, the one that opened not on Main Street but against the poorest part of town. She went into the grounds and to the mess halls and pressed her nose against the screens and watched the soldiers eat. They sat at long tables calling to each other through food-stuffed mouths.

"Hey bud, pass the coffee!"   8

"Give me the ham!"   9

"Yeah, give me the beans!"   10

After the soldiers were through the cooks came out and scolded Chonita, and then   11
they gave her packages with things to eat.

Chonita's mother did our washing, in gratefulness—as my mother put it—for the   12
use of a vacant lot of my grandfather's which was a couple of blocks down the street. On the lot was an old one-room shack which had been a shed long ago, and this Chonita's father had patched up with flattened-out pieces of tin. He was a laborer. Ever since the end of the border troubles there had been a development boom in the Valley, and Chonita's father was getting his share of the good times. Clearing brush and building irrigation ditches he sometimes pulled down as much as six dollars a week. He drank a good deal of it up, it was true. But corn was just a few cents a bushel in those days. He was the breadwinner, you might say, while Chonita furnished the luxuries.

Chonita was a poet too. I had just moved into the neighborhood when a boy came   13
up to me and said, "Come on! Let's go hear Chonita make a speech."

She was already on top of the alley fence when we got there, a scrawny little girl of   14
about nine, her bare dirty feet clinging to the fence almost like hands. A dozen other kids were there below her, waiting. Some were boys I knew at school; five or six were her younger brothers and sisters.

"Speech! Speech!" they all cried. "Let Chonita make a speech! Talk in English,   15
Chonita!"

They were grinning and nudging each other except for her brothers and sisters,   16
who looked up at her with proud serious faces. She gazed out beyond us all with a grand, distant air and then she spoke.

"Give me the hammon and the beans!" she yelled. "Give me the hammon and the   17
beans!"

She leaped off the fence and everybody cheered and told her how good it was and   18
how she could talk English better than the teachers at the grammar school.

I thought it was a pretty poor joke. Every evening almost, they would make her get   19
up on the fence and yell, "Give me the hammon and the beans!" And everybody would cheer and make her think she was talking English. As for me, I would wait there until she got it over with so we could play at something else. I wondered how long it would be before they got tired of it all. I never did find out because just about that time I got the chills and fever, and when I got up and around Chonita wasn't there anymore.

In later years I thought of her a lot, especially during the thirties when I was grow-   20
ing up. Those years would have been just made for her. Many's the time I have seen her in my mind's eyes, in the picket lines demanding not bread, not cake, but the hammon and the beans. But it didn't work out that way.

One night Doctor Zapata came into our kitchen through the back door. He set his ²¹ bag on the table and said to my father, who had opened the door for him, "Well, she is dead."

My father flinched. "What was it?" he asked. ²²

The doctor had gone to the window and he stood with his back to us, looking out ²³ toward the light of Fort Jones. "Pneumonia, flu, malnutrition, worms, the evil eye," he said without turning around. "What the hell difference does it make?"

"I wish I had known how sick she was," my father said in a very mild tone. "Not ²⁴ that it's really my affair, but I wish I had."

The doctor snorted and shook his head. ²⁵

My mother came in and I asked her who was dead. She told me. It made me feel ²⁶ strange but I did not cry. My mother put her arm around my shoulders. "She is in Heaven now," she said. "She is happy."

I shrugged her arm away and sat down in one of the kitchen chairs. ²⁷

"They're like animals," the doctor was saying. He turned round suddenly and his ²⁸ eyes glistened in the light. "Do you know what that brute of a father was doing when I left? He was laughing! Drinking and laughing with his friends."

"There's no telling what the poor man feels," my mother said. ²⁹

My father made a deprecatory gesture. "It wasn't his daughter anyway." ³⁰

"No?" the doctor said. He sounded interested. ³¹

"This is the woman's second husband," my father explained. "First one died before ³² the girl was born, shot and hanged from a mesquite limb. He was working too close to the tracks the day the Olmito train was derailed."

"You know what?" the doctor said. "In classical times they did things better. Take ³³ Troy, for instance. After they stormed the city they grabbed the babies by the heels and dashed them against the wall. That was more humane."

My father smiled. "You sound very radical. You sound just like your relative down ³⁴ there in Morelos."

"No relative of mine," the doctor said. "I'm a conservative, the son of a conservative, ³⁵ and you know that I wouldn't be here except for that little detail."

"Habit," my father said. "Pure habit, pure tradition. You're a radical at heart." ³⁶

"It depends on how you define radicalism," the doctor answered. "People tend to ³⁷ use words too loosely. A dentist could be called a radical, I suppose. He pulls up things by the roots."

My father chuckled. ³⁸

"Any bandit in Mexico nowadays can give himself a political label," the doctor went ³⁹ on, "and that makes him respectable. He's a leader of the people."

"Take Villa, now—" my father began. ⁴⁰

"Villa was a different type of man," the doctor broke in. ⁴¹

"I don't see any difference." ⁴²

The doctor came over to the table and sat down. "Now look at it this way," he ⁴³ began, his finger in front of my father's face. My father threw back his head and laughed.

"You'd better go to bed and rest," my mother told me. "You're not completely well, ⁴⁴ you know."

So I went to bed, but I didn't go to sleep, not right away. I lay there for a long time ⁴⁵ while behind my darkened eyelids Emiliano Zapata's cavalry charged down to the broad Santee, where there were grave men with hoary hairs. I was still awake at eleven when the cold voice of the bugle went gliding in and out of the dark like something that couldn't find its way back to wherever it had been. I thought of Chonita in Heaven, and I saw her in her torn and dirty dress, with a pair of bright wings attached, flying round and round like a butterfly shouting, "Give me the hammon and the beans!"

Then I cried. And whether it was the bugle, or whether it was Chonita or what, to 46 this day I do not know. But cry I did, and I felt much better after that.

QUESTIONS FOR DISCUSSION

1. At the beginning of this story, Parédes skillfully leads the reader through a typical day in Jonesville. How does he do this?
2. Why does he do this?
3. Recall what you learned about describing a place in Chapter 8. What techniques does Parédes use to establish his setting?
4. What is the significance of the fact that Chonita is the only one who goes to Fort Jones?
5. What do we know about the way Chonita was treated by others? Does this information cast any light on her character?
6. Compare Chonita to the other children the narrator mentions. What does this comparison tell us about her?
7. What function does the talk between the doctor and the narrator's father serve? What does it tell us about Chonita?
8. What does this discussion reveal about the doctor? About the time in which this story is set?
9. The story tells of two communities—two worlds. What are they?
10. How does the title help introduce these two worlds? Why does Chonita demand "the hammon and the beans" rather than "the ham and beans"?

THINKING CRITICALLY

1. In paragraph 9, the narrator says he thought the thirties "would have been just made for" Chonita; he is referring to the Great Depression of the 1930s. Read a little about this period in your library. Then explain what this statement means.
2. Why is Chonita so important to this story? How does she help reveal the story's theme? Make notes in the margins to explain Chonita's role.
3. At the story's end, the narrator imagines a Mexican revolutionary charging down a river in South Carolina during the American Revolution. Write a paragraph explaining what this has to do with the story's theme. Before you begin, make notes in the margins to explain historical events relating to this question.

SUGGESTIONS FOR JOURNAL ENTRIES

1. Chonita is a symbol of defiance against the poverty and ignorance the narrator sees around him. As such, she becomes a source of inspiration. Think of someone like Chonita in your life. Answer the journalists' questions to explain how he or she has inspired you.
2. Underline passages in the story that demonstrate Chonita's courage. Then freewrite for about five minutes to discuss someone you know who is equally

courageous. You might even want to narrate a brief story from his or her life that illustrates this quality.

3. The narrator seems to live in two worlds. Is this also true of you or of someone you know well? If so, list details that describe each of these worlds. Your journal entry should contain two different and complete lists.

The Son from America

Isaac Bashevis Singer

One of the most popular short story writers in America, Isaac Bashevis Singer (1904–1991) composed his works in Yiddish, his first language, then translated them into English. Born in Poland, the country in which this story takes place, Singer immigrated to the United States in 1935. He wrote regularly for the Jewish Daily Forward *and* The New Yorker *magazine. In 1978, he won the Nobel Prize in literature.*

Like many of Singer's other works, "The Son from America" deals with the isolation and the nobility of old age. It appears in A Crown of Feathers, *a collection of short stories that received the National Book Award.*

LOOKING AHEAD

1. The story takes place at about the turn of the century, a time when Russia controlled part of Poland. The characters in this story were driven out of their homes in Russia and forced to settle in Poland as a result of the "pogroms," the severe persecution of Jews by the government of the czar (the Russian emperor). Warsaw, mentioned in paragraph 5, is Poland's capital.
2. The story's setting reveals a great deal about its characters and theme. Keep a sharp lookout for details about Lentshin, the town in which the story takes place, and about the home of Berl and Berlcha, the main characters.
3. The story's theme can be seen most clearly in the differences between the two worlds: the old world of Europe and the new world of America.

VOCABULARY

circumcision	Religious ceremony in which the foreskin of a male infant's penis is surgically removed.
contours	Outline.
Gentile	Non-Jewish person.
hinterland	Remote region.
Kaddish	Prayer for the dead.
Messiah	Deliverer or savior of the Jewish people sent by God as promised in the scriptures.
squiresses	Wealthy women, women landowners.
synagogue	Temple, house of worship.
Talmud	Collection of sacred writings.
Torah	Body of Jewish literature, both written and oral, that contains the sacred laws and teachings of the religion.
Yiddish	Language spoken by Jews in eastern Europe.

The Son from
America | *I s a a c   B a s h e v i s   S i n g e r*

The village of Lentshin was tiny—a sandy marketplace where the peasants of the   1
area met once a week. It was surrounded by little huts with thatched roofs or
shingles green with moss. The chimneys looked like pots. Between the huts there were
fields, where the owners planted vegetables or pastured their goats.

In the smallest of these huts lived old Berl, a man in his eighties, and his wife, who   2
was called Berlcha (wife of Berl). Old Berl was one of the Jews who had been driven
from their villages in Russia and had settled in Poland. In Lentshin, they mocked the
mistakes he made while praying aloud. He spoke with a sharp "r." He was short, broad-
shouldered, and had a small white beard, and summer and winter he wore a sheepskin
hat, a padded cotton jacket, and stout boots. He walked slowly, shuffling his feet. He had
a half acre of field, a cow, a goat, and chickens.

The couple had a son, Samuel, who had gone to America forty years ago. It was said   3
in Lentshin that he became a millionaire there. Every month, the Lentshin letter carrier
brought old Berl a money order and a letter that no one could read because many of the
words were English. How much money Samuel sent his parents remained a secret. Three
times a year, Berl and his wife went on foot to Zakroczym and cashed the money orders
there. But they never seemed to use the money. What for? The garden, the cow, and
the goat provided most of their needs. Besides, Berlcha sold chickens and eggs, and from
these there was enough to buy flour for bread.

No one cared to know where Berl kept the money that his son sent him. There were   4
no thieves in Lentshin. The hut consisted of one room, which contained all their belong-
ings: the table, the shelf for meat, the shelf for milk foods, the two beds, and the clay
oven. Sometimes the chickens roosted in the woodshed and sometimes, when it was
cold, in a coop near the oven. The goat, too, found shelter inside when the weather was
bad. The more prosperous villagers had kerosene lamps, but Berl and his wife did not
believe in newfangled gadgets. What was wrong with a wick in a dish of oil? Only for
the Sabbath would Berlcha buy three tallow candles at the store. In summer, the couple
got up at sunrise and retired with the chickens. In the long winter evenings, Berlcha
spun flax at her spinning wheel and Berl sat beside her in the silence of those who enjoy
their rest.

Once in a while when Berl came home from the synagogue after evening prayers, he   5
brought news to his wife. In Warsaw there were strikers who demanded that the czar
abdicate. A heretic by the name of Dr. Herzl had come up with the idea that Jews should
settle again in Palestine. Berlcha listened and shook her bonneted head. Her face was
yellowish and wrinkled like a cabbage leaf. There were bluish sacks under her eyes. She
was half deaf. Berl had to repeat each word he said to her. She would say, "The things
that happen in the big cities!"

Here in Lentshin nothing happened except usual events: a cow gave birth to a calf,   6
a young couple had a circumcision party, or a girl was born and there was no party.
Occasionally, someone died. Lentshin had no cemetery, and the corpse had to be taken
to Zakroczym. Actually, Lentshin had become a village with few young people. The
young men left for Zakroczym, for Nowy Dwor, for Warsaw, and sometimes for the

United States. Like Samuel's, their letters were illegible, the Yiddish mixed with the languages of the countries where they were now living. They sent photographs in which the men wore top hats and the women fancy dresses like squiresses.

Berl and Berlcha also received such photographs. But their eyes were failing and   7
neither he nor she had glasses. They could barely make out the pictures. Samuel had sons and daughters with Gentile names—and grandchildren who had married and had their own offspring. Their names were so strange that Berl and Berlcha could never remember them. But what difference do names make? America was far, far away on the other side of the ocean, at the edge of the world. A Talmud teacher who came to Lentshin had said that Americans walk with their heads down and their feet up. Berl and Berlcha could not grasp this. How was it possible? But since the teacher said so it must be true. Berlcha pondered for some time and then she said, "One can get accustomed to everything."

And so it remained. From too much thinking—God forbid—one may lose one's   8
wits.

One Friday morning, when Berlcha was kneading the dough for the Sabbath loaves,   9
the door opened and a nobleman entered. He was so tall that he had to bend down to get through the door. He wore a beaver hat and a cloak bordered with fur. He was followed by Chazkel, the coachman from Zakroczym, who carried two leather valises with brass locks. In astonishment Berlcha raised her eyes.

The nobleman looked around and said to the coachman in Yiddish, "Here it is." He   10
took out a silver ruble and paid him. The coachman tried to hand him change but he said, "You can go now."

When the coachman closed the door, the nobleman said, "Mother, it's me, your son   11
Samuel—Sam."

Berlcha heard the words and her legs grew numb. Her hands, to which pieces of   12
dough were sticking, lost their power. The nobleman hugged her, kissed her forehead, both her cheeks. Berlcha began to cackle like a hen, "My son!" At that moment Berl came in from the woodshed, his arms piled with logs. The goat followed him. When he saw a nobleman kissing his wife, Berl dropped the wood and exclaimed, "What is this?"

The nobleman let go of Berlcha and embraced Berl. "Father!"   13

For a long time Berl was unable to utter a sound. He wanted to recite holy words   14
that he had read in the Yiddish Bible, but he could remember nothing. Then he asked, "Are you Samuel?"

"Yes, Father, I am Samuel."   15

"Well, peace be with you." Berl grasped his son's hand. He was still not sure that he   16
was not being fooled. Samuel wasn't as tall and heavy as this man, but then Berl reminded himself that Samuel was only fifteen years old when he had left home. He must have grown in that faraway country. Berl asked, "Why didn't you let us know you were coming?"

"Didn't you receive my cable?" Samuel asked.   17

Berl did not know what a cable was.   18

Berlcha had scraped the dough from her hands and enfolded her son. He kissed her   19
again and asked, "Mother, didn't you receive a cable?"

"What? If I lived to see this, I am happy to die," Berlcha said, amazed by her own   20 words. Berl, too, was amazed. These were just the words he would have said earlier if he had been able to remember. After a while Berl came to himself and said, "Pescha, you will have to make a double Sabbath pudding in addition to the stew."

It was years since Berl had called Berlcha by her given name. When he wanted to 21 address her, he would say, "Listen," or "Say." It is the young or those from the big cities who call a wife by her name. Only now did Berlcha begin to cry. Yellow tears ran from her eyes, and everything became dim. Then she called out, "It's Friday—I have to prepare for the Sabbath." Yes, she had to knead the dough and braid the loaves. With such a guest, she had to make a larger Sabbath stew. The winter day is short and she must hurry.

Her son understood what was worrying her, because he said, "Mother, I will help 22 you."

Berlcha wanted to laugh, but a choked sob came out. "What are you saying? God 23 forbid."

The nobleman took off his cloak and jacket and remained in his vest, on which 24 hung a solid-gold watch chain. He rolled up his sleeves and came to the trough. "Mother, I was a baker for many years in New York," he said, and he began to knead the dough.

"What! You are my darling son who will say Kaddish for me." She wept raspingly. 25 Her strength left her, and she slumped onto the bed.

Berl said, "Women will always be women." And he went to the shed to get more 26 wood. The goat sat down near the oven; she gazed with surprise at this strange man— his height and his bizarre clothes.

The neighbors had heard the good news that Berl's son had arrived from America 27 and they came to greet him. The women began to help Berlcha prepare for the Sabbath. Some laughed, some cried. The room was full of people, as at a wedding. They asked Berl's son, "What is new in America?" And Berl's son answered, "America is all right."

"Do Jews make a living?" 28

"One eats white bread there on weekdays." 29

"Do they remain Jews?" 30

"I am not a Gentile." 31

After Berlcha blessed the candles, father and son went to the little synagogue across 32 the street. A new snow had fallen. The son took large steps, but Berl warned him, "Slow down."

In the synagogue the Jews recited "Let Us Exult" and "Come, My Groom." All the 33 time, the snow outside kept falling. After prayers, when Berl and Samuel left the Holy Place, the village was unrecognizable. Everything was covered with snow. One could see only the contours of the roofs and the candles in the windows. Samuel said, "Nothing has changed here."

Berlcha had prepared gefilte fish, chicken soup with rice, meat, carrot stew. Berl 34 recited the benediction over a glass of ritual wine. The family ate and drank, and when it grew quiet for a while one could hear the chirping of the house cricket. The son talked a lot, but Berl and Berlcha understood little. His Yiddish was different and contained foreign words.

After the final blessing Samuel asked, "Father, what did you do with all the money 35 I sent you?"

Berl raised his white brows. "It's here."   36

"Didn't you put it in a bank?"   37

"There is no bank in Lentshin."   38

"Where do you keep it?"   39

Berl hesitated. "One is not allowed to touch money on the Sabbath, but I will show   40
you." He crouched beside the bed and began to shove something heavy. A boot
appeared. Its top was stuffed with straw. Berl removed the straw and the son saw that
the boot was full of gold coins. He lifted it.

"Father, this is a treasure!" he called out.   41

"Well."   42

"Why didn't you spend it?"   43

"On what? Thank God, we have everything."   44

"Why didn't you travel somewhere?"   45

"Where to? This is our home."   46

The son asked one question after the other, but Berl's answer was always the same: 47
they wanted for nothing. The garden, the cow, the goat, the chickens provided them with
all they needed. The son said, "If thieves knew about this, your lives wouldn't be safe."

"There are no thieves here."   48

"What will happen to the money?"   49

"You take it."   50

Slowly, Berl and Berlcha grew accustomed to their son and his American Yiddish.   51
Berlcha could hear him better now. She even recognized his voice. He was saying, "Perhaps we should build a larger synagogue."

"The synagogue is big enough," Berl replied.   52

"Perhaps a home for old people."   53

"No one sleeps in the street."   54

The next day after the Sabbath meal was eaten, a Gentile from Zakroczym brought   55
a paper—it was the cable. Berl and Berlcha lay down for a nap. They soon began to
snore. The goat, too, dozed off. The son put on his cloak and his hat and went for a
walk. He strode with his long legs across the marketplace. He stretched out a hand and
touched a roof. He wanted to smoke a cigar, but he remembered it was forbidden on
the Sabbath. He had a desire to talk to someone, but it seemed that the whole of
Lentshin was asleep. He entered the synagogue. An old man was sitting there, reciting
psalms. Samuel asked, "Are you praying?"

"What else is there to do when one gets old?"   56

"Do you make a living?"   57

The old man did not understand the meaning of these words. He smiled, showing   58
his empty gums, and then he said, "If God gives health, one keeps on living."

Samuel returned home. Dusk had fallen. Berl went to the synagogue for the evening   59
prayers and the son remained with his mother. The room was filled with shadows.

Berlcha began to recite in a solemn singsong, "God of Abraham, Isaac, and Jacob,   60
defend the poor people of Israel and Thy name. The Holy Sabbath is departing; the welcome week is coming to us. Let it be one of health, wealth and good deeds."

"Mother, you don't need to pray for wealth," Samuel said. "You are wealthy   61
already."

Berlcha did not hear—or pretended not to. Her face had turned into a cluster of 62
shadows.

In the twilight Samuel put his hand into his jacket pocket and touched his pass- 63
port, his checkbook, his letters of credit. He had come here with big plans. He had a
valise filled with presents for his parents. He wanted to bestow gifts on the village. He
brought not only his own money but funds from the Lentshin Society in New York,
which had organized a ball for the benefit of the village. But this village in the hinterland
needed nothing. From the synagogue one could hear hoarse chanting. The cricket, silent
all day, started again its chirping. Berlcha began to sway and utter holy rhymes inherited
from mothers and grandmothers:

> Thy holy sheep
> In mercy keep,
> In Torah and good deeds;
> Provide for all their needs,
> Shoes, clothes, and bread
> And the Messiah's tread.

QUESTIONS FOR DISCUSSION

1. What does the story's setting reveal about Berl and Berlcha and about their standard of living?
2. Why didn't they learn about the coming of their son until after he arrived? What does this tell you about their village?
3. Singer includes details about the kind of life the son leads in America. What are these details, and what do they show us about the son?
4. There are indications that Berl and Berlcha have led very hard lives. What are some of these indications?
5. What role does dialogue play in the story? Does it convey information about characters? Does it move the plot along? Does it reveal the story's theme? Explain your answers by pointing to specific passages in the story.

THINKING CRITICALLY

1. Despite their problems, Berl and Berlcha are content; in fact, they refuse to spend the money their son has sent. What is the source of their contentment?
2. Despite his wealth, the son from America worries about various things. What is the source of his concern?
3. Do Berl and Berlcha remind you of any other people you have read about thus far? For example, in what way are they like Scamacca's Oma in Chapter 8?

SUGGESTIONS FOR JOURNAL ENTRIES

1. Berl and Berlcha are set on finding happiness (or contentment) despite the hardships of life. In Chapter 10, Edgar Lee Masters's Lucinda Matlock also possessed this positive attitude. If you've ever known or read about anyone else like this, write a brief journal entry about a memorable event in this person's life that illustrates how courageous he or she is.
2. Explain your personal reaction to the characters in Singer's story. How do you feel about Berl, Berlcha, and their son?
3. This is a story in which religious principles and a belief in God are extremely important. Recall an incident in which your belief in a moral, ethical, or religious principle had a significant effect on you or on someone you know well. Sketch out a few details about the story and explain why the principle in question was important.

A Worn Path

Eudora Welty

Like all great writers, Pulitzer Prize–winning Eudora Welty relies on her powers of observation to write about what she knows best. Born in Jackson, Mississippi, she sets her stories in the rural South, where she has lived most of her life.

Many of Welty's characters seem eccentric, even bizarre, and they remain stuck in our minds and hearts long after we read about them. Their stories can be comical, disturbing, and touching all at the same time. But often the dignity of the human spirit shines through so brightly that we can't help being inspired by the experience.

Looking Ahead

1. The major character in this story, Phoenix Jackson, gets her first name from a mythical bird that became a symbol of rebirth. According to myth, the phoenix would live for 500 years and then burn itself into a pile of ashes from which another phoenix would arise.
2. We learn a great deal about Phoenix Jackson by what she does in this story. Try to analyze each of her actions as you make your way through the plot.
3. Look closely at the dialogue that old Phoenix uses when she talks to herself, to the animals, and to the other natural objects along the way. Incidentally, you'll notice that Welty has realistically captured the natural rhythm and sound of her speech, complete with regional pronunciation and grammatical errors.
4. As you've learned in Chapter 9, what we come to know about a character from other people in the story may be just as important as what the narrator says. Phoenix meets a few people during the story, each of whom helps reveal something important about her.

Vocabulary

appointed	Assigned.
enduring	Lasting.
frailest	Most delicate.
grave	Somber, sad.
illuminated	Lit up.
limber	Agile, flexible.
meditative	Thoughtful, prayerful.
pullets	Young hens.
ravine	Gorge.
rouse	Awaken, stir up.

A Worn Path | *Eudora Welty*

It was December—a bright frozen day in the early morning. Far out in the country 1 there was an old Negro woman with her head tied in a red rag, coming along a path through the pinewoods. Her name was Phoenix Jackson. She was very old and small and she walked slowly in the dark pine shadows, moving a little from side to side in her steps, with the balanced heaviness and lightness of a pendulum in a grandfather clock. She carried a thin, small cane made from an umbrella, and with this she kept tapping the frozen earth in front of her. This made a grave and persistent noise in the still air, that seemed meditative like the chirping of a solitary little bird.

She wore a dark striped dress reaching down to her shoe tops, and an equally long 2 apron of bleached sugar sacks, with a full pocket: all neat and tidy, but every time she took a step she might have fallen over her shoe-laces, which dragged from her unlaced shoes. She looked straight ahead. Her eyes were blue with age. Her skin had a pattern all its own of numberless branching wrinkles and as though a whole little tree stood in the middle of her forehead, but a golden color ran underneath, and the two knobs of her cheeks were illuminated by a yellow burning under the dark. Under the red rag her hair came down on her neck in the frailest of ringlets, still black, and with an odor like copper.

Now and then there was a quivering in the thicket. Old Phoenix said, "Out of my 3 way, all you foxes, owls, beetles, jack rabbits, coons, and wild animals! . . . Keep out from under these feet, little bob-whites. . . . Keep the big wild hogs out of my path. Don't let none of those come running my direction. I got a long way." Under her small black-freckled hand her cane, limber as a buggy whip, would switch at the brush as if to rouse up any hiding things.

On she went. The woods were deep and still. The sun made the pine needles almost 4 too bright to look at, up where the wind rocked. The cones dropped as light as feathers. Down in the hollow was the mourning dove—it was not too late for him.

The path ran up a hill. "Seem like there is chains about my feet, time I get this far," 5 she said, in the voice of argument old people keep to use with themselves. "Something always take a hold of me on this hill—pleads I should stay."

After she got to the top she turned and gave a full, severe look behind her where she 6 had come. "Up through pines," she said at length. "Now down through oaks."

Her eyes opened their widest, and she started down gently. But before she got to 7 the bottom of the hill a bush caught her dress.

Her fingers were busy and intent, but her skirts were full and long, so that before 8 she could pull them free in one place they were caught in another. It was not possible to allow the dress to tear. "I in the thorny bush," she said. "Thorns, you doing your appointed work. Never want to let folks pass—no sir. Old eyes thought you was a pretty little *green* bush."

Finally, trembling all over, she stood free, and after a moment dared to stoop for her 9 cane.

"Sun so high!" she cried, leaning back and looking, while the thick tears went over 10 her eyes. "The time getting all gone here."

At the foot of this hill was a place where a log was laid across the creek. 11

"Now comes the trial," said Phoenix. 12

Putting her right foot out, she mounted the log and shut her eyes. Lifting her skirt, 13 leveling her cane fiercely before her, like a festival figure in some parade, she began to march across. Then she opened her eyes and she was safe on the other side.

"I wasn't as old as I thought," she said. 14

But she sat down to rest. She spread her skirts on the bank around her and folded 15 her hands over her knees. Up above her was a tree in a pearly cloud of mistletoe. She did not dare to close her eyes, and when a little boy brought her a little plate with a slice of marble-cake on it she spoke to him. "That would be acceptable," she said. But when she went to take it there was just her own hand in the air.

So she left that tree, and had to go through a barbed-wire fence. There she had to 16 creep and crawl, spreading her knees and stretching her fingers like a baby trying to climb the steps. But she talked loudly to herself: she could not let her dress be torn now, so late in the day, and she could not pay for having her arm or her leg sawed off if she got caught fast where she was.

At last she was safe through the fence and risen up out in the clearing. Big dead 17 trees, like black men with one arm, were standing in the purple stalks of the withered cotton field. There sat a buzzard.

"Who you watching?" 18

In the furrow she made her way along. 19

"Glad this not the season for bulls," she said, looking sideways, "and the good Lord 20 made his snakes to curl up and sleep in the winter. A pleasure I don't see no two-headed snake coming around that tree, where it come once. It took a while to get by him, back in the summer."

She passed through the old cotton and went into a field of dead corn. It whispered 21 and shook and was taller than her head. "Through the maze now," she said, for there was no path.

Then there was something tall, black, and skinny there, moving before her. 22

At first she took it for a man. It could have been a man dancing in the field. But 23 she stood still and listened, and it did not make a sound. It was as silent as a ghost.

"Ghost," she said sharply, "who be you the ghost of? For I have heard of nary death 24 close by."

But there was no answer—only the ragged dancing in the wind. 25

She shut her eyes, reached out her hand, and touched a sleeve. She found a coat 26 and inside that an emptiness, cold as ice.

"You scarecrow," she said. Her face lighted. "I ought to be shut up for good," she 27 said with laughter. "My senses is gone. I too old. I the oldest people I ever know. Dance, old scarecrow," she said, "while I dancing with you."

She kicked her foot over the furrow, and with mouth drawn down, shook her head 28 once or twice in a little strutting way. Some husks blew down and whirled in streamers about her skirts.

Then she went on, parting her way from side to side with the cane, through the 29 whispering field. At last she came to the end, to a wagon track where the silver grass blew between the red ruts. The quail were walking around like pullets, seeming all dainty and unseen.

"Walk pretty," she said. "This the easy place. This the easy going."   30

She followed the track, swaying through the quiet bare fields, through the little   31
strings of trees silver in their dead leaves, past cabins silver from weather, with the doors
and windows boarded shut, all like old women under a spell sitting there. "I walking in
their sleep," she said, nodding her head vigorously.

In a ravine she went where a spring was silently flowing through a hollow log. Old   32
Phoenix bent and drank. "Sweet-gum makes the water sweet," she said, and drank more.
"Nobody know who made this well, for it was here when I was born."

The track crossed a swampy part where the moss hung as white as lace from every   33
limb. "Sleep on, alligators, and blow you bubbles." Then the track went into the road.

Deep, deep the road went down between the high green-colored banks. Overhead   34
the live-oaks met, and it was as dark as a cave.

A black dog with a lolling tongue came up out of the weeds by the ditch. She was   35
meditating, and not ready, and when he came at her she only hit him a little with her
cane. Over she went in the ditch, like a little puff of milkweed.

Down there, her senses drifted away. A dream visited her, and she reached her hand   36
up, but nothing reached down and gave her a pull. So she lay there and presently went
to talking. "Old woman," she said to herself, "that black dog come up out of the weeds
to stall you off, and now there he sitting on his fine tail, smiling at you."

A white man finally came along and found her—a hunter, a young man, with his   37
dog on a chain.

"Well, Granny!" he laughed. "What are you doing there?"   38

"Lying on my back like a June-bug waiting to be turned over, mister," she said,   39
reaching up her hand.

He lifted her up, gave her a swing in the air, and set her down, "Anything broken,   40
Granny?"

"No sir, them old dead weeds is springy enough," said Phoenix, when she had got   41
her breath. "I thank you for your trouble."

"Where do you live, Granny?" he asked, while the two dogs were growling at each   42
other.

"Away back yonder, sir, behind the ridge. You can't even see it from here."   43

"On your way home?"   44

"No, sir, I going to town."   45

"Why, that's too far! That's as far as I walk when I come out myself, and I get some-   46
thing for my trouble." He patted the stuffed bag he carried, and there hung down a little
closed claw. It was one of the bob-whites, with its beak hooked bitterly to show it was
dead. "Now you go on home, Granny!"

"I bound to go to town, mister," said Phoenix. "The time come around."   47

He gave another laugh, filling the whole landscape. "I know you old colored people!   48
Wouldn't miss going to town to see Santa Claus!"

But something held Old Phoenix very still. The deep lines in her face went into a   49
fierce and different radiation. Without warning, she had seen with her own eyes a flashing nickel fall out of the man's pocket onto the ground.

"How old are you, Granny?" he was saying.   50

"There is no telling, mister," she said, "no telling."   51

Then she gave a little cry and clapped her hands and said, "Git on away from here,   52
dog! Look! Look at that dog!" She laughed as if in admiration. "He ain't scared of
nobody. He a big black dog." She whispered, "Sic him!"

"Watch me get rid of that cur," said the man. "Sic him, Pete! Sic him!"   53

Phoenix heard the dogs fighting, and heard the man running and throwing sticks.   54
She even heard a gunshot. But she was slowly bending forward by that time, further and
further forward, the lids stretched down over her eyes, as if she were doing this in her
sleep. Her chin was lowered almost to her knees. The yellow palm of her hand came
out from the fold of her apron. Her fingers slid down and along the ground under the
piece of money with the grace and care they would have in lifting an egg from under a
sitting hen. Then she slowly straightened up, she stood erect, and the nickel was in her
apron pocket. A bird flew by. Her lips moved. "God watching me the whole time. I come
to stealing."

The man came back, and his own dog panted about them. "Well, I scared him off   55
that time," he said, and then he laughed and lifted his gun and pointed it at Phoenix.

She stood straight and faced him.   56

"Doesn't the gun scare you?" he said, still pointing it.   57

"No, sir, I seen plenty go off closer by, in my day, and for less than what I done,"   58
she said, holding utterly still.

He smiled, and shouldered the gun. "Well, Granny," he said, "you must be a hun-   59
dred years old, and scared of nothing. I'd give you a dime if I had any money with me.
But you take my advice and stay home, and nothing will happen to you."

"I bound to go on my way, mister," said Phoenix. She inclined her head in the red   60
rag. Then they went in different directions, but she could hear the gun shooting again
and again over the hill.

She walked on. The shadows hung from the oak trees to the road like curtains.   61
Then she smelled wood-smoke, and smelled the river, and she saw a steeple and the
cabins on their steep steps. Dozens of little black children whirled around her. There
ahead was Natchez shining. Bells were ringing. She walked on.

In the paved city it was Christmas time. There were red and green electric lights   62
strung and crisscrossed everywhere, and all turned on in the daytime. Old Phoenix
would have been lost if she had not distrusted her eyesight and depended on her feet to
know where to take her.

She paused quietly on the sidewalk where people were passing by. A lady came   63
along in the crowd, carrying an armful of red-, green-, and silver-wrapped presents; she
gave off perfume like the red roses in hot summer, and Phoenix stopped her.

"Please, missy, will you lace up my shoe?" She held up her foot.   64

"What do you want, Grandma?"   65

"See my shoe," said Phoenix. "Do all right for out in the country, but wouldn't look   66
right to go in a big building."

"Stand still then, Grandma," said the lady. She put her packages down on the side-   67
walk beside her and laced and tied both shoes tightly.

"Can't lace 'em with a cane," said Phoenix. "Thank you, missy. I doesn't mind ask-   68
ing a nice lady to tie up my shoe, when I gets out on the street."

Moving slowly and from side to side, she went into the big building and into a   69
tower of steps, where she walked up and around and around until her feet knew to stop.

She entered a door, and there she saw nailed up on the wall the document that had been stamped with the gold seal and framed in the gold frame, which matched the dream that was hung up in her head. 70

"Here I be," she said. There was a fixed and ceremonial stiffness over her body. 71

"A charity case, I suppose," said an attendant who sat at the desk before her. 72

But Phoenix only looked above her head. There was sweat on her face, the wrinkles in her skin shone like a bright net. 73

"Speak up, Grandma," the woman said. "What's your name? We must have your history, you know. Have you been here before? What seems to be the trouble with you?" 74

Old Phoenix only gave a twitch to her face as if a fly were bothering her. 75

"Are you deaf?" cried the attendant. 76

But then the nurse came in. 77

"Oh, that's just old Aunt Phoenix," she said. "She doesn't come for herself—she has a little grandson. She makes these trips just as regular as clockwork. She lives away back off the Old Natchez Trace." She bent down. "Well, Aunt Phoenix, why don't you just take a seat? We won't keep you standing after your long trip." She pointed. 78

The old woman sat down, bolt upright in the chair. 79

"Now, how is the boy?" asked the nurse. 80

Old Phoenix did not speak. 81

"I said, how is the boy?" 82

But Phoenix only waited and stared straight ahead, her face very solemn and withdrawn into rigidity. 83

"Is his throat any better?" asked the nurse. "Aunt Phoenix, don't you hear me? Is your grandson's throat any better since the last time you came for the medicine?" 84

With her hands on her knees, the old woman waited, silent, erect and motionless, just as if she were in armour. 85

"You mustn't take up our time this way, Aunt Phoenix," the nurse said. "Tell us quickly about your grandson, and get it over. He isn't dead, is he?" 86

At last there came a flicker and then a flame of comprehension across her face, and she spoke. 87

"My grandson. It was my memory had left me. There I sat and forgot why I made my long trip." 88

"Forgot?" The nurse frowned. "After you came so far?" 89

Then Phoenix was like an old woman begging a dignified forgiveness for waking up frightened in the night. "I never did go to school, I was too old at the Surrender," she said in a soft voice. "I'm an old woman without an education. It was my memory fail me. My little grandson, he is just the same, and I forgot it in the coming." 90

"Throat never heals, does it?" said the nurse, speaking in a loud, sure voice to Old Phoenix. By now she had a card with something written on it, a little list. "Yes. Swallowed lye. When was it—January—two-three years ago—" 91

Phoenix spoke unasked now. "No, missy, he not dead, he just the same. Every little while his throat begin to close up again, and he not able to swallow. He not get his breath. He not able to help himself. So the time come around, and I go on another trip for the soothing medicine." 92

"All right. The doctor said as long as you came to get it, you could have it," said the nurse. "But it's an obstinate case." 93

"My little grandson, he sit up there in the house all wrapped up, waiting by him-   94
self," Phoenix went on. "We is the only two left in the world. He suffer and it don't
seem to put him back at all. He got a sweet look. He going to last. He wear a little patch
quilt and peep out holding his mouth open like a little bird. I remember so plain now. I
not going to forget him again, no, the whole enduring time. I could tell him from all
the others in creation."

"All right." The nurse was trying to hush her now. She brought her a bottle of med-   95
icine. "Charity," she said, making a check mark in a book.

Old Phoenix held the bottle close to her eyes and then carefully put it into her   96
pocket.

"I thank you," she said.   97

"It's Christmas time, Grandma," said the attendant. "Could I give you a few pennies   98
out of my purse?"

"Five pennies is a nickel," said Phoenix stiffly.   99

"Here's a nickel," said the attendant.   100

Phoenix rose carefully and held out her hand. She received the nickel and then   101
fished the other nickel out of her pocket and laid it beside the new one. She stared at her
palm closely, with her head on one side.

Then she gave a tap with her cane on the floor.   102

"This is what come to me to do," she said. "I going to the store and buy my child a   103
little windmill they sells, made out of paper. He going to find it hard to believe there
such a thing in the world. I'll march myself back where he waiting, holding it straight up
in this hand."

She lifted her free hand, gave a little nod, turned round, and walked out of the doc-   104
tor's office. Then her slow step began on the stairs, going down.

QUESTIONS FOR DISCUSSION

1. Welty provides numerous vivid and exciting details to establish the story's setting. Why does she spend so much time describing the country through which Phoenix has to travel?
2. Phoenix's comments to the animals, trees, and other natural objects on her journey might be an indication that she is going mad or that she is a very colorful character with a vivid imagination. What do you think?
3. One thing is for sure: Phoenix is a survivor. What in the story shows us that she is persistent? What signs are there that Phoenix is, in fact, quite clever?
4. What do the people whom she encounters reveal about Phoenix through their conversations with her?

THINKING CRITICALLY

1. Is Phoenix Jackson appropriately named? In what ways is she like the phoenix? Start this assignment by reading a little about the phoenix in an encyclopedia or other reference book recommended by your librarian. Then reread "A Worn Path" and write notes in the margins that point out similarities between Phoenix Jackson and that mythical bird.
2. How might you react to Phoenix Jackson if you met her on a forest path, on a city street, or in a clinic?

SUGGESTIONS FOR JOURNAL ENTRIES

1. "A Worn Path" dramatizes the strength, courage, and selflessness of Phoenix Jackson. Do you know someone who displays similar qualities? Use the focused-freewriting method to recall an incident from his or her life that illustrates nobility of character.
2. Discuss the emotions you felt when you learned the reason for Phoenix's long journey.
3. If you saw Phoenix on the street corner, you might take her for a poor, lonely eccentric to be pitied by those who lead more fortunate lives. In what ways would "A Worn Path" disprove your theory?

SUGGESTIONS FOR SUSTAINED WRITING

1. Jackson's "Charles" is about a boy who creates an imaginary classmate to get his parents' attention. Have you ever had an imaginary friend? If so, tell the story of one "adventure" in which he or she played an important role and which would help readers understand why you created this companion. Before you begin, look for useful facts and insights in the journal notes you made after reading "Charles."

   In your first drafts, write your story in detail, telling as much as you can about your imaginary friend's actions and personality. Use dialogue if it will make your story more believable. Then, read the best of your rough drafts; ask what the story says about the reason(s) you created this companion. Put your answer into a thesis statement that appears in an introductory paragraph. Follow this introduction with the story you just wrote.

   Then, revise your paper once more. Add details to illustrate or prove your thesis; remove details that don't relate to the thesis, that don't help you explain why you created your imaginary friend. Finally, as with all assignments, edit your work carefully.

2. Some people refuse to accept their "fate" and fight to better themselves. In Parédes' "The Hammon and the Beans," Chonita defies hunger, poverty, and ignorance. Even though she is defeated in the end, she still becomes a source of inspiration for the narrator and for the story's readers.

   If you answered the first of the journal suggestions after this story, you have already gathered information about an individual whose spirit may have inspired you in some way. Turn your notes into an essay that does two things:

   • Explains what qualities in your subject make him or her an inspiration.
   • Shows how he or she has inspired you.

   Develop each part through narration. Tell a story or stories that will show readers the inspirational side of your subject and that will explain how his or her influence helped you.

   Before you begin drafting your paper, however, write a preliminary thesis statement that will state your central idea clearly. Keep this thesis in mind as you develop your project. You can always revise it near the end of the process, when the time comes to rewrite and edit.

   In any case, make several drafts. Add details as you go along, including those that describe setting. Use dialogue if it helps make your essay clearer and more effective.

3. Some of the characters you have read about in this chapter demonstrate positive and even courageous outlooks on life. Write a story about a person you know whose outlook is clearly positive. Narrate one or two events from your subject's life to show that you and your readers might draw inspiration from his or her

example. If possible, begin by expanding the journal notes you made after reading "The Hammon and the Beans," "The Son from America," and "A Worn Path."

Include enough details in the events you narrate to convince readers that what you are saying about your subject is true. A good way to do this is to write several drafts of your work, adding relevant details as you go along. When you are satisfied that you have enough information, write a statement that, based upon the events you have just recalled, sums up your subject's attitude about life and explains why you find that attitude so admirable. Make this statement your thesis, and include it in a well-written introduction or conclusion. Finally, make sure your paper is well organized, contains vivid and concrete language, and is free of distracting errors.

4. In "A Worn Path," Welty tells the moving story of a woman who might have lived in her hometown. In "The Hammon and the Beans" and in "The Son from America," the authors set their stories in places like those in which they grew up. Whether these stories are true is not important. What matters is that writers often rely on their knowledge of familiar places—their homes—to make their writing more *realistic*.

Write a true or made-up story set in your county, town, or neighborhood, or in any location you know well. Like Parédes, Singer, and Welty, make your story realistic and vivid by using concrete details to describe its setting and its people.

One way to gather information for this project is to visit the location in which your story will be set. Keep a sharp lookout for details that reveal the character of the place and its people. As you take notes, remember to rely on your senses and to name the things you see so that readers will recognize what you are describing. For example, Welty mentions the pines, oaks, and sweet-gums Phoenix sees in the forest. She also talks about the vulture the old woman encounters and the bob-whites the hunter has killed.

You can include such details as you go through the process of drafting and revising. Once you are satisfied that you have produced an interesting and well-developed paper, review your writing once more to correct errors in grammar, punctuation, and spelling, which will reduce its effectiveness.

5. The selections in this chapter show that admirable people make interesting characters in fiction. Try your hand at writing a short story that includes a main character based upon someone you know and respect greatly. Tell your story in a way that shows why this person deserves admiration. In other words, use what you know about your subject's personality to predict how well he or she will react to problems, situations, and people in the world of the story.

One way to start is to recall an exciting, tragic, frightening, or otherwise dramatic event you learned about on television, read about in a newspaper, or experienced yourself. More or less, use this event as the outline of your story, but change the plot so that the person you admire becomes its main character. Have fun predicting how this new main character will react to the story's people, problems, and events. However, remember that you want to show how admirable your subject is. To do this, you might need to change the story and its outcome. So be bold and creative! Alter the original plot as much as you like to achieve your purpose.

Before you begin writing, consult your journal, especially the entries for Singer's "The Son from America" and Welty's "A Worn Path." Before you stop writing, remember that short stories require as much revision and editing as other types of assignments.

6. As a variation on the suggestion above, use the plot of one of the stories in this chapter as inspiration for a short story of your own.

Borrow the general outline of the original story and, if you like, some of its minor characters. However, replace the main characters with those based upon people you know or upon those you create in your imagination. Write your own dialogue, describe the setting in your own words, and add characters you think will make the story more interesting. As a matter of fact, change things as much as you like to give your work the theme and purpose you want.

For example, the setting for "A Worn Path" might become a large city like Philadelphia, Atlanta, Dallas, or San Francisco. And Phoenix Jackson might be replaced by an old woman from your neighborhood or even by a member of your family. In any case, make sure the words you use are your own. Don't borrow vocabulary from the story on which you are basing yours.

You can have great fun with this assignment, so be as imaginative as you like. Of course, you owe it to yourself and your readers to follow the same careful process of drafting, revising, and editing you use when writing a formal essay.

EXPOSITION
AND
PERSUASION

Many new writers begin to develop their skills by practicing the kinds of writing in Sections Three and Four, description and narration. As you learned in previous chapters, description and narration usually involve writing about subjects that are concrete and, often, very specific—people, places, events, or objects that the reader can picture or understand easily. The primary purpose of description, of course, is to explain what someone or something looked like, sounded like, and so forth. The primary purpose of narration is simply to tell what happened, although many short stories and narrative essays do a great deal more.

At times, however, new writers face the challenge of discussing abstract ideas that can't be explained through narration and description alone. They may even be asked to support opinions, take convincing stands on controversial issues, or urge their readers to action. In such cases, they must rely on a variety of methods of development and techniques associated with exposition and persuasion. *Exposition* is writing that explains. *Persuasion* is writing that proves or convinces.

Each essay in Chapters 13, 14, and 15 explains an abstract idea by using illustration, comparison and contrast, or process analysis as its *primary* method of development. However, these selections also rely on other methods explained earlier in this book (see Chapter 3). The persuasive essays in Chapter 16, which support an opinion or urge readers to act, also use a variety of techniques. In fact, most writers of exposition and persuasion combine methods to develop ideas clearly and convincingly. Comparison-and-contrast papers frequently contain definitions, anecdotes, and examples; process analyses include accurate, sometimes vivid, descriptions; and illustration essays sometimes use comparisons, anecdotes, and descriptions. Persuasive writing is usually developed through examples, statistics, and other factual details, but anecdotes, comparisons, definitions, and descriptions also make useful tools for persuasion.

Whatever your purpose and however you choose to develop ideas, you will have to know your subject well, you will have to include enough accurate information to make your writing convincing, and you will have to present that information in a way that is clear and easy to follow.

437

Explaining Through Illustration

One of the most popular ways to explain an idea is illustration, a method of development you read about in Chapter 3. Illustration uses examples to turn an idea that is general, abstract, or hard to understand into something readers can recognize and, therefore, grasp more easily. As the word implies, an illustration is a concrete and specific picture of an idea that would otherwise have remained vague and undefined.

For instance, if you wanted a clearer and more definitive notion of what your friend meant when she claimed to have met several "interesting characters" since coming to school, you might ask her to describe a few of those "characters" specifically and to show you in what ways they were "interesting." Each of the people she discussed would then serve as an illustration or picture of what she meant by the abstract word "interesting."

Explaining Through Comparison and Contrast

This method of development involves pointing out similarities and/or differences between two people, objects, places, experiences, ways of doing something, and the like. Writers compare (point out similarities between) and contrast (point out differences between) two things to make one or both more recognizable or understandable to their readers. Let's say you want to explain a computer monitor to someone who has never seen one. You might compare it with a television set. After all, both have glass screens on which electronic images appear. To make your explanation more complete and accurate, however, you might also need to contrast these two devices by pointing out that only on television can one watch a baseball game, a soap opera, or reruns of *I Love Lucy*. Contrast also comes in handy when you want to explain why you believe one thing is better than another. For example, "Watch the Cart!" an essay in the introduction to Chapter 14, points out differences to explain why the author thinks women are more adept at grocery shopping than men.

There are many reasons for comparing or contrasting the subjects you wish to write about. Whatever your purpose, you may find that comparing or contrasting will help you bring abstract ideas into sharper focus and make them more concrete than if you had discussed each of your subjects separately.

Explaining Through Process Analysis

Process analysis is used in scientific writing to help readers understand both natural and technical processes such as the formation of rain clouds, the circulation of blood through the body, or the workings of a CD player. However, it also has a place in non-scientific writing. For example, you might want to use process analysis to explain how U.S. Presidents are elected, how money is transferred from one bank to another electronically, or even how your Aunt Millie manages to turn the most solemn occasion into a party!

Process analysis is also useful when you need to provide the reader with directions or instructions to complete a specific task. Subjects for such essays include "how to change the brakes on a Ford Mustang," "how to bake lasagna," or even "how to get to school from the center of town."

In each of these examples, the writer is assigning him- or herself the task of explaining, as specifically and as clearly as possible, an idea that might be very new and unfamiliar to the reader. And, in each case, the essay will focus on "how to do something" or "how something is done."

Though it may often seem deceptively simple, writing a process paper is often a painstaking task and must be approached carefully. Remember that your readers might be totally unfamiliar with what you're explaining and will need a great deal of information to follow the process easily and to understand it thoroughly.

As a matter of fact, the need to be clear and concrete often causes writers of process analysis to rely on other methods of development as well. Among them are narration, description, illustration, and comparison and contrast. Of these, writers of process analysis rely most heavily on narration. After all, a process is a story. Like narratives, process papers are often organized in chronological order and explain a series of events. Unlike narratives, however, process essays don't simply tell *what* happens; they also explain *how* something happens or *how* something should be done.

P E R S U A D I N G

Persuasion is the attempt to convince readers that your position on an issue is valid. Sometimes it even involves urging them to take an action supported by the evidence you have presented.

To be persuasive, you will find that it is necessary to explain reasons or ideas thoroughly and clearly. Therefore, exposition is always involved in persuasion, and many of the methods of development you will use to explain an idea will also come in handy when you need to defend an opinion or take a stand.

After reading Chapter 16, you will have a better idea about how to use illustration, contrast, narration, and the like as tools for presenting evidence that will convince readers your point of view has merit. You should also have a clearer notion of the kind of analytical reasoning writers of persuasion use to think through complex issues and to draw logical conclusions. Two kinds of reasoning, *deduction* and *induction,* play important roles in building an *argument,* the heart of any persuasive paper. Chapter 16 will show you how to combine such thinking with convincing evidence to construct an effective argument.

Of course, logical arguments are not enough to convince some readers, especially those whose opinions on a subject are the very opposite of yours or whose lack of excitement about an issue makes them unwilling to act. In such cases, you may have to go beyond pure argument and appeal to their emotions, their pride, their values. Whatever you are trying to prove and whatever kind of audience you face, the selections in Chapter 16 will help you begin developing the expertise to write persuasively on almost any topic.

Essays that illustrate, that compare and contrast, that explain processes, or that persuade are only a few of the types of assignments you will read and write as you continue your education. Nevertheless, they will teach you the important skills of organization and development that are the foundation upon which to build success as a college writer.

ILLUSTRATION

You have learned that the most interesting and effective writing uses specific and concrete details to *show* rather than to *tell* the reader something. One of the best ways to show your readers what you mean is to fill your writing with clear, relevant examples. Examples are also referred to as *illustrations*. They act as pictures—concrete representations—of the abstract idea you are trying to explain, and they make your writing easier to understand and more convincing to your readers. In fact, illustration can be used as the primary method to develop a thesis.

Effective illustrations can help you make reference to specific people, places, and things—concrete realities that your readers will recognize or understand easily. Say that you want to convince them that your 1996 "Wizbang" is an economical car. Instead of being content to rely on their understanding of a vague word like "economical," you decide to provide examples that show exactly what you think this term means. Therefore, you explain that the Wizbang gets about 65 miles per gallon around town, that its purchase price is $4000 less than its least expensive competitor's, and that it needs only one $50 tune-up every 40,000 miles. Now that's economical!

Several types of examples are discussed below. The important thing to remember is that the examples you choose must relate to and be appropriate to the idea you're illustrating. For instance, you probably wouldn't cite statistics about the Wizbang's safety record if you wanted to impress your readers with how inexpensive the car is to own and operate.

SPECIFIC FACTS, INSTANCES, OR OCCURRENCES

A good way to get examples into your writing is to use specific facts, instances, or occurrences relating to the idea you are explaining. Let's say you want to prove that the Wizbang does not perform well in bad weather. You can say it stalled twice during a recent rainstorm or that it did not start when the temperature fell below freezing last week. If you want to show that people in your town are community-minded, you might mention that they recently opened a shelter for the homeless, that they have organized a meals-on-wheels program for the elderly, or that they have increased their contributions to the United Way campaign in each of the last five years. If you want to prove that the 1960s were years of turmoil, you can recall the assassinations of John and Robert Kennedy and Martin Luther King, Jr., the antiwar marches, and the urban riots.

Several selections in this chapter use specific facts, instances, or occurrences to develop ideas. Edwin Way Teale's "Winter Folklore," contains fascinating instances of superstitions regarding the coming of winter. Grace Lukawska's "Wolf" is full of revealing facts about this animal. Specific instances and occurrences can also be found in Irina Groza's "Growing Up in Rumania" and in John Naisbitt and Patricia Aburdene's "The Culture of Cuisine."

STATISTICS

Mathematical figures, or statistics, can also be included to strengthen your readers' understanding of an abstract idea. If you want to prove that the cost of living in your hometown has increased dramatically over the last five years, you might explain that the price of a three-bedroom home has increased by about 30 percent, from $100,000 to $130,000, that real estate taxes have doubled from an average of $1500 per family to $3000 per family, and that the cost of utilities has nearly tripled, with each household now spending about $120 per month on heat and electricity. John Naisbitt and Patricia Aburdene's "The Culture of Cuisine," which you can read later in this chapter, makes excellent use of statistics to show that, across the globe, people from very different cultures are falling in love with each other's cooking. Philip K. Howard's "The Death of Common Sense" also uses statistics.

SPECIFIC PEOPLE, PLACES, OR THINGS

Mentioning specific people, places, and things familiar to the reader can also help you make abstract ideas easier to understand and more convincing. If you want to explain that the American South is famous for the Presidents and statespeople it has produced, you might bring up George Washington, Thomas Jefferson, Henry Clay, Lyndon Johnson, Martin Luther King, and Jimmy Carter. If you need to convince readers that your city is a great place to have fun, you will probably mention its amusement park, professional football stadium, brand-new children's zoo and aquarium, community swimming pool, camp grounds, and public golf courses. Specific people, places, and things are mentioned throughout Philip K. Howard's "The Death of Common Sense."

ANECDOTES

As you probably know, anecdotes are brief, informative stories that develop an idea or drive home a point. They are similar to and serve the same purpose as specific instances and occurrences, and they are sometimes used with such illustrations to develop an idea more fully. However, anecdotes often appear in greater detail than other types of examples. Look for anecdotes especially in Irina Groza's "Growing Up in Rumania" and Philip K. Howard's "The Death of Common Sense."

VISUALIZING EXAMPLES

The following paragraphs are from Alleen Pace Nilsen's "Sexism in English: A 1990's Update." They explain interesting facts about etymology, the origins of words.

States her thesis
|·|\·|in American culture a woman is valued for the attractiveness and sexiness of her body, while a man is valued for his physical strength and accomplishments. A woman is sexy; a man is successful.

A persuasive piece of evidence supporting this view are the eponyms—words that have come from someone's

Creates an interesting contrast
name—found in English. [After researching this subject] I had a two-and-a-half-inch stack of cards taken from men's names, but less than a half-inch stack from women's names, and most of those came from Greek mythology. In works that came into American English

Uses specific instances
since we separated from Britain, there are many eponyms based on the names of famous American men: bartlett pear, boysenberry, diesel engine, franklin stove, ferris wheel, gatling gun, mason jar, sideburns, sousaphone, schick test, and winchester rifle. The only

Mentions specific people
common eponyms taken from American women's names are Alice blue (after Alice Roosevelt Longworth), bloomers (after Amelia Jenks Bloomer) and Mae West jacket (after the buxom actress). Two out of the three feminine eponyms relate closely to a woman's physical anatomy, while the masculine eponyms (except for *sideburns* after General Burnsides) have nothing to do with the

namesake's body, but instead honor the man for an accomplishment of some kind.

Although in Greek mythology women played a bigger

Mentions
specific
mythological
figures;
mentions
things
readers
will
recognize

role than they did in the biblical stories of the
Judeo Christian cultures. /./.\ the same tendency to think of
women in relation to sexuality is seen in the eponyms
aphrodisiac from Aphrodite, the Greek name for the
goddess of love and beauty, and venereal disease, from
Venus, the Roman name for Aphrodite.

Restates
thesis.

Tells an
anecdote

Another interesting word from Greek mythology is
Amazon. According to Greek folk etymology, the *a* means
"without" as in *atypical* or *amoral* while *mazon* comes
from *mazos*, meaning breast as still seen in *mastectomy*.
In the Greek legend, Amazon women cut off their right
breasts so that they could better shoot their bows.
Apparently, the story tellers had a feeling that for
women to play the active, "masculine" role that the
Amazons adopted for themselves, they had to trade in
part of their femininity.

REVISING ILLUSTRATION ESSAYS

Before writing "Wolf," student Grace Lukawska had completed a great deal of prewriting in her journal to get started. When she finished her first draft, however, she realized she would have to add more detail and restructure her essay to make her point effectively. By the time she finished she had written several drafts, but the final product shows that careful revision is always worth the effort. Read these paragraphs from two versions of the complete paper, which appears in this chapter. Information in parentheses refers to Candace Savage's *Wolves*, a book in which Lukawska researched facts about her subject.

Lukawska—Rough Draft

Make
introduction
more
interesting?

There are still popular misconceptions of the wolf as
predator. Many people think that wolves kill for
pleasure or just to show their dominance over other

Include vivid details and examples to explain misconceptions?

animals. However, the truth is that wolves are very fascinating and intelligent.

Their intelligence manifests itself in their behavior. Wolves belong to a group of animals who live in hierarchical groups. According to Candace Savage, a large, well organized pack consists of an upper class—1/M parents, a middle class—1/M uncles and aunts, a lower class—1/M children, and finally "helpers" who are

For what? Explain?

inexperienced hunters and who depend on the pack (55). Their role is to baby-sit youngsters while the other wolves are hunting (62).

Another example of wolves' aptitude is clear communication. The leader of the group, usually the male, establishes regulations so that each animal knows whom it can boss and to whom it must subject. For

Does this relate to communication?

instance, a middle-class wolf must obey the leader's orders; children and helpers must subject to their relatives. These rules help to prevent fights or disagreements in packs. Furthermore, wolves have their

Say more about their language? Use examples?

own language which is based on different sound levels in their voices. For example, according to Savage, a whimper indicates a friendly attitude; snarls convey warnings and admonitions (58).

Lukawska—Final Draft

For centuries, popular misconceptions have pictured the wolf as a terrifying predator that kills for

Creates vivid images that serve as

pleasure. The name itself calls up nasty images: the glutton who "wolfs" down his food; the werewolf, who,

examples | during a full moon, grows hair all over his body, howls into the night, and claws beautiful maidens to death.

Mentions specific story, which readers may recognize | Even in fairy tales like "Little Red Riding Hood," the wolf is pictured as shrewd and bloodthirsty. But is the wolf really a cold-blooded killer? Not at all; the wolf

Makes thesis clearer, stronger | is a magnificent animal who displays many of the characteristics we value in human beings.

The intelligence of the wolf manifests itself in its behavior. The wolf's society is well organized and

Mentions title of Savage's book | hierarchical. According to Candace Savage, author of *Wolves*, a pack consists of an upper class--parents, a middle class--uncles and aunts, a lower class--children, and finally "helpers" who are inexperienced hunters and

Becomes more specific | who depend upon the pack for their food (55). Their role is to baby-sit youngsters while the other wolves are hunting (62). Like humans, wolves practice adoption. If parents die, their children are cared for by another family.

New paragraph explains behavior, not communication | The leader of the group, usually a male, establishes regulations so that each animal knows whom it can boss and to whom it must submit. For instance, a middle-class wolf must obey the leader's orders; children and helpers must submit to their relatives. This rule helps prevent disagreements and fights.

Creates a new paragraph to discuss communication. Expands her discussion! | Another indication of the wolf's intelligence is the ability to communicate. Wolves have their own language, which is based on the use of different intonations. According to Savage, a whimper communicates friendship, snarls convey warnings and admonishments, and a "special chirplike tone expresses sexual interest" (58). Like dogs, wolves also use gestures and facial expressions to communicate. By moving their foreheads, mouths, ears, and eyes, they express their emotions and announce their ranks. Frightened wolves keep their teeth covered, "eyes slightly closed, ears flat to the head" (Savage 55). They also bend their legs and tuck in their tails. Wolves that are self-confident, on the other hand, point their ears forward and bare their teeth. Wolves of the highest rank reveal their positions by keeping their tails and ears up and by looking directly into the eyes of other animals. Members of the pack show respect for them; like dogs, they keep their ears tucked in, their heads down, and their legs slightly bent.

Uses description to create examples

Includes concrete, specific vocabulary

PRACTICING ILLUSTRATION

Examples can be defined as concrete signs of abstract ideas. Below are several topic sentences expressing such ideas. Use the spaces below each to write a paragraph relating to each sentence. Develop your paragraph by using at least three examples of the kinds you have just read about. First, however, make a quick list of the examples you will use on a sheet of scratch paper. You can discuss them in detail when it comes time to write the paragraph.

Feel free to reword these sentences any way you like.

1. Wherever you go these days, people seem to be recycling.

_____

_____

_____

_____

_____

_____

_____

_____

_____

2. Some people I know are very materialistic.

_____

_____

_____

_____

_____

_____

_____

_____

_____

3. A friend of mine often engages in self-destructive behavior.

_____

_____

_____

_____

_____

_____

_____

_____

_____

4. _____ succeeds at whatever sport (or other type of activity)he (or
　　　(name a person)
she) pursues.

_____

_____

_____

_____

_____

_____

_____

_____

_____

5. Electronic devices play important roles in the modern home.

_____

_____

_____

_____

_____

_____

_____

_____

6. People in my town seem to be getting richer and richer (or poorer and poorer).

_____

_____

_____

_____

_____

_____

_____

_____

The illustrations found throughout this chapter make the abstract ideas they explain more interesting, more believable, and more easily understood. Keep this in mind as you read the essays that follow and especially as you begin to use illustration in your own writing.

Winter Folklore*

Edwin Way Teale

A writer for Popular Science *magazine, Edwin Way Teale (1899–1980) combined his talents as an essayist and a photographer to explain the wonder of the natural world. His best-remembered works are books describing the seasons. Among them is* Wandering Through Winter, *from which "Winter Folklore" is taken and for which Teale was awarded a Pulitzer Prize.*

LOOKING AHEAD

This selection uses several specific instances to explain an idea. That idea is made clear and convincing because of the careful detail Teale uses to build each of these illustrations.

VOCABULARY

abundant	Plentiful.
credulous	Gullible, willing to believe or trust too easily.
folklore	Traditional knowledge or beliefs of a people handed down from generation to generation.
gird	Prepare, fortify, strengthen.
Ozarks	Mountain range in Arkansas, Missouri, and Oklahoma.
severe	Harsh, extreme, very difficult.

*Editor's title

Winter Folklore | *Edwin Way Teale*

In the folklore of the country, numerous superstitions relate to winter weather. Back-country farmers examine their corn husks—the thicker the husk, the colder the winter. They watch the acorn crop—the more acorns, the more severe the season. They observe where white-faced hornets place their paper nests—the higher they are, the deeper will be the snow. They examine the size and shape and color of the spleens of butchered hogs for clues to the severity of the season. They keep track of the blooming of dogwood in the spring—the more abundant the blooms, the more bitter the cold in January. When chipmunks carry their tails high and squirrels have heavier fur and mice come into country houses early in the fall, the superstitious gird themselves for a long, hard winter. Without any scientific basis, a wider-than-usual black band on a woolly-bear caterpillar is accepted as a sign that winter will arrive early and stay late. Even the way a cat sits beside the stove carries its message to the credulous. According to a belief once widely held in the Ozarks, a cat sitting with its tail to the fire indicates very cold weather is on the way.

QUESTIONS FOR DISCUSSION

1. From what you read here, what can you conclude about Teale's attitude toward country folklore?
2. In Looking Ahead, you learned that Teale's main idea is convincing because of the many detailed examples he uses to explain it. Which examples do you find most convincing? Why?
3. How does Teale maintain unity in this paragraph? Where does he express his central idea?

THINKING CRITICALLY

1. Are some superstitions based on logic? For example, we avoid walking under ladders in order not to get splattered with paint or hit by a falling object. Think of two or three other examples, and explain them in writing.
2. Teale concentrates on country people, but all sorts of people are superstitious. Think about a superstition held by a group of people or type of person you know well. Discuss this superstition and the people who observe it in a paragraph or two. For example, focus on city people, college students, athletes, gamblers, children, the elderly, or members of a particular trade or profession.

SUGGESTIONS FOR JOURNAL ENTRIES

1. Make a list of short sentences or phrases about popular beliefs you associate with a particular time of year, a holiday, or a celebration. For instance, put down what you know about the folklore of spring or summer, about popular beliefs associated with Halloween or Valentine's Day, or about rituals and traditions people follow on birthdays or wedding days.
2. Think of a superstition you once held but have now given up. Use focused freewriting to explain what you believed in and why you believed in it. Then, give at least one example to show how that belief affected the way you lived your life. If you don't want to write about yourself, write about a superstitious friend, relative, or neighbor.

   Another way to approach this assignment is to write about a phobia—an irrational but very real fear—that you or someone you know suffers from. Show how this fear affects you or the person you are writing about. Examples include fear of heights (acrophobia), fear of closed spaces (claustrophobia), fear of open places (agoraphobia), and fear of water (hydrophobia). But there are many more.

The Culture of Cuisine

John Naisbitt and Patricia Aburdene

John Naisbitt and Patricia Aburdene have been called "futurists." Working closely with leaders in government, business, and science, they try to describe the future effects of important trends and developments in politics, manufacturing, the environment, education, economics, popular culture, and other fields. In 1982, Naisbitt published Megatrends, *which discusses new directions for American society in the 1980s. It was so successful that he and Aburdene followed up with* Megatrends 2000 *in 1990. "The Culture of Cuisine" is taken from this book.*

Looking Ahead

1. The authors develop the main idea of this selection by using illustrations like those you learned about in the chapter's introduction. Try spotting various kinds of examples as you read "The Culture of Cuisine."
2. Much of the information in this selection is expressed in direct quotations from people Naisbitt and Aburdene interviewed or from written materials they researched. As such, you can use "The Culture of Cuisine" as a model for putting quoted material into your own work.

Vocabulary

armadillo	Animal common in the American Southwest; it has skin that resembles armor.
chic	Stylish.
confectioneries	Places that sell sweets.
cravings	Desires, yearnings.
cuisine	Style or type of cooking or of food preparation.
delicacies	Treats, rare and delicious foods.
exotic	Interesting because it is unfamiliar or foreign.
gusto	Interest, excitement, zeal.
symbol	Sign, representation.

The Culture of Cuisine

John Naisbitt and Patricia Aburdene

West Los Angeles is the home of Gurume, a Japanese-run restaurant whose   1
speciality—Gurume chicken—is Oriental chopped chicken and green beans
in an Italian marinara sauce, served over spaghetti, with Japanese cabbage salad, Texas
toast, and Louisiana Tabasco sauce. It is a symbol of what is happening to world lifestyle
and cuisine.

We are tasting one another's cuisines with great gusto. Americans are exporting   2
seafood delicacies to Japan, Tex-Mex is all the rage in Paris, and the United States is
importing sushi bars as if they were Toyotas.

"Three years ago the world had never tasted soft-shells [crabs] and now we export   3
to twenty-two countries," said Terrence Conway, owner of the John T. Handy Company, a Chesapeake Bay firm that in 1986 exported 270,000 pounds of crabs, mainly to
Japan. (In 1988 the company was bought by a Japanese firm.)

Tex-Mex cuisine is prepared kosher in Israel, where former Houstonian Barry Rit-   4
man's Chili's restaurant comes complete with a Lone Star beer sign, armadillo art, and
cactus garden.

"There just wasn't anyplace here to buy the tacos, chili, or chips I ate back in   5
Texas," says Ritman, who satisfied his Southwest cravings while introducing Israelis to
tacos, tortillas, and margaritas.

In 1985 San Antonio-based Papa Maya, one of a handful of Tex-Mex restaurants in   6
Paris, received the city's Best Foreign Food award. Since then Tex-Mex has become
Paris's hot new exotic cuisine. Chic young Parisians now fill the house at La Perla, Café
Pacifico, and the Studio.

There were 19,364 Oriental restaurants in the United States in 1988, according to   7
RE-COUNT, a service of the Restaurant Consulting Group, Inc., in Evanston, Illinois.
Oriental restaurant growth outpaces all other restaurant categories, having increased 10
percent just in 1987 and 1988 while restaurants grew 4 percent overall, says RE-
COUNT.

In 1975 there were only about 300 sushi bars in the United States; by 1980 there   8
were more than 1,500, reports *Palate Pleasers,* the first Japanese food magazine for
Americans printed in the United States. Today there are thousands.

"At least five to ten new sushi bars open in New York City and Los Angeles every   9
month," according to Susan Hirano of *Palate Pleasers.* And the sushi craze has broken
out of the big city.

You can order sushi in American beef country: Des Moines, Iowa; Wichita, Kansas;   10
and Omaha, Nebraska. The Japanese Steak House, in Grand Rapids, Michigan, boasts a
floating sushi bar. The Kroger supermarket in Buckhead, Georgia, sells sushi. More
adventurous Georgians order the octopus and eel.

If Americans are crazy about sushi, the Japanese have shown they have an all-Amer-   11
ican sweet tooth. Tokyo is overflowing with the latest American confectioneries: Häa-
gen-Dazs, Famous Amos, Mrs. Field's, and David's Cookies stores. Even lesser-known
outlets like Steve's and Hobson's ice-cream shops are open in Tokyo.

In the United States ethnic food is one of the hottest segments in the restaurant   12 business. Eating out in Middle America used to mean steak and potatoes. Now it is Mexican, Chinese, Korean, Afghan, and Ethiopian. Between 1982 and 1986 overall restaurant traffic in the United States increased 10 percent, but Asian restaurants saw business grow 54 percent, Mexican restaurants 43 percent, and Italian restaurants 26 percent. In a one-block area of the Adams Morgan neighborhood of Washington, D.C., you can eat Ethiopian, Jamaican, Italian, Mexican, French, Salvadorean, Japanese, Chinese, Caribbean, Indian, or American.

QUESTIONS FOR DISCUSSION

1. Why is Gurume chicken "a symbol of what is happening to world lifestyle and cuisine" (paragraph 1)?
2. What evidence do Naisbitt and Aburdene give to illustrate that American cuisine is becoming popular across the globe?
3. What statistics do they include to show that the American appetite for foreign food is growing?
4. Does this selection make use of contrast? For what purpose?
5. Find examples of figurative language in "The Culture of Cuisine."
6. Naisbitt and Aburdene mention brand names. They also include names of places, businesses, restaurants, and organizations. Does doing this make their writing more convincing than if they had left those names out? Explain.
7. Why do they bother to mention that we can "order sushi in American beef country" (paragraph 10)? Why do they tell us we can buy it in a supermarket in Buckhead, Georgia?
8. Is the introduction to this selection effective? Defend your answer.

THINKING CRITICALLY

1. Have some fun imagining a dish that contains foods and ingredients from three or more very different cuisines. For example, try an English pot pie filled with Mexican rice and chicken, topped with Italian mozzarella cheese and tomato sauce, and served with sliced cucumbers in a Hungarian cream sauce.
2. What is the strangest type of food you have ever eaten? Think of a lunch you had at an ethnic restaurant or a dinner you ate at the home of a person who learned to cook in a culture very different from yours. Describe the dish or the entire meal in detail. Then ask yourself why you thought it was so strange.

SUGGESTIONS FOR JOURNAL ENTRIES

1. Are Americans becoming more international in their cooking and eating? Make a list of the foods you like that originated in another country. Then make a list of foods you like that you are *sure* originated in America. If you have trouble gathering information, brainstorm about this topic with a few classmates or friends. Before you begin, try to guess which list will be longer.
2. Do you agree that people the world over are sharing in each other's cultures? Make a list of things—consumer products, foods, sports, types of art or music, customs or traditions, trends or fads, and the like—that are popular in America but originated elsewhere. For example, mention sushi from Japan, the sauna bath from Scandinavia, or various types of music from Africa, the Caribbean, and other parts of the world.

Wolf

Grace Lukawska

Born in Boleslawiec, Poland, Grace Lukawska came to the United States in 1986. After studying English for speakers of other languages, she enrolled in a developmental writing course in which she wrote this paper. In Poland, Lukawska had seen many television specials on wild animals. When asked to write about a fascinating animal, she immediately thought of the wolf. Lukawska is studying to become a medical assistant.

LOOKING AHEAD

1. The author develops this essay with examples, but she also uses comparison and description.
2. Pay particular attention to the essay's organization. Consider what Lukawska has done to keep it focused and well organized.
3. "Getting Started" explains that summarizing written materials is a good way to gather information. Another is to quote directly from a source. Lukawska summarizes and quotes directly from Candace Savage's *Wolves*. She credits this book by indicating in parentheses the pages from which she took information. These entries are called parenthetical citations. She also provides full bibliographical information about the book at the end of her paper.

VOCABULARY

admonishments	Condemnations, rebukes.
attribute	Associate with, blame for.
glutton	Someone who eats too much.
hierarchical	Arranged by rank or importance.
manifests	Shows.
misconceptions	Incorrect opinions.
intonations	Levels of sound, pitches.
solidarity	Unity, mutual support, togetherness.

Wolf | *Grace Lukawska*

For centuries, popular misconceptions have pictured the wolf as a terrifying 1
predator that kills for pleasure. The name itself calls up nasty images: the glutton who "wolfs" down his food; the werewolf, who, during a full moon, grows hair all
over his body, howls into the night, and claws beautiful maidens to death. Even in fairy
tales like "Little Red Riding Hood," the wolf is pictured as shrewd and bloodthirsty. But
is the wolf really a cold-blooded killer? Not at all; the wolf is a magnificent animal who
displays many of the characteristics we value in human beings.

The intelligence of the wolf manifests itself in its behavior. The wolf's society is well 2
organized and hierarchical. According to Candace Savage, author of *Wolves,* a pack consists of an upper class—parents, a middle class—uncles and aunts, a lower class—children, and finally "helpers" who are inexperienced hunters and who depend upon the
pack for their food (55). Their role is to baby-sit youngsters while the other wolves are
hunting (62). Like humans, wolves practice adoption. If parents die, their children are
cared for by another family.

The leader of the group, usually a male, establishes regulations so that each animal 3
knows whom it can boss and to whom it must submit. For instance, a middle-class wolf
must obey the leader's orders; children and helpers must submit to their relatives. This
rule helps prevent disagreements and fights.

Another indication of the wolf's intelligence is the ability to communicate. Wolves 4
have their own language, which is based on the use of different intonations. According
to Savage, a whimper communicates friendship, snarls convey warnings and admonish-
ments, and a "special chirplike tone expresses sexual interest" (58). Like dogs, wolves
also use gestures and facial expressions to communicate. By moving their foreheads,
mouths, ears, and eyes, they express their emotions and announce their ranks. Frightened wolves keep their teeth covered, "eyes slightly closed, ears flat to the head" (Savage
55). They also bend their legs and tuck in their tails. Wolves that are self-confident, on
the other hand, point their ears forward and bare their teeth. Wolves of the highest rank
reveal their positions by keeping their tails and ears up and by looking directly into the
eyes of other animals. Members of the pack show respect for them; like dogs, they keep
their ears tucked in, their heads down, and their legs slightly bent.

Like people, wolves are sociable. In a group, they constantly check one another by 5
sniffing. To show affection, they nuzzle each other as if to kiss. To express hostility,
they lick their cheeks, wag their tails, howl, and even stick out their tongues. This kind
of behavior serves not only to locate companions outside the pack but also to mark their
territory and tell enemies of the family's solidarity (Savage 59).

Regardless of rank or age, wolves enjoy playing games with other members of their 6
pack. Even the leader, who may appear to be aggressive and ruthless, takes an active
part in these activities, which include chasing one another and rolling over. Another
sign of intelligence, such exercises not only give them pleasure, but they also help them
keep physically fit.

Wolves are natural-born strategists and planners. Hunting a large animal like a deer 7
or moose is very dangerous for a single wolf. Therefore, they hunt in groups. After locating a herd, one might act as a decoy to draw males away from the herd while the rest

single out and attack the victim. Wolves kill only weak or sick animals, and they never kill more than they need. In case there is any excess, leftovers are buried near their dens.

The reputation from which wolves suffer is undeserved and unfair. Wolves can be violent, and they are terrifying hunters. But they kill only to feed and protect their families; they never commit distinctly "human" crimes such as murder, theft, and rape. Wolves are not bloodthirsty monsters that should be feared and eradicated. They are magnificent animals, and they deserve their place on earth.

WORKS CITED

SAVAGE, CANDACE. *Wolves*. San Francisco: Sierra Club, 1980.

QUESTIONS FOR DISCUSSION

1. In Looking Ahead, you were asked what the author did to keep this essay focused and organized. What is the essay's thesis? What techniques does she use to maintain unity and coherence?
2. What kind of examples does Lukawska rely on most in this essay? Does she ever refer to specific persons, places, or things?
3. Where in this essay does she use comparison?
4. Where does she create verbal images? Why are they so effective?
5. What techniques for writing introductions and conclusions has Lukawska used? (Check Chapter 4 if you need to review these techniques.)

THINKING CRITICALLY

1. Consider another animal that has a bad reputation: a rat, a snake, a bat, a pig, a spider, or some other unpopular beast. Then in a paragraph or two discuss the positive qualities of this animal. For example, many people hate and fear rats, but laboratory rats play an important role in medical research.
2. Reread Lukawska's introduction. Then list other examples that would illustrate the popular misconception of wolves as bloodthirsty monsters.
3. The author suggests that human beings can sometimes be more beastly than the beasts. What does she mean? Do you agree? Can you provide some examples?

SUGGESTIONS FOR JOURNAL ENTRIES

1. Think of an animal or species of animal you know well—your Siamese cat or all domestic cats, the neighbor's German shepherd or all shepherds, a bird that often visits your backyard or all common birds. List important things you know about this creature—anything that would provide clues about its behavior, lifestyle, or personality.

    Then ask yourself what this information tells you. Draw three or more general conclusions about the animal from the details you have listed. Write these conclusions in the form of topic sentences for paragraphs that you might later develop in an essay.
2. Are human families as well organized and as close as the wolf family? Think of your own family. Then write a paragraph in which you use illustrations to evaluate the kind of family to which you belong. Perhaps the best types of illustrations to use are anecdotes taken from your own experiences.

Growing Up in Rumania

Irina Groza

When Irina Groza was a girl, Rumania was a Communist country, where personal freedom and economic opportunity were in short supply. Like other countries behind the iron curtain, Rumania made it difficult for people to leave. But Groza was one of the lucky ones, and she was able to immigrate to the United States. Today, she is studying for her associate's degree in nursing in addition to raising a family and working full-time.

Looking Ahead

1. Groza shows that personal experience can be a rich source of illustrations to develop an abstract idea. She fills her essay with specific instances and anecdotes that explain how horrible life in Rumania had become under a tyrannical and incompetent government.
2. Several types of writing can be used together to make a successful essay. Groza relies heavily on examples but also includes narrative and descriptive details.
3. In 1990, Communist governments across eastern Europe fell from power. In Rumania, dictator Nicolae Ceauşescu, his wife, and several members of his government were tried and executed for crimes against the people they had oppressed for over thirty years.

Vocabulary

brutalize	Treat cruelly or violently.
classics	Important and lasting works of literature.
compliance	Submission, agreement.
cult	Excessive or unnatural devotion to a person or idea.
egomania	Extreme pride and self-concern.
flawed	Defective, faulty.
ideology	Ideas, beliefs, philosophy.
impoverishing	Making poor.
indoctrinate	Drill into, force to believe.
inflicted	Imposed.
jeopardy	Danger, risk.
magnitude	Size, extent.
prey on	Persecute, attack, victimize.
purge	Remove, eliminate.
regime	Government, rule.
stature	Standing, reputation.
suppress	Dominate, control.

Growing Up in Rumania

Irina Groza

I grew up in a beautiful Transylvanian city called Arad, just a few miles from the   1
Hungarian border. In the mid-fifties, when I was born, Rumania was still recovering from the Second World War, and people were working hard to rebuild their country. I was in the third grade when our beloved president, Gheorghe Gheorghiu-Dej, died. He was succeeded by Nicolae Ceauşescu, a young and ambitious general who promised us a bright future. At his election, no one was able to foresee the magnitude of his egomania, ruthlessness, and incompetence. The tyranny that followed nearly destroyed Rumania and inflicted widespread suffering on its people for many years.

At the beginning of Ceauşescu's presidency, life was still good. I remember going   2
into town with my mother. The streets were busy places, filled with people who were smiling and laughing as they went about their business. The shops contained plenty of food; people stood in line only to buy fresh milk and bread. Slowly, however, certain foods began to disappear from store shelves and counters. It became much harder to get meat and fresh vegetables. Consumer goods such as clothing and small appliances became scarce. I heard my mother complain about the new president, but as a child I did not find these problems significant.

Then I started noticing a change in our school books. National heroes like Michael   3
Eminescu and George Cosbuc, who had once been glorified, were deleted from our history texts. George Enescu and other great Rumanian writers, artists, and musicians, who had been the symbols of our culture, were hardly mentioned. Classics were removed from our school library, and its shelves were overloaded with books about the new president and his regime. He was portrayed as a hero of the people who had fought for Communism, but he was a hero we had never heard of before. School children had to take courses in politics designed to indoctrinate them with Ceauşescu's diseased ideology. We were forced to memorize his speeches, which were full of lies about the progress and prosperity his government had brought to Rumania. Before long this sickening personality cult became obvious to everyone, and we knew that our country and our culture were being polluted by this madman.

Before long, new laws restricting people's personal freedom were put into effect.   4
One of these prohibited travel outside the country, and Rumanians found themselves prisoners in their own country. Another law required every family to have at least four children. Ceauşescu believed that increasing the population would make Rumania powerful and increase his stature in the world. All contraceptives were removed from the shelves, and doctors who performed abortions were severely punished. But many people could not afford to support large families and were forced to turn their children over to state orphanages. As shown in recent news releases, these places were badly run and unsanitary. In fact, many of the children housed there contracted AIDS.

In another attempt to suppress the people and to destroy their spirit, the govern-   5
ment began a campaign to discourage church attendance. Celebrations of religious holidays were prohibited, and people who openly expressed their faith put themselves in jeopardy. One day a police officer stopped me and ridiculed me in front of my friends because I was wearing a cross around my neck. I felt embarrassed and angry, but there

was nothing I could do. I had heard that many people had been beaten by the police, and we lived in constant fear of them. Those who continued to oppose the system were thrown into jail or put into mental institutions.

As soon as Ceauşescu took office, he began to purge those in the government who 6 might oppose him, and he surrounded himself with his supporters. He also established the *Securitate,* a secret police force, which drew to its ranks many misfits who were greedy for power and who had the stomach to swallow the government's lies. No special training was required of these people, just blind compliance to the will of the regime and a desire to brutalize people. Members of the *Securitate* were privileged: they shopped in their own well-supplied stores, and their salaries were about six times those of medical doctors.

The *Securitate* was Ceauşescu's tool for holding down opposition to a regime that 7 the people knew was a miserable failure and that had succeeded only in impoverishing the country and subjecting us to extreme economic hardship. People worked hard, but the lines at food stores became longer and longer. There were severe shortages of meat, milk, butter, flour, soap, detergent, toothpaste, gasoline, and medical supplies. No one could understand why a country that was so rich in natural resources and that possessed so many acres of fertile farmland was unable to feed its people or supply them with simple necessities.

One reason was that Ceauşescu had broken the people's spirit. Another had to do 8 with his insane plan to crowd Rumania's growing population into large cities. On the outskirts of Arad were many private homes, each of which sat on land of between half an acre and an acre. One year, the government decided to take this land from us and to build high-rise apartments on it. Neither we nor our neighbors got paid for our property. On top of everything else, we had to clear the land ourselves by cutting down our many fruit trees. Up to that point, we had been able to supplement our food with the fruits and vegetables we grew in our garden and with the animals we raised. But then the situation became desperate, and we were barely able to feed ourselves. The president's iron hand was felt by everyone, and hatred of him grew in everybody's heart.

Like everyone else, I missed the necessities that Ceauşescu's flawed economic policy 9 had taken from us. But I did not realize how badly the government had mismanaged its finances and how corrupt it had become until my mother became ill. Already retired by the time I left high school, she was suffering from high blood pressure and had a heart condition. In an emergency, when I had to call an ambulance, I was told to lie about my mother's age. Medical emergency squads had been instructed not to pick up retired people. If they were left to die, the government would no longer have to pay their pensions.

As the economic crisis got worse and shortages of important supplies increased, the 10 crime rate began to soar. Alcohol abuse became a problem, as did theft, burglary, and assault. But the *Securitate* were busy searching for people who committed political crimes, and real criminals were given a free hand to prey on decent people. In fact, the police often paid common criminals to act as their informants.

I was seventeen and still in high school when I started working in a huge textile 11 factory. Once in the factory, no one was able to leave before quitting time unless he or she got a special pass from the boss. Every two weeks, we had to stay late to attend

Communist Party indoctrination sessions. During these absurd meetings, the factory doors were locked, and no one was permitted to leave.

Our regular work week was six days long, but my boss often required us to work on 12 Sundays as well. In the beginning, I refused the overtime, reminding the boss that, according to our constitution, I had to work only six days a week. He in turn reminded me that if I refused overtime I could be assigned to the worst area in the factory. At this point, I had no choice but to accept the overtime, which paid the same wages as work on any other day.

Each day before we left the factory, we had to go through a room where women 13 guards body-searched us. One day, a guard thought that I was acting suspiciously and brought me to a special room where she asked me to remove all my clothes to see if I was hiding stolen material. I could not have concealed much under the thin summer dress I was wearing. She knew that because she had already body-searched me and had found nothing. I refused to obey. To clear myself, I called on another guard to search me again. At that moment, I felt embarrassment and outrage; I knew that the guard's purpose was only to exercise her power by humiliating whomever she wanted to.

My story is not unique. Ceauşescu's government tried to strip all Rumanians of their 14 dignity, pride, and freedom. Everyone suffered in some way, and everyone has a personal tragedy to tell. As for me, I could not continue to live under the constant humiliation and the severe restrictions on personal freedom that I have described. I remember looking at the birds and envying them because they were free to go anywhere in the world.

I promised myself I would never have children in Rumania because I did not want 15 them to suffer as I had. In 1977, with the help of a brother who was living in the United States, I had the opportunity to leave. The day I emigrated, the course of my life changed for the better though my heart broke for those I left behind. Now, however, new hope blossoms for Rumania. In December 1990, as part of the overthrow of corrupt Communist governments across eastern Europe, the people deposed the Ceauşescu regime and established a democracy.

QUESTIONS FOR DISCUSSION

1. Find Groza's thesis statement. What are the three main points she makes about Ceauşescu's government?
2. Which examples in this essay do you think best illustrate each of those three points?
3. How does Groza explain that Rumania, a land rich in natural resources, was unable to feed its people?
4. What kind of people did the Ceauşescu government employ to carry out its policies? What examples of such people does Groza provide?
5. Why does she include details about life in Rumania before Ceauşescu came to power?
6. How does Groza show that life in Rumania was difficult for other people as well as for her?

THINKING CRITICALLY

1. In what way is this essay similar to Scamacca's "Oma," a selection that appears in Chapter 9? Does it discuss similar ideas? What might a conversation between Oma and Irina Groza be about?
2. Does this essay discuss ideas similar to those in Howard's "The Death of Common Sense," which appears next? On what points might Groza and Howard find agreement?

SUGGESTIONS FOR JOURNAL ENTRIES

1. The government Groza describes is monstrous. Have you ever lived under, read about, or heard about a government that suppresses personal freedom and keeps its people in fear and poverty as Rumania did? If so, use focused freewriting to record one or two well-developed examples of how that government treats or treated its people.

    Another way to approach this assignment is to interview a person who has lived under a dictatorship. Find out what freedoms and opportunities your subject was denied, and explain his or her reaction to living in a country with such a government.

2. A major difference between a democracy and the place Groza describes is the freedom to criticize the government. Think of a law, policy, or practice of the government—federal, state, *or* local—with which you disagree. Brainstorm with others who share your opinion. Together, discuss the way(s) this law, policy, or practice affects people you know. Then, write down reasons it should be changed. If this topic doesn't interest you, focus on a school policy or regulation you want changed.

The Death of Common Sense

Philip K. Howard

This essay, which appeared in Reader's Digest, *was excerpted in 1995 from a book by the same title. The book's subtitle, which reveals much about its contents, is* How Law Is Suffocating America. *The author is an attorney who has done a great deal of research on the effect of the growing mass of government regulations on every segment of American society.*

LOOKING AHEAD

1. This essay contains a variety of examples: specific instances and occurrences, statistics, and anecdotes. It also mentions familiar persons, places and things. Look for such examples as you read it.
2. Find places where Howard uses dialogue. Ask yourself how this helps him make his point.

VOCABULARY

abode	Home, residence.
citing	Criticizing, finding fault with, penalizing.
deplorable	Terrible, distressing.
dictates	Rules, regulations.
edifice	Building.
explicitly	Clearly, in an outspoken manner.
frailty	Weakness, fragility.
idiosyncrasy	Individuality, oddity, irregularity.
mammoth	Huge.
pH	A measurement of acidity or alkalinity used in chemistry.
Providence	Heaven.
specific gravity	The mass of a volume of a substance as compared to the mass of an equal volume of water.
saris	A kind of dress worn by many women in India and Pakistan

The Death of
Common Sense | Philip K. Howard

In the winter of 1988, Mother Teresa's nuns of the Missionaries of Charity walked   1
through the snow in the South Bronx in their saris and sandals looking for abandoned buildings to convert into homeless shelters. They found two, which New York
City offered them at $1 each. The nuns set aside $500,000 for the reconstruction. Then,
for a year and a half, they went from hearing room to hearing room seeking approval for
the project.

Providence, however, was no match for law. New York's building code requires an   2
elevator in all new or renovated multiple-story buildings of this type. Installing an elevator would add upward of $100,000 to the cost. Mother Teresa didn't want to devote
that much money to something that wouldn't really help the poor. But the nuns were
told the law could not be waived even if an elevator did not make sense.

The plan for the shelter was abandoned. In a polite letter to the city, the nuns noted   3
that the episode "served to educate us about the law and its many complexities."

What the law required offends common sense. After all, there are probably over   4
100,000 walk-up apartment buildings in New York. But the law, aspiring to the perfect
abode, dictates a model home or no home.

Today, laws control much of our lives: fixing potholes, running schools, regulat-   5
ing day-care centers and the workplace, cleaning up the environment—and deciding
whether Mother Teresa gets a building permit.

Our regulatory system has become an instruction manual, telling us exactly what to   6
do and how to do it. The laws have expanded like floodwaters breaking through a
dike—drowning the society we intended to protect.

In 1993, at Long Island's John Marshall Elementary School, the local fire chief   7
appeared around Halloween dressed as Officer McGruff, the police dog that promotes
safety. He noticed all the student art tacked to the walls. Within days, McGruff had done
his duty: the art was gone.

Why? The New York State fire code addresses this public hazard explicitly: 8
"[S]tudent-prepared artwork . . . [must be] at least two feet from the ceilings and ten feet
from exit doors and . . . not exceed 20 percent of the wall area."

No one had ever heard of a fire caused by children's art. The school superinten-   9
dent, accused of permitting a legal violation, suggested that he had used a rule of thumb
"on how much to decorate."

Liz Skinner, a first-grade teacher, was confused: "The *essence* of primary education   10
is that children show pride in their work." Now, said one observer, the school looked
"about as inviting as a bomb shelter."

Government has imposed fire codes for centuries. But only our age has succeeded in   11
barring children's art from school walls.

Safety also was the goal of Congress when in 1970 it created the Occupational Safety   12
and Health Administration. For 25 years OSHA has been hard at work, producing over
4000 detailed rules that dictate everything from the ideal height of railings (42 inches)
to how much a plank can stick out from a temporary scaffold (no more than 12 inches).
American industry has spent several hundred billion dollars to comply with OSHA's
rules. All this must have done some good.

It hasn't. The rate of workdays missed due to injury is about the same as in 1973. A   13
tour through the Glen-Gery brick factory near Reading, PA, indicates why.

People have been making bricks more or less the same way for thousands of years.   14
No hidden hazards have ever been identified. But OSHA inspectors periodically visit the
Glen-Gery factory and walk around with measuring tapes. They are especially interested
in railings, citing Glen-Gery for having railings of the wrong height.

Glen-Gery has never had a mishap related to railings. But inspectors won't discuss   15
if a violation actually has anything to do with safety. They are just traffic cops looking
for violations. "We've done basically everything they asked for the last 20 years," says
Bob Hrasok, Glen-Gery's full-time manager in charge of regulatory compliance.

As a result, warnings are posted everywhere. For example, a large "Hazardous Mate-   16
rial" sign was placed on one side of a storage shed—holding sand. OSHA categorizes
sand as a hazardous material because sand—identical to the beach sand you and I sun-
bathe on—contains a mineral called silica, which some scientists believe under some
conditions might cause cancer.

In 1994, Glen-Gery was required to include with shipments of brick a form describ-   17
ing, for the benefit of workers, how to identify a brick (a "granular solid, essentially odor-
less," in a "wide range of colors") and giving its specific gravity (approximately 2.6). In
fact, OSHA issued 19,233 citations in 1994 for not keeping its forms correctly. According
to one expert, filling out these forms takes Americans 54 million hours per year.

Solid, objective rules, like the precise height of railings, satisfy lawmakers' longing   18
for certainty. Human activity, however, cannot be so neatly categorized. And the more
precise the rule, the less sensible the law.

Until recently, Dutch Noteboom, 73, owned a small meat-packing plant in Spring-   19
field, OR. The U.S. Department of Agriculture (USDA) had one full-time inspector on
the premises and one supervisor who visited regularly. This level of attention is somewhat surprising, since Noteboom had only four employees. But the rules required it.
Every day the inspector sat there, "often talking on the phone," says Noteboom. But
they always found time to cite him for a violation: one was for "loose paint located 20
feet from any animal."

"I was swimming in paper work," says Noteboom. "You should have seen all the   20
USDA manuals. The regulations drove me out of business."

The Soviets tried to run their country like a puppeteer pulling millions of strings. In   21
our country, government's laws have become like millions of tripwires, preventing us
from doing the sensible thing.

On the banks of the Mississippi River in Minneapolis, a mountain of 75,000 tons of   22
lime sludge was built up over 60 years, the byproduct of a nearby plant. By the early
1980s, it sat in the path of a proposed highway.

Government rules designate any material with a pH of over 12.5 as "hazardous   23
waste." That may generally make sense, but not for lime, which is used to improve the
environment by lowering the acidity of land and water.

The mountain of lime, whose alkalinity was also raised by dampness, had a pH of   24
12.7. The highway was stopped dead in its tracks for many months because Minnesota
had no licensed hazardous-waste-disposal site for the lime. Eventually, it was pushed
onto adjoining land, where, with the help of the sun, it dried its way into lawfulness.

People tend to have their own way of doing things. But law, trying to make sure 25 nothing ever goes wrong, doesn't respect the idiosyncrasy of human accomplishment. It sets forth the approved methods, in black and white, and that's that. When law notices people doing it differently, it mashes them flat.

Gary Crissey and a partner have run a tiny coffee shop in New York's Little Italy 26 for years. Recently, some customers were dismayed when served with disposable plates and forks. Crissey explained that restaurant inspectors had stopped by and told him the law would not let him operate if he continued to wash dishes by hand. The code requires an automatic dishwasher or a chemical process. But the idea of using chemicals was unappealing, and Crissey's coffee shop is so small that it has no room for a dishwasher. The only solution was disposables. Now everything is plastic.

Today we have a world in which people argue not about right and wrong, but about 27 whether something was done the right way. With enough procedures, it's argued, no bureaucrat will ever again put his hand in the till. And so, by 1994, the Defense Department was spending almost half as much on procedures for travel reimbursement ($1.5 billion) as on travel itself ($3.5 billion).

Plato argued that good people do not need laws to tell them to act responsibly, 28 while bad people will find a way around law. By pretending procedure will get rid of corruption, we have succeeded only in humiliating honest people and have provided a cover of darkness and complexity for the bad.

By the mid-1980s, Brooklyn's Carroll Street Bridge, built in 1889, was in disrepair. 29 The city budgeted $3.5 million for an overhaul. Under procurement procedures, the renovation was estimated to take seven years.

But with the bridge's 100th anniversary approaching, Sam Schwartz, the chief engi- 30 neer responsible for bridges, thought the bridge should be fixed in time for a centennial party. Eleven months later, at a cost of $2.5 million, the bridge had been fixed. Practically the entire neighborhood participated in the centennial party, by all accounts a wonderful affair.

For his leadership in completing the job in one-seventh of the time and at 70 per- 31 cent of budget, Schwartz received a reprimand.

Our modern legal system has achieved the worst of all worlds: a system of regula- 32 tion that goes too far—while it also does too little. A number of years ago, two workers were asphyxiated in a Liberal, KS, meat-packing plant while checking on a giant vat of animal blood. OSHA did virtually nothing. Stretched thin giving out citations for improper railing height, OSHA reinspected only once in eight years a plant that had admittedly "deplorable" conditions.

Then three more workers died—at the same plant. The government response? A 33 nationwide rule requiring atmospheric testing devices in confined work spaces, though many of them have had no previous problems.

Most such legal dictates are stacked on top of the prior year's laws and rules. The 34 result is a mammoth legal edifice: federal statutes and rules now total about 100 million words. The Federal Register, a daily report of new and proposed regulations, increased from 15,000 pages in the final year of John F. Kennedy's Presidency to over 68,000 pages in the second year of Bill Clinton's.

Whenever the rules are eased, however, America's energy and good sense pour in 35 like sunlight through opened blinds. After the 1994 earthquake in Los Angeles toppled freeways, Gov. Pete Wilson suspended the thick book of procedural guidelines and gave incentives for speedy work.

From law's perspective, the Los Angeles repair project was a nightmare of potential abuse. The process wasn't completely objective; almost nothing was spelled out to the last detail. When disagreements occurred, private contractors and state bureaucrats had to work them out. Rather than specifying every iron rod, state inspectors took responsibility for checking that the work complied with general standards. The result? Instead of a 2 1/2-year trudge through government process, the Santa Monica Freeway was rebuilt in 64 days to a higher standard than the old one. 36

"I'm proud," said Dwayne Barth, a construction supervisor. "It feels good having a stake in rebuilding L.A." 37

When the rule book got tossed, all that was left was responsibility. No one decided to spite Mother Teresa. It was the law. No one wants to take down children's art. It's the law. 38

"The idea of law," Yale professor Grant Gilmore cautioned in 1977, has been "ridiculously oversold." 39

The rules, procedures and rights smothering us are aspects of a legal technique that promises a permanent fix for human frailty. This legal experiment, we learn every time we encounter it, hasn't worked out. Modern law has not protected us from stupidity and caprice, but has made stupidity and caprice dominant features of society. 40

Energy and resourcefulness are what was great about America. Let judgment and personal conviction be important again. Relying on ourselves—rather than the law—to provide answers is not a new ideology. It's just common sense. 41

Questions for Discussion

1. What is Howard's purpose? What is his thesis? Why did he use illustration to develop it? Would explaining how various laws came into being (process analysis) have been a good way to proceed?
2. Where does Howard cite statistics? Where does he use anecdotes?
3. How does his quoting people affected by over-regulation help him achieve his purpose?
4. You know that it is not uncommon to find several methods of development in one essay. Where in this essay do you find comparison?
5. Where does Howard make use of figurative language? What does it say about his attitude toward his subject?
6. Howard's examples refer to a variety of regulations, occupations, people, and sections of the country. Explain how this variety contributes to the essay's success.

Thinking Critically

1. Read Glazer's "The Right to Be Let Alone" in Chapter 16. Explain the similarities between Glazer's ideas and Howard's in a short paragraph.
2. Is Howard against all government regulation? From what he has said, determine the kinds of regulations he might support to ensure workers' safety, to protect the environment, to maintain bridges, to keep schools safe, and so on. Reread the essay and make notes about such regulations in the margins. Then explain one of your examples in a well-developed paragraph.
3. Use the double-entry (summary/response) method you learned about in "Getting Started" to analyze and respond to three or four paragraphs in this essay. Don't be afraid to express your disagreement with anything Howard says. If you need to review how a double-entry notebook works, reread pages 5–6.

Suggestions for Journal Entries

1. List three laws or rules enforced by your college, community, or state that offend common sense. Then, brainstorm with a friend; gather details to show that these regulations should be changed to meet the needs for which they were intended. If you can't find a partner, do some freewriting or listing on your own.
2. Think of some rules enforced by your college, community, or state that make sense and that meet the needs for which they were intended. List them, and then explain briefly why you think they should not be changed.

3. Howard claims "people have their own way of doing things. But law, trying to make sure nothing ever goes wrong, doesn't respect the idiosyncrasy of human accomplishment." Freewrite for five minutes to explain what he means. Then list three examples to show that people who "break the rules"—who follow their own dreams instead of doing what they are told—sometimes accomplish a great deal. Take your examples from your own experiences, observations, or reading.

SUGGESTIONS FOR SUSTAINED WRITING

1. Take any *simple* idea or statement of fact that you know a lot about. Prove this idea or statement in an essay of four or five paragraphs by using examples like the kinds you have learned about. Start by writing a preliminary thesis that expresses the idea or fact plainly. For instance:

   Winters in my state can be *treacherous.*
   The hurricane that smashed into town last summer *devastated our community.*
   A student's life is *hectic.*
   Doing your own sewing (carpentry, plumbing, car repair, typing, or the like) can *save you a lot of money.*
   Casual sex can be *harmful to your health.*

   The main point in each statement is in italics. As you know, the main point in a thesis is what an essay should focus on. Keep this in mind as you write your first draft. Then, review your paper to determine whether each example you have included relates directly to your main point. If not, replace it with a better example or revise your thesis. Add other examples to develop your main point even further as you complete later drafts.

   When the time comes to correct spelling, punctuation, and grammar, check for coherence and clarity as well. Strengthen connections between sentences and paragraphs. Replace words and phrases that seem vague, general, or dull with more concrete, specific, and colorful choices.

2. Look back to the journal entries you made after reading Edwin Way Teale's "Winter Folklore." You may have begun writing about an irrational belief—superstition or fear—that you or someone you know has experienced. Use this information in an essay with a thesis that sums up how this belief affected the life of the person you are writing about.

   Include specific instances and anecdotes to illustrate your thesis. For example, say you are claustrophobic—afraid of being closed in. You can begin with a thesis that explains how difficult, embarrassing, and costly your fear makes getting around a big city. To illustrate this idea, you might explain how scared you become in rooms without windows, how loudly friends laugh when you climb twenty flights of stairs just to avoid the elevator, and how often you spend the extra money for a taxi so you won't have to ride a crowded bus. You might even write an anecdote or two about being trapped in an elevator or a closet.

   One way to end this essay is to explain how you or the person you are writing about overcame or plans to overcome this fear or superstition. Other techniques for writing conclusions are discussed in Chapter 4.

   To make your paper convincing, develop your examples vividly and completely. As you rewrite and edit, make sure you have included details and vocabulary that will show how dramatically your subject was affected by the fear or superstition you are discussing.

3. Is the world shrinking as John Naisbitt and Patricia Aburdene suggest? Review your responses to the Suggestions for Journal Entries after "The Culture of Cuisine." Use them as inspiration for an essay explaining that the products, ideas, or customs of another land or culture have found a home in America.

   Limit your paper to a country or culture you know a lot about, perhaps the one your family came from. Discuss examples of food, automobiles, films, styles and works of music, games and sports, furniture, clothing, social customs, holidays, religious practices, and so on.

   This is a good opportunity to use specific instances and occurrences or to mention specific objects. Include as many as you can in your first draft. As you revise your paper, try making your point even stronger with statistics.

   Of course, your college librarian can help you find special information, but you can draw on your own observations, knowledge, and experience. Let's say you write about Mexico. You might explain that three of the five health-food restaurants where you eat feature Mexican food because it is nutritious and low in fat; that ten of the twenty buildings on your campus use styles and materials from Mexico; that techniques for making textiles and ceramics invented by Mexicans have been adopted by a company you work for; and that a show of contemporary paintings, silverwork, and pottery from Mexico is touring your state.

4. If you responded to the first of the Suggestions for Journal Entries after Lukawska's "Wolf," you have already written three topic sentences that express conclusions about the behavior or "personality" of a particular animal or species of animal.

   Use these topic sentences in the body paragraphs of an essay that, like "Wolf," expresses your views on the character of this animal. Develop these paragraphs with illustrations. Perhaps some of the information in your journal will serve this purpose. Then, summarize in one statement the ideas expressed in your topic sentences; make this your essay's thesis.

   After completing your first draft, return to your paper and insert additional details and examples that will make it more convincing and clear. In your third draft, work on creating an effective introduction; like Lukawska, try using a startling remark or challenging a widely held opinion. In your conclusion, rephrase your thesis or look to the future. Then, revise the entire paper once more to improve word usage and sentence structure. End this careful process by editing for grammar and by proofreading.

5. Have you ever lived in a land whose government was a dictatorship? Do you know someone who did? Write an essay that uses examples from personal experience—yours or someone else's—to explain what living in that country was like.

   Collect information before starting your first draft. If you are writing about yourself, brainstorm with a family member who remembers as much about that time in your life as you do. If you are writing about someone else, try interviewing this person to gather examples about the kind of life he or she endured. In addition, read your response to the first journal suggestion after Irina Groza's "Growing Up in Rumania."

   Like Groza, use anecdotes and specific instances to explain what the government did to limit people's personal and economic freedom. Your essay doesn't have to be as long as hers, but it should be filled with examples that show how difficult living under a dictatorship can be.

Groza cared enough about her readers and her subject to complete the writing process step-by-step. She made several drafts, each of which developed her thesis in greater and more startling detail. Then she revised and edited her work to make sure it was well-organized, coherent, and free of mechanical errors. Follow her example.

6. As an alternative to suggestion 5, write a letter to the editor of a local or college newspaper complaining about a law, regulation, policy, or practice in your community or on campus. Using examples from personal experience, explain why you are against it; show how negatively it affects you and others in your town or school.

    Let's say your college library closes on Saturdays and Sundays. You decide to explain that this policy is hard on students who can't go to the library at other times. To develop your central idea, you might:

    - Talk about the long trips to other libraries you and friends are forced to make on weekends.
    - Discuss your many attempts to find a quiet place to study on Sunday afternoons.
    - Explain that ten of the twenty students in your history class didn't finish their midterm essays on time because they could not get information they needed.

    You are trying to convince your reader of a particular opinion. So, pack your letter with examples, but remember that each example should relate directly to that opinion. As always, state your point clearly in a thesis.

    Begin this assignment by looking to the journal responses you made after reading Groza's "Growing Up in Rumania" and Howard's "The Death of Common Sense." That information might help you complete the first draft of your letter. Once again be thorough and careful when revising and editing your work.

7. Do some of the rules and regulations enforced by your college, community, or state offend common sense? Or do most laws that govern you seem reasonable? Take one or the other side of this issue, or argue that some laws make sense while others are ridiculous. Either way, prove your point by discussing three or four laws, rules, or regulations as examples.

    In any case, make your central idea clear from the very beginning. For example, argue that common sense, practicality, and the people's best interests should determine law—not some abstract theory or impractical principle. Then, in the body of the essay, show how the rules and regulations you are discussing meet or fail to meet this standard. If you are arguing both sides of the issue, make sure you discuss examples of both reasonable and unreasonable laws.

    Before you begin, check the notes you made in your journal after reading "The Death of Common Sense." They should provide useful facts, insights, and examples with which to develop your paper. As always, apply common sense to your writing: revise, edit, and proofread.

COMPARISON AND CONTRAST

Comparison and contrast are methods of organizing and developing ideas by pointing out similarities and differences between subjects.

A comparison essay identifies similarities between subjects that on the *surface* appear to be quite different; for instance, Tom Wolfe's "Columbus and the Moon" in this chapter compares Columbus's voyages with the U.S. space program. A contrast essay identifies differences between subjects that on the *surface* appear to be very much alike; usually, these subjects belong to the same general class or are of the same type. Such is the case in Cowley's "Temptations of Old Age," an essay that discusses how two different types of people face the challenges of aging.

Contrast can also be used to explain the pros and cons of a particular question. In "The Militiaman, the Yuppie, and Me," Carolyn Swalina presents two sides to the gun-control issue. Swalina's tone is sarcastic and designed in part to amuse us, but her essay shows that contrast can serve as an effective tool for debate. For example, you might use it to discuss the pros and cons of living in a particular city, the advantages and disadvantages of getting married, or the strengths and weaknesses of your college basketball team. Explaining what you like and dislike about going to college, working at the supermarket, or visiting relatives will also make a good contrast paper. You might even discuss why you both loved and hated a certain film, television program, concert, or novel.

ORGANIZING COMPARISON/ CONTRAST PAPERS

One of the greatest advantages of using comparison or contrast is the simplicity with which it allows you to organize information. In fact, putting together a successful comparison or contrast essay doesn't have to be difficult if you follow either of the two standard methods of organization: point-by-point or subject-by-subject.

Which of the two methods for organizing a comparison-or-contrast paper is better for you? That depends on your topic and your purpose. The subject-by-subject method of organization is often used in short essays. You can see it in Hal Borland's "Hunger Moon," a selection containing just two paragraphs that reveal very different views of the eastern moon in February. The point-by-point method, on the other hand, works well with essays that compare or contrast several qualities or characteristics of two subjects. This arrangement allows readers to digest a large body of information bit by bit. As such, it helps eliminate the risk that readers will forget what you said in the first half of your essay before they finish the second half! Tom Wolfe's "Columbus and the Moon" uses the point-by-point pattern.

VISUALIZING METHODS OF COMPARISON

THE POINT-BY-POINT METHOD

Using the point-by-point method, you compare or contrast one aspect or characteristic of both subjects, often in the same paragraph, before moving on to the next point in another paragraph. For example, if you were showing how economical your 1996 Wizbang automobile is by contrasting it to the 1996 Roadhog, your essay might be organized like this:

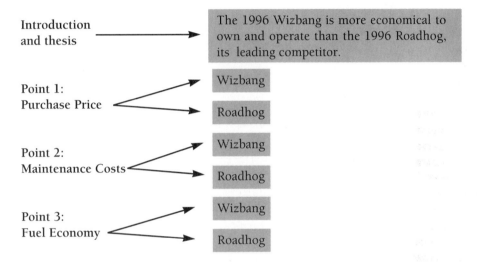

THE SUBJECT-BY-SUBJECT METHOD

Using the subject-by-subject method, you discuss *one* subject completely before going on to compare or contrast it with another subject in the second half of the essay. For example, you might outline the essay about the Wizbang and its competitor like this:

Introduction
and thesis

> The 1996 Wizbang is more economical to own and operate than the 1996 Roadhog, its leading competitor.

Subject 1: The Wizbang

- Purchase Price
- Maintenance Costs
- Fuel Economy

Subject 2: The Roadhog

- Purchase Price
- Maintenance Costs
- Fuel Economy

SEEING THE PATTERN IN A COMPARISON/CONTRAST PAPER

Student James Langley's "Watch the Cart!" which appears below, discusses differences between male and female shoppers. It follows the point-by-point pattern, which is common in longer essays. Notes in the left margin explain how Langley organized his paper. Notes on the right explain how he developed it.

States thesis
There is nothing similar to the way men and women shop for groceries. Believe me, I know because I work in a **Establishes his expertise** major supermarket. After watching scores of people shop for food day in and day out, I have become an expert on the habits of American consumers. I have noticed many things about them, but nothing stands out more clearly than the differences between men and women.

Point 1: How men search for a product
First of all, men never know where anything is. Nine **Begins with topic sentence** times out of ten, it will be a man who asks an employee to find a product for him. I don't know how many guys come up to me in the course of a night to ask me where something is, but 50% of those who do invariably return **Includes a statistic** to me in five minutes still unaware of the product's location. Men have no sense of direction in a supermarket. It's as if they're locked up in some life-**Uses a simile** sized maze. It has always been my contention that men who shop should be provided with specially trained dogs to sniff out the products they desire. It would certainly save me valuable time too often wasted as I explain for the tenth time that soup is in aisle 9.

Point 1: How women search for a product
Women on the other hand, rarely ask for an item's **Begins with topic sentence** location. When they do, it is usually for an obscure product only they have heard of and whose name only they can pronounce. Whenever a woman asks me where some

such items is, I always tell her to go to aisle 11—the ⟨Uses an example⟩

dog-food aisle. Send a man there, and he'll forget what

he was looking for and just buy the dog food out of

desperation. Send a woman there, and she'll be back in

five minutes with the product in hand, thanking me for

locating it for her.

Point 2:
How quicky
men and
women shop

Another difference between men and women is that ⟨Begins with topic sentence⟩

women shop at speeds that would get them tickets on

freeways, while men shop with the speed of a dead snail.

A woman can get her shopping done in the same amount of

time every time she goes. A man who shops just as often

gets worse and worse every time.

Point 3:
How well
men and
women
manipulate
carts

The biggest difference between the sexes in regard to ⟨Begins with topic sentence⟩

shopping, however, involves the manipulation of carts. A

woman guides a cart through the store so fluidly and

effortlessly that her movements are almost poetic. Men

are an entirely different story. A man with a shopping

cart is a menace to anyone within two aisles of him. Men

bounce their carts off display cases, sideswipe their ⟨Creates a vivid image⟩

fellow patrons and create havoc wherever they go. They

have no idea of how to control the direction of carts.

To a man, a shopping cart is a crazed metal monster ⟨Uses a metaphor⟩

designed to embarrass and harass him.

Conclusion
refers to
thesis and
re-states
essay's main
points

Overall, then, women are far more proficient

shoppers than men. They are efficient, speedy and

graceful; men are slow and clumsy. I know these things

because I work in a supermarket. I also know these

things because I am a man.

REVISING COMPARISON/CONTRAST PAPERS

Carolyn Swalina's "The Militiaman, the Yuppie, and Me" contrasts two extreme positions on the issue of gun control. To do this, Swalina created a conversation between two men on each side of the issue. She also managed to reveal some of her own thoughts on gun control and on the zealots involved in this debate. Paragraphs from her rough and final drafts appear below. They show the importance of making sure each side in a pro-and-con paper is developed adequately. They also show that revising to remove unneeded words makes writing more efficient. Swalina's essay appears later in this chapter.

Swalina—Rough Draft

As I sat there just sipping coffee, two men at a nearby table began to **?** catch my attention. One of them was a large man wearing camouflage pants and a black tee shirt; he pounded his fist on the table for emphasis **?** as

Describe this man?

he spoke to his companion. I labelled the two of these

Remove unneeded words?

men the "militiaman" and the "yuppie."

"Listen, there are a lot of crazies out there in this world of ours," said the militiaman. "Besides, having guns is our constitutional right."

"Ever read the second amendment?" said the militiaman. Washington and the rest of those guys knew what they were doing; they saw what happened when you

Combine with previous paragraph? Remove unneeded words

let the government have all the firepower. The feds will bother you whenever they feel like it. At least, if I still have my guns, they'll think twice before knocking down my door with a tank in the middle of the night."

Allow him more time to explain his opinion on this point?

"I'd rather have a cop knock down my door than some crazy with a gun," said the yuppie.

"Either way, you should have a gun to defend yourself," insisted the militiaman.

Swalina—Final Draft

As I sat there sipping coffee, two men at a nearby table caught my attention. One of them, a large man wearing camouflage pants and a black tee shirt, pounded his fist on the table as he spoke to his companion, who was wearing khaki slacks, penny loafers, and a button-down shirt. He was sipping club soda. I labelled them the "militiaman" and the "yuppie."

Has removed unneeded words

Describes the yuppie

"Listen, there are a lot of crazies out there," said the militiaman. "Besides, having guns is our constitutional right. Ever read the Second Amendment? It gives us the right 'to keep and bear arms.' Washington and the rest of those guys knew what they were doing; they saw what happened when you let the government have all the firepower. The feds will bother you whenever they feel like it. At least, if I still have my guns, they'll think twice before knocking down my door with a tank in the middle of the night."

Adds information via a quotation

Has combined paragraphs to eliminate unneeded words

"Yes, I've read the Constitution," said the yuppie. "And the Second Amendment is about 'a well regulated militia,' not private ownership. Besides, I'd rather have a cop knock down my door than some crazy with a gun."

Adds new information to explain yuppie's opinion

"Either way, you should have a gun to defend yourself," insisted the militiaman.

"Who were these guys?" I wondered. "Constitutional lawyers? And what were the chances that the government would drive a tank through my front door?"

Includes her own opinions in the essay for clarity, interest.

PRACTICING COMPARISON AND CONTRAST

In the spaces provided, write paragraphs that respond to any four of the following items. Remember that comparison explains similarities while contrast explains differences.

Before you start writing a paragraph, gather details for it and make a rough draft. Before you begin your final draft, make sure the paragraph has a topic sentence.

1. Compare caring for a child and caring for an animal.

_____

_____

_____

_____

_____

_____

2. Compare writing papers for English class and preparing for a mathematics test.

_____

_____

_____

_____

_____

_____

_____

3. Compare the cooking of two different cultures. For instance, compare Chinese with Italian, Indian with Mexican, Caribbean with Japanese, or Eastern European with American.

_____

_____

_____

_____

_____

_____

_____

4. Compare someone you know (perhaps yourself) to an animal. Start by writing
   "_____ is a snake" or "_____ is a work horse."

   _____

   _____

   _____

   _____

   _____

   _____

5. Contrast your work or study habits with those of a friend.

   _____

   _____

   _____

   _____

   _____

   _____

6. Contrast the ways you and your parents (sister, brother, or other relative) view sex
   (marriage, education, religion, money, or your friends).

   _____

   _____

   _____

   _____

   _____

   _____

7. Contrast two hobbies you pursue, two sports you play or follow, or two jobs you
   have held.

   _____

   _____

   _____

   _____

   _____

   _____

8. Contrast two pieces of music, films, paintings, books, or television shows that are about similar subjects or that have similar purposes.

_____

_____

_____

_____

_____

_____

As you just learned, how you organize a comparison or contrast essay depends on your topic and on the reason you are writing about it. In general, there is no absolutely right or wrong method for arranging the details in such a paper. Sometimes you may simply want to use the pattern you find easier. Just remember that comparing and contrasting are powerful tools for discovering ideas and expressing them effectively. In fact, the very act of pointing out similarities and differences may lead to important discoveries about your subjects that will make your writing richer in detail and more interesting.

Hunger Moon

Hal Borland

"Hunger Moon" is one of the many columns on nature and the outdoors that Hal Borland (1900–1978) published in the Sunday New York Times.

LOOKING AHEAD

Borland uses language that is both concrete and vivid. He develops this essay with carefully chosen nouns and adjectives and with exciting images and figures of speech.

VOCABULARY

awe	Combination of deep respect and fear.
burnished	Polished, shining.
charred	Burned, blackened by fire.
constellations	Groups of bright stars that take the shapes of animals, objects, and mythological people.
sequins	Small, shiny disks used as decorations on clothing.
stark	Sharp, clear.
strewing	Scattering, spreading, sprinkling.
traceries	Elegant patterns of lines like those seen in a large church window.

Hunger Moon   │ *H a l   B o r l a n d*

To see the full moon as it rose in the brittle eastern sky last night was to know both awe and shivering wonder. It was round as a medallion, bright as burnished brass, and its light had no more warmth than the frost cloud of a man's breath. It was a false and lifeless sun that made false daylight of the night. It killed the lesser stars and reduced the constellations to fundamentals. It burned the darkness with neither heat nor smoke, strewing the snow with charred skeletons of the naked trees. No wonder the Indians knew the February full moon as the Hunger Moon.

Yet, as it mounted the icy sky the moon set stark patterns of beauty. Footsteps in the snow became laced traceries of purple shadows. Starless ponds of night sky lay in the meadows' hollows. Roads became black velvet ribbons with winking frost sequins. Pines became whispering flocks of huge, dark birds on the hilltop and pasture cedars were black candle flames. Warm-windowed houses and frost-roofed barns were all twins, each with its counterpart beside it on the snow. And no man walked alone as he hurried toward warmth and shelter.

QUESTIONS FOR DISCUSSION

1. Earlier you learned that this selection uses the subject-by-subject method to present two views of the February moon. Explain these two views.
2. What does Borland's calling the moon a "false and lifeless sun" (paragraph 1) tell us about his subject?
3. Explain what he means when he says that the moon "killed the lesser stars and reduced the constellations to fundamentals" (paragraph 1).
4. Explain the image in the last two sentences.

THINKING CRITICALLY

1. Pick out at least four metaphors in this essay, and explain them in your own words.
2. Reread Borland's "January Wind," which appears in Chapter 6. What similarities do you see between it and "Hunger Moon"?

SUGGESTIONS FOR JOURNAL ENTRIES

1. Make two lists of details that reveal your feelings about a particular time: a season or month of the year, a day of the week, a time of day, your birthday, or a specific holiday. This is a pro-and-con assignment. In the first list, tell what you like about the time you are writing about. In the second, tell what you dislike about it.
2. Spend five minutes freewriting on the things you dislike about a job, task, or assignment you complete regularly at home, school, or work. After a short break, freewrite for another five minutes and discuss what, if anything, you like about this activity or explain why you think it should be done.

Rafters

Butler E. Brewton

Dr. Butler E. Brewton is a full professor at Montclair State University, where he teaches creative writing and modern American poetry. His work has appeared in many publications including the New York Times. He won first prize in Essence magazine's poetry contest and has been poet-in-residence for the New Jersey State Council on the Arts. In 1995, Brewton published Rafters and Other Poems.

More recently Brewton travelled in the South recapturing, through photography and writing, sights and sounds of a rich folk culture that he once knew. The farm in "Rafters" is in South Carolina.

LOOKING AHEAD

1. Finding a poem in a chapter on comparison/contrast is not common, yet "Rafters" proves that this type of writing can communicate strong feelings as well as explain abstract ideas.
2. Ask yourself what pattern (point-by-point or subject-by-subject) the poem's organization most closely resembles.
3. Brewton, like many other poets, is very careful about the words he chooses. Find examples of words you think have special meanings.

VOCABULARY

sprouts   Early growth or shoots of a plant.
stoops   Front steps to a city house, usually brick, stone, or concrete. (Used in some Eastern cities, "stoops" is from the Dutch word for steps.)

Rafters | *Butler E. Brewton*

The barn,
Gray and rotten where
The edges touch the wet earth,
Is filled to the rafters with things
We put away from one year to the next,

And out in the field,   6
Half hidden by the wild sprouts,
Is the old plow my father left
The last year he planted the crop
We all deserted, never harvesting
What the sweat was meant for,

But left one by one for the factories,   12
Taking wives and husbands to make
Homes where the work was good
In the cities.

I think about the hot summer streets   16
When we sat on the cement stoops
Drinking beer on paydays
While the children grew farther
From our reach and one day
So far they could not hear
The sound of our voice calling
Through the night.

And I know now that what   24
We came for we didn't get,
And we have put away whatever
Plans we had.

I will leave the city   28
And try to pull the old plow
Out of the land,
Fix the bottom of the barn
With aged hands.

QUESTIONS FOR DISCUSSION

1. How would you describe the speaker's attitude toward the city? Toward the country?
2. What pattern used in comparison/contrast does the poem's organization most closely resemble?
3. Besides contrast, what method of development does the poem use?
4. Where in this work does the poet paint verbal images?
5. Why does Brewton use the word "stoops"; why didn't he just use the more common "steps"? What other evidence do you find to show that Brewton is careful about word choice?

THINKING CRITICALLY

1. What things other than life in the city and in the country are being contrasted here? Make notes in the margins of the poem to record your answers.
2. Stanzas 2, 4, and 6 are very powerful. Use the double-entry method to summarize and respond to them in your notebook or journal. (Getting Started on pages 5–6 explains double entries.)
3. What things might be stored in the rafters of the barn? Are these things symbols for the speaker? Of what?

SUGGESTIONS FOR JOURNAL ENTRIES

1. Have you ever made a big change in your life that you regretted? Explain that change in a sentence or two. Then, list details to explain its effects on you. Like Brewton, include details that relate to you both **before** and **after** the change. In fact, try organizing your information under those two headings.
2. Make a journal entry about a change in your life that turned out well. Follow the advice in item 1.
3. Brewton describes a place he knew from childhood. Pick a place you have known for a long time and list details that show how different it is today from your first memories of it. For example, write about your former street, neighborhood, or hometown. Remember that your purpose is to contrast, so make two different lists.

Temptations of Old Age*

Malcolm Cowley

Malcolm Cowley (1898–1989) was a writer, editor, literary critic, and historian noted for his energy and productivity even until his death at 90. In the last decade of his life, Cowley wrote The View from 80, *a book that explains his very positive attitude toward aging and that offers excellent advice about the latter stages of life. Another selection from* The View from 80 *appears in Chapter 7.*

Looking Ahead

1. This selection is from a chapter of Cowley's book that discusses several temptations of old age and explains ways to avoid them. Among these temptations are greed, vanity, and a desire to escape life's problems through alcohol. But the greatest temptation, as shown in the following paragraphs, is "simply giving up."
2. Renoir, mentioned in paragraph 4, was a French painter of the nineteenth and twentieth centuries. Goya was a Spanish painter of the eighteenth and nineteenth centuries.

Vocabulary

ailments	Illnesses, disorders, diseases.
compelling	Convincing, strong, valid.
distinguished	Well-respected.
distraction	Amusement, diversion.
infirmities	Illnesses, weaknesses, ailments.
lithographs	Prints.
outwitted	Outsmarted, outmaneuvered.
Rolls-Royce	Expensive British automobile.
senility	Forgetfulness and decrease in mental powers affecting some elderly people.
stoical	Brave, uncomplaining.
unvanquished	Undefeated.

*Editor's title

Temptations of Old Age
| Malcolm Cowley

N ot whiskey or cooking sherry but simply giving up is the greatest temptation of 1
age. It is something different from a stoical acceptance of infirmities, which is
something to be admired.

The givers-up see no reason for working. Sometimes they lie in bed all day when 2
moving about would still be possible, if difficult. I had a friend, a distinguished poet,
who surrendered in that fashion. The doctors tried to stir him to action, but he refused
to leave his room. Another friend, once a successful artist, stopped painting when his
eyes began to fail. His doctor made the mistake of telling him that he suffered from a
fatal disease. He then lost interest in everything except the splendid Rolls-Royce,
acquired in his prosperous days, that stood in the garage. Daily he wiped the dust from
its hood. He couldn't drive it on the road any longer, but he used to sit in the driver's
seat, start the motor, then back the Rolls out of the garage and drive it in again, back
twenty feet and forward twenty feet; that was his only distraction.

I haven't the right to blame those who surrender, not being able to put myself inside 3
their minds or bodies. Often they must have compelling reasons, physical or moral. Not
only do they suffer from a variety of ailments, but also they are made to feel that they no
longer have a function in the community. Their families and neighbors don't ask them
for advice, don't really listen when they speak, don't call on them for efforts. One notes
that there are not a few recoveries from apparent senility when that situation changes. If
it doesn't change, old persons may decide that efforts are useless. I sympathize with
their problems, but the men and women I envy are those who accept old age as a series
of challenges.

For such persons, every new infirmity is an enemy to be outwitted, an obstacle to be 4
overcome by force of will. They enjoy each little victory over themselves, and sometimes they win a major success. Renoir was one of them. He continued painting, and
magnificently, for years after he was crippled by arthritis; the brush had to be strapped
to his arm. "You don't need your hand to paint," he said. Goya was another of the
unvanquished. At 72 he retired as an official painter of the Spanish court and decided to
work only for himself. His later years were those of the famous "black paintings" in
which he let his imagination run (and also of the lithographs, then a new technique). At
78 he escaped a reign of terror in Spain by fleeing to Bordeaux. He was deaf and his
eyes were failing; in order to work he had to wear several pairs of spectacles, one over
another, and then use a magnifying glass; but he was producing splendid work in a
totally new style. At 80 he drew an ancient man propped on two sticks, with a mass of
white hair and beard hiding his face and with the inscription "I am still learning."

"Eighty years old!" the great Catholic poet Paul Claudel wrote in his journal. "No 5
eyes left, no ears, no teeth, no legs, no wind! And when all is said and done, how aston-
ishingly well one does without them!"

QUESTIONS FOR DISCUSSION

1. Pick out particularly vivid verbs and adjectives in this selection.
2. Where does Cowley signal a transition from one subject to another?
3. Various methods can be combined to develop one idea. Where in this piece does Cowley use examples?
4. Do you think the conclusion of this selection is effective? Why or why not? If necessary, review ways to write conclusions in Chapter 4.
5. Why, according to the author, do some elderly people simply give up?
6. What does he mean when he says that others see "every new infirmity" as "an obstacle to be overcome by force of will" (paragraph 4)?

THINKING CRITICALLY

1. Cowley quotes directly from the "unvanquished." Why doesn't he also quote from "those who surrender"?
2. This selection uses the subject-by-subject pattern. Why does the author begin with the "givers-up" and not end with them? Should he have discussed Renoir, Goya, and Claudel first?
3. Would "Temptations of Old Age" have been better organized point-by-point? Why or why not?

SUGGESTIONS FOR JOURNAL ENTRIES

1. What Cowley says might apply to folks of all ages. Do you know someone who seems to face all the challenges life has to offer? Spend five minutes freewriting about the way this person reacts to such challenges. Then do the same for someone you might call a "giver-up." Try to include facts about their lives that will describe their personalities.
2. In what way are you like the people in your family who have come before you? Think about a parent, grandparent, great-aunt, or other older relative. Use listing or focused freewriting to explain what is similar about your personalities, interests, lifestyles, or your opinions about music, politics, other people, or anything else you can think of.

The Militiaman, the Yuppie, and Me

Carolyn Swalina

Carolyn Swalina has studied literature and communications at Wilkes University and the University of Maine. She is currently working on her doctorate in special education at the University of California at Berkeley. Her purpose in this essay is to contrast two extreme views on an issue that in the last few years has been the subject of much debate. She uses the point-by-point method in a fictional dialogue between a pro-gun and an anti-gun advocate. Swalina also creates a persona or speaker to express her own, more moderate views on the subject.

LOOKING AHEAD

1. "Sal Monella's Brew and Burger," the name of the place in which the dialogue takes place, contains a pun, a play on words. *Salmonella* is a bacteria that causes food poisoning. Using this word sets a humorous and ironic (tongue-in-cheek) tone. Thus, we know from the beginning that what is being said—by the militiaman and the yuppie, at least—does not reflect the author's point of view.
2. The characters in this dialogue quote from the Second Amendment to the U.S. Constitution: "A well regulated Militia, being necessary to the security of a free State, the right of the people to keep and bear Arms shall not be infringed [restricted]."

VOCABULARY

camouflage	Type of military clothing worn when hiding in woods or brush. Usually brown and green to blend in with other natural colors.
impaired	Limited, diminished, damaged.
law-abiding	Obeying the law.
militiaman	A member of one of a private armed, military-like group. Such groups have no connection with the U.S. government.
raving	Very enthusiastic about; it can also mean irrational or delirious. Obviously, both meanings apply in this essay.
scopes	Optical devices fitted on rifles for long-range shooting.
yuppie	An acronym (word made up of the first letters of a title) that means *young urban professional.*

The Militiaman, the
Yuppie, and Me   *Carolyn Swalina*

Just before I left school the other night, my journalism professor asked me to   1
write an editorial about gun control for the college newspaper. It would be due
the next day.

When I got home at 10:30 P.M. I decided I could think better if I relaxed a bit at Sal   2
Monella's Brew and Burger around the corner. As I sat there sipping coffee, two men at
a nearby table caught my attention. One of them, a large man wearing camouflage pants
and a black tee shirt, pounded his fist on the table as he spoke to his companion, who
was wearing khaki slacks, penny loafers, and a button-down shirt. He was sipping club
soda. I labelled them the "militiaman" and the "yuppie."

"Listen, there are a lot of crazies out there," said the militiaman. "Besides, having   3
guns is our constitutional right. Ever read the Second Amendment? It gives us the right
'to keep and bear arms.' Washington and the rest of those guys knew what they were
doing; they saw what happened when you let the government have all the firepower.
The feds will bother you whenever they feel like it. At least, if I still have my guns,
they'll think twice before knocking down my door with a tank in the middle of the
night."

"Yes, I've read the Constitution," said the yuppie. "And the Second Amendment is   4
about 'a well regulated militia,' not private ownership. Besides, I'd rather have a cop
knock down my door than some crazy with a gun."

"Either way, you should have a gun to defend yourself," insisted the militiaman.   5

"Who were these guys?" I wondered. "Constitutional lawyers? And what were the   6
chances that the government would drive a tank through my front door?"

"If guns are banned, what makes you think they're just gonna go away?" the mili-   7
tiaman asked. "Sure, law-abiding citizens will turn theirs in, but what about street gangs
and muggers? The only ones with guns will be cops and criminals. No, I'm not going to
give up my guns until you can prove that all the criminals and crazies have given up
theirs. And it's not just me! Everyone in my militia feels the same."

"What's wrong with cops having guns?" I said under my breath.   8

"Yes, but there are simply too many guns," responded the yuppie, sipping his club   9
soda. "I went to visit my mother at the retirement home last week, and she was raving
about a seminar she attended on rifle scopes for the visually impaired. She says her hit-
to-miss ratio has improved 100% because of those new scopes. They even come in
designer colors."

"What do you mean, designer colors?" I thought. "Scopes for the visually impaired?   10
And what's your mother doing in a rest home if she can still shoot?"

"Good for Mom. She's a true American. She'll go down fighting," said the militiaman pushing his glass aside. "The government keeps taking away people's rights. Look   11
at Waco. Just a few people who want to live in peace and harmony, and the government
comes in with heavy artillery to take their guns away."

"Yes, but if you don't have guns, the government won't bother you. After all, we   12
are a country of law. Guns are dangerous, and it's the government's responsibility to
protect us from them. The best way to do that is to outlaw all of them."

"So," I thought, "what if someone decides to outlaw fast cars, baseball bats, and 13 kitchen knives? Will people who own those things be criminals too?"

"But owning a gun is part of American manhood," said the man in the tee-shirt. 14 "What would John Wayne or Clint Eastwood do without their guns?"

John Wayne and Clint Eastwood? I saw Hollywood images of the Alamo and 15 Custer's last stand. But they had nothing to do with real people I knew who use guns to scare away groundhogs and skunks, to hunt, or to protect themselves in rural areas where the nearest police are miles away.

"Ah, their movies are just propaganda," said the yuppie. "They have nothing to do 16 with the real problem of violence in this society."

The militiaman sneered; the yuppie turned red. He looked up for a moment trying 17 to think about what to say next. "Let me tell you about the cold, hard facts. My son got shot on the playground because he wouldn't give some kid his homework. I've been shot twice: once on the highway after I brake-checked some guy who was tailgaiting me and once when I didn't make change fast enough when boarding a bus. When I walk up my street, I dodge bullets like I'm in a war zone. Sometimes I think I was safer in the army."

"You were," I finally broke in. "You had a gun when you were in the army." 18

"No kidding," continued the yuppie staring at me. "My mailman has a gun, the lady 19 who runs the news stand has a gun, and just last week I saw a semi-automatic hanging in the back window of an ice cream truck. I did, I tell you; I did."

As he finished, I began to think that there might be some merit in outlawing club 20 soda.

I paid for my coffee and walked out into the night air. The editorial was still due. 21 My visit to Sal Monella's hadn't been very fruitful, but it convinced me that, perhaps, there are a lot of "crazies" out there.

QUESTIONS FOR DISCUSSION

1. What differences do you see in the personalities of the militiaman and the yuppie? How does Swalina communicate these differences?
2. What is the speaker's attitude toward these men?
3. How does she expose the extremism in the yuppie's anti-gun stance?
4. How does she expose the extremism in the arguments of the militiaman?
5. Why does the author have the militiaman quote one part of the Second Amendment and the yuppie quote the other part? Why didn't she allow one man to quote the whole thing?
6. Do some of the arguments the militiaman and the yuppie use sound familiar? Which ones have you heard before?
7. In what other ways has Swalina made the debate seem believable? For example, does she ever use proper nouns?
8. What is Swalina's central idea?

THINKING CRITICALLY

1. Summarize the speaker's views on gun control. Begin by writing notes in the margins where her remarks appear. Then, use your notes to develop a short paragraph that explains her point of view.
2. Use the double-entry journal method to analyze the comments of the militiaman and the yuppie. Remember that this method requires summary and response. So, draw a line down the center of a piece of paper. On one side, summarize what each man says on each point discussed. On the other side, record your reactions to each of the ideas you summarized.
3. Mundie's "The Mentally Ill and Human Experimentation: Perfect Together," a student essay in Chapter 5, also uses irony. Compare and contrast that selection with Swalina's.

SUGGESTIONS FOR JOURNAL ENTRIES

1. Think of other arguments for or against gun control. List them in your journal.
2. Make two lists of arguments—pro and con—that you might use when presenting opposing sides of a controversial question. You can choose an issue in the national media, such as reforming the welfare system, testing student athletes for drugs, enforcing the death penalty, or limiting immigration. Then again, you might discuss something specific to your community or campus. For example, present arguments for and against requiring students to take certain courses or charging them athletic, activity, parking, and other fees along with tuition.

Columbus and the Moon

Tom Wolfe

Tom Wolfe is the author of The Right Stuff, *a book about the U.S. space program that was made into a major motion picture. He is also widely known as a writer of books and articles in which he demonstrates a powerful talent for social criticism.*

"Columbus and the Moon" compares Columbus's voyages with the exploration of space by the National Aeronautics and Space Administration (NASA).

LOOKING AHEAD

1. At the end of paragraph 5, Wolfe writes that some of the spinoffs of the space program were "not a giant step for mankind." This is a reference to what Neil Armstrong said when he set foot on the lunar surface in 1969: "That's one small step for a man, and one giant leap for mankind."
2. Neil Armstrong, Michael Collins, and Buzz Aldrin were on the Apollo 11 mission, which made the first landing on the moon.

VOCABULARY

albeit	Although, though.
appropriations	Financing, money.
awed	Amazed.
evangelical	Religious fundamentalist.
ignominy	Shame, disgrace.
lurid	Racy, suggestive, strange.
psychic phenomena	Extrasensory objects or events.
quest	Search.
testy	Irritable.
traumatized	Shocked, emotionally confused.

Columbus and the
Moon   *Tom Wolfe*

The National Aeronautics and Space Administration's moon landing 10 years ago   1
today was a Government project, but then so was Columbus's voyage to America in 1492. The Government, in Columbus's case, was the Spanish Court of Ferdinand
and Isabella. Spain was engaged in a sea race with Portugal in much the same way that
the United States would be caught up in a space race with the Soviet Union four and a
half centuries later.

The race in 1492 was to create the first shipping lane to Asia. The Portuguese expe-   2
ditions had always sailed east, around the southern tip of Africa. Columbus decided to
head due west, across open ocean, a scheme that was feasible only thanks to a recent
invention—the magnetic ship's compass. Until then ships had stayed close to the great
land masses even for the longest voyages. Likewise, it was only thanks to an invention of
the 1940's and early 1950's, the high-speed electronic computer, that NASA would even
consider propelling astronauts out of the Earth's orbit and toward the moon.

Both NASA and Columbus made not one but a series of voyages. NASA landed men   3
on six different parts of the moon. Columbus made four voyages to different parts of
what he remained convinced was the east coast of Asia. As a result both NASA and
Columbus had to keep coming back to the Government with their hands out, pleading
for refinancing. In each case the reply of the Government became, after a few years:
"This is all very impressive, but what earthly good is it to anyone back home?"

Columbus was reduced to making the most desperate claims. When he first reached   4
land in 1492 at San Salvador, off Cuba, he expected to find gold, or at least spices. The
Arawak Indians were awed by the strangers and their ships, which they believed had
descended from the sky, and they presented them with their most prized possessions,
live parrots and balls of cotton. Columbus soon set them digging for gold, which didn't
exist. So he brought back reports of fabulous riches in the form of manpower; which is
to say, slaves. He was not speaking of the Arawaks, however. With the exception of
criminals and prisoners of war, he was supposed to civilize all natives and convert them
to Christianity. He was talking about the Carib Indians, who were cannibals and therefore qualified as criminals. The Caribs would fight down to the last unbroken bone
rather than endure captivity, and few ever survived the voyages back to Spain. By the
end of Columbus's second voyage, in 1496, the Government was becoming testy. A great
deal of wealth was going into voyages to Asia, and very little was coming back. Columbus made his men swear to return to Spain saying that they had not only reached the
Asian mainland, they had heard Japanese spoken.

Likewise by the early 1970's, it was clear that the moon was in economic terms   5
pretty much what it looked like from Earth, a gray rock. NASA, in the quest for appro-
priations, was reduced to publicizing the "spinoffs" of the space program. These
included Teflon-coated frying pans, a ballpoint pen that would write in a weightless
environment, and a computerized biosensor system that would enable doctors to treat
heart patients without making house calls. On the whole, not a giant step for mankind.

In 1493, after his first voyage, Columbus had ridden through Barcelona at the side   6
of King Ferdinand in the position once occupied by Ferdinand's late son, Juan. By 1500,

the bad-mouthing of Columbus had reached the point where he was put in chains at the conclusion of his third voyage and returned to Spain in disgrace. NASA suffered no such ignominy, of course, but by July 20, 1974, the fifth anniversary of the landing of Apollo 11, things were grim enough. The public had become gloriously bored by space exploration. The fifth anniversary celebration consisted mainly of about 200 souls, mostly NASA people, sitting on folding chairs underneath a camp meeting canopy on the marble prairie outside the old Smithsonian Air Museum in Washington listening to speeches by Neil Armstrong, Michael Collins, and Buzz Aldrin and watching the caloric waves ripple.

Extraordinary rumors had begun to circulate about the astronauts. The most lurid 7 said that trips to the moon, and even into earth orbit, had so traumatized the men, they had fallen victim to religious and spiritualist manias or plain madness. (Of the total 73 astronauts chosen, one, Aldrin, is known to have suffered from depression, rooted, as his own memoir makes clear, in matters that had nothing to do with space flight. Two teamed up in an evangelical organization, and one set up a foundation for the scientific study of psychic phenomena—interests the three of them had developed long before they flew in space.) The NASA budget, meanwhile, had been reduced to the light-bill level.

Columbus died in 1509, nearly broke and stripped of most of his honors as Spain's 8 Admiral of the Ocean, a title he preferred. It was only later that history began to look upon him not as an adventurer who had tried and failed to bring home gold—but as a man with a supernatural sense of destiny, whose true glory was his willingness to plunge into the unknown, including the remotest parts of the universe he could hope to reach.

NASA still lives, albeit in reduced circumstances, and whether or not history will 9 treat NASA like the admiral is hard to say.

The idea that the exploration of the rest of the universe is its own reward is not 10 very popular, and NASA is forced to keep talking about things such as bigger communications satellites that will enable live television transmission of European soccer games at a fraction of the current cost. Such notions as "building a bridge to the stars for mankind" do not light up the sky today—but may yet.

QUESTIONS FOR DISCUSSION

1. What is the central idea of this essay?
2. What are some of the similarities between Columbus's voyages and NASA's space program that Wolfe identifies?
3. Wolfe uses anecdotes about Columbus and about the space program to help explain the similarities between the two. Which anecdotes show that both Columbus and NASA had trouble with finances? Which explain the loss of popularity that both suffered?
4. In what way were Columbus's "desperate claims" about the new world (paragraph 4) like NASA's publicizing the " 'spinoffs' of the space program" (paragraph 5)? What were some of these spinoffs?
5. What transitional words and expressions does Wolfe use to keep his essay coherent and easy to read?
6. How did Columbus's career end? What does Wolfe predict for NASA?

THINKING CRITICALLY

1. Reread Langley's "Watch the Cart!" in the chapter's introduction (pages 478–479). The notes in the margins label each of the points Langley develops through contrast. Make such notes in the margins of "Columbus and the Moon," which is also organized point-by-point.
2. Why should we continue funding NASA? Try to imagine what new information, materials, or processes useful to life on earth we might learn from more space exploration. Make a written list of these things.
3. In what ways, other than through direct funding by the United States government, might we keep the space program going?

SUGGESTIONS FOR JOURNAL ENTRIES

1. One important use of comparison is to let readers discover startling new things about familiar subjects. List a few facts and ideas that this essay taught you about the space program. Then mention a few things it taught you about Columbus.
2. Wolfe's essay compares two great programs of exploration from two very different centuries. Jot down some notes about how people from different times have coped with the same problems or accomplished the same tasks.

   For example, list similarities between the way you celebrate a traditional holiday (Thanksgiving, Christmas, Chanukah, the Fourth of July) and the way your grandparents did. Or consider how people now and long ago have coped with the same type of misfortune (the death of a loved one, the loss of a job) or have marked important events in their lives such as marriage, the birth of a child, or the purchase of a home.

SUGGESTIONS FOR SUSTAINED WRITING

1. The first of the Suggestions for Journal Entries after Hal Borland's "Hunger Moon" asks that you make two lists revealing what you like and dislike about a particular time: a season or month of the year, a day of the week, a time of day, your birthday, a special holiday, for example. Write this information in your journal if you haven't done so already. Then, use it to begin a short essay that explains your mixed feelings about your topic.

   A good way to organize this essay is subject by subject. Write a rough draft divided into two sections. In the first, explain what you like about this time; develop each of your reasons in a separate paragraph. In the second section, explain what you dislike about it; again, develop each reason in its own paragraph. Then, read this draft carefully to decide whether you need to add detail or to improve coherence in and between paragraphs. Make these changes when you rewrite your paper.

   Once you have a draft that is well developed and organized, summarize your overall or dominant reaction to your topic in a thesis. Do you like this time more than you dislike it? Is the opposite true? Or is it just impossible to decide? However you answer, put your thesis in an attention-grabbing introduction. Then write an effective conclusion. You can review how to write introductions and conclusions in Chapter 4. Finally, revise the entire paper once more and edit it thoroughly.

2. Use the advice in the previous suggestion to write an essay that might be entitled "It Was the Best of Times; It Was the Worst of Times." Pick an important period in your life about which you have both positive and negative memories. A time during which you had to make changes in your lifestyle or ideas might provide interesting details. Here are a few examples: your first term in a new school; the summer you started working; the time you got braces on your teeth or a cast on your broken leg; your first weeks in the military; the semester you learned to love math; your first year of marriage; the day your child began to walk; the months you spent recovering from an illness or operation.

3. Did you respond to items 1 or 2 in the suggestions for journal writing after "Rafters" by Butler Brewton? If you did, you have probably gathered information about an important change in your life. Expand your notes into a full-length essay about an event or development in your life that you are happy about or that you regret.

   Begin by briefly narrating the event or explaining the development. Then, show how it affected you. To do this effectively, describe your personality or lifestyle **before** and **after** the change. You can use either the point-by-point or the subject-by-subject method to organize this part of the paper.

   Begin the project by writing a preliminary thesis statement summarizing the effects or consequences of the change on you. Be aware that this statement will probably change a few times as you move through the process of drafting and revising your essay. Once you are sure you have a well-organized and well-developed final draft, put the finishing touches on your paper by correcting errors that might reduce its effectiveness or distract your readers.

4. In talking about people who are eighty, Malcolm Cowley describes two different types: those who fight on and those who give up. But we see these types in every generation, even our own. In fact, you may have begun discussing such people in your journal. Use these notes in an essay about people you know who fit Cowley's personality types: those who face life bravely and those who just give up.

   On the other hand, if you don't like this topic, you can start from scratch and choose your own basis for contrast. For example, discuss two very different types of students: those who are serious about getting an education and those who are not. Here's an example of a thesis for such a paper:

   > While serious students study hard, do extra reading, and compare
   > notes with classmates, those who just want to get by spend much of
   > their time playing cards or watching television!

   Cowley uses the subject-by-subject method; you might want to do the same. However you decide to organize your essay, discuss two or three people you know as examples of *each* personality type. Begin with a rough draft, adding details with each revision to make your paper clearer and more convincing. In the process, include an effective introduction and conclusion.

   Then, rewrite your paper once more. Make sure it has a clear thesis, it is easy to follow, and it is free of mistakes in grammar, punctuation, spelling, and the like.

5. Follow Carolyn Swalina's example. Write an essay in which you contrast two extreme views on a controversial subject about which you gathered details in your journal after reading "The Militiaman, the Yuppie, and Me."

   If you want, pattern your paper on Swalina's, and use the point-by-point method. To do this, focus on three or four major points; present two opposing opinions on each point before moving on to the next point. On the other hand, you can use the subject-by subject method by presenting all the arguments on one side of the issue before discussing the arguments on the other side. Either way, remember that, like Swalina, you are exposing two very extreme views. And like Swalina, you may want to express a third, more moderate and more reasonable view of your own. You can conclude your essay with this view by expressing it in a thesis statement near the end of your paper.

   This is a complicated assignment. To do it well, you will have to revise your work several times. And any assignment that demands that much work, also deserves to be edited and proofread conscientiously.

6. In "Columbus and the Moon," Tom Wolfe drew similarities between the discovery of the New World and NASA's exploration of outer space. Consider similarities between the way people from different times have:

- Celebrated an important holiday (Christmas, Chanukah, Thanksgiving);
- Coped with the same types of misfortune (the death of a loved one, the loss of a job); or
- Marked the same major events in their lives (marriage, the birth of a child, the purchase of a home).

Now, write an essay explaining these similarities in detail. When you draft and revise your paper, make sure it has a clear thesis and is well organized. Use either the subject-by-subject or point-by-point method. Improve coherence, clarity, and development as you go along. Then, put the finishing touches on your work by correcting distracting mechanical errors.

As with other assignments, you may have already begun gathering information in your journal. So, before you begin writing, review the notes you made after reading Wolfe's essay.

7. What was your hometown, neighborhood, or street like when you were a child, and what is it like now? Has it changed for the better or for the worse?

Describe important changes in a well-developed essay that uses the subject-by-subject method. If you want, begin by describing what the place was like before, then discuss what it has become. Rely on your senses, and use language that is specific, vivid, and concrete. Examples of such language are found throughout this chapter but especially in the work of Borland, Brewton, and Cowley. Other selections that describe places and things well appear in Chapter 8.

As you write your first draft, focus on a thesis that expresses your approval or disapproval of the changes you have seen. Put that thesis in your introduction or conclusion. Here are two examples:

What's happened to the downtown area in the last ten years has convinced me that even the most rundown city can be saved.

What's happened to Elm Street in recent years has made me an opponent of urban renewal.

If you responded to the third journal suggestion after Brewton's "Rafters," you might already have the information and inspiration to begin this project.

PROCESS ANALYSIS

Like illustration and comparison and contrast, process analysis is a way to explain complex ideas and abstract concepts. It can be used to show how something works or how something happens. It also comes in handy when you want to give readers instructions.

ORGANIZATION, PURPOSE, AND THESIS

Process explanations are organized in chronological order, much like narrative essays and short stories. In narration, however, the writer's purpose is to tell *what* happens. In process analysis, it is to explain *how* something happens (or happened) or *how* it is done.

You would be explaining a process if you wrote an essay discussing how the body uses oxygen, how electric light bulbs work, how a CD player produces sound, or how the Grand Canyon was formed. An example of such an essay in this chapter is Mildred Mastin Pace's "The Making of a Mummy."

As you can tell from the titles and topics above, process analysis is an important tool in scientific writing. But it can also be applied to topics in history, sociology, economics, the arts, and other subjects. For example, a process paper might be a good way to explain how the U.S. Constitution was ratified, how the stock market works, how people celebrate a holiday or tradition, or how a particular type of music developed. As Kenneth Kohler shows in "How I Came Out to My Parents," this type of writing can even explain how people deal with important personal issues.

Process analysis is also used in the writing of instructions. Scientists, doctors, engineers, and computer experts, for example, must often write careful directions to show their readers how to use a tool or machine, how to complete a procedure safely, how to conduct a test to achieve accurate results, or how to run complicated computer software. As a beginning writer, you might want to discuss a more limited subject by showing your readers how to change a tire, hang wallpaper, stop smoking, lose weight, study for a math exam, or accomplish another important task or goal. In this chapter, selections that instruct readers are Florence Pettit's "Sharpening Your Jackknife or Pocketknife" and Triena Milden's "So You Want to Flunk Out of College," which appears in the introduction.

The thesis in a process analysis essay is usually a statement of purpose; it explains why a process is important, why it occurs or occurred, or why it should be completed. For example, if you want to explain how to change the oil in a car, you might begin by saying that changing oil regularly can extend the engine's life. In addition to a statement of purpose, writers often begin with a broad summary or overview of the process so that readers can understand how each step relates to the whole procedure and to its purpose.

CLARITY AND DIRECTNESS

As with all types of writing, clarity and directness are important in process writing. You must explain the various steps in your process specifically and carefully enough that even readers who are unfamiliar with the subject will be able to follow each step easily. To be clear and to maintain your readers' interest, keep the following in mind:

1. *Use clear, simple language:* Use words that your readers will have no trouble understanding. If you *must* use terms your readers are not familiar with, provide a brief definition or description. Depending on how much your readers know about how to change a tire, for example, you might have to describe what a lug wrench looks like before you explain how to use it.

2. *Use the clearest, simplest organization:* Whenever possible, arrange the steps of your process in chronological order. In addition, use plenty of connective words and phrases between paragraphs (especially to show the passage of time); this will keep your writing coherent and easy to follow.

3. *Mention equipment and supplies:* Let readers know what equipment, tools, supplies, and other materials are involved in the process. Define or describe items that might be unfamiliar to them. If you are giving instructions, list these materials *before* you start explaining the steps in your process. Otherwise, the reader will have to stop in mid-process to find a needed item. This can be frustrating and time consuming.

4. *Discuss each step separately:* Reserve an entire paragraph for each step in the process; this is especially important when giving instructions. Explaining more than one step at a time can confuse readers and cause you to leave out important information.

5. *Discuss simultaneous steps separately:* If you need to explain two or more steps that occur at the same time, write about these steps in separate paragraphs. To maintain coherence between paragraphs, use connective elements like "At the same time," "Meanwhile," and "During this stage of the process."

6. *Give all the necessary information:* Always provide enough information to develop each step in the process adequately, and don't forget the small, important details. For instance, if you're explaining how to change the oil in a car, remember to tell your readers to wait for the engine to cool off before loosening the oil-pan nut; otherwise, the oil could severely burn their hands.

7. *Use the right verb tense:* If you're explaining a recurring process (one that happens over and over again), use the present tense. In writing about how your student government works, for instance, say that "the representatives *are elected* by fellow students and *meet* together every Friday afternoon." but if you're writing about a process that is over and done with, such as how one individual ran for election, use the past tense.

8. *Use direct commands:* When giving instructions, make each step clear and brief by simply telling the reader to do it (that is, by using the imperative mood). For example, don't say, "The first thing to do is to apply the handbrake." Instead, be more direct: "First, apply the handbrake."

VISUALIZING PROCESS ANALYSIS

The following diagram illustrates how you might organize the instructions on removing a flat tire. Transitions are underlined.

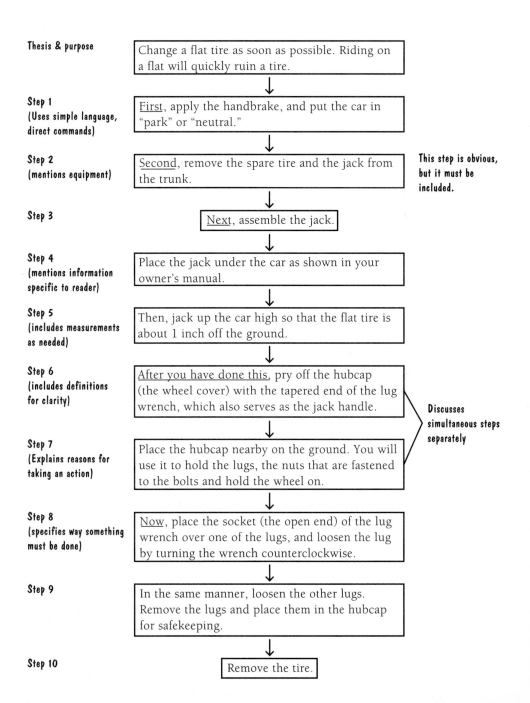

Thesis & purpose

Change a flat tire as soon as possible. Riding on a flat will quickly ruin a tire.

Step 1
(Uses simple language, direct commands)

First, apply the handbrake, and put the car in "park" or "neutral."

Step 2
(mentions equipment)

Second, remove the spare tire and the jack from the trunk.

This step is obvious, but it must be included.

Step 3

Next, assemble the jack.

Step 4
(mentions information specific to reader)

Place the jack under the car as shown in your owner's manual.

Step 5
(includes measurements as needed)

Then, jack up the car high so that the flat tire is about 1 inch off the ground.

Step 6
(includes definitions for clarity)

After you have done this, pry off the hubcap (the wheel cover) with the tapered end of the lug wrench, which also serves as the jack handle.

Discusses simultaneous steps separately

Step 7
(Explains reasons for taking an action)

Place the hubcap nearby on the ground. You will use it to hold the lugs, the nuts that are fastened to the bolts and hold the wheel on.

Step 8
(specifies way something must be done)

Now, place the socket (the open end) of the lug wrench over one of the lugs, and loosen the lug by turning the wrench counterclockwise.

Step 9

In the same manner, loosen the other lugs. Remove the lugs and place them in the hubcap for safekeeping.

Step 10

Remove the tire.

SEEING THE PATTERN IN A PROCESS ANALYSIS PAPER

The following essay, "So You Want to Flunk Out of College," takes a humorous approach to a serious issue. Student author Triena Milden uses irony by arguing the opposite of what she believes. Nonetheless, her tongue-in-cheek essay illustrates several techniques important to process analysis.

Flunking out of college is a relatively easy task. It requires little effort and might even be considered fun. [**States thesis**] Though it is hard to imagine why anyone would purposely try to flunk out of college, many people accomplish this task easily. In fact, whatever the reason one might want to flunk out of college, the process is quite simple. [**Uses present tense**]

[**Uses transitions for clear, simple organization**] First, do not show up for classes very often. It is important, however, to show up occasionally to find out when tests will be scheduled; the importance of this will become apparent later in this essay. [**Uses direct commands**] When in class, never raise your hand to ask questions and never volunteer any answers to the teacher's questions. If the teacher calls on you, either answer incorrectly or say "I don't know." Be sure your tone of voice conveys your lack of interest.

[**Discusses each step separately**] Another thing to avoid is homework. There are two reasons for this. First and most important, completing homework assignments only reinforces information learned earlier, thereby contributing to higher test scores. Second, although teachers credit homework as only part [**Provides all necessary information**] of the total grade, every little bit of credit hurts. Therefore, make sure that the teacher is aware that you are not doing your homework. You can do so by making certain that the teacher sees you writing down the answers as the homework is discussed in class.

The next area, tests, can be handled in two ways.

Uses simple language They can either not be taken, or they can be failed. If you do not take them, you run the risk of receiving an "incomplete" rather than a failing grade. In order to flunk out of college, failing grades are preferable.

Continues to use direct commands Therefore, make sure to take and fail all exams. Incidentally, this is where attendance and homework can really affect performance. Attending class and doing homework regularly can be detrimental to obtaining poor test scores.

Since you won't know the correct answers to test questions, make sure to choose those that are as absurd as possible without being obvious. Even if you guess a few correctly, your overall grade will be an *F* as long as the majority of your answers are wrong. By the way,

Keeps to the present tense one sure way to receive that cherished zero is to be caught cheating: all teachers promise a zero for this.

The same ideas pertain to any reports or term papers that you are assigned. If you fail to turn them in, you

Provides all necessary information might get an "incomplete." Therefore, hand in all papers, especially if they're poorly written. Make sure to use poor organization, to present information in a confused manner, and to write on the wrong topic whenever you can. The paper should be handwritten, not typed, and barely legible. Misspellings should be plentiful and as noticeable as possible. Smudged ink or dirty pages add a nice touch to the finished product. Finally, try to get caught plagiarizing.

By following these few simple suggestions, you will be assured of a failing grade. Try not to make it too obvious that your purpose is to fail. However, if a

Ends with a memorable conclusion

teacher shows concern and offers help, be sure to exhibit a poor attitude as you refuse. Should you decide to put extra effort into failing, you may even finish at the bottom of the class. Someone has to finish last. Why not you?

REVISING PROCESS ANALYSIS PAPERS

When Kenneth Kohler wrote the first draft of "How I Came Out to My Parents," he used narration. Later, he decided that telling what happened was less important than explaining how it happened. Paragraphs from the draft and revision of his paper show how he changed his narrative into process analysis. They also show that he added information, removed unnecessary words and details, and combined sentences to make his writing more efficient. The entire essay appears later.

Kohler—Early Draft

My struggle to "come out of the closet" grew out of several needs. First, I had a need to be closer to my parents and to share my life with them. Second, I had a **Combine these two reasons?** need to be honest with them about who I really was. And **Is "And" needed?** third, I needed to let them know that there was someone special in my life. By coming out to my parents, I would

Remove? Isn't this clear already? risk alienation and rejection for the hope that they **Save for later paragraph?** would gain a little more understanding of the man whom they called their son.

. . .

I had no idea how my parents might react when I came out to them. I knew that if my parents reacted violently or negatively it could take years to heal the damage **Wordy? Remove**

Repeats
ideas from
above.
Remove?

that would be done by their reaction. It was a chance I

had to take. I had to risk telling them my deepest

secret in an attempt to get closer to them. It was a

risk my brother never had to take.

unnecessary
words?

Do readers
need to
know this?

Kohler—Final Draft

My struggle to "come out of the closet" grew out of

several needs. First, I wanted to be closer with my

parents and to be honest about who I was. Second, I

needed to let them know that there was someone special

in my life. Finally, I had agreed to speak at my church

about being gay, and I felt it important to tell my

parents about my lifestyle before informing my

congregation.

Combines
ideas

Has
removed
ideas that
belong in
a later
paragraph

Adds
information
to strengthen
and clarify
purpose

. . .

I had no idea how they might react when I came out to

them. I knew that if they responded violently or

negatively it could take years to heal the damage. I

also knew that I might never see them again. It was for

this reason that I had avoided coming out to them

before. However, because of my pending public

announcement, the time had come to let them know.

Has
removed
unnecessary
words,
details

Adds
information
important
to purpose

I planned what I had to say carefully. Something so

important could not simply be announced and forgotten. I

had actually begun to prepare for this moment years

before by reading as much as I could about homosexuality

and by talking to gay friends. It was necessary for me

to accept myself as a gay man before expecting others to

Step 1

Adds a
paragraph
to trace
steps in
the process

```
do so. I had to develop a positive self-image, and this
took several years. Then, in the week prior to my
```

```
announcement, I began to rehearse my lines. I made

notes for various approaches I could take. I wanted to

feel secure in my delivery and didn't want to appear

ashamed of my lifestyle. "Why should I be?" I thought. I

had never felt differently. I imagined my parents' every

reaction and tried to predict my responses. I even

prepared myself for the worst, afraid they would tell me

to "Get out and never come back!"
```

Step 3

PRACTICING PROCESS ANALYSIS

Reread Visualizing Process Analysis on page 507. Use the method you see there to list instructions on doing a simple task. Write these steps in the boxes below, one step per box. Be complete; if you need more boxes, draw them on a piece of paper. As always, make a rough draft first. Here are examples of the task you might write about.

How to brush your teeth
How to make a pot of coffee
How to address an envelope
How to make out a check
How to start a car
How to take a two-minute shower
How to do laundry in a washing machine
How to heat leftovers in a microwave

State Task's Purpose

Step 1

Step 2

Step 3

Step 4

Step 5

Step 6

Step 7

Step 8

Enjoy the four selections that follow. They are well written and should provide you with effective examples of the techniques found in writing that makes good use of process analysis.

Sharpening Your Jackknife or Pocketknife

Florence H. Pettit

Noted for her clear and engaging style, Florence H. Pettit is the author of a number of books for young readers. "Sharpening Your Jackknife or Pocketknife" is from How to Make Whirligigs and Whimmy Diddles and Other American Folkcraft Objects. *This fascinating book explains how to make replicas of dolls, toys, blankets, and other objects used by Native Americans and Eskimos as well as by early European settlers in this hemisphere.*

"Sharpening Your Jackknife or Pocketknife" is typical of the writing found in the best technical or maintenance manuals. It is prose that has a clear and practical purpose and that remains direct and easy to follow throughout.

L OOKING AHEAD

It is important to mention tools, supplies, and materials the reader will need to complete a task. As you read this paragraph, circle things required for sharpening a knife.

V OCABULARY

burr	Rough spot that sticks up from a sharpened surface.
chisel	Tool used to shape wood.
gouge	Type of chisel with a rounded blade.
oval	Egg shape.
strop	Leather strap used for sharpening.

Sharpening Your Jackknife or Pocketknife

Florence H. Pettit

If you have never done any whittling or wood carving before, the first skill to learn is how to sharpen your knife. You may be surprised to learn that even a brand-new knife needs sharpening. Knives are never sold honed (finely sharpened), although some gouges and chisels are. It is essential to learn the firm stroke on the stone that will keep your blades sharp. The sharpening stone must be fixed in place on the table, so that it will not move around. You can do this by placing a piece of rubber inner tube or a thin piece of foam rubber under it. Or you can tack four strips of wood, if you have a rough worktable, to frame the stone and hold it in place. Put a generous puddle of oil on the stone—this will soon disappear into the surface of a new stone, and you will need to keep adding more oil. Press the knife blade flat against the stone in the puddle of oil, using your index finger. Whichever way the cutting edge of the knife faces is the side of the blade that should get a little more pressure. Move the blade around three or four times in a narrow oval about the size of your fingernail, going *counterclockwise* when the sharp edge is facing right. Now turn the blade over in the same spot on the stone, press hard, and move it around the small oval *clockwise*, with more pressure on the cutting edge that faces left. Repeat the ovals, flipping the knife blade over six or seven times, and applying lighter pressure to the blade the last two times. Wipe the blade clean with a piece of rag or tissue and rub it flat on the piece of leather strop at least twice on each side. Stroke *away* from the cutting edge to remove the little burr of metal that may be left on the blade.

QUESTIONS FOR DISCUSSION

1. Writers often begin describing a process by explaining its purpose. Why, according to Pettit, is learning how to sharpen a knife important?
2. What tools and materials does Pettit tell us we'll need to sharpen a knife properly?
3. List the steps involved in sharpening a jackknife or pocketknife.
4. Identify connective words and phrases (transitions) in this selection.
5. "Sharpening Your Jackknife or Pocketknife" is written in the imperative mood, using direct commands. Find examples of such commands.

THINKING CRITICALLY

1. What other things found around the house often need sharpening, tuning, or adjusting? Think through the process by actually doing it; then, write down its steps.
2. Make notes in the margins of Pettit's paragraph to mark similarities between it and Milden's "So You Want to Flunk Out of College," found in the chapter's introduction. Then, explain the differences between these selections.

SUGGESTIONS FOR JOURNAL ENTRIES

1. Think about a simple process that you've had to complete at home, at work, or at school. For instance, recall the steps you went through the last time you painted a wall, cooked macaroni and cheese, cut grass, set the table for dinner, ironed a load of laundry, or got dressed for an important date. Make a list of the tools, equipment, utensils, ingredients, and/or materials you needed to complete this process.
2. After brainstorming with a friend, write a paragraph that briefly discusses steps you go through to complete a common process such as shopping for groceries, polishing shoes, or getting a child ready for bed. You might start by reviewing what you wrote when responding to the Practicing Process Analysis exercise on pages 512–513.

The Measure of Eratosthenes

Carl Sagan

A professor of astronomy at Cornell University, Carl Sagan has worked on a number of NASA projects and has completed extensive research on the possibility of life on other planets. He has done much to popularize the study of science and is especially well known as a result of having hosted the public television series Cosmos. *Among his most widely read books are* The Dragons of Eden, *for which he won the Pulitzer Prize in 1977,* Broca's Brain, *and* Cosmos.

Sagan published "The Measure of Eratosthenes" (er-uh-TAHS-thuh-neez) to honor an ancient Greek thinker who, seventeen centuries before Columbus, accurately measured the Earth and proved that it was round.

L OOKING A HEAD

1. In paragraph 4, Sagan claims that "in almost everything, Eratosthenes was 'alpha.' " Alpha is the first letter of the Greek alphabet.
2. Papyrus, mentioned in paragraph 5, is a plant from which paper was made in ancient times.

V OCABULARY

cataract	Large waterfall.
circumference	Distance around a circle or globe.
compelling	Difficult to ignore.
deduced	Concluded, discovered.
inclined	Slanted.
intergalactic	Between galaxies.
intersect	Cross.
musings	Thoughts.
pronounced	Significant.
randomly	By chance.

The Measure of Eratosthenes | *Carl Sagan*

The earth is a place. It is by no means the only place. It is not even a typical place. No planet or star or galaxy can be typical, because the cosmos is mostly empty. The only typical place is within the vast, cold, universal vacuum, the everlasting night of intergalactic space, a place so strange and desolate that, by comparison, planets and stars and galaxies seem achingly rare and lovely.

If we were randomly inserted into the cosmos, the chance that we would find ourselves on or near a planet would be less than one in a billion trillion trillion (10^{33}, a one followed by 33 zeros). In everyday life, such odds are called compelling. Worlds are precious.

The discovery that the earth is a *little* world was made, as so many important human discoveries were, in the ancient Near East, in a time some humans call the third century B.C., in the greatest metropolis of the age, the Egyptian city of Alexandria.

Here there lived a man named Eratosthenes. One of his envious contemporaries called him "beta," the second letter of the Greek alphabet, because, he said, Eratosthenes was the world's second best in everything. But it seems clear that, in almost everything, Eratosthenes was "alpha."

He was an astronomer, historian, geographer, philosopher, poet, theater critic, and mathematician. His writings ranged from "Astronomy" to "On Freedom from Pain." He was also the director of the great library of Alexandria, where one day he read, in a papyrus book, that in the southern frontier outpost of Syene (now Aswan), near the first cataract of the Nile, at noon on June 21 vertical sticks cast no shadows. On the summer solstice, the longest day of the year, as the hours crept toward midday, the shadows of the temple columns grew shorter. At noon, they were gone. A reflection of the sun could then be seen in the water at the bottom of a deep well. The sun was directly overhead.

It was an observation that someone else might easily have ignored. Sticks, shadows, reflections in wells, the position of the sun—of what possible importance could such simple, everyday matters be? But Eratosthenes was a scientist, and his musings on these commonplaces changed the world: in a way, they made the world.

Eratosthenes had the presence of mind to do an experiment—actually to observe whether *in Alexandria* vertical sticks cast shadows near noon on June 21. And, he discovered, sticks do.

Eratosthenes asked himself how, at the same moment, a stick in Syene could cast no shadow and a stick in Alexandria, far to the north, could cast a pronounced shadow.

Consider a map of ancient Egypt with two vertical sticks of equal length, one stuck in Alexandria, the other in Syene. Suppose that, at a certain moment, neither stick casts any shadow at all. This is perfectly easy to understand—provided the earth is flat. The sun would then be directly overhead. If the two sticks cast shadows of equal length, that also would make sense on a flat earth: the sun's rays would then be inclined at the same angle to the two sticks. But how could it be that at the same instant there was no shadow at Syene and a substantial shadow at Alexandria?

The only possible answer, he saw, was that the surface of the earth is curved. Not only that: the greater the curvature, the greater the difference in the shadow lengths. The sun is so far away that its rays are parallel when they reach the earth. Sticks placed at different angles to the sun's rays cast shadows of different lengths. For the observed difference in the shadow lengths, the distance between Alexandria and Syene had to be about seven degrees along the surface of the earth; that is, if you imagine the sticks extending down to the center of the earth, they would intersect there at an angle of seven degrees.

Seven degrees is something like one-fiftieth of 360 degrees, the full circumference of 11
the earth. Eratosthenes knew that the distance between Alexandria and Syene was approximately 800 kilometers, because he had hired a man to pace it out.

Eight hundred kilometers times 50 is 40,000 kilometers; so that must be the cir- 12
cumference of the earth. (Or, if you like to measure things in miles, the distance between Alexandria and Syene is about 500 miles, and 500 miles times 50 is 25,000 miles.)

This is the right answer. 13

Eratosthenes' only tools were sticks, eyes, feet, and brains, plus a taste for experi- 14
ment. With them he deduced the circumference of the earth with an error of only a few percent, a remarkable achievement for 2,200 years ago. He was the first person accurately to measure the size of a planet.

QUESTIONS FOR DISCUSSION

1. What does paragraph 6 tell us about the purpose for which Sagan wrote this essay?
2. Where does Sagan refer to the scientific process of making observations and of drawing conclusions from those observations?
3. Where does Sagan define important terms?
4. You have read that each step in a process should be discussed thoroughly. In what paragraph or paragraphs does Sagan's essay illustrate this principle?
5. Does this essay list separate steps in a process one by one? Explain your answer.
6. What methods of development, other than process analysis, does Sagan use?

THINKING CRITICALLY

1. Why does the author tell us so much about the life of Eratosthenes? Explain your answer in a short paragraph.
2. Make notes in the margins that explain each step in the process by which Eratosthenes measured the earth's circumference. Then put your notes into a well-organized paragraph.

SUGGESTIONS FOR JOURNAL ENTRIES

1. Make a brief, informal list of steps you might use to explain how a simple machine or natural process works. Pick something you have had experience with or know a lot about. Here are examples:

MACHINE	PROCESS
Sling shot	Circulation of the blood
Bow and arrow	Formation of rain clouds
Bottle opener	Photosynthesis
Cork screw	Osmosis
Food blender	Pollination of flowers by bees
Pliers	Transmission of a particular disease
Water wheel	Movement of the tides
Fishing reel	Formation of a fossil

2. Follow the advice in Suggestion 1 for a process that human beings have learned or invented to survive or to improve the quality of their lives. Examples include the process by which a broken bone is set, artificial respiration is given, an

incandescent bulb turns electricity into light, solar energy is used to heat a house, a serious disease is treated, or a food crop is grown or harvested.

3. Read about a scientist or inventor in an encyclopedia or other library reference book. Then, list steps he or she used to discover a scientific principle or to invent an important technique or product. Among those you might read about are Archimedes, Galen, Copernicus, Galileo, Kepler, Newton, Harvey, Galvani, Faraday, Pasteur, Curie, Marconi, Carver, Edison, Einstein, Bohr, and Fermi.

How I Came Out to My Parents

Kenneth Kohler

When his freshman English instructor encouraged the class to "write from the heart," Ken Kohler decided to explain how he accomplished one of the most difficult and meaningful tasks in his life—telling his parents he was gay. Kohler's recollection of the process by which he came to the decision and finally confronted his parents shows how deeply concerned he was about their feelings and about the kind of relationship he would have with them once they knew of his sexual preference.

This essay represents the best of what process writers can achieve, for it combines the author's emotional commitment to his subject with clear, logical analysis. Ken Kohler is now a computer programmer completing his master's degree.

LOOKING AHEAD

1. Like other process essays, "How I Came Out to My Parents" is organized as a narrative. But this is not just another story. What is really important here is not *what* happened, but *how* it happened—the agony Kohler endured to tell his family about his homosexuality.
2. This selection is divided into two sections. The first explains how Kohler made the decision and found the courage to tell his parents he was gay. The second discusses the results of that decision.

VOCABULARY

acknowledged	Admitted.
acutely	Greatly, sharply.
alienation	State of loneliness, exclusion.
congregation	Church members.
disclosure	Announcement, revelation.
irreparably	Beyond repair.
pending	Upcoming, expected.
predict	Know ahead of time.
rejection	Disapproval.

How I Came Out to My Parents

Kenneth Kohler

Being a minority within your own family can be a source of conflict. I had always 1
known that I was different from my brother and my sister. My parents, too, may
have sensed the difference, but they never acknowledged it to me. For many years, I
had struggled with the idea of letting them know how different I was from my older
brother. I was gay and didn't know how they would react if they ever found out.

My struggle to "come out of the closet" grew out of several needs. First, I wanted to 2
be closer with my parents and to be honest about who I was. Second, I needed to let
them know that there was someone special in my life. Finally, I had agreed to speak at
my church about being gay, and I felt it important to tell my parents about my lifestyle
before informing my congregation.

Rejection was my greatest fear. At the time, I had friends who had not spoken to 3
their families for years after revealing they were gay. Their parents could not understand how their children could be "fags" or "dykes." These were terms their families
had previously applied only to strangers. Some friends even told me about the violent
reactions their families had had to the news. One of them said his father chased him
around the house with a butcher knife. I had also known people who had used their
homosexuality as a weapon against their families. Never did I want to hurt my parents;
I merely wanted to break down the barriers between us.

I had no idea how they might react when I came out to them. I knew that if they 4
responded violently or negatively it could take years to heal the damage. I also knew
that I might never see them again. It was for this reason that I had avoided coming out
to them before. However, because of my pending public announcement, the time had
come to let them know.

I planned what I had to say carefully. Something so important could not simply be 5
announced and forgotten. I had actually begun to prepare for this moment years before
by reading as much as I could about homosexuality and by talking to gay friends. It was
necessary for me to accept myself as a gay man before expecting others to do so. I had to
develop a positive self-image, and this took several years. Then, in the week prior to my
announcement, I began to rehearse my lines. I made notes for various approaches I
could take. I wanted to feel secure in my delivery and didn't want to appear ashamed of
my lifestyle. "Why should I be?" I thought. I had never felt differently. I imagined my
parents' every reaction and tried to predict my responses. I even prepared myself for the
worst, afraid they would tell me to "Get out and never come back!"

I also knew it was possible that none of the negative things that had happened to my
friends would happen to me. In fact, I thought my parents might have already suspected 6
I was gay. After all, I had been living with a man for three years. My partner at the time
said, "They probably already know about you, the way you swish around!" I knew he
could be right, but I was still afraid. Would my disclosure actually draw me closer to
them as I had hoped, or would it push me away? Would they accept my partner as they
had in the past? How would I cope with the loss of their love? These were just a few of
the many questions that swept through my mind as I called my mother to ask if I could
visit and talk about something important.

My heart was racing and my palms were sweating as I stopped the car in front of 7
their house. I turned off the ignition, took a deep breath, and stepped out. "This is it," I
thought. "This is what I've been thinking about doing for years." The walk to the front
door had never seemed so long. I was acutely aware of my heartbeat pounding in my
ears. My breath seemed suspended in the frigid February night air. Time seemed to stop
as I nervously straightened my jacket, threw my shoulders back, swallowed hard, and
opened the front door.

My father was sitting in the recliner watching the television. My mother was folding 8
laundry. "Hi, how are you doing?" I said, trying to hide my nervousness. They both
looked up and smiled. As I walked over to give each of them a hug, I wondered if they
would ever smile at me again.

I took off my coat, sat down next to my mother, and began to help her fold the 9
laundry. We talked about how fast my niece was growing up. While we spoke, I tried to
form the words that I feared would hurt them irreparably, but I realized there was only
one way to say it. "Mom. Dad. I've been thinking about telling you this for some time
now." I swallowed hard and took a good look at them. "I'm not telling you this because
I want to hurt you. I love you. Please try to understand." I paused and took a deep
breath. "I'm gay."

There was silence. Finally, with much hesitation, my mother asked, "Are you sure?" 10

There was still no response from my father. I wondered what was racing through his 11
head. His silence was deeper than I could remember. Again my mother spoke. "Are you
happy?"

"Yes," I replied with hesitation. I was not sure what would happen next. I could 12
almost hear the silent screams that I imagined howling in each of them.

"Well," she paused, "you've always been good to us, and you've never given us any 13
problems."

"Here it comes," I thought, "the guilt trip." 14

"I guess if you're happy," she continued slowly as if weighing every word, "then I'll 15
try to understand."

A smile spread over my face as I leaned over and gave her a long, warm hug. Never 16
had I felt so close to her. It was only then that my father piped up, "I hope you aren't
sleeping with someone new every night." I assured him that I wasn't as I gave him a
hug.

"You know, it's funny," my mother said. "We always thought your friend was gay, 17
but we didn't know you were." I tried hard to keep from laughing as I thought of my
partner's remarks. Deep down, I suspected that they had always known but had denied it.

When I explained that I was going to speak at my church about what it was like to 18
be gay, my mother's brow became dark and furrowed. "Do you think you should? What
if you lose your job? What if someone tries to hurt you?" she responded.

I tried to assure her that everything would be all right, but I really had no idea what 19
might happen. Of course, I knew my parents would struggle with my gayness just as I
had, but I was overjoyed that they were asking such questions. A great burden had been
lifted from my shoulders; I felt like laughing and dancing around the room. I realized I
no longer had to hide my private life, to change pronouns, or to avoid questions about
whom I was dating. More important, I had discovered how deeply my parents loved me.

QUESTIONS FOR DISCUSSION

1. Why did Kohler feel the need to "come out of the closet"?
2. Discuss the fears he dealt with before deciding to tell his parents he was gay.
3. What steps did he take to prepare *himself* for the moment when he would tell his parents he was gay?
4. What steps did he take to prepare his *parents* for this moment? Should he have done more to get them ready?
5. Why does the author tell us how the parents of his friends reacted when they announced they were gay? Does including this information help him explain a process?

THINKING CRITICALLY

1. What do you think about the response of Kohler's parents to his announcement? What does it reveal about them?
2. This essay and Sagan's "The Measure of Eratosthenes" tell us how something was done. What other similarities do you find between these selections? Make notes in the margins of Kohler's essay to identify them.
3. Had Kohler asked you for advice about approaching his parents, what would you have told him? Put your comments in the form of a letter.

SUGGESTIONS FOR JOURNAL ENTRIES

1. Recall a time when you told someone something he or she did not want to hear. Perhaps you had to tell your parents that you wrecked the family car, to persuade a sweetheart that your relationship was over, or to inform a friend or relative that a loved one had died. Freewrite for about five minutes to explain how hard this was.
2. Kohler's decision to tell his parents he was gay came from a strong desire to be honest with them. Write about a time when you needed to reveal something about yourself to a loved one who might find it difficult to accept. List a few steps that explain how you did this.

The Making of a Mummy

Mildred Mastin Pace

A graduate of Cornell University, Mildred Mastin Pace won fame as a radio and magazine writer in the 1930s and 1940s. However, her reputation rests on her books for young people. Among the most important of these are Wrapped for Eternity, *from which this selection is taken, and* The Pyramids. *Both reflect her interest in ancient Egypt.*

L OOKING A HEAD

1. Ancient Egyptians believed in life after death. One of their greatest concerns was that, left untreated, the body would decay and be unable to rejoin the soul in the "other world." Thus, they developed mummification, a process to preserve corpses.
2. The Egyptians pictured the god Horus (paragraph 22) as a falcon. As the story goes, Horus lost an eye in battle. After it was restored, it became a symbol for healing and was represented by "amulets," charms that protected the wearer.

V OCABULARY

abhorrence	Loathing, disgust, hatred.
adze	Tool for shaping wood.
bier	Platform on which a coffin is carried.
deftly	Skillfully.
derision	Scorn, contempt, ridicule.
dirges	Funeral songs.
disheveled	Untidy, in disorder or disarray.
interludes	Episodes, occurrences.
intoned	Sang.
jackal	Wild dog.
loathsome	Detestable, disgusting.
lustration	Cleansing.
resin	Preservative.
sarcophagus	Coffin of stone.
unguents	Creams, ointments.
viscera	Vital organs.

The Making of a Mummy

Mildred Mastin Pace

I t would take about ten weeks to create the mummy. During that period the fam- 1
ily would remain, as much as possible, in their home, in seclusion, chanting
dirges and mourning their loss.

The place where the body was taken for mummification was a large tent. Some- 2
times the embalmers' workshops were in permanent buildings. But in this country of
heat and sun and almost no rain, tents were practical. They could be moved easily when
necessary, and were more comfortable for the embalmers to work in than the walled
and confined space of a building.

The tent had cooled off during the night, and when the priests and workers gath- 3
ered to begin their job, the air was pleasant.

The body, freshly bathed, was laid out on a long, narrow table, high enough so that 4
those administering to the body need not bend over.

Beneath the table stood four stone jars, each about a foot high. These were the 5
Canopic jars and later they would hold the embalmed larger organs of the man's body:
the intestines, liver, stomach, lungs. The lid of each jar was topped with a figure carved
of stone: one the head of a man, one a dog's head, one the head of a jackal, and one the
head of a hawk.

The priest who was in charge of the embalming represented the god Anubis, who 6
presided over mummification and was the guardian of the tombs. Since this god had
the body of a man and the head of a jackal, this one priest wore a head mask of a jackal.

The priests were all freshly shaven; their heads, their faces—even their bodies 7
beneath the fine, crisp linen robes—had been shaved to remove all hair. Led by the
priest in the jackal mask, they intoned chants that announced the start of the work and
the ritual.

The first actual step toward mummification was about to begin. This was the 8
removal of the brain.

A specialist, highly skilled in his work, approached the head of the corpse. In his 9
hand he held a long, slender hooklike instrument. Deftly he pushed this up one nos-
tril, and working in a circular movement, he broke through the ethmoid bone, up into
the cavity of the brain.

Withdrawing the hooklike instrument, he chose another. This one was a narrow, 10
spirally twisted rod that had a small spoonlike tip. Pushing this up into the cranial cavity, he began, slowly, bit by bit, to draw out the brain through the nose, discarding each
piece as he went along.

This was an operation of skill and patience. When at long last he was finished, sat- 11
isfied that all of the brain had been removed from the cranial cavity, leaving it clean and
clear, he prepared to leave. His job was done, and he was pleased to have done it well.
Once in a while a clumsy operator crushed a bone or broke the nose, disfiguring the
face forever. But he had completed the delicate operation leaving the strong bone structure, the well-shaped face, as it had been when he started.

Now the mouth was cleansed and in it were placed wads of linen soaked in sweet 12
oils. The nostrils were cleansed and plugged with wax. The face was coated with a

resinous paste. A small piece of linen was placed over each eye, and the eyelids drawn over them.

The body was now ready for the second important operation toward mummifica- 13 tion. This was the removal of the viscera from the body cavity.

The man who was to perform this operation stood outside the tent, waiting to be 14 called in. He held in his hand a fairly large, flat black stone, one edge of which was honed to razor sharpness. It was called an Ethiopian stone. His job was not a pleasant one, and gruesome to watch. Hence the other workers and the priests held him in abhorrence.

As he waited, the priest wearing the jackal mask approached the body, which had 15 been turned slightly on its right side, exposing the left flank. The tent throbbed with the sound of the soft, rhythmic chantings of the priests.

The jackal head bent toward the body, and the masked priest dipped a small rush 16 pen into a pot of ink, then drew on the left side of the body a spindle-shaped line about five inches long.

The priest stepped back and the man with the stone was called in. Following the 17 line the priest had drawn, he cut, with great strength, through skin and flesh. Then, reaching through the incision, he severed and removed each organ: the stomach, liver, kidneys, lungs, intestines.

Only the heart was left in place. It was thought to be the seat of intelligence and 18 feeling, and so must remain forever intact within the body.

The other vital organs would be wrapped in resin-soaked cloth and each placed in 19 the proper Canopic jar. Their lids sealed on with wax, the jars would be set aside to await the day of burial.

His loathsome job finished, the man fled from the tent, followed by shouts of deri- 20 sion and contempt from all the others. He was considered unclean, and their angry out-cries, the curses they called down on him, would rid the tent of his taint.

The priests, the embalmers, might pretend to despise him. But they all knew his 21 job was an important one. Left in place, the internal organs would deteriorate rapidly, making the drying out of the body and successful mummification impossible.

The body cavity was cleansed with palm wine. The incision was pulled together, 22 and a priest performed the ritual of placing on it a wax plate bearing the all-powerful symbol, the Eye of Horus. For a wealthier man the plate might have been of silver, or even of gold. But in any case, always, the Eye of Horus was depicted on it. Next, thin wires of gold were fastened around each fingernail and toenail to keep them in place. And once again the corpse was bathed.

The body was now ready to be dried out. 23

The powder called natron came from the Libyan Desert. It was known to be a great 24 drying agent and had cleansing and purification powers as well. Laid out on a fresh, clean mat woven of plant fibers, the body was covered with natron. In the hot, dry atmosphere, with the heat of the sun to help, day after day the drying-out process in the natron went on.

The day came when the body was wholly dry—the skin stretched on the firm frame 25 of bone, the face thin but still the face of the man who had died.

The body was very light when the men lifted it onto a high table. It was bathed once 26 more. It was anointed with ointments and rubbed with sweet-smelling spices and herbs.

Priests now poured out libations—liquid that symbolically restored moisture to the body. They lighted incense, which they burned—also symbolically—to restore the body's warmth and odor. 27

The body was ready to be wrapped. 28

About 150 yards of linen cloth had been prepared, torn into strips of varying widths. On some of the bandages the man's name was written. Thus his identity would be preserved. On some there were figures of the gods and on others were religious writings and words of magic. All of these would give the man help and power when he reached the other world. 29

The bandaging was intricate, and those doing the work were highly skilled. But only the priests knew where the magical bandages, with their words of power, should be placed. Only the priests knew the words to be chanted when the man's ring was placed on his finger, the gold earrings hung in his ears. Only the priests could direct where, amongst the bandages, the amulets should be hidden to protect the deceased on his journey into the next world. 30

So as the bandaging began, and as it went on, there were frequent interludes when the wrapping ceased while the priests, with great ceremony, intoned their words of wisdom and chanted religious formulas. 31

Thus the wrapping, with its wealth of religious significance, took some time. And seventy days elapsed between the day of the man's death and the day when the wrapping was finished. On that day the mummy was taken back to the house of mourning where the man had died. 32

From the house the final procession set forth. The mummy, in its elaborately painted mummiform coffin, lay upon a lion-headed bier which was placed on a sledge drawn by men and oxen. Walking before the sledge, on each side, were two women who impersonated the goddess Isis and her sister goddess, Nephthys, guardians of the dead. Behind the bier came another sledge, drawn by men. On this was a chest that held the four Canopic jars. 33

The women mourners followed, wailing in grief, their hair disheveled. Then came the men mourners, beating their breasts in sorrow. Behind the mourners were the servants, carrying the objects the dead man would need for living in the other world: chests filled with clothes, toilet articles, jars of salves and unguents, and some of his favorite possessions. Others bore the funerary furniture: a bed, a chair, small stools. 34

When the procession reached the entrance of the tomb, the mummy was taken from its bier and set in a standing position on a mound of sand, facing the mourners. 35

While the mourners watched and waited, the priests began the long, complicated series of rituals that would assure the man success on his long journey into the next world. Small vessels of burning incense were waved, rites of purification, lustration, were performed. The ceremonies went on and on. Finally came the most complex and important rite of all, known as the Opening of the Mouth. 36

One priest, holding a miniature *adze* that possessed special mystical powers, approached the mummy. To the chanting of religious formulas, he touched the mummy's head: the eyes, to open them so the man could see; the ears, so he could hear; the mouth, so he could speak; the jaws, so he could eat. 37

He could now live in the other world as he had on earth. He would need the con- 38 tents of his carved chests, the furniture placed in his tomb, the food and drink that would be provided for him.

Even as the coffined body, sealed in its sarcophagus, was being placed in its tomb, the man's journey into the next world had begun. 39

The mourners, weary from their hot and dusty procession to the tomb and the long-lasting ceremonies that followed, were now ready to enjoy the great feast that had been prepared for them. Knowing that the dead man was on his way to a second happy life that would never end, they partook of a joyous banquet. The foods were the finest, the wines and beer plentiful. There were entertainers and musicians, and guests sang songs in praise of the man just buried. 40

The mourning was over. 41

QUESTIONS FOR DISCUSSION

1. What were the major steps in the process of mummification?
2. Why did the priests only "pretend to despise" the one who removed the "internal organs" (paragraph 21)?
3. Why was the heart not removed from the corpse?
4. Why did the mourners enjoy a "joyous banquet" after the mummy was in the tomb?
5. What transitional devices did you find in this essay?
6. Where does Pace use description? Is her writing too descriptive?
7. What would be a good thesis statement for this essay?

THINKING CRITICALLY

1. This essay and Sagan's "The Measure of Eratosthenes" explain how something was done. What other similarities do you find between them? Make notes in the margins of Pace's essay to identify them.
2. Make a list of evidence from this essay to show that the civilization of ancient Egypt was technologically advanced for its time.

SUGGESTIONS FOR JOURNAL ENTRIES

1. What similarities do you see between the funeral rights of the ancient Egyptians and modern funeral rites you know about? List as many of these similarities as you can.
2. Recall a wake or funeral you attended. Use listing or freewriting to discuss things we do to mourn or bury the dead. The process differs from religion to religion and from family to family, so write only about traditions, ceremonies, and rites about which you have personal knowledge.

SUGGESTIONS FOR SUSTAINED WRITING

1. Florence Pettit's "Sharpening Your Jackknife or Pocketknife" explains how to do a common chore. If you read this selection, use your journal notes to begin drafting an essay that provides instructions on how to complete a simple but important task.

   Make your paper as detailed as you can so that even someone with no knowledge of the process can follow it. The best way to do this is to write about a task you are familiar with, something you do often or regularly. Try to pick a simple activity, one that has only a few steps and that can be covered thoroughly in a short paper. Stay away from topics like "how to paint a house," "how to raise prize-winning dogs," or "how to improve your health." Instead, explain "how to prepare the walls of a small bedroom for painting," "how to bathe a cocker spaniel," or "how to fight a cold."

   Like Pettit, begin by explaining why the process is important or how your readers will benefit from your instructions. Describe any tools or supplies needed to complete the job in your introduction as well.

   After completing two or three drafts, try putting your instructions to the test if possible. Ask a friend or classmate to read and follow them *exactly* as written. If he or she has trouble, add information or revise your instructions to make them clearer or more logical. Then, edit your work to remove distracting errors in grammar, spelling, and the like.

2. Triena Milden takes an ironic or tongue-in-cheek approach to academic studies in "So You Want to Flunk Out of College," which appears in the chapter's introduction (pages 508–509.) You too may be able to provide advice to help someone fail at something important. Write an ironic but complete set of instructions for this purpose. Put them in a letter to someone you know well.

   If you follow Milden's lead, begin your letter by explaining how hard or easy it is to fail at the task you are discussing. Somewhere in your letter, perhaps in the introduction or conclusion, you might also explain why anyone would want to fail at it in the first place! In any case, revise and edit your letter to make sure it's clear, easy-to-follow, and fun to read!

3. If suggestion 2 doesn't appeal to you, write an essay that explains how *not* to do something. Here are some topics you might choose:

   How not to study for an important exam
   How not to do laundry
   How not to light a barbecue grill
   How not to start exercising
   How not to lie to your parents, children, spouse, or sweetheart
   How not to drive a car if you want it to last
   How not to become depressed when life gets difficult
   How not to become addicted to tobacco, drugs, alcohol, or other substances
   How not to get hooked on watching TV or any other activity

You can take a serious or a humorous approach, but you don't have to explain the correct way to do the thing you're discussing. Just include enough detail to convince your readers that not doing something correctly can produce unhappy results.

4. Item 2 in the Suggestions for Journal Entries after "The Measure of Eratosthenes" asks you to list steps in a process that human beings have learned or invented to survive or to improve the quality of their lives. If you did not respond to that suggestion, do so now.

    Use your list as the outline to an essay that fully explains the process. Write your first draft by following this outline. As you revise, develop each step in greater detail until you are sure the process is clear and complete. When you are ready to write an introduction, discuss the reason or reasons this process is important, thereby giving your essay an identifiable purpose and focus. In other words, let your readers know from the very start that the essay is worth their time.

    As you edit your final draft, check for coherence—adding connectives and linking pronouns as necessary. Then proofread.

5. Ken Kohler's "How I Came Out to My Parents" explains the painful process of telling people a truth they might not want to hear. Have you ever been in a similar situation? Did you ever have to confess that you smashed up the family car, misplaced an important document or tool at work, or lost your younger brother in a shopping mall? Have you ever said good-bye to a loved one or told somebody a close relative or friend died?

    Write an essay explaining how you did what had to be done. As you draft and rewrite, include details to show how painful the process was. Remember that this is not simply a narrative. Don't just say that you got the courage to face the situation or that you overcame emotional hurdles. Show *how* you did these things step by step.

    You can begin by explaining how you got yourself ready. Next, recall the things you did to prepare your listener(s) for the news. Then, tell how you made the announcement, and describe the way your listener(s) reacted. Finally, like Kohler, explain how you felt when the experience was over.

    Check your journal for notes that will help you get started. As you write your paper, remember that Kohler's essay is so powerful because he revised and edited it carefully. Do the same with yours.

6. Mildred Mastin Pace's "The Making of a Mummy" traces the steps in an ancient funeral rite. One of the Suggestions for Journal Entries that accompanies this piece asks you to recall a wake or funeral you attended and to list important steps you observed in the way your friends, family, or community mourns and buries the dead. Use these notes to write the first draft of an essay that explains one way people today grieve the loss of loved ones.

    If you need to add detail to later drafts, try brainstorming with or interviewing family members who can provide additional information. Since the process of grieving differs from religion to religion, culture to culture, and family to family, discuss only those traditions, ceremonies, and rites about which you have personal knowledge. Use your introduction or conclusion to explain what the rites you are describing reveal about the people who practice them.

7. If you have been able to stick to a diet, get a good grade on a test, quit smoking, or achieve another important personal goal, provide a few suggestions to help others do the same. You can put your suggestions in an essay that several people might want to read. Then again, you might write a letter to an individual in particular need of your advice. If you address one person, explain ways in which your suggestions can be applied to his or her life specifically.

One way to introduce your paper or letter is with an overview that explains how difficult or easy the task is and that reveals the benefits of following your instructions. A good thesis might go like this: "Kicking the nicotine habit requires courage, willpower, and perseverance, but it will help you live longer, breathe easier, and smell better!"

Once you have provided enough detail in the body of your paper or letter to develop the thesis, review your work carefully. Be sure you have used vocabulary that is interesting and convincing. When it comes time to edit the final draft, ask yourself whether you have maintained coherence in and between paragraphs. If not, add transitions, include linking pronouns, or repeat words and ideas as necessary.

Persuasion

All writers of persuasion have one thing in common: they want to convince their readers. How they do this differs depending upon their purpose and their audience.

Beginning with an Argument

At the heart of all persuasive writing is a good argument. Of course, an argument does not have to be a loud and excited discussion of a controversial issue. In fact, when it comes to writing, argumentation is just the attempt to prove a point or support an opinion through logic and concrete evidence.

Two types of thinking are used in argumentation: *induction* and *deduction*. Both support an opinion or belief the writer expresses in a *conclusion*.

Inductive thinking involves collecting separate facts, reasons, or other pieces of evidence and then drawing a conclusion from that information. Say you come down with a case of food poisoning—cramps, vomiting, a headache, the works! When you call the other five people with whom you shared a pot of stew the night before, each tells the same horrible story about cramps, vomiting, and so on. It's safe to say the stew made you sick! That's your *conclusion*. Support for that conclusion comes in the form of six separate tales of woe!

As a matter of fact, induction is the kind of thinking behind the conclusion-and-support method of developing paragraphs and essays, which is explained in Chapter 3. In papers developed through this method, the conclusion is often expressed in a formal thesis statement. A good example is Naisbitt and Aburdene's "The Culture of Cuisine" in Chapter 13. The authors state their thesis early: "We [various world cultures] are tasting each other's cuisine with great gusto." This is their *conclusion*. The rest of the essay is developed with *supportive evidence* (examples) from which the authors drew that conclusion.

While induction involves drawing a general idea from specific pieces of evidence, deduction moves from the general to the specific. Using deduction, writers start with a general statement or idea they believe their readers will agree with. Next, they apply a specific case or example to that statement. Finally, they draw a conclusion from the two. You would be using deduction if you argued:

General statement: All full-time students can use the college exercise room free of charge.
Specific case: I am a full-time student.
Conclusion: Therefore, I can use the college exercise room free of charge.

Diane Ravitch uses deductive reasoning to organize "The Decline and Fall of Teaching History," which appears later in this chapter. Ravitch's argument goes something like this:

General statement: Making political decisions that will keep democracy strong requires a knowledge of history.
Specific case: Many Americans know little about history.
Conclusion: To make political decisions that will keep our democracy strong, Americans must learn more about history.

Induction and deduction are two different ways of reasoning, but they almost always complement each other. In fact, logical and well-supported arguments often reflect both types of thinking.

DEVELOPING IDEAS IN AN ARGUMENT

Back in Chapter 3 you learned that, whether your purpose is to explain or persuade, you can choose several ways to develop a piece of writing. One of the most popular is *conclusion and support,* the method you just read about. As the essays in this chapter show, writers of persuasion often use a combination of methods to develop evidence that proves a point or supports an opinion. For example, in "The Decline and Fall of Teaching History," Diane Ravitch develops the ideas in her deductive argument by including both convincing anecdotes and the hard facts she has researched. She also quotes experts in the field: college history teachers. This is known as appealing to authority and is used successfully by Barry Glazer who, in "The Right to Be Let Alone," makes specific reference to the Constitution and quotes Supreme Court Justice Louis Brandeis.

Rob Teir's "Fight Drug Use with Tests" also uses this technique, as well as statistics and comparison, to create a tightly woven argument. Jack G. Shaheen relies on illustration, comparison, the cause-and-effect method, narration, and even analogy to argue for a change in the media's portrayal of Arabs.

The most important thing to remember about an effective argument is that it is *both* logical and well supported. You can use inductive reasoning, deductive reasoning, or both, but your argument must be reasonable and easy to follow. You can support ideas with examples, facts, statistics, the knowledge or opinions of experts, analogies, comparisons, definitions, first-hand observations, and the like. But your writing must contain enough supportive information to be clear, convincing, and easily understood.

GOING BEYOND ARGUMENT

You just learned that persuasive writing is aimed at convincing and that at the heart of persuasion is argument: the use of logic and evidence to support an opinion. Sometimes, you will simply want to convince readers that your stand on a controversial issue has merit or that a conclusion you have drawn about a complex question is correct. In such cases, a reasoned argument supported by concrete detail will be enough. When you need to change people's attitudes or urge them to action, however, logic and evidence alone may not get the job done. Therefore, while remaining clear-headed and fair, you might also appeal to the readers' self-interest, emotions, pride, and personal values.

Let's say your college is having a problem with litter. The dean asks you to write a letter to fellow students persuading them that they can help by cleaning up after themselves in the cafeteria and by keeping litter out of classrooms, lounges, and parking lots. You begin by explaining that keeping the college clean is easy and inexpensive if everyone pitches in and that a clean campus is a pleasant place to study. But those arguments appeal to reason, and they alone might not convince your readers to change their behavior.

Therefore, you continue by appealing to your audience's self-interest. The dirtier the campus, you argue, the more money the college will have to pay for janitorial services, thereby increasing tuition. You can also appeal to their sense of community and their self-image by explaining that the way students behave reveals much about their respect—or lack of it—for the college, for professors, for classmates, and for themselves.

If you are dealing with a group that is especially hard to convince, ask them to put themselves in the shoes of other students, faculty, and visitors—not to mention the janitors—who enter the cafeteria to find tables covered with soiled paper plates and napkins, half-eaten sandwiches, and dirty coffee cups. Express your disgust over cigarette butts and glass bottles dropped from cars in the parking lots. Complain about cans, yogurt containers, and waste paper left in lounges. In the process, use colorful figures of speech: ask your readers not to turn the place into an "academic pigsty"; or compare the cafeteria at day's end to a "small village that has been looted and trashed by an invading army." If that doesn't work, appeal to their pride by reminding them that they are college adults, not adolescents who lack table manners.

ADDRESSING OPPOSING ARGUMENTS

At the beginning of this chapter, you learned that how persuasive writers go about their work depends upon their purpose and their audience. In some cases, your readers may be sensitive about certain opinions that you believe are perfectly reasonable and that you can defend through logical argument. Say you are trying to convince bargain-hunting consumers that there should be no limit on the number of foreign cars we import. You might simply argue that competition keeps prices down. But what if your audience is a group of unemployed U.S. auto workers? Your job will be far more complicated, and you will first have to show that free, fair, and open trade can benefit workers worldwide.

At times, however, you will address readers whose opinions are the very opposite of yours, and you will be forced to discuss their point of view before defending your own. In some cases, you may be able to show that the opposing argument is weak, illogical, or untrue. In others, you will have to admit that it has merit while explaining that yours makes even better sense.

Let's say you believe cars should come equipped with back-seat air bags. You know your readers can argue that air bags add a lot to the price of a new car. Therefore, you begin by admitting this fact, but you argue that saving lives is more important than saving money. As such, you are able to answer a serious objection that, otherwise, would have lingered in your readers' minds. Now, you can develop your argument by including statistics about the many lives air bags saved and by showing that drivers whose cars have air bags pay lower insurance rates than other drivers. You might even appeal to your readers' emotions by describing what happens to people in the front and back seats of a car during a collision.

VISUALIZING STRATEGIES FOR PERSUASION

Read the following editorial, published in *USA Today* on March 28, 1995. Then, look over the two diagrams that follow it and that show how it uses both deduction and induction. An essay expressing an opposing view, from the same issue of *USA Today,* appears later in this chapter.

DRUG TESTS FAIL SCHOOLS

Imagine you wanted to go out for your company's softball team and your boss told you: "Pee in this cup—in front of me." 1

Most adults would consider such a demand outrageous. Yet, that's what some public schools were demanding from student athletes in the war against drugs when 12-year-old James Acton came along in 1991. 2

The would-be seventh-grade football player put a damper on such demands. First, he told Vernonia, OR public school officials that he wouldn't go along. Then he went to court. His claim: The district's drug tests—required of all those trying out for sports—violate Fourth Amendment rights to privacy. 3

Last year, a federal appeals court in San Francisco agreed. In doing so, it made such testing illegal in nine Western states under its jurisdiction. And it discouraged schools elsewhere from starting testing programs until the Supreme Court rules on the case. 4

Today, the high court hears arguments. And if students, schools and taxpayers are lucky, it will kill all such required drug tests for student athletes by next fall. 5

Drug testing can be smart, when it's conducted to protect public safety and security, as with transportation workers and drug enforcement agents. And it may even be sensible when it's done to ensure role models, such as professional and college athletes, don't abuse narcotics. 6

But it wastes money and violates rights when forced upon thousands of youngsters. 7

Vernonia began its program mostly because of increased disciplinary problems. 8

But school officials chose not to focus on the problem kids. They lassoed mostly innocent ones. Of 500 students tested in 4 1/2 years, a mere 12 tested positive, not many for a district claiming huge problems. 9

And who paid for the willy-nilly testing? Not local folks, but deficit-riddled Uncle Sam through the federal drug-free schools program. Vernonia's cut: $7,500 a year. 10

History shows there's a fairer way. Teen drug use was cut substantially during the 1980s, not because a few schools tested students for drugs but because most taught students the dangers of abuse and involved parents in their programs. 11

Schools should do the same today. They should call parents of kids suspected of drug use and get permission for any testing. 12

That would save money, focus the drug fight on those causing problems and not invade the privacy of innocent kids whose only crime is trying out for a sport. 13

Deduction in "Drug Tests Fail Schools"

As you have learned, deduction moves from general to specific. The process starts with a general statement, to which a specific case or example is applied. Then, a conclusion is drawn from these two. Here's how deduction works in "Drug Tests Fail Schools":

General statement: Drug testing should be permitted only to protect public safety or to ensure that role models don't abuse drugs (paragraph 6).
Specific case or example: Forcing students to test for drugs only wastes money and violates rights; it does not protect public safety (paragraph 7).
Conclusion: Therefore, forcing students to take drug tests should be stopped.

Induction in "Drug Tests Fail Schools"

Earlier you read that induction is the basis of the conclusion-and-support method for developing a paper. Support for a conclusion comes in the form of evidence or reasons behind it. Here's how induction works in "Drug Tests Fail Schools":

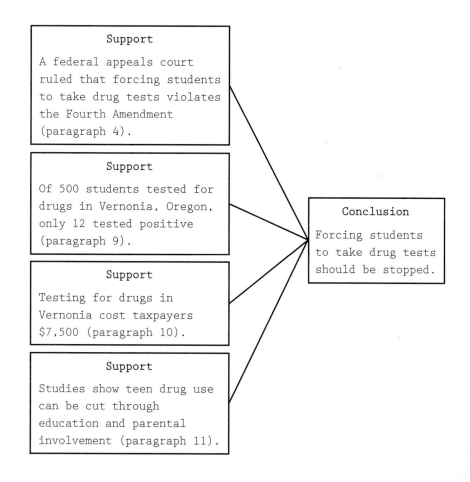

Support

A federal appeals court ruled that forcing students to take drug tests violates the Fourth Amendment (paragraph 4).

Support

Of 500 students tested for drugs in Vernonia, Oregon, only 12 tested positive (paragraph 9).

Support

Testing for drugs in Vernonia cost taxpayers $7,500 (paragraph 10).

Support

Studies show teen drug use can be cut through education and parental involvement (paragraph 11).

Conclusion

Forcing students to take drug tests should be stopped.

REVISING PERSUASION PAPERS

Writing persuasion papers requires logical and clear thinking, but most of all it takes hard work. Barry Glazer, a student whose essay appears in this chapter, wrote several drafts of a paper on individual rights before he arrived at a version with which he was satisfied. His rough draft contained the germ of an idea and several good examples, but by the time Glazer wrote his final draft, the paper had been transformed into a first-rate opinion paper. Indeed, even the title had changed.

Glazer—Rough Draft

It Ain't Nobody's Business but My Own

**Help?
In what
way?** Government is supposed to help people, not hurt them. Those we elect to public office are there to make things better for everyone. However, many of them are doing

**What kinds
of things?** things that annoy and frighten me. If I am not hurting anybody, the government should stay out of my private

**Expand?
Clarify?** affairs. What I do, if it isn't causing anyone else harm, is no one's business but my own.

**Support
this
claim!** If I have a terminal disease, I should be allowed to kill myself or get a doctor to help me do so.

**They don't?
Support this
claim!** If I am driving home late at night the police have no right to stop me just because I am young and look suspicious. Recently, I was walking around the block at three in the morning and the police stopped and questioned me. Yet, all I was doing was taking a late-night stroll.

. . . .

**What
kinds of
things?** Yes, we need government to take care of important things. But the government and the police should stay out of people's lives when it is none of their business. They should just leave us alone.

Glazer—Final Draft

The Right to Be Let Alone] **Revises title**

Appeals to authority
Government is the instrument of the people, says the United States Constitution. Those to whom the people entrust power are charged with maintaining justice, promoting the general welfare, and securing the blessings of liberty for us all.

Explains how government "is supposed to help people"

Explains what he meant by 'things that annoy and frighten me"
Recent newspaper opinion polls, however, suggest that many Americans are dissatisfied with the men and women running our communities, our states, and our nation. More and more of us have come to believe that our leaders are isolated from the realities ordinary people face. We fear we are losing control.

Instead of helping to alleviate this feeling of impotence, however, politicians and bureaucrats continue to make and enforce regulations that constrain our lives and constrict our freedoms. To help people regain a rightful measure of control, government—¶ whether national, state, or local—¶ should stay out of our private lives whenever possible.

Appeals to authority
As Supreme Court Justice Louis Brandeis noted, Americans treasure their "right to be let alone."

Supports claim with convincing details
There is no reason for the government to interfere in our lives if our behavior does not adversely affect others or if there is no immediate necessity for such interference. Were I in the painful throes of terminal cancer or facing the horror of Alzheimer's Disease, I

Appeals to emotions

should be allowed to kill myself. Faced with the

agonizing degeneration of my memory and personality, I would probably want to end my life in my own way. But the government says this is illegal. Indeed, were I to call upon a doctor to assist me on this final quest, she would stand a good chance of being charged with murder.

Supports claim by appealing to authority

The government should also stay out of an individual's life if there is no reason to believe he is doing wrong. The Bill of Rights protects us from unlawful searches and seizures. Yet, if I drive home from work in the early morning, I stand a reasonable chance of being stopped without cause at a police roadblock.

Appeals to readers' self-interest and personal values

While armed, uniformed officers shine flashlights in my face, I can be subjected to questions about my destination and point of origin. I can be told to produce my papers and to step out of my car. I can be made to endure the embarrassment of performing tricks to prove my sobriety.

Appeals to emotions

Allowing the police such powers is hardly in keeping with our government's mission to promote justice, security, and liberty.

. . . .

Supports preceding statement

Clearly, government is a necessity. Without it, we would face anarchy. Yet, those who roam the halls of power should remember from where their power originates and should find ways to reduce the burden of unnecessary regulations heaped on the backs of the American people.

Appeals to emotions

PRACTICING STRATEGIES FOR PERSUASION

1. **Practice Deduction**: Read each of the following general statements. Then, think of a specific case or example that applies to it. Next, draw a conclusion from the two. Write your responses in the spaces provided.

   a. General statement: Students who have had three years of high school mathematics can enroll in Math 101.

   Specific case:_____

   _____

   _____

   Conclusion:_____

   _____

   b. General statement: Students who commute to the college by car must buy parking decals.

   Specific case:_____

   _____

   _____

   Conclusion:_____

   _____

   c. General statement: Cars more than five years old must be inspected once per year.

   Specific case:_____

   _____

   _____

   Conclusion:_____

   _____

   d. General statement: People whose families have a history of heart disease should have annual coronary examinations.

   Specific case:_____

   _____

   _____

Conclusion:_____

_____

e. General statement: People who don't vote should not complain about the way government is run.

Specific case:_____

_____

_____

Conclusion:_____

_____

2. **Practice Induction:** Read each of the supportive statements below. Then, using induction, draw a general conclusion from it. Write that conclusion in the spaces provided.

a. Support: None of the restaurants on the east side of town offers meals for under $30.
Support: The east side is full of luxury high-rise apartment buildings.
Support: The east side has no discount clothing, drug, or grocery stores.

Conclusion: _____

_____

_____

b. Support: Students who attend Prof. Villa's class regularly have a good chance of passing her tests.
Support: Prof. Villa encourages students to come to her office for extra help.
Support: Prof. Villa's assignments are clear and practical.

Conclusion:_____

_____

_____

c. Support: The lock on the door had been broken.
Support: I couldn't find my jewelry.
Support: Furniture, pictures, and pillows in the living room had been moved.

Conclusion:_____

_____

_____

d. Support: Serena seemed to drag herself into the apartment and turned on the light.

Support: There were circles under her eyes.

Support: In about five minutes, the apartment was dark again.

Conclusion:_____

_____

_____

e. Support: Miguel Hernandez plans to attend medical school after getting his bachelor's degree in biology.

Support: His sister wants to become a dentist.

Support: His brother is enrolled in a five-year program in architecture.

Conclusion:_____

_____

_____

In the last few pages, you have read a lot about how to write persuasively. As with all kinds of writing, the most important ingredient in persuasion is your knowledge of the subject. Think of yourself as a lawyer. To argue a case or defend a client effectively, you will need to know the evidence well. Otherwise, you will have a hard time convincing judge or jury. Wise readers approach new opinions cautiously. Some will be open to persuasion. Others may even be eager to accept your point of view. But all will expect you to present evidence logically, clearly, and convincingly before they make your opinions their own.

The Right to Be Let Alone

Barry Glazer

Barry Glazer became interested in writing when he enrolled in a basic-skills composition class during his first semester in college. He went on to major in history and English, to become editor of his college newspaper, and to take a bachelor's degree. He now directs a tutoring program for developing writers and is planning to start a career in teaching after completing his studies in graduate school.

LOOKING AHEAD

1. This essay is logical, clear, and well developed, but it goes beyond pure argument and often appeals to the emotions.
2. Glazer organizes his work around three principles by which he would restrict the government's ability to interfere with our lives. Identify these principles as you read "The Right to Be Let Alone."
3. Louis Brandeis, mentioned in paragraph 2, was associate justice of the United States Supreme Court (1916–1939). He was a champion of individual rights.

VOCABULARY

adversely	Negatively.
alleviate	Reduce, lessen, relieve.
anarchy	Chaos, disorder, lawlessness.
bureaucrats	Government officials.
constrain	Restrain, hold in check, bind.
constrict	Bind, choke, squeeze.
endure	Suffer, bear, submit to.
entrust	Give to for safekeeping.
impotence	Lack of power.
reflect	Think.
refrain from	Stop, cease, avoid.
throes	Agony, pain.

The Right to Be Let Alone
Barry Glazer

Government is the instrument of the people, says the United States Constitu- 1
tion. Those to whom the people entrust power are charged with maintaining
justice, promoting the general welfare, and securing the blessings of liberty for us all.
Recent newspaper opinion polls, however, suggest that many Americans are dissatisfied
with the men and women running our communities, our states, and our nation. More
and more of us have come to believe that our leaders are isolated from the realities ordinary people face. We fear we are losing control.

Instead of helping to alleviate this feeling of impotence, however, politicians and 2
bureaucrats continue to make and enforce regulations that constrain our lives and constrict our freedoms. To help people regain a rightful measure of control, government—
whether national, state, or local—should stay out of our private lives whenever possible.
As Supreme Court Justice Louis Brandeis noted, Americans treasure their "right to be let
alone."

There is no reason for the government to interfere in our lives if our behavior does 3
not adversely affect others or if there is no immediate necessity for such interference.
Were I in the painful throes of terminal cancer or facing the horror of Alzheimer's disease, I should be allowed to kill myself. Faced with the agonizing degeneration of my
memory and personality, I would probably want to end my life in my own way. But the
government says this is illegal. Indeed, were I to call upon a doctor to assist me on this
final quest, she would stand a good chance of being charged with murder.

The government should also stay out of an individual's life if there is no reason to 4
believe he is doing wrong. The Bill of Rights protects us from unlawful searches and
seizures. Yet if I drive home from work in the early morning, I stand a reasonable chance
of being stopped without cause at a police roadblock. While armed, uniformed officers
shine flashlights in my face, I can be subjected to questions about my destination and
point of origin. I can be told to produce my papers and to step out of my car. I can be
made to endure the embarrassment of performing tricks to prove my sobriety. Allowing
the police such powers is hardly in keeping with our government's mission to promote
justice, security, and liberty.

Finally, the government should refrain from creating unnecessary burdens for the 5
American people. It should stay out of a person's private business if such involvement
burdens the individual unnecessarily or unfairly. Recently, my faithful dog Linda was
dying. Because of years of abuse at the hands of her previous owner, she was no longer
able to walk and had to be carried in my arms. At that time, the dog warden knocked on
my door and threatened me with fines for my continued refusal to license the animal.
When I told him that Linda was unable to walk, let alone leave my property, he threatened to return with the police.

Similarly, when I wanted to convert my garage into a den, I was overwhelmed by 6
official red tape. The cost of construction permits and of measures to meet complex
building codes cost more than the lumber, wall board, and other supplies for the project. Another example of governmental red tape became evident when I attempted to
enroll in a Japanese language course at a community college. I was told the state

required that I take a mathematics placement test or pass a course in elementary algebra first!

Clearly, government is a necessity. Without it, we would face anarchy. Yet those 7 who roam the halls of power should remember from where their power originates and should find ways to reduce the burden of unnecessary regulations heaped on the backs of the American people.

QUESTIONS FOR DISCUSSION

1. What one sentence in this essay best expresses Glazer's purpose and central idea?
2. In Looking Ahead, you learned that the author defends three principles by which he would limit government interference. What are these principles?
3. What method of development does Glazer rely on most?
4. Pick out vocabulary that appeals to the readers' emotions.
5. Why does Glazer bother to tell that Justice Brandeis is the source of the quotation in paragraph 2 (and of the essay's title)?
6. Find examples of deductive and inductive reasoning in this essay.
7. Where does the author address an argument that an opponent might use to dispute his?

THINKING CRITICALLY

1. What side would Barry Glazer take in the debate over mandatory testing of school-age athletes as expressed in "Drug Tests Fail Schools" and "Fight Drug Use with Tests"? Support your answer with reference to "The Right to Be Let Alone" and these other two selections.
2. Read or reread "The Militiaman, the Yuppie, and Me" in Chapter 14. Then imagine what Glazer might argue in regard to the gun-control issue.

SUGGESTIONS FOR JOURNAL ENTRIES

1. Glazer calls up several examples from experiences similar to those you or people like you might have had. Use focused freewriting to narrate an incident that explains how a government rule or regulation interferes with the right of privacy. Interpret the word "government" broadly; write about the federal, state, local, or college regulation you most disagree with. You might even address a rule followed by your family, your athletic team, or other group to which you belong.
2. Play the role of Glazer's opponent by responding to at least one of the examples he uses to support his thesis. Explain why requiring licenses for all dogs is reasonable; why strict building codes are important; why the police should have the right to stop and question drivers without cause; why doctors should not be allowed to help terminally ill patients commit suicide; or why states should set academic standards in public colleges.
3. Even if you agree with Glazer, you may know of instances in which people welcome government "interference." List as many examples of such beneficial interference as you can.

Fight Drug Use with Tests

Rob Teir

This opinion piece appeared as an opposing view to "Drug Tests Fail Schools" in USA Today on March 28, 1995. The author represents the American Alliance for Rights and Responsibilities.

LOOKING AHEAD

1. In order to fully appreciate what Teir is saying, review "Drug Tests Fail Schools," which appears in this chapter's introduction. Then, as you read "Fight Drug Use with Tests," look for places where Teir responds to arguments from that other essay.
2. Look for examples of both inductive and deductive thinking in Teir's essay.

VOCABULARY

adolescent	A youngster, juvenile.
deter	Discourage, prevent.
enhancing	Improving.
integrity	Soundness, wholeness, righteousness.
intrusions	Invasions, infringements.
steroids	Dangerous drugs taken by some athletes to increase strength and performance.
susceptible	Open to, vulnerable to.

Fight Drug Use with Tests

Rob Teir

Participation in high school sports is not a constitutional right. Rather, it is a 1
privilege, paid for by taxpayers, open to students who promise to meet certain conduct requirements on and off the field. One of these promises is to refrain from using drugs.

Drug use is a serious problem among high school students. Studies show that as 2
many as 500,000 high school students use muscle-pumping, life-destroying substances such as steroids. Many more use illegal drugs, which cause discipline problems and set the stage for lifelong addictions.

Drug testing works to deter and identify use. That is why drug testing is required to 3
compete in the Olympics, the National Collegiate Athletic Association and the National Football League. Since drug testing was instituted by these organizations, use of performance-enhancing drugs has been greatly reduced. We should want nothing less in schools.

Indeed, many athletes support testing programs, and no wonder. Without testing, 4
athletes have to choose between drug use and a competitive disadvantage on the field.

Those who challenge the need for drug testing may be forgetting what it is like to be 5
an adolescent. Peer pressure is enormous, and one of the few effective counterweights is the fear of being caught. More importantly, once drug use is identified, a school can reach out to the student before he or she gets addicted—or arrested.

Because of the incredible demands to perform well, high school athletes, like those 6
in college, are particularly susceptible to the temptations of drugs. Athletes are also role models for other students, who agree to all kinds of intrusions on their privacy, including sharing locker rooms and undergoing complete physical exams. Neither drug testing nor these requirements violate the Fourth Amendment.

For 25 years, public schools have been run by federal judges and civil libertarians, 7
with results everyone can see. It is time to return decisions on how to run public schools to locally accountable officials.

There is nothing unconstitutional about asking those who gain the advantages of 8
school-sponsored athletics to contribute to the safety of other players, the integrity of the game and their own well-being. The Supreme Court should leave these programs alone.

QUESTIONS FOR DISCUSSION

1. Teir uses deduction in paragraph 1. What is his general statement? What specific case or example does he apply to it?
2. What is the implied conclusion he draws from paragraph 1?
3. Where is inductive thinking evident in this essay?
4. You learned earlier that several methods of development can be applied to persuasion. Where does Teir use comparison?
5. What attempt does the author make to answer opposing arguments? Is he convincing?
6. What is Teir driving at in paragraph 7 when he mentions "results everyone can see"?

THINKING CRITICALLY

1. Teir and the author of "Drug Tests Fail Schools" disagree on a number of fundamental points. What are those points? Look especially at paragraphs 6 and 8 in "Fight Drug Use with Tests."
2. Use the double-entry notebook method discussed in "Getting Started" to analyze each of the paragraphs in this essay. As you recall, this method involves drawing a line down the center of a piece of notebook paper, then summarizing the author's comments on the left and recording your response to those comments on the right.
3. How did the U.S. Supreme Court finally rule on this issue? Find and read newspaper reports of the court's decision (late June, 1995) in your college library.

SUGGESTIONS FOR JOURNAL ENTRIES

1. How do you stand on the issue of testing school athletes for drugs? Write a paragraph that expresses your opinion. If you like, use direct quotations from "Drug Tests Fail Schools" or "Fight Drug Use with Tests" or both.
2. Make two lists—one of arguments for, the other of arguments against—a college, state, national, or world issue important to you. You can brainstorm with two or three friends to generate ideas. Here are examples of the kinds of issues you might address:

   • Testing drivers for drugs or alcohol via random highway spot-checks.
   • Testing pilots, bus drivers, and other public-transportation operators for drugs or alcohol.
   • Testing health workers for HIV or other infectious diseases.

- Denying additional welfare support to unwed mothers after they have had their first child.
- Raising tuitions so that colleges can hire and keep qualified faculty, buy needed equipment, and maintain first-rate facilities.
- Requiring non-science or non-engineering majors to complete courses in math and science in order to graduate from college.

The Media's Image of Arabs

Jack G. Shaheen

Jack Shaheen's parents came to the United States from Lebanon, a country with a large Arabic population. Although he focuses on the stereotype through which the American media pictures Arabs, Shaheen helps us understand the danger in all stereotyping regardless of the group. This essay first appeared in Newsweek *in 1988.*

L OOKING AHEAD

1. In paragraph 3, Shaheen creates an analogy by calling TV wrestling "that great American morality play." Used in the Middle Ages to teach people morality, such plays portrayed the forces of good and of evil battling for possession of someone's soul.
2. In paragraph 5, Shaheen asks if it is "easier for a camel to go through the eye of a needle" than for the media to portray Arabs fairly. This is a variation on the New Testament's "It is easier for a camel to pass through the eye of a needle than for one who is rich to enter the kingdom of God."
3. The Semites, mentioned in paragraph 8, are people of the eastern Mediterranean; both Jews and Arabs are Semites. At the end of this paragraph, Shaheen asks that we "retire the stereotypical Arab to a media Valhalla." In Nordic mythology, Valhalla was a heaven to which warriors killed in battle were sent.

V OCABULARY

caricatures	Images or pictures that exaggerate and poke fun at the subject's features or qualities.
cliché	Saying so overused it becomes boring and often meaningless.
conspires	Schemes, connives.
deplore	Criticize, lament.
mosques	Muslim houses of worship.
neutralize	Act as balance to, counteract.
nurtures	Feeds, nourishes.
prevail	Predominate, command our attention.
swarthy	Dark-skinned.

The Media's Image of Arabs

Jack G. Shaheen

A merica's bogyman is the Arab. Until the nightly news brought us TV pictures of   1
Palestinian boys being punched and beaten, almost all portraits of Arabs seen in
America were dangerously threatening. Arabs were either billionaires or bombers—
rarely victims. They were hardly ever seen as ordinary people practicing law, driving
taxis, singing lullabies or healing the sick. Though TV news may portray them more
sympathetically now, the absence of positive media images nurtures suspicion and
stereotype. As an Arab-American, I have found that ugly caricatures have had an enduring impact on my family.

I was sheltered from prejudicial portraits at first. My parents came from Lebanon in   2
the 1920s; they met and married in America. Our home in the steel city of Clairton, PA,
was a center for ethnic sharing—black, white, Jew and gentile. There was only one
major source of media images then, at the State movie theater where I was lucky enough
to get a part-time job as an usher. But in the late 1940s, Westerns and war movies were
popular, not Middle Eastern dramas. Memories of World War II were fresh, and the
screen heavies were the Japanese and the Germans. True to the cliché of the times, the
only good Indian was a dead Indian. But when I mimicked or mocked the bad guys, my
mother cautioned me. She explained that stereotypes blur our vision and corrupt the
imagination. "Have compassion for all people, Jackie," she said. "This way, you'll learn
to experience the joy of accepting people as they are, and not as they appear in films.
Stereotypes hurt."

Mother was right. I can remember the Saturday afternoon when my son, Michael,   3
who was seven, and my daughter, Michele, six, suddenly called out: "Daddy, Daddy,
they've got some bad Arabs on TV." They were watching that great American morality
play, TV wrestling. Akbar the Great, who liked to hear the cracking of bones, and Abdul-
lah the Butcher, a dirty fighter who liked to inflict pain, were pinning their foes with
"camel locks." From that day on, I knew I had to try to neutralize the media caricatures.

It hasn't been easy. With my children, I have watched animated heroes Heckle and   4
Jeckle pull the rug from under "Ali Boo-Boo, the Desert Rat," and Laverne and Shirley
stop "Sheik Ha-Mean-Ie" from conquering "the U.S. and the world." I have read comic
books like the "Fantastic Four" and "G.I. Combat" whose characters have sketched
Arabs as "lowlifes" and "human hyenas." Negative stereotypes were everywhere. A dictionary informed my youngsters that an Arab is a "vagabond, drifter, hobo and vagrant."
Whatever happened, my wife wondered, to Aladdin's good genie?

To a child, the world is simple: good versus evil. But my children and others with   5
Arab roots grew up without ever having seen a humane Arab on the silver screen, someone to pattern their lives after. Is it easier for a camel to go through the eye of a needle
than for a screen Arab to appear as a genuine human being?

Hollywood producers must have an instant Ali Baba kit that contains scimitars,   6
veils, sunglasses and such Arab clothing as *chadors* and *kufiyahs*. In the mythical "Ay-
rabland," oil wells, tents, mosques, goats and shepherds prevail. Between the sand
dunes, the camera focuses on a mock-up of a palace from "Arabian Nights"—or a military air base. Recent movies suggest that Americans are at war with Arabs, forgetting

the fact that out of 21 Arab nations, America is friendly with 19 of them. And in "Wanted Dead or Alive," a movie that starred Gene Simmons, the leader of the rock group Kiss, the war comes home when an Arab terrorist comes to the United States dressed as a rabbi and, among other things, conspires with Arab-Americans to poison the people of Los Angeles. The movie was released last year.

The Arab remains American culture's favorite whipping boy. In his memoirs, Terrel 7 Bell, Ronald Reagan's first secretary of education, writes about an "apparent bias among mid-level, right-wing staffers at the White House" who dismissed Arabs as "sand niggers." Sadly, the racial slurs continue. At a recent teacher's conference, I met a woman from Sioux Falls, S.D., who told me about the persistence of discrimination. She was in the process of adopting a baby when an agency staffer warned her that the infant had a problem. When she asked whether the child was mentally ill, or physically handicapped, there was silence. Finally, the worker said: "The baby is Jordanian."

To me, the Arab demon of today is much like the Jewish demon of yesterday. We 8 deplore the false portrait of Jews as a swarthy menace. Yet a similar portrait has been accepted and transferred to another group of Semites—the Arabs. Print and broadcast journalists have started to challenge this stereotype. They are now revealing more humane images of Palestinian Arabs, a people who traditionally suffered from the myth that Palestinian equals terrorist. Others could follow that lead and retire the stereotypical Arab to a media Valhalla.

It would be a step in the right direction if movie and TV producers developed char- 9 acters modeled after real-life Arab-Americans. We could then see a White House correspondent like Helen Thomas, whose father came from Lebanon, in "The Golden Girls," a heart surgeon patterned after Dr. Michael DeBakey on "St. Elsewhere," or a Syrian-American playing tournament chess like Yasser Seirawan, the Seattle grandmaster.

Politicians, too, should speak out against the cardboard caricatures. They should 10 refer to Arabs as friends, not just as moderates. And religious leaders could state that Islam like Christianity and Judaism maintains that all mankind is one family in the care of God. When all imagemakers rightfully begin to treat Arabs and all other minorities with respect and dignity, we may begin to unlearn our prejudices.

QUESTIONS FOR
DISCUSSION

1. Shaheen draws the evidence for his argument from personal experience, observation, and reading. Identify examples of information that come from each of these sources.
2. Why does the author tell us that "the Arab demon of today is much like the Jewish demon of yesterday" (paragraph 8)? What other comparison does he make, and how does it contribute to his argument?
3. Why does he recall what his mother said when he "mimicked or mocked the bad guys" (paragraph 2) of movies in the 1940s?
4. As you learned in Looking Ahead, paragraph 3 contains an analogy. In what other paragraph does the author place an analogy?
5. Shaheen could have directed his remarks to Arab-American readers, but he chose to address a far more comprehensive audience. How do we know that?
6. Is this selection pure argument, or does it appeal to the emotions as well? Explain.
7. Shaheen concludes by asking politicians and religious leaders to speak out against negative stereotyping. Is his ending appropriate to an essay that criticizes the media?

THINKING CRITICALLY

1. This essay was written several years ago. Is its message still current? As you begin thinking, recall that immediately after the bombing of the federal building in Oklahoma City in 1995, some law enforcement officials and members of the media speculated that this was the work of Arab terrorists. In a few days, of course, the world learned conclusively that no one of Arab nationality or descent had anything to do with it.
2. Shaheen attacks the media, at least on its portrayal of Arabs. On what issues would *you* criticize the television, movie, or music industries? On what issues might you applaud them?

SUGGESTIONS FOR
JOURNAL ENTRIES

1. Describe the way movies, television, music videos, radio, billboards, newspapers, and popular magazines portray a particular ethnic group. Is the portrait of this group flattering or negative? Examples of a group you might write about include African-Americans, Jews, Hispanics, Native Americans, Asian Indians, Chinese, Poles, Hungarians, Russians, Scandinavians, Italians, or even white Anglo-Saxon Protestants. Good ways to gather details for this journal entry are focused freewriting and brainstorming.

2. Not all stereotyping is based on race, religion, or ethnic background. Members of certain occupations—police officers and politicians, for example—sometimes suffer from bad media images. As a matter of fact, some of the worst stereotyping is based on age, sex, or sexual preference. Think about a group of people—other than a racial, religious, or ethnic group—that you think suffers from an unfair and inaccurate media image. Use focused freewriting or listing to gather examples of the way these people are portrayed on television, in movies, and so forth. Groups you might want to choose from:

Housewives	Secretaries
Teachers	Factory workers
Beauticians	Bachelors
Senior citizens	College students
Homosexuals	Husbands
Grandparents	Intellectuals
Scientists	Athletes
Auto mechanics	Nurses
Musicians	Single women

The Decline and Fall of Teaching History

Diane Ravitch

Diane Ravitch teaches at Columbia University's Teachers College and, with Chester E. Finn, wrote What Do Our 17-Year-Olds Know? *Ravitch and Finn believe the teaching of literature and history needs significant improvement. One of their suggestions is that all high school students complete at least two years of world history. As you learned in the introduction to this chapter, Ravitch argues that, without an increased emphasis on the study of history, American voters will find it harder and harder to make the independent and informed judgments required to keep our democracy strong.*

Looking Ahead

1. The essay's title recalls Edward Gibbon's *The History of the Decline and Fall of the Roman Empire*, written in the eighteenth century.
2. Ravitch establishes her expertise by presenting results of a nationwide study she conducted. She also relies on the expert testimony of other college history professors, whose opinions she quotes directly.
3. This selection uses methods to write effective introductions that you probably read about in Chapter 4. Look for them in the first two paragraphs.

Vocabulary

abysmal	Terribly low and empty (like a huge pit or cavern).
assessment	Evaluation.
causation	Relationship between causes and effects, study of why events occur.
chronology	History, series of events in time.
civics	Study of how government works.
collaboration	Cooperation, joint effort.
derives	Issues or originates from.
eminent	Famous, important, distinguished.
evolved	Developed, grew.
indifference	Lack of interest.
perspective	Point of view, way of looking at something.
premise	Principle or assumption upon which actions, ideas, or other principles are based.
sequenced	In an order, in a continuous series.
vocational	Occupational.

The Decline and
Fall of Teaching
History   *Diane Ravitch*

During the past generation, the amount of time devoted to historical studies in   1
American public schools has steadily decreased. About 25 years ago, most public high-school youths studied one year of world history and one of American history,
but today, most study only one year of ours. In contrast, the state schools of many other
Western nations require the subject to be studied almost every year. In France, for
example, all students, not just the college-bound, follow a carefully sequenced program
of history, civics and geography every year from the seventh grade through the twelfth
grade.

Does it matter if Americans are ignorant of their past? Does it matter if the general   2
public knows little of the individuals, the events and the movements that shaped our
nation? The fundamental premise of our democratic form of government is that political
power derives from the informed consent of the people. Informed consent requires a
citizenry that is rational and knowledgeable. If our system is to remain free and democratic, citizens should know not only how to judge candidates and their competing
claims but how our institutions evolved. An understanding of history does not lead
everyone to the same conclusions, but it does equip people with the knowledge to reach
independent judgments on current issues. Without historical perspective, voters are
more likely to be swayed by emotional appeals, by stirring commercials, or by little more
than a candidate's good looks or charisma.

Because of my interest as a historian of education in the condition of the study of   3
history, I have been involved during the last year, in collaboration with the National
Assessment of Educational Progress, in planning a countrywide study of what 17-year-
olds know about American history. In addition, my contacts with college students during the last year and discussions with other historians have led me to believe that there
is cause for concern.

On the college lecture circuit this past year, I visited some 30 campuses, ranging   4
from large public universities to small private liberal-arts colleges. Repeatedly, I was
astonished by questions from able students about the most elementary facts of American
history. At one urban Minnesota university, none of the 30 students in a course on ethnic relations had ever heard of the Supreme Court's Brown v. Board of Education decision of 1954, which held racial segregation in public schools unconstitutional. At a university in the Pacific Northwest, a professor of education publicly insisted that
high-school students should concentrate on vocational preparation and athletics, since
they had the rest of their lives to learn subjects like history "on their own time."

The shock of encountering college students who did not recognize the names of emi-   5
nent figures like Jane Addams or W.E.B. Du Bois led me to conduct an informal, unscien-
tific survey of professors who teach history to undergraduates. "My students are not stu-
pid, but they have an abysmal background in American, or any other kind of, history,"
said Thomas Kessner, who teaches American history at Kingsborough Community College
in Brooklyn. "They never heard of Daniel Webster; don't understand the Constitution;
don't know the difference between the Republican and Democratic parties."

This gloomy assessment was echoed by Naomi Miller, chairman of the history 6
department at Hunter College in New York. "My students have no historical knowledge
on which to draw when they enter college," she said. "They have no point of reference
for understanding World War I, the Treaty of Versailles or the Holocaust." More than
ignorance of the past, however, she finds an indifference to dates and chronology or
causation. "They think that everything is subjective. They have plenty of attitudes and
opinions, but they lack the knowledge to analyze a problem." Professor Miller believes
that "we are in danger of bringing up a generation without historical memory. This is a
dangerous situation."

QUESTIONS FOR DISCUSSION

1. What does the author mean by "informed consent," and why is learning history important to keeping our system of government "free and democratic"?
2. In the introduction to this chapter, you learned that Ravitch uses deductive reasoning. You also learned that writers often use both deduction and induction in the same piece. Find an example of inductive reasoning in this essay.
3. In several instances, the author relies on the testimony of experts to support her thesis. However, the professor of education quoted in paragraph 4 opposes her point of view. Why does she bother to quote this person?
4. The words of her colleagues provide the author with examples that show how little some students know about history. Are these examples convincing? Why or why not?
5. Where does Ravitch use rhetorical questions? Where does she use contrast? How do such techniques help her achieve her purpose?
6. This essay contains clear thinking and convincing logic. Does it ever appeal to our emotions?
7. Is the introduction effective? Why or why not?

THINKING CRITICALLY

1. What can you say to dispute the claim that students should learn history "on their own time"? What, if anything, can you say to support this claim?
2. Reread paragraphs 4, 5, and 6. Make sure you fully understand all of the historical allusions (references) they contain. If not, look them up in an encyclopedia or other library reference tool.

SUGGESTIONS FOR JOURNAL ENTRIES

1. Other than history, what do you think high school and college students should learn more about? Rely on your own experiences, brainstorm with a few classmates, or interview one or two professors to compile a list of the academic subjects or skills with which young people should become more familiar. Then, briefly list reasons students should study or practice each of them.
2. A strong democracy relies on the "informed consent" of its people, Ravitch believes. Given the important political and social concerns of our day, what specific problems or issues do you think American voters should be reading and learning more about? Mention the three or four you believe are most important; then, briefly explain and defend your choices. In other words, include a few details that might convince others they should be as concerned about these issues as you are.

SUGGESTIONS FOR SUSTAINED WRITING

1. Like Barry Glazer, many of us have strong opinions about the right of privacy. Perhaps you discussed some of your own in your journal after reading "The Right to Be Let Alone."

   Write an essay arguing that some government regulations interfere unnecessarily with the way we live. Use examples of federal, state, or local laws you think limit our freedom. If you interpret the word "government" broadly, you can even focus on rules enforced by your college, your family, or another group to which you belong.

   One way to introduce this essay is to show readers that you are reasonable. Begin by admitting that some rules are necessary and should be fully enforced. For example, voice your support for tough laws against child abuse, rape, and drunk driving. At the end of your introduction, however, state your thesis forcefully: explain that some rules enforced by the government, by your family, or by another group are inappropriate and should be abolished. Then, like Glazer, develop your essay with examples from your experiences or from those of people you know or have read about.

   Read your first draft carefully, adding detail as you go along to make your opinions clear and convincing. In later drafts, try including language and information that appeal to the readers' emotions. Then, edit your work thoroughly.

2. Read "The Right to Be Let Alone" again. Then, write an essay in which you play Glazer's opponent. Argue that, while some government regulations are inappropriate, the ones he criticizes should be strictly enforced.

   One way to organize your paper is to defend the regulations Glazer attacks in the same order he presented them. As such, you might outline the body of your essay like this:

   Terminally ill patients should not have the right to commit suicide.
   Police have the right to stop and question motorists at random.
   Pets should be licensed.
   Strict building codes are necessary.
   Colleges should enforce academic requirements.

   Develop each of these points in concrete and convincing detail using any of the methods mentioned earlier in this chapter. After completing several drafts, write a conclusion that restates your thesis or that uses one of the methods for closing explained in Chapter 4. As always, be sure your final draft is organized and edited well.

3. If you responded to journal Suggestion 2 after Teir's "Fight Drug Use with Tests," you have probably gathered information about two sides of a question that you find interesting and important. Read your notes carefully. Then, add information you might have learned since making your journal entries.

Now, turn your notes into the rough draft of an essay that argues for only one side of that question. As you learned earlier, it is often a good idea to address opposing arguments before expressing your own views. You can do this by exposing those arguments as unsupported, illogical, or untrue; or you can admit that they have some value while arguing that yours make even better sense. Either way, begin by discussing and dismissing opposing arguments. Then, devote the bulk of your essay to supporting your own point of view.

Revise your paper several times, adding information as needed, and make sure your opinion is clear, logical, and well supported. Conclude your work on this project with meticulous editing and proofreading.

4. If you responded to Shaheen's "The Media's Image of Arabs" in your journal, you may have begun discussing the way television, radio, movies, magazines, and the like portray a particular group. Express your reaction to this treatment in a preliminary thesis statement for a persuasive essay. Depending upon the details you have already gathered, you might write a preliminary thesis like this:

> Green-haired carpenters can expect nothing but ridicule from the media.

Now, draft an essay containing three or four detailed illustrations of what you mean. For instance, discuss magazines, movies, television shows and commercials, and billboard advertisements in which "green-haired carpenters" are ridiculed. End your essay like Shaheen ends his: offer the media advice about how to correct its stereotype of the people you have discussed.

As you rewrite your paper, add details and revise your thesis statement as needed. Edit your best draft for problems in grammar and mechanics.

5. Write a letter to the producers or sponsors of a television show you think unfairly stereotypes people on the basis of age, race, religion, nationality, profession, gender, or sexual preference. Analyze various episodes of the show. Provide details about the characters, plots, dialogue, and issues presented to support your view that the group in question is being treated unfairly.

Then, persuade your readers to make some changes. You can start with the logical approach. For example, explain that many people no longer tolerate unfair stereotyping and that continuing this practice will reduce the show's viewing audience. However, you can also appeal to your readers' sense of fairness and responsibility. Like Shaheen, for example, you might explain that, as "imagemakers," they have an important role in molding the character of our society.

As you go through the process of writing, rewriting, and polishing, make sure to provide evidence and use language that will persuade your readers to change their approach. You might find useful materials in the journal entries you made after reading Shaheen's "The Media's Image of Arabs."

6. The first suggestion for a journal entry after Ravitch's "The Decline and Fall of Teaching History" asked you to name skills or subjects other than history that students should learn more about. Now, gather more information about the subject or skill in your list that you believe is most important.

   Turn these notes into a letter or opinion paper for publication in your college or community newspaper. Your purpose is to persuade faculty, students, or anyone interested in education that high school and college curricula should put greater emphasis on the subject or skill you are discussing. Let's say you wish you knew more about music. You can argue that students be required to take courses in music history or appreciation, that more money be budgeted for school bands, and that every student have the chance to learn a musical instrument.

   As you know, a good source of evidence for any persuasive paper is the testimony of experts. You can gather such testimony by interviewing professors on your campus who teach the subject you are discussing or who share your opinion. Of course, you might also draw convincing evidence from your own experiences and from those of classmates.

   Though a reasoned argument may be the best way to approach this assignment, don't rule out an appeal to the emotions as well. For instance, after drafting the body of your paper, write an introduction that uses startling language and information to dramatize the need for the changes you propose. In your conclusion, include vocabulary that will move your readers to action. In any case, revise and edit your work carefully before submitting it for publication.

abstract language   Words that represent ideas rather than things we can see, hear, smell, feel, or taste. The word "love" is abstract, but the word "kiss" is concrete because we can perceive it with one or more of our five senses. (See Chapters 5 and 6.)

allusion   A passing reference to a person, place, event, thing, or idea with which the reader may be familiar. Allusions can be used to add detail, clarify important points, or set the tone of an essay, a poem, or a short story. Allusions can be found in Kuralt's "Wanderlust" (Chapter 10).

analogy   A method by which a writer points out similarities between two things that, on the surface, seem quite different. Analogies are most often used to make abstract or unfamiliar ideas clearer and more concrete. Chapters 3 and 4 contain examples of analogy.

anecdote   A brief, sometimes humorous story used to illustrate or develop a specific point. (See Chapters 9 and 13.)

argument   A type of persuasive writing that relies on logic and concrete evidence to prove a point or support an opinion. (See Chapter 16.)

central idea   The idea that conveys a writer's main point about a subject. It may be stated explicitly or implied. Also known as the "main idea" or "controlling idea," it determines the kinds and amount of detail needed to develop a piece of writing adequately. (See Chapter 1.)

chronological order   The arrangement of material in order of time. (See Section Four.)

coherence   The principle that writers observe in making certain that there are logical connections between the ideas and details in one sentence or paragraph and those in the next. (See Chapter 2.)

conclusion   A paragraph or series of paragraphs that ends an essay. Conclusions often restate the writer's central idea or summarize important points used to develop that idea. (See Chapter 4.) A conclusion can also be defined as a principle, opinion, or belief a writer supports or defends by using convincing information. (See Chapters 3 and 16.)

concrete language   Words that represent material things—things we can perceive with our five senses. (See abstract language above, and see Chapters 5 and 6.)

coordination   A technique used to express ideas of equal importance in the same sentence. To this end, writers often use compound sentences, which are composed of two independent (main) clauses connected with a coordinating conjunction. "Four students earned scholarships, but only three accepted them" is a compound sentence. (See Chapter 7.)

deduction   A kind of reasoning used to build an argument. Deductive thinking draws conclusions by applying specific cases or examples to general principles, rules, or ideas. You would be thinking deductively if you wrote:
All students must pay tuition.
I am a student.
Therefore, I must pay tuition. (See Chapter 16.)

details   Specific facts or pieces of information that a writer uses to develop ideas.

emphasis   The placing of stress on important ideas by controlling sentence structure through coordination, subordination, and parallelism. (See Chapter 7.)

figurative language (figures of speech)   Words or phrases that explain abstract ideas by comparing them to concrete realities the reader will recognize easily. Analogy, metaphor, simile, and personification are types of figurative language. (See Chapter 6.)

image   A verbal picture made up of sensory details. It expresses a general idea's meaning clearly and concretely. (See Chapter 5.)

induction   A kind of reasoning used to build an argument. Inductive thinking draws general conclusions from specific facts or pieces of evidence. If you heard the wind howling, saw the sky turning black, and spotted several ominous clouds on the horizon, you might rightly conclude that a storm was on its way. (See Chapter 16.)

introduction   A paragraph or series of paragraphs that begins an essay. It often contains a writer's central idea in the form of a thesis statement. (See Chapter 4.)

irony   A technique used by writers to communicate the very opposite of what their words mean. Irony is often used to create humor. An effective example of irony can be found in Milden's "So You Want to Flunk Out of College," which appears in the introduction to Chapter 15.

linking pronouns   Pronouns that make reference to nouns that have come before (antecedents). They are one of the ways to maintain coherence in and between paragraphs. (See Chapter 2.)

main point   The point that a writer focuses on in a thesis or topic sentence. (See Chapter 1.)

metaphor   A figure of speech that, like a simile, creates a comparison between two things in order to make the explanation of one of them clearer. Unlike a simile, a metaphor does not use "like" or "as." "The man is a pig" is a metaphor. (See Chapter 6.)

parallelism   A method to express facts and ideas of equal importance in the same sentence and thereby to give them added emphasis. Sentences that are parallel express items of equal importance in the same grammatical form. (See Chapter 7.)

personification   A figure of speech that writers use to discuss animals, plants, and inanimate objects in terms normally associated with human beings: for example, "Our neighborhoods are the *soul* of the city." (See Chapter 6.)

persuasion   A type of writing that supports an opinion, proves a point, or convinces the reader to act. (See Chapters 3 and 16.)

point of view   The perspective from which a narrative is told. Stories that use the first-person point of view are told by a narrator who is involved in the action and who uses words like "I," "me," and "we" to explain what happened. Stories that use the third-person point of view are told by a narrator who may or may not be involved in the action and who uses words like "he," "she," and "they" to explain what happened. (See Chapters 10, 11, and 12.)

simile   A figure of speech that, like a metaphor, compares two things for the sake of clarity and emphasis. Unlike a metaphor, however, a simile uses "like" or "as." "Samantha runs like a deer" is a simile. (See Chapter 6.)

subordination   A technique used to emphasize one idea over another by expressing the more important idea in the sentence's main clause and the other in its subordinate clause. (See Chapter 7.)

thesis statement   A clear and explicit statement of an essay's central idea. It often appears in an introductory paragraph but is sometimes found later in the essay. (See Chapter 1.)

topic sentence   A clear and explicit statement of a paragraph's central idea. (See Chapter 1.)

transitions (connectives)   Words or phrases used to make clear and direct connections between sentences and paragraphs, thereby maintaining coherence. (See Chapter 2.)

unity   The principle that writers observe in making certain that all the information in an essay or paragraph relates directly to the central idea, which is often expressed in a thesis statement or topic sentence. (See Chapter 2.)

ᴀCKNOWLEDGMENTS

ALBRECHT, ERNEST. From "Sawdust" by Ernest Albrecht. Reprinted by permission of the author.

ARONOWITZ, PAUL. "A Brother's Dream" by Paul Aronowitz, *the New York Times Magazine,* January 24, 1988. Copyright © 1988 by The New York Times Company. Reprinted by permission.

BALDWIN, JAMES. From "Sonny's Blues" © 1965 by James Baldwin. Copyright renewed. Collected in *Going to Meet the Man,* published by Vintage Books. Reprinted with the permission of The James Baldwin Estate.

BERRY, WENDELL. Excerpt from "Waste" from *What Are People For?* by Wendell Berry. Copyright © 1990 by Wendell Berry. Reprinted by permission of North Point Press, a division of Farrar, Straus & Giroux, Inc.

BISHOP, ELIZABETH. "Filling Station" from *The Complete Poems* 1927–1979 by Elizabeth Bishop. Copyright © 1983 by Alice Helen Methfessel. Reprinted by permission of Farrar, Straus & Giroux, Inc.

BORLAND, HAL. From "January Wind" and "Hunger Moon" by Hal Borland in *Hal Borland's Twelve Moons of the Year* Reprinted by permission of Frances Collin, Literary Agent. Copyright © 1979 by Barbara Dodge Borland, as executor of the estate of Hal Borland.

BREWTON, BUTLER E. "Rafters" from *Rafters and Other Poems* by Butler E. Brewton. (Basking Ridge, NJ: Sunbelt Books, 1995). Reprinted by permission of the author.

BRITT, SUZANNE. "I Wants To Go To The Prose" from *Newsweek.* Copyright © 1977 by Suzanne Britt. Reprinted by permission.

BURTON, SANDRA. "Condolences, It's a Girl" by Sandra Burton in *Time,* Fall 1990. Copyright © 1990 by Time, Inc. Reprinted by permission.

CARSON, RACHEL L. Excerpt from *The Sea Around Us.* Copyright © 1950, 1951, 1961 by Rachel L. Carson, renewed 1979, 1989 by Roger Christie. Reprinted by permission of Oxford University Press, Inc.

CARVER, RAYMOND. From *Fires* by Raymond Carver, copyright © 1983. Reprinted by permission of Capra Press, Santa Barbara.

CIARDI, JOHN L. "Dawn Watch" from *Manner of Speaking* by John L. Ciardi. Copyright © 1972 Rutgers University Press, New Brunswick, New Jersey. Reprinted by permission of The Ciardi Family Publishing Trust.

CIRILLI, MARIA. "Echoes" by Maria Cirilli. Reprinted by permission of the author.

COUSINS, NORMAN. Reprinted from *Anatomy of an Illness* by Norman Cousins, with the permission of W. W. Norton & Company, Inc. Copyright © 1979 by W. W. Norton & Company, Inc.

COWAN, RUTH SCHWARTZ. "Less Work for Mother?" from *American Heritage of Science and Technology,* Spring 1987. © Forbes Inc., 1992. Reprinted by permission of *American Heritage Magazine,* a division of Forbes, Inc.

COWLEY, MALCOLM. "The View from 80" from *Life,* December 1978. Reprinted by permission of The Estate of Malcolm Cowley.

CULLEN, IDA M. Reprinted by permission of GRM Associates, Inc., Agents for the Estate of Ida M. Cullen. From the book *Color* by Countee Cullen. Copyright © 1925 by Harper & Brothers; copyright renewed 1953 by Ida M. Cullen.

CUTFORTH, RENÉ. From "Padre Blaisdell and the Refugee Children" by René Cutforth in *The Korean Reporter* by Allan Wingate, 1952. Reprinted by permission.

DICKINSON, LYNDA. Excerpt from *Victims of Vanity* by Lynda Dickinson, 1989. Reprinted by permission of Gordon Soules Book Publishers, Inc.

DIGLIO, DEBORAH. "Lessons Learned" by Deborah Diglio. Reprinted by permission of the author.

DI PASQUALE, ANITA. "The Transformation of Maria Fernandez" by Anita Di Pasquale. Reprinted by permission of the author.

di PASQUALE, EMANUEL. "Joy of An Immigrant, a Thanksgiving" and "Old Man Timichenko" copyright © 1989 by Emanuel di Pasquale. ("Joy of an Immigrant" originally published in M.C. Livingston [Ed.], *Thanksgiving Poems.*) Reprinted from *Genesis* by Emanuel di Pasquale, with the permission of BOA Editions, Ltd., 92 Park Ave., Brockport, NY 14420.

DIAZ-TALTY, LOIS. "The Day I Was Fat" by Lois Diaz-Talty. Reprinted by permission of the author.

DILLARD, ANNIE. "In The Jungle" from *Teaching a Stone to Talk* by Annie Dillard. Copyright © 1982 by Annie Dillard. Reprinted by permission of HarperCollins Publishers, Inc.

DOUBILET, DAVID. "Ballet with Stingrays" from *National Geographic,* January 1989. Reprinted by permission of The National Geographic Society.

ELLISON, RALPH. From "Battle Royal" in *Invisible Man* by Ralph Ellison. Copyright © 1947, 1948, 1952 by Ralph Ellison. Copyright renewed 1975, 1976, 1980 by Ralph Ellison. Reprinted by permission of Random House, Inc.

FRANKE, LINDA BIRD. "The Ambivalence of Abortion" by Linda Bird Franke from *the New York TImes,* 1981. Reprinted by permission of the author.

FULGHUM, ROBERT. "I Was Just Wondering" from *All I Really Need to Know I Learned in Kindergarten.* Copyright © 1986, 1988 by Robert Fulghum. Reprinted by permission of Villard Books, a division of Random House, Inc.

GANSBERG, MARTIN. "38 Who Saw Murder Didn't Call the Police" from *the New York Times,* March 17, 1964. Copyright © 1964 by The New York Times Company. Reprinted by permisison.

GARFITT, ROGER. "Bogota, Columbia" by Roger Garfitt from "Notes from Abroad," *Granta Magazine,* Vol. 29, Winter, 1989. Reprinted by permission of Jane Turnbull Literary Agent.

GAYLIN, WILLARD. Excerpt from *The Rage Within,* 1984. © 1984 by Dr. Willard Gaylin. Reprinted by permission of The William Morris Agency, Inc., on behalf of the author.

GLAZER, BARRY. "The Right to Be Let Alone" by Barry Glazer. Reprinted by permission of the author.

GONZALEZ, LOUIS. "Music" by Louis Gonzalez. Reprinted by permission of the author.

GROZA, IRINA. "Growing Up in Rumania" by Irina Groza. Reprinted by permission of the author.

GWINN, MARY ANN. "A Deathly Call of the Wild" from *the Seattle Times*. Reprinted by permission of *the Seattle Times*.

HAMILL, PETE. From *A Drinking Life* by Pete Hamill. Copyright © 1994 by Deidre Enterprise, Inc. By permission of Little, Brown and Company.

HARRIS, SYDNEY J. "How to Keep Air Clean" from *For the Time Being* Copyright © 1972 by Sydney J. Harris. Copyright © 1969, 1970, 1971, 1972 by Publishers-Hall Syndicate. Reprinted by permission of Houghton Mifflin Company. All rights reserved.

HAYDEN, ROBERT. "Those Winter Sundays" is reprinted from *Angle of Ascent* by Robert Hayden with the permission of Liveright Publishing Corporation. Copyright © 1966 by Robert Hayden.

HIGHET, GILBERT. "The Subway Station" from *Talents and Geniuses* by Gilbert Highet. Copyright © 1957 by Gilbert Highet, renewed. Reprinted by permission Curtis Brown Ltd.

HOWARD, PHILIP K. "The Death of Common Sense", as appeared in *The Reader's Digest,* April 1995. From the book *The Death of Commom Sense,* © 1994 by Philip K. Howard. Reprinted with permission of Reader's Digest and Random House, Inc.

JACKSON, SHIRLEY. "Charles" from *The Lottery and Other Stories* by Shirley Jackson. Copyright © 1949 by Shirley Jackson. Copyright renewed © 1977 by Laurence Hyman, Barry Hyman, Mrs. Sarah Webster and Mrs. Joane Schnurer. Reprinted by permission of Farrar, Straus & Giroux, Inc.

KAZIN, ALFRED. Excerpt from "The Kitchen" in *A Walker in the City*, copyright 1951 and renewed 1979 by Alfred Kazin, reprinted by permission of Harcourt Brace & Company.

KELLER, JAMES. "Exile and Return" by James Keller. Reprinted by permission of the author. Kenny, Maurice. "Going Home" from *Between Two Rivers: Selected Poems*. Reprinted by permission of White Pine Press.

KING, JR., MARTIN LUTHER. "I Have A Dream" by Martin Luther King, Jr. Copyright © 1963 by Martin Luther King, Jr. copyright renewed 1991 by Coretta Scott King. Reprinted by arrangement with The Heirs to the Estate of Martin Luther King, Jr., c/o Joan Daves Agency as agent for the proprietor.

KINGSTON, MAXINE HONG. From *The Woman Warrior* by Maxine Hong Kingston. Copyright 1975, 1976 by Maxine Hong Kingston. Reprinted by permission of Alfred A. Knopf, Inc.

KOHLER, KENNETH. "How I Came Out to My Parents" by Kenneth Kohler. Reprinted by permission of the author.

KURALT, CHARLES. "Wanderlust" is reprinted by permission of The Putnam Publishing Group from *Life on the Road* by Charles Kuralt. Copyright © 1990 by Charles Kuralt.

LANGLEY, JAMES. "Watch the Cart!" by James Langley. Reprinted by permission of the author.

LAURENCE, MARGARET. From "Where the World Began" in *Heart of a Stranger* by Margaret Laurence. Copyright © 1976 by Margaret Laurence. Reprinted by permission of New End Inc.

LEE, LI-YOUNG. "The Gift" copyright © 1986, by Li-Young Lee. Reprinted from *Rose,* by Li-Young Lee, with the permission of BOA Editions, Ltd., 92 Park Ave., Brockport NY 14420.

LEGUIN, URSULA K. "The Ones Who Walk Away from Omelas" from *New Dimensions 3*. Copyright © 1973 by Ursula K. LeGuin. Reprinted by permission of the author and her agent, Virginia Kidd.

LEWIS, ANTHONY. "The System Worked" from *the New York Times,* 1979. Copyright © 1979 by The New York Times Company. Reprinted by permission.

LOUIS-FERDINAND, GINA K. "Is Justice Served?" by Gina K. Louis-Ferdinand. Reprinted by permission of the author.

LUKAWSKA, GRACE. "Wolf" by Grace Lukawska. Reprinted by permission of the author.

MAILER, NORMAN. From "The Death of Benny Paret" by Norman Mailer in *The Presidential Papers*. Copyright 1963. Reprinted by permission.

MANNING, MARY. "A Visit to Belfast" from *The Atlantic Monthly,* 1972. Reprinted by permission.

MARIUS, ROBERT. "Writing and its Rewards" and "Writing Things Down." Copyright Richard Marius. Reprinted by permission of the author.

MASSIE, ROBERT K. From *Peter The Great* by Robert K. Massie. Copyright © 1980 by ROBERT K. MASSIE. Reprinted by permission of Alfred A. Knopf, Inc.

MASTERS, EDGAR LEE. "Lucinda Matlock" and "Margaret Fuller Slack" from *Spoon River Anthology*. Originally published by Macmillan Publishing Company. Reprinted by permission of Ellen C. Masters.

MATTHIESSEN, PETER. From *The Snow Leopard* by Peter Matthiessen. Copyright © 1978 by Peter Matthiessen. Used by permission of Viking Penguin, a division of Penguin Books USA Inc.

MCPHEE, JOHN. Excerpt from "The Woods from Hog Wallow" from *The Pine Barrens* by John McPhee. Copyright © 1968 by John McPhee. Reprinted by permission of Farrar, Straus & Giroux, Inc. Published in Canada by Macfarlane, Walter and Ross, Toronto and reprinted by permission.

MILDEN, TRIENA. "So You Want to Flunk Out of College" by Triena Milden. Reprinted by permission of the author.

MOWAT, FARLEY. Excerpt from *People of the Deer* by Farley Mowat. Copyright © 1951, 1952 by Farley Mowat, Ltd. By permission of Little, Brown and Company.

MULLER, GILBERT AND HARVEY WIENER, "On Writing" from A SHORT PROSE READER 4th edition. Reprinted by permission of McGraw-Hill, Inc.

MUNDIE, NANCY J. "The Mentally Ill and Human Experimentation: Perfect Together" by Nancy J. Mundie. Reprinted by permission of the author.

NAISBITT, JOHN AND PATRICIA ABURDENE. From *Megatrends 2000* by John Naisbitt and Patricia Aburdene. Copyright © 1990 by Megatrends Ltd. By permission of William Morrow & Company, Inc.

NILSEN, ALLEEN PACE. From "Sexism in English: A 1990's Update" by Alleen Pace Nilsen. Reprinted by permission of the author.

PACE, MILDRED MASTIN. "The Story of the Egyptian Mummy " from *Wrapped for Eternity* by Mildred Mastin Pace. Copyright © 1974. Reprinted by permission of Susan Mastin Scott, Executor for the Estate of Mildred Mastin Pace.

PARÉDES, AMÉRICO. "The Hammon and the Beans" is reprinted with permission from the publisher of *The Hammon and the Beans and Other Stories* by Américo Parédes. (Houston: Arte Publico Press - University of Houston, 1994).

PARSHALL, GERALD. "Freeing the Survivors" by Gerald Parshall in *U.S. News & World Report*, April 3, 1995. Copyright, April 3, 1995, *U.S. News & World Report*. Reprinted by permission.

PETTIT, FLORENCE H. "Sharpening Your Jackknife or Pocketknife" by Florence H. Pettit in *How to Make Whirligigs and Whimmy Diddles and Other American Folkcraft Objects*. Copyright 1972 by Florence H. Pettit. Reprinted by permission of the author.

PICKERING, SAMUEL. "Faith of the Father" from *Still Life* © 1990 by University Press of New England. Reprinted by permission.

POTTER, MEG. "The Shopping Bag Ladies" by Meg Potter. Reprinted by permission of the author.

RAINIE, HARRISON. "The Buried Sounds of Children Crying" by Harrison Rainie from *U.S. News & World Report*. Copyright, May 1, 1995, U.S. News & World Report. Reprinted by permission.

ROBERTS, ROBIN. From "Strike Out Little League" by Robin Roberts in *Newsweek,* 1975. Reprinted by permission of the author.

ROLAND, DANIEL. From "Which Side of the Fence" by Daniel Roland. Reprinted by permission of the author.

ROMERO, LEO. "What the Gossips Saw" from *Agua Negra* by Leo Romero. Copyright © 1981 by Leo Romero. Reprinted by permission of Ahsahta Press at Boise State University.

ROSE, KENNETH JON. From "2001 Space Shuttle" from *Travel & Leisure,* November 1979. © 1979 Jon Kenneth Rose. Reprinted by permission of Travel & Leisure and the author. All rights reserved.

ROSE, PHYLLIS. "Mothers and Fathers" from *Never Say Good-Bye* by Phyllis Rose. Copyright © 1984, 1985, 1986, 1987, 1988, 1989, 1990 by Phyllis Rose. Reprinted by permission of Georges Borchardt, Inc. for the author.

RUSSELL, BERTRAND. "What I Have Lived For" from *Autobiography* by Bertrand Russell. Reprinted by permission of Routledge.

RYAN, MICHAEL. From "They Track the Deadliest Viruses" by Michael Ryan in *Parade Magazine,* April 23, 1995. Reprinted by permission.

SAGAN, CARL. "The Measure of Eratosthenes" from *Harvard Magazine,* September/October 1980. Copyright © 1980 by Harvard Magazine. Reprinted by permission of Harvard Magazine and the author.

SAGAN, CARL. From "The Nuclear Winter" by Carl Sagan. Reprinted by permission of the author.

SANDBURG, CARL. Excerpts from *Abraham Lincoln - The Prairie Years,* Volume I by Carl Sandburg, copyright 1926 by Harcourt Brace & Company and renewed 1953 by Carl Sandburg, reprinted by permission of the publisher.

SCAMACCA, MARIA. "Oma: Portrait of a Heroine" by Maria Scamacca. Reprinted by permission of the author.

SCHROF, JOANNIE M. "The Last Safe Haven" from *U.S. News & World Report*, December 26, 1994. Reprinted by permission.

SCHWARTZ, ADRIENNE. "The Colossus in the Kitchen" by Adrienne Schwartz. Reprinted by permission of the author.

SELZER, RICHARD. From *A Mask on the Face of Death* by Richard Selzer. Copyright © 1987 by Richard Selzer. Reprinted by permission of Georges Borchardt, Inc. for the author.

SHABECOFF, PHILIP. "Congress Again Confronts Hazards of Killer Chemicals" by Philip Shabecoff from *the New York Times*, October 11, 1987. Copyright © 1987 by The New York Times Company. Reprinted by permission.

SHAHEEN, JACK. "The Media's Image of Arabs" by Jack Shaheen from *Newsweek,* 1988. Reprinted by permission of the author.

SIMETI, MARY TAYLOR, *On Persephone's Island: A Sicilian Journal*. New York: Alfred A. Knopf, Inc., 1986.

SINGER, ISAAC BASHEVIS. "The Son from America" from *A Crown of Feathers* by Isaac Bashevis Singer. Copyright © 1973 by Isaac Bashevis Singer. Reprinted by permission of Farrar, Straus & Giroux, Inc.

STEINBECK, JOHN. "Flight", copyright 1938, renewed © 1966 by John Steinbeck from *The Long Valley* by John Steinbeck. Used by permission of Viking Penguin, a division of Penguin Books USA Inc.

STEINBECK, JOHN. From *America and Americans* by John Steinbeck. Copyright © 1966 by John Steinbeck, text. Copyright © 1966 by Viking Penguin, photographs. Used by permission of Viking Penguin, a divison of Penguin Books USA Inc.

STEINBECK, JOHN. "The Chrysanthemums", copyright 1937, renewed © 1965 by John Steinbeck from *The Long Valley* by John Steinbeck. Used by permission of Viking Penguin, a division of Penguin Books USA Inc.

STENSRUD, ROCKWELL. "Who's on Third?" from Teaching Guide to the film series, *The Search for Solutions*. Reprinted by permission of the author.

SULLIVAN, JESSIE. "If at First You Do Not See. . ." by Jessie Sullivan. Reprinted by permission of the author.

SWALINA, CAROLYN. "The Militiaman, the Yuppie, and Me" by Carolyn Swalina. Reprinted by permission of the author.

TEIR, ROB. "Fight Drug Use With Tests" by Rob Teir in *USA Today,* March 28, 1995. Reprinted by permission of the author.

USA TODAY. "Drug Tests Fail Schools." Copyright 1995, *USA Today*. Reprinted by permission.

WAGNER, GAYE. "Death of an Officer" is reprinted by permission from the May/June 1995 *The American Enterprise,* published by the American Enterprise Institute in Washington, D.C.

WALLIS, CLAUDIA. From "How to Live to Be 200" by Claudia Wallis in *Time,* March 6, 1995. Copyright © 1995 Time, Inc. Reprinted by permission.

WALL STREET JOURNAL. From "Affirmative Reaction" in *the Wall Street Journal*, April 20, 1995. Reprinted by permission of The Wall Street Journal, © 1995 Dow Jones & Company, Inc. All Rights Reserved Worldwide.

WELTY, EUDORA. "A Worn Path" from *A Curtain of Green and Other Stories*, copyright 1941 and renewed 1969 by Eudora Welty, reprinted by permission of Harcourt Brace & Company.

WILLIAMS, WILLIAM CARLOS. Excerpt from *The Doctor Stories* by William Carlos Williams. Copyright 1938 by William Carlos Williams. Reprinted by permission of New Directions Publishing Corporation.

WITT, MICHAEL. "Gambling" by Michael Witt. Reprinted by permission of the author.Wnorowski, Alice. "A Longing" by Alice Wnorowski. Reprinted by permission of the author.

WOLFE, TOM. "Columbus and the Moon" from *the New York Times,* July 29, 1979. Copyright 1979 by Tom Wolfe. Reprinted by permission of Janklow & Nesbit for the author.

WONG, JADE SNOW. From "Uncle Kwok" in *Fifth Chinese Daughter* by Jade Snow Wong. Copyright © 1950/1989 by Jade Snow Wong. Used with permission of the University of Washington Press.

INDEX